i

The Torah: A Mechanical Translation

Leviticus

~~~~~~~~~~~~~~~~~~~~~~~~~~~~~~~~~~~~~~~

A new and unique method of translation that brings you a literal and faithful word-for-word translation of the Hebrew text through the English language.

By Jeff A. Benner

The Torah: A Mechanical Translation - Leviticus by Jeff A. Benner. ISBN 978-1-63868-009-3.

Published 2021 by Virtualbookworm.com Publishing Inc., P.O. Box 9949, College Station, TX 77845, US. ©2019, Jeff A. Benner. All rights reserved. Any part of this book may be copied without prior permission for educational purposes only.

Acknowledgments

A work of this size could never have been completed without the support of many people. I would first like to thank my wife, Denise, and our children for the encouragement and support they have given me over the years. I also want to thank my publisher, Bobby Bernshausen, and his wife, Angela, of Virtual Bookworm Publishing. They have always been there when I needed them and have been very helpful and encouraging with the publishing of my books. My thanks also goes out to Doris Dppel who has freely given of her time and energy to review and edit, not only this work, but many of my other works. I would also like to thank the following people who have provided of their valuable time to help with the editing of this work. Without all of these people, this book would not be the quality that it is now.

Abell, Harry ♦ Adjei, Alex ♦ Ammundsen, Ron ♦ Angel, Priscilla ♦ Arnold, Bill ♦ Arnold, Tracy ♦ Ashcom, Ingrid ♦ Atkins, Larry ♦ Barbier, Marcia ♦ Barna, Veronica ♦ Baynard, Jane E. ♦ Beale, Robert ♦ Beard, Lance ♦ Beaver, Kandy ♦ Beck, Charles ♦ Begley, Holly ♦ Benson, Robin ♦ Bilek, Diane ♦ Black, Robert ♦ Blair, J Michael ♦ Blankenship, Donnie ♦ Blasé, Kathy ♦ Blignaut, André ♦ Blue, Anisa ♦ Booth, Ellie ♦ Bornman, Neala ♦ Botha, Chrissie ♦ Bradshaw, Marc ♦ Bruno, Cheryl ♦ Burton, Todd ♦ Calpino, Michael ♦ Carmichael, Jim ♦ Chatham, Kyle ♦ Colling, Ron ♦ Compton, Sharri ♦ Conaway, Richard ♦ Corcoran, Geoffrey ♦ Corson, Rev. Jim ♦ Craig, LuAna ♦ Custer, Pam ♦ Daigle, Cyndi ♦ Daniels, Ardree ♦ de Beer, Suzanne ♦ de Caussin, Daniel ♦ Deuprey, Sue ♦ Dick, Jo Ann ♦ Donarodo, Rod ♦ Dunnett, Daniel D. ♦ Eichelberger, John ♦ Farcas, David ♦ Farcas, Ruth ♦ Felczak, Przemek ♦ Fier, Robert ♦ Finn, Ken ♦ Foisy, Steve M. ♦ Forsman, Devora ♦ Fortune, Tom ♦ Gador, Yakob ♦ Garcia, Ben ♦ Gates, Philip ♦ Geronimo, Leopoldo ♦ Giancarli, Anthony D. ♦ Kay, Glen ♦ Goblet, Jesse ♦ Gonzalez, Daniel ♦ Gonzalez, Janice ♦ Gould, Janet ♦ Gramm, Jim ♦ Gregory, Ronen ♦ Gunter, Rocquelle ♦ Haeffner, Adam ♦ Hamlett, Kathy ♦ Hayes, Gordon ♦ Healy, Dorothy ♦ Henderson, Robert ♦ Henning, Nadia ♦ Heperi, Dallin ♦ Higgins, Carol ♦ Holiday, Rose ♦ Howie, Jennifer H MacRae ♦ Hudson, Brian Keith ♦ Hunter, Myhrrhleine ♦ Irons, Jeanne M. ♦ Jacobsen, Amanda ♦ Janssen, Henry

♦ Jones, Tim ♦ Karunaratne, Herschel ♦ Kayaga, Angellah ♦ Keep, David ♦ Keller, Sandra S. ♦ Kempf, Julia ♦ Kern, Cory ♦ Kindall, Kathy ♦ Knox, Kevin P. ♦ Krueger, Frank R. ♦ Lambert, Jerry R. ♦ Law, Duncan ♦ Lee, Peggy ♦ Lee, Ronald ♦ Leisy, Paul Matthew ♦ Lema, Andrew ♦ Lenár, Jaroslav ♦ Longanecker, Ann-Marie Rael ♦ Lorin, R. ♦ Lurk, Paul ♦ Lyles, Dr. Don ♦ Lyman, Dave ♦ MacDougall, Doug ♦ MacIsaac, Edward ♦ Man, Ho Yep ♦ Maney, Mike ♦ McClusky, Michelle ♦ McKenzie, Frances ♦ McKenzie, James M. ♦ Morford, Thomas ♦ Morgado, Eric ♦ Mugisha, Albert ♦ Nawman, Nora ♦ Neff, John ♦ Nichols, Kathy ♦ Nielson, Josh ♦ Norris, Andrew ♦ Novelo, Emily ♦ O, Ricky and Jacki ♦ O'Connor, Elaine ♦ Odem, Bruce ♦ Oerder, Max ♦ O'Reilly, John ♦ Orme, Kenneth ♦ Palmer, Wesley ♦ Parker, Cindy ♦ Parker, Debra ♦ Patterson, Tim ♦ Paul, Leslie ♦ Peightal, David ♦ Peterson, Preston ♦ Phillips, Jean-Marc ♦ Phillips, Matthew ♦ Pollic, Gene ♦ Quigley, Donna ♦ Range, Katharine ♦ Riden, Debora ♦ Rivera, Carrie ♦ Robertson, Dan ♦ Rodriguez, Renny ♦ Rogers, Nathanael David ♦ Rose, Wesley "Dr. Ley" ♦ Rowland, Marilene ♦ Roy, Peter ♦ Rustici, Jan ♦ Saunders, Charles Jr. ♦ Schaper, Jeff ♦ Scott, Corey ♦ Sellmar, Mary ♦ Simcoke, Bob ♦ Skipper, Jason D. ♦ Smith, Terry ♦ Sovea, J.L. ♦ Stanley, Rashida ♦ Stolz, Frances ♦ Talbot, Randy ♦ Tenenbaum, Bruce A. ♦ Tercha, Diane ♦ Thomas, John P. ♦ Timmons, Ken ♦ Todd, Yvonne ♦ Tomausi, Sebastian ♦ Uyenaka, Stephanie ♦ Vallee, Lisa Anne ♦ Van Rooyen, Wernhard ♦ Walker, Gavin ♦ Walters, BJ ♦ Whetter, Dorothy ♦ Wilcoxson, Jewell H. Jr. ♦ Withrow, Charles ♦ Wofford, Matt ♦ Wood, Basil ♦ Worrell, Lynda ♦ Wu, Steve ♦ Wyckoff, Janet

The Book of Leviticus

Chapter 1

1:1 *and~he~will~*CALL.OUT(V) (וַיִּקְרָא *wai'yiq'ra*)[1] TO (אֶל *el*) Mosheh (מֹשֶׁה *mo'sheh*) *and~he~will~much~*SPEAK(V) (וַיְדַבֵּר *wai'da'beyr*) **YHWH** (יְהוָה *YHWH*) TO~him (אֵלָיו *ey'law*) from~TENT (מֵאֹהֶל *meyohel*) APPOINTED (מוֹעֵד *mo'eyd*) to~>~SAY(V) (לֵאמֹר *ley'mor*) **RMT:** and he called out to Mosheh, and **YHWH** spoke to him from the appointed tent saying,

1:2 *!(ms)~much~*SPEAK(V) (דַּבֵּר *da'beyr*) TO (אֶל *el*) SON~s (בְּנֵי *bê'ney*) Yisra'eyl (יִשְׂרָאֵל *yis'ra'eyl*) *and~you(ms)~did~*SAY(V) (וְאָמַרְתָּ *wê'a'mar'ta*) TO~them(m) (אֲלֵהֶם *a'ley'hem*) HUMAN (אָדָם *a'dam*) GIVEN.THAT (כִּי *ki*) *he~will~make~*COME.NEAR(V) (יַקְרִיב *yaq'riv*) from~you(mp) (מִכֶּם *mi'kem*) DONATION (קָרְבָּן *qar'ban*) to~**YHWH** (לַיהוָה *la'YHWH*) FROM (מִן *min*) the~BEAST (הַבְּהֵמָה *ha'be'hey'mah*) FROM (מִן *min*) the~CATTLE (הַבָּקָר *ha'ba'qar*) and~FROM (וּמִן *u'min*) the~FLOCKS (הַצֹּאן *ha'tson*) *you(mp)~will~make~*COME.NEAR(V) (תַּקְרִיבוּ *taq'ri'vu*) AT (אֶת *et*) DONATION~you(mp) (קָרְבַּנְכֶם *qar'ban'khem*) **RMT:** speak to the sons of Yisra'eyl, and you will say to them, each that will bring from you a donation to **YHWH**, from the beast, from the cattle, from the flocks, you will bring near your donation.

1:3 IF (אִם *im*) ASCENSION.OFFERING (עֹלָה *o'lah*) DONATION~him (קָרְבָּנוֹ *qar'ba'no*) FROM (מִן *min*) the~CATTLE (הַבָּקָר *ha'ba'qar*) MALE (זָכָר *za'khar*) WHOLE (תָּמִים *ta'mim*) *he~will~make~*COME.NEAR(V)~him (יַקְרִיבֶנּוּ *yaq'riy've'nu*) TO (אֶל *el*) OPENING (פֶּתַח *pe'tahh*) TENT (אֹהֶל *o'hel*) APPOINTED (מוֹעֵד *mo'eyd*) *he~will~make~*COME.NEAR(V) (יַקְרִיב *yaq'riv*) AT~him (אֹתוֹ *o'to*) to~SELF-WILL~him (לִרְצֹנוֹ *lir'tso'no*) to~FACE~s (לִפְנֵי *liph'ney*) **YHWH** (יְהוָה *YHWH*) **RMT:** If his donation is an ascension offering from the cattle, it will be a whole male, he will bring him near to the opening of the appointed tent, he will bring him near for his self-will, to the face of **YHWH**,

---

[1] The Hebrew name for the third book of the Torah is *vaiyiqra* (and he called), the first word in the book.

1:4 <u>and~he~did~SUPPORT</u>[(V)] (וְסָמַךְ *wê'sa'makh*) <u>HAND~him</u> (יָדוֹ *ya'do*) <u>UPON</u> (עַל *al*) <u>HEAD</u> (רֹאשׁ *rosh*) <u>the~ASCENSION.OFFERING</u> (הָעֹלָה *ha'o'lah*) <u>and~he~did~be~ACCEPT</u>[(V)] (וְנִרְצָה *wê'nir'tsah*) <u>to~ him</u> (לוֹ *lo*) <u>to~>~much~COVER</u>[(V)] (לְכַפֵּר *lê'kha'peyr*) <u>UPON~him</u> (עָלָיו *a'law*) **RMT:** and he will support his hand upon the head of the ascension offering, and he will be acceptable to him[2], for making a covering upon him,

1:5 <u>and~he~did~SLAY</u>[(V)] (וְשָׁחַט *wê'sha'hhat*) <u>AT</u> (אֶת *et*) <u>SON</u> (בֶּן *ben*) <u>the~CATTLE</u> (הַבָּקָר *ha'ba'qar*) <u>to~FACE~s</u> (לִפְנֵי *liph'ney*) **YHWH** (יְהֹוָה *YHWH*) <u>and~they~did~make~COME.NEAR</u>[(V)] (וְהִקְרִיבוּ *wê'hiq'ri'vu*) <u>SON~s</u> (בְּנֵי *bê'ney*) <u>Aharon</u> (אַהֲרֹן *a'ha'ron*) <u>the~ ADMINISTRATOR~s</u> (הַכֹּהֲנִים *ha'ko'ha'nim*) <u>AT</u> (אֶת *et*) <u>the~BLOOD</u> (הַדָּם *ha'dam*) <u>and~they~did~SPRINKLE</u>[(V)] (וְזָרְקוּ *wê'zar'qu*) <u>AT</u> (אֶת *et*) <u>the~BLOOD</u> (הַדָּם *ha'dam*) <u>UPON</u> (עַל *al*) <u>the~ALTAR</u> (הַמִּזְבֵּחַ *ha'miz'bey'ahh*) <u>ALL.AROUND</u> (סָבִיב *sa'viv*) <u>WHICH</u> (אֲשֶׁר *a'sher*) <u>OPENING</u> (פֶּתַח *pe'tahh*) <u>TENT</u> (אֹהֶל *o'hel*) <u>APPOINTED</u> (מוֹעֵד *mo'eyd*) **RMT:** and he will slay the son of the cattle to the face of **YHWH**, and the sons of Aharon, the administrators, will bring near the blood, and they will sprinkle the blood upon the altar all around where the opening of the appointed tent is,

1:6 <u>and~he~did~make~STRIP.OFF</u>[(V)] (וְהִפְשִׁיט *wê'hiph'shit*) <u>AT</u> (אֶת *et*) <u>the~ASCENSION.OFFERING</u> (הָעֹלָה *ha'o'lah*) <u>and~he~did~much~ DIVIDE.INTO.PIECES</u>[(V)] (וְנִתַּח *wê'ni'tahh*) <u>AT~her</u> (אֹתָהּ *o'tah*) <u>to~ PIECE~s~her</u> (לִנְתָחֶיהָ *lin'ta'hhey'ah*) **RMT:** and he will strip off the ascension offering, and he will divide her into pieces to her pieces,

1:7 <u>and~they~did~GIVE</u>[(V)] (וְנָתְנוּ *wê'nat'nu*) <u>SON~s</u> (בְּנֵי *bê'ney*) <u>Aharon</u> (אַהֲרֹן *a'ha'ron*) <u>the~ADMINISTRATOR</u> (הַכֹּהֵן *ha'ko'heyn*) <u>FIRE</u> (אֵשׁ *eysh*) <u>UPON</u> (עַל *al*) <u>the~ALTAR</u> (הַמִּזְבֵּחַ *ha'miz'bey'ahh*) <u>and~they~did~ARRANGE</u>[(V)] (וְעָרְכוּ *wê'ar'khu*) <u>TREE~s</u> (עֵצִים *ey'tsim*) <u>UPON</u> (עַל *al*) <u>the~FIRE</u> (הָאֵשׁ *ha'eysh*) **RMT:** and the sons of Aharon, the administrators, will give fire upon the altar, and they will arrange the wood upon the fire,

1:8 <u>and~they~did~ARRANGE</u>[(V)] (וְעָרְכוּ *wê'ar'khu*) <u>SON~s</u> (בְּנֵי *bê'ney*) <u>Aharon</u> (אַהֲרֹן *a'ha'ron*) <u>the~ADMINISTRATOR~s</u> (הַכֹּהֲנִים *ha'ko'ha'nim*) <u>AT</u> (אֶת *eyt*) <u>the~PIECE~s</u> (הַנְּתָחִים *han'ta'hhim*) <u>AT</u>

---

[2] If the "to" is referring to **YHWH**, then this should be translated as "to him," but if the "to" is referring to the one bringing the sacrifice it should be translated as "for him."

(אֵת *et*) the~HEAD (הָרֹאשׁ *ha'rosh*) and~AT (וְאֵת *wê'et*) the~SUET (הַפָּדֶר *ha'pa'der*) UPON (עַל *al*) the~TREE~s (הָעֵצִים *ha'eytsim*) WHICH (אֲשֶׁר *a'sher*) UPON (עַל־ *al*) the~FIRE (הָאֵשׁ *ha'eysh*) WHICH (אֲשֶׁר *a'sher*) UPON (עַל *al*) the~ALTAR (הַמִּזְבֵּחַ *ha'miz'bey'ahh*) **RMT:** and the sons of Aharon, the administrators, will arrange the pieces, the head, the suet, upon the wood, which is upon the fire, which is upon the altar,

1:9 and~INSIDE~him (וְקִרְבּוֹ *wê'qir'bo*) and~LEG~s~him (וּכְרָעָיו *ukh'ra'aw*) he~will~BATHE(V) (יִרְחַץ *yir'hhats*) in~the~WATER~s2 (בַּמָּיִם *ba'ma'yim*) and~he~did~make~BURN.INCENSE(V) (וְהִקְטִיר *wê'hiq'tir*) the~ADMINISTRATOR (הַכֹּהֵן *ha'ko'heyn*) AT (אֵת *et*) the~ALL (הַכֹּל *ha'kol*) the~ALTAR~unto (הַמִּזְבֵּחָה *ha'miz'bey'hhah*) ASCENSION.OFFERING (עֹלָה *o'lah*) FIRE.OFFERING (אִשֵּׁה *i'sheyh*) AROMA (רֵיחַ *rey'ahh*) SWEET (נִיחוֹחַ *ni'hho'ahh*) to~YHWH (לַיהוָה *la'YHWH*) **RMT:** and he will bathe his insides and his legs in the waters, and the administrator will burn it all as incense upon the altar, an ascension offering of a fire offering, a sweet aroma to **YHWH**,

1:10 and~IF (וְאִם *wê'im*) FRCM (מִן *min*) the~FLOCKS (הַצֹּאן *ha'tson*) DONATION~him (קָרְבָּנוֹ *qar'ba'no*) FROM (מִן *min*) the~SHEEP~s (הַכְּשָׂבִים *hak'sa'vim*) OR (אוֹ *o*) FROM (מִן *min*) the~SHE-GOAT~s (הָעִזִּים *ha'i'zim*) to~ASCENSION.OFFERING (לְעֹלָה *lê'lah*) MALE (זָכָר *za'khar*) WHOLE (תָּמִים *ta'mim*) he~will~make~COME.NEAR(V)~him (יַקְרִיבֶנּוּ *yaq'riy've'nu*) **RMT:** and if the donation is from the flocks, from the sheep or from the she-goats, for an ascension offering, it will be a whole male, he will bring him near,

1:11 and~he~did~SLAY(V) (וְשָׁחַט *wê'sha'hhat*) AT~him (אֹתוֹ *o'to*) UPON (עַל *al*) MIDSECT.ON (יֶרֶךְ *ye'rekh*) the~ALTAR (הַמִּזְבֵּחַ *ha'miz'bey'ahh*) NORTH~unto (צָפֹנָה *tsa'pho'nah*) to~FACE~s (לִפְנֵי *liph'ney*) YHWH (יְהוָה *YHWH*) and~they~did~SPRINKLE(V) (וְזָרְקוּ *wê'zar'qu*) SON~s (בְּנֵי *bê'ney*) Aharon (אַהֲרֹן *a'ha'ron*) the~ADMINISTRATOR~s (הַכֹּהֲנִים *ha'ko'ha'nim*) AT (אֵת *et*) BLOOD~him (דָּמוֹ *da'mo*) UPON (עַל *al*) the~ALTAR (הַמִּזְבֵּחַ *ha'miz'bey'ahh*) ALL.AROUND (סָבִיב *sa'viv*) **RMT:** and he will slay him upon the midsection of the altar unto the north, to the face of **YHWH**, and the sons of Aharon, the administrators, will sprinkle his blood upon the altar all around,

1:12 and~he~did~much~DIVIDE.INTO.PIECES(V) (וְנִתַּח *wê'ni'tahh*) AT~him (אֹתוֹ *o'to*) tc~PIECE~s~him (לִנְתָחָיו *lin'ta'hhaw*) and~AT

3

(וְאֵת wê'et) HEAD~him (רֹאשׁוֹ ro'sho) and~AT (וְאֵת wê'et) SUET~
him (פִּדְרוֹ pid'ro) and~he~did~ARRANGE[(V)] (וְעָרַךְ wê'a'rekh) the~
ADMINISTRATOR (הַכֹּהֵן ha'ko'heyn) AT~them[(m)] (אֹתָם o'tam) UPON
(עַל al) the~TREE~s (הָעֵצִים ha'eytsim) WHICH (אֲשֶׁר a'sher) UPON
(עַל al) the~FIRE (הָאֵשׁ ha'eysh) WHICH (אֲשֶׁר a'sher) UPON (עַל al)
the~ALTAR (הַמִּזְבֵּחַ ha'miz'bey'ahh) **RMT:** and he will divide him into
pieces to his pieces, and his head and his suet, and the administrator
will arrange them upon the wood, which is upon the fire, which is
upon the altar,

1:13 and~the~INSIDE (וְהַקֶּרֶב wê'ha'qe'rev) and~the~LEG~s2
(וְהַכְּרָעַיִם wê'hak'ra'a'im) he~will~BATHE[(V)] (יִרְחַץ yir'hhats) in~the~
WATER~s2 (בַּמָּיִם ba'ma'yim) and~he~did~make~COME.NEAR[(V)]
(וְהִקְרִיב wê'hiq'riv) the~ADMINISTRATOR (הַכֹּהֵן ha'ko'heyn) AT (אֶת
et) the~ALL (הַכֹּל ha'kol) and~he~did~make~BURN.INCENSE[(V)]
(וְהִקְטִיר wê'hiq'tir) the~ALTAR~unto (הַמִּזְבֵּחָה ha'miz'bey'hhah)
ASCENSION.OFFERING (עֹלָה o'lah) HE (הוּא hu) FIRE.OFFERING
(אִשֵּׁה i'sheyh) AROMA (רֵיחַ rey'ahh) SWEET (נִיחֹחַ ni'hho'ahh) to~
YHWH (לַיהוָה la'YHWH) **RMT:** and he will bathe the insides and the
legs in the waters, and the administrator will bring near all, and he
will burn it as incense upon the altar, an ascension offering, he is a
fire offering, a sweet aroma to **YHWH**,

1:14 and~IF (וְאִם wê'im) FROM (מִן min) the~FLYER (הָעוֹף ha'oph)
ASCENSION.OFFERING (עֹלָה o'lah) DONATION~him (קָרְבָּנוֹ
qar'ba'no) to~**YHWH** (לַיהוָה la'YHWH) and~he~did~make~
COME.NEAR[(V)] (וְהִקְרִיב wê'hiq'riv) FROM (מִן min) the~
TURTLEDOVE~s (הַתֹּרִים ha'to'rim) OR (אוֹ o) FROM (מִן min) SON~s
(בְּנֵי bê'ney) the~DOVE (הַיּוֹנָה hai'yo'nah) AT (אֶת et) DONATION~
him (קָרְבָּנוֹ qar'ba'no) **RMT:** and if the ascension offering is from the
flyers, his donation to **YHWH**, then he will bring near from the
turtledoves or from the sons of the doves his donation,

1:15 and~he~did~make~COME.NEAR[(V)]~him (וְהִקְרִיבוֹ wê'hiq'ri'vo)
the~ADMINISTRATOR (הַכֹּהֵן ha'ko'heyn) TO (אֶל el) the~ALTAR
(הַמִּזְבֵּחַ ha'miz'bey'ahh) and~he~did~SNAP.OFF[(V)] (וּמָלַק u'ma'laq)
AT (אֶת et) HEAD~him (רֹאשׁוֹ ro'sho) and~he~did~make~
BURN.INCENSE[(V)] (וְהִקְטִיר wê'hiq'tir) the~ALTAR~unto (הַמִּזְבֵּחָה
ha'miz'bey'hhah) and~he~did~be~DRAIN[(V)] (וְנִמְצָה wê'nim'tsah)
BLOOD~him (דָּמוֹ da'mo) UPON (עַל al) WALL (קִיר qir) the~ALTAR
(הַמִּזְבֵּחַ ha'miz'bey'ahh) **RMT:** and the administrator will bring him
near to the altar, and he will snap off his head, and he will burn it as

incense upon the altar, and his blood will be drained upon the wall of the altar,

1:16 and~he~did~make~TURN.ASIDE^(V) (וְהֵסִיר) *wê'hey'sir*) AT (אֶת) *et*) CROP~him (מֻרְאָתוֹ) *mur'ɔ'to*) in~PLUMAGE~her (בְּנֹצָתָהּ) *bê'no'tsa'tah*) and~he~did~make~THROW.OUT^(V) (וְהִשְׁלִיךְ) *wê'hish'likh*) AT~her (אֹתָהּ) *o'tah*) BESIDE (אֵצֶל) *ey'tsel*) the~ALTAR (הַמִּזְבֵּחַ) *ha'miz'bey'ahh*) EAST~unto (קֵדְמָה) *qeyd'mah*) TO (אֶל) *el*) AREA (מְקוֹם) *mê'qom*) the~FATNESS (הַדָּשֶׁן) *ha'da'shen*) **RMT:** and he will remove his³ crop with her plumage, and he will throw her out beside the altar unto the east, to the area of the fatness,

1:17 and~he~did~much~SPLIT.IN.TWO^(V) (וְשִׁסַּע) *wê'shi'sa*) AT~him (אֹתוֹ) *o'to*) in~WING~s~him (בִכְנָפָיו) *vikh'na'phaw*) NOT (לֹא) *lo*) he~ will~make~SEPARATE^(V) (יַבְדִּיל) *yav'dil*) and~he~did~make~ BURN.INCENSE^(V) (וְהִקְטִיר) *wê'hiq'tir*) AT~him (אֹתוֹ) *o'to*) the~ ADMINISTRATOR (הַכֹּהֵן) *ha'ko'heyn*) the~ALTAR~unto (הַמִּזְבֵּחָה) *ha'miz'bey'hhah*) UPON (עַל) *al*) the~TREE~s (הָעֵצִים) *ha'eytsim*) WHICH (אֲשֶׁר) *a'sher*) UPON (עַל) *al*) the~FIRE (הָאֵשׁ) *ha'eysh*) ASCENSION.OFFERING (עֹלָה) *o'lah*) HE (הוּא) *hu*) FIRE.OFFERING (אִשֶּׁה) *i'sheyh*) AROMA (רֵיחַ) *rey'ahh*) SWEET (נִיחֹחַ) *ni'hho'ahh*) to~ **YHWH** (לַיהֹוָה) *la'YHWH*) **RMT:** and he will split him in two by his wings, he will not separate, and the administrator will burn him as incense upon the altar, upon the wood, which is upon the fire, an ascension offering, he is a fire offering, a sweet aroma to **YHWH**,

Chapter 2

2:1 and~SOUL (וְנֶפֶשׁ) *wê'ne'phesh*) GIVEN.THAT (כִּי) *ki*) she~will~ make~COME.NEAR^(V) (תַקְרִיב) *taq'riv*) DONATION (קָרְבַּן) *qar'ban*) DEPOSIT (מִנְחָה) *min'hhah*) to~**YHWH** (לַיהֹוָה) *la'YHWH*) FLOUR (סֹלֶת) *so'let*) he~will~EXIST^(V) (יִהְיֶה) *yih'yeh*) DONATION~him (קָרְבָּנוֹ) *qar'ba'no*) and~he~did~POUR.DOWN^(V) (וְיָצַק) *wê'ya'tsaq*) UPON~her (עָלֶיהָ) *a'ley'ah*) OIL (שֶׁמֶן) *she'men*) and~he~did~GIVE^(V) (וְנָתַן) *wê'na'tan*) UPON~her (עָלֶיהָ) *a'ley'ah*) FRANKINCENSE (לְבֹנָה) *lê'vo'nah*) **RMT:** and a soul that will bring near a donation of deposit

---

³ The turtledove and dove are feminine words in Hebrew, therefore the pronoun "him" appears to be in error and should be "her" (compare with the next word-her plumage).

for **YHWH**, flour will exist as his donation, and he will pour down upon her oil, and he will give upon her frankincense,

2:2 and~he~did~make~COME^(V)~her (וֶהֱבִיאָהּ we'he'vi'ah) TO (אֶל el) SON~s (בְּנֵי bê'ney) Aharon (אַהֲרֹן a'ha'ron) the~ADMINISTRATOR~s (הַכֹּהֲנִים ha'ko'ha'nim) and~he~did~GRASP^(V) (וְקָמַץ wê'qa'mats) from~THERE (מִשָּׁם mi'sham) FILLING (מְלֹא mê'lo) HANDFUL~him (קֻמְצוֹ qum'tso) from~FLOUR~her (מִסָּלְתָּהּ mi'sal'tah) and~from~OIL (וּמִשַּׁמְנָהּ u'mi'sham'nah) UPON (עַל al) ALL (כָּל kol) to~FRANKINCENSE~her (לְבֹנָתָהּ lê'vo'na'tah) and~he~did~make~BURN.INCENSE^(V) (וְהִקְטִיר wê'hiq'tir) the~ADMINISTRATOR (הַכֹּהֵן ha'ko'heyn) AT (אֵת et) MEMORIAL~her (אַזְכָּרָתָהּ az'ka'ra'tah) the~ALTAR~unto (הַמִּזְבֵּחָה ha'miz'bey'hhah) FIRE.OFFERING (אִשֶּׁה i'sheyh) AROMA (רֵיחַ rey'ahh) SWEET (נִיחֹחַ ni'hho'ahh) to~YHWH (לַיהוָה la'YHWH) **RMT:** and he will bring her to the sons of Aharon, the administrators, and he will grasp from there, filling his handful from her flour and from the oil upon all for her frankincense, and the administrator will burn her memorial as incense upon the altar, a fire offering, a sweet aroma to **YHWH**,

2:3 and~the~be~LEAVE.BEHIND^(V)~ing^(fs) (וְהַנּוֹתֶרֶת wê'ha'no'te'ret) FROM (מִן min) the~DEPOSIT (הַמִּנְחָה ha'min'hhah) to~Aharon (לְאַהֲרֹן lê'a'ha'ron) and~to~SON~s~him (וּלְבָנָיו ul'va'naw) SPECIAL (קֹדֶשׁ qo'desh) SPECIAL~s (קָדָשִׁים qa'da'shim) from~FIRE.OFFERING~s (מֵאִשֵּׁי mey'l'shey) **YHWH** (יְהוָה YHWH) **RMT:** and from the deposit being left behind, it belongs to Aharon and to his sons, it is a special of specials[4] from the fire offerings of **YHWH**,

2:4 and~GIVEN.THAT (וְכִי wê'khi) you^(ms)~will~make~COME.NEAR^(V) (תַקְרִב taq'riv) DONATION (קָרְבַּן qar'ban) DEPOSIT (מִנְחָה min'hhah) BAKED (מַאֲפֵה ma'a'pheyh) OVEN (תַנּוּר ta'nur) FLOUR (סֹלֶת so'let) PIERCED.BREAD~s (חַלּוֹת hha'lot) UNLEAVENED.BREAD~s (מַצֹּת ma'tsot) MIX^(V)~ed^(fp) (בְּלוּלֹת bê'lu'lot) in~the~OIL (בַּשֶּׁמֶן ba'she'men) and~THIN.BREAD~s (וּרְקִיקֵי ur'qi'qey) UNLEAVENED.BREAD~s (מַצּוֹת ma'tsot) SMEAR^(V)~ed^(mp) (מְשֻׁחִים mê'shu'hhim) in~the~OIL (בַּשָּׁמֶן ba'sha'men) **RMT:** and, given that you will bring near a donation of deposit, oven baked, flour of unleavened pierced breads mixed with the oil and unleavened thin breads smeared with the oil,

---

[4] The phrase "special of specials" means a "very special thing, one or place."

2:5 and~IF (וְאִם wê'im) DEPOSIT (מִנְחָה min'hhah) UPON (עַל al) the~PAN (הַמַּחֲבַת ha'ma'hha'vat) DONATION~you^(ms) (קׇרְבָּנֶ֫ךָ qar'ba'ne'kha) FLOUR (סֹלֶת so'let) MIX^(v)~ed^(fs) (בְּלוּלָה bê'lu'lah) in~ the~OIL (בַשֶּׁמֶן va'she'men) UNLEAVENED.BREAD (מַצָּה ma'tsah) she~will~EXIST^(v) (תִּהְיֶה tih'yeh) **RMT:** and if your donation is a deposit upon the pan, flour mixed with the oil, she will be unleavened bread.

2:6 >~CRUMBLE^(v) (פָּתוֹת pa'tot) AT~her (אֹתָהּ o'tah) FRAGMENT~s (פִּתִּים pi'tim) and~you^(ms)~did~POUR.DOWN^(v) (וְיָצַקְתָּ wê'ya'tsaq'ta) UPON~her (עָלֶ֫יהָ a'ley'ah) OIL (שָׁמֶן sha'men) DEPOSIT (מִנְחָה min'hhah) SHE (הִוא hi) **RMT:** Crumble her fragments, and you will pour down upon her oil, she is a deposit,

2:7 and~IF (וְאִם wê'im) DEPOSIT (מִנְחַת mi'ne'hhat) BOILING.POT (מַרְחֶשֶׁת mar'hhe'shet) DONATION~you^(ms) (קׇרְבָּנֶ֫ךָ qar'ba'ne'kha) FLOUR (סֹלֶת so'let) in~the~OIL (בַשֶּׁמֶן ba'she'men) she~will~be~ DO^(v) (תֵּעָשֶׂה tey'a'seh) **RMT:** and if your donation is a deposit of the boiling pot, the flour will be made with the oil,

2:8 and~you^(ms)~did~make~COME^(v) (וְהֵבֵאתָ wê'hey'vey'ta) AT (אֵת et) the~DEPOSIT (הַמִּנְחָה na'min'hhah) WHICH (אֲשֶׁר a'sher) he~ will~be~DO^(v) (יֵעָשֶׂה yey'a'seh) from~THESE (מֵאֵ֫לֶּה mey'ey'leh) to~ **YHWH** (לַיהוָה la'YHWH) and~he~did~make~COME.NEAR^(v)~her (וְהִקְרִיבָהּ wê'hiq'ri'vah) TO (אֶל el) the~ADMINISTRATOR (הַכֹּהֵן ha'ko'heyn) and~he~did~make~DRAW.NEAR^(v)~her (וְהִגִּישָׁהּ wê'hi'gi'shah) TO (אֶל el) the~ALTAR (הַמִּזְבֵּחַ ha'miz'bey'ahh) **RMT:** and you will bring the deposit, which he will make from these, to **YHWH**, and he will bring it near to the administrator, and he will draw her near to the altar,

2:9 and~he~did~make~RAISE.UP^(v) (וְהֵרִים wê'hey'rim) the~ ADMINISTRATOR (הַכֹּהֵן ha'ko'heyn) FROM (מִן min) the~DEPOSIT (הַמִּנְחָה ha'min'hhah) AT (אֵת et) MEMORIAL~her (אַזְכָּרָתָהּ az'ka'ra'tah) and~he~did~make~BURN.INCENSE^(v) (וְהִקְטִיר wê'hiq'tir) the~ALTAR~unto (הַמִּזְבֵּ֫חָה ha'miz'bey'hhah) FIRE.OFFERING (אִשֵּׁה i'sheyh) AROMA (רֵיחַ rey'ahh) SWEET (נִיחֹחַ ni'hho'ahh) to~**YHWH** (לַיהוָה la'YHWH) **RMT:** and the administrator will raise her memorial up from the deposit, and he will burn incense upon the altar, a fire offering, a sweet aroma to **YHWH**,

2:10 and~the~be~LEAVE.BEHIND^(v)~ing^(fs) (וְהַנּוֹתֶ֫רֶת wê'ha'no'te'ret) FROM (מִן min) the~DEPOSIT (הַמִּנְחָה ha'min'hhah) to~Aharon

(לְאַהֲרֹן *lê'a'ha'ron*) and~to~SON~s~him (וּלְבָנָיו *ul'va'naw*) SPECIAL (קֹדֶשׁ *qo'desh*) SPECIAL~s (קָדָשִׁים *qa'da'shim*) from~ FIRE.OFFERING~s (מֵאִשֵּׁי *mey'l'shey*) **YHWH** (יְהוָה *YHWH*) **RMT:** and from the deposit being left behind, it belongs to Aharon and to his sons, it is a special of specials[5] from the fire offerings of **YHWH**.

2:11 ALL (כָּל *kol*) the~DEPOSIT (הַמִּנְחָה *ha'min'hhah*) WHICH (אֲשֶׁר *a'sher*) you(mp)~will~make~COME.NEAR(V) (תַּקְרִיבוּ *taq'ri'vu*) to~ **YHWH** (לַיהוָה *la'YHWH*) NOT (לֹא *lo*) you(ms)~will~DO(V) (תֵעָשֶׂה *tey'a'seh*) LEAVENED.BREAD (חָמֵץ *hha'meyts*) GIVEN.THAT (כִּי *ki*) ALL (כָל *khol*) LEAVEN (שְׂאֹר *sê'or*) and~ALL (וְכָל *wê'khol*) HONEY (דְּבַשׁ *dê'vash*) NOT (לֹא *lo*) you(mp)~will~make~BURN.INCENSE(V) (תַקְטִירוּ *taq'ti'ru*) FROM~him (מִמֶּנּוּ *mi'me'nu*) FIRE.OFFERING (אִשֶּׁה *i'sheh*) to~**YHWH** (לַיהוָה *la'YHWH*) **RMT:** All the deposit, which you will bring near to **YHWH**, you will not make leavened bread, given that you will not burn any leaven or any honey as incense from him, a fire offering for **YHWH**.

2:12 DONATION (קָרְבַּן *qar'ban*) SUMMIT (רֵאשִׁית *rey'shit*) you(mp)~ will~make~COME.NEAR(V) (תַּקְרִיבוּ *taq'ri'vu*) AT~them(m) (אֹתָם *o'tam*) to~**YHWH** (לַיהוָה *la'YHWH*) and~TO (וְאֶל *wê'el*) the~ALTAR (הַמִּזְבֵּחַ *ha'miz'bey'ahh*) NOT (לֹא *lo*) they(m)~will~GO.UP(V) (יַעֲלוּ *ya'a'lu*) to~AROMA (לְרֵיחַ *lê'rey'ahh*) SWEET (נִיחֹחַ *ni'hho'ahh*) **RMT:** The donation of the summit[6], you will bring them near to **YHWH** and to the altar, they will not go up[7] for a sweet aroma,

2:13 and~ALL (וְכָל *wê'khol*) DONATION (קָרְבַּן *qar'ban*) DEPOSIT~ you(ms) (מִנְחָתְךָ *min'hha'te'kha*) in~the~SALT (בַּמֶּלַח *ba'me'lahh*) you(ms)~will~SEASON(V) (תִּמְלָח *tim'lahh*) and~NOT (וְלֹא *wê'lo*) you(ms)~will~make~CEASE(V) (תַשְׁבִּית *tash'bit*) SALT (מֶלַח *me'lahh*) COVENANT (בְּרִית *bê'rit*) Elohiym~you(ms) (אֱלֹהֶיךָ *e'lo'hey'kha*) from~UPON (מֵעַל *mey'al*) DEPOSIT~you(ms) (מִנְחָתֶךָ *min'hha'te'kha*) UPON (עַל *al*) ALL (כָּל *kol*) DONATION~you(ms) (קָרְבָּנְךָ *qar'ban'kha*) you(ms)~will~make~COME.NEAR(V) (תַּקְרִיב *taq'riv*) SALT (מֶלַח *me'lahh*) **RMT:** and all the donations of your deposit you will season with salt, and you will not cease the salt of the covenant of your

---

[5] The phrase "special of specials" means a "very special thing, one or place."

[6] The "summit" may be the "best" or the "first" of the produce.

[7] In the sense of not being burned on the fire.

Elohiym from upon your deposit, upon all your donations you will bring near with salt,

2:14 and~IF (וְאִם wê'im) you(ms)~will~make~COME.NEAR(V) (תַּקְרִיב taq'riv) DEPOSIT (מִנְחַת mi'ne'hhat) FIRST-FRUIT~s (בִּכּוּרִים bi'ku'rim) to~YHWH (לַיהוָה 'a'YHWH) GREEN.GRAIN (אָבִיב a'viv) DRY(V)~ed(ms) (קָלוּי qa'lui) in~the~FIRE (בָּאֵשׁ ba'eysh) BEATEN.GRAIN (גֶּרֶשׂ ge'res) PLANTATION (כַּרְמֶל kar'mel) you(ms)~will~make~COME.NEAR(V) (תַּקְרִיב taq'riv) AT (אֵת eyt) DEPOSIT (מִנְחַת mi'ne'hhat) FIRST-FRUIT~s~you(ms) (בִּכּוּרֶיךָ bi'ku'rey'kha) **RMT:** and if you will bring near a deposit of the first-fruits for YHWH, it will be green grain dried by the fire, beaten grain of the plantation, you will bring near the deposit of your first-fruits,

2:15 and~you(ms)~did~GIVE(V) (וְנָתַתָּ wê'na'ta'ta) UPON~her (עָלֶיהָ a'ley'ah) OIL (שֶׁמֶן she'men) and~you(ms)~did~PLACE(V) (וְשַׂמְתָּ wê'sam'ta) UPON~her (עָלֶיהָ a'ley'ah) FRANKINCENSE (לְבֹנָה lê'vo'nah) DEPOSIT (מִנְחָה min'hhah) SHE (הִוא hi) **RMT:** and you will give upon her oil, and you will place upon her frankincense, she is a deposit,

2:16 and~he~did~make~BURN.INCENSE(V) (וְהִקְטִיר wê'hiq'tir) the~ADMINISTRATOR (הַכֹּהֵן ha'ko'heyn) AT (אֵת et) MEMORIAL~her (אַזְכָּרָתָהּ az'ka'ra'tah) from~BEATEN.GRAIN~her (מִגִּרְשָׂהּ mi'gir'sah) and~from~OIL (וּמִשַּׁמְנָהּ u'mi'sham'nah) UPON (עַל al) ALL (כָּל kol) to~FRANKINCENSE~her (לְבֹנָתָהּ lê'vo'na'tah) FIRE.OFFERING (אִשֶּׁה i'sheh) to~YHWH (לַיהוָה la'YHWH) **RMT:** and the administrator will make incense with her memorial, from her beaten grain and from the oil, with all of her frankincense, a fire offering for YHWH,

Chapter 3

3:1 and~IF (וְאִם wê'im) SACRIFICE (זֶבַח ze'vahh) OFFERING.OF.RESTITUTION~s (שְׁלָמִים shê'la'mim) DONATION~him (קָרְבָּנוֹ qar'ba'no) IF (אִם im) FROM (מִן min) the~CATTLE (הַבָּקָר ha'ba'qar) HE (הוּא hu) make~COME.NEAR(V)~ing(ms) (מַקְרִיב maq'riv) IF (אִם im) MALE (זָכָר za'khar) IF (אִם im) FEMALE (נְקֵבָה nê'qey'vah) WHOLE (תָּמִים ta'mim) he~will~make~COME.NEAR(V)~him (יַקְרִיבֶנּוּ yaq'riy've'nu) to~FACE~s (לִפְנֵי liph'ney) YHWH (יְהוָה YHWH) **RMT:** and if his donation is a sacrifice of offerings of restitution, if he is bringing near from the cattle, if a male or a female, a whole one, he will bring him near to the face of YHWH,

9

3:2 and~he~did~SUPPORT^(V) (וְסָמַךְ wê'sa'makh) <u>HAND~him</u> (יָדוֹ ya'do) <u>UPON</u> (עַל al) <u>HEAD</u> (רֹאשׁ rosh) <u>DONATION~him</u> (קָרְבָּנוֹ qar'ba'no) and~he~did~SLAY^(V)~him (וּשְׁחָטוֹ ush'hha'to) <u>OPENING</u> (פֶּתַח pe'tahh) <u>TENT</u> (אֹהֶל o'hel) <u>APPOINTED</u> (מוֹעֵד mo'eyd) and~ they~did~SPRINKLE^(V) (וְזָרְקוּ wê'zar'qu) <u>SON~s</u> (בְּנֵי bê'ney) Aharon (אַהֲרֹן a'ha'ron) the~ADMINISTRATOR~s (הַכֹּהֲנִים ha'ko'ha'nim) <u>AT</u> (אֶת et) the~BLOOD (הַדָּם ha'dam) <u>UPON</u> (עַל al) the~ALTAR (הַמִּזְבֵּחַ ha'miz'bey'ahh) <u>ALL.AROUND</u> (סָבִיב sa'viv) **RMT:** and he will support his hand upon the head of his donation and he will slay him at the opening of the appointed tent, and the sons of Aharon, the administrators, will sprinkle the blood upon the altar all around,

3:3 and~he~did~make~COME.NEAR^(V) (וְהִקְרִיב wê'hiq'riv) <u>from~</u> SACRIFICE (מִזֶּבַח mi'ze'vahh) the~OFFERING.OF.RESTITUTION~s (הַשְּׁלָמִים ha'she'la'mim) <u>FIRE.OFFERING</u> (אִשֶּׁה i'sheh) to~**YHWH** (לַיהוָה la'YHWH) <u>AT</u> (אֶת et) the~FAT (הַחֵלֶב ha'hhey'lev) the~ much~COVER.OVER^(V)~ing^(ms) (הַמְכַסֶּה ham'kha'seh) <u>AT</u> (אֶת et) the~ INSIDE (הַקֶּרֶב ha'qe'rev) and~AT (וְאֵת wê'eyt) <u>ALL</u> (כָּל kol) the~FAT (הַחֵלֶב ha'hhey'lev) <u>WHICH</u> (אֲשֶׁר a'sher) <u>UPON</u> (עַל al) the~INSIDE (הַקֶּרֶב ha'qe'rev) **RMT:** and he will bring near, from the sacrifice of the offerings of restitution, a fire offering for **YHWH**, the fat covering, the inside and all the fat which is upon the inside,

3:4 and~AT (וְאֵת wê'eyt) <u>TWO</u> (שְׁתֵּי shê'tey) the~KIDNEY~s (הַכְּלָיֹת hak'la'yot) and~AT (וְאֵת wê'et) the~FAT (הַחֵלֶב ha'hhey'lev) <u>WHICH</u> (אֲשֶׁר a'sher) UPON~them^(f) (עֲלֵהֶן a'ley'hen) <u>WHICH</u> (אֲשֶׁר a'sher) <u>UPON</u> (עַל al) the~HIP~s (הַכְּסָלִים hak'sa'lim) and~AT (וְאֵת wê'et) the~LOBE (הַיֹּתֶרֶת hai'yo'te'ret) <u>UPON</u> (עַל al) the~HEAVY (הַכָּבֵד ha'ka'veyd) <u>UPON</u> (עַל al) the~KIDNEY~s (הַכְּלָיוֹת hak'la'yot) he~ will~make~TURN.ASIDE^(V)~her (יְסִירֶנָּה yê'si're'nah) **RMT:** and the two kidneys and the fat, which is upon them, which is upon the hips, and the lobe upon the heavy one[8] with the kidneys he will remove,

3:5 and~they~did~make~BURN.INCENSE^(V) (וְהִקְטִירוּ wê'hiq'ti'ru) AT~him (אֹתוֹ o'to) SON~s (בְנֵי vê'ney) Aharon (אַהֲרֹן a'ha'ron) the~ ALTAR~unto (הַמִּזְבֵּחָה ha'miz'bey'hhah) <u>UPON</u> (עַל al) the~ ASCENSION.OFFERING (הָעֹלָה ha'o'lah) <u>WHICH</u> (אֲשֶׁר a'sher) <u>UPON</u> (עַל al) the~TREE~s (הָעֵצִים ha'eytsim) <u>WHICH</u> (אֲשֶׁר a'sher) <u>UPON</u> (עַל al) the~FIRE (הָאֵשׁ ha'eysh) <u>FIRE.OFFERING</u> (אִשֵּׁה i'sheyh) AROMA (רֵיחַ rey'ahh) <u>SWEET</u> (נִיחֹחַ ni'hho'ahh) to~**YHWH** (לַיהוָה la'YHWH)

---

[8] "The heavy one" is the "liver," the heaviest organ of the body.

la'YHWH) **RMT:** and the sons of Aharon will burn him as incense upon the altar upon the ascension offering, which is upon the wood, which is upon the fire, a fire offering, a sweet aroma to **YHWH,**

3:6 and~IF (וְאִם *wê'im*) FROM (מִן *min*) the~FLOCKS (הַצֹּאן *ha'tson*) DONATION~him (קָרְבָּנוֹ *qar'ba'no*) to~SACRIFICE (לְזֶבַח *lê'ze'vahh*) OFFERING.OF.RESTITUTION~s (שְׁלָמִים *shê'la'mim*) to~YHWH (לַיהוָה *la'YHWH*) MALE (זָכָר *za'khar*) OR (אוֹ *o*) FEMALE (נְקֵבָה *nê'qey'vah*) WHOLE (תָּמִים *ta'mim*) he~will~make~COME.NEAR[(V)]~him (יַקְרִיבֶנּוּ *yaq'riy've'nu*) **RMT:** and if his donation is from the flocks for a sacrifice of offerings of restitution to **YHWH,** it will be a whole male or female, he will bring him near.

3:7 IF (אִם *im*) SHEEP (כֶּשֶׂב *ke'sev*) HE (הוּא *hu*) make~ COME.NEAR[(V)]~ing[(ms)] (מַקְרִיב *maq'riv*) AT (אֶת *et*) DONATION~him (קָרְבָּנוֹ *qar'ba'no*) and~he~did~make~COME.NEAR[(V)] (וְהִקְרִיב *wê'hiq'riv*) AT~him (אֹתוֹ *o'to*) to~FACE~s (לִפְנֵי *liph'ney*) **YHWH** (יְהוָה *YHWH*) **RMT:** If he is bringing near a sheep for his donation, he will bring him near to the face of **YHWH,**

3:8 and~he~did~SUPPORT[·(V)] (וְסָמַךְ *wê'sa'makh*) AT (אֶת *et*) HAND~ him (יָדוֹ *ya'do*) UPON (עַל *al*) HEAD (רֹאשׁ *rosh*) DONATION~him (קָרְבָּנוֹ *qar'ba'no*) and~he~did~SLAY[(V)] (וְשָׁחַט *wê'sha'hhat*) AT~him (אֹתוֹ *o'to*) to~FACE~s (לִפְנֵי *liph'ney*) TENT (אֹהֶל *o'hel*) APPOINTED (מוֹעֵד *mo'eyd*) and~they~did~SPRINKLE[(V)] (וְזָרְקוּ *wê'zar'qu*) SON~s (בְּנֵי *bê'ney*) Aharon (אַהֲרֹן *a'ha'ron*) AT (אֶת *et*) BLOOD~him (דָּמוֹ *da'mo*) UPON (עַל *al*) the~ALTAR (הַמִּזְבֵּחַ *ha'miz'bey'ahh*) ALL.AROUND (סָבִיב *sa'viv*) **RMT:** and he will support his hand upon the head of his donation, and he will slay him to the face of the appointed tent, and the sons of Aharon will sprinkle his blood upon the altar all around,

3:9 and~he~did~make~COME.NEAR[(V)] (וְהִקְרִיב *wê'hiq'riv*) from~ SACRIFICE (מִזֶּבַח *mi'ze'vahh*) the~OFFERING.OF.RESTITUTION~s (הַשְּׁלָמִים *ha'she'la'mim*) FIRE.OFFERING (אִשֶּׁה *i'sheh*) to~YHWH (לַיהוָה *la'YHWH*) FAT~him (חֶלְבּוֹ *hhel'bo*) the~RUMP (הָאַלְיָה *ha'al'yah*) WHOLE (תְמִימָה *tê'mi'mah*) to~ALONGSIDE (לְעֻמַּת *lê'u'mat*) the~SPINE (הֶעָצֶה *he'a'tseh*) he~will~make~TURN.ASIDE[(V)]~ her (יְסִירֶנָּה *yê'si're'nah*) and~AT (וְאֶת *wê'et*) the~FAT (הַחֵלֶב *ha'hhey'lev*) the~much~COVER.OVER[(V)]~ing[(ms)] (הַמְכַסֶּה *ham'kha'seh*) AT (אֶת *et*) the~INSIDE (הַקֶּרֶב *ha'qe'rev*) and~AT (וְאֵת *wê'eyt*) ALL (כָּל *kol*) the~FAT (הַחֵלֶב *ha'hhey'lev*) WHICH (אֲשֶׁר *a'sher*) UPON (עַל *al*) the~INSIDE (הַקֶּרֶב *ha'qe'rev*) **RMT:** and he will bring near, from the sacrifice of the offerings of restitution, a fire offering for **YHWH**, his fat, the rump, everything alongside the spine he will remove and the fat covering the inside and all the fat which is upon the inside,

3:10 and~AT (וְאֵת wê'eyt) TWO (שְׁתֵּי shê'tey) the~KIDNEY~s (הַכְּלָיֹת hak'la'yot) and~AT (וְאֵת wê'et) the~FAT (הַחֵלֶב ha'hhey'lev) WHICH (אֲשֶׁר a'sher) UPON~them[f] (עֲלֵהֶן a'ley'hen) WHICH (אֲשֶׁר a'sher) UPON (עַל al) the~HIP~s (הַכְּסָלִים hak'sa'lim) and~AT (וְאֵת wê'et) the~LOBE (הַיֹּתֶרֶת hai'yo'te'ret) UPON (עַל al) the~HEAVY (הַכָּבֵד ha'ka'veyd) UPON (עַל al) the~KIDNEY~s (הַכְּלָיֹת hak'la'yot) he~will~make~TURN.ASIDE[V]~her (יְסִירֶנָּה yê'si're'nah) **RMT:** and the two kidneys and the fat, which is upon them, which is upon the hips, and the lobe upon the heavy one[9] with the kidneys he will remove,

3:11 and~he~did~make~BURN.INCENSE[V]~him (וְהִקְטִירוֹ wê'hiq'ti'ro) the~ADMINISTRATOR (הַכֹּהֵן ha'ko'heyn) the~ALTAR~unto (הַמִּזְבֵּחָה ha'miz'bey'hhah) BREAD (לֶחֶם le'hhem) FIRE.OFFERING (אִשֶּׁה i'sheh) to~**YHWH** (לַיהוָה la'YHWH) **RMT:** and the administrator will burn him as incense upon the altar, it is a bread offering to **YHWH**,

3:12 and~IF (וְאִם wê'im) SHE-GOAT (עֵז eyz) DONATION~him (קָרְבָּנוֹ qar'ba'no) and~he~did~make~COME.NEAR[V]~him (וְהִקְרִיבוֹ wê'hiq'ri'vo) to~FACE~s (לִפְנֵי liph'ney) **YHWH** (יְהוָה YHWH) **RMT:** and if his donation is a she-goat, he will bring him near to the face of **YHWH**,

3:13 and~he~did~SUPPORT[V] (וְסָמַךְ wê'sa'makh) AT (אֶת et) HAND~him (יָדוֹ ya'do) UPON (עַל al) HEAD~him (רֹאשׁוֹ ro'sho) and~he~did~SLAY[V] (וְשָׁחַט wê'sha'hhat) AT~him (אֹתוֹ o'to) to~FACE~s (לִפְנֵי liph'ney) TENT (אֹהֶל o'hel) APPOINTED (מוֹעֵד mo'eyd) and~they~did~SPRINKLE[V] (וְזָרְקוּ wê'zar'qu) SON~s (בְּנֵי bê'ney) Aharon (אַהֲרֹן a'ha'ron) AT (אֶת et) BLOOD~him (דָּמוֹ da'mo) UPON (עַל al) the~ALTAR (הַמִּזְבֵּחַ ha'miz'bey'ahh) ALL.AROUND (סָבִיב sa'viv) **RMT:** and he will support his hand upon his head, and he will slay him to the face of the appointed tent, and the sons of Aharon will sprinkle his blood upon the altar all around,

3:14 and~he~did~make~COME.NEAR[V] (וְהִקְרִיב wê'hiq'riv) FROM~him (מִמֶּנּוּ mi'me'nu) DONATION~him (קָרְבָּנוֹ qar'ba'no)

---

[9] "The heavy one" is the "liver," the heaviest organ of the body.

FIRE.OFFERING (אִשֶּׁה i'sheh) to~**YHWH** (לַיהוָה la'YHWH) AT (אֶת et) the~FAT (הַחֵלֶב ha'hhey'lev) the~*much*~COVER.OVER(V)~ing(ms) (הַמְכַסֶּה ham'kha'seh) AT (אֶת et) the~INSIDE (הַקֶּרֶב ha'qe'rev) and~AT (וְאֵת we'eyt) ALL (כָּל kol) the~FAT (הַחֵלֶב ha'hhey'lev) WHICH (אֲשֶׁר a'sher) UPON (עַל al) the~INSIDE (הַקֶּרֶב ha'qe'rev) **RMT:** and he will bring near from him his donation, a fire offering to **YHWH**, the fat covering, the inside, and all the fat which is upon the inside,

3:15 and~AT (וְאֵת we'eyt) TWO (שְׁתֵּי shê'tey) the~KIDNEY~s (הַכְּלָיֹת hak'la'yot) and~AT (וְאֵת we'et) the~FAT (הַחֵלֶב ha'hhey'lev) WHICH (אֲשֶׁר a'sher) UPON~them(f) (עֲלֵהֶן a'ley'hen) WHICH (אֲשֶׁר a'sher) UPON (עַל al) the~HIP~s (הַכְּסָלִים hak'sa'lim) and~AT (וְאֵת we'et) the~LOBE (הַיֹּתֶרֶת hai'yo'te'ret) UPON (עַל al) the~HEAVY (הַכָּבֵד ha'ka'veyd) UPON (עַל al) the~KIDNEY~s (הַכְּלָיֹת hak'la'yot) he~will~make~TURN.ASIDE(V)~her (יְסִירֶנָּה yê'si're'nah) **RMT:** and the two kidneys and the fat which is upon them, which is upon the hips, and the lobe upon the heavy one[10] with the kidneys, he will remove,

3:16 and~*he~did~make*~BURN.INCENSE(V)~them(m) (וְהִקְטִירָם wê'hiq'ti'ram) the~ADMINISTRATOR (הַכֹּהֵן ha'ko'heyn) the~ALTAR~ unto (הַמִּזְבֵּחָה ha'miz'bey'hhah) BREAD (לֶחֶם le'hhem) FIRE.OFFERING (אִשֶּׁה i'sheh) to~AROMA (לְרֵיחַ lê'rey'ahh) SWEET (נִיחֹחַ ni'hho'ahh) ALL (כָּל kol) FAT (חֵלֶב hhey'lev) to~**YHWH** (לַיהוָה la'YHWH) **RMT:** and the administrator will burn them as incense upon the altar, it is a bread offering for a sweet aroma, all the fat is for **YHWH**.

3:17 CUSTOM (חֻקַּת hhu'qat) DISTANT (עוֹלָם o'lam) to~ GENERATION~s~you(mp) (לְדֹרֹתֵיכֶם lê'do'ro'tey'khem) in~ALL (בְּכֹל bê'khol) SETTLING~s~you(mp) (מוֹשְׁבֹתֵיכֶם mosh'vo'tey'khem) ALL (כָּל kol) FAT (חֵלֶב hhey'lev) and~ALL (וְכָל wê'khol) BLOOD (דָּם dam) NOT (לֹא lo) you(mp)~will~EAT(V) (תֹאכֵלוּ to'khey'lu) **RMT:** It is a distant custom for your generations in all your settlings, you will not eat any of the fat or any of the blood,

---

[10] Meaning the "liver," the heaviest organ in the body.

Chapter 4

4:1 and~he~will~much~SPEAK^(V) (וַיְדַבֵּר *wai'da'beyr*) **YHWH** (יְהוָה YHWH) <u>TO</u> (אֶל *el*) <u>Mosheh</u> (מֹשֶׁה *mo'sheh*) <u>to~>~SAY</u>^(V) (לֵאמֹר *ley'mor*) **RMT:** and **YHWH** spoke to Mosheh saying,

4:2 *!^(ms)~much~SPEAK*^(V) (דַּבֵּר *da'beyr*) <u>TO</u> (אֶל *el*) <u>SON~s</u> (בְּנֵי *bê'ney*) <u>Yisra'eyl</u> (יִשְׂרָאֵל *yis'ra'eyl*) <u>to~>~SAY</u>^(V) (לֵאמֹר *ley'mor*) <u>SOUL</u> (נֶפֶשׁ *ne'phesh*) <u>GIVEN.THAT</u> (כִּי *ki*) *she~will~FAIL*^(V) (תֶחֱטָא *te'hhe'ta*) <u>in~</u> <u>ERROR</u> (בִשְׁגָגָה *vish'ga'gah*) <u>from~ALL</u> (מִכֹּל *mi'kol*) <u>DIRECTIVE~s</u> (מִצְוֹת *mits'ot*) **YHWH** (יְהוָה YHWH) <u>WHICH</u> (אֲשֶׁר *a'sher*) <u>NOT</u> (לֹא *lo*) *they^(f)~will~be~DO*^(V) (תֵעָשֶׂינָה *tey'a'sey'nah*) and~he~did~DO^(V) (וְעָשָׂה *wê'a'sah*) <u>from~UNIT</u> (מֵאַחַת *mey'a'hhat*) <u>from~THEY</u>^(f) (מֵהֵנָּה *mey'hey'nah*) **RMT:** speak to the sons of Yisra'eyl saying, a soul that will fail with an error from any of the directives of **YHWH**, which were not done, and he will do from one of them.

4:3 <u>IF</u> (אִם *im*) the~ADMINISTRATOR (הַכֹּהֵן *ha'ko'heyn*) the~ SMEARED (הַמָּשִׁיחַ *ha'ma'shi'ahh*) he~will~FAIL^(V) (יֶחֱטָא *ye'hhe'ta*) to~GUILTINESS (לְאַשְׁמַת *lê'ash'mat*) the~PEOPLE (הָעָם *ha'am*) and~ he~did~make~COME.NEAR^(V) (וְהִקְרִיב *wê'hiq'riv*) <u>UPON</u> (עַל *al*) <u>FAILURE~him</u> (חַטָּאתוֹ *hha'ta'to*) <u>WHICH</u> (אֲשֶׁר *a'sher*) he~did~FAIL^(V) (חָטָא *hha'ta*) <u>BULL</u> (פַּר *par*) <u>SON</u> (בֶּן *ben*) <u>CATTLE</u> (בָּקָר *ba'qar*) <u>WHOLE</u> (תָּמִים *ta'mim*) <u>to~YHWH</u> (לַיהוָה *la'YHWH*) <u>to~FAILURE</u> (לְחַטָּאת *lê'hha'tat*) **RMT:** If the smeared administrator will fail, it will be guiltiness of the people, and he will bring near, for his failure because he failed, a bull son, a whole cattle to **YHWH** for the failure,

4:4 and~he~did~make~COME^(V) (וְהֵבִיא *wê'hey'vi*) <u>AT</u> (אֶת *et*) the~ BULL (הַפָּר *ha'par*) <u>TO</u> (אֶל *el*) <u>OPENING</u> (פֶּתַח *pe'tahh*) <u>TENT</u> (אֹהֶל *o'hel*) <u>APPOINTED</u> (מוֹעֵד *mo'eyd*) to~FACE~s (לִפְנֵי *liph'ney*) **YHWH** (יְהוָה YHWH) and~he~did~SUPPORT^(V) (וְסָמַךְ *wê'sa'makh*) <u>AT</u> (אֶת *et*) <u>HAND~him</u> (יָדוֹ *ya'do*) <u>UPON</u> (עַל *al*) <u>HEAD</u> (רֹאשׁ *rosh*) the~BULL (הַפָּר *ha'par*) and~he~did~SLAY^(V) (וְשָׁחַט *wê'sha'hhat*) <u>AT</u> (אֶת *et*) the~BULL (הַפָּר *ha'par*) to~FACE~s (לִפְנֵי *liph'ney*) **YHWH** (יְהוָה YHWH) **RMT:** and he will bring the bull to the opening of the appointed tent, to the face of **YHWH**, and he will support his hand upon the head of the bull, and he will slay the bull to the face of **YHWH**,

4:5 and~he~did~TAKE^(V) (וְלָקַח *wê'la'qahh*) the~ADMINISTRATOR (הַכֹּהֵן *ha'ko'heyn*) the~SMEARED (הַמָּשִׁיחַ *ha'ma'shi'ahh*) <u>from~</u> <u>BLOOD</u> (מִדַּם *mi'dam*) the~BULL (הַפָּר *ha'par*) and~he~did~make~

COME^(V) (וְהֵבִיא *wê'hey'vi*) AT~him (אֹתוֹ *o'to*) TO (אֶל *el*) TENT (אֹהֶל *o'hel*) APPOINTED (מוֹעֵד *mo'eyd*) **RMT:** and the smeared administrator will take from the blood of the bull and he will bring him to the appointed tent,

4:6 and~he~did~DIP^(V) (יְטָבַל *wê'ta'val*) the~ADMINISTRATOR (הַכֹּהֵן *ha'ko'heyn*) AT (אֶת *et*) FINGER~him (אֶצְבָּעוֹ *ets'ba'o*) in~the~BLOOD (בַּדָּם *ba'dam*) and~he~did~make~SPATTER^(V) (וְהִזָּה *wê'hi'zah*) FROM (מִן *min*) the~BLOOD (הַדָּם *ha'dam*) SEVEN (שֶׁבַע *she'va*) FOOTSTEP~s (פְּעָמִים *pê'a'mim*) to~FACE~s (לִפְנֵי *liph'ney*) **YHWH** (יְהוָה *YHWH*) AT (אֶת *et*) FACE~s (פְּנֵי *pê'ney*) TENT.CURTAIN (פָּרֹכֶת *pa'ro'khet*) the~SPECIAL (הַקֹּדֶשׁ *ha'qo'desh*) **RMT:** and the administrator will dip his finger in the blood and he will spatter from the blood seven times to the face of **YHWH**, at the face of the special tent curtain,

4:7 and~he~did~GIVE^(V) (וְנָתַן *wê'na'tan*) the~ADMINISTRATOR (הַכֹּהֵן *ha'ko'heyn*) FROM (מִן *min*) the~BLOOD (הַדָּם *ha'dam*) UPON (עַל *al*) HORN~s (קַרְנוֹת *qər'not*) ALTAR (מִזְבַּח *miz'bahh*) INCENSE.SMOKE (קְטֹרֶת *qê'to'ret*) the~AROMATIC.SPICE~s (הַסַּמִּים *ha'sa'mim*) to~FACE~s (לִפְנֵי *liph'ney*) **YHWH** (יְהוָה *YHWH*) WHICH (אֲשֶׁר *a'sher*) in~TENT (בְּאֹהֶל *bê'o'hel*) APPOINTED (מוֹעֵד *mo'eyd*) and~AT (וְאֵת *wê'eyt*) ALL (כָּל *kol*) BLOOD (דַּם *dam*) the~BULL (הַפָּר *ha'par*) he~will~POUR.OUT^(V) (יִשְׁפֹּךְ *yish'pokh*) TO (אֶל *el*) BOTTOM.BASE (יְסוֹד *yê'sod*) ALTAR (מִזְבַּח *miz'bahh*) the~ ASCENSION.OFFERING (הָעֹלָה *ha'o'lah*) WHICH (אֲשֶׁר *a'sher*) OPENING (פֶּתַח *pe'tahh*) TENT (אֹהֶל *o'hel*) APPOINTED (מוֹעֵד *mo'eyd*) **RMT:** and the administrator will place from the blood upon the horns of the altar of incense smoke of the aromatic spices to the face of **YHWH**, which is in the appointed tent, and he will pour out all the blood of the bull to the bottom base of the altar of the ascension offering, which is at the opening of the appointed tent,

4:8 and~AT (וְאֶת *wê'et*) ALL (כָּל *kol*) FAT (חֵלֶב *hhey'lev*) BULL (פַּר *par*) the~FAILURE (הַחַטָּאת *ha'hha'tat*) he~will~make~RAISE.UP^(V) (יָרִים *ya'rim*) FROM~him (מִמֶּנּוּ *mi'me'nu*) AT (אֶת *et*) the~FAT (הַחֵלֶב *ha'hhey'lev*) the~much~COVER.OVER^(V)~ing^(ms) (הַמְכַסֶּה *ham'kha'seh*) UPON (עַל *al*) the~INSIDE (הַקֶּרֶב *ha'qe'rev*) and~AT (וְאֵת *wê'eyt*) ALL (כָּל *kol*) the~FAT (הַחֵלֶב *ha'hhey'lev*) WHICH (אֲשֶׁר *a'sher*) UPON (עַל *al*) the~INSIDE (הַקֶּרֶב *ha'qe'rev*) **RMT:** and he will raise up all the fat of the bull of the failure, the fat of the covering upon the insides and all the fat which is upon the insides,

15

4:9 <u>and~AT</u> (וְאֵת *wê'eyt*) <u>TWO</u> (שְׁתֵּי *shê'tey*) <u>the~KIDNEY~s</u> (הַכְּלָיֹת *hak'la'yot*) <u>and~AT</u> (וְאֵת *wê'et*) <u>the~FAT</u> (הַחֵלֶב *ha'hhey'lev*) <u>WHICH</u> (אֲשֶׁר *a'sher*) <u>UPON~them</u>[f] (עֲלֵיהֶן *a'ley'hen*) <u>WHICH</u> (אֲשֶׁר *a'sher*) <u>UPON</u> (עַל *al*) <u>the~HIP~s</u> (הַכְּסָלִים *hak'sa'lim*) <u>and~AT</u> (וְאֵת *wê'et*) <u>the~LOBE</u> (הַיֹּתֶרֶת *hai'yo'te'ret*) <u>UPON</u> (עַל *al*) <u>the~HEAVY</u> (הַכָּבֵד *ha'ka'veyd*) <u>UPON</u> (עַל *al*) <u>the~KIDNEY~s</u> (הַכְּלָיוֹת *hak'la'yot*) <u>he~will~make~TURN.ASIDE</u>[V]<u>~her</u> (יְסִירֶנָּה *yê'si're'nah*) **RMT:** and the two kidneys and the fat, which is upon them, which is upon the hips, and the lobe upon the heavy one[11] with the kidneys he will remove.

4:10 <u>like~WHICH</u> (כַּאֲשֶׁר *ka'a'sheyr*) <u>they</u>[m]<u>~will~make~RAISE.UP</u>[V] (יוּרַם *yu'ram*) <u>from~OX</u> (מִשּׁוֹר *mi'shor*) <u>SACRIFICE</u> (זֶבַח *ze'vahh*) <u>the~OFFERING.OF.RESTITUTION~s</u> (הַשְּׁלָמִים *ha'she'la'mim*) <u>and~he~did~make~BURN.INCENSE</u>[V]<u>~them</u>[m] (וְהִקְטִירָם *wê'hiq'ti'ram*) <u>the~ADMINISTRATOR</u> (הַכֹּהֵן *ha'ko'heyn*) <u>UPON</u> (עַל *al*) <u>ALTAR</u> (מִזְבַּח *miz'bahh*) <u>the~ASCENSION.OFFERING</u> (הָעֹלָה *ha'o'lah*) **RMT:** Just as they were raised up from the ox of the sacrifice of the offerings of restitution, and the administrator will burn them as incense upon the altar of the ascension offering,

4:11 <u>and~AT</u> (וְאֵת *wê'et*) <u>SKIN</u> (עוֹר *or*) <u>the~BULL</u> (הַפָּר *ha'par*) <u>and~AT</u> (וְאֵת *wê'et*) <u>ALL</u> (כָּל *kol*) <u>FLESH~him</u> (בְּשָׂרוֹ *bê'sar'o*) <u>UPON</u> (עַל *al*) <u>HEAD~him</u> (רֹאשׁוֹ *ro'sho*) <u>and~UPON</u> (וְעַל *wê'al*) <u>LEG~s~him</u> (כְּרָעָיו *kê'ra'aw*) <u>and~INSIDE~him</u> (וְקִרְבּוֹ *wê'qir'bo*) <u>and~DUNG~him</u> (וּפִרְשׁוֹ *u'phir'sho*) **RMT:** and the skin of the bull and all his flesh upon his head and upon his legs and his inside and his dung,

4:12 <u>and~he~did~make~GO.OUT</u>[V] (וְהוֹצִיא *wê'ho'tsi*) <u>AT</u> (אֵת *et*) <u>ALL</u> (כָּל *kol*) <u>the~BULL</u> (הַפָּר *ha'par*) <u>TO</u> (אֶל *el*) <u>from~OUTSIDE</u> (מִחוּץ *mi'hhuts*) <u>to~the~CAMP</u> (לַמַּחֲנֶה *la'ma'hha'neh*) <u>TO</u> (אֶל *el*) <u>AREA</u> (מָקוֹם *ma'qom*) <u>CLEAN</u> (טָהוֹר *ta'hor*) <u>TO</u> (אֶל *el*) <u>POUR.OUT</u>[V]<u>~ing</u>[ms] (שֶׁפֶךְ *she'phekh*) <u>the~FATNESS</u> (הַדֶּשֶׁן *ha'de'shen*) <u>and~he~did~CREMATE</u>[V] (וְשָׂרַף *wê'sa'raph*) <u>AT~him</u> (אֹתוֹ *o'to*) <u>UPON</u> (עַל *al*) <u>TREE~s</u> (עֵצִים *ey'tsim*) <u>in~the~FIRE</u> (בָּאֵשׁ *ba'eysh*) <u>UPON</u> (עַל *al*) <u>POUR.OUT</u>[V]<u>~ing</u>[ms] (שֶׁפֶךְ *she'phekh*) <u>the~FATNESS</u> (הַדֶּשֶׁן *ha'de'shen*) <u>he~will~be~CREMATE</u>[V] (יִשָּׂרֵף *yi'sa'reyph*) **RMT:** and he will bring out all of the bull to the outside of the camp, to the clean area for pouring out the fatness, and he will cremate him upon the wood with the fire, upon the pouring out of the fatness he will be cremated,

---

[11] The "liver," which is the heaviest organ in the body.

4:13 <u>and~IF</u> (וְאִם wê'im) <u>ALL</u> (כָּל kol) <u>COMPANY</u> (עֲדַת a'dat) <u>Yisra'eyl</u> (יִשְׂרָאֵל yis'ra'eyl) _they(m)~will~GO.ASTRAY_(V) (יִשְׁגּוּ yish'gu) _and~he~did~be~BE.OUT.OF.SIGHT_(V) (וְנֶעְלַם wê'ne'lam) <u>WORD</u> (דָּבָר da'var) <u>from~EYE~s2</u> (מֵעֵינֵי mey'ey'ney) <u>the~ASSEMBLY</u> (הַקָּהָל ha'qa'hal) _and~they~did~DO_(V) (וְעָשׂוּ wê'a'su) <u>UNIT</u> (אַחַת a'hhat) <u>from~ALL</u> (מִכָּל mi'kol) <u>DIRECTIVE~s</u> (מִצְוֹת mits'ot) **YHWH** (יְהוָה YHWH) <u>WHICH</u> (אֲשֶׁר a'sher) <u>NOT</u> (לֹא lo) _they(f)~will~be~DO_(V) (תֵעָשֶׂינָה tey'a'sey'nah)[12] _and~they~did~BE.GUILTY_(V) (וְאָשֵׁמוּ wê'a'shey'mu) **RMT:** and if all the company of Yisra'eyl will go astray, and a word[13] was out of sight from the eyes of the assembly, and they did anyone of the directives of **YHWH**, which was not to be done, then they will be guilty,

4:14 _and~she~did~be~KNOW_(V) (וְנוֹדְעָה wê'nod'ah) <u>the~FAILURE</u> (הַחַטָּאת ha'hha'tat) <u>WHICH</u> (אֲשֶׁר a'sher) _they~did~FAIL_(V) (חָטְאוּ hhat'u) <u>UPON~her</u> (עָלֶיהָ a'ley'ah) _and~they~did~make~COME.NEAR_(V) (וְהִקְרִיבוּ wê'hiq'ri'vu) <u>the~ASSEMBLY</u> (הַקָּהָל ha'qa'hal) <u>BULL</u> (פַּר par) <u>SON</u> (בֶּן ben) <u>CATTLE</u> (בָּקָר ba'qar) <u>to~FAILURE</u> (לְחַטָּאת lê'hha'tat) _and~they~did~make~COME_(V) (וְהֵבִיאוּ wê'hey'vi'u) <u>AT~him</u> (אֹתוֹ o'to) <u>to~FACE~s</u> (לִפְנֵי liph'ney) <u>TENT</u> (אֹהֶל o'hel) <u>APPOINTED</u> (מוֹעֵד mo'eyd) **RMT:** and the failure, which they failed, will be known upon her, and the assembly will bring near a son of a bull of the cattle for the failure, and they will bring him to the face of the appointed tent,

4:15 _and~they~did~SUPPORT_(V) (וְסָמְכוּ wê'sam'khu) <u>BEARD~s</u> (זִקְנֵי ziq'ney) <u>the~COMPANY</u> (הָעֵדָה ha'ey'dah) <u>AT</u> (אֶת et) <u>HAND~s2~them(m)</u> (יְדֵיהֶם yê'dey'hem) <u>UPON</u> (עַל al) <u>HEAD</u> (רֹאשׁ rosh) <u>the~BULL</u> (הַפָּר ha'par) <u>to~FACE~s</u> (לִפְנֵי liph'ney) **YHWH** (יְהוָה YHWH) _and~he~did~SLAY_(V) (וְשָׁחַט wê'sha'hhat) <u>AT</u> (אֶת et) <u>the~BULL</u> (הַפָּר ha'par) <u>to~FACE~s</u> (לִפְנֵי liph'ney) **YHWH** (יְהוָה YHWH) **RMT:** and the bearded ones will support the company with their hands upon the head of the bull to the face of **YHWH**, and they will slay the bull to the face of **YHWH**,

4:16 _and~he~did~make~COME_(V) (וְהֵבִיא wê'hey'vi) <u>the~ADMINISTRATOR</u> (הַכֹּהֵן ha'ko'heyn) <u>the~SMEARED</u> (הַמָּשִׁיחַ ha'ma'shi'ahh) <u>from~BLOOD</u> (מִדַּם mi'dam) <u>the~BULL</u> (הַפָּר ha'par)

---

[12] The "they," identified as feminine plural, is referring to the directives, a feminine plural noun (compare with verse 22).

[13] This Hebrew word may also mean "matter."

TO (אֶל el) TENT (אֹהֶל o'hel) APPOINTED (מוֹעֵד mo'eyd) **RMT:** and the smeared administrator will bring the blood from the bull to the appointed tent,

4:17 and~he~did~DIP^(V) (וְטָבַל wê'ta'val) the~ADMINISTRATOR (הַכֹּהֵן ha'ko'heyn) FINGER~him (אֶצְבָּעוֹ ets'ba'o) FROM (מִן min) the~BLOOD (הַדָּם ha'dam) and~he~did~make~SPATTER^(V) (וְהִזָּה wê'hi'zah) SEVEN (שֶׁבַע she'va) FOOTSTEP~s (פְּעָמִים pê'a'mim) to~ FACE~s (לִפְנֵי liph'ney) YHWH (יְהֹוָה YHWH) AT (אֵת eyt) FACE~s (פְּנֵי pê'ney) the~TENT.CURTAIN (הַפָּרֹכֶת ha'pa'ro'khet) **RMT:** and the administrator will dip his finger in the blood and he will spatter it seven times to the face of **YHWH**, at the face of the tent curtain,

4:18 and~FROM (וּמִן u'min) the~BLOOD (הַדָּם ha'dam) he~will~ GIVE^(V) (יִתֵּן yi'teyn) UPON (עַל al) HORN~s (קַרְנֹת qar'not) the~ ALTAR (הַמִּזְבֵּחַ ha'miz'bey'ahh) WHICH (אֲשֶׁר a'sher) to~FACE~s (לִפְנֵי liph'ney) YHWH (יְהֹוָה YHWH) WHICH (אֲשֶׁר a'sher) in~TENT (בְּאֹהֶל bê'o'hel) APPOINTED (מוֹעֵד mo'eyd) and~AT (וְאֵת wê'eyt) ALL (כָּל kol) the~BLOOD (הַדָּם ha'dam) he~will~POUR.OUT^(V) (יִשְׁפֹּךְ yish'pokh) TO (אֶל el) BOTTOM.BASE (יְסוֹד yê'sod) ALTAR (מִזְבַּח miz'bahh) the~ASCENSION.OFFERING (הָעֹלָה ha'o'lah) WHICH (אֲשֶׁר a'sher) OPENING (פֶּתַח pe'tahh) TENT (אֹהֶל o'hel) APPOINTED (מוֹעֵד mo'eyd) **RMT:** and from the blood, he will place it upon the horns of the altar, which is to the face of **YHWH**, which is in the appointed tent, and he will pour out all the blood to the bottom base of the altar of the ascension offering, which is at the opening of the appointed tent,

4:19 and~AT (וְאֵת wê'eyt) ALL (כָּל kol) FAT~him (חֶלְבּוֹ hhel'bo) he~ will~make~RAISE.UP^(V) (יָרִים ya'rim) FROM~him (מִמֶּנּוּ mi'me'nu) and~he~did~make~BURN.INCENSE^(V) (וְהִקְטִיר wê'hiq'tir) the~ ALTAR~unto (הַמִּזְבֵּחָה ha'miz'bey'hhah) **RMT:** and he will raise up all his fat from him, and he will burn it as incense upon the altar,

4:20 and~he~did~DO^(V) (וְעָשָׂה wê'a'sah) to~the~BULL (לַפָּר la'par) like~WHICH (כַּאֲשֶׁר ka'a'sheyr) he~did~DO^(V) (עָשָׂה a'sah) to~BULL (לְפַר lê'phar) the~FAILURE (הַחַטָּאת ha'hha'tat) SO (כֵּן keyn) he~ will~DO^(V) (יַעֲשֶׂה ya'a'seh) to~him (לֹו lo) and~he~did~much~ COVER^(V) (וְכִפֶּר wê'khi'per) UPON~them^(m) (עֲלֵהֶם a'ley'hem) the~ ADMINISTRATOR (הַכֹּהֵן ha'ko'heyn) and~he~did~be~FORGIVE^(V) (וְנִסְלַח wê'nis'lahh) to~them^(m) (לָהֶם la'hem) **RMT:** and he will do to the bull just as he did to the bull of the failure, so he will do to him, and the administrator will make a covering upon them and he will be forgiven for them,

4:21 and~*he~did~make*~GO.OUT[V] (וְהוֹצִיא *wê'ho'tsi*) AT (אֶת *et*) the~BULL (הַפָּר *ha'par*) TO (אֶל *el*) from~OUTSIDE (מִחוּץ *mi'hhuts*) to~the~CAMP (לַמַּחֲנֶה *la'ma'hha'neh*) and~*he~did~*CREMATE[V] (וְשָׂרַף *wê'sa'raph*) AT~him (אֹתוֹ *o'to*) like~WHICH (כַּאֲשֶׁר *ka'a'sheyr*) *he~did~*CREMATE[V] (שָׂרַף *sa'raph*) AT (אֵת *eyt*) the~BULL (הַפָּר *ha'par*) the~FIRST (הָרִאשׁוֹן *ha'ri'shon*) FAILURE (חַטַּאת *hha'tat*) the~ASSEMBLY (הַקָּהָל *ha'qa'hal*) HE (הוּא *hu*) **RMT:** and he will bring out the bull to the outside of the camp, and he will cremate him just as he cremated the first bull, he is the failure of the assembly.

4:22 WHICH (אֲשֶׁר *a'sher*) CAPTAIN (נָשִׂיא *na'si*) *he~will~*FAIL[V] (יֶחֱטָא *ye'hhe'ta*) and~*he~did~*DO[V] (וְעָשָׂה *wê'a'sah*) UNIT (אַחַת *a'hhat*) from~ALL (מִכֹּל *mi'kol*) DIRECTIVE~s (מִצְוֹת *mits'ot*) **YHWH** (יְהוָה *YHWH*) Elohiym~him (אֱלֹהָיו *e'lo'haw*) WHICH (אֲשֶׁר *a'sher*) NOT (לֹא *lo*) *they(f)~will~be~*DO[V] (תֵעָשֶׂינָה *tey'a'sey'nah*) in~ERROR (בִּשְׁגָגָה *bish'ga'gah*) and~*he~did~*BE.GUILTY[V] (וְאָשֵׁם *wê'a'sheym*) **RMT:** When a captain fails, and he does one of any of the directives of **YHWH** his Elohiym, which was not to be done in error, then he is guilty.

4:23 OR (אוֹ *o*) *he~did~be~make~*KNOW[V] (הוֹדַע *ho'da*) TO~him (אֵלָיו *ey'law*) FAILURE~him (חַטָּאתוֹ *hha'ta'to*) WHICH (אֲשֶׁר *a'sher*) *he~did~*FAIL[V] (חָטָא *hha'ta*) in~her (בָּהּ *bah*) and~*he~did~make~*COME[V] (וְהֵבִיא *wê'hey'vi*) AT (אֶת *et*) DONATION~him (קָרְבָּנוֹ *qar'ba'no*) HAIRY.GOAT (שְׂעִיר *sê'ir*) SHE-GOAT~s (עִזִּים *i'zim*) MALE (זָכָר *za'khar*) WHOLE (תָּמִים *ta'mim*) **RMT:** Or if his failure, which he failed in her, is made known to him, then he will bring his donation, a hairy goat of the she-goats, a whole male,

4:24 and~*he~did~*SUPPORT[V] (וְסָמַךְ *wê'sa'makh*) HAND~him (יָדוֹ *ya'do*) UPON (עַל *al*) HEAD (רֹאשׁ *rosh*) the~HAIRY.GOAT (הַשָּׂעִיר *ha'sa'ir*) and~*he~did~*SLAY[V] (וְשָׁחַט *wê'sha'hhat*) AT~him (אֹתוֹ *o'to*) in~AREA (בִּמְקוֹם *bim qom*) WHICH (אֲשֶׁר *a'sher*) *he~will~*SLAY[V] (יִשְׁחַט *yish'hhat*) AT (אֶת *et*) the~ASCENSION.OFFERING (הָעֹלָה *ha'o'lah*) to~FACE~s (לִפְנֵי *liph'ney*) **YHWH** (יְהוָה *YHWH*) FAILURE (חַטָּאת *hha'tat*) HE (הוּא *hu*) **RMT:** and he will support his hand upon the head of the hairy goat, and he will slay him in the area which he slays the ascension offering, to the face of **YHWH**, he is the failure,

19

4:25 <u>and~he~did~TAKE</u>^(V) (וְלָקַח *wê'la'qahh*) <u>the~ADMINISTRATOR</u> (הַכֹּהֵן *ha'ko'heyn*) <u>from~BLOOD</u> (מִדַּם *mi'dam*) <u>the~FAILURE</u> (הַחַטָּאת *ha'hha'tat*) <u>in~FINGER~him</u> (בְּאֶצְבָּעוֹ *bê'ets'ba'o*) <u>and~he~ did~GIVE</u>^(V) (וְנָתַן *wê'na'tan*) <u>UPON</u> (עַל *al*) <u>HORN~s</u> (קַרְנֹת *qar'not*) <u>ALTAR</u> (מִזְבַּח *miz'bahh*) <u>the~ASCENSION.OFFERING</u> (הָעֹלָה *ha'o'lah*) <u>and~AT</u> (וְאֶת *wê'et*) <u>BLOOD~him</u> (דָּמוֹ *da'mo*) <u>he~will~POUR.OUT</u>^(V) (יִשְׁפֹּךְ *yish'pokh*) <u>TO</u> (אֶל *el*) <u>BOTTOM.BASE</u> (יְסוֹד *yê'sod*) <u>ALTAR</u> (מִזְבַּח *miz'bahh*) <u>the~ASCENSION.OFFERING</u> (הָעֹלָה *ha'o'lah*)
RMT: and the administrator will take from the blood of the failure with his finger, and he will place it upon the horns of the altar of the ascension offering, and he will pour out his blood to the bottom base of the altar of the ascension offering,

4:26 <u>and~AT</u> (וְאֶת *wê'et*) <u>ALL</u> (כָּל *kol*) <u>FAT~him</u> (חֶלְבּוֹ *hhel'bo*) *he~ did~make~BURN.INCENSE*^(V) (יַקְטִיר *yaq'tir*) <u>the~ALTAR~unto</u> (הַמִּזְבֵּחָה *ha'miz'bey'hhah*) <u>like~FAT</u> (כְּחֵלֶב *kê'hhey'lev*) <u>SACRIFICE</u> (זֶבַח *ze'vahh*) <u>the~OFFERING.OF.RESTITUTION~s</u> (הַשְּׁלָמִים *ha'she'la'mim*) <u>and~he~did~much~COVER</u>^(V) (וְכִפֶּר *wê'khi'per*) <u>UPON~him</u> (עָלָיו *a'law*) <u>the~ADMINISTRATOR</u> (הַכֹּהֵן *ha'ko'heyn*) <u>from~FAILURE~him</u> (מֵחַטָּאתוֹ *mey'hha'ta'to*) *and~he~did~be~ FORGIVE*^(V) (וְנִסְלַח *wê'nis'lahh*) <u>to~him</u> (לוֹ *lo*) **RMT:** and he will burn all his fat as incense upon the altar, like the fat of the sacrifice of the offerings of restitution, and the administrator will make a covering upon him because of his failure, and he will be forgiven for him,

4:27 <u>and~IF</u> (וְאִם *wê'im*) <u>SOUL</u> (נֶפֶשׁ *ne'phesh*) <u>UNIT</u> (אַחַת *a'hhat*) *she~will~FAIL*^(V) (תֶּחֱטָא *te'hhe'ta*) <u>in~ERROR</u> (בִשְׁגָגָה *vish'ga'gah*) <u>from~PEOPLE</u> (מֵעַם *mey'am*) <u>the~LAND</u> (הָאָרֶץ *ha'a'rets*) <u>in~></u> *DO*^(V)~her (בַּעֲשֹׂתָהּ *ba'a'so'tah*) <u>UNIT</u> (אַחַת *a'hhat*) <u>from~ DIRECTIVE~s</u> (מִמִּצְוֹת *mi'mits'wot*) **YHWH** (יְהוָה *YHWH*) <u>WHICH</u> (אֲשֶׁר *a'sher*) <u>NOT</u> (לֹא *lo*) *they^(f)~will~be~DO*^(V) (תֵעָשֶׂינָה *tey'a'sey'nah*) <u>and~he~did~BE.GUILTY</u>^(V) (וְאָשֵׁם *wê'a'sheym*)
RMT: and if one soul from the people of the land will fail with an error, by doing one of the directives of **YHWH** which was not to be done, then he will be guilty.

4:28 <u>OR</u> (אוֹ *o*) *he~did~be~make~KNOW*^(V) (הוֹדַע *ho'da*) <u>TO~him</u> (אֵלָיו *ey'law*) <u>FAILURE~him</u> (חַטָּאתוֹ *hha'ta'to*) <u>WHICH</u> (אֲשֶׁר *a'sher*) *he~did~FAIL*^(V) (חָטָא *hha'ta*) *and~he~did~make~COME*^(V) (וְהֵבִיא *wê'hey'vi*) <u>DONATION~him</u> (קָרְבָּנוֹ *qar'ba'no*) <u>HAIRY.GOAT</u> (שְׂעִירַת *sê'i'rat*) <u>SHE-GOAT~s</u> (עִזִּים *i'zim*) <u>WHOLE</u> (תְּמִימָה *tê'mi'mah*) <u>FEMALE</u> (נְקֵבָה *nê'qey'vah*) <u>UPON</u> (עַל *al*) <u>FAILURE~him</u> (חַטָּאתוֹ

hha'ta'to) <u>WHICH</u> (אֲשֶׁר *a'sher*) *he~did~*<u>FAIL</u>^(V) (חָטָא *hha'ta*)
RMT: Or his failure is made known to him, which he failed, and he brings his donation, a hairy goat of the she-goats, a whole female for his failure which he failed,

4:29 <u>and~*he~did~*SUPPORT</u>^(\) (וְסָמַךְ *wê'sa'makh*) <u>AT</u> (אֶת *et*)
<u>HAND~him</u> (יָדוֹ *ya'do*) <u>UPON</u> (עַל *al*) <u>HEAD</u> (רֹאשׁ *rosh*) <u>the~FAILURE</u>
(הַחַטָּאת *ha'hha'tat*) <u>and~*he~did~*SLAY</u>^(V) (וְשָׁחַט *wê'sha'hhat*) <u>AT</u>
(אֶת *et*) <u>the~FAILURE</u> (הַחַטָּאת *ha'hha'tat*) <u>in~AREA</u> (בִּמְקוֹם
bim'qom) <u>the~ASCENSION.OFFERING</u> (הָעֹלָה *ha'o'lah*) **RMT:** and he will support his hand upon the head of the failure, and he will slay the failure in the area of the ascension offering,

4:30 <u>and~*he~did~*TAKE</u>^(V) (וְלָקַח *wê'la'qahh*) <u>the~ADMINISTRATOR</u>
(הַכֹּהֵן *ha'ko'heyn*) <u>from~BLOOD~her</u> (מִדָּמָהּ *mi'da'mah*) <u>in~</u>
<u>FINGER~him</u> (בְּאֶצְבָּעוֹ *bê'ets'ba'o*) <u>and~*he~did~*GIVE</u>^(V) (וְנָתַן
wê'na'tan) <u>UPON</u> (עַל *al*) <u>HORN~s</u> (קַרְנֹת *qar'not*) <u>ALTAR</u> (מִזְבַּח
miz'bahh) <u>the~ASCENSION.OFFERING</u> (הָעֹלָה *ha'o'lah*) <u>and~AT</u> (וְאֶת
wê'et) <u>ALL</u> (כָּל *kol*) <u>BLOOD~her</u> (דָּמָהּ *da'mah*) *he~will~*<u>POUR.OUT</u>^(V)
(יִשְׁפֹּךְ *yish'pokh*) <u>TO</u> (אֶל *el*) <u>BOTTOM.BASE</u> (יְסוֹד *yê'sod*) <u>the~</u>
<u>ALTAR</u> (הַמִּזְבֵּחַ *ha'miz'bey'ahh*) **RMT:** and the administrator will take from her blood and he will place it upon the horns of the altar of the ascension offering, and he will pour out her blood to the bottom base of the altar,

4:31 <u>and~AT</u> (וְאֶת *wê'et*) <u>ALL</u> (כָּל *kol*) <u>FAT~her</u> (חֶלְבָּהּ *hhel'bah*) *he~*
will~make~<u>TURN.ASIDE</u>^(V) (יָסִיר *ya'sir*) <u>like~WHICH</u> (כַּאֲשֶׁר
ka'a'sheyr) *he~did~be~make~*<u>TURN.ASIDE</u>^(V) (הוּסַר *hu'sar*) <u>FAT</u> (חֵלֶב
hhey'lev) <u>from~UPON</u> (מֵעַל *mey'al*) <u>SACRIFICE</u> (זֶבַח *ze'vahh*) <u>the~</u>
<u>OFFERING.OF.RESTITUTION~s</u> (הַשְּׁלָמִים *ha'she'la'mim*) <u>and~*he~did~*</u>
make~<u>BURN.INCENSE</u>^(V) (וְהִקְטִיר *wê'hiq'tir*) <u>the~ADMINISTRATOR</u>
(הַכֹּהֵן *ha'ko'heyn*) <u>the~ALTAR~unto</u> (הַמִּזְבֵּחָה *ha'miz'bey'hhah*) <u>to~</u>
<u>AROMA</u> (לְרֵיחַ *lê'rey'ahh*) <u>SWEET</u> (נִיחֹחַ *ni'hho'ahh*) <u>to~**YHWH**</u>
(לַיהוָה *la'YHWH*) <u>and~*he~did~*much~COVER</u>^(V) (וְכִפֶּר *wê'khi'per*)
<u>UPON~him</u> (עָלָיו *a'law*) <u>the~ADMINISTRATOR</u> (הַכֹּהֵן *ha'ko'heyn*)
<u>and~*he~did~*be~FORGIVE</u>^(V) (וְנִסְלַח *wê'nis'lahh*) <u>to~him</u> (לוֹ *lo*)
RMT: and he will remove all her fat just as he removed the fat from upon the sacrifice of the offerings of restitution, and the administrator will burn it as incense upon the altar for a sweet aroma to **YHWH**, and the administrator will make a covering upon him and he will be forgiven for him,

4:32 and~IF (אִם wê'im) SHEEP (כֶּבֶשׂ ke'ves) _he~will~make~_
COME(V) (יָבִיא ya'vi) DONATION~him (קָרְבָּנוֹ qar'ba'no) to~FAILURE
(לְחַטָּאת lê'hha'tat) FEMALE (נְקֵבָה nê'qey'vah) WHOLE (תְמִימָה
tê'mi'mah) _he~will~make~COME_(V)~_her_ (יְבִיאֶנָּה yê'vi'e'nah)
RMT: and if he will bring a sheep for his donation for the failure, a
whole female he will bring,

4:33 and~_he~did~SUPPORT_(V) (וְסָמַךְ wê'sa'makh) AT (אֶת et)
HAND~him (יָדוֹ ya'do) UPON (עַל al) HEAD (ראשׁ rosh) the~FAILURE
(הַחַטָּאת ha'hha'tat) and~_he~did~SLAY_(V) (וְשָׁחַט wê'sha'hhat) AT~
her (אֹתָהּ o'tah) to~FAILURE (לְחַטָּאת lê'hha'tat) in~AREA (בִּמְקוֹם
bim'qom) WHICH (אֲשֶׁר a'sher) _he~will~SLAY_(V) (יִשְׁחַט yish'hhat) AT
(אֶת et) the~ASCENSION.OFFERING (הָעֹלָה ha'o'lah) **RMT:** and he
will support his hand upon the head of the failure, and he will slay
her for the failure in the area which the ascension offering is slain,

4:34 and~_he~did~TAKE_(V) (וְלָקַח wê'la'qahh) the~ADMINISTRATOR
(הַכֹּהֵן ha'ko'heyn) from~BLOOD (מִדַּם mi'dam) the~FAILURE
(הַחַטָּאת ha'hha'tat) in~FINGER~him (בְּאֶצְבָּעוֹ bê'ets'ba'o) and~_he~_
did~GIVE(V) (וְנָתַן wê'na'tan) UPON (עַל al) HORN~s (קַרְנֹת qar'not)
ALTAR (מִזְבַּח miz'bahh) the~ASCENSION.OFFERING (הָעֹלָה ha'o'lah)
and~AT (וְאֶת wê'et) ALL (כָּל kol) BLOOD~her (דָּמָהּ da'mah) _he~_
will~POUR.OUT(V) (יִשְׁפֹּךְ yish'pokh) TO (אֶל el) BOTTOM.BASE (יְסוֹד
yê'sod) the~ALTAR (הַמִּזְבֵּחַ ha'miz'bey'ahh) **RMT:** and the
administrator will take from the blood of the failure with his finger,
and he will place it upon the horns of the altar of the ascension
offering, and he will pour out all her blood to the bottom base of the
altar,

4:35 and~AT (וְאֶת wê'et) ALL (כָּל kol) FAT~her (חֶלְבָּהּ hhel'bah) _he~_
will~make~TURN.ASIDE(V) (יָסִיר ya'sir) like~WHICH (כַּאֲשֶׁר
ka'a'sheyr) _he~will~be~make~TURN.ASIDE_(V) (יוּסַר yu'sar) FAT (חֵלֶב
hhey'lev) the~SHEEP (הַכֶּשֶׂב ha'ke'sev) from~SACRIFICE (מִזֶּבַח
mi'ze'vahh) the~OFFERING.OF.RESTITUTION~s (הַשְּׁלָמִים
ha'she'la'mim) and~_he~did~make~BURN.INCENSE_(V) (וְהִקְטִיר
wê'hiq'tir) the~ADMINISTRATOR (הַכֹּהֵן ha'ko'heyn) AT~them(m)
(אֹתָם o'tam) the~ALTAR~unto (הַמִּזְבֵּחָה ha'miz'bey'hhah) UPON (עַל
al) FIRE.OFFERING~s (אִשֵּׁי i'shey) **YHWH** (יְהוָה YHWH) and~_he~did~_
much~COVER(V) (וְכִפֶּר wê'khi'per) UPON~him (עָלָיו a'law) the~
ADMINISTRATOR (הַכֹּהֵן ha'ko'heyn) UPON (עַל al) FAILURE~him
(חַטָּאתוֹ hha'ta'to) WHICH (אֲשֶׁר a'sher) _he~did~FAIL_(V) (חָטָא
hha'ta) and~_he~did~be~FORGIVE_(V) (וְנִסְלַח wê'nis'lahh) to~him (לוֹ
lo)

lo) **RMT:** and he will remove all her fat just as he removed the fat of the sheep from the sacrifice of the offerings of restitution, and the administrator will burn them as incense upon the altar, fire offerings of **YHWH**, and the administrator will make a covering upon him and his failure which he failed, and he will be forgiven for him,

Chapter 5

5:1 and~SOUL (וְנֶפֶשׁ *wê'ne'phesh*) GIVEN.THAT (כִּי *ki*) *she~will~* FAIL[(V)] (תֶחֱטָא *te'hhe'ta*) and~she~did~HEAR[(V)] (וְשָׁמְעָה *wê'sham'ah*) VOICE (קוֹל *qol*) OATH (אָלָה *a'lah*) and~HE (וְהוּא *wê'hu*) WITNESS (עֵד *eyd*) OR (אוֹ *o*) *he~did~*SEE[(V)] (רָאָה *ra'ah*) OR (אוֹ *o*) *he~did~* KNOW[(V)] (יָדָע *ya'da*) IF (אִם *im*) NOT (לוֹא *lo*) *he~will~make~* BE.FACE.TO.FACE[(V)] (יַגִּיד *yc'gid*) and~he~did~LIFT.UP[(V)] (וְנָשָׂא *wê'na'sa*) TWISTEDNESS~him (עֲוֹנוֹ *a'o'no*) **RMT:** and a soul that will fail and will hear the voice of an oath and he[14] is a witness, whether he saw or knew, if he will not tell, then he will lift up his twistedness.

5:2 OR (אוֹ *o*) SOUL (נֶפֶשׁ *ne'phesh*) WHICH (אֲשֶׁר *a'sher*) *she~will~* TOUCH[(V)] (תִּגַּע *ti'ga*) in~ALL (בְּכָל *bê'khol*) WORD (דָּבָר *da'var*) DIRTY (טָמֵא *ta'mey*) OR (אוֹ *o*) in~CARCASS (בְּנִבְלַת *vê'niv'lat*) LIVING (חַיָּה *hhai'yah*) DIRTY (טְמֵאָה *tê'mey'ah*) OR (אוֹ *o*) in~CARCASS (בְּנִבְלַת *bê'niv'lat*) BEAST (בְּהֵמָה *bê'hey'mah*) DIRTY (טְמֵאָה *tê'mey'ah*) OR (אוֹ *o*) in~CARCASS (בְּנִבְלַת *bê'niv'lat*) SWARMER (שֶׁרֶץ *she'rets*) DIRTY (טָמֵא *ta'mey*) and~ne~did~be~BE.OUT.OF.SIGHT[(V)] (וְנֶעְלַם *wê'ne'lam*) FROM~him (מִמֶּנּוּ *mi'me'nu*) and~HE (וְהוּא *wê'hu*) DIRTY (טָמֵא *ta'mey*) and~he~did~BE.GUILTY[(V)] (וְאָשֵׁם *wê'a'sheym*) **RMT:** Or a soul which will touch any word[15] of dirtiness, or a carcass of a dirty living one, or a carcass of a dirty living[16] one, or the carcass of a dirty swarmer, and he was out of sight from him, then he is dirty and he will be guilty.

5:3 OR (אוֹ *o*) GIVEN.THAT (כִּי *khi*) *he~will~*TOUCH[(V)] (יִגַּע *yiga*) in~ DIRTY (בְּטֻמְאַת *bê'tum'at*) HUMAN (אָדָם *a'dam*) to~ALL (לְכֹל *lê'khol*) DIRTY~him (טֻמְאָתוֹ *tu'm'a'to*) WHICH (אֲשֶׁר *a'sher*) *he~will~* BE.DIRTY[(V)] (יִטְמָא *yit'ma*) in~her (בָּהּ *bah*) and~he~did~be~ BE.OUT.OF.SIGHT[(V)] (וְנֶעְלַם *wê'ne'lam*) FROM~him (מִמֶּנּוּ *mi'me'nu*)

---

[14] The gender of the subject changes from feminine to masculine.
[15] This Hebrew word can also mean a "thing."
[16] A euphemism for a "creature."

and~HE (וְהוּא *wê'hu*) he~did~KNOW^(V) (יָדַע *ya'da*) and~he~did~ BE.GUILTY^(V) (וְאָשֵׁם *wê'a'sheym*) **RMT:** Or if he will touch a dirty human, for all of his dirtiness, which he is dirty for, and he will be out of sight from him, and he knew, then he will be guilty.

5:4 OR (אוֹ *o*) SOUL (נֶפֶשׁ *ne'phesh*) GIVEN.THAT (כִּי *ki*) she~will~be~ SWEAR^(V) (תִשָּׁבַע *ti'sha'va*) to~>~much~UTTER^(V) (לְבַטֵּא *lê'va'tey*) in~ LIP~s2 (בִשְׂפָתַיִם *vis'pha'ta'yim*) to~>~make~BE.DYSFUNCTIONAL^(V) (לְהָרַע *lê'ha'ra*) OR (אוֹ *o*) to~>~make~DO.WELL^(V) (לְהֵיטִיב *lê'hey'tiv*) to~ALL (לְכֹל *lê'khol*) WHICH (אֲשֶׁר *a'sher*) he~will~much~ UTTER^(V) (יְבַטֵּא *yê'va'tey*) the~HUMAN (הָאָדָם *ha'a'dam*) in~ SWEARING (בִּשְׁבֻעָה *bish'vu'ah*) and~he~did~be~BE.OUT.OF.SIGHT^(V) (וְנֶעְלַם *wê'ne'lam*) FROM~him (מִמֶּנּוּ *mi'me'nu*) and~HE (וְהוּא *wê'hu*) he~did~KNOW^(V) (יָדַע *ya'da*) and~he~did~BE.GUILTY^(V) (וְאָשֵׁם *wê'a'sheym*) to~UNIT (לְאַחַת *lê'a'hhat*) from~THESE (מֵאֵלֶּה *mey'ey'leh*) **RMT:** Or a soul that will swear by uttering with lips to make dysfunctional or make well, for all which the human will utter with a swearing, and he be out of sight from him, and he knew, then he will be guilty to one of these,

5:5 and~he~did~EXIST^(V) (וְהָיָה *wê'hai'yah*) GIVEN.THAT (כִי *khi*) he~ will~BE.GUILTY^(V) (יֶאְשַׁם *ye'e'sham*) to~UNIT (לְאַחַת *lê'a'hhat*) from~THESE (מֵאֵלֶּה *mey'ey'leh*) and~he~did~self~ THROW.THE.HAND^(V) (וְהִתְוַדָּה *wê'hit'wa'dah*) WHICH (אֲשֶׁר *a'sher*) he~did~FAIL^(V) (חָטָא *hha'ta*) UPON~her (עָלֶיהָ *a'ley'ah*) **RMT:** and it will come to pass when he is guilty to one of these, and he will confess what he failed upon her,

5:6 and~he~did~make~COME^(V) (וְהֵבִיא *wê'hey'vi*) AT (אֶת *et*) GUILT~him (אֲשָׁמוֹ *a'sha'mo*) to~**YHWH** (לַיהוָה *la'YHWH*) UPON (עַל *al*) FAILURE~him (חַטָּאתוֹ *hha'ta'to*) WHICH (אֲשֶׁר *a'sher*) he~did~ FAIL^(V) (חָטָא *hha'ta*) FEMALE (נְקֵבָה *nê'qey'vah*) FROM (מִן *min*) the~FLOCKS (הַצֹּאן *ha'tson*) SHEEP (כִּשְׂבָּה *kis'bah*) OR (אוֹ *o*) HAIRY.GOAT (שְׂעִירַת *sê'i'rat*) SHE-GOAT~s (עִזִּים *i'zim*) to~FAILURE (לְחַטָּאת *lê'hha'tat*) and~he~did~much~COVER^(V) (וְכִפֶּר *wê'khi'per*) UPON~him (עָלָיו *a'law*) the~ADMINISTRATOR (הַכֹּהֵן *ha'ko'heyn*) from~FAILURE~him (מֵחַטָּאתוֹ *mey'hha'ta'to*) **RMT:** and he will bring his guilt to **YHWH** because of his failure, which he failed, a female from the flocks of sheep or a hairy goat of the she-goats for the failure, and the administrator will make a covering upon him because of his failure,

5:7 and~IF (וְאִם wê'im) NOT (לֹא lo) *she~will~make~TOUCH*(V) (תַגִּיע ta'gi) HAND~him (יָדוֹ ya'do) SUFFICIENT (דֵּי dey) RAM (שֶׂה seh) and~*he~did~make~COME*(V) (וְהֵבִיא wê'hey'vi) AT (אֶת et) GUILT~ him (אֲשָׁמוֹ a'sha'mo) WHICH (אֲשֶׁר a'sher) *he~did~FAIL*(V) (חָטָא hha'ta) TWO (שְׁתֵּי shê'tey) TURTLEDOVE~s (תֹרִים to'rim) OR (אוֹ o) TWO (שְׁנֵי shê'ney) SON~s (בְנֵי vê'ney) DOVE (יוֹנָה yo'nah) to~ **YHWH** (לַיהוָה la'YHWH) UNIT (אֶחָד e'hhad) to~FAILURE (לְחַטָּאת lê'hha'tat) and~UNIT (וְאֶחָד wê'e'hhad) to~ASCENSION.OFFERING (לְעֹלָה lê'lah) **RMT:** and if his hand cannot sufficiently touch[17] a ram, then he will bring his guilt, which he failed, two turtledoves or two sons of the dove to YHWH, one for a failure and one for an ascension offering,

5:8 and~*he~did~make~COME*(V) (וְהֵבִיא wê'hey'vi) AT~them(m) (אֹתָם o'tam) TO (אֶל el) the~ADMINISTRATOR (הַכֹּהֵן ha'ko'heyn) and~*he~ did~make~COME.NEAR*(V) (וְהִקְרִיב wê'hiq'riv) AT (אֶת et) WHICH (אֲשֶׁר a'sher) to~the~FAILURE (לַחַטָּאת la'hha'tat) FIRST (רִאשׁוֹנָה ri'sho'nah) and~*he~did~SNAP.OFF*(V) (וּמָלַק u'ma'laq) AT (אֶת et) HEAD~him (רֹאשׁוֹ ro'sho) from~FOREFRONT (מִמּוּל mi'mul) NECK~ him (עָרְפּוֹ ar'po) and~NOT (וְלֹא wê'lo) *he~will~make~SEPARATE*(V) (יַבְדִּיל yav'dil) **RMT:** and he will bring them to the administrator, and he will bring near what is for the failure first, and he will snap off his head from the forefront of his neck and he will not separate it,

5:9 and~*he~did~make~SPATTER*(V) (וְהִזָּה wê'hi'zah) from~BLOOD (מִדַּם mi'dam) the~FAILURE (הַחַטָּאת ha'hha'tat) UPON (עַל al) WALL (קִיר qir) the~ALTAR (הַמִּזְבֵּחַ ha'miz'bey'ahh) and~the~be~ REMAIN(V)~ing(ms) (וְהַנִּשְׁאָר wê'ha'nish'ar) in~the~BLOOD (בַּדָּם ba'dam) *he~will~be~DRAIN*(V) (יִמָּצֵה yi'ma'tseyh) TO (אֶל el) BOTTOM.BASE (יְסוֹד yê'sod) the~ALTAR (הַמִּזְבֵּחַ ha'miz'bey'ahh) FAILURE (חַטָּאת hha'tat) HE (הוּא hu) **RMT:** and he will spatter from the blood of the failure upon the wall of the altar, and the remaining blood will be drained to the bottom base of the altar, he is the failure,

5:10 and~AT (וְאֶת wê'et) the~SECOND (הַשֵּׁנִי ha'shey'ni) *he~will~ DO*(V) (יַעֲשֶׂה ya'a'seh) ASCENSION.OFFERING (עֹלָה o'lah) like~the~ DECISION (כַּמִּשְׁפָּט ka'mish'pat) and~*he~did~much~COVER*(V) (וְכִפֶּר wê'khi'per) UPON~him (עָלָיו a'law) the~ADMINISTRATOR (הַכֹּהֵן ha'ko'heyn) from~FAILURE~him (מֵחַטָּאתוֹ mey'hha'ta'to) WHICH

---

[17] To touch in the sense of being able to afford.

(אֲשֶׁר a'sher) <u>he~did~</u>FAIL^(V) (חָטָא hha'ta) <u>and~he~did~be~</u>
<u>FORGIVE</u>^(V) (וְנִסְלַח wê'nis'lahh) <u>to~</u>him (לוֹ lo) **RMT:** and he will do
the second as an ascension offering, according to the decision, and
the administrator will make a covering upon him because of his
failure, which he failed, and he will be forgiven for him,

5:11 <u>and~</u>IF (וְאִם wê'im) <u>NOT</u> (לֹא lo) <u>she~will~make~</u>OVERTAKE^(V)
(תַּשִּׂיג ta'sig) <u>HAND~</u>him (יָדוֹ ya'do) <u>to~</u>TWO (לִשְׁתֵּי lish'tey)
<u>TURTLEDOVE~s</u> (תֹרִים to'rim) <u>OR</u> (אוֹ o) <u>to~</u>TWO (לִשְׁנֵי lish'ney)
<u>SON~s</u> (בְנֵי vê'ney) <u>DOVE</u> (יוֹנָה yo'nah) <u>and~he~did~make~</u>COME^(V)
(וְהֵבִיא wê'hey'vi) <u>AT</u> (אֶת et) <u>DONATION~</u>him (קָרְבָּנוֹ qar'ba'no)
<u>WHICH</u> (אֲשֶׁר a'sher) <u>he~did~</u>FAIL^(V) (חָטָא hha'ta) <u>TENTH</u> (עֲשִׂירִת
a'si'rit) <u>the~EYPHAH</u> (הָאֵפָה ha'ey'phah) <u>FLOUR</u> (סֹלֶת so'let) <u>to~</u>
<u>FAILURE</u> (לְחַטָּאת lê'hha'tat) <u>NOT</u> (לֹא lo) <u>he~will~</u>PLACE^(V) (יָשִׂים
ya'sim) <u>UPON~</u>her (עָלֶיהָ a'ley'ah) <u>OIL</u> (שֶׁמֶן she'men) <u>and~NOT</u> (וְלֹא
wê'lo) <u>he~will~</u>GIVE^(V) (יִתֵּן yi'teyn) <u>UPON~</u>her (עָלֶיהָ a'ley'ah)
<u>FRANKINCENSE</u> (לְבֹנָה lê'vo'nah) <u>GIVEN.THAT</u> (כִּי ki) <u>FAILURE</u> (חַטָּאת
hha'tat) <u>SHE</u> (הִיא hi)[18] **RMT:** and if his hand is not able to overtake[19]
two turtledoves or two sons of the dove, then he will bring his
donation, because he failed, a tenth of an eyphah of flour for the
failure, he will not place oil upon her, and he will not give
frankincense upon her, given that she is the failure,

5:12 <u>and~he~did~make~</u>COME^(V)<u>~her</u> (וֶהֱבִיאָהּ we'he'vi'ah) <u>TO</u> (אֶל
el) <u>the~ADMINISTRATOR</u> (הַכֹּהֵן ha'ko'heyn) <u>and~he~did~</u>GRASP^(V)
(וְקָמַץ wê'qa'mats) <u>the~ADMINISTRATOR</u> (הַכֹּהֵן ha'ko'heyn) <u>FROM~</u>
her (מִמֶּנָה mi'me'nah) <u>FILLING</u> (מְלוֹא mê'lo) <u>HANDFUL~</u>him (קֻמְצוֹ
qum'tso) <u>AT</u> (אֶת et) <u>MEMORIAL~</u>her (אַזְכָּרָתָה az'ka'ra'tah) <u>and~</u>
<u>he~did~make~</u>BURN.INCENSE^(V) (וְהִקְטִיר wê'hiq'tir) <u>the~ALTAR~</u>
<u>unto</u> (הַמִּזְבֵּחָה ha'miz'bey'hhah) <u>UPON</u> (עַל al) <u>FIRE.OFFERING~s</u>
(אִשֵּׁי i'shey) <u>**YHWH**</u> (יְהוָה YHWH) <u>FAILURE</u> (חַטָּאת hha'tat) <u>SHE</u> (הוּא
hi) **RMT:** and he will bring her to the administrator, and the
administrator will grasp from her a filling of his handful, it is a
memorial, and he will burn it as incense upon the altar upon the fire
offerings of **YHWH**, she is the failure,

5:13 <u>and~he~did~much~</u>COVER^(V) (וְכִפֶּר wê'khi'per) <u>UPON~</u>him (עָלָיו
a'law) <u>the~ADMINISTRATOR</u> (הַכֹּהֵן ha'ko'heyn) <u>UPON</u> (עַל al)
<u>FAILURE~</u>him (חַטָאתוֹ hha'ta'to) <u>WHICH</u> (אֲשֶׁר a'sher) <u>he~did~</u>FAIL^(V)

---

[18] *Leningrad Codex:* הוא
[19] To overtake in the sense of acquiring.

(מֵאֵלֶּה *mey'ey'leh*) from~THESE (מֵאַחַת *mey'a'hhat*) from~UNIT (חָטָא *hha'ta*) and~he~did~be~FORGIVE[V] (וְנִסְלַח *wê'nis'lahh*) to~him (לוֹ *lo*) and~she~did~EXIST[V] (וְהָיְתָה *wê'hai'tah*) to~the~ ADMINISTRATOR (לַכֹּהֵן *la'ko'heyn*) like~the~DEPOSIT (כַּמִּנְחָה *ka'min'hhah*) **RMT:** and the administrator will make a covering upon him, upon his failure, because he failed, from one of these, and he will be forgiven for him, and she will exist for the administrator as the deposit,

5:14 and~he~will~much~SPEAK[V] (וַיְדַבֵּר *wai'da'beyr*) **YHWH** (יְהוָה *YHWH*) TO (אֶל *el*) Mosheh (מֹשֶׁה *mo'sheh*) to~>~SAY[V] (לֵּאמֹר *ley'mor*) **RMT:** and YHWH spoke to Mosheh saying,

5:15 SOUL (נֶפֶשׁ *ne'phesh*) GIVEN.THAT (כִּי *ki*) she~will~ TRANSGRESS[V] (תִמְעֹל *tim'ol*) TRANSGRESSION (מַעַל *ma'al*) and~ FAILURE (וְחָטְאָה *wê'hhat'ah*) in~ERROR (בִּשְׁגָגָה *bish'ga'gah*) from~ SPECIAL~s (מִקָּדְשֵׁי *mi'qad'shey*) **YHWH** (יְהוָה *YHWH*) and~he~did~ make~COME[V] (וְהֵבִיא *wê'hey'vi*) AT (אֶת *et*) GUILT~him (אֲשָׁמוֹ *a'sha'mo*) to~YHWH (לַיהוָה *la'YHWH*) BUCK (אַיִל *a'yil*) WHOLE (תָּמִים *ta'mim*) FROM (מִן *min*) the~FLOCKS (הַצֹּאן *ha'tson*) in~ ARRANGEMENT~you[ms] (בְּעֶרְכְּךָ *bê'er'ke'kha*) SILVER (כֶּסֶף *ke'seph*) SHEQEL~s (שְׁקָלִים *shê'qa'lim*) in~SHEQEL (בְּשֶׁקֶל *bê'she'qel*) the~ SPECIAL (הַקֹּדֶשׁ *ha'qo'desh*) to~GUILT (לְאָשָׁם *lê'a'sham*) **RMT:** a soul that will transgress a transgression and is a failure in error from the special ones of **YHWH**, then he will bring his guilt to **YHWH**, a whole buck from the flocks, with your arrangement of silver sheqels, with the special sheqel for the guilt,

5:16 and~AT (וְאֵת *wê'eyt*) WHICH (אֲשֶׁר *a'sher*) he~did~FAIL[V] (חָטָא *hha'ta*) FROM (מִן *min*) the~SPECIAL (הַקֹּדֶשׁ *ha'qo'desh*) he~will~ much~MAKE.RESTITUTION[V] (יְשַׁלֵּם *yê'sha'leym*) and~AT (וְאֵת *wê'et*) FIFTH~him (חֲמִישִׁתוֹ *hha'mi'shi'to*) he~will~make~ADD[V] (יוֹסֵף *yo'seyph*) UPON~him (עָלָיו *a'law*) and~he~did~GIVE[V] (וְנָתַן *wê'na'tan*) AT~him (אֹתוֹ *o'to*) to~the~ADMINISTRATOR (לַכֹּהֵן *la'ko'heyn*) and~the~ADMINISTRATOR (וְהַכֹּהֵן *wê'ha'ko'heyn*) he~ will~much~COVER[V] (יְכַפֵּר *yê'kha'peyr*) UPON~him (עָלָיו *a'law*) in~ BUCK (בְּאֵיל *bê'eyl*) the~GUILT (הָאָשָׁם *ha'a'sham*) and~he~did~be~ FORGIVE[V] (וְנִסְלַח *wê'nis'lahh*) to~him (לוֹ *lo*) **RMT:** and he will make restitution for when he failed by the special thing, and he will cause to add his fifth upon him, and he will give him to the administrator, and the administrator will make a covering upon him with the buck of the guilt, and he will be forgiven for him,

5:17 and~IF (וְאִם *wê'im*) SOUL (נֶפֶשׁ *ne'phesh*) GIVEN.THAT (כִּי *ki*) she~will~FAIL[V] (תֶחֱטָא *te'hhe'ta*) and~she~did~DO[V] (וְעָשְׂתָה *wê'as'tah*) UNIT (אַחַת *a'hhat*) from~ALL (מִכָּל *mi'kol*) DIRECTIVE~s (מִצְוֹת *mits'ot*) YHWH (יְהוָה *YHWH*) WHICH (אֲשֶׁר *a'sher*) NOT (לֹא *lo*) they[f]~will~be~DO[V] (תֵעָשֶׂינָה *tey'a'sey'nah*) and~NOT (וְלֹא *wê'lo*) he~did~KNOW[V] (יָדַע *ya'da*) and~he~did~BE.GUILTY[V] (וְאָשֵׁם *wê'a'sheym*) and~he~did~LIFT.UP[V] (וְנָשָׂא *wê'na'sa*) TWISTEDNESS~him (עֲוֹנוֹ *a'o'no*) **RMT:** and if a soul that failed and did one of any of the directives of **YHWH**, which was not to be done, and he did not know, then he will be guilty and he will lift up his twistedness,

5:18 and~he~did~make~COME[V] (וְהֵבִיא *wê'hey'vi*) BUCK (אַיִל *a'yil*) WHOLE (תָּמִים *ta'mim*) FROM (מִן *min*) the~FLOCKS (הַצֹּאן *ha'tson*) in~ARRANGEMENT~you[ms] (בְּעֶרְכְּךָ *bê'er'ke'kha*) to~GUILT (לְאָשָׁם *lê'a'sham*) TO (אֶל *el*) the~ADMINISTRATOR (הַכֹּהֵן *ha'ko'heyn*) and~he~did~much~COVER[V] (וְכִפֶּר *wê'khi'per*) UPON~him (עָלָיו *a'law*) the~ADMINISTRATOR (הַכֹּהֵן *ha'ko'heyn*) UPON (עַל *al*) ERROR~him (שִׁגְגָתוֹ *shig'ga'to*) WHICH (אֲשֶׁר *a'sher*) he~did~ERR[V] (שָׁגַג *sha'gag*) and~HE (וְהוּא *wê'hu*) NOT (לֹא *lo*) he~did~KNOW[V] (יָדַע *ya'da*) and~he~did~be~FORGIVE[V] (וְנִסְלַח *wê'nis'lahh*) to~him (לוֹ *lo*) **RMT:** and he will bring a whole buck from the flocks, with your arrangement for the guilt, to the administrator, and the administrator will make a covering upon him concerning his error, which her erred and he did not know, and he will be forgiven for him.

5:19 GUILT (אָשָׁם *a'sham*) HE (הוּא *hu*) >~BE.GUILTY[V] (אָשֹׁם *a'shom*) he~did~BE.GUILTY[V] (אָשַׁם *a'sham*) to~YHWH (לַיהוָה *la'YHWH*) **RMT:** It is guilt, he is very guilty to **YHWH**,

5:20 (06:1) and~he~will~much~SPEAK[V] (וַיְדַבֵּר *wai'da'beyr*) YHWH (יְהוָה *YHWH*) TO (אֶל *el*) Mosheh (מֹשֶׁה *mo'sheh*) to~>~SAY[V] (לֵאמֹר *ley'mor*) **RMT:** and **YHWH** spoke to Mosheh saying,

5:21 (06:2) SOUL (נֶפֶשׁ *ne'phesh*) GIVEN.THAT (כִּי *ki*) she~will~FAIL[V] (תֶחֱטָא *te'hhe'ta*) and~she~did~TRANSGRESS[V] (וּמָעֲלָה *u'ma'a'lah*) TRANSGRESSION (מַעַל *ma'al*) in~YHWH (בַּיהוָה *ba'YHWH*) and~he~did~much~DENY[V] (וְכִחֵשׁ *wê'khi'hheysh*) in~the~NEIGHBOR~him (בַּעֲמִיתוֹ *ba'a'mi'to*) in~DEPOSITED (בְּפִקָּדוֹן *bê'phi'qa'don*) OR (אוֹ *o*) in~SECURITY.DEPOSIT (בִתְשׂוּמֶת *vit'su'met*) HAND (יָד *yad*) OR (אוֹ *o*) in~PLUCKING (בְגָזֵל *vê'ga'zeyl*) OR (אוֹ *o*) he~did~OPPRESS[V] (עָשַׁק *a'shaq*) AT (אֶת *et*) NEIGHBOR~him (עֲמִיתוֹ *a'mi'to*) **RMT:** a soul that fails and transgresses a transgression with **YHWH**, and he lies to his

28

neighbor about a deposit or security deposit of the hand or with plucking or oppresses his neighbor.

5:22 (06:3) <u>OR</u> (אוֹ *o*) <u>he~did~FIND</u>$^{(V)}$ (מָצָא *ma'tsa*) <u>LOST.THING</u> (אֲבֵדָה *a'vey'dah*) <u>and~he~did~much~DENY</u>$^{(V)}$ (וְכִחֶשׁ *wê'khi'hhesh*) <u>in~her</u> (בָּהּ *bah*) <u>and~he~did~be~SWEAR</u>$^{(V)}$ (וְנִשְׁבַּע *wê'nish'ba*) <u>UPON</u> (עַל *al*) <u>FALSE</u> (שָׁקֶר *sha'qer*) <u>UPON</u> (עַל *al*) <u>UNIT</u> (אַחַת *a'hhat*) <u>from~ALL</u> (מִכֹּל *mi'kol*) <u>WHICH</u> (אֲשֶׁר *a'sher*) <u>he~will~DO</u>$^{(V)}$ (יַעֲשֶׂה *ya'a'seh*) <u>the~HUMAN</u> (הָאָדָם *ha'a'dam*) <u>to~>~FAIL</u>$^{(V)}$ (לַחֲטֹא *la'hha'to*) <u>in~them</u>$^{(f)}$ (בָהֵנָּה *va'hey'nah*) **RMT:** Or he finds a lost thing and he lies about her, and he swears according to falsehood, anyone of the things which the human did, it is for failing in them,

5:23 (06:4) <u>and~he~did~EXIST</u>$^{(V)}$ (וְהָיָה *wê'hai'yah*) <u>GIVEN.THAT</u> (כִּי *ki*) <u>he~will~FAIL</u>$^{(V)}$ (יֶחֱטָא *ye'hhe'ta*) <u>and~he~did~BE.GUILTY</u>$^{(V)}$ (וְאָשֵׁם *wê'a'sheym*) <u>and~he~did~make~TURN.BACK</u>$^{(V)}$ (וְהֵשִׁיב *wê'hey'shiv*) <u>AT</u> (אֶת *et*) <u>the~PLUCKED</u> (הַגְּזֵלָה *hag'zey'lah*) <u>WHICH</u> (אֲשֶׁר *a'sher*) <u>he~did~PLUCK.AWAY</u>$^{(V)}$ (גָּזָל *ga'zal*) <u>OR</u> (אוֹ *o*) <u>AT</u> (אֶת *et*) <u>the~OPPRESSION</u> (הָעֹשֶׁק *ha'o'sheq*) <u>WHICH</u> (אֲשֶׁר *a'sher*) <u>he~did~OPPRESS</u>$^{(V)}$ (עָשָׁק *a'shaq*) <u>OR</u> (אוֹ *o*) <u>AT</u> (אֶת *et*) <u>the~DEPOSITED</u> (הַפִּקָּדוֹן *ha'pi'qa'don*) <u>WHICH</u> (אֲשֶׁר *a'sher*) <u>he~did~be~make~REGISTER</u>$^{(V)}$ (הָפְקַד *haph'qad*) <u>AT~him</u> (אִתּוֹ *i'to*) <u>OR</u> (אוֹ *o*) <u>AT</u> (אֶת *et*) <u>the~LOST.THING</u> (הָאֲבֵדָה *ha'a'vey'dah*) <u>WHICH</u> (אֲשֶׁר *a'sher*) <u>he~did~FIND</u>$^{(V)}$ (מָצָא *ma'tsa*) **RMT:** and it will come to pass, given that he failed and he is guilty, and he returns the plucked thing which he plucked, or the oppression which he oppressed, or the deposited thing which he set over him, or the lost thing which he found.

5:24 (06:5) <u>OR</u> (אוֹ *o*) <u>from~ALL</u> (מִכֹּל *mi'kol*) <u>WHICH</u> (אֲשֶׁר *a'sher*) <u>he~will~be~SWEAR</u>$^{(V)}$ (יִשָּׁבַע *yi'sha'va*) <u>UPON~him</u> (עָלָיו *a'law*) <u>to~the~FALSE</u> (לַשֶּׁקֶר *la'she'qer*) <u>and~he~did~much~MAKE.RESTITUTION</u>$^{(V)}$ (וְשִׁלַּם *wê'shi'lam*) <u>AT~him</u> (אֹתוֹ *o'to*) <u>in~HEAD~him</u> (בְּרֹאשׁוֹ *bê'ro'sho*) <u>and~FIFTH~s~him</u> (וַחֲמִשִׁתָיו *wa'hha'mi'shi'taw*) <u>he~will~make~ADD</u>$^{(V)}$ (יֹסֵף *yo'seyph*) <u>UPON~him</u> (עָלָיו *a'law*) <u>to~the~WHICH</u> (לַאֲשֶׁר *la'a'sheyr*) <u>HE</u> (הוּא *hu*) <u>to~him</u> (לוֹ *lo*) <u>he~will~GIVE</u>$^{(V)}$<u>~him</u> (יִתְּנֶנּוּ *yit'ne'nu*) <u>in~DAY</u> (בְּיוֹם *bê'yom*) <u>GUILTINESS~him</u> (אַשְׁמָתוֹ *ash'ma'to*) **RMT:** Or from all which he will swear according to the falsehood, and he will make his restitution with his head[20], and he will cause his fifths to be added upon him, he will give him that which belongs to him in the day of his guiltiness,

---

[20] Meaning "with his principle."

5:25 (06:6) <u>and~AT</u> (וְאֶת wê'et) <u>GUILT~him</u> (אֲשָׁמוֹ a'sha'mo) _he~ will~make~COME_^(V) (יָבִיא ya'vi) <u>to~**YHWH**</u> (לַיהוָה la'YHWH) <u>BUCK</u> (אַיִל a'yil) <u>WHOLE</u> (תָּמִים ta'mim) <u>FROM</u> (מִן min) <u>the~FLOCKS</u> (הַצֹּאן ha'tson) <u>in~ARRANGEMENT~you</u>^(ms) (בְּעֶרְכְּךָ bê'er'ke'kha) <u>to~ GUILT</u> (לְאָשָׁם lê'a'sham) <u>TO</u> (אֶל el) <u>the~ADMINISTRATOR</u> (הַכֹּהֵן ha'ko'heyn) **RMT:** and he will bring his guilt to **YHWH**, a whole buck from the flocks with your arrangement for the guilt, to the administrator,

5:26 (06:7) <u>and~he~did~much~COVER</u>^(V) (וְכִפֶּר wê'khi'per) <u>UPON~ him</u> (עָלָיו a'law) <u>the~ADMINISTRATOR</u> (הַכֹּהֵן ha'ko'heyn) <u>to~ FACE~s</u> (לִפְנֵי liph'ney) **YHWH** (יְהוָה YHWH) <u>and~he~did~be~ FORGIVE</u>^(V) (וְנִסְלַח wê'nis'lahh) <u>to~him</u> (לוֹ lo) <u>UPON</u> (עַל al) <u>UNIT</u> (אַחַת a'hhat) <u>from~ALL</u> (מִכֹּל mi'kol) <u>WHICH</u> (אֲשֶׁר a'sher) _he~will~ DO_^(V) (יַעֲשֶׂה ya'a'seh) <u>to~GUILTINESS</u> (לְאַשְׁמָה lê'ash'mah) <u>in~her</u> (בָהּ vah) **RMT:** and the administrator will make a covering upon him to the face of **YHWH**, and he will be forgiven for him upon anyone from which he does for guiltiness with her,

Chapter 6

6:1 (06:8) _and~he~will~much~SPEAK_^(V) (וַיְדַבֵּר wai'da'beyr) **YHWH** (יְהוָה YHWH) <u>TO</u> (אֶל el) <u>Mosheh</u> (מֹשֶׁה mo'sheh) _to~>~SAY_^(V) (לֵאמֹר ley'mor) **RMT:** and **YHWH** spoke to Mosheh saying,

6:2 (06:9) _!_^(ms)_~much~DIRECT_^(V) (צַו tsaw) <u>AT</u> (אֶת et) <u>Aharon</u> (אַהֲרֹן a'ha'ron) <u>and~AT</u> (וְאֶת wê'et) <u>SON~s~him</u> (בָּנָיו ba'naw) _to~>~SAY_^(V) (לֵאמֹר ley'mor) <u>THIS</u> (זֹאת zot) <u>TEACHING</u> (תּוֹרַת to'rat) <u>the~ ASCENSION.OFFERING</u> (הָעֹלָה ha'o'lah) <u>SHE</u> (הִוא hi) <u>the~ ASCENSION.OFFERING</u> (הָעֹלָה ha'o'lah) <u>UPON</u> (עַל al) <u>SMOLDERING.FIRE</u> (מוֹקְדָה moq'dah) <u>UPON</u> (עַל al) <u>the~ALTAR</u> (הַמִּזְבֵּחַ ha'miz'bey'ahh) <u>ALL</u> (כָּל kol) <u>the~NIGHT</u> (הַלַּיְלָה ha'lai'lah) <u>UNTIL</u> (עַד ad) <u>the~MORNING</u> (הַבֹּקֶר ha'bo'qer) <u>and~FIRE</u> (וְאֵשׁ wê'eysh) <u>the~ALTAR</u> (הַמִּזְבֵּחַ ha'miz'bey'ahh) _she~will~be~make~ SMOLDER_^(V) (תּוּקַד tu'qad) <u>in~him</u> (בּוֹ bo) **RMT:** direct Aharon and his sons to say, this is the teaching of the ascension offering, she is the rising upon the smoldering fire upon the altar all the night until the morning, and the fire of the altar will be smoldering in her,

6:3 (06:10) _and~he~did~WEAR_^(V) (וְלָבַשׁ wê'la'vash) <u>the~ ADMINISTRATOR</u> (הַכֹּהֵן ha'ko'heyn) <u>LONG.GARMENT~him</u> (מִדּוֹ mi'do) <u>STRAND</u> (בַד vad) <u>and~UNDERGARMENT~s</u> (וּמִכְנְסֵי

u'mikh'ne'sey) STRAND (בַד vad) *he~will~*WEAR[V] (יִלְבָּשׁ yil'bash)
UPON (עַל al) FLESH~him (בְּשָׂרוֹ bê'sar'o) *and~he~did~make~*
RAISE.UP[V] (וְהֵרִים wê'hey'rim) AT (אֵת et) the~FATNESS (הַדֶּשֶׁן
ha'de'shen) WHICH (אֲשֶׁר a'sher) *she~will~*EAT[V] (תֹּאכַל to'khal)
the~FIRE (הָאֵשׁ ha'eysh) AT (אֵת et) the~ASCENSION.OFFERING
(הָעֹלָה ha'o'lah) UPON (עַל al) the~ALTAR (הַמִּזְבֵּחַ ha'miz'bey'ahh)
*and~he~did~*PLACE[V]~him (וְשָׂמוֹ wê'sa'mo) BESIDE (אֵצֶל ey'tsel)
the~ALTAR (הַמִּזְבֵּחַ ha'miz'bey'ahh) **RMT:** and the administrator will
wear his long garment of strand, and he will wear undergarments of
strand upon his flesh, and he will raise up the fatness which the fire
will eat with the ascension offering upon the altar, and he will place
him beside the altar,

6:4 (06:11) *and~he~did~*STRIP.OFF[V] (וּפָשַׁט u'pha'shat) AT (אֵת et)
GARMENT~s~him (בְּגָדָיו bê'ga'daw) *and~he~did~*WEAR[V] (וְלָבַשׁ
wê'la'vash) GARMENT~s (בְּגָדִים bê'ga'dim) OTHER~s (אֲחֵרִים
a'hhey'rim) *and~he~did~make~*GO.OUT[V] (וְהוֹצִיא wê'ho'tsi) AT (אֵת
et) the~FATNESS (הַדֶּשֶׁן ha'de'shen) TO (אֶל el) from~OUTSIDE (מִחוּץ
mi'hhuts) to~the~CAMP (לַמַּחֲנֶה la'ma'hha'neh) TO (אֶל el) AREA
(מָקוֹם ma'qom) CLEAN (טָהוֹר ta'hor) **RMT:** and he will strip off his
garments and he will wear other garments, and he will bring out the
fatness to the outside of the camp to the clean area,

6:5 (06:12) *and~the~*FIRE (וְהָאֵשׁ wê'ha'eysh) UPON (עַל al) the~
ALTAR (הַמִּזְבֵּחַ ha'miz'bey'ahh) *she~will~be~make~*SMOLDER[V]
(תּוּקַד tu'qad) in~him (בּוֹ bo) NOT (לֹא lo) *she~will~*QUENCH[V]
(תִכְבֶּה tikh'beh) *and~he~did~much~*BURN[V] (וּבִעֵר u'vi'eyr) UPON~
her (עָלֶיהָ a'ley'ah) the~ADMINISTRATOR (הַכֹּהֵן ha'ko'heyn) TREE~s
(עֵצִים ey'tsim) in~the~MORNING (בַּבֹּקֶר ba'bo'qer) in~the~
MORNING (בַּבֹּקֶר ba'bo'qer) *and~he~did~*ARRANGE[V] (וְעָרַךְ
wê'a'rekh) UPON~her (עָלֶיהָ a'ley'ah) the~ASCENSION.OFFERING
(הָעֹלָה ha'o'lah) *and~he~did~make~*BURN.INCENSE[V]
(וְהִקְטִיר wê'hiq'tir) UPON~her (עָלֶיהָ a'ley'ah) FAT~s (חֶלְבֵי hhel'vey) the~
OFFERING.OF.RESTITUTION~s (הַשְּׁלָמִים ha'she'la'mim) **RMT:** and
the fire upon the altar will be made to smolder in him, she will not
be quenched, and the administrator will burn upon her wood every
morning, and he will arrange upon her the ascension offering and he
will make the fats of the offerings of restitution burn as incense
upon her.

6:6 (06:13) FIRE (אֵשׁ eysh) CONTINUALLY (תָּמִיד ta'mid) *she~will~
be~make~*SMOLDER[V] (תּוּקַד tu'qad) UPON (עַל al) the~ALTAR

(הַמִּזְבֵּחַ ha'miz'bey'ahh) NOT (לֹא lo) she~will~QUENCH[V] (תִכְבֶּה tikh'veh) **RMT:** The fire will be made to smolder continually upon the altar, she will not be quenched,

6:7 (06:14) and~THIS (וְזֹאת wê'zot) TEACHING (תּוֹרַת to'rat) the~ DEPOSIT (הַמִּנְחָה ha'min'hhah) !(ms)~make~COME.NEAR[V] הַקְרֵב haq'reyv) AT~her (אֹתָהּ o'tah) SON~s (בְּנֵי bê'ney) Aharon (אַהֲרֹן a'ha'ron) to~FACE~s (לִפְנֵי liph'ney) **YHWH** (יְהוָה YHWH) TO (אֶל el) FACE~s (פְּנֵי pê'ney) the~ALTAR (הַמִּזְבֵּחַ ha'miz'bey'ahh) **RMT:** and this is the teaching of the deposit, the sons of Aharon will bring her near to the face of **YHWH**, to the face of the altar,

6:8 (06:15) and~he~did~make~RAISE.UP[V] (וְהֵרִים wê'hey'rim) FROM~him (מִמֶּנּוּ mi'me'nu) in~HANDFUL~him (בְּקֻמְצוֹ bê'qum'tso) from~FLOUR (מִסֹּלֶת mi'so'let) the~DEPOSIT (הַמִּנְחָה ha'min'hhah) and~from~OIL (וּמִשַּׁמְנָהּ u'mi'sham'nah) and~AT (וְאֵת wê'eyt) ALL (כָּל kol) the~FRANKINCENSE (הַלְּבֹנָה hal'vo'nah) WHICH (אֲשֶׁר a'sher) UPON (עַל al) the~DEPOSIT (הַמִּנְחָה ha'min'hhah) and~he~ did~make~BURN.INCENSE[V] (וְהִקְטִיר wê'hiq'tir) the~ALTAR (הַמִּזְבֵּחַ ha'miz'bey'ahh) AROMA (רֵיחַ rey'ahh) SWEET (נִיחֹחַ ni'hho'ahh) MEMORIAL~her (אַזְכָּרָתָהּ az'ka'ra'tah) to~YHWH (לַיהוָה la'YHWH) **RMT:** and he will raise up from him with his handful from the flour of the deposit, and from the oil and all the frankincense which is upon the deposit, and he will burn it as incense upon the altar, a sweet aroma, her memorial to **YHWH**,

6:9 (06:16) and~the~be~LEAVE.BEHIND[V]~ing(fs) (וְהַנּוֹתֶרֶת wê'ha'no'te'ret) FROM~her (מִמֶּנָּה mi'me'nah) they(m)~will~EAT[V] (יֹאכְלוּ yokh'lu) Aharon (אַהֲרֹן a'ha'ron) and~SON~s~him (וּבָנָיו u'va'naw) UNLEAVENED.BREAD~s (מַצּוֹת ma'tsot) she~will~be~ EAT[V] (תֵּאָכֵל tey'a'kheyl) in~AREA (בְּמָקוֹם bê'ma'qom) UNIQUE (קָדֹשׁ qa'dosh) in~COURTYARD (בַּחָצֵר ba'hha'tsar) TENT (אֹהֶל o'hel) APPOINTED (מוֹעֵד mo'eyd) they(m)~will~EAT[V]~her (יֹאכְלוּהָ yokh'lu'ah) **RMT:** and Aharon and his sons will eat the one being left behind from her, she will be eaten with unleavened breads in the unique area, in the courtyard of the appointed tent they will eat her.

6:10 (06:17) NOT (לֹא lo) she~will~be~BAKE[V] (תֵאָפֶה tey'a'pheh) LEAVENED.BREAD (חָמֵץ hha'meyts) DISTRIBUTION~them(m) חֶלְקָם hhel'qam) I~did~GIVE[V] (נָתַתִּי na'ta'ti) AT~her (אֹתָהּ o'tah) from~ FIRE.OFFERING~s~me (מֵאִשָּׁי mey'i'shai) SPECIAL (קֹדֶשׁ qo'desh) SPECIAL~s (קָדָשִׁים qa'da'shim) SHE (הִוא hi) like~the~FAILURE (כַּחַטָּאת ka'hha'tat) and~like~GUILT (וְכָאָשָׁם wê'kha'a'sham)

RMT: Leavened bread will not be baked, I gave her for their distribution, from my fire offerings, she is a special of specials[21], like the failure and like the guilt.

6:11 (06:18) ALL (כָּל *kol*) MALE (זָכָר *za'khar*) in~SON~s (בִּבְנֵי *biv'ney*) Aharon (אַהֲרֹן *a'ha'ron*) he~will~EAT[(V)]~her (יֹאכְלֶנָּה *yo'kha'le'nah*) CUSTOM (חָק *hhoq*) DISTANT (עוֹלָם *o'lam*) to~ GENERATION~s~you[(mp)] (לְדֹרֹתֵיכֶם *lê'do'ro'tey'khem*) from~ FIRE.OFFERING~s (מֵאִשֵּׁי *mey'I'shey*) **YHWH** (יְהוָה *YHWH*) ALL (כֹּל *kol*) WHICH (אֲשֶׁר *a'sher*) he~will~TOUCH[(V)] (יִגַּע *yiga*) in~them[(m)] (בָּהֶם *ba'hem*) he~will~SET.APART[(V)] (יִקְדָּשׁ *yiq'dash*) **RMT:** Every male among the sons of Aharon will eat her, it is a custom of a distant time for your generations, it is from the fire offerings of **YHWH**, all that touch them, he will set apart,

6:12 (06:19) and~he~will~much~SPEAK[(V)] (וַיְדַבֵּר *wai'da'beyr*) **YHWH** (יְהוָה *YHWH*) TO (אֶל *el*) Mosheh (מֹשֶׁה *mo'sheh*) to~>~SAY[(V)] (לֵּאמֹר *ley'mor*) **RMT:** and **YHWH** spoke to Mosheh saying,

6:13 (06:20) THIS (זֶה *zeh*) DONATION (קָרְבַּן *qar'ban*) Aharon (אַהֲרֹן *a'ha'ron*) and~SON~s~him (וּבָנָיו *u'va'naw*) WHICH (אֲשֶׁר *a'sher*) they[(m)]~will~make~COME.NEAR[(V)] (יַקְרִיבוּ *yaq'ri'vu*) to~**YHWH** (לַיהוָה *la'YHWH*) in~DAY (בְּיוֹם *bê'yom*) >~be~SMEAR[(V)] (הִמָּשַׁח *hi'ma'shahh*) AT~him (אֹתוֹ *o'to*) TENTH (עֲשִׂירִת *a'si'rit*) the~EYPHAH (הָאֵיפָה *ha'ey'phah*) FLOUR (סֹלֶת *so'let*) DEPOSIT (מִנְחָה *min'hhah*) CONTINUALLY (תָּמִיד *ta'mid*) ONE.HALF~her (מַחֲצִיתָהּ *ma'hha'tsi'tah*) in~the~MORNING (בַּבֹּקֶר *ba'bo'qer*) and~ONE.HALF~ her (וּמַחֲצִיתָהּ *u'ma'hha'tsi'tah*) in~the~EVENING (בָּעָרֶב *ba'a'rev*) **RMT:** this is the donation of Aharon and his sons which they will bring near to **YHWH** in the day he is being smeared, a tenth of the eyphah of flour, a continual deposit, one half of her in the morning and one of her in the evening.

6:14 (06:21) UPON (עַל *ci*) PAN (מַחֲבַת *ma'hha'vat*) in~the~OIL (בַּשֶּׁמֶן *ba'she'men*) she~will~be~DO[(V)] (תֵּעָשֶׂה *tey'a'seh*) be~make~ FRY[(V)]~ing[(fs)] (מֻרְבֶּכֶת *mur'be'khet*) you[(ms)]~will~make~COME[(V)]~her (תְּבִיאֶנָּה *tê'vi'e'nah*) COOKED~s (תֻּפִינֵי *tu'phi'ney*) DEPOSIT (מִנְחַת *mi'ne'hhat*) FRAGMENT~s (פִּתִּים *pi'tim*) you[(ms)]~will~make~ COME.NEAR[(V)] (תַּקְרִיב *taq'riv*) AROMA (רֵיחַ *rey'ahh*) SWEET (נִיחֹחַ *ni'hho'ahh*) to~**YHWH** (לַיהוָה *la'YHWH*) **RMT:** She will be made with

---

[21] The phrase "special of specials" means a "very special thing, one or place."

the oil upon the pan, being fried you will bring her, you will bring near the cooked things of the deposit of fragments, it is a sweet aroma to **YHWH**,

6:15 (06:22) and~the~ADMINISTRATOR (וְהַכֹּהֵן *wê'ha'ko'heyn*) the~ SMEARED (הַמָּשִׁיחַ *ha'ma'shi'ahh*) UNDER~him (תַּחְתָּיו *tahh'taw*) from~SON~s~him (מִבָּנָיו *mi'ba'naw*) he~will~DO(V) (יַעֲשֶׂה *ya'a'seh*) AT~her (אֹתָהּ *o'tah*) CUSTOM (חָק *hhaq*) DISTANT (עוֹלָם *o'lam*) to~ **YHWH** (לַיהוָה *la'YHWH*) ENTIRELY (כָּלִיל *ka'lil*) she~will~be~make~ BURN.INCENSE(V) (תָּקְטָר *taq'tar*) **RMT:** and the smeared administrator under him from his sons will make her, it is a custom of a distant time to **YHWH**, she will be entirely burned as incense,

6:16 (06:23) and~ALL (וְכָל *wê'khol*) DEPOSIT (מִנְחַת *mi'ne'hhat*) ADMINISTRATOR (כֹּהֵן *ko'heyn*) ENTIRELY (כָּלִיל *ka'lil*) she~will~ EXIST(V) (תִּהְיֶה *tih'yeh*) NOT (לֹא *lo*) she~will~be~EAT(V) (תֵאָכֵל *tey'a'kheyl*) **RMT:** and every deposit of the administrator will entirely exist, she will not be eaten,

6:17 (06:24) and~he~will~much~SPEAK(V) (וַיְדַבֵּר *wai'da'beyr*) **YHWH** (יְהוָה *YHWH*) TO (אֶל *el*) Mosheh (מֹשֶׁה *mo'sheh*) to~>~SAY(V) (לֵּאמֹר *ley'mor*) **RMT:** and **YHWH** spoke to Mosheh saying,

6:18 (06:25) !(ms)~much~SPEAK(V) (דַּבֵּר *da'beyr*) TO (אֶל *el*) Aharon (אַהֲרֹן *a'ha'ron*) and~TO (וְאֶל *wê'el*) SON~s~him (בָּנָיו *ba'naw*) to~ >~SAY(V) (לֵאמֹר *ley'mor*) THIS (זֹאת *zot*) TEACHING (תּוֹרַת *to'rat*) the~FAILURE (הַחַטָּאת *ha'hha'tat*) in~AREA (בִּמְקוֹם *bim'qom*) WHICH (אֲשֶׁר *a'sher*) you(ms)~will~SLAY(V) (תִּשָּׁחֵט *ti'sha'hheyt*) the~ ASCENSION.OFFERING (הָעֹלָה *ha'o'lah*) you(ms)~will~SLAY(V) (תִּשָּׁחֵט *ti'sha'hheyt*) the~FAILURE (הַחַטָּאת *ha'hha'tat*) to~FACE~s (לִפְנֵי *liph'ney*) **YHWH** (יְהוָה *YHWH*) SPECIAL (קֹדֶשׁ *qo'desh*) SPECIAL~s (קָדָשִׁים *qa'da'shim*) SHE (הִוא *hi*) **RMT:** speak to Aharon and to his sons saying, this is the teaching of the failure in the area which you will slay the ascension offering, you will slay the failure to the face of **YHWH**, she is a special of specials[22].

6:19 (06:26) the~ADMINISTRATOR (הַכֹּהֵן *ha'ko'heyn*) the~much~ FAIL(V)~ing(ms) (הַמְחַטֵּא *ham'hha'tey*) AT~her (אֹתָהּ *o'tah*) he~will~ EAT(V)~her (יֹאכְלֶנָּה *yo'kha'le'nah*) in~AREA (בְּמָקוֹם *bê'ma'qom*) UNIQUE (קָדֹשׁ *qa'dosh*) she~will~be~EAT(V) (תֵאָכֵל *tey'a'kheyl*) in~

---

[22] The phrase "special of specials" means a "very special thing, one or place."

COURTYARD (בֶּחָצַר) ba'hha'tsar) ‾ENT (אֹהֶל) o'hel) APPOINTED (מוֹעֵד mo'eyd) **RMT:** The administrator, the one bearing the blame with her, will eat her in the unique area, she will be eaten in the courtyard of the appointed tent.

6:20 (06:27) ALL (כֹּל kol) WHICH (אֲשֶׁר a'sher) he~will~TOUCH⁽ᵛ⁾ (יִגַּע yiga) in~FLESH~her (בִּבְשָׂרָהּ biv'sa'rah) he~will~SET.APART⁽ᵛ⁾ (יִקְדָּשׁ yiq'dash) and~WHICH (וַאֲשֶׁר wa'a'sher) he~will~SPATTER⁽ᵛ⁾ (יִזֶּה yi'zeh) from~BLOOD~her (מִדָּמָהּ mi'da'mah) UPON (עַל al) the~ GARMENT (הַבֶּגֶד ha'be'ged) WHICH (אֲשֶׁר a'sher) he~will~ SPATTER⁽ᵛ⁾ (יִזֶּה yi'zeh) UPON~her (עָלֶיהָ a'ley'ah) you⁽ᵐᵖ⁾~will~ much~WASH⁽ᵛ⁾ (תְּכַבֵּס tê'kha'beys) in~AREA (בְּמָקוֹם bê'ma'qom) UNIQUE (קָדֹשׁ qa'dosh) **RMT:** Anything that touches her flesh will be set apart, and when he will spatter her blood upon the garment, when he will spatter upon her, you will wash it in the unique area,

6:21 (06:28) and~UTENSIL (וּכְלִי ukh'li) CLAY (חֶרֶשׂ hhe'res) WHICH (אֲשֶׁר a'sher) she~will~be~much~BOIL⁽ᵛ⁾ (תְּבֻשַּׁל tê'vu'shal) in~him (בּוֹ bo) he~will~be~CRACK⁽ᵛ⁾ (יִשָּׁבֵר yi'sha'veyr) and~IF (וְאִם wê'im) in~UTENSIL (בִּכְלִי bikh'li) COPPER (נְחֹשֶׁת nê'hho'shet) she~did~be~ much~BOIL⁽ᵛ⁾ (בֻּשָּׁלָה bu'sha'lah) and~he~did~be~much~SCOUR⁽ᵛ⁾ (וּמֹרַק u'mo'raq) and~he~did~be~much~FLUSH⁽ᵛ⁾ (וְשֻׁטַּף wê'shu'taph) in~the~WATER~s2 (בַּמָּיִם ba'ma'yim) **RMT:** and the utensil of clay which she is being boiled in will be cracked, or if she is being boiled in a utensil of copper, then he will be scoured and he will be flushed in the waters.

6:22 (06:29) ALL (כָּל kol) MALE (זָכָר za'khar) in~the~ ADMINISTRATOR~s (בַּכֹּהֲנִים ba'ko'ha'nim) he~will~EAT⁽ᵛ⁾ (יֹאכַל yo'khal) AT~her (אֹתָהּ o'tah) SPECIAL (קֹדֶשׁ qo'desh) SPECIAL~s (קָדָשִׁים qa'da'shim) SHE (הוּא hi) **RMT:** All the males among the administrators will eat her, she is a special of specials[23],

6:23 (06:30) and~ALL (וְכָל wê'khol) FAILURE (חַטָּאת hha'tat) WHICH (אֲשֶׁר a'sher) he~will~be~make~COME⁽ᵛ⁾ (יוּבָא yu'va) from~BLOOD~ her (מִדָּמָהּ mi'da'mah) TO (אֶל el) TENT (אֹהֶל o'hel) APPOINTED (מוֹעֵד mo'eyd) to~>~much~COVER⁽ᵛ⁾ (לְכַפֵּר lê'kha'peyr) in~the~ SPECIAL (בַּקֹּדֶשׁ ba'qo'desh) NOT (לֹא lo) she~will~be~EAT⁽ᵛ⁾ (תֵאָכֵל tey'a'kheyl) in~the~FIRE (בָּאֵשׁ ba'eysh) you⁽ᵐˢ⁾~will~CREMATE⁽ᵛ⁾ (תִּשָּׂרֵף ti'sa'reyph) **RMT:** and every failure which he will bring from

---

[23] The phrase "special of specials" means a "very special thing, one or place."

her blood to the appointed tent to make a covering in the special place will not be eaten in the fire, you will cremate it,

Chapter 7

7:1 and~THIS (וְזֹאת *wê'zot*) TEACHING (תּוֹרַת *to'rat*) the~GUILT (הָאָשָׁם *ha'a'sham*) SPECIAL (קֹדֶשׁ *qo'desh*) SPECIAL~s (קָדָשִׁים *qa'da'shim*) HE (הוּא *hu*) **RMT:** and this is the teaching of the guilt, he is a special of specials[24].

7:2 in~AREA (בִּמְקוֹם *bim'qom*) WHICH (אֲשֶׁר *a'sher*) he~will~ SLAY[(V)]~him (יִשְׁחֲטוּ *yish'hha'tu*) AT (אֶת *et*) the~ ASCENSION.OFFERING (הָעֹלָה *ha'o'lah*) he~will~SLAY[(V)]~him (יִשְׁחֲטוּ *yish'hha'tu*) AT (אֶת *et*) the~GUILT (הָאָשָׁם *ha'a'sham*) and~AT (וְאֶת *wê'et*) BLOOD~him (דָּמוֹ *da'mo*) he~will~SPRINKLE[(V)] (יִזְרֹק *yiz'roq*) UPON (עַל *al*) the~ALTAR (הַמִּזְבֵּחַ *ha'miz'bey'ahh*) ALL.AROUND (סָבִיב *sa'viv*) **RMT:** In the area where he will slay the ascension offering he will slay the guilt offering, he will sprinkle his blood upon the altar all around,

7:3 and~AT (וְאֶת *wê'eyt*) ALL (כָּל *kol*) FAT~him (חֶלְבּוֹ *hhel'bo*) he~ will~make~COME.NEAR[(V)] (יַקְרִיב *yaq'riv*) FROM~him (מִמֶּנּוּ *mi'me'nu*) AT (אֶת *eyt*) the~RUMP (הָאַלְיָה *ha'al'yah*) and~AT (וְאֶת *wê'et*) the~FAT (הַחֵלֶב *ha'hhey'lev*) the~much~COVER.OVER[(V)]~ ing[(ms)] (הַמְכַסֶּה *ham'kha'seh*) AT (אֶת *et*) the~INSIDE (הַקֶּרֶב *ha'qe'rev*) **RMT:** and he will bring all his fat near, the rump, the fat covering, the insides,

7:4 and~AT (וְאֵת *wê'eyt*) TWO (שְׁתֵּי *shê'tey*) the~KIDNEY~s (הַכְּלָיֹת *hak'la'yot*) and~AT (וְאֶת *wê'et*) the~FAT (הַחֵלֶב *ha'hhey'lev*) WHICH (אֲשֶׁר *a'sher*) UPON~them[(f)] (עֲלֵיהֶן *a'ley'hen*) WHICH (אֲשֶׁר *a'sher*) UPON (עַל *al*) the~HIP~s (הַכְּסָלִים *hak'sa'lim*) and~AT (וְאֶת *wê'et*) the~LOBE (הַיֹּתֶרֶת *hai'yo'te'ret*) UPON (עַל *al*) the~HEAVY (הַכָּבֵד *ha'ka'veyd*) UPON (עַל *al*) the~KIDNEY~s (הַכְּלָיֹת *hak'la'yot*) he~will~ make~TURN.ASIDE[(V)]~her (יְסִירֶנָּה *yê'si're'nah*) **RMT:** and the two

---

[24] The phrase "special of specials" means a "very special thing, one or place."

kidneys and the fat which is upon them which is upon the hips, and the lobe upon the heavy one[25] with the kidneys he will remove,

7:5 and~*he~did~make*~BURN.INCENSE[(V)] (וְהִקְטִיר wê'hiq'tir) AT~ them[(m)] (אֹתָם o'tam) the~ADMINISTRATOR (הַכֹּהֵן ha'ko'heyn) the~ ALTAR~unto (הַמִּזְבֵּחָה ha'miz'bey'hhah) FIRE.OFFERING (אִשֶּׁה i'sheh) to~YHWH (לַיהוָה la'YHWH) GUILT (אָשָׁם a'sham) HE (הוא hu) **RMT:** and the administrator will burn them as incense upon the altar, a fire offering to **YHWH**, he is the guilt.

7:6 ALL (כָּל kol) MALE (זָכָר za'khar) in~the~ADMINISTRATOR~s (בַּכֹּהֲנִים ba'ko'ha'nim) *he~will*~EAT[(V)]~him (יֹאכְלֶנּוּ yo'khe'le'nu) in~ AREA (בְּמָקוֹם bê'ma'qom) UNIQUE (קָדוֹשׁ qa'dosh) *he~will~be*~ EAT[(V)] (יֵאָכֵל yey'a'kheyl) SPECIAL (קֹדֶשׁ qo'desh) SPECIAL~s (קָדָשִׁים qa'da'shim) HE (הוא hu) **RMT:** All the males with the administrators will eat him, he is a special of specials[26].

7:7 like~the~FAILURE (כַּחַטָּאת ka'hha'tat) like~GUILT (כָּאָשָׁם ka'a'sham) TEACHING (תּוֹרָה to'rah) UNIT (אַחַת a'hhot) to~them[(m)] (לָהֶם la'hem) the~ADMINISTRATOR (הַכֹּהֵן ha'ko'heyn) WHICH (אֲשֶׁר a'sher) *he~will~much~*COVER[(V)] (יְכַפֶּר yê'kha'per) in~him (בּוֹ bo) to~ him (לוֹ lo) *he~will*~EXIST[(V)] (יִהְיֶה yih'yeh) **RMT:** Like the failure, like the guilt, it is one teaching for them, the administrator, which will make a covering with him, it will exist for him,

7:8 and~the~ADMINISTRATOR (וְהַכֹּהֵן wê'ha'ko'heyn) the~*make~* COME.NEAR[(V)]~*ing*[(ms)] (הַמַּקְרִיב ha'maq'riv) AT (אֶת et) ASCENSION.OFFERING (עֹלַת o'lat) MAN (אִישׁ ish) SKIN (עוֹר or) the~ ASCENSION.OFFERING (הָעֹלָה ha'o'lah) WHICH (אֲשֶׁר a'sher) *he~ did~make~*COME.NEAR[(V)] (הִקְרִיב hiq'riv) to~the~ADMINISTRATOR (לַכֹּהֵן la'ko'heyn) to~him (לוֹ lo) *he~will*~EXIST[(V)] (יִהְיֶה yih'yeh) **RMT:** and the administrator bringing near the ascension offering of a man, the skin of the ascension offering, which he brought near to the administrator, he will exist for him,

7:9 and~ALL (וְכָל wê'khol) DEPOSIT (מִנְחָה min'hhah) WHICH (אֲשֶׁר a'sher) *she~will~be~*BAKE[(V)] (תֵּאָפֶה tey'a'pheh) in~the~OVEN (בַּתַּנּוּר

---

[25] The phrase "lobe upon the heavy one" may be written incorrectly and should read "upon the heavy lobe" (see Exodus 29:22 and Leviticus 8:16).

[26] The phrase "special of specials" means a "very special thing, one or place."

ba'ta'nur) and~ALL (וְכָל *wê'khol*) *he~did~be~*DO[(V)] (נַעֲשָׂה *na'a'sah*) in~the~BOILING.POT (בַּמַּרְחֶשֶׁת *va'mar'hhe'shet*) and~UPON (וְעַל *wê'al*) PAN (מַחֲבַת *ma'hha'vat*) to~the~ADMINISTRATOR (לַכֹּהֵן *la'ko'heyn*) the~*make~*COME.NEAR[(V)]~*ing*[(ms)] (הַמַּקְרִיב *ha'maq'riv*) AT~her (אֹתָהּ *o'tah*) to~him (לוֹ *lo*) *she~will~*EXIST[(V)] (תִהְיֶה *tih'yeh*) **RMT:** and all the deposits, which will be baked in the oven, and all that was made in the boiling pot and upon the pan, belongs to the administrator, the one bringing her, she will exist for him,

7:10 and~ALL (וְכָל *wê'khol*) DEPOSIT (מִנְחָה *min'hhah*) MIX[(V)]~*ed*[(fs)] (בְלוּלָה *vê'lu'lah*) in~the~OIL (בַשֶּׁמֶן *va'she'men*) and~DRIED.OUT (וַחֲרֵבָה *wa'hha'rey'vah*) to~ALL (לְכָל *lê'khol*) SON~s (בְּנֵי *bê'ney*) Aharon (אַהֲרֹן *a'ha'ron*) *she~will~*EXIST[(V)] (תִהְיֶה *tih'yeh*) MAN (אִישׁ *ish*) like~BROTHER~him (כְּאָחִיו *kê'a'hhiw*) **RMT:** and all the deposits mixed in the oil and dried out, belong to all the sons of Aharon, she will exist each like his brother,

7:11 and~THIS (וְזֹאת *wê'zot*) TEACHING (תּוֹרַת *to'rat*) SACRIFICE (זֶבַח *ze'vahh*) the~*OFFERING.OF.RESTITUTION~s* (הַשְּׁלָמִים *ha'she'la'mim*) WHICH (אֲשֶׁר *a'sher*) *he~will~make~*COME.NEAR[(V)] (יַקְרִיב *yaq'riv*) to~YHWH (לַיהֹוָה *la'YHWH*) **RMT:** and this is the teaching of the sacrifice, the offerings of restitution, which he will bring near to **YHWH**.

7:12 IF (אִם *im*) UPON (עַל *al*) THANKS (תּוֹדָה *to'dah*) *he~will~make~*COME.NEAR[(V)]~*him* (יַקְרִיבֶנּוּ *yaq'riy've'nu*) and~*he~did~make~*COME.NEAR[(V)] (וְהִקְרִיב *wê'hiq'riv*) UPON (עַל *al*) SACRIFICE (זֶבַח *ze'vahh*) the~THANKS (הַתּוֹדָה *ha'to'dah*) PIERCED.BREAD~s (חַלּוֹת *hha'lot*) UNLEAVENED.BREAD~s (מַצּוֹת *ma'tsot*) MIX[(V)]~*ed*[(fp)] (בְּלוּלֹת *bê'lu'lot*) in~the~OIL (בַּשֶּׁמֶן *ba'she'men*) and~THIN.BREAD~s (וּרְקִיקֵי *ur'qi'qey*) UNLEAVENED.BREAD~s (מַצּוֹת *ma'tsot*) SMEAR[(V)]~*ed*[(mp)] (מְשֻׁחִים *mê'shu'hhim*) in~the~OIL (בַּשָּׁמֶן *ba'sha'men*) and~FLOUR (וְסֹלֶת *wê'so'let*) *be~make~*FRY[(V)]~*ing*[(fs)] (מֻרְבֶּכֶת *mur'be'khet*) PIERCED.BREAD~s (חַלֹּת *hha'lot*) MIX[(V)]~*ed*[(fp)] (בְּלוּלֹת *bê'lu'lot*) in~the~OIL (בַּשָּׁמֶן *ba'sha'men*) **RMT:** If it is for thanks, he will bring him near, and he will bring it near upon the sacrifice of the thanks, pierced unleavened breads mixed in the oil, and thin unleavened breads smeared with oil, and flour being fried, pierced breads mixed with the oil.

7:13 UPON (עַל *al*) PIERCED.BREAD~s (חַלֹּת *hha'lot*) BREAD (לֶחֶם *le'hhem*) LEAVENED.BREAD (חָמֵץ *hha'meyts*) *he~will~make~*COME.NEAR[(V)] (יַקְרִיב *yaq'riv*) DONATION~him (קָרְבָּנוֹ *qar'ba'no*)

UPON (עַל *al*) SACRIFICE (זֶבַח *ze'vahh*) THANKS (תּוֹדַת *to'dat*) OFFERING.OF.RESTITUTION~s~him (שְׁלָמָיו *shê'la'maw*) **RMT:** Upon the pierced breads is leavened bread, he will bring near his donation upon the sacrifice of thanks, it is his offerings of restitution,

7:14 and~he~did~make~COME.NEAR(V) (וְהִקְרִיב *wê'hiq'riv*) FROM~ him (מִמֶּנּוּ *mi'me'nu*) UNIT (אֶחָד *e'hhad*) from~ALL (מִכָּל *mi'kol*) DONATION (קָרְבָּן *qar'ban*) OFFERING (תְּרוּמָה *tê'ru'mah*) to~**YHWH** (לַיהוָה *la'YHWH*) to~the~ADMINISTRATOR (לַכֹּהֵן *la'ko'heyn*) the~ SPRINKLE(V)~ing(ms) (הַזֹּרֵק *ha'zo'reyq*) AT (אֶת *et*) BLOOD (דַּם *dam*) the~OFFERING.OF.RESTITUTION~s (הַשְּׁלָמִים *ha'she'la'mim*) to~him (לוֹ *lo*) he~will~EXIST(V) (יִהְיֶה *yih'yeh*) **RMT:** and he will bring near from himself a unit from all the donation offerings to **YHWH**, it will belong to the administrator, the one sprinkling the blood of the offerings of restitution, he will exist for him,

7:15 and~FLESH (וּבְשַׂר *uv'sar*) SACRIFICE (זֶבַח *ze'vahh*) THANKS (תּוֹדַת *to'dat*) OFFERING.OF.RESTITUTION~s~him (שְׁלָמָיו *shê'la'maw*) in~DAY (בְּיוֹם *bê'yom*) DONATION~him (קָרְבָּנוֹ *qar'ba'no*) he~will~be~EAT(V) (יֵאָכֵל *yey'a'kheyl*) NOT (לֹא *lo*) he~ will~make~REST(V) (יַנִּיחַ *ya'ni'ahh*) FROM~him (מִמֶּנּוּ *mi'me'nu*) UNTIL (עַד *ad*) MORNING (בֹּקֶר *bo'qer*) **RMT:** and the flesh of the sacrifice of thanks is his offerings of restitution, in the day his donation will be eaten, he will not leave any from him until morning,

7:16 and~IF (וְאִם *wê'im*) VOW (נֶדֶר *ne'der*) OR (אוֹ *o*) FREEWILL.OFFERING (נְדָבָה *nê'da'vah*) SACRIFICE (זֶבַח *ze'vahh*) DONATION~him (קָרְבָּנוֹ *qar'ba'no*) in~DAY (בְּיוֹם *bê'yom*) >~make~ COME.NEAR(V)~him (הַקְרִיבוֹ *haq'ri'vo*) AT (אֶת *et*) SACRIFICE~him (זִבְחוֹ *ziv'hho*) he~will~be~EAT(V) (יֵאָכֵל *yey'a'kheyl*) and~from~ MORROW (וּמִמָּחֳרָת *u'mi'ma'hha'rat*) and~the~be~ LEAVE.BEHIND(V)~ing(ms) (וְהַנּוֹתָר *wê'ha'no'tar*) FROM~him (מִמֶּנּוּ *mi'me'nu*) he~will~be~EAT(V) (יֵאָכֵל *yey'a'kheyl*) **RMT:** but if the sacrifice of his donation is a vow or freewill offering, in the day his sacrifice is brought near, he will be eaten, and that being left behind from him on the morrow, he will be eaten,

7:17 and~the~be~LEAVE.BEHIND(V)~ing(ms) (וְהַנּוֹתָר *wê'ha'no'tar*) from~FLESH (מִבְּשַׂר *mi'be'sar*) the~SACRIFICE (הַזָּבַח *ha'za'vahh*) in~ the~DAY (בַּיּוֹם *ba'yom*) the~THIRD (הַשְּׁלִישִׁי *hash'li'shi*) in~the~FIRE (בָּאֵשׁ *ba'eysh*) he~will~be~CREMATE(V) (יִשָּׂרֵף *yi'sa'reyph*) **RMT:** and that being left behind from the flesh of the sacrifice in the third day, will be cremated in the fire,

7:18 and~IF (וְאִם wê'im) the~>~be~EAT⁽ᵛ⁾ (הֵאָכֹל hey'a'khol) he~
will~be~EAT⁽ᵛ⁾ (יֵאָכֵל yey'a'kheyl) from~FLESH (מִבְּשַׂר mi'be'sar)
SACRIFICE (זֶבַח ze'vahh) OFFERING.OF.RESTITUTION~s~him (שְׁלָמָיו
shê'la'maw) in~the~DAY (בַּיוֹם ba'yom) the~THIRD (הַשְּׁלִישִׁי
hash'li'shi) NOT (לֹא lo) he~will~be~ACCEPT⁽ᵛ⁾ (יֵרָצֶה yey'ra'tseh)
the~make~COME.NEAR⁽ᵛ⁾~ing⁽ᵐˢ⁾ (הַמַּקְרִיב ha'maq'riv) AT~him (אֹתוֹ
o'to) NOT (לֹא lo) he~will~be~THINK⁽ᵛ⁾ (יֵחָשֵׁב yey'hha'sheyv) to~him
(לוֹ lo) FOUL (פִּגּוּל pi'gul) he~will~EXIST⁽ᵛ⁾ (יִהְיֶה yih'yeh) and~the~
SOUL (וְהַנֶּפֶשׁ wê'ha'ne'phesh) the~EAT⁽ᵛ⁾~ing⁽ᶠˢ⁾ (הָאֹכֶלֶת
ha'o'khe'let) FROM~him (מִמֶּנּוּ mi'me'nu) TWISTEDNESS~her (עֲוֹנָהּ
a'o'nah) she~will~LIFT.UP⁽ᵛ⁾ (תִּשָּׂא ti'sa) **RMT:** and if the flesh of the
sacrifice of his offerings of restitution will surely be eaten in the third
day, the one bringing him near will not be accepted, he will not be
considered, he will exist foul, and the soul eating from him will lift up
her twistedness,

7:19 and~the~FLESH (וְהַבָּשָׂר wê'ha'ba'sar) WHICH (אֲשֶׁר a'sher) he~
will~TOUCH⁽ᵛ⁾ (יִגַּע yiga) in~ALL (בְּכָל bê'khol) DIRTY (טָמֵא ta'mey)
NOT (לֹא lo) he~will~be~EAT⁽ᵛ⁾ (יֵאָכֵל yey'a'kheyl) in~the~FIRE (בָּאֵשׁ
ba'eysh) he~will~be~CREMATE⁽ᵛ⁾ (יִשָּׂרֵף yi'sa'reyph) and~the~FLESH
(וְהַבָּשָׂר wê'ha'ba'sar) ALL (כָּל kol) CLEAN (טָהוֹר ta'hor) he~will~
EAT⁽ᵛ⁾ (יֹאכַל yo'khal) FLESH (בָּשָׂר ba'sar) **RMT:** and the flesh which
touches any dirty thing will not be eaten, he will be cremated in the
fire, and the flesh of all clean things, he will eat the flesh,

7:20 and~the~SOUL (וְהַנֶּפֶשׁ wê'ha'ne'phesh) WHICH (אֲשֶׁר a'sher)
she~will~EAT⁽ᵛ⁾ (תֹּאכַל to'khal) FLESH (בָּשָׂר ba'sar) from~SACRIFICE
(מִזֶּבַח mi'ze'vahh) the~OFFERING.OF.RESTITUTION~s (הַשְּׁלָמִים
ha'she'la'mim) WHICH (אֲשֶׁר a'sher) to~**YHWH** (לַיהוָה la'YHWH)
and~DIRTY~him (וְטֻמְאָתוֹ wê'tum'a'to) UPON~him (עָלָיו a'law)
and~she~did~be~CUT⁽ᵛ⁾ (וְנִכְרְתָה wê'nikh're'tah) the~SOUL (הַנֶּפֶשׁ
ha'ne'phesh) the~SHE (הַהִוא ha'hi) from~PEOPLE~s~her (מֵעַמֶּיהָ
mey'a'mey'ah) **RMT:** and the soul which will eat flesh from the
sacrifice of the offerings of restitution which belongs to **YHWH**, then
his dirtiness is upon him, and that soul will be cut from her people,

7:21 and~SOUL (וְנֶפֶשׁ wê'ne'phesh) GIVEN.THAT (כִּי ki) she~will~
TOUCH⁽ᵛ⁾ (תִגַּע ti'ga) in~ALL (בְּכָל bê'khol) DIRTY (טָמֵא ta'mey) in~
DIRTY (בְּטֻמְאַת bê'tum'at) HUMAN (אָדָם a'dam) OR (אוֹ o) in~
BEAST (בִּבְהֵמָה biv'hey'mah) DIRTY (טְמֵאָה tê'mey'ah) OR (אוֹ o) in~
ALL (בְּכָל bê'khol) FILTHY (שֶׁקֶץ she'qets) DIRTY (טָמֵא ta'mey) and~
he~did~EAT⁽ᵛ⁾ (וְאָכַל wê'a'khal) from~FLESH (מִבְּשַׂר mi'be'sar)

SACRIFICE (זֶבַח ze'vahh) the~OFFERING.OF.RESTITUTION~s (הַשְּׁלָמִים ha'she'la'mim) WHICH (אֲשֶׁר a'sher) to~YHWH (לַיהוָה la'YHWH) and~she~did~be~CUT[V] (וְנִכְרְתָה wê'nikh're'tah) the~ SOUL (הַנֶּפֶשׁ ha'ne'phesh) the~SHE (הַהִוא ha'hi) from~PEOPLE~s~ her (מֵעַמֶּיהָ mey'a'mey'ah) RMT: and the soul that will touch any dirty thing, a dirty human or dirty beast or any filthy dirty thing, and ate from the flesh of the sacrifice of the offerings of restitution, which belong to YHWH, then that soul will be cut from her people,

7:22 and~he~will~much~SPEAK[V] (וַיְדַבֵּר wai'da'beyr) YHWH (יְהוָה YHWH) TO (אֶל el) Mosheh (מֹשֶׁה mo'sheh) to~>~SAY[V] (לֵאמֹר ley'mor) RMT: and YHWH spoke to Mosheh saying,

7:23 !^(ms)~much~SPEAK[V] (דַּבֵּר da'beyr) TO (אֶל el) SON~s (בְּנֵי bê'ney) Yisra'eyl (יִשְׂרָאֵל yis'ra'eyl) to~>~SAY[V] (לֵאמֹר ley'mor) ALL (כָּל kol) FAT (חֵלֶב hhey'lev) OX (שׁוֹר shor) and~SHEEP (וְכֶשֶׂב wê'khe'sev) and~SHE-GOAT (וָעֵז wa'eyz) NOT (לֹא lo) you^(mp)~will~ EAT[V] (תֹאכֵלוּ to'khey'lu) RMT: speak to the sons of Yisra'eyl saying, all the fat of the ox and sheep and she-goats you will not eat,

7:24 and~FAT (וְחֵלֶב wê'hhey'lev) CARCASS (נְבֵלָה nê'vey'lah) and~ FAT (וְחֵלֶב wê'hhey'lev) TORN (טְרֵפָה tê'rey'phah) he~will~be~DO[V] (יֵעָשֶׂה yey'a'seh) to~ALL (לְכָל lê'khol) BUSINESS (מְלָאכָה mê'la'khah) and~>~EAT[V] (וְאָכֹל wê'a'khol) NOT (לֹא lo) you^(mp)~ will~EAT[V]~him (תֹאכְלֻהוּ to'khe'lu'hu) RMT: and the fat of a carcass and the fat of a torn thing will be done for any business, but you must not eat him,

7:25 GIVEN.THAT (כִּי ki) ALL (כָּל kol) EAT[V]~ing^(ms) (אֹכֵל o'kheyl) FAT (חֵלֶב hhey'lev) FROM (מִן min) the~BEAST (הַבְּהֵמָה ha'be'hey'mah) WHICH (אֲשֶׁר a'sher) he~will~make~COME.NEAR[V] (יַקְרִיב yaq'riv) FROM~her (מִמֶּנָּה mi'me'nah) FIRE.OFFERING (אִשֶּׁה i'sheh) to~YHWH (לַיהוָה la'YHWH) and~she~did~be~CUT[V] (וְנִכְרְתָה wê'nikh're'tah) the~SOUL (הַנֶּפֶשׁ ha'ne'phesh) the~EAT[V]~ing^(fs) (הָאֹכֶלֶת ha'o'khe'let) from~PEOPLE~s~her (מֵעַמֶּיהָ mey'a'mey'ah) RMT: given that all eating the fat from the beast, which is brought near from the fire offering to YHWH, and the soul that is eating will be cut from her people,

7:26 and~ALL (וְכָל wê'khol) BLOOD (דָּם dam) NOT (לֹא lo) you^(mp)~ will~EAT[V] (תֹאכְלוּ to'khe'lu) in~ALL (בְּכֹל bê'khol) SETTLING~s~ you^(mp) (מוֹשְׁבֹתֵיכֶם mosh'vo'tey'khem) to~the~FLYER (לָעוֹף la'oph) and~to~the~BEAST (וְלַבְּהֵמָה wê'la'be'hey'mah) RMT: and all the blood, belonging to the flyer or to the beast, you will not eat in all your settlings.

7:27 <u>ALL</u> (כָּל *kol*) <u>SOUL</u> (נֶפֶשׁ *ne'phesh*) <u>WHICH</u> (אֲשֶׁר *a'sher*) *she~will~*EAT^(V) (תֹאכַל *to'khal*) <u>ALL</u> (כָּל *kol*) <u>BLOOD</u> (דָם *dam*) and~*she~did~be~*CUT^(V) (וְנִכְרְתָה *wê'nikh're'tah*) the~SOUL (הַנֶּפֶשׁ *ha'ne'phesh*) the~SHE (הַהִוא *ha'hi*) from~PEOPLE~s~her (מֵעַמֶּיהָ *mey'a'mey'ah*) **RMT:** Any soul which will eat any blood, then that soul will be cut from her people,

7:28 and~*he~will~much~*SPEAK^(V) (וַיְדַבֵּר *wai'da'beyr*) **YHWH** (יְהֹוָה *YHWH*) <u>TO</u> (אֶל *el*) <u>Mosheh</u> (מֹשֶׁה *mo'sheh*) to~>~SAY^(V) (לֵאמֹר *ley'mor*) **RMT:** and **YHWH** spoke to Mosheh saying,

7:29 !^(ms)~*much~*SPEAK^(V) (דַּבֵּר *da'beyr*) <u>TO</u> (אֶל *el*) <u>SON~s</u> (בְּנֵי *bê'ney*) <u>Yisra'eyl</u> (יִשְׂרָאֵל *yis'ra'eyl*) to~>~SAY^(V) (לֵאמֹר *ley'mor*) the~*make~*COME.NEAR^(V)~*ing*^(ms) (הַמַּקְרִיב *ha'maq'riv*) <u>AT</u> (אֶת *et*) <u>SACRIFICE</u> (זֶבַח *ze'vahh*) <u>OFFERING.OF.RESTITUTION~s~him</u> (שְׁלָמָיו *shê'la'maw*) to~**YHWH** (לַיהֹוָה *la'YHWH*) <u>he~will~make~</u>COME^(V) (יָבִיא *ya'vi*) <u>AT</u> (אֶת *et*) <u>DONATION~him</u> (קָרְבָּנוֹ *qar'ba'no*) to~**YHWH** (לַיהֹוָה *la'YHWH*) <u>from~SACRIFICE</u> (מִזֶּבַח *mi'ze'vahh*) <u>OFFERING.OF.RESTITUTION~s~him</u> (שְׁלָמָיו *shê'la'maw*) **RMT:** speak to the sons of Yisra'eyl saying, the one bringing near a sacrifice of his offering of restitution to **YHWH**, he will bring his donation to **YHWH** from the sacrifice of his offerings of restitution.

7:30 <u>HAND~s2~him</u> (יָדָיו *ya'daw*) they^(f)~*will~make~*COME^(V) (תְּבִיאֶינָה *tê'vi'ey'nah*) <u>AT</u> (אֶת *eyt*) <u>FIRE.OFFERING~s</u> (אִשֵּׁי *i'shey*) **YHWH** (יְהֹוָה *YHWH*) <u>AT</u> (אֶת *et*) the~FAT (הַחֵלֶב *ha'hhey'lev*) <u>UPON</u> (עַל *al*) the~CHEST (הֶחָזֶה *he'hha'zeh*) <u>he~will~make~</u>COME^(V)~him (יְבִיאֶנּוּ *yê'vi'e'nu*) <u>AT</u> (אֶת *eyt*) the~CHEST (הֶחָזֶה *he'hha'zeh*) to~>~*make~*WAVE^(V) (לְהָנִיף *lê'ha'niph*) AT~him (אֹתוֹ *o'to*) <u>WAVING</u> (תְּנוּפָה *tê'nu'phah*) to~FACE~s (לִפְנֵי *liph'ney*) **YHWH** (יְהֹוָה *YHWH*) **RMT:** His hands will bring the fire offerings of **YHWH**, the fat upon the chest he will bring with the chest, to make him wave, a waving to the face of **YHWH**,

7:31 and~*he~did~make~*BURN.INCENSE^(V) (וְהִקְטִיר *wê'hiq'tir*) the~<u>ADMINISTRATOR</u> (הַכֹּהֵן *ha'ko'heyn*) <u>AT</u> (אֶת *et*) the~FAT (הַחֵלֶב *ha'hhey'lev*) the~ALTAR~unto (הַמִּזְבֵּחָה *ha'miz'bey'hhah*) and~*he~did~*EXIST^(V) (וְהָיָה *wê'hai'yah*) the~CHEST (הֶחָזֶה *he'hha'zeh*) to~<u>Aharon</u> (לְאַהֲרֹן *lê'a'ha'ron*) and~to~SON~s~him (וּלְבָנָיו *ul'va'naw*)

RMT: and the administrator will make the fat burn as incense upon the altar, and the chest will exist for Aharon and for his sons,

7:32 <u>and~AT</u> (וְאֵת֙ *wê'eyt*) <u>THIGH</u> (שֹׁ֖וק *shoq*) <u>the~RIGHT.HAND</u> (הַיָּמִ֑ין *hai'ya'min*) *you^(mp)~will~*<u>GIVE</u>^(V) (תִּתְּנ֥וּ *tit'nu*) <u>OFFERING</u> (תְרוּמָ֖ה *tê'ru'mah*) <u>to~the~ADMINISTRATOR</u> (לַכֹּהֵ֑ן *la'ko'heyn*) <u>from~SACRIFICE~s</u> (מִזִּבְחֵ֖י *mi'ziv'hhey*) <u>OFFERING.OF.RESTITUTION~s~you^(mp)</u> (שַׁלְמֵיכֶֽם *shal'mey'khem*) **RMT:** and the right thigh you will give as an offering to the administrator from the sacrifices of your offerings of restitution.

7:33 <u>the~*make~*COME.NEAR^(√)*~ing^(ms)*</u> (הַמַּקְרִ֞יב *ha'maq'riv*) <u>AT</u> (אֶת־ *et*) <u>BLOOD</u> (דַּ֤ם *dam*) <u>the~OFFERING.OF.RESTITUTION~s</u> (הַשְּׁלָמִים֙ *ha'she'la'mim*) <u>and~AT</u> (וְאֶת־ *wê'et*) <u>the~FAT</u> (הַחֵ֔לֶב *ha'hhey'lev*) <u>from~SON~s</u> (מִבְּנֵ֖י *mi'be'ney*) <u>Aharon</u> (אַהֲרֹ֑ן *a'ha'ron*) <u>to~him</u> (ל֥וֹ *lo*) *she~will~*<u>EXIST</u>^(V) (תִהְיֶ֛ה *tih'yeh*) <u>THIGH</u> (שֹׁ֥וק *shoq*) <u>the~RIGHT.HAND</u> (הַיָּמִ֖ין *hai'ya'min*) <u>to~SHARE</u> (לְמָנָֽה *lê'ma'nah*) **RMT:** The one from the sons of Aharon bringing near the blood of the offerings of restitution, and the fat, the right thigh will exist for him for a share,

7:34 <u>GIVEN.THAT</u> (כִּי֩ *ki*) <u>AT</u> (אֶת־ *et*) <u>CHEST</u> (חֲזֵ֨ה *hha'zeyh*) <u>the~WAVING</u> (הַתְּנוּפָ֜ה *hat'nu'phah*) <u>and~AT</u> (וְאֵ֣ת *wê'eyt*) <u>THIGH</u> (שֹׁ֣וק *shoq*) <u>the~OFFERING</u> (הַתְּרוּמָ֗ה *hat'ru'mah*) *I~did~*<u>TAKE</u>^(V) (לָקַ֙חְתִּי֙ *la'qahh'ti*) <u>from~AT</u> (מֵאֵת֙ *mey'eyt*) <u>SON~s</u> (בְּנֵ֣י *bê'ney*) <u>Yisra'eyl</u> (יִשְׂרָאֵ֔ל *yis'ra'eyl*) <u>from~SACRIFICE~s</u> (מִזִּבְחֵ֖י *mi'ziv'hhey*) <u>OFFERING.OF.RESTITUTION~s~them^(m)</u> (שַׁלְמֵיהֶ֑ם *shal'mey'hem*) <u>and~*I~will~*GIVE</u>^(V) (וָאֶתֵּ֣ן *wa'e'teyn*) <u>AT~them^(m)</u> (אֹתָ֡ם *o'tam*) <u>to~Aharon</u> (לְאַהֲרֹ֣ן *lê'a'ha'ron*) <u>the~ADMINISTRATOR</u> (הַכֹּהֵן֩ *ha'ko'heyn*) <u>and~to~SON~s~him</u> (וּלְבָנָ֨יו *ul'va'naw*) <u>to~CUSTOM</u> (לְחָק־ *lê'hhaq*) <u>DISTANT</u> (עֹולָ֜ם *o'lam*) <u>from~AT</u> (מֵאֵת֙ *mey'eyt*) <u>SON~s</u> (בְּנֵ֣י *bê'ney*) <u>Yisra'eyl</u> (יִשְׂרָאֵֽל *yis'ra'eyl*) **RMT:** given that the chest of the waving and the thigh of the offering, I took from the sons of Yisra'eyl from the sacrifices of their offerings of restitution, and I will give them to Aharon the administrator and to his sons from the sons of Yisra'eyl for a distant custom.

7:35 <u>THIS</u> (זֹ֣את *zot*) <u>OINTMENT</u> (מִשְׁחַ֤ת *mish'hhat*) <u>Aharon</u> (אַהֲרֹן֙ *a'ha'ron*) <u>and~OINTMENT</u> (וּמִשְׁחַ֣ת *u'mish'hhat*) <u>SON~s~him</u> (בָּנָ֔יו *ba'naw*) <u>from~FIRE.OFFERING~s</u> (מֵאִשֵּׁ֖י *mey'l'shey*) <u>YHWH</u> (יְהוָ֑ה *YHWH*) <u>in~DAY</u> (בְּיוֹם֙ *bê'yom*) <u>he~did~*make~*COME.NEAR</u>^(V) (הִקְרִ֣יב *hiq'riv*) <u>AT~them^(fm)</u> (אֹתָ֔ם *o'tam*) <u>to~>~much~ADORN</u>^(V) (לְכַהֵ֖ן *lê'kha'heyn*) <u>to~YHWH</u> (לַיהוָֽה *la'YHWH*) **RMT:** This is the ointment of Aharon and the ointment of his sons from the fire offerings of **YHWH**, in the day he brought them near to be adorned for **YHWH**.

7:36 <u>WHICH</u> (אֲשֶׁר *a'sher*) <u>he~did~much~DIRECT</u>^(V) (צִוָּה *tsi'wah*) **YHWH** (יְהוָה *YHWH*) <u>to~>~GIVE</u>^(V) (לָתֵת *la'teyt*) <u>to~them</u>^(m) (לָהֶם *la'hem*) <u>in~DAY</u> (בְּיוֹם *bê'yom*) <u>>~SMEAR</u>^(V)~him (מָשְׁחוֹ *mash'hho*) <u>AT~them</u>^(m) (אֹתָם *o'tam*) <u>from~AT</u> (מֵאֵת *mey'eyt*) <u>SON~s</u> (בְּנֵי *bê'ney*) <u>Yisra'eyl</u> (יִשְׂרָאֵל *yis'ra'eyl*) <u>CUSTOM</u> (חֻקַּת *hhu'qat*) <u>DISTANT</u> (עוֹלָם *o'lam*) <u>to~GENERATION~s~them</u>^(m) (לְדֹרֹתָם *lê'do'ro'tam*) **RMT:** Which **YHWH** directed to give to them in the day of his smearing them from the sons of Yisra'eyl, a distant custom for their generations.

7:37 <u>THIS</u> (זֹאת *zot*) <u>the~TEACHING</u> (הַתּוֹרָה *ha'to'rah*) <u>to~the~ASCENSION.OFFERING</u> (לָעֹלָה *la'o'lah*) <u>to~the~DEPOSIT</u> (לַמִּנְחָה *la'min'hhah*) <u>and~to~the~FAILURE</u> (וְלַחַטָּאת *wê'la'hha'tat*) <u>and~to~the~GUILT</u> (וְלָאָשָׁם *wê'la'a'sham*) <u>and~to~the~SETTING~s</u> (וְלַמִּלּוּאִים *wê'la'mi'lu'im*) <u>and~to~SACRIFICE</u> (וּלְזֶבַח *ul'ze'vahh*) <u>the~OFFERING.OF.RESTITUTION~s</u> (הַשְּׁלָמִים *ha'she'la'mim*) **RMT:** This is the teaching for the ascension offering, for the deposit and for the failure and for the guilt and for the settings and for the sacrifice of offerings of restitution.

7:38 <u>WHICH</u> (אֲשֶׁר *a'sher*) <u>he~did~much~DIRECT</u>^(V) (צִוָּה *tsi'wah*) **YHWH** (יְהוָה *YHWH*) <u>AT</u> (אֶת *et*) <u>Mosheh</u> (מֹשֶׁה *mo'sheh*) <u>in~HILL</u> (בְּהַר *bê'har*) <u>Sinai</u> (סִינַי *si'nai*) <u>in~DAY</u> (בְּיוֹם *bê'yom*) <u>>~much~DIRECT</u>^(V)~him (צַוֹּתוֹ *tsa'wo'to*) <u>AT</u> (אֶת *et*) <u>SON~s</u> (בְּנֵי *bê'ney*) <u>Yisra'eyl</u> (יִשְׂרָאֵל *yis'ra'eyl*) <u>to~>~make~COME.NEAR</u>^(V) (לְהַקְרִיב *lê'haq'riv*) <u>AT</u> (אֶת *et*) <u>DONATION~s~them</u>^(m) (קָרְבְּנֵיהֶם *qar'be'ney'hem*) <u>to~YHWH</u> (לַיהוָה *la'YHWH*) <u>in~WILDERNESS</u> (בְּמִדְבַּר *bê'mid'bar*) <u>Sinai</u> (סִינָי *si'nai*) **RMT:** Which **YHWH** directed Mosheh in the hill of Sinai in the day of his directing the sons of Yisra'eyl to bring near their donations to **YHWH** in the wilderness of Sinai,

Chapter 8

8:1 <u>and~he~will~much~SPEAK</u>^(V) (וַיְדַבֵּר *wai'da'beyr*) **YHWH** (יְהוָה *YHWH*) <u>TO</u> (אֶל *el*) <u>Mosheh</u> (מֹשֶׁה *mo'sheh*) <u>to~>~SAY</u>^(V) (לֵאמֹר *ley'mor*) **RMT:** and **YHWH** spoke to Mosheh saying,

8:2 <u>I</u>^(ms)~TAKE^(V) (קַח *qahh*) <u>AT</u> (אֶת *et*) <u>Aharon</u> (אַהֲרֹן *a'ha'ron*) <u>and~AT</u> (וְאֵת *wê'et*) <u>SON~s~him</u> (בָּנָיו *ba'naw*) <u>AT~him</u> (אִתּוֹ *i'to*) <u>and~AT</u>

44

(וְאֵת wê'eyt) the~GARMENT~s (הַבְּגָדִים ha'be'ga'dim) and~AT (וְאֵת wê'eyt) OIL (שֶׁמֶן she'men) the~OINTMENT (הַמִּשְׁחָה ha'mish'hhah) and~AT (וְאֵת wê'eyt) BULL (פַּר par) the~FAILURE (הַחַטָּאת ha'hha'tat) and~AT (וְאֵת wê'eyt) TWO (שְׁנֵי shê'ney) the~BUCK~s (הָאֵילִים ha'ey'lim) and~AT (וְאֵת wê'eyt) WICKER.BASKET (סַל sal) the~UNLEAVENED.BREAD~s (הַמַּצּוֹת ha'ma'tsot) **RMT:** take Aharon and his sons with him and the garments and the oil of ointment and the bull of failure and two bucks and the wicker basket of unleavened breads,

8:3 and~AT (וְאֵת wê'eyt) ALL (כָּל kol) the~COMPANY (הָעֵדָה ha'ey'dah) !*(mp)~make~*ASSEMBLE[(V)] (הַקְהֵל haq'heyl) TO (אֶל el) OPENING (פֶּתַח pe'tahh) TENT (אֹהֶל o'hel) APPOINTED (מוֹעֵד mo'eyd) **RMT:** and cause to assemble all the company to the opening of the appointed tent,

8:4 and~he~will~DO[(V)] (וַיַּעַשׂ wai'ya'as) Mosheh (מֹשֶׁה mo'sheh) like~WHICH (כַּאֲשֶׁר ka'a'sheyr) he~did~much~DIRECT[(V)] (צִוָּה tsi'wah) **YHWH** (יְהוָה YHWH) AT~him (אֹתוֹ o'to) and~she~will~ASSEMBLE[(V)] (וַתִּקָּהֵל wa'ti'qa'heyl) the~COMPANY (הָעֵדָה ha'ey'dah) TO (אֶל el) OPENING (פֶּתַח pe'tahh) TENT (אֹהֶל o'hel) APPOINTED (מוֹעֵד mo'eyd) **RMT:** and Mosheh did just as **YHWH** directed him, and the company assembled to the opening of the appointed tent,

8:5 and~he~will~SAY[(V)] (וַיֹּאמֶר wai'yo'mer) Mosheh (מֹשֶׁה mo'sheh) TO (אֶל el) the~COMPANY (הָעֵדָה ha'ey'dah) THIS (זֶה zeh) the~WORD (הַדָּבָר ha'da'var) WHICH (אֲשֶׁר a'sher) he~did~much~DIRECT[(V)] (צִוָּה tsi'wah) **YHWH** (יְהוָה YHWH) to~>~DO[(V)] (לַעֲשׂוֹת la'a'sot) **RMT:** and Mosheh said to the company, this is the word which **YHWH** directed to do,

8:6 and~he~will~make~COME.NEAR[(V)] (וַיַּקְרֵב wai'yaq'reyv) Mosheh (מֹשֶׁה mo'sheh) AT (אֶת et) Aharon (אַהֲרֹן a'ha'ron) and~AT (וְאֵת wê'et) SON~s~him (בָּנָיו ba'naw) and~he~will~BATHE[(V)] (וַיִּרְחַץ wai'yir'hhats) AT~them[(m)] (אֹתָם o'tam) in~the~WATER~s2 (בַּמָּיִם ba'ma'yim) **RMT:** and Mosheh brought near Aharon and his sons and he bathed them in the waters,

8:7 and~he~will~GIVE[(V)] (וַיִּתֵּן wai'yi'teyn) UPON~him (עָלָיו a'law) AT (אֶת et) the~TUNIC (הַכֻּתֹּנֶת ha'ku'to'net) and~he~will~GIRD.UP[(V)] (וַיַּחְגֹּר wai'yahh'gor) AT~him (אֹתוֹ o'to) in~SASH (בָּאַבְנֵט ba'av'neyt) and~he~will~make~WEAR[(V)] (וַיַּלְבֵּשׁ wai'yal'beysh) AT~

him (אֹתוֹ o'to) AT (אֶת et) the~CLOAK (הַמְּעִיל ham'il) and~he~will~ GIVE[V] (וַיִּתֵּן wai'yi'teyn) UPON~him (עָלָיו a'law) AT (אֶת et) the~ EPHOD (הָאֵפֹד ha'ey'phod) and~he~will~GIRD.UP[V] (וַיַּחְגֹּר wai'yahh'gor) AT~him (אֹתוֹ o'to) in~DECORATIVE.BAND (בְּחֵשֶׁב bê'hhey'shev) the~EPHOD (הָאֵפֹד ha'ey'phod) and~he~will~GIRD[V] (וַיֶּאְפֹּד wai'ye'pod) to~him (לוֹ lo) in~him (בּוֹ bo) **RMT:** and he placed upon him the tunic, and he girded him up with a sash, and he caused him to wear the cloak, and he placed upon him the Ephod, and he girded him up with the decorative band of the Ephod, and he girded for him with him,

8:8 and~he~will~PLACE[V] (וַיָּשֶׂם wai'ya'sem) UPON~him (עָלָיו a'law) AT (אֶת et) the~BREASTPLATE (הַחֹשֶׁן ha'hho'shen) and~he~will~ GIVE[V] (וַיִּתֵּן wai'yi'teyn) TO (אֶל el) the~BREASTPLATE (הַחֹשֶׁן ha'hho'shen) AT (אֶת et) the~Uriym (הָאוּרִים ha'u'rim) and~AT (וְאֶת wê'et) the~Tumiym (הַתֻּמִּים ha'tu'mim) **RMT:** and he placed upon him the breastplate, and he placed on the breastplate the Uriym and the Tumiym,

8:9 and~he~will~PLACE[V] (וַיָּשֶׂם wai'ya'sem) AT (אֶת et) the~ TURBAN (הַמִּצְנֶפֶת ha'mits'ne'phet) UPON (עַל al) HEAD~him (רֹאשׁוֹ ro'sho) and~he~will~PLACE[V] (וַיָּשֶׂם wai'ya'sem) UPON (עַל al) the~ TURBAN (הַמִּצְנֶפֶת ha'mits'ne'phet) TO (אֶל el) FOREFRONT (מוּל mul) FACE~s~him (פָּנָיו pa'naw) AT (אֶת eyt) BLOSSOM (צִיץ tsits) the~GOLD (הַזָּהָב ha'za'hav) DEDICATION (נֵזֶר ney'zer) the~SPECIAL (הַקֹּדֶשׁ ha'qo'desh) like~WHICH (כַּאֲשֶׁר ka'a'sheyr) he~did~much~ DIRECT[V] (צִוָּה tsi'wah) **YHWH** (יְהֹוָה YHWH) AT (אֶת et) Mosheh (מֹשֶׁה mo'sheh) **RMT:** and he placed the turban upon his head, and he placed upon the turban, to the forefront of his face, the gold blossom, the special thing of dedication[27], just as **YHWH** directed Mosheh,

8:10 and~he~will~TAKE[V] (וַיִּקַּח wai'yi'qahh) Mosheh (מֹשֶׁה mo'sheh) AT (אֶת et) OIL (שֶׁמֶן she'men) the~OINTMENT (הַמִּשְׁחָה ha'mish'hhah) and~he~will~SMEAR[V] (וַיִּמְשַׁח wai'yim'shahh) AT (אֶת et) the~DWELLING (הַמִּשְׁכָּן ha'mish'kan) and~AT (וְאֶת wê'et) ALL (כָּל kol) WHICH (אֲשֶׁר a'sher) in~him (בּוֹ bo) and~he~will~much~ SET.APART[V] (וַיְקַדֵּשׁ wai'qa'deysh) AT~them[m] (אֹתָם o'tam) **RMT:** and Mosheh took the oil of ointment and he smeared the dwelling and all which was in him, and he set them apart,

---

[27] That is a "crown."

8:11 and~_he~will~make~_SPATTER ^(V) (וַיַּז _wai'yaz_) <u>FROM~him</u> מִמֶּנּוּ (_mi'me'nu_) <u>UPON</u> עַל (_al_) <u>the~ALTAR</u> הַמִּזְבֵּחַ (_ha'miz'bey'ahh_) <u>SEVEN</u> (שֶׁבַע _she'va_) <u>FOOTSTEP</u>~s פְּעָמִים (_pê'a'mim_) and~_he~will~_SMEAR^(V) (וַיִּמְשַׁח _wai'yim'shahh_) <u>AT</u> אֶת (_et_) <u>the~ALTAR</u> הַמִּזְבֵּחַ (_ha'miz'bey'ahh_) <u>and~AT</u> (וְאֶת _wê et_) <u>ALL</u> כָּל (_kol_) <u>UTENSIL~s~him</u> (כֵּלָיו _key'law_) <u>and~AT</u> (וְאֶת _wê'et_) <u>the~CAULDRON</u> הַכִּיּוֹר (_ha'ki'yor_) and~AT (וְאֶת _wê'et_) <u>BASE~him</u> כַּנּוֹ (_ka'no_) to~>~much~ <u>SET.APART</u>^(V)~them^(m) לְקַדְּשָׁם (_lê'qad'sham_) **RMT:** and he spattered some of him upon the altar seven times, and he smeared the altar and all his utensils and the cauldron and his base to set them apart,

8:12 and~_he~will~_POUR.DOWN^(V) (וַיִּצֹק _wai'yi'tsoq_) <u>from~OIL</u> מִשֶּׁמֶן (_mi'she'men_) <u>the~OINTMENT</u> הַמִּשְׁחָה (_ha'mish'hhah_) <u>UPON</u> עַל (_al_) <u>HEAD</u> רֹאשׁ (_rosh_) <u>Aharon</u> אַהֲרֹן (_a'ha'ron_) and~_he~will~_SMEAR^(V) (וַיִּמְשַׁח _wai'yim'shahh_) <u>AT~him</u> אֹתוֹ (_o'to_) to~>~much~ <u>SET.APART</u>^(V)~him לְקַדְּשׁוֹ (_lê'qad'sho_) **RMT:** and he poured down some of the oil of ointment upon the head of Aharon, and he smeared him to set him apart,

8:13 and~_he~will~make~_COME.NEAR^(V) (וַיַּקְרֵב _wai'yaq'reyv_) <u>Mosheh</u> מֹשֶׁה (_mo'sheh_) <u>AT</u> (אֶת _et_) <u>SON~s</u> בְּנֵי (_bê'ney_) <u>Aharon</u> (אַהֲרֹן _a'ha'ron_) and~_he~will~make~_WEAR^(V)~them^(m) וַיַּלְבִּשֵׁם _wai'yal'bi'sheym_) <u>TUNIC</u>~s כֻּתֳּנֹת (_ku'ta'not_) and~_he~will~_GIRD.UP^(V) (וַיַּחְגֹּר _wai'yahh'gor_) <u>AT~them</u>^(m) (אֹתָם _o'tam_) <u>SASH</u> אַבְנֵט _av'neyt_) and~_he~will~_SADDLE^(V) (וַיַּחֲבֹשׁ _wai'ya'hha'vosh_) to~them^(m) לָהֶם (_la'hem_) <u>HEADDRESS</u>~s מִגְבָּעוֹת (_mig'ba'ot_) like~<u>WHICH</u> כַּאֲשֶׁר _ka'a'sheyr_) he~did~much~DIRECT^(V) צִוָּה (_tsi'wah_) **YHWH** יְהוָה (_YHWH_) <u>AT</u> אֶת (_et_) <u>Mosheh</u> (מֹשֶׁה _mo'sheh_) **RMT:** and Mosheh brought near the sons of Aharon, and he caused them to wear tunics, and he girded them up with a sash, and he saddled them with headdresses just as **YHWH** directed Mosheh,

8:14 and~_he~will~make~_DRAW.NEAR^(V) (וַיַּגֵּשׁ _wai'ya'geysh_) <u>AT</u> (אֵת _eyt_) <u>BULL</u> פַּר (_par_) <u>the~FAILURE</u> (הַחַטָּאת _ha'hha'tat_) and~_he~will~_SUPPORT^(V) (וַיִּסְמֹךְ _wai'yis'mokh_) <u>Aharon</u> אַהֲרֹן (_a'ha'ron_) and~ <u>SON~s~him</u> וּבָנָיו (_u'va'naw_) <u>AT</u> אֶת (_et_) <u>HAND~s2~them</u>^(m) יְדֵיהֶם (_yê'dey'hem_) <u>UPON</u> עַל (_al_) <u>HEAD</u> רֹאשׁ (_rosh_) <u>BULL</u> פַּר (_par_) <u>the~FAILURE</u> הַחַטָּאת (_ha'hha'tat_) **RMT:** and he drew near the bull of failure and Aharon and his sons supported their hands upon the head of the bull of failure,

8:15 and~_he~will~_SLAY^(V) (וַיִּשְׁחָט _wai'yish'hhat_) and~_he~will~_TAKE^(V) (וַיִּקַּח _wai'yi'qahh_) <u>Mosheh</u> מֹשֶׁה (_mo'sheh_) <u>AT</u> אֶת (_et_) <u>the~BLOOD</u>

(הַדָּם ha'dam) and~*he~will~*GIVE[V] (וַיִּתֵּן wai'yi'teyn) UPON (עַל al)
HORN~s (קַרְנוֹת qar'not) the~ALTAR (הַמִּזְבֵּחַ ha'miz'bey'ahh)
ALL.AROUND (סָבִיב sa'viv) in~FINGER~him (בְּאֶצְבָּעוֹ bê'ets'ba'o)
and~*he~will~*much~FAIL[V] (וַיְחַטֵּא wai'hha'tey) AT (אֶת et) the~
ALTAR (הַמִּזְבֵּחַ ha'miz'bey'ahh) and~AT (וְאֶת wê'et) the~BLOOD
(הַדָּם ha'dam) *he~did~*POUR.DOWN[V] (יָצַק ya'tsaq) TO (אֶל el)
BOTTOM.BASE (יְסוֹד yê'sod) the~ALTAR (הַמִּזְבֵּחַ ha'miz'bey'ahh)
and~*he~will~*much~SET.APART[V]~him (וַיְקַדְּשֵׁהוּ wai'qad'shey'hu)
to~>~much~COVER[V] (לְכַפֵּר lê'kha'peyr) UPON~him (עָלָיו a'law)
RMT: and he slew it, and Mosheh took the blood and placed it upon
the horns of the altar, all around, with his finger, and he purified the
altar, and he poured down the blood at the bottom base of the altar,
and he set him apart to make a covering over him,

8:16 and~*he~will~*TAKE[V] (וַיִּקַּח wai'yi'qahh) AT (אֶת et) ALL (כָּל
kol) the~FAT (הַחֵלֶב ha'hhey'lev) WHICH (אֲשֶׁר a'sher) UPON (עַל al)
the~INSIDE (הַקֶּרֶב ha'qe'rev) and~AT (וְאֶת wê'eyt) LOBE (יֹתֶרֶת
yo'te'ret) the~HEAVY (הַכָּבֵד ha'ka'veyd) and~AT (וְאֶת wê'et) TWO
(שְׁתֵּי shê'tey) the~KIDNEY~s (הַכְּלָיֹת hak'la'yot) and~AT (וְאֶת wê'et)
FAT~them[(f)] (חֶלְבְּהֶן hhel'be'hen) and~*he~will~*make~
BURN.INCENSE[V] (וַיַּקְטֵר wai'yaq'teyr) Mosheh (מֹשֶׁה mo'sheh) the~
ALTAR~unto (הַמִּזְבֵּחָה ha'miz'bey'hhah) **RMT:** and he took all the fat
which was upon the inside, and the heavy lobe[28], and the two
kidneys, and their fat, and Mosheh burned incense upon the altar,

8:17 and~AT (וְאֶת wê'et) the~BULL (הַפָּר ha'par) and~AT (וְאֶת
wê'et) SKIN~him (עֹרוֹ o'ro) and~AT (וְאֶת wê'et) FLESH~him (בְּשָׂרוֹ
bê'sar'o) and~AT (וְאֶת wê'et) DUNG~him (פִּרְשׁוֹ pir'sho) *he~did~*
CREMATE[V] (שָׂרַף sa'raph) in~the~FIRE (בָאֵשׁ ba'eysh) from~
OUTSIDE (מִחוּץ mi'hhuts) to~the~CAMP (לַמַּחֲנֶה la'ma'hha'neh)
like~WHICH (כַּאֲשֶׁר ka'a'sheyr) *he~did~*much~DIRECT[V] (צִוָּה
tsi'wah) **YHWH** (יְהֹוָה YHWH) AT (אֶת et) Mosheh (מֹשֶׁה mo'sheh)
RMT: and the bull and his skin and his flesh and his dung he
cremated in the fire outside the camp, just as **YHWH** directed
Mosheh,

8:18 and~*he~will~*make~COME.NEAR[V] (וַיַּקְרֵב wai'yaq'reyv) AT (אֵת
eyt) BUCK (אַיִל eyl) the~ASCENSION.OFFERING (הָעֹלָה ha'o'lah)
and~*they[(m)]~will~*SUPPORT[V] (וַיִּסְמְכוּ wai'yis'me'khu) Aharon (אַהֲרֹן
a'ha'ron) and~SON~s~him (וּבָנָיו u'va'naw) AT (אֶת et) HAND~s2~

---

[28] "The heavy lobe" is the liver, the heaviest organ in the body.

them[(m)] (יְדֵיהֶם *yê'dey'hem*) UPON (עַל *al*) HEAD (רֹאשׁ *rosh*) the~ BUCK (הָאָיִל *ha'a'yil*) **RMT:** and he brought near the buck of the ascension offering, and Aharon and his sons supported their hands upon the head of the buck,

8:19 and~*he~will~*SLAY[(V)] (וַיִּשְׁחָט *wai'yish'hhat*) and~*he~will~* SPRINKLE[(V)] (וַיִּזְרֹק *wai'yiz'roq*) Mosheh (מֹשֶׁה *mo'sheh*) AT (אֶת *et*) the~BLOOD (הַדָּם *ha'dam*) UPON (עַל *al*) the~ALTAR (הַמִּזְבֵּחַ *ha'miz'bey'ahh*) ALL.AROUND (סָבִיב *sa'viv*) **RMT:** and he slew it, and Mosheh sprinkled the blood upon the altar, all around,

8:20 and~AT (וְאֶת *wê'et*) the~BUCK (הָאָיִל *ha'a'yil*) *he~did~much~* DIVIDE.INTO.PIECES[(V)] (נִתַּח *n'tahh*) to~PIECE~s~him (לִנְתָחָיו *lin'ta'hhaw*) and~*he~will~make~*BURN.INCENSE[(V)] (וַיַּקְטֵר *wai'yaq'teyr*) Mosheh (מֹשֶׁה *mo'sheh*) AT (אֶת *et*) the~HEAD (הָרֹאשׁ *ha'rosh*) and~AT (וְאֶת *wê'et*) the~PIECE~s (הַנְּתָחִים *han'ta'hhim*) and~AT (וְאֶת *wê'et*) the~SUET (הַפָּדֶר *ha'pa'der*) **RMT:** and he divided the buck into pieces, according to his pieces, and Mosheh burned as incense the head and the pieces and the suet,

8:21 and~AT (וְאֶת *wê'et*) the~INSIDE (הַקֶּרֶב *ha'qe'rev*) and~AT (וְאֶת *wê'et*) the~LEG~s2 (הַכְּרָעַיִם *ha'ke'ra'a'yim*) *he~did~*BATHE[(V)] (רָחַץ *ra'hhats*) in~the~WATER~s2 (בַּמָּיִם *ba'ma'yim*) and~*he~will~make~* BURN.INCENSE[(V)] (וַיַּקְטֵר *wai'yaq'teyr*) Mosheh (מֹשֶׁה *mo'sheh*) AT (אֶת *et*) ALL (כָּל *kol*) the~BUCK (הָאָיִל *ha'a'yil*) the~ALTAR~unto (הַמִּזְבֵּחָה *ha'miz'bey'hhah*) ASCENSION.OFFERING (עֹלָה *o'lah*) HE (הוּא *hu*) to~AROMA (לְרֵיחַ *lê'rey'ahh*) SWEET (נִיחֹחַ *ni'hho'ahh*) FIRE.OFFERING (אִשֶּׁה *i'sheh*) HE (הוּא *hu*) to~**YHWH** (לַיהוָה *la'YHWH*) like~WHICH (כַּאֲשֶׁר *ka'a'sheyr*) *he~did~much~*DIRECT[(V)] (צִוָּה *tsi'wah*) **YHWH** (יְהוָה *YHWH*) AT (אֶת *et*) Mosheh (מֹשֶׁה *mo'sheh*) **RMT:** and the inside and the legs, and he bathed in the waters and Mosheh burned as incense all of the buck upon the altar, he was an ascension offering for a sweet aroma, he was a fire offering to **YHWH**, just as **YHWH** directed Mosheh,

8:22 and~*he~will~make~*COME.NEAR[(V)] (וַיַּקְרֵב *wai'yaq'reyv*) AT (אֶת *et*) the~BUCK (הָאָיִל *ha'a'yil*) the~SECOND (הַשֵּׁנִי *ha'shey'ni*) BUCK (אֵיל *eyl*) the~INSTALLATION~s (הַמִּלֻּאִים *ha'mi'lu'im*) and~*they*[(m)]~ *will~*SUPPORT[(V)] (וַיִּסְמְכוּ *wai'yis'me'khu*) Aharon (אַהֲרֹן *a'ha'ron*) and~SON~s~him (וּבָנָיו *u'va'naw*) AT (אֶת *et*) HAND~s2~them[(m)] (יְדֵיהֶם *yê'dey'hem*) UPON (עַל *al*) HEAD (רֹאשׁ *rosh*) the~BUCK (הָאָיִל *ha'a'yil*) **RMT:** and he brought near the second buck, the buck of installation, and Aharon and his sons supported their hands upon the head of the buck,

8:23 and~he~will~SLAY(V) (וַיִּשְׁחָט wai'yish'hhat) and~he~will~TAKE(V) (וַיִּקַּח wai'yi'qahh) Mosheh (מֹשֶׁה mo'sheh) from~BLOOD~him (מִדָּמוֹ mi'da'mo) and~he~will~GIVE(V) (וַיִּתֵּן wai'yi'teyn) UPON (עַל al) TIP (תְּנוּךְ tê'nukh) EAR (אֹזֶן o'zen) Aharon (אַהֲרֹן a'ha'ron) the~RIGHT (הַיְמָנִית hai'ma'nit) and~UPON (וְעַל wê'al) THUMB (בֹּהֶן bo'hen) HAND~him (יָדוֹ ya'do) the~RIGHT (הַיְמָנִית hai'ma'nit) and~UPON (וְעַל wê'al) THUMB (בֹּהֶן bo'hen) FOOT~him (רַגְלוֹ rag'lo) the~RIGHT (הַיְמָנִית hai'ma'nit) **RMT:** and he slew, and Mosheh took from his blood and he placed it upon the tip of the right ear of Aharon and upon the thumb of his right hand and upon the thumb of his right foot,

8:24 and~he~will~make~COME.NEAR(V) (וַיַּקְרֵב wai'yaq'reyv) AT (אֶת et) SON~s (בְּנֵי bê'ney) Aharon (אַהֲרֹן a'ha'ron) and~he~will~GIVE(V) (וַיִּתֵּן wai'yi'teyn) Mosheh (מֹשֶׁה mo'sheh) FROM (מִן min) the~BLOOD (הַדָּם ha'dam) UPON (עַל al) TIP (תְּנוּךְ tê'nukh) EAR~them(m) (אָזְנָם az'nam) the~RIGHT (הַיְמָנִית hai'ma'nit) and~UPON (וְעַל wê'al) THUMB (בֹּהֶן bo'hen) HAND~them(m) (יָדָם ya'dam) the~RIGHT (הַיְמָנִית hai'ma'nit) and~UPON (וְעַל wê'al) THUMB (בֹּהֶן bo'hen) FOOT~them(m) (רַגְלָם rag'lam) the~RIGHT (הַיְמָנִית hai'ma'nit) and~he~will~SPRINKLE(V) (וַיִּזְרֹק wai'yiz'roq) Mosheh (מֹשֶׁה mo'sheh) AT (אֶת et) the~BLOOD (הַדָּם ha'dam) UPON (עַל al) the~ALTAR (הַמִּזְבֵּחַ ha'miz'bey'ahh) ALL.AROUND (סָבִיב sa'viv) **RMT:** and he brought near the sons of Aharon and Mosheh placed some of the blood upon their right ear and upon the thumb of their right hand and upon the thumb of their right foot, and Mosheh sprinkled the blood upon the altar, all around,

8:25 and~he~will~TAKE(V) (וַיִּקַּח wai'yi'qahh) AT (אֶת et) the~FAT (הַחֵלֶב ha'hhey'lev) and~AT (וְאֶת wê'et) the~RUMP (הָאַלְיָה ha'al'yah) and~AT (וְאֶת wê'et) ALL (כָּל kol) the~FAT (הַחֵלֶב ha'hhey'lev) WHICH (אֲשֶׁר a'sher) UPON (עַל al) the~INSIDE (הַקֶּרֶב ha'qe'rev) and~AT (וְאֵת wê'eyt) LOBE (יֹתֶרֶת yo'te'ret) the~HEAVY (הַכָּבֵד ha'ka'veyd) and~AT (וְאֶת wê'et) TWO (שְׁתֵּי shê'tey) the~KIDNEY~s (הַכְּלָיֹת hak'la'yot) and~AT (וְאֶת wê'et) FAT~them(f) (חֶלְבְּהֶן hhel'be'hen) and~AT (וְאֵת wê'eyt) THIGH (שׁוֹק shoq) the~RIGHT.HAND (הַיָּמִין hai'ya'min) **RMT:** and he took the fat and the rump and all the fat which is upon the inside and the heavy lobe[29] and the two kidneys and their fat and the right thigh,

8:26 and~from~WICKER.BASKET (וּמִסַּל *u'mi'sal*) the~ UNLEAVENED.BREAD~s (הַמַּצּוֹת *ha'ma'tsot*) WHICH (אֲשֶׁר *a'sher*) to~FACE~s (לִפְנֵי *liph'ney*) **YHWH** (יְהוָה *YHWH*) he~did~TAKE[(V)] (לָקַח *la'qahh*) PIERCED.BREAD (חַלַּת *hha'lat*) UNLEAVENED.BREAD (מַצָּה *ma'tsah*) UNIT (אַחַת *a'hhat*) and~PIERCED.BREAD (וְחַלַּת *wê'hha'lat*) BREAD (לֶחֶם *le'hem*) OIL (שֶׁמֶן *she'men*) UNIT (אַחַת *a'hhat*) and~ THIN.BREAD (וְרָקִיק *wê'raqiq*) UNIT (אֶחָד *e'hhad*) and~he~will~ PLACE[(V)] (וַיָּשֶׂם *wai'ya'sem*) UPON (עַל *al*) the~FAT~s (הַחֲלָבִים *ha'hha'la'vim*) and~UPON (וְעַל *wê'al*) THIGH (שׁוֹק *shoq*) the~ RIGHT.HAND (הַיָּמִין *hai'ya'min*) **RMT:** and from the wicker basket of the unleavened breads, which is to the face of **YHWH**, he took one of the pierced unleavened bread, one of the pierced bread of oil, and one of the thin bread, and he placed upon the fats and upon the right thigh,

8:27 and~he~will~GIVE[(V)] (וַיִּתֵּן *wai'yi'teyn*) AT (אֶת *et*) the~ALL (הַכֹּל *ha'kol*) UPON (עַל *al*) PALM~s2 (כַּפֵּי *ka'pey*) Aharon (אַהֲרֹן *a'ha'ron*) and~UPON (וְעַל *wê'al*) PALM~s2 (כַּפֵּי *ka'pey*) SON~s~him (בָּנָיו *va'naw*) and~he~will~make~WAVE[(V)] (וַיָּנֶף *wai'ya'neph*) AT~them[(m)] (אֹתָם *o'tam*) WAVING (תְּנוּפָה *tê'nu'phah*) to~FACE~s (לִפְנֵי *liph'ney*) **YHWH** (יְהוָה *YHWH*) **RMT:** and he placed all of it upon the palms of Aharon and upon the palms of his sons, and he waved them, a waving to the face of **YHWH**,

8:28 and~he~will~TAKE[(V)] (וַיִּקַּח *wai'yi'qahh*) Mosheh (מֹשֶׁה *mo'sheh*) AT~them[(m)] (אֹתָם *o'tam*) from~UPON (מֵעַל *mey'al*) PALM~s2~them[(m)] (כַּפֵּיהֶם *ka'pey'hem*) and~he~will~make~ BURN.INCENSE[(V)] (וַיַּקְטֵר *wai'yaq'teyr*) the~ALTAR~unto (הַמִּזְבֵּחָה *ha'miz'bey'hhah*) UPON (עַל *al*) the~ASCENSION.OFFERING (הָעֹלָה *ha'o'lah*) INSTALLATION~s (מִלֻּאִים *mi'lu'im*) THEY[(m)] (הֵם *heym*) to~ AROMA (לְרֵיחַ *lê'rey'ahh*) SWEET (נִיחֹחַ *ni'hho'ahh*) FIRE.OFFERING (אִשֶּׁה *i'sheh*) HE (הוּא *hu*) to~**YHWH** (לַיהוָה *la'YHWH*) **RMT:** and Mosheh took them from upon their palms, and he burned it as incense upon the altar, upon the ascension offering of installation, they are for a sweet aroma, he is a fire offering to **YHWH**,

8:29 and~he~will~TAKE[(V)] (וַיִּקַּח *wai'yi'qahh*) Mosheh (מֹשֶׁה *mo'sheh*) AT (אֶת *et*) the~CHEST (הֶחָזֶה *he'hha'zeh*) and~he~will~

---

[29] "The heavy lobe" is the liver, the heaviest organ in the body.

make~WAVE[(V)]~him (וַיְנִיפֵהוּ *wai'ni'phey'hu*) WAVING (תְּנוּפָה *tê'nu'phah*) to~FACE~s (לִפְנֵי *liph'ney*) **YHWH** (יְהוָה *YHWH*) from~ BUCK (מֵאֵיל *mey'eyl*) the~INSTALLATION~s (הַמִּלֻּאִים *ha'mi'lu'im*) to~Mosheh (לְמֹשֶׁה *lê'mo'sheh*) he~did~EXIST[(V)] (הָיָה *hai'yah*) to~ SHARE (לְמָנָה *lê'ma'nah*) like~WHICH (כַּאֲשֶׁר *ka'a'sheyr*) he~did~ _much_~DIRECT[(V)] (צִוָּה *tsi'wah*) **YHWH** (יְהוָה *YHWH*) AT (אֶת *et*) Mosheh (מֹשֶׁה *mo'sheh*) **RMT:** and Mosheh took the chest, and he waved him, a waving to the face of **YHWH**, from the buck of installation, belonging to Mosheh, he existed for a share, just as **YHWH** directed Mosheh,

8:30 and~he~will~TAKE[(V)] (וַיִּקַּח *wai'yi'qahh*) Mosheh (מֹשֶׁה *mo'sheh*) from~OIL (מִשֶּׁמֶן *mi'she'men*) the~OINTMENT (הַמִּשְׁחָה *ha'mish'hhah*) and~FROM (וּמִן *u'min*) the~BLOOD (הַדָּם *ha'dam*) WHICH (אֲשֶׁר *a'sher*) UPON (עַל *al*) the~ALTAR (הַמִּזְבֵּחַ *ha'miz'bey'ahh*) and~he~will~make~SPATTER[(V)] (וַיַּז *wai'yaz*) UPON (עַל *al*) Aharon (אַהֲרֹן *a'ha'ron*) UPON (עַל *al*) GARMENT~s~him (בְּגָדָיו *bê'ga'daw*) and~UPON (וְעַל *wê'al*) SON~s~him (בָּנָיו *ba'naw*) and~UPON (וְעַל *wê'al*) GARMENT~s (בִּגְדֵי *big'dey*) SON~s~him (בָּנָיו *va'naw*) AT~him (אִתּוֹ *i'to*) and~he~will~much~SET.APART[(V)] (וַיְקַדֵּשׁ *wai'qa'deysh*) AT (אֶת *et*) Aharon (אַהֲרֹן *a'ha'ron*) AT (אֶת *et*) GARMENT~s~him (בְּגָדָיו *bê'ga'daw*) and~AT (וְאֶת *wê'et*) SON~s~ him (בָּנָיו *ba'naw*) and~AT (וְאֶת *wê'et*) GARMENT~s (בִּגְדֵי *big'dey*) SON~s~him (בָּנָיו *va'naw*) AT~him (אִתּוֹ *i'to*) **RMT:** and Mosheh took some of the oil of ointment and from the blood, which was upon the altar, and he spattered it upon Aharon, upon his garments and upon his sons and upon the garments of his sons with him, and he set apart Aharon, his garments and his sons and the garments of his sons with him,

8:31 and~he~will~SAY[(V)] (וַיֹּאמֶר *wai'yo'mer*) Mosheh (מֹשֶׁה *mo'sheh*) TO (אֶל *el*) Aharon (אַהֲרֹן *a'ha'ron*) and~TO (וְאֶל *wê'el*) SON~s~him (בָּנָיו *ba'naw*) _![(mp)]_~much~BOIL[(V)] (בַּשְּׁלוּ *bash'lu*) AT (אֶת *et*) the~FLESH (הַבָּשָׂר *ha'ba'sar*) OPENING (פֶּתַח *pe'tahh*) TENT (אֹהֶל *o'hel*) APPOINTED (מוֹעֵד *mo'eyd*) and~THERE (וְשָׁם *wê'sham*) you[(mp)]~will~EAT[(V)] (תֹּאכְלוּ *tokh'lu*) AT~him (אֹתוֹ *o'to*) and~AT (וְאֶת *wê'et*) the~BREAD (הַלֶּחֶם *ha'le'hhem*) WHICH (אֲשֶׁר *a'sher*) in~ WICKER.BASKET (בְּסַל *bê'sal*) the~INSTALLATION~s (הַמִּלֻּאִים *ha'mi'lu'im*) like~WHICH (כַּאֲשֶׁר *ka'a'sheyr*) I~did~much~DIRECT[(V)] (צִוֵּיתִי *tsi'wey'ti*) to~>~SAY[(V)] (לֵאמֹר *ley'mor*) Aharon (אַהֲרֹן *a'ha'ron*) and~SON~s~him (וּבָנָיו *u'va'naw*) they[(m)]~will~EAT[(V)]~him

(יֹאכְלֻהוּ *yokh'lu'hu*) **RMT:** and Mosheh said to Aharon and to his sons, boil the flesh at the opening of the appointed tent and there you will eat him and the bread which is in the wicker basket of installation, just as I directed, saying, Aharon and his sons will eat him,

8:32 and~the~*be*~LEAVE.BEHIND⁽ᴺ⁾~*ing*⁽ᵐˢ⁾ (וְהַנּוֹתָר *wê'ha'no'tar*) in~ the~FLESH (בַּבָּשָׂר *ba'ba'sar*) and~in~the~BREAD (וּבַלָּחֶם *u'va'la'hhem*) in~the~FIRE (בָּאֵשׁ *ba'eysh*) you⁽ᵐᵖ⁾~will~CREMATE⁽ⱽ⁾ (תִּשְׂרֹפוּ *tis'ro'phu*) **RMT:** and that being left behind of the flesh and of the bread, you will cremate in the fire,

8:33 and~from~OPENING (וּמִפֶּתַח *u'mi'pe'tahh*) TENT (אֹהֶל *o'hel*) APPOINTED (מוֹעֵד *mo'eyd*) NOT (לֹא *lo*) you⁽ᵐᵖ⁾~will~GO.OUT⁽ⱽ⁾ (תֵּצְאוּ *teyts'u*) SEVEN (שִׁבְעַת *shiv'at*) DAY~s (יָמִים *ya'mim*) UNTIL (עַד *ad*) DAY (יוֹם *yom*) >~FILL⁽ⱽ⁾ (מְלֹאת *mê'lot*) DAY~s (יְמֵי *yê'mey*) INSTALLATION~s~you⁽ᵐᵖ⁾ (מִלֻּאֵיכֶם *mi'lu'ey'khem*) GIVEN.THAT (כִּי *ki*) SEVEN (שִׁבְעַת *shiv'at*) DAY~s (יָמִים *ya'mim*) he~will~much~FILL⁽ⱽ⁾ (יְמַלֵּא *yê'ma'ley*) AT (אֶת *et*) HAND~you⁽ᵐᵖ⁾ (יֶדְכֶם *yed'khem*) **RMT:** and from the opening of the appointed tent you will not go out seven days, until the day of fillings, the days of your installation, given that seven days he will fill your hand[30].

8:34 like~WHICH (כַּאֲשֶׁר *ka'a'sheyr*) he~did~DO⁽ⱽ⁾ (עָשָׂה *a'sah*) in~ the~DAY (בַּיּוֹם *ba'yom*) the~THIS (הַזֶּה *ha'zeh*) he~did~much~ DIRECT⁽ⱽ⁾ (צִוָּה *tsi'wah*) **YHWH** (יְהוָה *YHWH*) to~>~DO⁽ⱽ⁾ (לַעֲשֹׂת *la'a'sot*) to~>~much~COVER⁽ⱽ⁾ (לְכַפֵּר *lê'kha'peyr*) UPON~you⁽ᵐᵖ⁾ (עֲלֵיכֶם *a'ley'khem*) **RMT:** Just as is done in this day, YHWH directed to do, to make a covering upon you,

8:35 and~OPENING (וּפֶתַח *u'phe'tahh*) TENT (אֹהֶל *o'hel*) APPOINTED (מוֹעֵד *mo'eyd*) you⁽ᵐᵖ⁾~will~SETTLE⁽ⱽ⁾ (תֵּשְׁבוּ *teysh'vu*) DAYTIME (יוֹמָם *yo'mam*) and~NIGHT (וָלַיְלָה *wa'lai'lah*) SEVEN (שִׁבְעַת *shiv'at*) DAY~s (יָמִים *ya'mim*) and~you⁽ᵐᵖ⁾~did~SAFEGUARD⁽ⱽ⁾ (וּשְׁמַרְתֶּם *ush'mar'tem*) AT (אֶת *et*) CHARGE (מִשְׁמֶרֶת *mish'me'ret*) **YHWH** (יְהוָה *YHWH*) and~NOT (וְלֹא *wê'lo*) you⁽ᵐᵖ⁾~will~DIE⁽ⱽ⁾ (תָמוּתוּ *ta'mu'tu*) GIVEN.THAT (כִּי *ki* SO (כֵן *kheyn*)[31] I~did~be~much~

---

[30] To "fill the hand" is an idiom of uncertain meaning, but the same phrase is used in Akkadian to mean the placing of a relevant tool or insignia (such as a scepter for a king) in the hand of one being installed in a high office.

[31] The phrase "GIVEN.THAT SO" means "since."

DIRECT^(V) (צִוֵּיתִי *tsu'wey'ti*) **RMT:** and the opening of the appointed tent you will settle day and night seven days, and you will safeguard the charge of **YHWH**, and you will not die, since I directed,

8:36 and~*he*~*will*~DO^(V) (וַיַּעַשׂ *wai'ya'as*) Aharon (אַהֲרֹן *a'ha'ron*) and~SON~s~him (וּבָנָיו *u'va'naw*) AT (אֵת *eyt*) ALL (כָּל *kol*) the~ WORD~s (הַדְּבָרִים *ha'de'va'rim*) WHICH (אֲשֶׁר *a'sher*) *he~did~ much*~DIRECT^(V) (צִוָּה *tsi'wah*) **YHWH** (יְהוָה *YHWH*) in~HAND (בְּיַד *bê'yad*) Mosheh (מֹשֶׁה *mo'sheh*) **RMT:** and Aharon did, and his sons, all the words that **YHWH** directed, by the hand of Mosheh,

Chapter 9

9:1 and~*he*~*will*~EXIST^(V) (וַיְהִי *wai'hi*) in~the~DAY (בַּיּוֹם *ba'yom*) the~EIGHTH (הַשְּׁמִינִי *hash'mini*) *he~did~*CALL.OUT^(V) (קָרָא *qa'ra*) Mosheh (מֹשֶׁה *mo'sheh*) to~Aharon (לְאַהֲרֹן *lê'a'ha'ron*) and~to~ SON~s~him (וּלְבָנָיו *ul'va'naw*) and~to~BEARD~s (וּלְזִקְנֵי *ul'ziq'ney*) Yisra'eyl (יִשְׂרָאֵל *yis'ra'eyl*) **RMT:** and it came to pass in the eighth day, Mosheh called out to Aharon and to his sons and to the bearded ones of Yisra'eyl,

9:2 and~*he*~*will*~SAY^(V) (וַיֹּאמֶר *wai'yo'mer*) TO (אֶל *el*) Aharon (אַהֲרֹן *a'ha'ron*) !^(ms)~TAKE^(V) (קַח *qahh*) to~you^(ms) (לְךָ *lê'kha*) BULLOCK (עֵגֶל *ey'gel*) SON (בֶּן *ben*) CATTLE (בָּקָר *ba'qar*) to~FAILURE (לְחַטָּאת *lê'hha'tat*) and~BUCK (וְאַיִל *wê'a'yil*) to~ASCENSION.OFFERING (לְעֹלָה *lê'lah*) WHOLE~s (תְּמִימִם *tê'mi'mim*) and~ !^(ms)~*make*~ COME.NEAR^(V) (וְהַקְרֵב *wê'haq'reyv*) to~FACE~s (לִפְנֵי *liph'ney*) **YHWH** (יְהוָה *YHWH*) **RMT:** and he said to Aharon, take for you a bullock, a son of the cattle, for the failure, and a buck for the ascension offering, whole ones, and bring near to the face of **YHWH**,

9:3 and~TO (וְאֶל *wê'el*) SON~s (בְּנֵי *bê'ney*) Yisra'eyl (יִשְׂרָאֵל *yis'ra'eyl*) you^(ms)~*will*~*much*~SPEAK^(V) (תְּדַבֵּר *tê'da'beyr*) to~>~SAY^(V) (לֵאמֹר *ley'mor*) !^(mp)~TAKE^(V) (קְחוּ *qê'hhu*) HAIRY.GOAT (שְׂעִיר *sê'ir*) SHE-GOAT~s (עִזִּים *i'zim*) to~FAILURE (לְחַטָּאת *lê'hha'tat*) and~ BULLOCK (וְעֵגֶל *wê'ey'gel*) and~SHEEP (וָכֶבֶשׂ *wa'khe'ves*) SON~s (בְּנֵי *bê'ney*) YEAR (שָׁנָה *sha'nah*) WHOLE~s (תְּמִימִם *tê'mi'mim*) to~ ASCENSION.OFFERING (לְעֹלָה *lê'lah*) **RMT:** and to the sons of Yisra'eyl you will speak saying, take a hairy goat of the she-goats for the failure, and a bullock and a sheep, sons of a year[32], whole ones, for the ascension offering,

9:4 and~OX (וְשׁוֹר *wê'shor*) and~BUCK (וָאַיִל *wa'a'yil*) to~ OFFERING.OF.RESTITUTION~s (לִשְׁלָמִים *lish'la'mim*) to~>~ SACRIFICE[(V)] (לִזְבֹּחַ *liz'bo'ahh*) to~FACE~s (לִפְנֵי *liph'ney*) **YHWH** (יְהוָה *YHWH*) and~DEPOSIT (וּמִנְחָה *u'min'hhah*) MIX[(V)]~ed[(fs)] (בְּלוּלָה *bê'lu'lah*) in~the~OIL (בַשֶּׁמֶן *va'sha'men*) GIVEN.THAT (כִּי *ki*) the~ DAY (הַיּוֹם *hai'yom*) **YHWH** (יְהוָה *YHWH*) he~did~be~SEE[(V)] (נִרְאָה *nir'ah*) TO~you[(mp)] (אֲלֵיכֶם *a'ley'khem*) **RMT:** and an ox and a buck for the offering of restitution, for a sacrifice to the face of **YHWH**, and a deposit mixed in the oil, given that today **YHWH** appeared to you,

9:5 and~they[(m)]~will~TAKE[(V)] (וַיִּקְחוּ *wai'yiq'hhu*) AT (אֵת *eyt*) WHICH (אֲשֶׁר *a'sher*) he~did~much~DIRECT[(V)] (צִוָּה *tsi'wah*) Mosheh (מֹשֶׁה *mo'sheh*) TO (אֶל *el*) FACE~s (פְּנֵי *pê'ney*) TENT (אֹהֶל *o'hel*) APPOINTED (מוֹעֵד *mo'eyd*) and~they[(m)]~will~COME.NEAR[(V)] (וַיִּקְרְבוּ *wai'yiq're'vu*) ALL (כָּל *kol*) the~COMPANY (הָעֵדָה *ha'ey'dah*) and~ they[(m)]~will~STAND[(V)] (וַיַּעַמְדוּ *wai'ya'am'du*) to~FACE~s (לִפְנֵי *liph'ney*) **YHWH** (יְהוָה *YHWH*) **RMT:** and they took what Mosheh directed to the face of the appointed tent, and all the company came near, and they stood to the face of **YHWH**,

9:6 and~he~will~SAY[(V)] (וַיֹּאמֶר *wai'yo'mer*) Mosheh (מֹשֶׁה *mo'sheh*) THIS (זֶה *zeh*) the~WORD (הַדָּבָר *ha'da'var*) WHICH (אֲשֶׁר *a'sher*) he~did~much~DIRECT[(V)] (צִוָּה *tsi'wah*) **YHWH** (יְהוָה *YHWH*) you[(mp)]~ will~DO[(V)] (תַּעֲשׂוּ *ta'a'su*) and~he~will~be~SEE[(V)] (וְיֵרָא *wê'yey'ra*) TO~you[(mp)] (אֲלֵיכֶם *a'ley'khem*) ARMAMENT (כְּבוֹד *kê'vod*) **YHWH** (יְהוָה *YHWH*) **RMT:** and Mosheh said, this is the word that **YHWH** directed you to do, and the armament of **YHWH** appeared to you,

9:7 and~he~will~SAY[(V)] (וַיֹּאמֶר *wai'yo'mer*) Mosheh (מֹשֶׁה *mo'sheh*) TO (אֶל *el*) Aharon (אַהֲרֹן *a'ha'ron*) ![(ms)]~COME.NEAR[(V)] (קְרַב *qê'rav*) TO (אֶל *el*) the~ALTAR (הַמִּזְבֵּחַ *ha'miz'bey'ahh*) and~![(ms)]~DO[(V)] (וַעֲשֵׂה *wa'a'seyh*) AT (אֶת *et*) FAILURE~you[(ms)] (חַטָּאתְךָ *hha'ta'te'kha*) and~AT (וְאֶת *wê'et*) ASCENSION.OFFERING~you[(ms)] (עֹלָתֶךָ *o'la'te'kha*) and~![(ms)]~much~COVER[(V)] (וְכַפֵּר *wê'kha'peyr*) in~ UNTIL~you[(ms)] (בַּעַדְךָ *ba'ad'kha*) and~in~UNTIL (וּבְעַד *uv'ad*) the~ PEOPLE (הָעָם *ha'am*) and~![(ms)]~DO[(V)] (וַעֲשֵׂה *wa'a'seyh*) AT (אֶת *et*) DONATION (קָרְבַּן *qar'ban*) the~PEOPLE (הָעָם *ha'am*) and~![(ms)]~

---

[32] "Son of a year" is an idiom for "one year old."

*much~*COVER^(V) (וְכִפֶּר *wê'kha'peyr*) in~UNTIL~them^(m) (בַּעֲדָם *ba'a'dam*) like~WHICH (כַּאֲשֶׁר *ka'a'sheyr*) *he~did~much~*DIRECT^(V) (צִוָּה *tsi'wah*) **YHWH** (יְהוָה *YHWH*) **RMT:** and Mosheh said to Aharon, come near to the altar and do your failure and your ascension offering and make a covering on behalf of yourself and on behalf of the people, and do the donation of the people, and make a covering on their behalf, just as **YHWH** directed,

9:8 *and~he~will~*COME.NEAR^(V) (וַיִּקְרַב *wai'yiq'rav*) Aharon (אַהֲרֹן *a'ha'ron*) TO (אֶל *el*) the~ALTAR (הַמִּזְבֵּחַ *ha'miz'bey'ahh*) *and~he~will~*SLAY^(V) (וַיִּשְׁחַט *wai'yish'hhat*) AT (אֶת *et*) BULLOCK (עֵגֶל *ey'gel*) the~FAILURE (הַחַטָּאת *ha'hha'tat*) WHICH (אֲשֶׁר *a'sher*) to~him (לוֹ *lo*) **RMT:** and Aharon came near to the altar, and he slew the bullock of the failure, which belonged to him,

9:9 *and~they^(m)~will~make~*COME.NEAR^(V) (וַיַּקְרִבוּ *wai'yaq'ri'vu*) SON~s (בְּנֵי *bê'ney*) Aharon (אַהֲרֹן *a'ha'ron*) AT (אֶת *et*) the~BLOOD (הַדָּם *ha'dam*) TO~him (אֵלָיו *ey'law*) *and~he~will~*DIP^(V) (וַיִּטְבֹּל *wai'yit'bol*) FINGER~him (אֶצְבָּעוֹ *ets'ba'o*) in~the~BLOOD (בַּדָּם *ba'dam*) *and~he~will~*GIVE^(V) (וַיִּתֵּן *wai'yi'teyn*) UPON (עַל *al*) HORN~s (קַרְנוֹת *qar'not*) the~ALTAR (הַמִּזְבֵּחַ *ha'miz'bey'ahh*) and~ AT (וְאֶת *wê'et*) the~BLOOD (הַדָּם *ha'dam*) *he~did~*POUR.DOWN^(V) (יָצַק *ya'tsaq*) TO (אֶל *el*) BOTTOM.BASE (יְסוֹד *yê'sod*) the~ALTAR (הַמִּזְבֵּחַ *ha'miz'bey'ahh*) **RMT:** and the sons of Aharon brought near the blood to him, and he dipped his finger in the blood, and he placed it upon the horns of the altar, and he poured down the blood to the bottom base of the altar,

9:10 *and~AT* (וְאֶת *wê'et*) the~FAT (הַחֵלֶב *ha'hhey'lev*) *and~AT* (וְאֶת *wê'et*) the~KIDNEY~s (הַכְּלָיֹת *hak'la'yot*) *and~AT* (וְאֶת *wê'et*) the~ LOBE (הַיֹּתֶרֶת *hai'yo'te'ret*) FROM (מִן *min*) the~HEAVY (הַכָּבֵד *ha'ka'veyd*) FROM (מִן *min*) the~FAILURE (הַחַטָּאת *ha'hha'tat*) *he~ did~make~*BURN.INCENSE^(V) (הִקְטִיר *hiq'tir*) the~ALTAR~unto (הַמִּזְבֵּחָה *ha'miz'bey'hhah*) like~WHICH (כַּאֲשֶׁר *ka'a'sheyr*) *he~did~ much~*DIRECT^(V) (צִוָּה *tsi'wah*) **YHWH** (יְהוָה *YHWH*) AT (אֶת *et*) Mosheh (מֹשֶׁה *mo'sheh*) **RMT:** and the fat and the kidneys and the heavy lobe[33] from the failure, he burned as incense upon the altar, just as **YHWH** directed Mosheh,

9:11 *and~AT* (וְאֶת *wê'et*) the~FLESH (הַבָּשָׂר *ha'ba'sar*) *and~AT* (וְאֶת *wê'et*) the~SKIN (הָעוֹר *ha'or*) *he~did~*CREMATE^(V) (שָׂרַף *sa'raph*) in~

---

[33] "The heavy lobe" is the liver, the heaviest organ in the body.

the~FIRE (בָּאֵשׁ <u>ba'eysh</u>) <u>from~OUTSIDE</u> (מִחוּץ <u>mi'hhuts</u>) <u>to~the~</u>
<u>CAMP</u> (לַמַּחֲנֶה <u>la'ma'hha'neh</u>) **RMT:** and the flesh and the skin he
cremated in the fire outside the camp,

9:12 <u>and~he~will~SLAY</u>^(V) (וַיִּשְׁחַט <u>wai'yish'hhat</u>) <u>AT</u> (אֶת <u>et</u>) <u>the~</u>
<u>ASCENSION.OFFERING</u> (הָעֹלָה <u>ha'o'lah</u>) <u>and~they^(m)~will~make~</u>
<u>FIND</u>^(V) (וַיַּמְצִאוּ <u>wai'yam'tsi'u</u>) <u>SON~s</u> (בְּנֵי <u>bê'ney</u>) <u>Aharon</u> אַהֲרֹן
<u>a'ha'ron</u>) <u>TO~him</u> (אֵלָיו <u>ey'law</u>) <u>AT</u> (אֶת <u>et</u>) <u>the~BLOOD</u> (הַדָּם
<u>ha'dam</u>) <u>and~he~will~SPRINKLE</u>^(V)~<u>him</u> (וַיִּזְרְקֵהוּ <u>wai'yiz're'qey'hu</u>)
<u>UPON</u> (עַל <u>al</u>) <u>the~ALTAR</u> (הַמִּזְבֵּחַ <u>ha'miz'bey'ahh</u>) <u>ALL.AROUND</u>
(סָבִיב <u>sa'viv</u>) **RMT:** and he slew the ascension offering, and the sons
of Aharon revealed to him the blood, and he sprinkled him upon the
altar all around,

9:13 <u>and~AT</u> (וְאֶת <u>wê'et</u>) <u>the~ASCENSION.OFFERING</u> (הָעֹלָה
<u>ha'o'lah</u>) <u>they~did~make~FIND</u>^(V) (הִמְצִיאוּ <u>him'tsi'u</u>) <u>TO~him</u> אֵלָיו
<u>ey'law</u>) <u>to~PIECE~s~her</u> (לִנְתָחֶיהָ <u>lin'ta'hhey'ah</u>) <u>and~AT</u> (וְאֶת <u>wê'et</u>)
<u>the~HEAD</u> (הָרֹאשׁ <u>ha'rosh</u>) <u>and~he~will~make~BURN.INCENSE</u>^(V)
(וַיַּקְטֵר <u>wai'yaq'teyr</u>) <u>UPON</u> (עַל <u>al</u>) <u>the~ALTAR</u> (הַמִּזְבֵּחַ
<u>ha'miz'bey'ahh</u>) **RMT:** and they revealed the ascension offering to
him, to her pieces and the head, and he burned it as incense upon
the altar,

9:14 <u>and~he~will~BATHE</u>^(V) (וַיִּרְחַץ <u>wai'yir'hhats</u>) <u>AT</u> (אֶת <u>et</u>) <u>the~</u>
<u>INSIDE</u> (הַקֶּרֶב <u>ha'qe'rev</u>) <u>and~AT</u> (וְאֶת <u>wê'et</u>) <u>the~LEG~s2</u> (הַכְּרָעַיִם
<u>hak'ra'a'yim</u>) <u>and~he~will~make~BURN.INCENSE</u>^(V) (וַיַּקְטֵר
<u>wai'yaq'teyr</u>) <u>UPON</u> (עַל <u>al</u>) <u>the~ASCENSION.OFFERING</u> (הָעֹלָה
<u>ha'o'lah</u>) <u>the~ALTAR~unto</u> (הַמִּזְבֵּחָה <u>ha'miz'bey'hhah</u>) **RMT:** and he
bathed the insides and the legs, and he burned them as incense
upon the ascension offering, unto the altar,

9:15 <u>and~he~will~make~COME.NEAR</u>^(V) (וַיַּקְרֵב <u>wai'yaq'reyv</u>) <u>AT</u> אֵת
<u>eyt</u>) <u>DONATION</u> (קָרְבַּן <u>qar'ban</u>) <u>the~PEOPLE</u> (הָעָם <u>ha'am</u>) <u>and~he~</u>
<u>will~TAKE</u>^(V) (וַיִּקַּח <u>wai'yi'qahh</u>) <u>AT</u> (אֶת <u>et</u>) <u>HAIRY.GOAT</u> (שְׂעִיר <u>sê'ir</u>)
<u>the~FAILURE</u> (הַחַטָּאת <u>ha'hha'tat</u>) <u>WHICH</u> (אֲשֶׁר <u>a'sher</u>) <u>to~the~</u>
<u>PEOPLE</u> (לָעָם <u>la'am</u>) <u>and~he~will~SLAY</u>^(V)~<u>him</u> (וַיִּשְׁחָטֵהוּ
<u>wai'yish'hha'tey'hu</u>) <u>and~he~will~much~FAIL</u>^(V)~<u>him</u> (וַיְחַטְּאֵהוּ
<u>wai'hhat'ey'hu</u>) <u>like~the~FIRST</u> (כָּרִאשׁוֹן <u>ka'ri'shon</u>) **RMT:** and he
brought near the donation of the people, and he took the hairy goat,
the failure, which belonged to the people, and slew him, and he bore
the blame with him like the first one,

9:16 and~he~will~make~COME.NEAR^(V) (וַיַּקְרֵב *wai'yaq'reyv*) AT (אֶת־ *et*) the~ASCENSION.OFFERING (הָעֹלָה *ha'o'lah*) and~he~will~DO^(V)~ her (וַיַּעֲשֶׂהָ *wai'ya'a'se'ah*) like~the~DECISION (כַּמִּשְׁפָּט *ka'mish'pat*) **RMT:** and he brought near the ascension offering, and he did her according to the decision,

9:17 and~he~will~make~COME.NEAR^(V) (וַיַּקְרֵב *wai'yaq'reyv*) AT (אֶת־ *et*) the~DEPOSIT (הַמִּנְחָה *ha'min'hhah*) and~he~will~much~FILL^(V) (וַיְמַלֵּא *wai'ma'ley*) PALM~him (כַפּוֹ *kha'po*) FROM~her (מִמֶּנָּה *mi'me'nah*) and~he~will~make~BURN.INCENSE^(V) (וַיַּקְטֵר *wai'yaq'teyr*) UPON (עַל *al*) the~ALTAR (הַמִּזְבֵּחַ *ha'miz'bey'ahh*) from~to~STRAND (מִלְּבַד *mi'le'vad*)³⁴ ASCENSION.OFFERING (עֹלַת *o'lat*) the~MORNING (הַבֹּקֶר *ha'bo'qer*) **RMT:** and he brought near the deposit, and he filled his palm from her, and he burned it as incense upon the altar apart from the ascension offering of the morning,

9:18 and~he~will~SLAY^(V) (וַיִּשְׁחַט *wai'yish'hhat*) AT (אֶת־ *et*) the~OX (הַשּׁוֹר *ha'shor*) and~AT (וְאֶת־ *wê'et*) the~BUCK (הָאַיִל *ha'a'yil*) SACRIFICE (זֶבַח *ze'vahh*) the~OFFERING.OF.RESTITUTION~s (הַשְּׁלָמִים *ha'she'la'mim*) WHICH (אֲשֶׁר *a'sher*) to~the~PEOPLE (לָעָם *la'am*) and~they^(m)~will~make~FIND^(V) (וַיַּמְצִאוּ *wai'yam'tsi'u*) SON~s (בְּנֵי *bê'ney*) Aharon (אַהֲרֹן *a'ha'ron*) AT (אֶת־ *et*) the~BLOOD (הַדָּם *ha'dam*) TO~him (אֵלָיו *ey'law*) and~he~will~SPRINKLE^(V)~him (וַיִּזְרְקֵהוּ *wai'yiz're'qey'hu*) UPON (עַל *al*) the~ALTAR (הַמִּזְבֵּחַ *ha'miz'bey'ahh*) ALL.AROUND (סָבִיב *sa'viv*) **RMT:** and he slew the ox and the buck of the sacrifice of the offerings of restitution, which belonged to the people, and the sons of Aharon revealed the blood to him, and he sprinkled him upon the altar, all around,

9:19 and~AT (וְאֶת־ *wê'et*) the~FAT~s (הַחֲלָבִים *ha'hha'la'vim*) FROM (מִן *min*) the~OX (הַשּׁוֹר *ha'shor*) and~FROM (וּמִן *u'min*) the~BUCK (הָאַיִל *ha'a'yil*) the~RUMP (הָאַלְיָה *ha'al'yah*) and~the~much~ COVER.OVER^(V)~ing^(ms) (וְהַמְכַסֶּה *wê'ham'kha'seh*) and~the~ KIDNEY~s (הַכְּלָיֹת *wê'hak'la'yot*) and~LOBE (וְיֹתֶרֶת *wê'yo'te'ret*) the~HEAVY (הַכָּבֵד *ha'ka'veyd*) **RMT:** and the fats from the ox and from the buck the rump, and what is covering over the kidneys and the lobe of the heavy lobe³⁵,

---

³⁴ An idiom meaning "apart from."

³⁵ "The heavy lobe" is the liver, the heaviest organ in the body.

9:20 and~*they*(m)~*will*~PLACE(V) (וַיָּשִׂימוּ *wai'ya'si'mu*) AT (אֶת *et*) the~FAT~s (הַחֲלָבִים *ha'hha'la'vim*) UPON (עַל *al*) the~CHEST (הֶחָזוֹת *he'hha'zot*) and~*he*~*will*~*make*~BURN.INCENSE(V) (וַיַּקְטֵר *wai'yaq'teyr*) the~FAT~s (הַחֲלָבִים *ha'hha'la'vim*) the~ALTAR~unto (הַמִּזְבֵּחָה *ha'miz'bey'hhah*) **RMT:** and they placed the fats upon the chest, and he made the fats burn as incense unto the altar,

9:21 and~AT (וְאֵת *wê'eyt*) the~CHEST (הֶחָזוֹת *he'hha'zot*) and~AT (וְאֵת *wê'eyt*) THIGH (שׁוֹק *shoq*) the~RIGHT.HAND (הַיָּמִין *hai'ya'min*) he~*did*~*make*~WAVE(V) (הֵנִיף *hey'niph*) Aharon (אַהֲרֹן *a'ha'ron*) WAVING (תְּנוּפָה *tê'nu'phah*) to~FACE~s (לִפְנֵי *liph'ney*) **YHWH** (יְהוָה *YHWH*) like~WHICH (כַּאֲשֶׁר *ka'a'sheyr*) he~*did*~much~DIRECT(V) (צִוָּה *tsi'wah*) Mosheh (מֹשֶׁה *mo'sheh*) **RMT:** and the chest and the right thigh Aharon waved a waving to the face of **YHWH**, just as Mosheh directed,

9:22 and~*he*~*will*~LIFT.UP(V) (וַיִּשָּׂא *wai'yi'sa*) Aharon (אַהֲרֹן *a'ha'ron*) AT (אֶת *et*) HAND~him (יָדוֹ *ya'do*)[36] TO (אֶל *el*) the~PEOPLE (הָעָם *ha'am*) and~*he*~*will*~much~KNEEL(V)~them(m) (וַיְבָרְכֵם *wai'var'kheym*) and~*he*~*will*~GO.DOWN(V) (וַיֵּרֶד *wai'yey'red*) from~>~DO(V) (מֵעֲשֹׂת *mey'a'sot*) the~FAILURE (הַחַטָּאת *ha'hha'tat*) and~the~ASCENSION.OFFERING (וְהָעֹלָה *wê'ha'o'lah*) and~the~OFFERING.OF.RESTITUTION~s (וְהַשְּׁלָמִים *wê'hash'la'mim*) **RMT:** and Aharon lifted up his hand to the people, and he exalted them, and he went down from doing the failure and the ascension offering and the offerings of restitution,

9:23 and~*he*~*will*~COME(N) (וַיָּבֹא *wai'ya'vo*) Mosheh (מֹשֶׁה *mo'sheh*) and~Aharon (וְאַהֲרֹן *wê'a'ha'ron*) TO (אֶל *el*) TENT (אֹהֶל *o'hel*) APPOINTED (מוֹעֵד *mo'eyd*) and~*they*(m)~*will*~GO.OUT(V) (וַיֵּצְאוּ *wai'yeyts'u*) and~*they*(m)~*will*~much~KNEEL(V) (וַיְבָרְכוּ *wai'va'ra'khu*) AT (אֶת *et*) the~PEOPLE (הָעָם *ha'am*) and~*he*~*will*~be~SEE(V) (וַיֵּרָא *wai'yey'ra*) ARMAMENT (כְּבוֹד *khê'vod*) **YHWH** (יְהוָה *YHWH*) TO (אֶל *el*) ALL (כָּל *kol*) the~PEOPLE (הָעָם *ha'am*) **RMT:** and Mosheh came, and Aharon, to the appointed tent, and they went out and they exalted the people, and the armament of **YHWH** appeared to all the people,

9:24 and~*she*~*will*~GO.OUT(V) (וַתֵּצֵא *wa'tey'tsey*) FIRE (אֵשׁ *eysh*) from~to~FACE~s (מִלִּפְנֵי *mi'liph'ney*) **YHWH** (יְהוָה *YHWH*) and~*she*~*will*~EAT(V) (וַתֹּאכַל *wa'to'khal*) UPON (עַל *al*) the~ALTAR (הַמִּזְבֵּחַ *ha'miz'bey'hha*)

---

[36] *Qere* = יָדָיו.

59

ha'miz'bey'ahh) <u>AT</u> (אֶת *et*) the~ASCENSION.OFFERING (הָעֹלָה)
ha'o'lah) <u>and~AT</u> (וְאֶת *wê'et*) <u>the~FAT~s</u> (הַחֲלָבִים *ha'hha'la'vim*)
<u>and~he~will~SEE^(V)</u> (וַיַּרְא *wai'yar*) <u>ALL</u> (כָּל *kol*) the~PEOPLE (הָעָם)
ha'am) <u>and~they^(m)~will~SHOUT.ALOUD^(V)</u> (וַיָּרֹנּוּ *wai'ya'ro'nu*) <u>and~</u>
<u>they^(m)~will~FALL^(V)</u> (וַיִּפְּלוּ *wai'yip'lu*) <u>UPON</u> (עַל *al*) <u>FACE~s~them^(m)</u>
(פְּנֵיהֶם *pê'ney'hem*) **RMT:** and a fire came out from before the face
of **YHWH**, and she ate the ascension offering and the fats upon the
altar, and all the people saw, and they shouted aloud and they fell
upon their faces,

Chapter 10

10:1 <u>and~they^(m)~will~TAKE^(V)</u> (וַיִּקְחוּ *wai'yiq'hhu*) <u>SON~s</u> (בְנֵי)
vê'ney) <u>Aharon</u> (אַהֲרֹן *a'ha'ron*) <u>Nadav</u> (נָדָב *na'dav*) <u>and~Aviyhu</u>
(וַאֲבִיהוּא *wa'a'vi'hu*) <u>MAN</u> (אִישׁ *ish*) <u>FIRE.PAN~him</u> מַחְתָּתוֹ
mahh'ta'to) <u>and~they^(m)~will~GIVE^(V)</u> (וַיִּתְּנוּ *wai'yit'nu*) <u>in~them^(f)</u>
(בָהֵן *va'heyn*) <u>FIRE</u> (אֵשׁ *eysh*) <u>and~they^(m)~will~PLACE^(V)</u> (וַיָּשִׂימוּ
wai'ya'si'mu) <u>UPON~her</u> (עָלֶיהָ *a'ley'ah*) <u>INCENSE.SMOKE</u> (קְטֹרֶת
qê'to'ret) <u>and~they^(m)~will~make~COME.NEAR^(V)</u> (וַיַּקְרִבוּ
wai'yaq'ri'vu)³⁷ <u>to~FACE~s</u> (לִפְנֵי *liph'ney*) **YHWH** (יְהוָה *YHWH*) <u>FIRE</u>
(אֵשׁ *eysh*) <u>BE.STRANGE^(V)~ing^(fs)</u> (זָרָה *za'rah*) <u>WHICH</u> (אֲשֶׁר *a'sher*)
<u>NOT</u> (לֹא *lo*) <u>he~did~much~DIRECT^(V)</u> (צִוָּה *tsi'wah*) <u>AT~them^(m)</u> אֹתָם)
o'tam) **RMT:** and the sons of Aharon, Nadav and Aviyhu, each took
his fire pan, and they placed fire in them, and they placed incense
smoke upon her, and they brought strange fire near to the face of
YHWH, which he did not direct them,

10:2 <u>and~she~will~GO.OUT^(V)</u> (וַתֵּצֵא *wa'tey'tsey*) <u>FIRE</u> (אֵשׁ *eysh*)
<u>from~to~FACE~s</u> (מִלִּפְנֵי *mi'liph'ney*) **YHWH** (יְהוָה *YHWH*) <u>and~she~</u>
<u>will~EAT^(V)</u> (וַתֹּאכַל *wa'to'khal*) <u>AT~them^(m)</u> (אוֹתָם *o'tam*) <u>and~</u>
<u>they^(m)~will~DIE^(V)</u> (וַיָּמֻתוּ *wai'ya'mu'tu*) <u>to~FACE~s</u> (לִפְנֵי *liph'ney*)
YHWH (יְהוָה *YHWH*) **RMT:** and fire went out from before the face of
YHWH and she at them and they died to the face of **YHWH**,

10:3 <u>and~he~will~SAY^(V)</u> (וַיֹּאמֶר *wai'yo'mer*) <u>Mosheh</u> (מֹשֶׁה
mo'sheh) <u>TO</u> (אֶל *el*) <u>Aharon</u> (אַהֲרֹן *a'ha'ron*) <u>HE</u> (הוּא *hu*) <u>WHICH</u>
(אֲשֶׁר *a'sher*) <u>he~did~much~SPEAK^(V)</u> (דִּבֶּר *di'ber*) **YHWH** (יְהוָה *YHWH*) <u>to~>~SAY^(V)</u> (לֵאמֹר *ley'mor*) <u>in~NEAR~s~me</u> (בִּקְרֹבַי
biq'ro'vai) <u>I~will~be~SET.APART^(V)</u> (אֶקָּדֵשׁ *e'qa'deysh*) <u>and~UPON</u>

---

³⁷ *Leningrad Codex:* ויקריבו

(וְעַל wê'al) FACE~s פְּנֵי pê'ney) AL כָּל khol) the~PEOPLE (הָעָם ha'am) I~will~be~BE.HEAVY(V) אֶכָּבֵד e'ka'veyd) and~he~will~ BE.SILENT(V) (וַיִּדֹּם wai'yi'dom) Aha-on אַהֲרֹן a'ha'ron) **RMT:** and Mosheh said to Aharon, this is what **YHWH** spoke, saying, with ones near me I will be set apart, and upon the face of all the people I will be heavy, and Aharon was silent,

10:4 and~he~will~CALL.OUT(V) וַיִּקְרָא wai'yiq'ra) Mosheh (מֹשֶׁה mo'sheh) TO אֶל el) Miysha'eyl מִישָׁאֵל mi'sha'eyl) and~TO (וְאֶל wê'el) El'tsaphan אֶלְצָפָן el'tsa'phan) SON~s בְּנֵי bê'ney) Uziy'eyl (עֻזִּיאֵל u'zi'eyl) UNCLE דֹּד dod' Aharon אַהֲרֹן a'ha'ron) and~he~ will~SAY(V) וַיֹּאמֶר wai'yo'mer) TO~them(m) אֲלֵהֶם a'ley'hem) !(mp)~ COME.NEAR(V) קִרְבוּ qir'vu) !(mᵖ)~LIFT.UP(V) שְׂאוּ sê'u) AT (אֶת et) BROTHER~s~you(mp) אֲחֵיכֶם a'hhey'khem) from~AT (מֵאֵת mey'eyt) FACE~s פְּנֵי pê'ney) the~SPECIAL הַקֹּדֶשׁ ha'qo'desh) TO (אֶל el) from~OUTSIDE (מִחוּץ mi'hhuts) to~the~CAMP לַמַּחֲנֶה la'ma'hha'neh) **RMT:** and Mosheh called out to Miysha'eyl and to El'tsaphan, the sons of Uziy'eyl, the uncle of Aharon, and said to them, come near, lift up your brothers from the face of the special place to the outside of the camp,

10:5 and~they(m)~will~COME.NEAR(V) וַיִּקְרְבוּ wai'yiq're'vu) and~ they(m)~will~LIFT.UP(V)~them(m) וַיִּשָּׂאֻם wai'yi'sa'um) in~TUNIC~s~ them(m) בְּכֻתֳּנֹתָם bê'khu'ta'no'tam) TO אֶל el) from~OUTSIDE מִחוּץ mi'hhuts) to~the~CAMP לַמַּחֲנֶה la'ma'hha'neh) like~WHICH כַּאֲשֶׁר ka'a'sheyr) he~did~much~SPEAK(V) דִּבֶּר di'ber) Mosheh (מֹשֶׁה mo'sheh) **RMT:** and they came near and they lifted them up with their tunics, to the outside of the camp, just as Mosheh spoke,

10:6 and~he~will~SAY(V) (וַיֹּאמֶר wai'yo'mer) Mosheh (מֹשֶׁה mo'sheh) TO אֶל el) Aharon אַהֲרֹן a'ha'ron) and~to~Elazar (וּלְאֶלְעָזָר ul'el'a'zar) and~to~Iytamar וּלְאִיתָמָר ul'i'ta'mar) SON~s~ him בָּנָיו ba'naw) HEAD~s~you(mp) רָאשֵׁיכֶם ra'shey'khem) DO.NOT (אַל al) you(mp)~will~LOOSE(V) תִּפְרָעוּ tiph'ra'u) and~GARMENT~s~ you(mp) וּבִגְדֵיכֶם u'vig'dey'khem) NOT (לֹא lo) you(mp)~will~RIP(V) תִּפְרֹמוּ tiph'ro'mu) and~NOT (וְלֹא wê'lo) you(mp)~will~DIE(V) תָמֻתוּ ta'mu'tu) and~UPON (וְעַל wê'al) ALL כָּל kol) the~COMPANY הָעֵדָה ha'ey'dah) he~will~SNAP(V) יִקְצֹף yiq'tsoph) and~BROTHER~s~ you(mp) וַאֲחֵיכֶם wa'a'hhey'khem) ALL כָּל kol) HOUSE (בֵּית beyt) Yisra'eyl יִשְׂרָאֵל yis'rc'eyl) they(m)~will~WEEP(V) יִבְכּוּ yiv'ku) AT (אֶת et) the~CREMATING הַשְּׂרֵפָה has'rey'phah) WHICH אֲשֶׁר a'sher) he~did~CREMATE(V) שָׂרָף sa'raph) **YHWH** יְהוָה YHWH) **RMT:** and

Mosheh said to Aharon, and to Elazar and to Iytamar, his sons, you will not loose your heads, and you will not rip your garments, and you will not die, and he will snap upon all the company, and your brothers, all the house of Yisra'eyl will weep the cremating, which **YHWH** cremated,

10:7 and~from~OPENING (וּמִפֶּתַח u'mi'pe'tahh) TENT (אֹהֶל o'hel) APPOINTED (מוֹעֵד mo'eyd) NOT (לֹא lo) you(mp)~will~GO.OUT(V) (תֵּצְאוּ teyts'u) OTHERWISE (פֶּן pen) you(mp)~will~DIE(V) (תָּמֻתוּ ta'mu'tu) GIVEN.THAT (כִּי ki) OIL (שֶׁמֶן she'men) OINTMENT (מִשְׁחַת mish'hhat) **YHWH** (יְהוָה YHWH) UPON~you(mp) (עֲלֵיכֶם a'ley'khem) and~they(m)~will~DO(V) (וַיַּעֲשׂוּ wai'ya'a'su) like~WORD (כִּדְבָר kid'var) Mosheh (מֹשֶׁה mo'sheh) **RMT:** and you will not go out from the opening of the appointed tent, otherwise you will die, given that the oil of ointment of **YHWH** is upon you, and they did according to the word of Mosheh,

10:8 and~*he~will~much*~SPEAK(V) (וַיְדַבֵּר wai'da'beyr) **YHWH** (יְהוָה YHWH) TO (אֶל el) Aharon (אַהֲרֹן a'ha'ron) to~>~SAY(V) (לֵאמֹר ley'mor) **RMT:** and **YHWH** spoke to Aharon saying,

10:9 WINE (יַיִן ya'yin) and~LIQUOR (וְשֵׁכָר wê'shey'khar) DO.NOT (אַל al) you(ms)~will~GULP(V) (תֵּשְׁתְּ teysh'te) YOU(ms) (אַתָּה a'tah) and~SON~s~you(ms) (וּבָנֶיךָ u'va'ney'kha) AT~you(fs) (אִתָּךְ i'takh) in~ >~COME(V)~you(mp) (בְּבֹאֲכֶם bê'vo'a'khem) TO (אֶל el) TENT (אֹהֶל o'hel) APPOINTED (מוֹעֵד mo'eyd) and~NOT (וְלֹא wê'lo) you(mp)~will~ DIE(V) (תָּמֻתוּ ta'mu'tu) CUSTOM (חֻקַּת hhu'qat) DISTANT (עוֹלָם o'lam) to~GENERATION~s~you(mp) (לְדֹרֹתֵיכֶם lê'do'ro'tey'khem) **RMT:** you will not gulp wine and liquor, you and your sons with you, when coming to the appointed tent, and you will not die, it is a distant custom for your generations,

10:10 and~to~>~*make*~SEPARATE(V) (וּלֲהַבְדִּיל u'la'hav'dil) BETWEEN (בֵּין beyn) the~SPECIAL (הַקֹּדֶשׁ ha'qo'desh) and~BETWEEN (וּבֵין u'veyn) the~ORDINARY (הַחֹל ha'hhol) and~BETWEEN (וּבֵין u'veyn) the~DIRTY (הַטָּמֵא ha'ta'mey) and~BETWEEN (וּבֵין u'veyn) the~ CLEAN (הַטָּהוֹר ha'ta'hor) **RMT:** and to make a separation between the special and the ordinary and between the dirty and the clean,

10:11 and~to~>~*make*~THROW(V) (וּלְהוֹרֹת ul'ho'rot) AT (אֶת et) SON~s (בְּנֵי bê'ney) Yisra'eyl (יִשְׂרָאֵל yis'ra'eyl) AT (אֵת eyt) ALL (כָּל kol) the~CUSTOM~s (הַחֻקִּים ha'hhu'qim) WHICH (אֲשֶׁר a'sher) he~ did~*much*~SPEAK(V) (דִּבֶּר di'ber) **YHWH** (יְהוָה YHWH) TO~them(m)

(אֲלֵיהֶם *a'ley'hem*) in~HAND (בְּיַד *bê'yad*) Mosheh (מֹשֶׁה *mo'sheh*)
RMT: and to teach the sons of Yisra'eyl all the customs that **YHWH**
spoke to them by the hand of Mosheh,

10:12 and~he~will~much~SPEAK(ⱽ) (וַיְדַבֵּר *wai'da'beyr*) Mosheh
(מֹשֶׁה *mo'sheh*) TO (אֶל *el*) Aharon (אַהֲרֹן *a'ha'ron*) and~TO (וְאֶל
wê'el) Elazar (אֶלְעָזָר *el'a'zar*) and~TO (וְאֶל *wê'el*) Iytamar (אִיתָמָר
i'ta'mar) SON~s~him (בָּנָיו *ba'naw*) the~be~LEAVE.BEHIND(ⱽ)~ing(mp)
(הַנּוֹתָרִים *ha'no'ta'rim*) !(mp)~TAKE(ⱽ) (קְחוּ *qê'hhu*) AT (אֶת *et*) the~
DEPOSIT (הַמִּנְחָה *ha'min'hhah*) the~be~LEAVE.BEHIND(ⱽ)~ing(fs)
(הַנּוֹתֶרֶת *ha'no'te'ret*) from~FIRE.OFFERING~s (מֵאִשֵּׁי *mey'I'shey*)
YHWH (יְהוָה *YHWH*) and~!(mp)~EAT(ⱽ)~him~& (וְאִכְלוּהָ *wê'ikh'lu'ah*)
UNLEAVENED.BREAD~s (מַצּוֹת *ma'tsot*) BESIDE (אֵצֶל *ey'tsel*) the~
ALTAR (הַמִּזְבֵּחַ *ha'miz'bey'ahh*) GIVEN.THAT (כִּי *ki*) SPECIAL (קֹדֶשׁ
qo'desh) SPECIAL~s (קָדָשִׁים *qa da'shim*) SHE (הוּא *hi*) **RMT:** and
Mosheh spoke to Aharon, and to Elazar and to Iytamar his sons, the
ones being left behind, take the deposit, the one being left behind
from the fire offerings of **YHWH**, and eat the unleavened breads
beside the altar, given that she is a special of specials[38],

10:13 and~you(mp)~did~EAT(ⱽ) (וַאֲכַלְתֶּם *wa'a'khal'tem*) AT~her (אֹתָהּ
o'tah) in~AREA (בְּמָקוֹם *bê'ma'qom*) UNIQUE (קָדֹשׁ *qa'dosh*)[39]
GIVEN.THAT (כִּי *ki*) CUSTOM~you(ms) (חָקְךָ *hha'qe'kha*) and~
CUSTOM (וְחָק *wê'hhaq*) SON~s~you(ms) (בָּנֶיךָ *ba'ney'kha*) SHE (הוּא
hi) from~FIRE.OFFERING~s (מֵאִשֵּׁי *mey'I'shey*) **YHWH** (יְהוָה *YHWH*)
GIVEN.THAT (כִּי *ki*) SO (כֵן *kheyn*)[40] I~did~be~much~DIRECT(ⱽ) (צֻוֵּיתִי
tsu'wey'ti) **RMT:** and you will eat her in the unique area, given that
she is your custom, and a custom of your sons, from the fire
offerings of **YHWH**, since I have been directed,

10:14 and~AT (וְאֵת *wê'eyt*) CHEST (חֲזֵה *hha'zeyh*) the~WAVING
(הַתְּנוּפָה *hat'nu'phah*) and~AT (וְאֵת *wê'eyt*) THIGH (שׁוֹק *shoq*) the~
OFFERING (הַתְּרוּמָה *hat'ru'mah*) you(mp)~will~EAT(ⱽ) (תֹּאכְלוּ *tokh'lu*)
in~AREA (בְּמָקוֹם *bê'ma'qom*) CLEAN (טָהוֹר *ta'hor*) YOU(ms) (אַתָּה
a'tah) and~SON~s~you(ms) (וּבָנֶיךָ *u'va'ney'kha*) and~DAUGHTER~s~
you(ms) (וּבְנֹתֶיךָ *uv'no'tey'kha*) AT~you(fs) (אִתָּךְ *i'takh*) GIVEN.THAT
(כִּי *ki*) CUSTOM~you(ms) (חָקְךָ *hha'qe'kha*) and~CUSTOM (וְחָק

---

[38] The phrase "special of specials" means a "very special thing, one
or place."

[39] *Leningrad Codex*: קדוש

[40] The phrase "GIVEN.THAT SO" means "since."

wê'hhaq) <u>SON~s~you</u>^(ms) (בָּנֶיךָ *ba'ney'kha*) <u>*they~did~be~*GIVE</u>^(V) (נִתְּנוּ
nit'nu) <u>from~SACRIFICE~s</u> (מִזִּבְחֵי *mi'ziv'hhey*)
<u>OFFERING.OF.RESTITUTION~s</u> (שַׁלְמֵי *shal'mey*) <u>SON~s</u> (בְּנֵי *bê'ney*)
<u>Yisra'eyl</u> (יִשְׂרָאֵל *yis'ra'eyl*) **RMT:** and the chest of the waving and the
thigh of the offering you will eat in the clean area, you and your sons
and your daughters with you, given that it is your custom and the
custom of your sons, they were given from the sacrifices of the
offerings of restitution of the sons of Yisra'eyl.

10:15 <u>THIGH</u> (שׁוֹק *shoq*) <u>the~OFFERING</u> (הַתְּרוּמָה *hat'ru'mah*) <u>and~</u>
<u>CHEST</u> (וַחֲזֵה *wa'hha'zeyh*) <u>the~WAVING</u> (הַתְּנוּפָה *hat'nu'phah*)
<u>UPON</u> (עַל *al*) <u>FIRE.OFFERING~s</u> (אִשֵּׁי *i'shey*) <u>the~FAT~s</u> (הַחֲלָבִים
ha'hha'la'vim) <u>*they*^(m)*~will~make~*COME</u>^(V) (יָבִיאוּ *ya'vi'u*) <u>to~>~</u>
<u>*make~*WAVE</u>^(V) (לְהָנִיף *lê'ha'niph*) <u>WAVING</u> (תְּנוּפָה *tê'nu'phah*) <u>to~</u>
<u>FACE~s</u> (לִפְנֵי *liph'ney*) **YHWH** (יְהוָה *YHWH*) <u>and~*he~did~*EXIST</u>^(V)
(וְהָיָה *wê'hai'yah*) <u>to~you</u>^(ms) (לְךָ *lê'kha*) <u>and~to~SON~s~you</u>^(ms)
(וּלְבָנֶיךָ *ul'va'ney'kha*) <u>AT~you</u>^(ms) (אִתָּךְ *it'kha*) <u>to~CUSTOM</u> (לְחָק
lê'hhaq) <u>DISTANT</u> (עוֹלָם *o'lam*) <u>like~WHICH</u> (כַּאֲשֶׁר *ka'a'sheyr*) <u>*he~*</u>
<u>*did~much~*DIRECT</u>^(V) (צִוָּה *tsi'wah*) **YHWH** (יְהוָה *YHWH*) **RMT:** The
thigh of the offering and the chest of the waving they will bring upon
the fire offerings of the fat, to make a waving to the face of **YHWH**,
and he will exist for you and for your sons with you, it is for a distant
custom just as **YHWH** directed,

10:16 <u>and~AT</u> (וְאֵת *wê'eyt*) <u>HAIRY.GOAT</u> (שְׂעִיר *sê'ir*) <u>the~FAILURE</u>
(הַחַטָּאת *ha'hha'tat*) <u>>~SEEK</u>^(V) (דָּרֹשׁ *da'rosh*) <u>*he~did~*SEEK</u>^(V)
da'rash) <u>Mosheh</u> (מֹשֶׁה *mo'sheh*) <u>and~LOOK</u> (וְהִנֵּה *wê'hin'neyh*) <u>*he~*</u>
<u>*did~be~much~*CREMATE</u>^(V) (שֹׂרָף *so'raph*) <u>and~*he~will~*SNAP</u>^(V)
(וַיִּקְצֹף *wai'yiq'tsoph*) <u>UPON</u> (עַל *al*) <u>Elazar</u> (אֶלְעָזָר *el'a'zar*) <u>and~</u>
<u>UPON</u> (וְעַל *wê'al*) <u>Iytamar</u> (אִיתָמָר *i'ta'mar*) <u>SON~s</u> (בְּנֵי *bê'ney*)
<u>Aharon</u> (אַהֲרֹן *a'ha'ron*) <u>the~*be~*LEAVE.BEHIND</u>^{(V)~}*ing*^(mp)
(הַנּוֹתָרִם *ha'no'ta'rim*) <u>to~>~SAY</u>^(V) (לֵאמֹר *ley'mor*) **RMT:** and Mosheh
diligently sought the hairy goat of the failure, and look, he was
cremated, and he snapped upon Elazar and upon Iytamar, the sons
of Aharon, the ones being left behind, saying,

10:17 <u>WHY</u> (מַדּוּעַ *ma'du'a*) <u>NOT</u> (לֹא *lo*) <u>*you*^(mp)*~did~*EAT</u>^(V)
a'khal'tem) <u>AT</u> (אֶת *et*) <u>the~FAILURE</u> (הַחַטָּאת *ha'hha'tat*) <u>in~AREA</u>
(בִּמְקוֹם *bim'qom*) <u>the~SPECIAL</u> (הַקֹּדֶשׁ *ha'qo'desh*) <u>GIVEN.THAT</u> (כִּי
ki) <u>SPECIAL</u> (קֹדֶשׁ *qo'desh*) <u>SPECIAL~s</u> (קָדָשִׁים *qa'da'shim*) <u>SHE</u> (הִוא
hi) <u>and~AT~her</u> (וְאֹתָהּ *wê'o'tah*) <u>*he~did~*GIVE</u>^(V) (נָתַן *na'tan*) <u>to~</u>
<u>you</u>^(mp) (לָכֶם *la'khem*) <u>to~>~LIFT.UP</u>^(V) (לָשֵׂאת *la'seyt*) <u>AT</u> (אֶת *et*)

TWISTEDNESS (עָוֹן a'won) the~COMPANY (הָעֵדָה ha'ey'dah) to~>~ much~COVER[V] (לְכַפֵּרׁ lê'kha'peyr) UPON~them[m] (עֲלֵיהֶם a'ley'hem) to~FACE~s (לִפְנֵי liph'ney) **YHWH** (יְהוָה YHWH) **RMT:** why did you not eat the failure in the special area, given that she was a special of specials[41], and he gave her to you to lift up the twistedness of the company to cover over them to the face of **YHWH**.

10:18 THOUGH (הֵן heyn) NOT (לֹא lo) he~did~be~make~COME[V] (הוּבָא hu'va) AT (אֶת et) BLOOD~her (דָּמָהּ da'mah) TO (אֶל el) the~ SPECIAL (הַקֹּדֶשׁ ha'qo'desh) FACE~s~unto (פְּנִימָה pê'ni'mah) >~ EAT[V] (אָכוֹל a'khol) you[mp]~will~EAT[V] (תֹּאכְלוּ tokh'lu) AT~her (אֹתָהּ o'tah) in~the~SPECIAL (בַּקֹּדֶשׁ ba'qo'desh) like~WHICH (כַּאֲשֶׁר ka'a'sheyr) I~did~much~DIRECT[V] (צִוֵּיתִי tsi'wey'ti) **RMT:** Though her blood was not brought to the special place within, you will surely eat her in the special place, just as I directed,

10:19 and~he~will~much~SPEAK[V] (וַיְדַבֵּר wai'da'beyr) Aharon (אַהֲרֹן a'ha'ron) TO (אֶל el) Mosheh (מֹשֶׁה mo'sheh) THOUGH (הֵן heyn) the~DAY (הַיּוֹם hai'yom) they~did~make~COME.NEAR[V] (הִקְרִיבוּ hiq'ri'vu) AT (אֶת et) FAILURE~them[m] (חַטָּאתָם hha'ta'tam) and~AT (וְאֶתׁ wê'et) ASCENSION.OFFERING~them[m] (עֹלָתָם o'la'tam) to~FACE~s (לִפְנֵי liph'ney) **YHWH** (יְהוָה YHWH) and~they[f]~will~CALL.OUT[V] (וַתִּקְרֶאנָה wa'tiq're'nah) AT~me (אֹתִי o'ti) like~THESE (כָּאֵלֶּה ka'ey'leh) and~I~did~EAT[V] (וְאָכַלְתִּי wê'a'khal'ti) FAILURE (חַטָּאת hha'tat) the~DAY (הַיּוֹם hai'yom) he~ will~DO.WELL[V] (הַיִּיטַב hai'yiy'tav) in~EYE~s2 (בְּעֵינֵי bê'ey'ney) **YHWH** (יְהוָה YHWH) **RMT:** and Aharon spoke to Mosheh, though today they brought near their failure and their ascension offering to the face of **YHWH**, and they[42] called me out like this, and I will eat the failure today, will it do well in the eyes of **YHWH**,

10:20 and~he~will~HEAR[V] (וַיִּשְׁמַע wai'yish'ma) Mosheh (מֹשֶׁה mo'sheh) and~he~will~DO.WELL[V] (וַיִּיטַב wai'yiy'tav) in~EYE~s2~ him (בְּעֵינָיו bê'ey'naw) **RMT:** and Mosheh heard and it did well in his eyes,

---

[41] The phrase "special of specials" means a "very special thing, one or place."

[42] As the "they" is the feminine plural pronoun, it is referring to the "failure" and the "ascension offering," not the sons of Aharon.

Chapter 11

11:1 <u>and~he~will~much~SPEAK</u>^(V) (וַיְדַבֵּר *wai'da'beyr*) **YHWH** (יְהוָה YHWH) <u>TO</u> (אֶל *el*) <u>Mosheh</u> (מֹשֶׁה *mo'sheh*) <u>and~TO</u> (וְאֶל *wê'el*) <u>Aharon</u> (אַהֲרֹן *a'ha'ron*) <u>to~>~SAY</u>^(V) (לֵאמֹר *ley'mor*) <u>TO~them</u>^(m) (אֲלֵהֶם *a'ley'hem*) **RMT:** and **YHWH** spoke to Mosheh and to Aharon, saying to them.

11:2 <u>!^(mp)~much~SPEAK</u>^(V) (דַּבְּרוּ *da'be'ru*) <u>TO</u> (אֶל *el*) <u>SON~s</u> (בְּנֵי *bê'ney*) <u>Yisra'eyl</u> (יִשְׂרָאֵל *yis'ra'eyl*) <u>to~>~SAY</u>^(V) (לֵאמֹר *ley'mor*) <u>THIS</u> (זֹאת *zot*) <u>the~LIVING</u> (הַחַיָּה *ha'hha'yah*) <u>WHICH</u> (אֲשֶׁר *a'sher*) <u>you</u>^(mp)~will~EAT^(V) (תֹּאכְלוּ *tokh'lu*) <u>from~ALL</u> (מִכָּל *mi'kol*) <u>the~BEAST</u> (הַבְּהֵמָה *ha'be'hey'mah*) <u>WHICH</u> (אֲשֶׁר *a'sher*) <u>UPON</u> (עַל *al*) <u>the~LAND</u> (הָאָרֶץ *ha'a'rets*) **RMT:** Speak to the sons of Yisra'eyl, saying, these are the living ones that you will eat from all the beasts which are upon the land.

11:3 <u>ALL</u> (כֹּל *kol*) <u>make~CLEAVE</u>^(V)~ing^(fs) (מַפְרֶסֶת *maph're'set*) <u>HOOF</u> (פַּרְסָה *par'sah*) <u>and~SPLIT.IN.TWO</u>^(V)~ing^(fs) (וְשֹׁסַעַת *wê'sho'sa'at*) <u>SPLITTING</u> (שֶׁסַע *she'sa*) <u>HOOF~s</u> (פְּרָסֹת *pê'ra'sot*) <u>make~GO.UP</u>^(V)~ing^(fs) (מַעֲלַת *ma'a'lat*) <u>CUD</u> (גֵּרָה *gey'rah*) <u>in~the~BEAST</u> (בַּבְּהֵמָה *ba'be'hey'mah*) <u>AT~her</u> (אֹתָהּ *o'tah*) <u>you</u>^(mp)~will~EAT^(V) (תֹּאכֵלוּ *to'khey'lu*) **RMT:** All being cleaved of the hoof, and splitting hoofs split in two, and making the cud go up among the beasts, you will eat her.

11:4 <u>SURELY</u> (אַךְ *akh*) <u>AT</u> (אֶת *et*) <u>THIS</u> (זֶה *zeh*) <u>NOT</u> (לֹא *lo*) <u>you</u>^(mp)~will~EAT^(V) (תֹאכְלוּ *to'khe'lu*) <u>from~make~GO.UP</u>^(V)~ing^(mp) (מִמַּעֲלֵי *mi'ma'a'ley*) <u>the~CUD</u> (הַגֵּרָה *ha'gey'rah*) <u>and~from~make~CLEAVE</u>^(V)~ing^(mp) (וּמִמַּפְרִיסֵי *u'mi'maph'ri'sey*)⁴³ <u>the~HOOF</u> (הַפַּרְסָה *ha'par'sah*) <u>AT</u> (אֶת *et*) <u>the~CAMEL</u> (הַגָּמָל *ha'ga'mal*) <u>GIVEN.THAT</u> (כִּי *ki*) <u>make~GO.UP</u>^(V)~ing^(fs) (מַעֲלֵה *ma'a'leyh*) <u>CUD</u> (גֵּרָה *gey'rah*) <u>HE</u> (הוּא *hu*) <u>and~HOOF</u> (וּפַרְסָה *u'phar'sah*) <u>WITHOUT~him</u> (אֵינֶנּוּ *ey'ne'nu*) <u>make~CLEAVE</u>^(V)~ing^(ms) (מַפְרִיס *maph'ris*) <u>DIRTY</u> (טָמֵא *ta'mey*) <u>HE</u> (הוּא *hu*) <u>to~you</u>^(mp) (לָכֶם *la'khem*) **RMT:** Surely of these you will not eat, from ones making the cud go up or from ones cleaving of the hoof, the camel, given that he is making the cud go up, but his hoof is without a cleaving, he is dirty to you,

11:5 <u>and~AT</u> (וְאֶת *wê'et*) <u>the~RABBIT</u> (הַשָּׁפָן *ha'sha'phan*) <u>GIVEN.THAT</u> (כִּי *ki*) <u>make~GO.UP</u>^(V)~ing^(fs) (מַעֲלֵה *ma'a'leyh*) <u>CUD</u>

---

⁴³ *Leningrad Codex:* וממפרסי

(גֵּרָה gey'rah) <u>HE</u> (הוּא hu) <u>and~HOOF</u> (וּפַרְסָה u'phar'sah) <u>NOT</u> (לֹא lo) <u>he~will~make~CLEAVE</u>(V) (יַפְרִיס yaph'ris) <u>DIRTY</u> (טָמֵא ta'mey) <u>HE</u> (הוּא hu) <u>to~you</u>(mp) (לָכֶם la'khem) **RMT:** and the rabbit, given that he is making the cud go up, but the hoof is not cleaved, he is dirty to you,

11:6 <u>and~AT</u> (וְאֶת wê'et) <u>the~HARE</u> (הָאַרְנֶבֶת ha'ar'ne've't) <u>GIVEN.THAT</u> (כִּי ki) <u>make~GO.UP</u>(V)~ing(fs) (מַעֲלַת ma'a'lat) <u>CUD</u> (גֵּרָה gey'rah) <u>SHE</u> (הִוא hi) <u>and~HOOF</u> (וּפַרְסָה u'phar'sah) <u>NOT</u> (לֹא lo) <u>she~did~make~CLEAVE</u>(V) (הִפְרִיסָה hiph'ri'sah) <u>DIRTY</u> (טְמֵאָה tê'mey'ah) <u>SHE</u> (הִוא hi) <u>to~you</u>(mp) (לָכֶם la'khem) **RMT:** and the hare, given that she is making the cud go up, but the hoof is not cleaved, she is dirty to you,

11:7 <u>and~AT</u> (וְאֶת wê'et) <u>the~SWINE</u> (הַחֲזִיר ha'hha'zir) <u>GIVEN.THAT</u> (כִּי ki) <u>make~CLEAVE</u>(V)~ing(ms) (מַפְרִיס maph'ris) <u>HOOF</u> (פַּרְסָה par'sah) <u>HE</u> (הוּא hu) <u>and~SPLIT.IN.TWO</u>(V)~ing(ms) (וְשֹׁסַע wê'sho'sa) <u>SPLITTING</u> (שֶׁסַע sne'sa) <u>HOOF</u> (פַּרְסָה par'sah) <u>and~HE</u> (וְהוּא wê'hu) <u>CUD</u> (גֵּרָה gey'rah) <u>NOT</u> (לֹא lo) <u>he~will~be~CHEW</u>(V) (יִגָּר yi'gar) <u>DIRTY</u> (טָמֵא ta'mey) <u>HE</u> (הוּא hu) <u>to~you</u>(mp) (לָכֶם la'khem) **RMT:** and the swine, given that he is cleaving the hoof and the split hoof is split in two, but he does not chew the cud, he is dirty to you.

11:8 <u>from~FLESH~them</u>(m) (מִבְּשָׂרָם mi'be'sa'ram) <u>NOT</u> (לֹא lo) <u>you</u>(mp)~<u>will~EAT</u>(V) (תֹאכֵלוּ to'khey'lu) <u>and~in~CARCASS~them</u>(m) (וּבְנִבְלָתָם uv'niv'la'tam) <u>NOT</u> (לֹא lo) <u>you</u>(mp)~<u>will~TOUCH</u>(V) (תִגָּעוּ ti'ga'u) <u>DIRTY~s</u> (טְמֵאִים tê'mey'im) <u>THEY</u>(m) (הֵם heym) <u>to~you</u>(mp) (לָכֶם la'khem) **RMT:** You will not eat from their flesh and you will not touch their carcass, they are dirty to you.

11:9 <u>AT</u> (אֶת et) <u>THIS</u> (זֶה zeh) <u>you</u>(mp)~<u>will~EAT</u>(V) (תֹאכְלוּ tokh'lu) <u>from~ALL</u> (מִכֹּל mi'kol) <u>WHICH</u> (אֲשֶׁר a'sher) <u>in~the~WATER~s2</u> (בַּמַּיִם ba'ma'yim) <u>ALL</u> (כֹּל kol) <u>WHICH</u> (אֲשֶׁר a'sher) <u>to~him</u> (לוֹ lo) <u>FIN</u> (סְנַפִּיר sê'na'pir) <u>and~SCALES</u> (וְקַשְׂקֶשֶׂת wê'qas'qe'set) <u>in~the~WATER~s2</u> (בַּמַּיִם ba'ma'yim) <u>in~the~SEA~s</u> (בַּיַּמִּים ba'ya'mim) <u>and~in~the~WADI~s</u> (וּבַנְּחָלִים u'van'hha'lim) <u>AT~them</u>(m) (אֹתָם o'tam) <u>you</u>(mp)~<u>will~EAT</u>(V) (תֹאכֵלוּ to'khey'lu) **RMT:** Of these you will eat, from all which are in the waters, all which have to him a fin and scales, in the waters, in the seas, in the wadis, them you will eat,

11:10 <u>and~ALL</u> (וְכֹל wê'khol) <u>WHICH</u> (אֲשֶׁר a'sher) <u>WITHOUT</u> (אֵין eyn) <u>to~him</u> (לוֹ lo) <u>FIN</u> (סְנַפִּיר sê'na'pir) <u>and~SCALES</u> (וְקַשְׂקֶשֶׂת

wê'qas'qe'set) <u>in~the~SEA~s</u> (בַּיַּמִּים *ba'ya'mim*) <u>and~in~the~</u>
<u>WADI~s</u> (וּבַנְּחָלִים *u'van'hha'lim*) <u>from~ALL</u> (מִכֹּל *mi'kol*) <u>SWARMER</u>
(שֶׁרֶץ *she'rets*) <u>the~WATER~s2</u> (הַמַּיִם *ha'ma'yim*) <u>and~from~ALL</u>
(וּמִכֹּל *u'mi'kol*) <u>SOUL</u> (נֶפֶשׁ *ne'phesh*) <u>the~LIVING</u> (הַחַיָּה *ha'hha'yah*)
<u>WHICH</u> (אֲשֶׁר *a'sher*) <u>in~the~WATER~s2</u> (בַּמַּיִם *ba'ma'yim*) <u>FILTHY</u>
(שֶׁקֶץ *she'qets*) <u>THEY</u>[(m)] (הֵם *heym*) <u>to~you</u>[(mp)] (לָכֶם *la'khem*)
RMT: and all which are without to him a fin and scales, in the seas
and in the wadis, from all the swarmers of the waters and from all
the living souls which are in the waters, they are filthy to you,

11:11 <u>and~FILTHY</u> (וְשֶׁקֶץ *wê'she'qets*) <u>they</u>[(m)]<u>~will~EXIST</u>[(V)] יִהְיוּ
yih'yu) <u>to~you</u>[(mp)] (לָכֶם *la'khem*) <u>from~FLESH~them</u>[(m)] מִבְּשָׂרָם
mi'be'sa'ram) <u>NOT</u> (לֹא *lo*) <u>you</u>[(mp)]<u>~will~EAT</u>[(V)] תֹאכֵלוּ) *to'khey'lu*)
<u>and~AT</u> (וְאֶת *wê'et*) <u>CARCASS~them</u>[(m)] (נִבְלָתָם *niv'la'tam*) <u>you</u>[(mp)]<u>~</u>
<u>will~much~DETEST</u>[(V)] (תְּשַׁקֵּצוּ *tê'sha'qey'tsu*) **RMT:** and they will
exist as filthy to you, you will not eat from their flesh and you will
detest their carcass.

11:12 <u>ALL</u> (כֹּל *kol*) <u>WHICH</u> (אֲשֶׁר *a'sher*) <u>WITHOUT</u> (אֵין *eyn*) <u>to~him</u>
(לוֹ *lo*) <u>FIN</u> (סְנַפִּיר *sê'na'pir*) <u>and~SCALES</u> (וְקַשְׂקֶשֶׂת *wê'qas'qe'set*)
<u>in~the~WATER~s2</u> (בַּמַּיִם *ba'ma'yim*) <u>FILTHY</u> (שֶׁקֶץ *she'qets*) <u>HE</u>
(הוּא *hu*) <u>to~you</u>[(mp)] (לָכֶם *la'khem*) **RMT:** All of them that are
without fins and scales in the waters, he is filthy to you,

11:13 <u>and~AT</u> (וְאֶת *wê'et*) <u>THESE</u> (אֵלֶּה *ey'leh*) <u>you</u>[(mp)]<u>~will~much~</u>
<u>DETEST</u>[(V)] (תְּשַׁקְּצוּ *tê'shaq'tsu*) <u>FROM</u> (מִן *min*) <u>the~FLYER</u> (הָעוֹף
ha'oph) <u>NOT</u> (לֹא *lo*) <u>they</u>[(m)]<u>~will~be~EAT</u>[(V)] (יֵאָכְלוּ *yey'akh'lu*)
<u>FILTHY</u> (שֶׁקֶץ *she'qets*) <u>THEY</u>[(m)] (הֵם *heym*) <u>AT</u> (אֶת *et*) <u>the~EAGLE</u>
(הַנֶּשֶׁר *ha'ne'sher*) <u>and~AT</u> (וְאֶת *wê'et*) <u>the~BEARDED.VULTURE</u>
(הַפֶּרֶס *ha'pe'res*) <u>and~AT</u> (וְאֶת *wê'eyt*) <u>the~OSPREY</u> (הָעָזְנִיָּה
ha'az'niy'yah) **RMT:** and these you will detest from the flyers, they
will not be eaten, they are filthy, the eagle, and the bearded vulture,
and the osprey,

11:14 <u>and~AT</u> (וְאֶת *wê'et*) <u>the~VULTURE</u> (הַדָּאָה *ha'da'ah*) <u>and~AT</u>
(וְאֶת *wê'et*) <u>the~HAWK</u> (הָאַיָּה *ha'ai'yah*) <u>to~KIND~her</u> לְמִינָהּ
lê'mi'nah) **RMT:** and the vulture, and the hawk to her kind.

11:15 <u>AT</u> (אֵת *eyt*) <u>ALL</u> (כָּל *kol*) <u>RAVEN</u> (עֹרֵב *o'reyv*) <u>to~KIND~him</u>
(לְמִינוֹ *lê'mi'no*) **RMT:** All raven to his kind,

11:16 <u>and~AT</u> (וְאֵת *wê'eyt*) <u>DAUGHTER</u> (בַּת *bat*) <u>the~OWL</u> (הַיַּעֲנָה
hai'ya'a'nah) <u>and~AT</u> (וְאֶת *wê'et*) <u>the~NIGHTHAWK</u> (הַתַּחְמָס
ha'tahh'mas) <u>and~AT</u> (וְאֶת *wê'et*) <u>the~SEAGULL</u> (הַשָּׁחַף

ha'sha'hhaph) and~AT (וְאֵת) wê'et) the~FALCON (הַנֵּץ ha'neyts) to~
KIND~him (לְמִינֵהוּ lê'mi'ney'hu) **RMT:** and the daughter of the owl[44],
and the nighthawk, and the seagull, and the falcon to his kind,

11:17 and~AT (וְאֶת) wê'et) the~LITTLE.OWL (הַכּוֹס ha'kos) and~AT
(וְאֶת) wê'et) the~CORMORANT (הַשָּׁלָךְ ha'sha'lakh) and~AT (וְאֶת)
wê'et) the~EARED.OWL (הַיַּנְשׁוּף hai'yan'shuph) **RMT:** and the little
owl, and the cormorant, and the eared owl,

11:18 and~AT (וְאֶת) wê'et) the~IBIS (הַתִּנְשֶׁמֶת ha'tin'she'met) and~
AT (וְאֶת) wê'et) the~PELICAN (הַקָּאָת ha'qa'at) and~AT (וְאֶת) wê'et)
the~GIER-EAGLE (הָרָחָם ha'ra'hnam) **RMT:** and the ibis, and the
pelican, and the gier-eagle,

11:19 and~AT (וְאֶת) wê'eyt) the~STORK (הַחֲסִידָה ha'hha'si'dah)
the~HERON (הָאֲנָפָה ha'a'na'p̄ah) to~KIND~her (לְמִינָהּ lê'mi'nah)
and~AT (וְאֶת) wê'et) the~GROUSE (הַדּוּכִיפַת ha'du'khi'phat) and~AT
(וְאֶת) wê'et) the~BAT (הָעֲטַלֵּף ha'a'ta'leyph) **RMT:** and the stork, the
heron to her kind, and the grouse, and the bat[45].

11:20 ALL (כֹּל kol) SWARMER (שֶׁרֶץ she'rets) the~FLYER (הָעוֹף
ha'oph) the~WALK$^{(V)}$~ing$^{(ms)}$ (הַהֹלֵךְ ha'ho'leykh) UPON (עַל al) FOUR
(אַרְבַּע ar'ba) FILTHY (שֶׁקֶץ s̩e'qets) HE (הוּא hu) to~you$^{(mp)}$ (לָכֶם
la'khem) **RMT:** All the swarmers of the flyers, the ones walking[46]
upon four, he is filthy to you.

11:21 SURELY (אַךְ akh) AT (אֶת et) THIS (זֶה zeh) you$^{(mp)}$~will~EAT$^{(V)}$
(תֹּאכְלוּ tokh'lu) from~ALL (מִכֹּל mi'kol) SWARMER (שֶׁרֶץ she'rets)
the~FLYER (הָעוֹף ha'oph) the~WALK$^{(V)}$~ing$^{(ms)}$ (הַהֹלֵךְ ha'ho'leykh)
UPON (עַל al) FOUR (אַרְבַּע ar'ba) WHICH (אֲשֶׁר a'sher) NOT (לֹא
lo)[47] LEG~s2 (כְרָעַיִם khê'ra'a'yim) from~UPWARD (מִמַּעַל mi'ma'al)
to~FOOT~s2~him (לְרַגְלָיו lê'rag'law) to~>~much~LEAP$^{(V)}$ (לְנַתֵּר

---

[44] The meaning of "daughter of the owl" is uncertain; most
translations ignore the word "daughter."

[45] Because all English translations identify this list of creatures as
"birds" (see verse 13), the addition of the "bat" has often been used
to show ignorance of the author of the text. However, as the
Hebrew word "oph" simply means "a creature that flies," the
addition of the bat is justifiable.

[46] The word "walking" also means "going," and may apply to flyers as
they "go" on two feet and with two wings.

[47] *Qere* = לוֹ (to him).

lê'na'teyr) in~them^(f) בָּהֵן *ba'heyn*) UPON (עַל *al*) the~LAND (הָאָרֶץ *ha'a'rets*) **RMT:** Surely of these you will eat, from all the swarmers of the flyers, the ones walking upon four, which have to him legs above his feet, to leap with them upon the land.

11:22 AT (אֶת *et*) THESE (אֵלֶּה *ey'leh*) from~them^(m) מֵהֶם *mey'hem*) *you*^(mp)*~will~EAT*^(V) תֹּאכֵלוּ *to'khey'lu*) AT (אֶת *et*) the~ SWARMING.LOCUST (הָאַרְבֶּה *ha'ar'beh*) to~KIND~him (לְמִינוֹ *lê'mi'no*) and~AT (וְאֶת *wê'et*) the~LOCUST (הַסָּלְעָם *ha'sal'am*) to~ KIND~him (לְמִינֵהוּ *lê'mi'ney'hu*) and~AT (וְאֶת *wê'et*) the~ LEAPING.LOCUST (הַחַרְגֹּל *ha'hhar'gol*) to~KIND~him (לְמִינֵהוּ *lê'mi'ney'hu*) and~AT (וְאֶת *wê'et*) the~GRASSHOPPER (הֶחָגָב *he'hha'gav*) to~KIND~him (לְמִינֵהוּ *lê'mi'ney'hu*) **RMT:** Of these from them you will eat, the swarming locust to his kind, and the locust to his kind, and the leaping locust to his kind, and the grasshopper to his kind,

11:23 and~ALL (וְכֹל *wê'khol*) SWARMER (שֶׁרֶץ *she'rets*) the~FLYER (הָעוֹף *ha'oph*) WHICH (אֲשֶׁר *a'sher*) to~him (לוֹ *lo*) FOUR (אַרְבַּע *ar'ba*) FOOT~s2 (רַגְלָיִם *rag'la'yim*) FILTHY (שֶׁקֶץ *she'qets*) HE (הוּא *hu*) to~you^(mp) (לָכֶם *la'khem*) **RMT:** and all the swarmers of the flyers which have to him four feet, he is filthy to you,

11:24 and~to~THESE (וּלְאֵלֶּה *ul'ey'leh*) *you*^(mp)*~will~self~BE.DIRTY*^(V) (תִּטַּמָּאוּ *ti'ta'ma'u*) ALL (כָּל *kol*) the~TOUCH^(V)~*ing*^(ms) הַנֹּגֵעַ *ha'no'gey'a*) in~CARCASS~them^(m) (בְּנִבְלָתָם *bê'niv'la'tam*) *he~will~ BE.DIRTY*^(V) (יִטְמָא *yit'ma*) UNTIL (עַד *ad*) the~EVENING (הָעֶרֶב *ha'a'rev*) **RMT:** and to these you will make yourself dirty, every touching with their carcass, he will be dirty until the evening,

11:25 and~ALL (וְכָל *wê'khol*) the~LIFT.UP^(V)~*ing*^(ms) הַנֹּשֵׂא *ha'no'sey*) from~CARCASS~them^(m) (מִנִּבְלָתָם *mi'niv'la'tam*) *he~will~WASH*^(V) (יְכַבֵּס *yê'kha'beys*) GARMENT~s~him (בְּגָדָיו *bê'ga'daw*) and~he~ *did~BE.DIRTY*^(V) (וְטָמֵא *wê'ta'mey*) UNTIL (עַד *ad*) the~EVENING (הָעֶרֶב *ha'a'rev*) **RMT:** and all the ones lifting up their carcass, he will wash his garments and he will be dirty until the evening.

11:26 to~ALL (לְכָל *lê'khol*) the~BEAST (הַבְּהֵמָה *ha'be'hey'mah*) WHICH (אֲשֶׁר *a'sher*) SHE (הִוא *hi*) *make~CLEAVE*^(V)~*ing*^(fs) מַפְרֶסֶת *maph're'set*) HOOF (פַּרְסָה *par'sah*) and~SPLITTING (וְשֶׁסַע *wê'she'sa*) WITHOUT~her (אֵינֶנָּה *ey'ne'nah*) SPLIT.IN.TWO^(V)~*ing*^(fs) (שֹׁסַעַת *sho'sa'at*) and~CUD (וְגֵרָה *wê'gey'rah*) WITHOUT~her (אֵינֶנָּה *ey'ne'nah*) *make~GO.UP*^(V)~*ing*^(fs) מַעֲלָה *ma'a'lah*) DIRTY~s (טְמֵאִים *ta'mey'im*) *tê'mey'im*) THEY^(m) (הֵם *heym*) to~you^(mp) (לָכֶם *la'khem*) ALL (כָּל *kol*) the~TOUCH^(V)~ing^(ms) (הַנֹּגֵעַ *ha'no'gey'a*) in~them^(m) (בָּהֶם *ba'hem*) *he~will~BE.DIRTY^(V)* (יִטְמָא *yit'ma*) **RMT:** To every beast which she is cleaving of the hoof and is not splitting in two and is not bringing up the cud, they are dirty for you, all the ones touching them will be dirty,

11:27 and~ALL (וְכֹל *wê'khol*) WALK^(V)~ing^(ms) (הוֹלֵךְ *ho'leykh*) UPON (עַל *al*) PALM~s2~him (כַּפָּיו *ka'paw*) in~ALL (בְּכָל *bê'khol*) the~ LIVING (הַחַיָּה *ha'hha'yah*) the~WALK^(V)~ing^(fs) (הַהֹלֶכֶת *ha'ho'le'khet*) UPON (עַל *al*) FOUR (אַרְבַּע *ar'ba*) DIRTY~s (טְמֵאִים *tê'mey'im*) THEY^(m) (הֵם *heym*) to~you^(mp) (לָכֶם *la'khem*) ALL (כָּל *kol*) the~ TOUCH^(V)~ing^(ms) (הַנֹּגֵעַ *ha'no'gey'a*) in~CARCASS~them^(m) (בְּנִבְלָתָם *bê'niv'la'tam*) *he~will~BE.DIRTY^(V)* (יִטְמָא *yit'ma*) UNTIL (עַד *ad*) the~ EVENING (הָעָרֶב *ha'a'rev*) **RMT:** and everyone walking upon his palms, among every living thing walking upon four, they are dirty for you, everyone touching their carcass will be dirty until the evening,

11:28 and~the~LIFT.UP^(V)~ing^(ms) (וְהַנֹּשֵׂא *wê'ha'no'sey*) AT (אֶת *et*) CARCASS~them^(m) (נִבְלָתָם *niv'la'tam*) *he~will~WASH^(V)* (יְכַבֵּס *yê'kha'beys*) GARMENT~s~him (בְּגָדָיו *bê'ga'daw*) and~*he~did~ BE.DIRTY^(V)* (וְטָמֵא *wê'ta'mey*) UNTIL (עַד *ad*) the~EVENING (הָעָרֶב *ha'a'rev*) DIRTY~s (טְמֵאִים *tê'mey'im*) THEY^(m) (הֵמָּה *hey'mah*) to~ you^(mp) (לָכֶם *la'khem*) **RMT:** and the one lifting up their carcass will wash his garments and he will be dirty until the evening, they are dirty to you,

11:29 and~THIS (וְזֶה *wê'zeh*) to~you^(mp) (לָכֶם *la'khem*) the~DIRTY (הַטָּמֵא *ha'ta'mey*) in~the~SWARMER (בַּשֶּׁרֶץ *ba'she'rets*) the~ SWARM^(V)~ing^(ms) (הַשֹּׁרֵץ *ha'sho'reyts*) UPON (עַל *al*) the~LAND (הָאָרֶץ *ha'a'rets*) the~WEASEL (הַחֹלֶד *ha'hho'led*) and~the~MOUSE (וְהָעַכְבָּר *wê'ha'akh'bar*) and~the~TORTOISE (וְהַצָּב *wê'ha'tsav*) to~ KIND~him (לְמִינֵהוּ *lê'mi'ney'hu*) **RMT:** and this is dirty to you among the swarmers swarming upon the land, the weasel and the mouse and the tortoise to his kind,

11:30 and~the~FERRET (וְהָאֲנָקָה *wê'ha'a'na'qah*) and~the~ CHAMELEON (וְהַכֹּחַ *wê'ha'ko'chh*) and~the~LIZARD (וְהַלְּטָאָה *wê'hal'ta'ah*) and~the~SNAIL (וְהַחֹמֶט *wê'ha'hho'met*) and~the~IBIS (וְהַתִּנְשָׁמֶת *wê'ha'tin'sha'met*) **RMT:** and the ferret and the chameleon and the lizard and the snail and the ibis.

11:31 THESE (אֵלֶּה ey'leh) the~DIRTY~s (הַטְּמֵאִים hat'mey'im) to~ you(mp) (לָכֶם la'khem) in~ALL (בְּכָל bê'khol) the~SWARMER (הַשָּׁרֶץ ha'sha'rets) ALL (כָּל kol) the~TOUCH(V)~ing(ms) (הַנֹּגֵעַ ha'no'gey'a) in~ them(m) (בָּהֶם ba'hem) in~DEATH~them(m) (בְּמֹתָם bê'mo'tam) he~ will~BE.DIRTY(V) (יִטְמָא yit'ma) UNTIL (עַד ad) the~EVENING (הָעָרֶב ha'a'rev) **RMT**: These are the dirty ones to you among all the swarmers, everyone touching them in their death will be dirty until evening,

11:32 and~ALL (וְכֹל wê'khol) WHICH (אֲשֶׁר a'sher) he~will~FALL(V) (יִפֹּל yi'pol) UPON~him (עָלָיו a'law) from~them(m) (מֵהֶם mey'hem) in~DEATH~them(m) (בְּמֹתָם bê'mo'tam) he~will~BE.DIRTY(V) (יִטְמָא yit'ma) from~ALL (מִכָּל mi'kol) UTENSIL (כְּלִי kê'li) TREE (עֵץ eyts) OR (אוֹ o) GARMENT (בֶגֶד ve'ged) OR (אוֹ o) SKIN (עוֹר or) OR (אוֹ o) SACK (שָׂק saq) ALL (כָּל kol) UTENSIL (כְּלִי kê'li) WHICH (אֲשֶׁר a'sher) he~will~be~DO(V) (יֵעָשֶׂה yey'a'seh) BUSINESS (מְלָאכָה mê'la'khah) in~them(m) (בָּהֶם ba'hem) in~the~WATER~s2 (בַּמַּיִם ba'ma'yim) he~ will~be~make~COME(V) (יוּבָא yu'va) and~he~did~BE.DIRTY(V) (וְטָמֵא wê'ta'mey) UNTIL (עַד ad) the~EVENING (הָעָרֶב ah'e'rev) and~he~ did~BE.CLEAN(V) (וְטָהֵר wê'ta'har) **RMT**: and all of them in their death which will fall upon him, he will be dirty, including any utensil of wood or garment or skin or sack, every utensil which will be done for business he will bring them in the waters, and he will be dirty until evening then he will be clean,

11:33 and~ALL (וְכָל wê'khol) UTENSIL (כְּלִי kê'li) CLAY (חֶרֶשׂ hhe'res) WHICH (אֲשֶׁר a'sher) he~will~FALL(V) (יִפֹּל yi'pol) from~them(m) (מֵהֶם mey'hem) TO (אֶל el) MIDST~him (תּוֹכוֹ to'kho) ALL (כֹּל kol) WHICH (אֲשֶׁר a'sher) in~MIDST~him (בְּתוֹכוֹ bê'to'kho) he~will~BE.DIRTY(V) (יִטְמָא yit'ma) and~AT~him (וְאֹתוֹ wê'o'to) you(mp)~will~CRACK(V) (תִּשְׁבֹּרוּ tish'bo'ru) **RMT**: and every utensil of clay which they will fall into his midst, all which is in his midst will be dirty and you will crack him.

11:34 from~ALL (מִכָּל mi'kol) the~FOODSTUFF (הָאֹכֶל ha'o'khel) WHICH (אֲשֶׁר a'sher) he~will~be~EAT(V) (יֵאָכֵל yey'a'kheyl) WHICH (אֲשֶׁר a'sher) he~will~COME(V) (יָבוֹא ya'vo) UPON~him (עָלָיו a'law) WATER~s2 (מַיִם ma'yim) he~will~BE.DIRTY(V) (יִטְמָא yit'ma) and~ ALL (וְכָל wê'khol) DRINKING (מַשְׁקֶה mash'qeh) WHICH (אֲשֶׁר a'sher) he~will~be~GULP(V) (יִשָּׁתֶה yi'sha'teh) in~ALL (בְּכָל bê'khol) UTENSIL (כְּלִי kê'li) he~will~BE.DIRTY(V) (יִטְמָא yit'ma) **RMT**: From all the foodstuff which will be eaten, which waters will come upon will be dirty, and all drink which can be gulped in every utensil will be dirty,

11:35 and~ALL (וְכֹל wê'khol) WHICH (אֲשֶׁר a'sher) he~will~FALL[V] (יִפֹּל yi'pol) from~CARCASS~them[m] (מִנִּבְלָתָם mi'niv'la'tam) UPON~ him (עָלָיו a'law) he~will~BE.DIRTY[V] (יִטְמָא yit'ma) OVEN (תַּנּוּר ta'nur) and~EARTHENWARE~s2 (וְכִירַיִם wê'khi'ra'yim) he~will~be~ much~BREAK.DOWN[V] (יֻתָּץ yu'tats) DIRTY~s (טְמֵאִים tê'mey'im) THEY[m] (הֵם heym) and~DIRTY~s (וּטְמֵאִים ut'mey'im) they[m]~will~ EXIST[V] (יִהְיוּ yih'yu) to~you[mp] (לָכֶם la'khem) **RMT:** and all which will fall from their carcass upon him will be dirty, oven and earthenware, he will be broken down, they are dirty, and they will exist as dirty things to you.

11:36 SURELY (אַךְ akh) from~the~EYE (מַעְיָן ma'yan) and~CISTERN (וּבוֹר u'vor) COLLECTION (מִקְוֵה miq'weh) WATER~s2 (מַיִם ma'yim) he~will~EXIST[V] (יִהְיֶה yih'yeh) CLEAN (טָהוֹר ta'hor) and~TOUCH[V]~ ing[ms] (וְנֹגֵעַ wê'no'gey'a) in~CARCASS~them[m] (בְּנִבְלָתָם bê'niv'la'tam) he~will~BE.DIRTY[V] (יִטְמָא yit'ma) **RMT:** Surely, from the eye[48] and cistern, a collection of waters, he will exist clean, but touching with their carcass he will be dirty,

11:37 and~GIVEN.THAT (וְכִי wê'khi) he~will~FALL[V] (יִפֹּל yi'pol) from~CARCASS~them[m] (מִנִּבְלָתָם mi'niv'la'tam) UPON (עַל al) ALL (כָּל kol) SEED (זֶרַע ze'ra) SOWN (זֵרוּעַ zey'ru) WHICH (אֲשֶׁר a'sher) he~will~be~SOW[V] (יִזָּרֵעַ yi'za'rey'a) CLEAN (טָהוֹר ta'hor) HE (הוּא hu) **RMT:** and if their carcass will fall upon any seed sown which will be sown, he is clean,

11:38 and~GIVEN.THAT (וְכִי wê'khi) he~GIVE[V]~ed[ms] (יֻתַּן yu'tan) WATER~s2 (מַיִם ma'yim) UPON (עַל al) SEED (זֶרַע ze'ra) and~he~ did~FALL[V] (וְנָפַל wê'na'phal) from~CARCASS~them[m] (מִנִּבְלָתָם mi'niv'la'tam) UPON~him (עָלָיו a'law) DIRTY (טָמֵא ta'mey) HE (הוּא hu) to~you[mp] (לָכֶם la'khem) **RMT:** and if he placed waters upon the seed, and their carcass fell upon him, he is dirty,

11:39 and~GIVEN.THAT (וְכִי wê'khi) he~will~DIE[V] (יָמוּת ya'mut) FROM (מִן min) the~BEAST (הַבְּהֵמָה ha'be'hey'mah) WHICH (אֲשֶׁר a'sher) SHE (הִיא hi) to~you[mp] (לָכֶם la'khem) to~FOOD (לְאָכְלָה lê'akh'lah) the~TOUCH[V]~ing[ms] (הַנֹּגֵעַ ha'no'gey'a) in~CARCASS~her (בְּנִבְלָתָהּ bê'niv'la'tah) he~will~BE.DIRTY[V] (יִטְמָא yit'ma) UNTIL (עַד

---

[48] That is, a fountain.

ad) the~EVENING (הָעָרֶב *ha'a'rev*) **RMT:** and if the beast, which belongs to you for food, dies, the one touching her carcass will be dirty until the evening,

11:40 and~the~EAT^(V)~*ing*^(ms) (וְהָאֹכֵל *wê'ha'o'kheyl*) from~CARCASS~ her (מִנִּבְלָתָהּ *mi'niv'la'tah*) he~will~WASH^(V) (יְכַבֵּס *yê'kha'beys*) GARMENT~s~him (בְּגָדָיו *bê'ga'daw*) and~he~did~BE.DIRTY^(V) (וְטָמֵא *wê'ta'mey*) UNTIL (עַד *ad*) the~EVENING (הָעָרֶב *ha'a'rev*) and~the~ LIFT.UP^(V)~*ing*^(ms) (וְהַנֹּשֵׂא *wê'ha'no'sey*) AT (אֶת *et*) CARCASS~her (נִבְלָתָהּ *niv'la'tah*) he~will~WASH^(V) (יְכַבֵּס *yê'kha'beys*) GARMENT~s~him (בְּגָדָיו *bê'ga'daw*) and~he~did~BE.DIRTY^(V) (וְטָמֵא *wê'ta'mey*) UNTIL (עַד *ad*) the~EVENING (הָעָרֶב *ha'a'rev*) **RMT:** and the one eating her carcass will wash his garments and he will be dirty until the evening, and the one lifting up her carcass will wash his garments and he will be dirty until the evening,

11:41 and~ALL (וְכָל *wê'khol*) the~SWARMER (הַשֶּׁרֶץ *ha'she'rets*) the~SWARM^(V)~*ing*^(ms) (הַשֹּׁרֵץ *ha'sho'reyts*) UPON (עַל *al*) the~LAND (הָאָרֶץ *ha'a'rets*) FILTHY (שֶׁקֶץ *she'qets*) HE (הוּא *hu*) NOT (לֹא *lo*) he~will~be~EAT^(V) (יֵאָכֵל *yey'a'kheyl*) **RMT:** and every swarming swarmer upon the land is filthy, he will not be eaten.

11:42 ALL (כֹּל *kol*) WALK^(V)~*ing*^(ms) (הוֹלֵךְ *ho'leykh*) UPON (עַל *al*) BELLY (גָּחוֹן *ga'hhon*) and~ALL (וְכֹל *wê'khol*) WALK^(V)~*ing*^(ms) (הוֹלֵךְ *ho'leykh*) UPON (עַל *al*) FOUR (אַרְבַּע *ar'ba*) UNTIL (עַד *ad*) ALL (כָּל *kol*) make~INCREASE^(V)~*ing*^(ms) (מַרְבֵּה *mar'beyh*) FOOT~s2 (רַגְלַיִם *rag'la'yim*) to~ALL (לְכָל *lê'khol*) the~SWARMER (הַשֶּׁרֶץ *ha'she'rets*) the~SWARM^(V)~*ing*^(ms) (הַשֹּׁרֵץ *ha'sho'reyts*) UPON (עַל *al*) the~LAND (הָאָרֶץ *ha'a'rets*) NOT (לֹא *lo*) you^(mp)~will~EAT^(V)~them^(m) (תֹאכְלוּם *to'khe'lum*) GIVEN.THAT (כִּי *ki*) FILTHY (שֶׁקֶץ *she'qets*) THEY^(m) (הֵם *heym*) **RMT:** All walking upon the belly and all walking upon four, as well as all making an increase of feet[49], for all the swarming swarmers upon the land, you will not eat them, given that they are filthy.

11:43 DO.NOT (אַל *al*) you^(mp)~will~much~DETEST^(V) (תְּשַׁקְּצוּ *tê'shaq'tsu*) AT (אֶת *et*) SOUL~s~you^(mp) (נַפְשֹׁתֵיכֶם *naph'sho'tey'khem*) in~ALL (בְּכָל *bê'khol*) the~SWARMER (הַשֶּׁרֶץ *ha'she'rets*) the~SWARM^(V)~*ing*^(ms) (הַשֹּׁרֵץ *ha'sho'reyts*) and~NOT (וְלֹא *wê'lo*) you^(mp)~will~make~self~BE.DIRTY^(V) (תִּטַּמְּאוּ *ti'tam'u*) in~ them^(m) (בָּהֶם *ba'hem*) and~you^(mp)~did~be~BE.DIRTY^(V) (וְנִטְמֵתֶם *wê'nit'me'tem*)

---

[49] The phrase "making an increase of feet" means "have many feet."

wê'nit'mey'tem) <u>in~them</u>[(m)] (בָּם *bam*) **RMT:** You will not detest your souls with all the swarming swarmers, and you will not make yourself be dirty with them, and you will be dirty with them,

11:44 <u>GIVEN.THAT</u> (כִּי *ki*) <u>I</u> (אֲנִי *a'ni*) **YHWH** (יְהֹוָה *YHWH*) <u>Elohiym~</u> <u>you</u>[(mp)] (אֱלֹהֵיכֶם *e'lo'hey'khem*) <u>and~you</u>[(mp)]<u>~did~self~SET.APART</u>[(V)] (וְהִתְקַדִּשְׁתֶּם *wê'hit'qa'dish'tem*) <u>and~you</u>[(mp)]<u>~did~EXIST</u>[(V)] (וִהְיִיתֶם *wih'yi'tem*) <u>UNIQUE~s</u> (קְדֹשִׁים *qê'do'shim*) <u>GIVEN.THAT</u> (כִּי *ki*) <u>UNIQUE</u> (קָדוֹשׁ *qa'dosh*) <u>I</u> (אֲנִי *a'ni*) <u>and~NOT</u> (וְלֹא *wê'lo*) <u>you</u>[(mp)]<u>~</u> <u>will~much~BE.DIRTY</u>[(V)] (תְטַמְּאוּ *tê'tam'u*) <u>AT</u> (אֶת *et*) <u>SOUL~s~you</u>[(mp)] (נַפְשֹׁתֵיכֶם *naph'sho'tey'khem*) <u>in~ALL</u> (בְּכָל *bê'khol*) <u>the~SWARMER</u> (הַשֶּׁרֶץ *ha'she'rets*) <u>the~TREAD</u>[(V)]<u>~ing</u>[(ms)] (הָרֹמֵשׂ *ha'ro'meys*) <u>UPON</u> (עַל *al*) <u>the~LAND</u> (הָאָרֶץ *ha'a rets*) **RMT:** given that I am **YHWH** your Elohiym and you will set yourself apart and you will exist as unique ones, given that I am unique, and you will not make your souls be dirty with all the treading swarmers upon the land,

11:45 <u>GIVEN.THAT</u> (כִּי *ki*) <u>I</u> (אֲנִי *a'ni*) **YHWH** (יְהֹוָה *YHWH*) <u>the~</u> <u>make~GO.UP</u>[(V)]<u>~ing</u>[(ms)] (הַמַּעֲלֶה *ha'ma'a'leh*) <u>AT~you</u>[(mp)] (אֶתְכֶם *et'khem*) <u>from~LAND</u> (מֵאֶרֶץ *mey'e'rets*) <u>Mits'rayim</u> (מִצְרַיִם *mits'ra'yim*) <u>to~>~EXIST</u>[(V)] (לִהְיֹת *lih'yot*) <u>to~you</u>[(mp)] (לָכֶם *la'khem*) <u>to~Elohiym</u> (לֵאלֹהִים *ley'lo'him*) <u>and~you</u>[(mp)]<u>~did~EXIST</u>[(V)] (וִהְיִיתֶם *wih'yi'tem*) <u>UNIQUE~s</u> (קְדֹשִׁים *qê'do'shim*) <u>GIVEN.THAT</u> (כִּי *ki*) <u>UNIQUE</u> (קָדוֹשׁ *qa'dosh*) <u>I</u> (אֲנִי *a'ni*) **RMT:** given that I am **YHWH**, the one making you go up from the land of Mits'rayim, to exist for you for Elohiym, and you will exist as unique ones, given that I am unique.

11:46 <u>THIS</u> (זֹאת *zot*) <u>TEACHING</u> (תּוֹרַת *to'rat*) <u>the~BEAST</u> (הַבְּהֵמָה *ha'be'hey'mah*) <u>and~the~FLYER</u> (וְהָעוֹף *wê'ha'oph*) <u>and~ALL</u> (וְכֹל *wê'khol*) <u>SOUL</u> (נֶפֶשׁ *ne'phesh*) <u>the~LIVING</u> (הַחַיָּה *ha'hha'yah*) <u>the~</u> <u>TREAD</u>[(V)]<u>~ing</u>[(fs)] (הָרֹמֶשֶׂת *ha'ro'me'set*) <u>in~the~WATER~s2</u> (בַּמַּיִם *ba'ma'yim*) <u>and~to~ALL</u> (וּלְכָל *ul'khol*) <u>SOUL</u> (נֶפֶשׁ *ne'phesh*) <u>the~</u> <u>SWARM</u>[(V)]<u>~ing</u>[(fs)] (הַשֹּׁרֶצֶת *ha'sho're'tset*) <u>UPON</u> (עַל *al*) <u>the~LAND</u> (הָאָרֶץ *ha'a'rets*) **RMT:** This is the teaching of the beast and the flyer and every living treading soul in the waters, and for every swarming soul upon the land.

11:47 <u>to~>~make~SEPARATE</u>[(V)] (לְהַבְדִּיל *lê'hav'dil*) <u>BETWEEN</u> (בֵּין *beyn*) <u>the~DIRTY</u> (הַטָּמֵא *ha'ta'mey*) <u>and~BETWEEN</u> (וּבֵין *u'veyn*) <u>the~CLEAN</u> (הַטָּהֹר *ha'ta'hor*) <u>and~BETWEEN</u> (וּבֵין *u'veyn*) <u>the~</u> <u>LIVING</u> (הַחַיָּה *ha'hha'yah*) <u>the~be~EAT</u>[(V)]<u>~ing</u>[(fs)] (הַנֶּאֱכֶלֶת *ha'ne'e'khe'let*) <u>and~BETWEEN</u> (וּבֵין *u'veyn*) <u>the~LIVING</u> (הַחַיָּה *ha'hha'yah*) ha'hha'yah) WHICH (אֲשֶׁר a'sher) NOT (לֹא lo) she~will~be~EAT(V) (תֵּאָכֵל tey'a'kheyl) **RMT:** For making a separation between the dirty and the clean and between the living thing to be eaten and the living thing which will not be eaten,

Chapter 12

12:1 and~he~will~much~SPEAK(V) (וַיְדַבֵּר wai'da'beyr) **YHWH** (יְהוָה YHWH) TO (אֶל el) Mosheh (מֹשֶׁה mo'sheh) to~>~SAY(V) (לֵּאמֹר ley'mor) **RMT:** and **YHWH** spoke to Mosheh, saying,

12:2 !(ms)~much~SPEAK(V) (דַּבֵּר da'beyr) TO (אֶל el) SON~s (בְּנֵי bê'ney) Yisra'eyl (יִשְׂרָאֵל yis'ra'eyl) to~>~SAY(V) (לֵאמֹר ley'mor) WOMAN (אִשָּׁה i'shah) GIVEN.THAT (כִּי ki) she~will~make~SOW(V) (תַזְרִיעַ taz'ri'a) and~she~did~BRING.FORTH(V) (וְיָלְדָה wê'yal'dah) MALE (זָכָר za'khar) and~she~did~BE.DIRTY(V) (וְטָמְאָה wê'tam'ah) SEVEN (שִׁבְעַת shiv'at) DAY~s (יָמִים ya'mim) like~DAY~s (כִּימֵי ki'mey) REMOVAL (נִדַּת ni'dat) >~ILL(V)~her (דְּוֺתָהּ dê'o'tah) she~will~BE.DIRTY(V) (תִּטְמָא tit'ma) **RMT:** speak to the sons of Yisra'eyl, saying, a woman that will produce and bring forth a male, then she will be dirty seven days, like the days of removal of her illness, she will be dirty,

12:3 and~in~the~DAY (וּבַיּוֹם u'vai'yom) the~EIGHTH (הַשְּׁמִינִי hash'mini) he~will~be~SNIP.OFF(V) (יִמּוֹל yi'mol) FLESH (בְּשַׂר bê'sar) FORESKIN~him (עָרְלָתוֹ ar'la'to) **RMT:** and in the eighth day, the flesh of his foreskin will be snipped off,

12:4 and~THREE~s (וּשְׁלֹשִׁים ush'lo'shim) DAY (יוֹם yom) and~THREE (וּשְׁלֹשֶׁת ush'lo'shet) DAY~s (יָמִים ya'mim) she~will~SETTLE(V) (תֵּשֵׁב tey'sheyv) in~BLOOD~s (בִּדְמֵי bid'mey) CLEAN (טָהֳרָה ta'ha'rah) in~ALL (בְּכָל bê'khol) SPECIAL (קֹדֶשׁ qo'desh) NOT (לֹא lo) she~will~TOUCH(V) (תִּגָּע ti'ga) and~TO (וְאֶל wê'el) the~SANCTUARY (הַמִּקְדָּשׁ ha'miq'dash) NOT (לֹא lo) she~will~COME(V) (תָבֹא ta'vo) UNTIL (עַד ad) >~FILL(V) (מְלֹאת mê'lot) DAY~s (יְמֵי yê'mey) CLEAN~her (טָהֳרָהּ ta'ha'rah) **RMT:** and thirty and three days she will settle in the bloodshed of the cleanliness, with all special things she will not touch, and she will not come to the sanctuary until the filling of the days of her cleanliness,

12:5 and~IF (וְאִם wê'im) FEMALE (נְקֵבָה nê'qey'vah) she~will~BRING.FORTH(V) (תֵלֵד tey'leyd) and~she~did~BE.DIRTY(V) (וְטָמְאָה wê'tam'ah) WEEK~s2 (שְׁבֻעַיִם shê'vu'a'yim) like~REMOVAL~her

(כְּנִדָּתָהּ kê'ni'da'tah) and~SIX~s (וְשִׁשִׁים wê'shi'shim) DAY (יוֹם yom) and~SIX (וְשֵׁשֶׁת wê'shey'shet) DAY~s (יָמִים ya'mim) she~will~ SETTLE^(V) (תֵּשֵׁב tey'sheyv) UPON (עַל al) BLOOD~s (דְּמֵי dê'mey) CLEAN (טָהֳרָה ta'ha'rah) **RMT:** and if she will bring forth a female, then she will be dirty two weeks, like her removal, and sixty and six days she will settle upon the bloodshed of cleanliness,

12:6 and~in~>~FILL^(V) (וּבִמְלֹאת u'vim'lot) DAY~s (יְמֵי yê'mey) CLEAN~her (טָהֳרָהּ ta'ha'rah) to~SON (לְבֵן lê'veyn) OR (אוֹ o) to~ DAUGHTER (לְבַת lê'vat) she~will~make~COME^(V) (תָּבִיא ta'vi) SHEEP (כֶּבֶשׂ ke'ves) SON (בֶּן ben) YEAR~him (שְׁנָתוֹ shê'na'to) to~ ASCENSION.OFFERING (לְעֹלָה lê'lah) and~SON (וּבֶן u'ven) DOVE (יוֹנָה yo'nah) OR (אוֹ o) TURTLEDOVE (תֹר tor) to~FAILURE (לְחַטָּאת lê'hha'tat) TO (אֶל el) OPENING (פֶּתַח pe'tahh) TENT (אֹהֶל o'hel) APPOINTED (מוֹעֵד mo'eyd) TO (אֶל el) the~ADMINISTRATOR (הַכֹּהֵן ha'ko'heyn) **RMT:** and in the filling of the days of her cleanliness for a son or for a daughter, she will bring a year old sheep for an ascension offering, a son of a dove or a turtledove for the failure, to the opening of the appointed tent, to the administrator,

12:7 and~he~did~make~COME.NEAR^(V)~him (וְהִקְרִיבוֹ wê'hiq'ri'vo) to~FACE~s (לִפְנֵי liph'ney) **YHWH** (יְהֹוָה YHWH) and~he~did~much~ COVER^(V) (וְכִפֶּר wê'khi'per) UPON~her (עָלֶיהָ a'ley'ah) and~she~did~ BE.CLEAN^(V) (וְטָהֲרָה wê'ta'ha'rah) from~FOUNTAIN (מִמְּקֹר mim'qor) BLOOD~s~her (דָּמֶיהָ da'mey'ah) THIS (זֹאת zot) TEACHING (תּוֹרַת to'rat) the~BRING.FORTH^(V)~ing^(fs) (הַיֹּלֶדֶת hai'yo'le'det) to~ the~MALE (לַזָּכָר la'za'khar) OR (אוֹ o) to~the~FEMALE (לַנְּקֵבָה lan'qey'vah) **RMT:** and he will bring him near to the face of **YHWH**, and he will make a covering upon her, and she will be clean from the fountain of her bloodshed, this is the teaching of the bringing forth for the male or for the female,

12:8 and~IF (וְאִם wê'im) NOT (לֹא lo) she~will~FIND^(V) (תִמְצָא tim'tsa) HAND~her (יָדָהּ ya'dah) SUFFICIENT (דֵּי dey) RAM (שֶׂה seh) and~she~did~TAKE^(V) (וְלָקְחָה wê'laq'hhah) TWO (שְׁתֵּי shê'tey) TURTLEDOVE~s (תֹרִים to'rim) OR (אוֹ o) TWO (שְׁנֵי shê'ney) SON~s (בְּנֵי bê'ney) DOVE (יוֹנָה yo'nah) UNIT (אֶחָד e'hhad) to~ ASCENSION.OFFERING (לְעֹלָה lê'lah) and~UNIT (וְאֶחָד wê'e'hhad) to~FAILURE (לְחַטָּאת lê'hha'tat) and~he~did~much~COVER^(V) (וְכִפֶּר wê'khi'per) UPON~her (עָלֶיהָ a'ley'ah) the~ADMINISTRATOR (הַכֹּהֵן ha'ko'heyn) and~she~did~BE.CLEAN^(V) (וְטָהֵרָה wê'ta'hey'rah) **RMT:** and if she does not find her hand sufficient with a ram, then she will take two turtledoves or two sons of a dove, one for the ascension offering and one for the failure, and the administrator will make a covering upon her and she will be clean,

Chapter 13

13:1 and~he~will~much~SPEAK^(V) (וַיְדַבֵּר *wai'da'beyr*) YHWH (יְהוָה **YHWH**) TO (אֶל *el*) Mosheh (מֹשֶׁה *mo'sheh*) and~TO (וְאֶל *wê'el*) Aharon (אַהֲרֹן *a'ha'ron*) to~>~SAY^(V) (לֵאמֹר *ley'mor*) **RMT:** and **YHWH** spoke to Mosheh and to Aharon, saying,

13:2 HUMAN (אָדָם *a'dam*) GIVEN.THAT (כִּי *ki*) he~will~EXIST^(V) (יִהְיֶה *yih'yeh*) in~SKIN (בְעוֹר *vê'or*) FLESH~him (בְשָׂרוֹ *bê'sar'o*) >~ LIFT.UP^(V) (שְׂאֵת *sê'eyt*) OR (אוֹ *o*) SCAB (סַפַּחַת *sa'pa'hhat*) OR (אוֹ *o*) BRIGHT.SPOT (בַהֶרֶת *va'he'ret*) and~he~did~EXIST^(V) (וְהָיָה *wê'hai'yah*) in~SKIN (בְעוֹר *vê'or*) FLESH~him (בְשָׂרוֹ *bê'sar'o*) to~ TOUCH (לְנֶגַע *lê'ne'ga*) INFECTION (צָרַעַת *tsa'ra'at*) and~he~did~be~ make~COME^(V) (וְהוּבָא *wê'hu'va*) TO (אֶל *el*) Aharon (אַהֲרֹן *a'ha'ron*) the~ADMINISTRATOR (הַכֹּהֵן *ha'ko'heyn*) OR (אוֹ *o*) TO (אֶל *el*) UNIT (אֶחָד *a'hhad*) from~SON~s~him (מִבָּנָיו *mi'ba'naw*) the~ ADMINISTRATOR~s (הַכֹּהֲנִים *ha'ko'ha'nim*) **RMT:** a human that has in the skin of his flesh a lifting up or a scab or a bright spot, and has in the skin of his flesh a plague of infection, then he will be brought to Aharon the administrator or to one of his sons the administrators,

13:3 and~he~did~SEE^(V) (וְרָאָה *wê'ra'ah*) the~ADMINISTRATOR (הַכֹּהֵן *ha'ko'heyn*) AT (אֶת *et*) the~TOUCH (הַנֶּגַע *ha'ne'ga*) in~SKIN (בְעוֹר *bê'or*) the~FLESH (הַבָּשָׂר *ha'ba'sar*) and~HAIR (וְשֵׂעָר *wê'sey'ar*) in~the~TOUCH (בַּנֶּגַע *ba'ne'ga*) he~did~OVERTURN^(V) (הָפַךְ *ha'phakh*) WHITE (לָבָן *la'van*) and~APPEARANCE (וּמַרְאֵה *u'mar'eyh*) the~TOUCH (הַנֶּגַע *ha'ne'ga*) SUNKEN (עָמֹק *a'moq*) from~SKIN (מֵעוֹר *mey'or*) FLESH~him (בְשָׂרוֹ *bê'sar'o*) TOUCH (נֶגַע *ne'ga*) INFECTION (צָרַעַת *tsa'ra'at*) HE (הוּא *hu*) and~he~did~SEE^(V)~him (וְרָאָהוּ *wê'ra'a'hu*) the~ADMINISTRATOR (הַכֹּהֵן *ha'ko'heyn*) and~he~did~ much~BE.DIRTY^(V) (וְטִמֵּא *wê'ti'mey*) AT~him (אֹתוֹ *o'to*) **RMT:** and the administrator will see the plague in the skin of the flesh, and a hair in the plague turned white, and the appearance of the plague is sunken from the skin of his flesh, he is the plague of infection, and the administrator will see him and he will declare him dirty,

13:4 and~IF (וְאִם *wê'im*) BRIGHT.SPOT (בַהֶרֶת *ba'he'ret*) WHITE (לְבָנָה *lê'va'nah*) SHE (הִוא *hi*) in~SKIN (בְעוֹר *bê'or*) FLESH~him (בְשָׂרוֹ)

bê'sar'o) and~SUNKEN (וְעָמֹק we'a'moq) WITHOUT (אֵין eyn)
APPEARANCE~her (מַרְאֶהָ mar'e'ah) FROM (מִן min) the~SKIN (הָעוֹר
ha'or) and~HAIR (וּשְׂעָרָה us'a'rah) NOT (לֹא lo) he~did~OVERTURN[V]
(הָפַךְ ha'phakh) WHITE (לָבָן la'van) and~he~did~make~SHUT[V]
(וְהִסְגִּיר wê'his'gir) the~ADMINISTRATOR (הַכֹּהֵן ha'ko'heyn) AT (אֶת
et) the~TOUCH (הַנֶּגַע ha'ne'ga) SEVEN (שִׁבְעַת shiv'at) DAY~s (יָמִים
ya'mim) **RMT:** and if the bright spot is white, she is in the skin of his
flesh and her appearance is not sunken from the skin and a hair is
not turned white, then the administrator will shut the plague seven
days,

13:5 and~he~did~SEE[V]~him (וְרָאָהוּ wê'ra'a'hu) the~
ADMINISTRATOR (הַכֹּהֵן ha'ko'heyn) in~the~DAY (בַּיּוֹם ba'yom) the~
SEVENTH (הַשְּׁבִיעִי hash'vi'i) and~LOOK (וְהִנֵּה wê'hin'neyh) the~
TOUCH (הַנֶּגַע ha'ne'ga) he~did~STAND[V] (עָמַד a'mad) in~EYE~s2~
him (בְּעֵינָיו bê'ey'naw) NOT (לֹא lo) he~did~SPREAD.ACROSS[V]
pha'sah) the~TOUCH (הַנֶּגַע ha'ne'ga) in~the~SKIN (בָּעוֹר ba'or) and~
he~did~make~SHUT[V]~him (וְהִסְגִּירוֹ wê'his'gi'ro) the~
ADMINISTRATOR (הַכֹּהֵן ha'ko'heyn) SEVEN (שִׁבְעַת shiv'at) DAY~s
(יָמִים ya'mim) SECOND (שֵׁנִית shey'nit) **RMT:** and the administrator
will see him in the seventh day and look, the plague stood in his
eyes, the plague did not spread across the skin, then the
administrator will cause him to be shut a second seven days,

13:6 and~he~did~SEE[V] (וְרָאָה wê'ra'ah) the~ADMINISTRATOR
(הַכֹּהֵן ha'ko'heyn) AT~him (אֹתוֹ o'to) in~the~DAY (בַּיּוֹם ba'yom)
the~SEVENTH (הַשְּׁבִיעִי hash'vi'i) SECOND (שֵׁנִית shey'nit) and~LOOK
(וְהִנֵּה wê'hin'neyh) DIMNESS (כֵּהָה key'hah) the~TOUCH (הַנֶּגַע
ha'ne'ga) and~NOT (וְלֹא wê'lo) he~did~SPREAD.ACROSS[V] (פָשָׂה
pha'sah) the~TOUCH (הַנֶּגַע ha'ne'ga) in~the~SKIN (בָּעוֹר ba'or) and~
he~did~much~BE.CLEAN[V]~him (וְטִהֲרוֹ wê'ti'ha'ro) the~
ADMINISTRATOR (הַכֹּהֵן ha'ko'heyn) SCAB (מִסְפַּחַת mis'pa'hhat) SHE
(הִיא hi)[50] and~he~did~much~WASH[V] (וְכִבֶּס wê'khi'bes)
GARMENT~s~him (בְּגָדָיו bê'ga'daw) and~he~did~BE.CLEAN[V] (וְטָהֵר
wê'ta'har) **RMT:** and the administrator will see him in the second
seventh day, and look, dimness of the plague and the plague did not
spread across the skin, then the administrator will declare him clean,
she is a scab, and he will wash his garments and he will be clean,

---

[50] *Leningrad Codex:* הִיא

13:7 and~IF (וְאִם wê'im) >~SPREAD.ACROSS[V] (פָּשֹׂה pa'soh) she~ will~SEIZE.HOLD[V] (תִפְשֶׂה tiph'seh) the~SCAB (הַמִּסְפַּחַת ha'mis'pa'hhat) in~the~SKIN (בָּעוֹר ba'or) AFTER (אַחֲרֵי a'hha'rey) >~ be~SEE[V]~him (הֵרָאֹתוֹ hey'ra'o'to) TO (אֶל el) the~ADMINISTRATOR (הַכֹּהֵן ha'ko'heyn) to~CLEAN~him (לְטָהֳרָתוֹ lê'ta'ha'ra'to) and~he~ did~be~SEE[V] (וְנִרְאָה wê'nir'ah) SECOND (שֵׁנִית shey'nit) TO (אֶל el) the~ADMINISTRATOR (הַכֹּהֵן ha'ko'heyn) **RMT:** but if spreading across, the scab of the skin will seize hold, after he appears to the administrator for his cleanliness, he will appear a second time to the administrator,

13:8 and~he~did~SEE[V] (וְרָאָה wê'ra'ah) the~ADMINISTRATOR (הַכֹּהֵן ha'ko'heyn) and~LOOK (וְהִנֵּה wê'hin'neyh) she~did~ SPREAD.ACROSS[V] (פָּשְׂתָה pas'tah) the~SCAB (הַמִּסְפַּחַת ha'mis'pa'hhat) in~the~SKIN (בָּעוֹר ba'or) and~he~did~much~ BE.DIRTY[V]~him (וְטִמְּאוֹ wê'tim'o) the~ADMINISTRATOR (הַכֹּהֵן ha'ko'heyn) INFECTION (צָרַעַת tsa'ra'at) SHE (הִוא hi) **RMT:** and the administrator will see, and look, the scab spread across the skin, and the administrator will declare him dirty, she is an infection.

13:9 TOUCH (נֶגַע ne'ga) INFECTION (צָרַעַת tsa'ra'at) GIVEN.THAT (כִּי ki) she~will~EXIST[V] (תִהְיֶה tih'yeh) in~HUMAN (בְּאָדָם bê'a'dam) and~he~did~be~make~COME[V] (וְהוּבָא wê'hu'va) TO (אֶל el) the~ ADMINISTRATOR (הַכֹּהֵן ha'ko'heyn) **RMT:** A plague of infection that exists in the human will be brought to the administrator,

13:10 and~he~did~SEE[V] (וְרָאָה wê'ra'ah) the~ADMINISTRATOR (הַכֹּהֵן ha'ko'heyn) and~LOOK (וְהִנֵּה wê'hin'neyh) >~LIFT.UP[V] (שְׂאֵת sê'eyt) WHITE (לְבָנָה lê'va'nah) in~the~SKIN (בָּעוֹר ba'or) and~SHE (וְהִיא wê'hi) she~did~OVERTURN[V] (הָפְכָה haph'khah) HAIR (שֵׂעָר sey'ar) WHITE (לָבָן la'van) and~REVIVING (וּמִחְיַת u'mihh'yat) FLESH (בָּשָׂר ba'sar) LIVING (חַי hhai) in~the~ELEVATION (בַּשְׂאֵת bas'eyt) **RMT:** and the administrator will see, and look, a lifting up of white on the skin, and the hair turned white, and a reviving[51] of the living flesh in the elevation[52].

13:11 INFECTION (צָרַעַת tsa'ra'at) be~SLEEP[V]~ing[fs] (נוֹשֶׁנֶת no'she'net) SHE (הִוא hi) in~SKIN (בְּעוֹר bê'or) FLESH~him (בְּשָׂרוֹ bê'sar'o) and~he~did~much~BE.DIRTY[V]~him (וְטִמְּאוֹ wê'tim'o) the~ ADMINISTRATOR (הַכֹּהֵן ha'ko'heyn) NOT (לֹא lo) he~will~make~

---

[51] Probably meaning "tender" or "raw."

[52] Probably meaning "swelling."

SHUT^(V)~him (יַסְגִּרֶנּוּ yas'gi're'nu) GIVEN.THAT (כִּי ki) DIRTY (טָמֵא ta'mey) HE (הוּא hu) **RMT:** It is an infection, she is sleeping in the skin of his flesh, and the administrator will declare him dirty, he will not cause him shut, given that he is dirty,

13:12 and~IF (וְאִם wê'im) >~BURST.OUT^(V) (פָּרוֹחַ pa'ro'ahh) she~will~BURST.OUT^(V) (תִּפְרַח tiph'rahh) the~INFECTION (הַצָּרַעַת ha'tsa'ra'at) in~the~SKIN (בָּעוֹר ba'or) and~she~did~much~COVER.OVER^(V) (וְכִסְּתָה wê'khis tah) the~INFECTION (הַצָּרַעַת ha'tsa'ra'at) AT (אֵת eyt) ALL (כָּל kol) SKIN (עוֹר or) the~TOUCH (הַנֶּגַע ha'ne'ga) from~HEAD~him (מֵרֹאשׁוֹ mey'ro'sho) and~UNTIL (וְעַד wê'ad) FOOT~s2~him (רַגְלָיו rag'law) to~ALL (לְכָל lê'khol) APPEARANCE (מַרְאֵה mar'eyh) EYE~s2 (עֵינֵי ey'ney) the~ADMINISTRATOR (הַכֹּהֵן ha'ko'heyn) **RMT:** and if the infection in the skin will completely burst out, and the infection will cover over all the skin of the plague, from his head to his feet to all the appearance of the eyes of the administrator[53],

13:13 and~he~did~SEE^(V) (וְרָאָה wê'ra'ah) the~ADMINISTRATOR (הַכֹּהֵן ha'ko'heyn) and~LOCK (וְהִנֵּה wê'hin'neyh) she~did~much~COVER.OVER^(V) (כִסְּתָה khis'tah) the~INFECTION (הַצָּרַעַת ha'tsa'ra'at) AT (אֶת et) ALL (כָּל kol) FLESH~him (בְּשָׂרוֹ bê'sar'o) and~he~did~much~BE.CLEAN^(V) (וְטִהַר wê'ti'har) AT (אֶת et) the~TOUCH (הַנֶּגַע ha'na'ga) ALL~him (כֻּלּוֹ ku'lo) he~did~OVERTURN^(V) (הָפַךְ ha'phakh) WHITE (לָבָן la'van) CLEAN (טָהוֹר ta'hor) HE (הוּא hu) **RMT:** and the administrator will see, and look, the infection covered over all his flesh, then the plague of all of him will be declared clean, he turned white, he is clean,

13:14 and~in~DAY (וּבְיוֹם uv'yom) >~be~SEE^(V) (הֵרָאוֹת hey'ra'ot) in~him (בּוֹ bo) FLESH (בָּשָׂר ba'sar) LIVING (חַי hhai) he~will~BE.DIRTY^(V) (יִטְמָא yit'ma) **RMT:** and in the day living[54] flesh appears in him, he will be dirty,

13:15 and~he~did~SEE^(V) (וְרָאָה wê'ra'ah) the~ADMINISTRATOR (הַכֹּהֵן ha'ko'heyn) AT (אֶת et) the~FLESH (הַבָּשָׂר ha'ba'sar) the~LIVING (הַחַי ha'hhai) and~he~did~much~BE.DIRTY^(V)~him (וְטִמְאוֹ wê'tim'o) the~FLESH (הַבָּשָׂר ha'ba'sar) the~LIVING (הַחַי ha'hhai) DIRTY (טָמֵא ta'mey) HE (הוּא hu) INFECTION (צָרַעַת tsa'ra'at) HE

---

[53] The phrase "to all the appearance of the eyes of the administrator" means "as far as the administrator can see."
[54] Probably meaning "tender" or "raw."

(הוּא *hu*) **RMT:** and the administrator will see the living flesh, and he will declare him dirty, the living flesh is dirty, he is an infection.

13:16 <u>OR</u> (אוֹ *o*) <u>GIVEN.THAT</u> (כִי *khi*) <u>*he~will~*TURN.BACK</u>^(V) (יָשׁוּב *ya'shuv*) <u>the~FLESH</u> (הַבָּשָׂר *ha'ba'sar*) <u>the~LIVING</u> (הַחַי *ha'hhai*) <u>and~he~did~be~OVERTURN</u>^(V) (וְנֶהְפַּךְ *wê'neh'pakh*) <u>to~Lavan</u> (לְלָבָן *lê'la'van*) <u>and~he~did~COME</u>^(V) (וּבָא *u'va*) <u>TO</u> (אֶל *el*) <u>the~ADMINISTRATOR</u> (הַכֹּהֵן *ha'ko'heyn*) **RMT:** Or, given that the living flesh will turn back, and he was turned to white, and he will come to the administrator,

13:17 <u>and~he~did~SEE</u>^(V)~him (וְרָאָהוּ *wê'ra'a'hu*) <u>the~ADMINISTRATOR</u> (הַכֹּהֵן *ha'ko'heyn*) <u>and~LOOK</u> (וְהִנֵּה *wê'hin'neyh*) <u>he~did~be~OVERTURN</u>^(V) (נֶהְפַּךְ *neh'pakh*) <u>the~TOUCH</u> (הַנֶּגַע *ha'ne'ga*) <u>to~WHITE</u> (לְלָבָן *lê'la'van*) <u>and~he~did~much~BE.CLEAN</u>^(V) (וְטִהַר *wê'ti'har*) <u>the~ADMINISTRATOR</u> (הַכֹּהֵן *ha'ko'heyn*) <u>AT</u> (אֶת *et*) <u>the~TOUCH</u> (הַנֶּגַע *ha'ne'ga*) <u>CLEAN</u> (טָהוֹר *ta'hor*) <u>HE</u> (הוּא *hu*) **RMT:** and the administrator will see him, and look, the plague was turned white, and the administrator will declare the plague clean, he is clean,

13:18 <u>and~FLESH</u> (וּבָשָׂר *u'va'sar*) <u>GIVEN.THAT</u> (כִּי *ki*) <u>*he~will~*EXIST</u>^(V) (יִהְיֶה *yih'yeh*) <u>in~him</u> (בוֹ *vo*) <u>in~SKIN~him</u> (בְעֹרוֹ *vê'o'ro*) <u>BOILS</u> (שְׁחִין *shê'hhin*) <u>and~he~did~be~HEAL</u>^(V) (וְנִרְפָּא *wê'nir'pa*) **RMT:** and the flesh that exists in him, in his skin are boils, and he will be healed,

13:19 <u>and~he~did~EXIST</u>^(V) (וְהָיָה *wê'hai'yah*) <u>in~AREA</u> (בִּמְקוֹם *bim'qom*) <u>the~BOILS</u> (הַשְּׁחִין *hash'hhin*) <u>>~LIFT.UP</u>^(V) (שְׂאֵת *sê'eyt*) <u>WHITE</u> (לְבָנָה *lê'va'nah*) <u>OR</u> (אוֹ *o*) <u>BRIGHT.SPOT</u> (בַהֶרֶת *va'he'ret*) <u>WHITE</u> (לְבָנָה *lê'va'nah*) <u>REDDISH</u> (אֲדַמְדָּמֶת *a'dam'da'met*) <u>and~he~did~be~SEE</u>^(V) (וְנִרְאָה *wê'nir'ah*) <u>TO</u> (אֶל *el*) <u>the~ADMINISTRATOR</u> (הַכֹּהֵן *ha'ko'heyn*) **RMT:** and in the place of the boils exists a lifting up of white, or a white reddish bright spot, then he will appear to the administrator,

13:20 <u>and~he~did~SEE</u>^(V) (וְרָאָה *wê'ra'ah*) <u>the~ADMINISTRATOR</u> (הַכֹּהֵן *ha'ko'heyn*) <u>and~LOOK</u> (וְהִנֵּה *wê'hin'neyh*) <u>APPEARANCE~her</u> (מַרְאֶהָ *mar'e'ah*) <u>LOW</u> (שָׁפָל *sha'phal*) <u>FROM</u> (מִן *min*) <u>the~SKIN</u> (הָעוֹר *ha'or*) <u>and~HAIR~her</u> (וּשְׂעָרָה *us'a'rah*) <u>he~did~OVERTURN</u>^(V) (הָפַךְ *ha'phakh*) <u>WHITE</u> (לָבָן *la'van*) <u>and~he~did~much~BE.DIRTY</u>^(V)~him (וְטִמְּאוֹ *wê'tim'o*) <u>the~ADMINISTRATOR</u> (הַכֹּהֵן *ha'ko'heyn*) <u>TOUCH</u> (נֶגַע *ne'ga*) <u>INFECTION</u> (צָרַעַת *tsa'ra'at*) <u>SHE</u> (הִוא *hi*) <u>in~the~</u>

BOILS (בַּשְּׁחִין) *bash'hhin*) *she~will~*BURST.OUT[V] (פָּרָחָה) *pa'ra'hhah*)
RMT: and the administrator will see, and look, her appearance is low
from the skin, and her hair turned white, then the administrator will
declare him dirty, she is a plague of infection, she will burst out in
the boils,

13:21 and~IF (וְאִם) *wê'im*) *he~will~*SEE[V]~her (יִרְאֶנָּה) *yir'e'nah*) the~
ADMINISTRATOR (הַכֹּהֵן) *ha'ko'heyn*) and~LOOK (וְהִנֵּה) *wê'hin'neyh*)
WITHOUT (אֵין) *eyn*) in~her (בָּהּ) *bah*) HAIR (שֵׂעָר) *sey'ar*) WHITE (לָבָן)
la'van) and~LOW (וּשְׁפָלָה) *ush'pha'lah*) WITHOUT~her (אֵינֶנָּה)
ey'ne'nah) FROM (מִן) *min*) the~SKIN (הָעוֹר) *ha'or*) and~SHE (וְהִיא)
wê'hi) DIMNESS (כֵהָה) *khey'hah*) and~he~did~make~SHUT[V]~him
(וְהִסְגִּירוֹ) *wê'his'gi'ro*) the~ADMINISTRATOR (הַכֹּהֵן) *ha'ko'heyn*)
SEVEN (שִׁבְעַת) *shiv'at*) DAY~s (יָמִים) *ya'mim*) **RMT:** and if the
administrator will see her, and look, no white hair is in her, and she
is not low from the skin, and she is dim, then the administrator will
cause him to shut seven days,

13:22 and~IF (וְאִם) *wê'im*) >~SPREAD.ACROSS[V] (פָּשֹה) *pa'soh*) *she~
will~*SEIZE.HOLD[V] (תִפְשֶׂה) *tiph'seh*) in~the~SKIN (בָּעוֹר) *ba'or*) and~
he~did~much~BE.DIRTY[V] (וְטִמֵּא) *wê'ti'mey*) the~ADMINISTRATOR
(הַכֹּהֵן) *ha'ko'heyn*) AT~him (אֹתוֹ) *o'to*) TOUCH (נֶגַע) *ne'ga*) SHE (הִוא)
hi) **RMT:** but if spreading across, seizing hold in the skin, then the
administrator will declare him dirty, she is a plague,

13:23 and~IF (וְאִם) *wê'im*) UNDER~s~her (תַּחְתֶּיהָ) *tahh'tey'ah*) *she~
will~*STAND[V] (תַעֲמֹד) *ta'a'mod*) the~BRIGHT.SPOT (הַבַּהֶרֶת)
ha'ba'he'ret) NOT (לֹא) *lo*) *she~did~*SPREAD.ACROSS[V] (פָשָׂתָה)
pha'sa'tah) SEARING (צָרֶבֶת) *tsa're'vet*) the~BOILS (הַשְּׁחִין) *hash'hhin*)
SHE (הִוא) *hi*) and~he~did~much~BE.CLEAN[V]~him (וְטִהֲרוֹ)
wê'ti'ha'ro) the~ADMINISTRATOR (הַכֹּהֵן) *ha'ko'heyn*) **RMT:** and if the
bright spot stands in her place, and does not spread across, she is
the searing boils, and the administrator will declare him clean.

13:24 OR (אוֹ) *o*) FLESH (בָשָׂר) *va'sar*) GIVEN.THAT (כִּי) *ki*) *he~will~*
EXIST[V] (יִהְיֶה) *yih'yeh*) in~SKIN~him (בְעֹרוֹ) *vê'o'ro*) SINGE.SCAR
(מִכְוַת) *mikh'wat*) FIRE (אֵשׁ) *eysh*) and~*she~did~*EXIST[V] (וְהָיְתָה)
wê'hai'tah) REVIVING (מִחְיַת) *mihh'yat*) the~SINGE.SCAR (הַמִּכְוָה)
ha'mikh'wah) BRIGHT.SPOT (בַּהֶרֶת) *ba'he'ret*) WHITE (לְבָנָה)
lê'va'nah) REDDISH (אֲדַמְדֶּמֶת) *a'dam'de'met*) OR (אוֹ) *o*) WHITE (לְבָנָה)
lê'va'nah) **RMT:** Or the flesh that exists in his skin is a singe scar of
fire, and the reviving of the singe scar exists as a bright spot, white
reddish or white,

13:25 and~*he~did*~SEE[(V)] (וְרָאָה *wê'ra'ah*) AT~her (אֹתָהּ *o'tah*) the~ ADMINISTRATOR (הַכֹּהֵן *ha'ko'heyn*) and~LOOK (וְהִנֵּה *wê'hin'neyh*) *he~did~be*~OVERTURN[(V)] (נֶהְפַּךְ *neh'pakh*) HAIR (שֵׂעָר *sey'ar*) WHITE (לָבָן *la'van*) in~the~BRIGHT.SPOT (בַּבַּהֶרֶת *ba'ba'he'ret*) and~ APPEARANCE~her (וּמַרְאֶהָ *u'mar'e'ah*) SUNKEN (עָמֹק *a'moq*) FROM (מִן *min*) the~SKIN (הָעוֹר *ha'or*) INFECTION (צָרַעַת *tsa'ra'at*) SHE (הִוא *hi*) in~the~SINGE.SCAR (בַּמִּכְוָה *ba'mikh'wah*) *she~will*~ BURST.OUT[(V)] (פָּרָחָה *pa'ra'hhah*) and~*he~did~much*~BE.DIRTY[(V)] (וְטִמֵּא *wê'ti'mey*) AT~him (אֹתוֹ *o'to*) the~ADMINISTRATOR (הַכֹּהֵן *ha'ko'heyn*) TOUCH (נֶגַע *ne'ga*) INFECTION (צָרַעַת *tsa'ra'at*) SHE (הִוא *hi*) **RMT:** then the administrator will see her, and look, the hair turned white in the bright spot, and her appearance is sunken from the skin, she is an infection, in the singe scar she will burst out, and the administrator will declare him dirty, she is a plague of infection,

13:26 and~IF (וְאִם *wê'im*) *he~will*~SEE[(V)]~her (יִרְאֶנָּה *yir'e'nah*) the~ ADMINISTRATOR (הַכֹּהֵן *ha'ko'heyn*) and~LOOK (וְהִנֵּה *wê'hin'neyh*) WITHOUT (אֵין *eyn*) in~the~BRIGHT.SPOT (בַּבֶּהֶרֶת *ba'be'he'ret*) HAIR (שֵׂעָר *sey'ar*) WHITE (לָבָן *la'van*) and~LOW (וּשְׁפָלָה *ush'pha'lah*) WITHOUT~her (אֵינֶנָּה *ey'ne'nah*) FROM (מִן *min*) the~ SKIN (הָעוֹר *ha'or*) and~SHE (וְהִוא *wê'hi*) DIMNESS (כֵהָה *khey'hah*) and~*he~did~make*~SHUT[(V)]~him (וְהִסְגִּירוֹ *wê'his'gi'ro*) the~ ADMINISTRATOR (הַכֹּהֵן *ha'ko'heyn*) SEVEN (שִׁבְעַת *shiv'at*) DAY~s (יָמִים *ya'mim*) **RMT:** and if the administrator will see her, and look, it is without a white hair in the bright spot, and she is not low from the skin, and she is dim, then the administrator will cause him to shut seven days,

13:27 and~*he~did*~SEE[(V)]~him (וְרָאָהוּ *wê'ra'a'hu*) the~ ADMINISTRATOR (הַכֹּהֵן *ha'ko'heyn*) in~the~DAY (בַּיּוֹם *ba'yom*) the~ SEVENTH (הַשְּׁבִיעִי *hash'vi'i*) IF (אִם *im*) >~SPREAD.ACROSS[(V)] (פשׂה *pa'soh*) *she~will*~SEIZE.HOLD[(V)] (תִפְשֶׂה *tiph'seh*) in~the~SKIN (בָּעוֹר *ba'or*) and~*he~did~much*~BE.DIRTY[(V)] (וְטִמֵּא *wê'ti'mey*) the~ ADMINISTRATOR (הַכֹּהֵן *ha'ko'heyn*) AT~him (אֹתוֹ *o'to*) TOUCH (נֶגַע *ne'ga*) INFECTION (צָרַעַת *tsa'ra'at*) SHE (הִוא *hi*) **RMT:** and the administrator will see him in the seventh day, if spreading across seizing hold in the skin, then the administrator will declare him dirty, she is a plague of infection,

13:28 and~IF (וְאִם *wê'im*) UNDER~s~her (תַחְתֶּיהָ *tahh'tey'ah*) *she~ will*~STAND[(V)] (תַעֲמֹד *ta'a'mod*) the~BRIGHT.SPOT (הַבֶּהֶרֶת *ha'ba'he'ret*) NOT (לֹא *lo*) *she~did*~SPREAD.ACROSS[(V)] (פָשְׂתָה *pas'tah*)

phas'tah) in~the~SKIN (בָעוֹר *va'or*) and~SHE (וְהִוא *wê'hi*) DIMNESS (כֵהָה *khey'hah*) >~LIFT.UP^(V) (שְׂאֵת *sê'eyt*) the~SINGE.SCAR (הַמִּכְוָה *ha'mikh'wah*) SHE (הִוא *hi*) and~he~did~much~BE.CLEAN^(V)~him (וְטִהֲרוֹ *wê'ti'ha'ro*) the~ADMINISTRATOR (הַכֹּהֵן *ha'ko'heyn*) GIVEN.THAT (כִּי *ki*) SEARING (צָרֶבֶת *tsa're'vet*) the~SINGE.SCAR (הַמִּכְוָה *ha'mikh'wah*) SHE (הִוא *hi*) **RMT:** and if the bright spot stands in her place, and does not spread across in the skin and she is dim, she is a lifting up of the singe scar, and the administrator will declare him clean, given that she is a searing of a singe scar,

13:29 and~MAN (וְאִישׁ *wê'ish*) OR (אוֹ *o*) WOMAN (אִשָּׁה *i'shah*) GIVEN.THAT (כִּי *ki*) he~will~EXIST^(V) (יִהְיֶה *yih'yeh*) in~him (בוֹ *vo*) TOUCH (נֶגַע *na'ga*) in~HEAD (בְּרֹאשׁ *bê'rosh*) OR (אוֹ *o*) in~BEARD (בְזָקָן *vê'za'qan*) **RMT:** and a man or woman that exists in him a plague in the head or in the beard,

13:30 and~he~did~SEE^(V) (וְרָאָה *wê'ra'ah*) the~ADMINISTRATOR (הַכֹּהֵן *ha'ko'heyn*) AT (אֶת *et*) the~TOUCH (הַנֶּגַע *ha'ne'ga*) and~ LOOK (וְהִנֵּה *wê'hin'neyh*) APPEARANCE~him (מַרְאֵהוּ *mar'ey'hu*) SUNKEN (עָמֹק *a'moq*) FROM (מִן *min*) the~SKIN (הָעוֹר *ha'or*) and~ in~him (וּבוֹ *u'vo*) HAIR (שֵׂעָר *sey'ar*) YELLOW (צָהֹב *tsa'hov*) SCRAWNY (דָּק *daq*) and~he~did~much~BE.DIRTY^(V) (וְטִמֵּא *wê'ti'mey*) AT~him (אֹתוֹ *o'to*) the~ADMINISTRATOR (הַכֹּהֵן *ha'ko'heyn*) ERUPTION (נֶתֶק *re'teq*) HE (הוּא *hu*) INFECTION (צָרַעַת *tsa'ra'at*) the~HEAD (הָרֹאשׁ *ha'rosh*) OR (אוֹ *o*) the~BEARD (הַזָּקָן *ha'za'qan*) HE (הוּא *hu*) **RMT:** and the administrator will see the plague, and look, his appearance is sunken from the skin, and a scrawny yellow hair is in him, and the administrator will declare him dirty, he is an eruption, he is an infection of the head or beard,

13:31 and~GIVEN.THAT (וְכִי *wê'khi*) he~will~SEE^(V) (יִרְאֶה *yir'eh*) the~ADMINISTRATOR (הַכֹּהֵן *ha'ko'heyn*) AT (אֶת *et*) TOUCH (נֶגַע *ne'ga*) the~ERUPTION (הַנֶּתֶק *ha'ne'teq*) and~LOOK (וְהִנֵּה *wê'hin'neyh*) WITHOUT (אֵין *eyn*) APPEARANCE~him (מַרְאֵהוּ *mar'ey'hu*) SUNKEN (עָמֹק *a'moq*) FROM (מִן *min*) the~SKIN (הָעוֹר *ha'or*) and~HAIR (וְשֵׂעָר *wê'sey'ar*) COAL (שָׁחֹר *sha'hhor*) WITHOUT (אֵין *eyn*) in~him (בוֹ *bo*) and~he~did~make~SHUT^(V) (וְהִסְגִּיר *wê'his'gir*) the~ADMINISTRATOR (הַכֹּהֵן *ha'ko'heyn*) AT (אֶת *et*) TOUCH (נֶגַע *ne'ga*) the~ERUPTION (הַנֶּתֶק *ha'ne'teq*) SEVEN (שִׁבְעַת *shiv'at*) DAY~s (יָמִים *ya'mim*) **RMT:** and, given that the administrator will see the plague of eruption, and look, his appearance is not sunken from the skin, and the hair is not black as coal in him, and the administrator will cause to shut the plague of eruption seven days,

13:32 and~he~did~SEE[V] (וְרָאָה wê'ra'ah) the~ADMINISTRATOR (הַכֹּהֵן ha'ko'heyn) AT (אֶת et) the~TOUCH (הַנֶּגַע ha'ne'ga) in~the~DAY (בַּיּוֹם ba'yom) the~SEVENTH (הַשְּׁבִיעִי hash'vi'i) and~LOOK (וְהִנֵּה wê'hin'neyh) NOT (לֹא lo) he~did~SPREAD.ACROSS[V] (פָשָׂה pha'sah) the~ERUPTION (הַנֶּתֶק ha'ne'teq) and~NOT (וְלֹא wê'lo) he~did~EXIST[V] (הָיָה hai'yah) in~him (בוֹ vo) HAIR (שֵׂעָר sey'ar) YELLOW (צָהֹב tsa'hov) and~APPEARANCE (וּמַרְאֵה u'mar'eyh) the~ERUPTION (הַנֶּתֶק ha'ne'teq) WITHOUT (אֵין eyn) SUNKEN (עָמֹק a'moq) FROM (מִן min) the~SKIN (הָעוֹר ha'or) **RMT:** and the administrator will see the plague in the seventh day, and look, the eruption did not spread across, and a yellow hair did not exist in him, and the appearance of the eruption was not sunken from the skin,

13:33 and~he~did~self~SHAVE[V] (וְהִתְגַּלָּח wê'hit'ga'lahh) and~AT (וְאֶת wê'et) the~ERUPTION (הַנֶּתֶק ha'ne'teq) NOT (לֹא lo) he~will~much~SHAVE[V] (יְגַלֵּחַ yê'ga'ley'ahh) and~he~did~make~SHUT[V] (וְהִסְגִּיר wê'his'gir) the~ADMINISTRATOR (הַכֹּהֵן ha'ko'heyn) AT (אֶת et) the~ERUPTION (הַנֶּתֶק ha'ne'teq) SEVEN (שִׁבְעַת shiv'at) DAY~s (יָמִים ya'mim) SECOND (שֵׁנִית shey'nit) **RMT:** and he will shave himself, but he will not shave the eruption, and the administrator will cause shut the eruption a second seven days,

13:34 and~he~did~SEE[V] (וְרָאָה wê'ra'ah) the~ADMINISTRATOR (הַכֹּהֵן ha'ko'heyn) AT (אֶת et) the~ERUPTION (הַנֶּתֶק ha'ne'teq) in~the~DAY (בַּיּוֹם ba'yom) the~SEVENTH (הַשְּׁבִיעִי hash'vi'i) and~LOOK (וְהִנֵּה wê'hin'neyh) NOT (לֹא lo) he~did~SPREAD.ACROSS[V] (פָשָׂה pha'sah) the~ERUPTION (הַנֶּתֶק ha'ne'teq) in~the~SKIN (בָּעוֹר ba'or) and~APPEARANCE~him (וּמַרְאֵהוּ u'mar'ey'hu) WITHOUT~him (אֵינֶנּוּ ey'ne'nu) SUNKEN (עָמֹק a'moq) FROM (מִן min) the~SKIN (הָעוֹר ha'or) and~he~did~much~BE.CLEAN[V] (וְטִהַר wê'ti'har) AT~him (אֹתוֹ o'to) the~ADMINISTRATOR (הַכֹּהֵן ha'ko'heyn) and~he~did~much~WASH[V] (וְכִבֶּס wê'khi'bes) GARMENT~s~him (בְּגָדָיו bê'ga'daw) and~he~did~BE.CLEAN[V] (וְטָהֵר wê'ta'har) **RMT:** and the administrator will see the eruption in the seventh day, and look, the eruption did not spread across in the skin, and his appearance is not sunken from the skin, and the administrator will declare him clean, and he will wash his garments and he will be clean,

13:35 and~IF (וְאִם wê'im) >~SPREAD.ACROSS[V] (פָשֹׂה pa'soh) he~will~SPREAD.ACROSS[V] (יִפְשֶׂה yiph'seh) the~ERUPTION (הַנֶּתֶק

ha'ne'teq) in~the~SKIN (בָּעוֹר ba'o.) AFTER (אַחֲרֵי a'hha'rey) CLEAN~
him (טָהֳרָתוֹ ta'ha'ra'to) **RMT:** but if the eruption completely spread
across in the skin after his cleaning,

13:36 and~*he~did~*SEE[V]~him (וְרָאָהוּ wê'ra'a'hu) the~
ADMINISTRATOR (הַכֹּהֵן ha'ko'heyn) and~LOOK (וְהִנֵּה wê'hin'neyh)
*he~did~*SPREAD.ACROSS[V] (פָּשָׂה *pa*'sah) the~ERUPTION (הַנֶּתֶק
ha'ne'teq) in~the~SKIN (בָּעוֹר ba'or) NOT (לֹא lo) *he~will~much~*
INVESTIGATE[V] (יְבַקֵּר yê'va'qeyr) the~ADMINISTRATOR (הַכֹּהֵן
ha'ko'heyn) to~the~HAIR (לַשֵּׂעָר la'sey'ar) the~YELLOW (הַצָּהֹב
ha'tsa'hov) DIRTY (טָמֵא ta'mey) HE (הוּא hu) **RMT:** then the
administrator will see him, and look, the eruption spread across in
the skin, the administrator will not investigate for the yellow hair, he
is dirty,

13:37 and~IF (וְאִם wê'im) in~EYE~s2~him (בְּעֵינָיו bê'ey'naw) *he~
did~*STAND[V] (עָמַד a'mad) the~ERUPTION (הַנֶּתֶק ha'ne'teq) and~
HAIR (וְשֵׂעָר wê'sey'ar) COAL (שָׁחֹר sha'hhor) *he~did~*SPRING.UP[V]
(צָמַח tsa'mahh) in~him (בּוֹ bo) *he~did~be~*HEAL[V] (נִרְפָּא nir'pa)
the~ERUPTION (הַנֶּתֶק ha'ne'teq) CLEAN (טָהוֹר ta'hor) HE (הוּא hu)
and~*he~did~much~*BE.CLEAN [V]~him (וְטִהֲרוֹ wê'ti'ha'ro) the~
ADMINISTRATOR (הַכֹּהֵן ha'ko'heyn) **RMT:** but if in his eyes the
eruption stands and a black as coal hair sprang up in him, the
eruption is healed, he is clean, and the administrator will declare him
clean,

13:38 and~MAN (וְאִישׁ wê'ish) OR (אוֹ o) WOMAN (אִשָּׁה i'shah)
GIVEN.THAT (כִּי ki) *he~will~*EXIST[V] (יִהְיֶה yih'yeh) in~SKIN (בְעוֹר
vê'or) FLESH~them[m] (בְשָׂרָם bê'sa'ram) BRIGHT.SPOT~s (בֶּהָרֹת
be'ha'rot) BRIGHT.SPOT~s (בֶּהָרֹת be'ha'rot)[55] WHITE~s (לְבָנֹת
lê'va'not) **RMT:** and a man or woman that exists in the skin of their
flesh white bright spots,

13:39 and~*he~did~*SEE[V] (וְרָאָה wê'ra'ah) the~ADMINISTRATOR
(הַכֹּהֵן ha'ko'heyn) and~LOOK (וְהִנֵּה wê'hin'neyh) in~SKIN (בְעוֹר
vê'or) FLESH~them[m] (בְשָׂרָם bê'sa'ram) BRIGHT.SPOT~s (בֶּהָרֹת
be'ha'rot) DIMNESS~s (כֵּהֹת key'hot) WHITE~s (לְבָנֹת lê'va'not)
RASH (בֹּהַק bo'haq) HE (הוּא hu) *he~did~*BURST.OUT[V] (פָּרַח
pa'rahh) in~the~SKIN (בָּעוֹר ba'or) CLEAN (טָהוֹר ta'hor) HE (הוּא hu)
RMT: and the administrator will see, and look, in the skin of their

---

[55] This Hebrew word may have been written twice by error or it is
doubled for emphasis.

flesh are dim white bright spots, he is a rash burst out in the skin, he is clean,

13:40 and~MAN (וְאִישׁ *wê'ish*) GIVEN.THAT (כִּי *ki*) he~will~be~ HAIR.FELL.OUT[(V)] (יִמָּרֵט *yi'ma'reyt*) HEAD~him (רֹאשׁוֹ *ro'sho*) BALD (קֵרֵחַ *qey'rey'ahh*) HE (הוּא *hu*) CLEAN (טָהוֹר *ta'hor*) HE (הוּא *hu*) **RMT:** and a man whose hair has fallen out of his head, he is bald, he is clean,

13:41 and~IF (וְאִם *wê'im*) from~EDGE (מִפְּאַת *mi'pe'at*) FACE~s~him (פָּנָיו *pa'naw*) he~will~be~HAIR.FELL.OUT[(V)] (יִמָּרֵט *yi'ma'reyt*) HEAD~him (רֹאשׁוֹ *ro'sho*) BARE.SPOT (גִּבֵּחַ *gi'bey'ahh*) HE (הוּא *hu*) CLEAN (טָהוֹר *ta'hor*) HE (הוּא *hu*) **RMT:** and if from the edge of his face the hair fell out of his head, he has a bald forehead, he is clean,

13:42 and~GIVEN.THAT (וְכִי *wê'khi*) he~will~EXIST[(V)] (יִהְיֶה *yih'yeh*) in~the~BALD.SPOT (בַקָּרַחַת *va'qa'ra'hhat*) OR (אוֹ *o*) in~the~ BARE.SPOT (בַגַּבַּחַת *va'ga'ba'hhat*) TOUCH (נֶגַע *ne'ga*) WHITE (לָבָן *la'van*) REDDISH (אֲדַמְדָּם *a'dam'dam*) INFECTION (צָרַעַת *tsa'ra'at*) BURST.OUT[(V)]~ing[(fs)] (פֹּרַחַת *po'ra'hhat*) SHE (הִוא *hi*) in~BALD.SPOT~ him (בְּקָרַחְתּוֹ *bê'qa'rahh'to*) OR (אוֹ *o*) in~BARE.SPOT~him (בְגַבַּחְתּוֹ *vê'ga'bahh'to*) **RMT:** and, given that a white reddish plague will exist with the baldness or with the bald forehead, she is an infection bursting out in his bald spot or in his bare spot,

13:43 and~he~did~SEE[(V)] (וְרָאָה *wê'ra'ah*) AT~him (אֹתוֹ *o'to*) the~ ADMINISTRATOR (הַכֹּהֵן *ha'ko'heyn*) and~LOOK (וְהִנֵּה *wê'hin'neyh*) >~LIFT.UP[(V)] (שְׂאֵת *sê'eyt*) the~TOUCH (הַנֶּגַע *ha'ne'ga*) WHITE (לְבָנָה *lê'va'nah*) REDDISH (אֲדַמְדֶּמֶת *a'dam'de'met*) in~BALD.SPOT~him (בְּקָרַחְתּוֹ *bê'qa'rahh'to*) OR (אוֹ *o*) in~BARE.SPOT~him (בְגַבַּחְתּוֹ *vê'ga'bahh'to*) like~APPEARANCE (כְּמַרְאֵה *kê'mar'eyh*) INFECTION (צָרַעַת *tsa'ra'at*) SKIN (עוֹר *or*) FLESH (בָּשָׂר *ba'sar*) **RMT:** and the administrator will see him, and look, the white reddish plague is lifted up in his bald spot or in his bare spot, like the appearance of an infection of the skin of the flesh,

13:44 MAN (אִישׁ *ish*) INFECT[(V)]~ed[(ms)] (צָרוּעַ *tsa'ru'a*) HE (הוּא *hu*) DIRTY (טָמֵא *ta'mey*) HE (הוּא *hu*) he~did~BE.DIRTY[(V)] (טָמֵא *ta'mey*) he~will~much~BE.DIRTY[(V)]~him (יְטַמְאֶנּוּ *yê'tam'e'nu*) the~ ADMINISTRATOR (הַכֹּהֵן *ha'ko'heyn*) in~HEAD~him (בְּרֹאשׁוֹ *bê'ro'sho*) TOUCH~him (נִגְעוֹ *nig'o*) **RMT:** He is an infected man, he is dirty, the administrator will declare him completely dirty, his plague is in his head,

13:45 and~the~INFECT(V)~ed(ms) (וְהַצָּרוּעַ wê'ha'tsa'ru'a) WHICH (אֲשֶׁר a'sher) in~him (בּוֹ bo) the~TOUCH (הַנֶּגַע ha'ne'ga) GARMENT~s~him (בְּגָדָיו bê'ga'daw) they(m)~will~EXIST(V) (יִהְיוּ yih'yu) RIP(V)~ed(mp) (פְרֻמִים phê'ru'mim) and~HEAD~him (וְרֹאשׁוֹ wê'ro'sho) he~will~EXIST(V) (יִהְיֶה yih'yeh) LOOSE(V)~ed(ms) (פָרוּעַ pha'ru'a) and~UPON (וְעַל wê'al) UPPER.LIP (שָׂפָם sa'pham) he~will~ ENWRAP(V) (יַעְטֶה ya'teh) and~he~did~BE.DIRTY(V) (וְטָמֵא wê'ta'mey) DIRTY (טָמֵא ta'mey) ne~will~CALL.OUT(V) (יִקְרָא yiq'ra) **RMT:** and the infected one, which the plague is in him, his garments will be ripped, and his head will be loosed[56], and upon the upper lip he will enwrap, and he will be very dirty, he will call out dirty.

13:46 ALL (כָּל kol) DAY~s (יְמֵי yê'mey) WHICH (אֲשֶׁר a'sher) the~ TOUCH (הַנֶּגַע ha'ne'ga) in~him (בּוֹ bo) he~will~BE.DIRTY(V) (יִטְמָא yit'ma) DIRTY (טָמֵא ta'mey) HE (הוּא hu) ALONE (בָּדָד ba'dad) he~ will~SETTLE(V) (יֵשֵׁב yey'sheyv) from~OUTSIDE (מִחוּץ mi'hhuts) to~ the~CAMP (לַמַּחֲנֶה la'ma'hha'neh) SETTLING~him (מוֹשָׁבוֹ mo'sha'vo) **RMT:** All the days which the plague is in him he will be dirty, he is dirty, he will settle alone, he will settle his settling outside of the camp,

13:47 and~the~GARMENT (וְהַבֶּגֶד wê'ha'be'ged) GIVEN.THAT (כִּי ki) he~will~EXIST(V) (יִהְיֶה yih'yeh) in~him (בוֹ vo) TOUCH (נֶגַע ne'ga) INFECTION (צָרַעַת tsa'ra'at) in~GARMENT (בְּבֶגֶד bê've'ged) WOOL (צֶמֶר tse'mer) OR (אוֹ o) in~GARMENT (בְּבֶגֶד bê've'ged) FLAX~s (פִּשְׁתִּים pish'tim) **RMT:** and the garment that the plague of infection exists in, in a garment of wool, or in a garment of flax.

13:48 OR (אוֹ o) in~WARP (בִשְׁתִי vish'tiy) OR (אוֹ o) in~MIXTURE (בְעֵרֶב vê'ey'rev) to~the~FLAX~s (לַפִּשְׁתִּים la'pish'tim) and~to~the~ WOOL (וְלַצָּמֶר wê'la'tsa'mer) OR (אוֹ o) in~SKIN (בָעוֹר vê'or) OR (אוֹ o) in~ALL (בְּכָל bê'khol) BUSINESS (מְלֶאכֶת mê'le'khet) SKIN (עוֹר or) **RMT:** Or in the warp or in the mixture[57], to the flax and to the wool, or in the skin or in any business of skin[58],

13:49 and~he~did~EXIST(V) (וְהָיָה wê'hai'yah) the~TOUCH (הַנֶּגַע ha'ne'ga) GREENISH (יְרַקְרַק yê'raq'raq) OR (אוֹ o) REDDISH (אֲדַמְדָּם a'dam'dam) in~the~GARMENT (בַּבֶּגֶד ba'be'ged) OR (אוֹ o) in~the~ SKIN (בָעוֹר va'or) OR (אוֹ o) in~the~WARP (בַשְּׁתִי vash'ti) OR (אוֹ o)

---

[56] That is, "uncovered" or "bare."

[57] That is the "woof."

[58] "Business of skin" is a person working with leather.

in~the~MIXTURE (בָּעֵרֶב *va'ey'rev*) OR (אוֹ *o*) in~ALL (בְכָל *vê'khol*) UTENSIL (כְּלִי *kê'li*) SKIN (עוֹר *or*) TOUCH (נֶגַע *ne'ga*) INFECTION (צָרַעַת *tsa'ra'at*) HE (הוּא *hu*) and~he~did~be~make~SEE^(V) (וְהָרְאָה *wê'har'ah*) AT (אֶת *et*) the~ADMINISTRATOR (הַכֹּהֵן *ha'ko'heyn*) **RMT:** but if the greenish or reddish plague exists in the garment or in the skin or in the warp or in the mixture or any utensil of skin, he is a plague of infection, and he will be caused to appear to the administrator,

13:50 and~he~did~SEE^(V) (וְרָאָה *wê'ra'ah*) the~ADMINISTRATOR (הַכֹּהֵן *ha'ko'heyn*) AT (אֶת *et*) the~TOUCH (הַנֶּגַע *ha'na'ga*) and~he~did~make~SHUT^(V) (וְהִסְגִּיר *wê'his'gir*) AT (אֶת *et*) the~TOUCH (הַנֶּגַע *ha'ne'ga*) SEVEN (שִׁבְעַת *shiv'at*) DAY~s (יָמִים *ya'mim*) **RMT:** and the administrator will see the plague, and he will cause the plague to be shut seven days,

13:51 and~he~did~SEE^(V) (וְרָאָה *wê'ra'ah*) AT (אֶת *et*) the~TOUCH (הַנֶּגַע *ha'ne'ga*) in~the~DAY (בַּיּוֹם *ba'yom*) the~SEVENTH (הַשְּׁבִיעִי *hash'vi'i*) GIVEN.THAT (כִּי *ki*) he~did~SPREAD.ACROSS^(V) (פָשָׂה *pha'sah*) the~TOUCH (הַנֶּגַע *ha'ne'ga*) in~the~GARMENT (בַּבֶּגֶד *ba'be'ged*) OR (אוֹ *o*) in~the~WARP (בַשְּׁתִי *vash'ti*) OR (אוֹ *o*) in~the~MIXTURE (בָעֵרֶב *va'ey'rev*) OR (אוֹ *o*) in~the~SKIN (בָעוֹר *va'or*) to~ALL (לְכֹל *lê'khol*) WHICH (אֲשֶׁר *a'sher*) he~will~be~DO^(V) (יֵעָשֶׂה *yey'a'seh*) the~SKIN (הָעוֹר *ha'or*) to~BUSINESS (לִמְלָאכָה *lim'la'khah*) INFECTION (צָרַעַת *tsa'ra'at*) make~IRRITATE^(V)~ing^(fs) (מַמְאֶרֶת *mam'e'ret*) the~TOUCH (הַנֶּגַע *ha'ne'ga*) DIRTY (טָמֵא *ta'mey*) HE (הוּא *hu*) **RMT:** and he will see the plague in the seventh day, given that the plague spread across in the garment, or in the warp or in the mixture or in the skin, to anything that will be done to the skin for business, the plague is an irritating infection, he is dirty,

13:52 and~he~did~CREMATE^(V) (וְשָׂרַף *wê'sa'raph*) AT (אֶת *et*) the~GARMENT (הַבֶּגֶד *ha'be'ged*) OR (אוֹ *o*) AT (אֶת *et*) the~WARP (הַשְּׁתִי *hash'ti*) OR (אוֹ *o*) AT (אֶת *et*) the~MIXTURE (הָעֵרֶב *ha'ey'rev*) in~the~WOOL (בַּצֶּמֶר *ba'tse'mer*) OR (אוֹ *o*) in~the~FLAX~s (בַּפִּשְׁתִּים *va'pish'tim*) OR (אוֹ *o*) AT (אֶת *et*) ALL (כָּל *kol*) UTENSIL (כְּלִי *kê'li*) the~SKIN (הָעוֹר *ha'or*) WHICH (אֲשֶׁר *a'sher*) he~will~EXIST^(V) (יִהְיֶה *yih'yeh*) in~him (בוֹ *vo*) the~TOUCH (הַנֶּגַע *ha'na'ga*) GIVEN.THAT (כִּי *ki*) INFECTION (צָרַעַת *tsa'ra'at*) make~IRRITATE^(V)~ing^(fs) (מַמְאֶרֶת *mam'e'ret*) SHE (הִוא *hi*) in~the~FIRE (בָּאֵשׁ *ba'eysh*) you^(ms)~will~CREMATE^(V) (תִּשָּׂרֵף *ti'sa'reyph*) **RMT:** and he will cremate the garment or the warp or the mixture, in the wool or in the flax, or any utensil of the skin that the plague exists in him, given that she is an irritating infection, you will cremate it in the fire,

13:53 and~IF (וְאִם *wê'im*) he~will~SEE[V] (יִרְאֶה *yir'eh*) the~ADMINISTRATOR (הַכֹּהֵן *ha'ko'heyn*) and~LOOK (וְהִנֵּה *wê'hin'neyh*) NOT (לֹא *lo*) he~did~SPREAD.ACROSS[V] (פָשָׂה *pha'sah*) the~TOUCH (הַנֶּגַע *ha'ne'ga*) in~the~GARMENT (בַּבֶּגֶד *ba'be'ged*) OR (אוֹ *o*) in~the~WARP (בַשְּׁתִי *vash'ti*) OR (אוֹ *o*) in~the~MIXTURE (בָעֵרֶב *va'ey'rev*) OR (אוֹ *o*) in~ALL (בְּכָל *bê'khol*) UTENSIL (כְּלִי *kê'li*) SKIN (עוֹר *or*) **RMT:** and the administrator will see, and look, if the plague did not spread across in the garment, or in the warp or in the mixture or in any utensil of skin,

13:54 and~he~did~much~DIRECT[V] (וְצִוָּה *wê'tsi'wah*) the~ADMINISTRATOR (הַכֹּהֵן *ha'ko'heyn*) and~they~did~much~WASH[V] (וְכִבְּסוּ *wê'khi'be'su*) AT (אֶת *eyt*) WHICH (אֲשֶׁר *a'sher*) in~him (בּוֹ *bo*) the~TOUCH (הַנָּגַע *ha'na'ga*) and~he~did~make~SHUT[V]~him (וְהִסְגִּירוֹ *wê'his'gi'ro*) SEVEN (שִׁבְעַת *shiv'at*) DAY~s (יָמִים *ya'mim*) SECOND (שֵׁנִית *shey'nit*) **RMT:** and the administrator will direct and they will wash the plague that is in him, and he will cause him to be shut a second seven days,

13:55 and~he~did~SEE[V] (וְרָאָה *wê'ra'ah*) the~ADMINISTRATOR (הַכֹּהֵן *ha'ko'heyn*) AFTER (אַחֲרֵי *a'hha'rey*) >~self~WASH[V] (הֻכַּבֵּס *hu'ka'beys*) AT (אֶת *et*) the~TOUCH (הַנֶּגַע *ha'ne'ga*) and~LOOK (וְהִנֵּה *wê'hin'neyh*) NOT (לֹא *lo*) he~did~OVERTURN[V] (הָפַךְ *ha'phakh*) the~TOUCH (הַנֶּגַע *ha'ne'ga*) AT (אֶת *et*) EYE~him (עֵינוֹ *ey'no*) and~the~TOUCH (וְהַנֶּגַע *wê'ha'ne'ga*) NOT (לֹא *lo*) he~did~SPREAD.ACROSS[V] (פָשָׂה *pha'sah*) DIRTY (טָמֵא *ta'mey*) HE (הוּא *hu*) in~the~FIRE (בָּאֵשׁ *ba'eysh*) you[mp]~will~CREMATE[V]~him (תִּשְׂרְפֶנּוּ *tis're'phe'nu*) PIT (פְּחֶתֶת *pê'hhe'tet*) SHE (הִיא *hi*) in~BALD.SPOT~him (בְּקָרַחְתּוֹ *bê'qa'rahh'to*) OR (אוֹ *o*) in~BARE.SPOT~him (בְגַבַּחְתּוֹ *vê'ga'bahh'to*) **RMT:** and the administrator will see after the plague is washed, and look, the plague did not overturn his eye[59], and the plague did not spread across, he is dirty, you will cremate him in the fire, she is a pit in his bald spot or in his bare spot,

13:56 and~IF (וְאִם *wê'im*) he~did~SEE[V] (רָאָה *ra'ah*) the~ADMINISTRATOR (הַכֹּהֵן *ha'ko'heyn*) and~LOOK (וְהִנֵּה *wê'hin'neyh*) DIMNESS (כֵּהָה *key'hah*) the~TOUCH (הַנֶּגַע *ha'ne'ga*) AFTER (אַחֲרֵי

---

[59] The phrase "did not overturn his eye" means "did not change color."

a'hha'rey) >~*self*~WASH(V) (הֻכַּבֵּס *hu'ka'beys*) AT~him (אֹתוֹ *o'to*)
and~*he~did*~TEAR(V) (וְקָרַע *wê'qa'ra*) AT~him (אֹתוֹ *o'to*) FROM (מִן
min) the~GARMENT (הַבֶּגֶד *ha'be'ged*) OR (אוֹ *o*) FROM (מִן *min*)
the~SKIN (הָעוֹר *ha'or*) OR (אוֹ *o*) FROM (מִן *min*) the~WARP (הַשְּׁתִי
hash'ti) OR (אוֹ *o*) FROM (מִן *min*) the~MIXTURE (הָעֵרֶב *ha'ey'rev*)
RMT: and the administrator will see, and look, if the plague is dim
after washing him, then he will tear him from the garment or from
the skin or from the warp or from the mixture,

13:57 and~IF (וְאִם *wê'im*) *she~will~be~*SEE(V) (תֵּרָאֶה *tey'ra'eh*)
YET.AGAIN (עוֹד *od*) in~the~GARMENT (בַּבֶּגֶד *ba'be'ged*) OR (אוֹ *o*)
in~the~WARP (בַשְּׁתִי *vash'ti*) OR (אוֹ *o*) in~the~MIXTURE (בָעֵרֶב
va'ey'rev) OR (אוֹ *o*) in~ALL (בְכָל *vê'khol*) UTENSIL (כְלִי *kê'li*) SKIN
(עוֹר *or*) BURST.OUT(V)~*ing*(fs) (פֹּרַחַת *po'ra'hhat*) SHE (הִוא *hi*) in~
the~FIRE (בָּאֵשׁ *ba'eysh*) you(mp)~*will~*CREMATE(V)~him (תִּשְׂרְפֶנּוּ
tis're'phe'nu) AT (אֵת *eyt*) WHICH (אֲשֶׁר *a'sher*) in~him (בּוֹ *bo*) the~
TOUCH (הַנָּגַע *ha'na'ga*) **RMT:** and if she[60] appears yet again in the
garment or in the warp or in the mixture or in any utensil of skin, she
is a bursting out, you will cremate what the plague is in the fire,

13:58 and~the~GARMENT (וְהַבֶּגֶד *wê'ha'be'ged*) OR (אוֹ *o*) the~
WARP (הַשְּׁתִי *hash'ti*) OR (אוֹ *o*) the~MIXTURE (הָעֵרֶב *ha'ey'rev*) OR
(אוֹ *o*) ALL (כָל *khol*) UTENSIL (כְלִי *kê'li*) the~SKIN (הָעוֹר *ha'or*)
WHICH (אֲשֶׁר *a'sher*) you(mp)~*will~much~*WASH(V) (תְכַבֵּס
tê'kha'beys) and~*he~did*~TURN.ASIDE(V) (וְסָר *wê'sar*) from~them(m)
(מֵהֶם *mey'hem*) the~TOUCH (הַנָּגַע *ha'na'ga*) and~*he~did*~be~
*much~*WASH(V) (וְכֻבַּס *wê'khu'bas*) SECOND (שֵׁנִית *shey'nit*) and~*he~*
did~BE.CLEAN(V) (וְטָהֵר *wê'ta'har*) **RMT:** and the garment or the
warp or the mixture or any utensil of skin, you will wash, and if the
plague turns aside from them, then he will be washed a second time,
and he will be clean.

13:59 THIS (זֹאת *zot*) TEACHING (תּוֹרַת *to'rat*) TOUCH (נֶגַע *ne'ga*)
INFECTION (צָרַעַת *tsa'ra'at*) GARMENT (בֶּגֶד *be'ged*) the~WOOL
(הַצֶּמֶר *ha'tse'mer*) OR (אוֹ *o*) the~FLAX~s (הַפִּשְׁתִּים *ha'pish'tim*) OR
(אוֹ *o*) the~WARP (הַשְּׁתִי *hash'ti*) OR (אוֹ *o*) the~MIXTURE (הָעֵרֶב
ha'ey'rev) OR (אוֹ *o*) ALL (כָּל *kol*) UTENSIL (כְלִי *kê'li*) SKIN (עוֹר *or*)
to~>~*much~*BE.CLEAN(V)~him (לְטַהֲרוֹ *lê'ta'ha'ro*) OR (אוֹ *o*) to~>~

---

[60] The Hebrew word TOUCH (plague) is a masculine noun. In verse 56
the masculine pronoun "him" is used for this word, but here, this
verb uses the feminine pronoun "she" and appears to be in error.

_much~_BE.DIRTY^(v)~him (לְטַמְּאוֹ _lê'ta'me'o_) **RMT:** This is the teaching of the plague of infection of a garment of wool or flax or the warp or the mixture or any utensil of skin, for his cleanliness or for his dirtiness,

Chapter 14

14:1 and~he~will~much~SPEAK^(v) (וַיְדַבֵּר _wai'da'beyr_) **YHWH** (יְהוָה YHWH) TO (אֶל _el_) Mosheh (מֹשֶׁה _mo'sheh_) to~>~SAY^(v) (לֵאמֹר _ley'mor_) **RMT:** and **YHWH** will speak to Mosheh saying,

14:2 THIS (זאת _zot_) _she~will~_EXIST^(v) (תִּהְיֶה _tih'yeh_) TEACHING (תּוֹרַת _to'rat_) the~be~much~INFECT^(v)~ing^(ms) (הַמְּצֹרָע _ham'tso'ra_) in~DAY (בְּיוֹם _bê'yom_) CLEAN~him (טָהֳרָתוֹ _ta'ha'ra'to_) and~he~did~ be~make~COME^(v) (וְהוּבָא _wé hu'va_) TO (אֶל _el_) the~ ADMINISTRATOR (הַכֹּהֵן _ha'ko'heyn_) **RMT:** this will be the teaching of the one being infected in the day of his cleanliness, and he will be brought to the administrator,

14:3 and~he~will~GO.OUT^(v) (וְיָצָא _wê'ya'tsa_) the~ADMINISTRATOR (הַכֹּהֵן _ha'ko'heyn_) TO (אֶל _el_) from~OUTSIDE (מִחוּץ _mi'hhuts_) to~ the~CAMP (לַמַּחֲנֶה _la'ma'hha'neh_) and~he~did~SEE^(v) (וְרָאָה _wê'ra'ah_) the~ADMINISTRATOR (הַכֹּהֵן _ha'ko'heyn_) and~LOOK (וְהִנֵּה _wê'hin'neyh_) _he~did~be~_HEAL^(v) (נִרְפָּא _nir'pa_) TOUCH (נֶגַע _ne'ga_) the~INFECTION (הַצָּרַעַת _ha'tsa'ra'at_) FROM (מִן _min_) the~INFECT^(v)~ ed^(ms) (הַצָּרוּעַ _ha'tsa'ru'a_) **RMT:** and the administrator will go out to the outside of the camp, and the administrator will see, and look, the plague infection was healed from the infected one,

14:4 and~he~did~much~DIRECT^(v) (וְצִוָּה _wê'tsi'wah_) the~ ADMINISTRATOR (הַכֹּהֵן _ha'ko'heyn_) and~he~did~TAKE^(v) (וְלָקַח _wê'la'qahh_) to~the~_make~_BE.CLEAN^(v)~ing^(ms) (לַמִּטַּהֵר _la'mi'ta'heyr_) TWO (שְׁתֵּי _shê'tey_) BIRD~s (צִפֳּרִים _tsi'pa'rim_) LIVING~s (חַיּוֹת _hhai'yot_) CLEAN~s (טְהֹרוֹת _tê'ho'rot_) and~TREE (וְעֵץ _wê'eyts_) CEDAR (אֶרֶז _e'rez_) and~SCARLET (וּשְׁנִי _ush'ni_) KERMES (תוֹלַעַת _to'al'at_) and~HYSSOP (וְאֵזֹב _wê'ey'zov_) **RMT:** and the administrator will direct, and the one being clean will take two living clean birds and cedar wood and scarlet of kermes and hyssop,

14:5 and~he~did~much~DIRECT^(v) (וְצִוָּה _wê'tsi'wah_) the~ ADMINISTRATOR (הַכֹּהֵן _ha'ko'heyn_) and~he~did~SLAY^(v) (וְשָׁחַט _wê'sha'hhat_) AT (אֶת _et_) the~BIRD (הַצִּפּוֹר _ha'tsi'por_) the~UNIT (הָאֶחָת _ha'e'hhat_) TO (אֶל _el_) UTENSIL (כְּלִי _kê'li_) CLAY (חֶרֶשׂ _hhe'res_) hhe'res) UPON (עַל al) WATER~s2 (מַיִם ma'yim) LIVING~s (חַיִּים hhai'yim) **RMT:** and the administrator will direct, and he will slay the one bird to a utensil of clay[61] upon living waters[62].

14:6 AT (אֶת et) the~BIRD (הַצִּפֹּר ha'tsi'por) the~LIVING (הַחַיָּה ha'hha'yah) he~will~TAKE[(V)] (יִקַּח yi'qahh) AT~her (אֹתָהּ o'tah) and~ AT (וְאֵת we'et) TREE (עֵץ eyts) the~CEDAR (הָאֶרֶז ha'e'rez) and~AT (וְאֵת we'et) SCARLET (שְׁנִי shê'ni) the~KERMES (הַתּוֹלַעַת ha'to'la'at) and~AT (וְאֵת we'et) the~HYSSOP (הָאֵזֹב ha'ey'zov) and~he~did~ DIP[(V)] (וְטָבַל we'ta'val) AT~them[(m)] (אוֹתָם o'tam) and~AT (וְאֵת we'eyt) the~BIRD (הַצִּפֹּר ha'tsi'por) the~LIVING (הַחַיָּה ha'hha'yah) in~BLOOD (בְּדַם bê'dam) the~BIRD (הַצִּפֹּר ha'tsi'por) the~SLAY[(V)]~ ed[(fs)] (הַשְּׁחֻטָה hash'hhu'tah) UPON (עַל al) the~WATER~s2 (הַמַּיִם ha'ma'yim) the~LIVING~s (הַחַיִּים ha'hhai'yim) **RMT:** He will take the living bird and the cedar wood and the scarlet kermes and the hyssop and he will dip them and the living bird in blood of the slain bird upon the living waters,

14:7 and~he~did~make~SPATTER[(V)] (וְהִזָּה wê'hi'zah) UPON (עַל al) to~the~make~BE.CLEAN[(V)]~ing[(ms)] (הַמִּטַּהֵר ha'mi'ta'heyr) FROM (מִן min) the~INFECTION (הַצָּרַעַת ha'tsa'ra'at) SEVEN (שֶׁבַע she'va) FOOTSTEP~s (פְּעָמִים pê'a'mim) and~he~did~much~BE.CLEAN[(V)]~him (וְטִהֲרוֹ wê'ti'ha'ro) and~he~did~much~SEND[(V)] (וְשִׁלַּח wê'shi'lahh) AT (אֶת et) the~BIRD (הַצִּפֹּר ha'tsi'por) the~LIVING (הַחַיָּה ha'hha'yah) UPON (עַל al) FACE~s (פְּנֵי pê'ney) the~FIELD (הַשָּׂדֶה ha'sa'deh) **RMT:** and he will spatter upon the ones being made clean from the infection seven times, then he will declare him clean and he will send the living bird upon the face of the field,

14:8 and~he~did~much~WASH[(V)] (וְכִבֶּס wê'khi'bes) to~the~make~ BE.CLEAN[(V)]~ing[(ms)] (הַמִּטַּהֵר ha'mi'ta'heyr) AT (אֶת et) GARMENT~s~ him (בְּגָדָיו bê'ga'daw) and~he~did~much~SHAVE[(V)] (וְגִלַּח wê'gi'lahh) AT (אֶת et) ALL (כָּל kol) HAIR~him (שְׂעָרוֹ sê'a'ro) and~ he~did~BATHE[(V)] (וְרָחַץ wê'ra'hhats) in~the~WATER~s2 (בַּמַּיִם ba'ma'yim) and~he~did~BE.CLEAN[(V)] (וְטָהֵר wê'ta'har) and~AFTER (וְאַחַר wê'a'hhar) he~will~COME[(V)] (יָבוֹא ya'vo) TO (אֶל el) the~ CAMP (הַמַּחֲנֶה ha'ma'hha'neh) and~he~did~SETTLE[(V)] (וְיָשַׁב wê'ya'shav) from~OUTSIDE (מִחוּץ mi'hhuts) to~TENT~him (לְאָהֳלוֹ lê'a'ha'lo) SEVEN (שִׁבְעַת shiv'at) DAY~s (יָמִים ya'mim) **RMT:** and he

---

[61] A "utensil of clay" is a clay vessel.
[62] Meaning "running."

will wash the garments of the one being made clean, and he will shave all his hair, and he will bathe in the waters and he will be clean, and after he will come to the camp and he will settle outside of his tent for seven days,

14:9 and~he~did~EXIST^(V) (וְהָיָה wê'hai'yah) in~the~DAY (בַיּום vai'yom) the~SEVENTH (הַשְּׁבִיעִי nash'vi'i) he~will~much~SHAVE^(V) (יְגַלַּח yê'ga'lahh) AT (אֶת et) ALL (כָּל kol) HAIR~him (שְׂעָרו sê'a'ro) AT (אֶת et) HEAD~him (ראשׁו ro'sho) and~AT (וְאֶת wê'et) BEARD~him (זְקָנו zê'qa'no) and~AT (וְאֶת wê'eyt) ARCH~s (גַּבֹּת ga'bot) EYE~s2~him (עֵינָיו ey'naw) and~AT (וְאֶת wê'et) ALL (כָּל kcl) HAIR~him (שְׂעָרו sê'a'ro) he~will~much~SHAVE^(V) (יְגַלֵּחַ yê'ga'ley'ahh) and~he~did~much~WASH^(V) (וְכִבֶּס wê'khi'bes) AT (אֶת et) GARMENT~s~him (בְּגָדָיו bê'ga'daw) and~he~did~BATHE^(V) (וְרָחַץ wê'ra'hhats) AT (אֶת et) FLESH~him (בְּשָׂרו bê'sar'o) in~the~WATER~s2 (בַּמַּיִם ba'ma'yim) and~he~aid~BE.CLEAN^(V) (וְטָהֵר wê'ta'har) **RMT:** and it will come to pass in the seventh day, he will shave all his hair, his head and his beard and the arches of his eyes, and all his hair he will shave, and he will wash his garments, and he will bathe his flesh in the waters and he will be clean,

14:10 and~in~the~DAY (וּבַיּום u'vai'yom) the~EIGHTH (הַשְּׁמִינִי hash'mini) he~will~TAKE^(V) (יִקַּח yi'qahh) TWO (שְׁנֵי shê'rey) SHEEP~s (כְבָשִׂים khê'va'sim) WHOLE~s (תְּמִימִם tê'mi'mim)⁶³ and~SHEEP (וְכַבְשָׂה wê'khav'sah) UNIT (אַחַת a'hhat) DAUGHTER (בַּת bat) YEAR~her (שְׁנָתָהּ shê'na'tah) WHOLE (תְּמִימָה tê'mi'mah) and~THREE (וּשְׁלֹשָׁה ush'lo'shah) ONE.TENTH~s (עֶשְׂרֹנִים es'ro'nim) FLOUR (סֹלֶת so'let) DEPOSIT (מִנְחָר min'hhah) MIX^(V)~ed^(fs) (בְּלוּלָה bê'lu'lah) in~the~OIL (בַשֶּׁמֶן va'she'men) and~LOG (וְלֹג wê'log) UNIT (אֶחָד e'hhad) OIL (שָׁמֶן sha'men) **RMT:** and in the eighth day he will take two whole sheep and one whole sheep, a daughter of a year, and three one-tenths of flour, it is a deposit, mixed in the oil of one log of oil,

14:11 and~he~did~make~STAND^(V) (וְהֶעֱמִיד wê'he'e'mid) the~ADMINISTRATOR (הַכֹּהֵן ha'ko'heyn) the~much~BE.CLEAN^(V)~ing^(ms) (הַמְטַהֵר ham'ta'heyr) AT (אֵת eyt) the~MAN (הָאִישׁ ha'ish) to~the~make~BE.CLEAN^(V)~ing^(ms) (הַמִּטַּהֵר ha'mi'ta'heyr) and~AT~them^(m) (וְאֹתָם wê'o'tam) to~FACE~s (לִפְנֵי liph'ney) **YHWH** (יְהוָה YHWH) OPENING (פֶּתַח pe'tahh) TENT (אֹהֶל o'hel) APPOINTED (מוֹעֵד mo'ed)

---

⁶³ *Leningrad Codex:* תמימם

mo'eyd) **RMT:** and the administrator, the one making clean, will make the man to be made clean, stand with them, to the face of **YHWH** at the opening of the appointed tent,

14:12 and~*he~did*~TAKE^(V) (וְלָקַח *wê'la'qahh*) the~ADMINISTRATOR (הַכֹּהֵן *ha'ko'heyn*) AT (אֶת *et*) the~SHEEP (הַכֶּבֶשׂ *ha'ke'ves*) the~ UNIT (הָאֶחָד *ha'e'hhad*) and~*he~did~make*~COME.NEAR^(V) (וְהִקְרִיב *wê'hiq'riv*) AT~him (אֹתוֹ *o'to*) to~GUILT (לְאָשָׁם *lê'a'sham*) and~AT (וְאֶת *wê'et*) LOG (לֹג *log*) the~OIL (הַשָּׁמֶן *ha'sha'men*) and~*he~did*~ WAVE^(V) (וְהֵנִיף *wê'hey'niph*) AT~them^(m) (אֹתָם *o'tam*) WAVING (תְּנוּפָה *tê'nu'phah*) to~FACE~s (לִפְנֵי *liph'ney*) **YHWH** (יְהוָה *YHWH*) **RMT:** and the administrator will take the one sheep and he will bring him near for guilt, and the log of oil, and he will wave them as a waving to the face of **YHWH**,

14:13 and~*he~did*~SLAY^(V) (וְשָׁחַט *wê'sha'hhat*) AT (אֶת *et*) the~ SHEEP (הַכֶּבֶשׂ *ha'ke'ves*) in~AREA (בִּמְקוֹם *bim'qom*) WHICH (אֲשֶׁר *a'sher*) *he~will*~SLAY^(V) (יִשְׁחַט *yish'hhat*) AT (אֶת *et*) the~FAILURE (הַחַטָּאת *ha'hha'tat*) and~AT (וְאֶת *wê'et*) the~ ASCENSION.OFFERING (הָעֹלָה *ha'o'lah*) in~AREA (בִּמְקוֹם *bim'qom*) the~SPECIAL (הַקֹּדֶשׁ *ha'qo'desh*) GIVEN.THAT (כִּי *ki*) like~the~ FAILURE (כַּחַטָּאת *ka'hha'tat*) the~GUILT (הָאָשָׁם *ha'a'sham*) HE (הוּא *hu*) to~the~ADMINISTRATOR (לַכֹּהֵן *la'ko'heyn*) SPECIAL (קֹדֶשׁ *qo'desh*) SPECIAL~s (קָדָשִׁים *qa'da'shim*) HE (הוּא *hu*) **RMT:** and he will slay the sheep in the area which he slays the failure and the ascension offering in the special area, given that he is like the failure of the guilt for the administrator, he is the special of specials⁶⁴,

14:14 and~*he~did*~TAKE^(V) (וְלָקַח *wê'la'qahh*) the~ADMINISTRATOR (הַכֹּהֵן *ha'ko'heyn*) from~BLOOD (מִדַּם *mi'dam*) the~GUILT (הָאָשָׁם *ha'a'sham*) and~*he~did*~GIVE^(V) (וְנָתַן *wê'na'tan*) the~ ADMINISTRATOR (הַכֹּהֵן *ha'ko'heyn*) UPON (עַל *al*) TIP (תְּנוּךְ *tê'nukh*) EAR (אֹזֶן *o'zen*) to~the~*make*~BE.CLEAN^{(V)~}*ing*^(ms) (הַמִּטַּהֵר *ha'mi'ta'heyr*) the~RIGHT (הַיְמָנִית *hai'ma'nit*) and~UPON (וְעַל *wê'al*) THUMB (בֹּהֶן *bo'hen*) HAND~him (יָדוֹ *ya'do*) the~RIGHT (הַיְמָנִית *hai'ma'nit*) and~UPON (וְעַל *wê'al*) THUMB (בֹּהֶן *bo'hen*) FOOT~him (רַגְלוֹ *rag'lo*) the~RIGHT (הַיְמָנִית *hai'ma'nit*) **RMT:** and the administrator will take from the blood of the guilt and the administrator will place it upon the tip of the right ear of the ones

---

⁶⁴ The phrase "special of specials" means a "very special thing, one or place."

being made clean, and upon the thumb of his right hand and upon the thumb of his right foot,

14:15 and~he~did~TAKE^(V) (וְלָקַח *wê'la'qahh*) the~ADMINISTRATOR (הַכֹּהֵן *ha'ko'heyn*) from~LOG (מִלֹּג *mi'log*) the~OIL (הַשֶּׁמֶן *ha'sha'men*) and~he~did~POUR.DOWN^(V) (וְיָצַק *wê'ya'tsaq*) UPON (עַל *al*) PALM (כַּף *kaph*) the~ADMINISTRATOR (הַכֹּהֵן *ha'ko'heyn*) the~LEFT.HAND (הַשְּׂמָאלִית *has'ma'lit*) **RMT:** and the administrator will take from the log of oil and he will pour down upon the palm of the left hand of the administrator,

14:16 and~he~did~DIP^(V) (וְטָבַל *wê'ta'val*) the~ADMINISTRATOR (הַכֹּהֵן *ha'ko'heyn*) AT (אֶת *et*) FINGER~him (אֶצְבָּעוֹ *ets'ba'o*) the~ RIGHT (הַיְמָנִית *hai'ma'nit*) FROM (מִן *min*) the~OIL (הַשֶּׁמֶן *ha'she'men*) WHICH (אֲשֶׁר *a'sher*) UPON (עַל *al*) PALM~him (כַּפּוֹ *ka'po*) the~LEFT.HAND (הַשְּׂמָאלִית *has'ma'lit*) and~he~did~make~ SPATTER^(V) (וְהִזָּה *wê'hi'zah*) FROM (מִן *min*) the~OIL (הַשֶּׁמֶן *ha'she'men*) in~FINGER~him (בְּאֶצְבָּעוֹ *bê'ets'ba'o*) SEVEN (שֶׁבַע *she'va*) FOOTSTEP~s (פְּעָמִים *pê'a'mim*) to~FACE~s (לִפְנֵי *liph'ney*) **YHWH** (יְהוָה *YHWH*) **RMT:** and the administrator will dip his right finger in the oil which is upon the palm of his left hand and he will spatter the oil on his finger seven times to the face of **YHWH**,

14:17 and~from~REMAINDER (וּמִיֶּתֶר *u'mi'ye'ter*) the~OIL (הַשֶּׁמֶן *ha'she'men*) WHICH (אֲשֶׁר *a'sher*) UPON (עַל *al*) PALM~him (כַּפּוֹ *ka'po*) he~will~GIVE^(V) (יִתֵּן *yi'teyn*) the~ADMINISTRATOR (הַכֹּהֵן *ha'ko'heyn*) UPON (עַל *al*) TIP (תְּנוּךְ *tê'nukh*) EAR (אֹזֶן *o'zen*) to~ the~make~BE.CLEAN^{(V)~ing(ms)} (הַמִּטַּהֵר *ha'mi'ta'heyr*) the~RIGHT (הַיְמָנִית *hai'ma'nit*) and~UPON (וְעַל *wê'al*) THUMB (בֹּהֶן *bo'hen*) HAND~him (יָדוֹ *ya'do*) the~RIGHT (הַיְמָנִית *hai'ma'nit*) and~UPON (וְעַל *wê'al*) THUMB (בֹּהֶן *bo'hen*) FOOT~him (רַגְלוֹ *rag'lo*) the~RIGHT (הַיְמָנִית *hai'ma'nit*) UPON (עַל *al*) BLOOD (דַּם *dam*) the~GUILT (הָאָשָׁם *ha'a'sham*) **RMT:** and from the remainder of the oil which is upon his palm, the administrator will place upon the tip of the right ear of the one being made clean, and upon the thumb of his right hand and upon the thumb of his right foot, upon the blood of the guilt,

14:18 and~the~be~LEAVE.BEHIND^{(V)~ing(ms)} (וְהַנּוֹתָר *wê'ha'no'tar*) in~the~OIL (בַּשֶּׁמֶן *ba'she'men*) WHICH (אֲשֶׁר *a'sher*) UPON (עַל *al*) PALM (כַּף *kaph*) the~ADMINISTRATOR (הַכֹּהֵן *ha'ko'heyn*) he~will~ GIVE^(V) (יִתֵּן *yi'teyn*) UPON (עַל *al*) HEAD (רֹאשׁ *rosh*) to~the~make~ BE.CLEAN^{(V)~ing(ms)} (הַמִּטַּהֵר *ha'mi'ta'heyr*) and~he~did~much~

COVER^(V) (וְכִפֶּר *wê'khi'per*) UPON~him (עָלָיו *a'law*) the~
ADMINISTRATOR (הַכֹּהֵן *ha'ko'heyn*) to~FACE~s (לִפְנֵי *liph'ney*)
YHWH (יְהוָה *YHWH*) **RMT:** and the oil that is left behind which is
upon the palm, the administrator will place it upon the head of the
one being made clean, and the administrator will make a covering
upon him to the face of **YHWH**,

14:19 and~he~did~DO^(V) (וְעָשָׂה *wê'a'sah*) the~ADMINISTRATOR
(הַכֹּהֵן *ha'ko'heyn*) AT (אֶת *et*) the~FAILURE (הַחַטָּאת *ha'hha'tat*)
and~he~did~much~COVER^(V) (וְכִפֶּר *wê'khi'per*) UPON (עַל *al*) to~
the~make~BE.CLEAN^(V)~ing^(ms) (הַמִּטַּהֵר *ha'mi'ta'heyr*) from~
DIRTY~s~him (מִטֻּמְאָתוֹ *mi'tum'a'to*) and~AFTER (וְאַחַר *wê'a'hhar*)
he~will~SLAY^(V) (יִשְׁחַט *yish'hhat*) AT (אֶת *et*) the~
ASCENSION.OFFERING (הָעֹלָה *ha'o'lah*) **RMT:** and the administrator
will do the failure and he will make a covering upon the ones being
made clean from his dirtiness, and after, he will slay the ascension
offering,

14:20 and~he~did~make~GO.UP^(V) (וְהֶעֱלָה *wê'he'e'lah*) the~
ADMINISTRATOR (הַכֹּהֵן *ha'ko'heyn*) AT (אֶת *et*) the~
ASCENSION.OFFERING (הָעֹלָה *ha'o'lah*) and~AT (וְאֶת *wê'et*) the~
DEPOSIT (הַמִּנְחָה *ha'min'hhah*) the~ALTAR~unto (הַמִּזְבֵּחָה
ha'miz'bey'hhah) and~he~did~much~COVER^(V) (וְכִפֶּר *wê'khi'per*)
UPON~him (עָלָיו *a'law*) the~ADMINISTRATOR (הַכֹּהֵן *ha'ko'heyn*)
and~he~did~BE.CLEAN^(V) (וְטָהֵר *wê'ta'har*) **RMT:** and the
administrator will make the ascension offering go up, and the
deposit, unto the altar, and the administrator will make restitution
upon him and he will be clean,

14:21 and~IF (וְאִם *wê'im*) HELPLESS (דַּל *dal*) HE (הוּא *hu*) and~
WITHOUT (וְאֵין *wê'eyn*) HAND~him (יָדוֹ *ya'do*) make~OVERTAKE^(V)~
ing^(fs) (מַשֶּׂגֶת *ma'se'get*) and~he~did~TAKE^(V) (וְלָקַח *wê'la'qahh*)
SHEEP (כֶּבֶשׂ *ke'ves*) UNIT (אֶחָד *e'hhad*) GUILT (אָשָׁם *a'sham*) to~
WAVING (לִתְנוּפָה *lit'nu'phah*) to~>~much~COVER^(V) (לְכַפֵּר
lê'kha'peyr) UPON~him (עָלָיו *a'law*) and~ONE.TENTH (וְעִשָּׂרוֹן
wê'i'sa'ron) FLOUR (סֹלֶת *so'let*) UNIT (אֶחָד *e'hhad*) MIX^(V)~ed^(ms)
(בָּלוּל *ba'lul*) in~the~OIL (בַּשֶּׁמֶן *ba'she'men*) to~DEPOSIT (לְמִנְחָה
lê'min'hhah) and~LOG (וְלֹג *wê'log*) OIL (שָׁמֶן *sha'men*) **RMT:** but if
he is helpless and his hand is unable to reach[65], then he will take one

---

[65] Meaning to "acquire possessions."

sheep, guilt for a waving to make a covering upon him, and one tenth of flour mixed in the oil for a deposit and a log of oil,

14:22 and~TWO (וּשְׁתֵּי *ush'tey*) <u>TURTLEDOVE~s</u> (תֹרִים *to'rim*) <u>OR</u> (אוֹ *o*) <u>TWO</u> (שְׁנֵי *shê'ney*) <u>SON~s</u> (בְּנֵי *bê'ney*) <u>DOVE</u> (יוֹנָה *yo'nah*) <u>WHICH</u> (אֲשֶׁר *a'sher*) *she~will~make~*OVERTAKE(V) (תַּשִּׂיג *ta'sig*) <u>HAND~him</u> (יָדוֹ *ya'do*) and~he~did~EXIST(V) (וְהָיָה *wê'hai'yah*) <u>UNIT</u> (אֶחָד *e'hhad*) <u>FAILURE</u> (חַטָּאת *hha'tat*) and~the~UNIT (וְהָאֶחָד *wê'ha'e'hhad*) <u>ASCENSION.OFFERING</u> (עֹלָה *o'lah*) **RMT:** and two turtledoves or two sons of a dove, which his hand will reach[66], and one will exist for a failure and the other one will be for an ascension offering,

14:23 and~he~did~make~COME(V) (וְהֵבִיא *wê'hey'vi*) <u>AT~them</u>(m) (אֹתָם *o'tam*) <u>in~the~DAY</u> (בַּיוֹם *ba'yom*) <u>the~EIGHTH</u> (הַשְּׁמִינִי *hash'mini*) <u>to~CLEAN~him</u> (לְטָהֳרָתוֹ *lê'ta'ho'ra'to*) <u>TO</u> (אֶל *el*) <u>the~ADMINISTRATOR</u> (הַכֹּהֵן *ha'ko'heyn*) <u>TO</u> (אֶל *el*) <u>OPENING</u> (פֶּתַח *pe'tahh*) <u>TENT</u> (אֹהֶל *o'hel*) <u>APPOINTED</u> (מוֹעֵד *mo'eyd*) <u>to~FACE~s</u> (לִפְנֵי *liph'ney*) **YHWH** (יְהוָה *YHWH*) **RMT:** and he will bring them in the eighth day for his cleanliness to the administrator to the opening of the appointed tent to the face of **YHWH**,

14:24 and~he~did~TAKE(V) (וְלָקַח *wê'la'qahh*) <u>the~ADMINISTRATOR</u> (הַכֹּהֵן *ha'ko'heyn*) <u>AT</u> (אֶת *et*) <u>SHEEP</u> (כֶּבֶשׂ *ke'ves*) <u>the~GUILT</u> (הָאָשָׁם *ha'a'sham*) and~AT (וְאֶת *wê'et*) <u>LOG</u> (לֹג *log*) <u>the~OIL</u> (הַשָּׁמֶן *ha'sha'men*) and~he~did~WAVE(V) (וְהֵנִיף *wê'hey'niph*) <u>AT~them</u>(m) (אֹתָם *o'tam*) <u>the~ADMINISTRATOR</u> (הַכֹּהֵן *ha'ko'heyn*) <u>WAVING</u> (תְּנוּפָה *tê'nu'phah*) <u>to~FACE~s</u> (לִפְנֵי *liph'ney*) **YHWH** (יְהוָה *YHWH*) **RMT:** and the administrator will take the sheep of the guilt and the log of the oil and the administrator will wave them, a waving to the face of **YHWH**,

14:25 and~he~did~SLAY(V) (וְשָׁחַט *wê'sha'hhat*) <u>AT</u> (אֶת *et*) <u>SHEEP</u> (כֶּבֶשׂ *ke'ves*) <u>the~GUILT</u> (הָאָשָׁם *ha'a'sham*) and~he~did~TAKE(V) (וְלָקַח *wê'la'qahh*) <u>the~ADMINISTRATOR</u> (הַכֹּהֵן *ha'ko'heyn*) <u>from~BLOOD</u> (מִדַּם *mi'dam*) <u>the~GUILT</u> (הָאָשָׁם *ha'a'sham*) and~he~did~GIVE(V) (וְנָתַן *wê'na'tan*) <u>UPON</u> (עַל *al*) <u>TIP</u> (תְּנוּךְ *tê'nukh*) <u>EAR</u> (אֹזֶן *o'zen*) to~the~make~BE.CLEAN(V)~ing(ms) (הַמִּטַּהֵר *ha'mi'ta'heyr*) <u>the~RIGHT</u> (הַיְמָנִית *hai'ma'nit*) and~UPON (וְעַל *wê'al*) <u>THUMB</u> (בֹּהֶן *bo'hen*) <u>HAND~him</u> (יָדוֹ *ya'do*) <u>the~RIGHT</u> (הַיְמָנִית *hai'ma'nit*) and~UPON (וְעַל *wê'al*) <u>THUMB</u> (בֹּהֶן *bo'hen*) <u>FOOT~him</u> (רַגְלוֹ *rag'lo*)

---

[66] Meaning "acquire."

the~RIGHT (הַיְמָנִית *hai'ma'nit*) **RMT:** and he will slay the sheep of the guilt and the administrator will take from the blood of the guilt and he will place it upon the tip of the right ear to the one being made clean and upon the thumb of his right hand and upon the thumb of his right foot,

14:26 and~FROM (וּמִן *u'min*) the~OIL (הַשֶּׁמֶן *ha'she'men*) he~will~POUR.DOWN[V] (יִצֹק *yi'tsoq*) the~ADMINISTRATOR (הַכֹּהֵן *ha'ko'heyn*) UPON (עַל *al*) PALM (כַּף *kaph*) the~ADMINISTRATOR (הַכֹּהֵן *ha'ko'heyn*) the~LEFT.HAND (הַשְּׂמָאלִית *has'ma'lit*) **RMT:** and from the oil, the administrator will pour down upon the palm of the left hand of the administrator,

14:27 and~he~did~make~SPATTER[V] (וְהִזָּה *wê'hi'zah*) the~ADMINISTRATOR (הַכֹּהֵן *ha'ko'heyn*) in~FINGER~him (בְּאֶצְבָּעוֹ *bê'ets'ba'o*) the~RIGHT (הַיְמָנִית *hai'ma'nit*) FROM (מִן *min*) the~OIL (הַשֶּׁמֶן *ha'she'men*) WHICH (אֲשֶׁר *a'sher*) UPON (עַל *al*) PALM~him (כַּפּוֹ *ka'po*) the~LEFT.HAND (הַשְּׂמָאלִית *has'ma'lit*) SEVEN (שֶׁבַע *she'va*) FOOTSTEP~s (פְּעָמִים *pê'a'mim*) to~FACE~s (לִפְנֵי *liph'ney*) YHWH (יְהוָה *YHWH*) **RMT:** and the administrator will spatter the oil, which is upon the palm of his left hand, on his right finger seven times to the face of **YHWH**,

14:28 and~he~did~GIVE[V] (וְנָתַן *wê'na'tan*) the~ADMINISTRATOR (הַכֹּהֵן *ha'ko'heyn*) FROM (מִן *min*) the~OIL (הַשֶּׁמֶן *ha'she'men*) WHICH (אֲשֶׁר *a'sher*) UPON (עַל *al*) PALM~him (כַּפּוֹ *ka'po*) UPON (עַל *al*) TIP (תְּנוּךְ *tê'nukh*) EAR (אֹזֶן *o'zen*) to~the~make~BE.CLEAN[V]~ing[ms] (הַמִּטַּהֵר *ha'mi'ta'heyr*) the~RIGHT (הַיְמָנִית *hai'ma'nit*) and~UPON (וְעַל *wê'al*) THUMB (בֹּהֶן *bo'hen*) HAND~him (יָדוֹ *ya'do*) the~RIGHT (הַיְמָנִית *hai'ma'nit*) and~UPON (וְעַל *wê'al*) THUMB (בֹּהֶן *bo'hen*) FOOT~him (רַגְלוֹ *rag'lo*) the~RIGHT (הַיְמָנִית *hai'ma'nit*) UPON (עַל *al*) AREA (מְקוֹם *mê'qom*) BLOOD (דַּם *dam*) the~GUILT (הָאָשָׁם *ha'a'sham*) **RMT:** and the administrator will place from the oil which is upon his palm upon the right ear of the one being made clean and upon the thumb of his right hand and upon the thumb of his right toe, upon the area of the blood of guilt,

14:29 and~the~be~LEAVE.BEHIND[V]~ing[ms] (וְהַנּוֹתָר *wê'ha'no'tar*) FROM (מִן *min*) the~OIL (הַשֶּׁמֶן *ha'she'men*) WHICH (אֲשֶׁר *a'sher*) UPON (עַל *al*) PALM (כַּף *kaph*) the~ADMINISTRATOR (הַכֹּהֵן *ha'ko'heyn*) he~will~GIVE[V] (יִתֵּן *yi'teyn*) UPON (עַל *al*) HEAD (רֹאשׁ *rosh*) to~the~make~BE.CLEAN[V]~ing[ms] (הַמִּטַּהֵר *ha'mi'ta'heyr*) to~>~much~COVER[V] (לְכַפֵּר *lê'kha'peyr*) UPON~him (עָלָיו *a'law*) to~

FACE~s (לִפְנֵי *liph'ney*) **YHWH** (יְהוָה *YHWH*) **RMT:** and the oil that is being left behind, which is upon the palm of the administrator, he will place it upon the head of the one being made clean to make a covering upon him to the face of **YHWH**,

14:30 and~he~did~DO^(V) (וְעָשָׂה *wê'a'sah*) AT (אֶת *et*) the~UNIT (הָאֶחָד *ha'e'hhad*) FROM (מִן *min*) the~TURTLEDOVE~s (הַתֹּרִים *ha'to'rim*) OR (אוֹ *o*) FROM (מִן *min*) SON~s (בְּנֵי *bê'ney*) the~DOVE (הַיּוֹנָה *hai'yo'nah*) from~WHICH (מֵאֲשֶׁר *mey'a'sher*) she~will~make~OVERTAKE^(V) (תַּשִּׂיג *ta'sig*) HAND~him (יָדוֹ *ya'do*) **RMT:** and he will do the one from the turtledoves or from the sons of the dove, from which his hand will reach.

14:31 AT (אֵת *eyt*) WHICH (אֲשֶׁר *a'sher*) she~will~make~OVERTAKE^(V) (תַּשִּׂיג *ta'sig*) HAND~him (יָדוֹ *ya'do*) AT (אֶת *et*) the~UNIT (הָאֶחָד *ha'e'hhad*) FAILURE (חַטָּאת *hha'tat*) and~AT (וְאֶת *wê'et*) the~UNIT (הָאֶחָד *ha'e'hhad*) ASCENSION.OFFERING (עֹלָה *o'lah*) UPON (עַל *al*) the~DEPOSIT (הַמִּנְחָה *ha'min'hhah*) and~he~did~much~COVER^(V) (וְכִפֶּר *wê'khi'per*) the~ADMINISTRATOR (הַכֹּהֵן *ha'ko'heyn*) UPON (עַל *al*) to~the~make~BE.CLEAN^{(V)~ing(ms)} (הַמִּטַּהֵר *ha'mi'ta'heyr*) to~FACE~s (לִפְנֵי *liph'ney*) **YHWH** (יְהוָה *YHWH*) **RMT:** That which his hand has reached is for the one failure and for the one ascension offering upon the deposit, and the administrator will make a covering upon the one being made clean to the face of **YHWH**.

14:32 THIS (זֹאת *zot*) TEACHING (תּוֹרַת *to'rat*) WHICH (אֲשֶׁר *a'sher*) in~him (בּוֹ *bo*) TOUCH (נֶגַע *ne'ga*) INFECTION (צָרַעַת *tsa'ra'at*) WHICH (אֲשֶׁר *a'sher*) NOT (לֹא *lo*) she~will~make~OVERTAKE^(V) (תַּשִּׂיג *ta'sig*) HAND~him (יָדוֹ *ya'do*) in~CLEANSING~him (בְּטָהֳרָתוֹ *bê'ta'ha'ra'to*) **RMT:** This is the teaching in who has a plague of infection in him, who is not able to reach[67] his hand for his cleansing,

14:33 and~he~will~much~SPEAK^(V) (וַיְדַבֵּר *wai'da'beyr*) **YHWH** (יְהוָה *YHWH*) TO (אֶל *el*) Mosheh (מֹשֶׁה *mo'sheh*) and~TO (וְאֶל *wê'el*) Aharon (אַהֲרֹן *a'ha'ron*) to~>~SAY^(V) (לֵאמֹר *ley'mor*) **RMT:** and **YHWH** spoke to Mosheh and to Aharon saying,

14:34 GIVEN.THAT (כִּי *ki*) you^(mp)~will~COME^(V) (תָבֹאוּ *ta'vo'u*) TO (אֶל *el*) LAND (אֶרֶץ *e'rets*) Kena'an (כְּנַעַן *kê'na'an*) WHICH (אֲשֶׁר *a'sher*) I (אֲנִי *a'ni*) GIVE^{(V)~ing(ms)} (נֹתֵן *no'teyn*) to~you^(mp) (לָכֶם *la'khem*)

---

[67] Meaning to "acquire" what is needed.

la'khem) to~HOLDINGS (לַאֲחֻזָּה *la'a'hhu'zah*) and~I~did~GIVE[V] (וְנָתַתִּי *wê'na'ta'ti*) TOUCH (נֶגַע *ne'ga*) INFECTION (צָרַעַת *tsa'ra'at*) in~HOUSE (בְּבֵית *bê'veyt*) LAND (אֶרֶץ *e'rets*) HOLDINGS~you[mp] (אֲחֻזַּתְכֶם *a'hhu'zat'khem*) **RMT:** given that you will come to the land of Kena'an which I am giving to you for a holdings, and I will give a plague of infection in a house of the land of your holdings,

14:35 and~he~did~COME[V] (וּבָא *u'va*) WHICH (אֲשֶׁר *a'sher*) to~him (לוֹ *lo*) the~HOUSE (הַבַּיִת *ha'ba'yit*) and~he~did~make~ BE.FACE.TO.FACE[V] (וְהִגִּיד *wê'hi'gid*) to~the~ADMINISTRATOR (לַכֹּהֵן *la'ko'heyn*) to~>~SAY[V] (לֵאמֹר *ley'mor*) like~TOUCH (כְּנֶגַע *kê'ne'ga*) he~did~be~SEE[V] (נִרְאָה *nir'ah*) to~me (לִי *li*) in~the~HOUSE (בַּבָּיִת *ba'ba'yit*) **RMT:** then the one who the house belongs to will come and he will tell it to the administrator saying, something like a plague was seen to me in the house,

14:36 and~he~did~much~DIRECT[V] (וְצִוָּה *wê'tsi'wah*) the~ ADMINISTRATOR (הַכֹּהֵן *ha'ko'heyn*) and~they~did~much~TURN[V] (וּפִנּוּ *u'phi'nu*) AT (אֶת *et*) the~HOUSE (הַבַּיִת *ha'ba'yit*) in~BEFORE (בְּטֶרֶם *bê'te'rem*) he~will~COME[V] (יָבֹא *ya'vo*) the~ ADMINISTRATOR (הַכֹּהֵן *ha'ko'heyn*) to~>~SEE[V] (לִרְאוֹת *lir'ot*) AT (אֶת *et*) the~TOUCH (הַנֶּגַע *ha'ne'ga*) and~NOT (וְלֹא *wê'lo*) he~will~ BE.DIRTY[V] (יִטְמָא *yit'ma*) ALL (כָּל *kol*) WHICH (אֲשֶׁר *a'sher*) in~the~ HOUSE (בַּבָּיִת *ba'ba'yit*) and~AFTER (וְאַחַר *wê'a'hhar*) SO (כֵּן *keyn*) he~will~COME[V] (יָבֹא *ya'vo*) the~ADMINISTRATOR (הַכֹּהֵן *ha'ko'heyn*) to~>~SEE[V] (לִרְאוֹת *lir'ot*) AT (אֶת *et*) the~HOUSE (הַבָּיִת *ha'ba'yit*) **RMT:** and the administrator will direct and they will clear out the house before the administrator comes to see the plague, and all that is in the house will not be dirty, and after that the administrator will come to see the house,

14:37 and~he~did~SEE[V] (וְרָאָה *wê'ra'ah*) AT (אֶת *et*) the~TOUCH (הַנֶּגַע *ha'ne'ga*) and~LOOK (וְהִנֵּה *wê'hin'neyh*) the~TOUCH (הַנֶּגַע *ha'ne'ga*) in~WALL~s (בְּקִירֹת *bê'qi'rot*) the~HOUSE (הַבַּיִת *ha'ba'yit*) SPOT~s (שְׁקַעֲרוּרֹת *shê'qa'a'ru'rot*) GREENISH~s (יְרַקְרַקֹּת *yêraq'ra'qot*) OR (אוֹ *o*) REDDISH~s (אֲדַמְדַּמֹת *a'dam'da'mot*) and~ APPEARANCE~s~them[f] (וּמַרְאֵיהֶן *u'mar'ey'hen*) LOW (שָׁפָל *sha'phal*) FROM (מִן *min*) the~WALL (הַקִּיר *ha'qir*) **RMT:** and he will see the plague, and look, the plague is in the walls of the house, greenish or reddish spots, and their appearance is lower from the wall,

14:38 and~he~will~GO.OUT^(V) (וְיָצָא *wê'ya'tsa*) the~
ADMINISTRATOR (הַכֹּהֵן *ha'ko'heyn*) FROM (מִן *min*) the~HOUSE
(הַבַּיִת *ha'ba'yit*) TO (אֶל *el*) OPENING (פֶּתַח *pe'tahh*) the~HOUSE
(הַבַּיִת *ha'ba'yit*) and~he~did~make~SHUT^(V) (וְהִסְגִּיר *wê'his'gir*) AT
(אֶת *et*) the~HOUSE (הַבַּיִת *ha'ba'yit*) SEVEN (שִׁבְעַת *shiv'at*) DAY~s
(יָמִים *ya'mim*) **RMT:** then the administrator will go out[68] from the
house to the opening of the house, and he will shut the house for
seven days,

14:39 and~he~did~TURN.BACK^(V) (וְשָׁב *wê'shav*) the~
ADMINISTRATOR (הַכֹּהֵן *ha'ko'heyn*) in~the~DAY (בַּיֹּום *ba'yom*) the~
SEVENTH (הַשְּׁבִיעִי *hash'vi'i*) and~he~did~SEE^(V) (וְרָאָה *wê'ra'ah*)
and~LOOK (וְהִנֵּה *wê'hin'neyh*) he~did~SPREAD.ACROSS^(V) (פָּשָׂה
pa'sah) the~TOUCH (הַנֶּגַע *ha'ʻe'ga*) in~WALL~s (בְּקִירֹת *bê'qi'rot*)
the~HOUSE (הַבָּיִת *ha'ba'yit*) **RMT:** and the administrator will return
in the seventh day and he will see, and look, the plague spread
across in the walls of the house,

14:40 and~he~did~much~DIRECT^(V) (וְצִוָּה *wê'tsi'wah*) the~
ADMINISTRATOR (הַכֹּהֵן *ha'ko'heyn*) and~they~did~much~
EXTRACT^(V) (וְחִלְּצוּ *wê'hhil'tsu*) AT (אֶת *et*) the~STONE~s (הָאֲבָנִים
ha'a'va'nim) WHICH (אֲשֶׁר *a'sher*) in~them^(f) (בָּהֵן *ba'heyn*) the~
TOUCH (הַנָּגַע *ha'na'ga*) and~they~did~make~THROW.OUT^(V)
(וְהִשְׁלִיכוּ *wê'hish'li'khu*) AT~them^(f) (אֶתְהֶן *et'hen*) TO (אֶל *el*) from~
OUTSIDE (מִחוּץ *mi'hhuts*) ־כ~the~CITY (לָעִיר *la'ir*) TO (אֶל *el*) AREA
(מָקֹום *ma'qom*) DIRTY (טָמֵא *ta'mey*) **RMT:** then the administrator
will direct, and they will extract the stones which have the plague in
them, and they will throw them out to the outside of the city, to the
dirty area,

14:41 and~AT (וְאֶת *wê'et*) the~HOUSE (הַבַּיִת *ha'ba'yit*) he~will~
make~SCRAPE.OFF^(V) (יַקְצִעַ *yaq'tsi'a*) from~HOUSE (מִבַּיִת *mi'ba'yit*)
ALL.AROUND (סָבִיב *sa'viv*) and~they~did~POUR.OUT^(V) (וְשָׁפְכוּ
wê'shaph'khu) AT (אֶת *et*) the~DIRT (הֶעָפָר *he'a'phar*) WHICH (אֲשֶׁר
a'sher) they~did~make~SCRAPE.OFF^(V) (הִקְצוּ *hiq'tsu*) TO (אֶל *el*)
from~OUTSIDE (מִחוּץ *mi'hhuts*) to~the~CITY (לָעִיר *la'ir*) TO (אֶל *el*)
AREA (מָקֹום *ma'qom*) DIRTY (טָמֵא *ta'mey*) **RMT:** and he will cause
the house to be scraped off from the inside and all around, and they

---

[68] This verb is written in the perfect tense, "and he went out," but
the context implies that this should be written in the imperfect
tense, "and he will go out."

will pour out the dirt which they caused to be scraped off to the outside of the city, to the dirty area,

14:42 and~they~did~TAKE(V) (וְלָקְחוּ *wê'laq'hhu*) STONE~s (אֲבָנִים *a'va'nim*) OTHER~s (אֲחֵרוֹת *a'hhey'rot*) and~they~did~make~ COME(V) (וְהֵבִיאוּ *wê'hey'vi'u*) TO (אֶל *el*) UNDER (תַּחַת *ta'hhat*) the~ STONE~s (הָאֲבָנִים *ha'a'va'nim*) and~DIRT (וְעָפָר *wê'a'phar*) OTHER (אַחֵר *a'hheyr*) he~will~TAKE(V) (יִקַּח *yi'qahh*) and~he~did~PLASTER(V) (וְטָח *wê'tahh*) AT (אֶת *et*) the~HOUSE (הַבָּיִת *ha'ba'yit*) **RMT:** and they will take other stones, and they will bring them to be in place of the stones, and he will take other dirt and he will plaster the house,

14:43 and~IF (וְאִם *wê'im*) he~will~TURN.BACK(V) (יָשׁוּב *ya'shuv*) the~TOUCH (הַנֶּגַע *ha'ne'ga*) and~he~did~BURST.OUT(V) (וּפָרַח *u'pha'rahh*) in~the~HOUSE (בַּבַּיִת *ba'ba'yit*) AFTER (אַחַר *a'hhar*) he~ did~much~EXTRACT(V) (חִלֵּץ *hhi'leyts*) AT (אֶת *et*) the~STONE~s (הָאֲבָנִים *ha'a'va'nim*) and~AFTER (וְאַחֲרֵי *wê'a'hha'rey*) >~make~ SCRAPE.OFF(V) (הִקְצוֹת *hiq'tsot*) AT (אֶת *et*) the~HOUSE (הַבָּיִת *ha'ba'yit*) and~AFTER (וְאַחֲרֵי *wê'a'hha'rey*) >~be~PLASTER(V) (הִטּוֹחַ *hi'to'ahh*) **RMT:** and if the plague return and he bursts out in the house after he extracted the stones and after the scraping off the house and after being plastered,

14:44 and~he~did~COME(V) (וּבָא *u'va*) the~ADMINISTRATOR (הַכֹּהֵן *ha'ko'heyn*) and~he~did~SEE(V) (וְרָאָה *wê'ra'ah*) and~LOOK (וְהִנֵּה *wê'hin'neyh*) he~did~SPREAD.ACROSS(V) (פָּשָׂה *pa'sah*) the~TOUCH (הַנֶּגַע *ha'ne'ga*) in~the~HOUSE (בַּבַּיִת *ba'ba'yit*) INFECTION (צָרַעַת *tsa'ra'at*) make~IRRITATE(V)~ing(fs) (מַמְאֶרֶת *mam'e'ret*) SHE (הִוא *hi*) in~the~HOUSE (בַּבַּיִת *ba'ba'yit*) DIRTY (טָמֵא *ta'mey*) HE (הוּא *hu*) **RMT:** and the administrator will come and he will see, and look, the plague spread across in the house, she[69] is an irritating infection, he[70] is dirty,

14:45 and~he~did~BREAK.DOWN(V) (וְנָתַץ *wê'na'tats*) AT (אֶת *et*) the~HOUSE (הַבָּיִת *ha'ba'yit*) AT (אֶת *et*) STONE~s~him (אֲבָנָיו *a'va'naw*) and~AT (וְאֶת *wê'et*) TREE~s~him (עֵצָיו *ey'tsaw*) and~AT (וְאֵת *wê'eyt*) ALL (כָּל *kol*) DIRT (עָפָר *a'phar*) the~HOUSE (הַבָּיִת *ha'ba'yit*) and~he~did~make~GO.OUT(V) (וְהוֹצִיא *wê'ho'tsi*) TO (אֶל *el*) from~OUTSIDE (מִחוּץ *mi'hhuts*) to~the~CITY (לָעִיר *la'ir*) TO (אֶל *el*)

---

[69] This pronoun is referring to "infection," the only feminine word in this verse.

[70] This pronoun is referring to the word "house."

el) AREA (מָקוֹם *ma'qom*) DIRTY (טָמֵא *ta'mey*) **RMT:** and he will break down the house, his stones, his wood, and all the dirt of the house, and he will bring it out to the outside of the city, to the dirty area,

14:46 and~the~COME(V)~ing(ms) (וְהַבָּא *wê'ha'ba*) TO (אֶל *el*) the~ HOUSE (הַבַּיִת *ha'ba'yit*) ALL (כָּל *kol*) DAY~s (יְמֵי *yê'mey*) he~did~ make~SHUT(V) (הִסְגִּיר *his'gir*) AT~him (אֹתוֹ *o'to*) he~will~BE.DIRTY(V) (יִטְמָא *yit'ma*) UNTIL (עַד *ad*) the~EVENING (הָעָרֶב *ha'a'rev*) **RMT:** and the one coming to the house all the days he caused him to be shut, he will be dirty until the evening,

14:47 and~the~LIE.DOWN(V)~i~g(ms) (וְהַשֹּׁכֵב *wê'ha'sho'kheyv*) in~ the~HOUSE (בַּבַּיִת *ba'ba'yit*) he~will~WASH(V) (יְכַבֵּס *yê'kha'beys*) AT (אֶת *et*) GARMENT~s~him (בְּגָדָיו *bê'ga'daw*) and~the~EAT(V)~ing(ms) (וְהָאֹכֵל *wê'ha'o'kheyl*) in~the~HOUSE (בַּבַּיִת *ba'ba'yit*) he~will~ WASH(V) (יְכַבֵּס *yê'kha'beys*) AT (אֶת *et*) GARMENT~s~him (בְּגָדָיו *bê'ga'daw*) **RMT:** and the one lying down in the house, he will wash his garments and the one eating in the house, he will wash his garments,

14:48 and~IF (וְאִם *wê'im*) !(ms)~COME(V) (בֹּא *bo*) he~will~COME(V) (יָבֹא *ya'vo*) the~ADMINISTRATOR (הַכֹּהֵן *ha'ko'heyn*) and~he~did~ SEE(V) (וְרָאָה *wê'ra'ah*) and~LOOK (וְהִנֵּה *wê'hin'neyh*) NOT (לֹא *lo*) he~did~SPREAD.ACROSS(V) (פָשָׂה *pha'sah*) the~TOUCH (הַנֶּגַע *ha'ne'ga*) in~the~HOUSE (בַּבַּיִת *ba'ba'yit*) AFTER (אַחֲרֵי *a'hha'rey*) >~ be~PLASTER(V) (הִטֹּחַ *hi'to'ahh*) AT (אֶת *et*) the~HOUSE (הַבַּיִת *ha'ba'yit*) and~he~did~much~BE.CLEAN(V) (וְטִהַר *wê'ti'har*) the~ ADMINISTRATOR (הַכֹּהֵן *ha'ko'heyn*) AT (אֶת *et*) the~HOUSE (הַבַּיִת *ha'ba'yit*) GIVEN.THAT (כִּי *ki*) he~did~be~HEAL(V) (נִרְפָּא *nir'pa*) the~ TOUCH (הַנֶּגַע *ha'na'ga*) **RMT:** and if the administrator certainly comes and he will see, and look, the plague did not spread across in the house after the house has been plastered, given that the plague was healed,

14:49 and~he~did~TAKE(V) (וְלָקַח *wê'la'qahh*) to~>~much~FAIL(V) (לְחַטֵּא *lê'hha'tey*) AT (אֶת *et*) the~HOUSE (הַבַּיִת *ha'ba'yit*) TWO (שְׁתֵּי *shê'tey*) BIRD~s (צִפֳּרִים *tsi'pa'rim*) and~TREE (וְעֵץ *wê'eyts*) CEDAR (אֶרֶז *e'rez*) and~SCARLET (וּשְׁנִי *ush'ni*) KERMES (תוֹלַעַת *to'al'at*) and~HYSSOP (וְאֵזֹב *wê'ey'zov*) **RMT:** and, for purifying the house, he will take two birds and a tree of cedar and a scarlet kermes and hyssop,

14:50 and~he~did~SLAY[V] (וְשָׁחַט wê'sha'hhat) AT (אֶת et) the~BIRD (הַצִּפֹּר ha'tsi'por) the~UNIT (הָאֶחָת ha'e'hhat) TO (אֶל el) UTENSIL (כְּלִי kê'li) CLAY (חֶרֶשׂ hhe'res) UPON (עַל al) WATER~s2 (מַיִם ma'yim) LIVING~s (חַיִּים hhai'yim) **RMT:** and he will slay the one bird in a utensil of clay upon living waters,

14:51 and~he~did~TAKE[V] (וְלָקַח wê'la'qahh) AT (אֶת et) TREE (עֵץ eyts) the~CEDAR (הָאֶרֶז ha'e'rez) and~AT (וְאֶת wê'et) the~HYSSOP (הָאֵזֹב ha'ey'zov) and~AT (וְאֵת wê'eyt) SCARLET (שְׁנִי shê'ni) the~KERMES (הַתּוֹלַעַת ha'to'la'at) and~AT (וְאֵת wê'eyt) the~BIRD (הַצִּפֹּר ha'tsi'por) the~LIVING (הַחַיָּה ha'hha'yah) and~he~did~DIP[V] (וְטָבַל wê'ta'val) AT~them[m] (אֹתָם o'tam) in~BLOOD (בְּדַם bê'dam) the~BIRD (הַצִּפֹּר ha'tsi'por) the~SLAY[V]~ed[fs] (הַשְּׁחוּטָה hash'hhu'tah) and~in~the~WATER~s2 (וּבַמַּיִם u'va'ma'yim) the~LIVING~s (הַחַיִּים ha'hhai'yim) and~he~did~make~SPATTER[V] (וְהִזָּה wê'hi'zah) TO (אֶל el) the~HOUSE (הַבַּיִת ha'ba'yit) SEVEN (שֶׁבַע she'va) FOOTSTEP~s (פְּעָמִים pê'a'mim) **RMT:** and he will take the tree of cedar and the hyssop and the scarlet kermes and the living bird, and he will dip them in the blood of the slain bird and the living waters, and he will spatter it on the house seven times,

14:52 and~he~did~much~FAIL[V] (וְחִטֵּא wê'hhi'tey) AT (אֶת et) the~HOUSE (הַבַּיִת ha'ba'yit) in~BLOOD (בְּדַם bê'dam) the~BIRD (הַצִּפּוֹר ha'tsi'por) and~in~the~WATER~s2 (וּבַמַּיִם u'va'ma'yim) the~LIVING~s (הַחַיִּים ha'hhai'yim) and~in~the~BIRD (וּבַצִּפֹּר u'va'tsi'por) the~LIVING (הַחַיָּה ha'hha'yah) and~in~TREE (וּבָעֵץ uv'eyts) the~CEDAR (הָאֶרֶז ha'e'rez) and~in~the~HYSSOP (וּבָאֵזֹב u'va'ey'zov) and~in~SCARLET (וּבִשְׁנִי u'vish'ni) the~KERMES (הַתּוֹלָעַת ha'to'la'at) **RMT:** and he will purify the house with the blood of the bird and with the living waters and with the living bird and with the cedar tree and with the hyssop and with the scarlet kermes,

14:53 and~he~did~much~SEND[V] (וְשִׁלַּח wê'shi'lahh) AT (אֶת et) the~BIRD (הַצִּפֹּר ha'tsi'por) the~LIVING (הַחַיָּה ha'hha'yah) TO (אֶל el) from~OUTSIDE (מִחוּץ mi'hhuts) to~the~CITY (לָעִיר la'ir) TO (אֶל el) FACE~s (פְּנֵי pê'ney) the~FIELD (הַשָּׂדֶה ha'sa'deh) and~he~did~much~COVER[V] (וְכִפֶּר wê'khi'per) UPON (עַל al) the~HOUSE (הַבַּיִת ha'ba'yit) and~he~did~BE.CLEAN[V] (וְטָהֵר wê'ta'har) **RMT:** and he will send the living bird to the outside of the city, to the face of the field, and he will make a covering upon the house, and he will be clean.

14:54 <u>THIS</u> (זאת *zot*) <u>the~TEACHING</u> (הַתּוֹרָה *ha'to'rah*) <u>to~ALL</u> (לְכָל *lê'khol*) <u>TOUCH</u> (נֶגַע *ne'ga*) <u>the~INFECTION</u> (הַצָּרָעַת *ha'tsa'ra'at*) <u>and~to~the~ERUPTION</u> (וְלַנָּתֶק *wê'la'na'teq*) **RMT:** This is the teaching for every plague of infection and for the eruption,

14:55 <u>and~to~INFECTION</u> (וּלְצָרַעַת *ul'tsa'ra'at*) <u>the~GARMENT</u> (הַבֶּגֶד *ha'be'ged*) <u>and~to~the~HOUSE</u> (וְלַבָּיִת *wê'la'ba'yit*) **RMT:** and for an infection of a garment and for the house,

14:56 <u>and~to~the~ELEVATION</u> (וְלַשְׂאֵת *wê'las'eyt*) <u>and~to~the~SCAB</u> (וְלַסַּפַּחַת *wê'la'sa'pa'hhat*) <u>and~to~the~BRIGHT.SPOT</u> (וְלַבֶּהָרֶת *wê'la'be'ha'ret*) **RMT:** and for the elevation and for the scab and for the bright spot.

14:57 <u>to~>~make~THROW</u>^(V) (לְהוֹרֹת *lê'ho'rot*) <u>in~DAY</u> (בְּיוֹם *bê'yom*) <u>the~DIRTY</u> (הַטָּמֵא *ha'ta'mey*) <u>and~in~DAY</u> (וּבְיוֹם *uv'yom*) <u>the~CLEAN</u> (הַטָּהֹר *ha'ta'hor*) <u>THIS</u> (זאת *zot*) <u>TEACHING</u> (תּוֹרַת *to'rat*) <u>the~INFECTION</u> (הַצָּרָעַת *ha'tsa'ra'at*) **RMT:** To teach in the day of dirtiness and in the day of cleanliness, this is the teaching of the infection[71],

Chapter 15

15:1 <u>and~he~will~much~SPEAK</u>^(V) (וַיְדַבֵּר *wai'da'beyr*) **YHWH** (יְהוָה YHWH) <u>TO</u> (אֶל *el*) <u>Mosheh</u> (מֹשֶׁה *mo'sheh*) <u>and~TO</u> (וְאֶל *wê'el*) <u>Aharon</u> (אַהֲרֹן *a'ha'ron*) <u>to~>~SAY</u>^(V) (לֵאמֹר *ley'mor*) **RMT:** and **YHWH** spoke to Mosheh and to Aharon saying,

15:2 <u>!^(mp)~much~SPEAK</u>^(V) (דַּבְּרוּ *da'be'ru*) <u>TO</u> (אֶל *el*) <u>SON~s</u> (בְּנֵי *bê'ney*) <u>Yisra'eyl</u> (יִשְׂרָאֵל *yis'ra'eyl*) <u>and~you^(mp)~did~SAY</u>^(V) (וַאֲמַרְתֶּם *wa'a'mar'tem*) <u>TO~them^(m)</u> (אֲלֵהֶם *a'ley'hem*) <u>MAN</u> (אִישׁ *ish*) <u>MAN</u> (אִישׁ *ish*) <u>GIVEN.THAT</u> (כִּי *ki*) <u>he~will~EXIST</u>^(V) (יִהְיֶה *yih'yeh*) <u>ISSUE</u>^(V)<u>~ing^(ms)</u> (זָב *zav*) <u>from~FLESH~him</u> (מִבְּשָׂרוֹ *mi'be'sa'ro*) <u>DISCHARGE~him</u> (זוֹבוֹ *zo'vo*) <u>DIRTY</u> (טָמֵא *ta'mey*) <u>HE</u> (הוּא *hu*) **RMT:** speak to the sons of Yisra'eyl and you will say to them, each man that exists with an issuing from a discharge of his flesh, he is dirty,

15:3 <u>and~THIS</u> (וְזאת *wê'zot*) <u>she~will~EXIST</u>^(V) (תִּהְיֶה *tih'yeh*) <u>DIRTY~him</u> (טֻמְאָתוֹ *tu'm'a'to*) <u>in~DISCHARGE~him</u> (בְּזוֹבוֹ *bê'zo'vo*)

---

[71] An alternate translation may be; "to teach when it is dirty and when it is clean, this is the teaching of the infection."

*he~did~*FLOW.OUT$^{(V)}$ (רָר *rar*) FLESH~him (בְּשָׂרוֹ *bê'sar'o*) AT (אֶת *et*) DISCHARGE~him (זוֹבוֹ *zo'vo*) OR (אוֹ *o*) *he~did~make~*SEAL$^{(V)}$ (הֶחְתִּים *hehh'tim*) FLESH~him (בְּשָׂרוֹ *bê'sar'o*) from~DISCHARGE~ him (מִזּוֹבוֹ *mi'zo'vo*) DIRTY~him (טֻמְאָתוֹ *tu'm'a'to*) SHE (הִוא *hi*) **RMT:** and this will be his dirtiness with his discharge, his flesh flowed out with his discharge or his flesh was sealed from his discharge, she is his dirtiness.

15:4 ALL (כָּל *kol*) the~LYING.PLACE (הַמִּשְׁכָּב *ha'mish'kav*) WHICH (אֲשֶׁר *a'sher*) *he~will~*LIE.DOWN$^{(V)}$ (יִשְׁכַּב *yish'kav*) UPON~him (עָלָיו *a'law*) the~ISSUE$^{(V)}$~*ing*$^{(ms)}$ (הַזָּב *ha'zav*)^{72} *he~will~*BE.DIRTY$^{(V)}$ (יִטְמָא *yit'ma*) and~ALL (וְכָל *wê'khol*) the~UTENSIL (הַכְּלִי *hak'li*) WHICH (אֲשֶׁר *a'sher*) *he~will~*SETTLE$^{(V)}$ (יֵשֵׁב *yey'sheyv*) UPON~him (עָלָיו *a'law*) *he~will~*BE.DIRTY$^{(V)}$ (יִטְמָא *yit'ma*) **RMT:** Every lying place where he lies down upon with the issuing, will be dirty, and every utensil which he settles upon will be dirty,

15:5 and~MAN (וְאִישׁ *wê'ish*) WHICH (אֲשֶׁר *a'sher*) *he~will~*TOUCH$^{(V)}$ (יִגַּע *yiga*) in~LYING.PLACE~him (בְּמִשְׁכָּבוֹ *bê'mish'ka'vo*) *he~will~*WASH$^{(V)}$ (יְכַבֵּס *yê'kha'beys*) GARMENT~s~him (בְּגָדָיו *bê'ga'daw*) and~*he~did~*BATHE$^{(V)}$ (וְרָחַץ *wê'ra'hhats*) in~the~WATER~s2 (בַּמַּיִם *ba'ma'yim*) and~*he~did~*BE.DIRTY$^{(V)}$ (וְטָמֵא *wê'ta'mey*) UNTIL (עַד *ad*) the~EVENING (הָעָרֶב *ha'a'rev*) **RMT:** and a man which touches his lying place will wash his garments and he will bathe in the waters and he will be dirty until evening,

15:6 and~the~SETTLE$^{(V)}$~*ing*$^{(ms)}$ (וְהַיֹּשֵׁב *wê'hai'yo'sheyv*) UPON (עַל *al*) the~UTENSIL (הַכְּלִי *hak'li*) WHICH (אֲשֶׁר *a'sher*) *he~will~*SETTLE$^{(V)}$ (יֵשֵׁב *yey'sheyv*) UPON~him (עָלָיו *a'law*) the~ISSUE$^{(V)}$~*ing*$^{(ms)}$ (הַזָּב *ha'zav*) *he~will~*WASH$^{(V)}$ (יְכַבֵּס *yê'kha'beys*) GARMENT~s~him (בְּגָדָיו *bê'ga'daw*) and~*he~did~*BATHE$^{(V)}$ (וְרָחַץ *wê'ra'hhats*) in~the~WATER~s2 (בַּמַּיִם *ba'ma'yim*) and~*he~did~*BE.DIRTY$^{(V)}$ (וְטָמֵא *wê'ta'mey*) UNTIL (עַד *ad*) the~EVENING (הָעָרֶב *ha'a'rev*) **RMT:** and the one settling upon the utensil, who settles upon him with an issuing, he will wash his garments and he will bathe in the waters and he will be dirty until the evening,

15:7 and~the~TOUCH$^{(V)}$~*ing*$^{(ms)}$ (וְהַנֹּגֵעַ *wê'ha'no'gey'a*) in~FLESH (בִּבְשַׂר *biv'sar*) the~ISSUE$^{(V)}$~*ing*$^{(ms)}$ (הַזָּב *ha'zav*) *he~will~*WASH$^{(V)}$ (יְכַבֵּס *yê'kha'beys*) GARMENT~s~him (בְּגָדָיו *bê'ga'daw*) and~*he~did~*BATHE$^{(V)}$ (וְרָחַץ *wê'ra'hhats*) in~the~WATER~s2 (בַּמַּיִם

---

^{72} This Hebrew word appears to be missing a preposition like "with."

ba'ma'yim) and~he~did~BE.DIRTY^(V) (וְטָמֵא wê'ta'mey) UNTIL (עַד ad) the~EVENING (הָעָרֶב ha'a'rev) **RMT**: and the one touching the flesh with the issuing, he will wash his garments and he will bathe in the waters and he will be dirty until the evening,

15:8 and~GIVEN.THAT (וְכִי wê'khi) >~SPIT^(V) (יָרֹק ya'roq) the~ ISSUE^(V)~ing^(ms) (הַזָּב ha'zav) in~the~CLEAN (בַּטָּהוֹר ba'ta'hor) and~ he~did~much~WASH^(V) (וְכִבֶּס wê'khi'bes) GARMENT~s~him (בְּגָדָיו bê'ga'daw) and~he~did~BATHE^(V) (וְרָחַץ wê'ra'hhats) in~the~ WATER~s2 (בַּמַּיִם ba'ma'yim) and~he~did~BE.DIRTY^(V) (וְטָמֵא wê'ta'mey) UNTIL (עַד ad) the~EVENING (הָעָרֶב ha'a'rev) **RMT**: and if the issuing spit on the clean one[73], then he will wash his garments and he will bathe in the waters and he will be dirty until the evening,

15:9 and~ALL (וְכָל wê'khol) the~SADDLE (הַמֶּרְכָּב ha'mer'kav) WHICH (אֲשֶׁר a'sher) he~will~RIDE^(V) (יִרְכַּב yir'kav) UPON~him (עָלָיו a'law) the~ISSUE^(V)~ing^(ms) (הַזָּב ha'zav) he~will~BE.DIRTY^(V) (יִטְמָא yit'ma) **RMT**: and every saddle which he rides upon with the issuing will be dirty,

15:10 and~ALL (וְכָל wê'khol) the~TOUCH^(V)~ing^(ms) (הַנֹּגֵעַ ha'no'gey'a) in~ALL (בְּכֹל bê'khol) WHICH (אֲשֶׁר a'sher) he~will~ EXIST^(V) (יִהְיֶה yih'yeh) UNDER~s~him (תַחְתָּיו tahh'taw) he~will~ BE.DIRTY^(V) (יִטְמָא yit'ma) UNTIL (עַד ad) the~EVENING (הָעָרֶב ha'a'rev) and~the~LIFT.UP^(V)~ing^(ms) (וְהַנּוֹשֵׂא wê'ha'no'sey) AT~ them^(m) (אוֹתָם o'tam) he~will~WASH^(V) (יְכַבֵּס yê'kha'beys) GARMENT~s~him (בְּגָדָיו bê'ga'daw) and~he~did~BATHE^(V) (וְרָחַץ wê'ra'hhats) in~the~WATER~s2 (בַּמַּיִם ba'ma'yim) and~he~did~ BE.DIRTY^(V) (וְטָמֵא wê'ta'mey) UNTIL (עַד ad) the~EVENING (הָעָרֶב ha'a'rev) **RMT**: and everyone touching anything which will exist under him will be dirty until the evening, and the one lifting them up will wash his garments and he will bathe in the waters and he will be dirty until the evening,

15:11 and~ALL (וְכֹל wê'khol) WHICH (אֲשֶׁר a'sher) he~will~TOUCH^(V) (יִגַּע yiga) in~him (בּוֹ bo) the~ISSUE^(V)~ing^(ms) (הַזָּב ha'zav) and~ HAND~s2~him (וְיָדָיו wê'ya'daw) NOT (לֹא lo) he~did~FLUSH^(V) (שָׁטַף sha'taph) in~the~WATER~s2 (בַּמַּיִם ba'ma'yim) and~he~did~much~ WASH^(V) (וְכִבֶּס wê'khi'bes) GARMENT~s~him (בְּגָדָיו bê'ga'daw) and~he~did~BATHE^(V) (וְרָחַץ wê'ra'hhats) in~the~WATER~s2 (בַּמַּיִם

---

[73] An alternate translation may be "and if the one with the issuing spits on a clean person."

ba'ma'yim) and~he~did~BE.DIRTY^(V) (וְטָמֵא wê'ta'mey) UNTIL (עַד ad) the~EVENING (הָעָֽרֶב ha'a'rev) **RMT:** and everyone he touches with the issuing and did not flush his hands in the waters, then he will wash his garments and he will bath in the waters and he will be dirty until the evening,

15:12 and~UTENSIL (וּכְלִי ukh'li) CLAY (חֶרֶשׂ hhe'res) WHICH (אֲשֶׁר a'sher) he~will~TOUCH^(V) (יִגַּע yiga) in~him (בּוֹ bo) the~ISSUE^(V)~ing^(ms) (הַזָּב ha'zav) he~will~be~CRACK^(V) (יִשָּׁבֵר yi'sha'veyr) and~ALL (וְכֹל wê'khol) UTENSIL (כְּלִי kê'li) TREE (עֵץ eyts) he~will~be~FLUSH^(V) (יִשָּׁטֵף yi'sha'teyph) in~the~WATER~s2 (בַּמָּֽיִם ba'ma'yim) **RMT:** and a utensil of clay which he touches with the issuing will be cracked and every utensil of wood will be flushed in the waters,

15:13 and~GIVEN.THAT (וְכִי wê'khi) he~will~BE.CLEAN^(V) (יִטְהַר yit'har) the~ISSUE^(V)~ing^(ms) (הַזָּב ha'zav) from~DISCHARGE~him (מִזּוֹבוֹ mi'zo'vo) and~he~did~COUNT^(V) (וְסָפַר wê'sa'phar) to~him (לוֹ lo) SEVEN (שִׁבְעַת shiv'at) DAY~s (יָמִים ya'mim) to~CLEAN~him (לְטָהֳרָתוֹ lê'ta'ha'ra'to) and~he~did~much~WASH^(V) (וְכִבֶּס wê'khi'bes) GARMENT~s~him (בְּגָדָיו bê'ga'daw) and~he~did~BATHE^(V) (וְרָחַץ wê'ra'hhats) FLESH~him (בְּשָׂרוֹ bê'sar'o) in~WATER~s2 (בְּמַיִם bê'ma'yim) LIVING~s (חַיִּים hhai'yim) and~he~did~BE.CLEAN^(V) (וְטָהֵר wê'ta'har) **RMT:** and if the one with the issuing will be clean from his discharge, then he will count to himself seven days for his cleanness, then he will wash his garments and he will bathe his flesh in living waters and he will be clean,

15:14 and~in~the~DAY (וּבַיּוֹם u'vai'yom) the~EIGHTH (הַשְּׁמִינִי hash'mini) he~will~TAKE^(V) (יִקַּח yi'qahh) to~him (לוֹ lo) TWO (שְׁתֵּי shê'tey) TURTLEDOVE~s (תֹרִים to'rim) OR (אוֹ o) TWO (שְׁנֵי shê'ney) SON~s (בְּנֵי bê'ney) DOVE (יוֹנָה yo'nah) and~he~did~COME^(V) (וּבָא u'va) to~FACE~s (לִפְנֵי liph'ney) **YHWH** (יְהוָה YHWH) TO (אֶל el) OPENING (פֶּתַח pe'tahh) TENT (אֹהֶל o'hel) APPOINTED (מוֹעֵד mo'eyd) and~he~did~GIVE^(V)~them^(m) (וּנְתָנָם un'ta'nam) TO (אֶל el) the~ADMINISTRATOR (הַכֹּהֵן ha'ko'heyn) **RMT:** and in the eighth day he will take for himself two turtledoves or two sons of the dove, and he will come to the face of **YHWH**, to the opening of the appointed tent, and he will give them to the administrator,

15:15 and~he~did~DO^(V) (וְעָשָׂה wê'a'sah) AT~them^(m) (אֹתָם o'tam) the~ADMINISTRATOR (הַכֹּהֵן ha'ko'heyn) UNIT (אֶחָד e'hhad) FAILURE (חַטָּאת hha'tat) and~the~UNIT (וְהָאֶחָד wê'ha'e'hhad) ASCENSION.OFFERING (עֹלָה o'lah) and~he~did~much~COVER^(V)

(וְכִפֶּר *wê'khi'per*) UPON~him (עָלָיו *a'law*) the~ADMINISTRATOR (הַכֹּהֵן *ha'ko'heyn*) to~FACE~s (לִפְנֵי *liph'ney*) YHWH (יְהֹוָה *YHWH*) from~DISCHARGE~him (מִזּוֹבוֹ *mi'zo'vo*) RMT: and the administrator will do them, one is the failure and the other one is the ascension offering, and the administrator will make a covering upon him, to the face of YHWH because of his discharge,

15:16 and~MAN (וְאִישׁ *wê'ish*) GIVEN.THAT (כִּי *ki*) she~will~ GO.OUT[V] (תֵצֵא *tey'tsey*) FROM~him (מִמֶּנּוּ *mi'me'nu*) LYING.DOWN (שִׁכְבַת *shikh'vat*) SEED (זָרַע *za'ra*) and~he~did~BATHE[V] (וְרָחַץ *wê'ra'hhats*) in~the~WATER~s2 (בַּמַּיִם *ba'ma'yim*) AT (אֶת *et*) ALL (כָּל *kol*) FLESH~him (בְּשָׂרוֹ *bê'sar'o*) and~he~did~BE.DIRTY[V] (וְטָמֵא *wê'ta'mey*) UNTIL (עַד *ad*) the~EVENING (הָעָרֶב *ha'a'rev*) RMT: and a man that has a lying down of seed[74] go out from him, then he will bathe all his flesh in the waters and he will be dirty until the evening,

15:17 and~ALL (וְכָל *wê'khol*) GARMENT (בֶּגֶד *be'ged*) and~ALL (וְכָל *wê'khol*) SKIN (עוֹר *or*) WHICH (אֲשֶׁר *a'sher*) he~will~EXIST[V] (יִהְיֶה *yih'yeh*) UPON~him (עָלָיו *a'law*) LYING.DOWN (שִׁכְבַת *shikh'vat*) SEED (זָרַע *za'ra*) and~he~did~be~much~WASH[V] (וְכֻבַּס *wê'khu'bas*) in~the~WATER~s2 (בַּמַּיִם *ba ma'yim*) and~he~did~BE.DIRTY[V] (וְטָמֵא *wê'ta'mey*) UNTIL (עַד *ad*) the~EVENING (הָעָרֶב *ha'a'rev*) RMT: and every garment and every skin which exists the lying down of seed upon him will be washed in the waters and will be dirty until the evening,

15:18 and~WOMAN (וְאִשָּׁה *wê'i'shah*) WHICH (אֲשֶׁר *a'sher*) he~will~ LIE.DOWN[V] (יִשְׁכַּב *yish'kav*) MAN (אִישׁ *ish*) AT~her (אֹתָהּ *o'tah*) LYING.DOWN (שִׁכְבַת *shikh'vat*) SEED (זָרַע *za'ra*) and~they~did~ BATHE[V] (וְרָחֲצוּ *wê'ra'hhc tsu*) in~the~WATER~s2 (בַמַּיִם *va'ma'yim*) and~they~did~BE.DIRTY[V] (וְטָמְאוּ *wê'tam'u*) UNTIL (עַד *ad*) the~ EVENING (הָעָרֶב *ha'a'rev*) RMT: and a woman that a man lies down with and has a laying down of seed, then they will bathe in the waters and they will be dirty until the evening,

15:19 and~WOMAN (וְאִשָּׁה *wê'i'shah*) GIVEN.THAT (כִּי *ki*) she~will~ EXIST[V] (תִהְיֶה *tih'yeh*) ISSUE[V]~ing[fs] (זָבָה *za'vah*) BLOOD (דָּם *dam*) he~will~EXIST[V] (יִהְיֶה *yih'yeh*) DISCHARGE~her (זֹבָהּ *zo'vah*) in~ FLESH~her (בִּבְשָׂרָהּ *biv'sa'rah*) SEVEN (שִׁבְעַת *shiv'at*) DAY~s (יָמִים *ya'mim*) she~will~EXIST[V] (תִהְיֶה *tih'yeh*) in~REMOVAL~her (בְנִדָּתָהּ *bê'ni'da'tah*)

---

[74] The "lying down of seed" is the emission of seed during copulation.

vê'ni'da'tah) <u>and~ALL</u> (וְכֹל *wê'khol*) <u>the~TOUCH</u>^(V)*~ing*^{*(ms)*} הַנֹּגֵעַ
ha'no'gey'a) <u>in~her</u> (בָּהּ *bah*) *he~will~*BE.DIRTY^(V) (יִטְמָא *yit'ma*)
<u>UNTIL</u> (עַד *ad*) <u>the~EVENING</u> (הָעָרֶב *ha'a'rev*) **RMT:** and a woman
that will have an issuing, the blood of her discharge is in her flesh,
she will exist seven days in her removal, and anyone touching her
will be dirty until evening,

15:20 <u>and~ALL</u> (וְכֹל *wê'khol*) <u>WHICH</u> (אֲשֶׁר *a'sher*) *she~will~*
<u>LIE.DOWN</u>^(V) (תִּשְׁכַּב *tish'kav*) <u>UPON~him</u> (עָלָיו *a'law*) <u>in~REMOVAL~</u>
<u>her</u> (בְּנִדָּתָהּ *bê'ni'da'tah*) *he~will~*BE.DIRTY^(V) (יִטְמָא *yit'ma*) <u>and~ALL</u>
(וְכֹל *wê'khol*) <u>WHICH</u> (אֲשֶׁר *a'sher*) *she~will~*SETTLE^(V) (תֵּשֵׁב
tey'sheyv) <u>UPON~him</u> (עָלָיו *a'law*) *he~will~*BE.DIRTY^(V) (יִטְמָא
yit'ma) **RMT:** and anything which she lays down upon in her removal
will be dirty, and anything which she settles upon will be dirty,

15:21 <u>and~ALL</u> (וְכֹל *wê'khol*) <u>the~TOUCH</u>^(V)*~ing*^{*(ms)*} הַנֹּגֵעַ
ha'no'gey'a) <u>in~LYING.PLACE~her</u> (בְּמִשְׁכָּבָהּ *bê'mish'ka'vah*) *he~will~*
<u>WASH</u>^(V) (יְכַבֵּס *yê'kha'beys*) <u>GARMENT~s~him</u> (בְּגָדָיו *bê'ga'daw*)
*and~he~did~*BATHE^(V) (וְרָחַץ *wê'ra'hhats*) <u>in~the~WATER~s2</u> (בַּמַּיִם
ba'ma'yim) *and~he~did~*BE.DIRTY^(V) (וְטָמֵא *wê'ta'mey*) <u>UNTIL</u> (עַד
ad) <u>the~EVENING</u> (הָעָרֶב *ha'a'rev*) **RMT:** and anyone touching her
lying place, he will wash his garments and he will bathe in the waters
and he will be dirty until the evening,

15:22 <u>and~ALL</u> (וְכֹל *wê'khol*) <u>the~TOUCH</u>^(V)*~ing*^{*(ms)*} הַנֹּגֵעַ
ha'no'gey'a) <u>in~ALL</u> (בְּכֹל *bê'khol*) <u>UTENSIL</u> (כְּלִי *kê'li*) <u>WHICH</u> (אֲשֶׁר
a'sher) *she~will~*SETTLE^(V) (תֵּשֵׁב *tey'sheyv*) <u>UPON~him</u> (עָלָיו *a'law*)
*he~will~*WASH^(V) (יְכַבֵּס *yê'kha'beys*) <u>GARMENT~s~him</u> (בְּגָדָיו
bê'ga'daw) *and~he~did~*BATHE^(V) (וְרָחַץ *wê'ra'hhats*) <u>in~the~</u>
<u>WATER~s2</u> (בַּמַּיִם *ba'ma'yim*) *and~he~did~*BE.DIRTY^(V) (וְטָמֵא
wê'ta'mey) <u>UNTIL</u> (עַד *ad*) <u>the~EVENING</u> (הָעָרֶב *ha'a'rev*) **RMT:** and
anyone touching any utensil which she settled upon, he will wash his
garments and he will bathe in the waters and he will be dirty until
the evening,

15:23 <u>and~IF</u> (וְאִם *wê'im*) <u>UPON</u> (עַל *al*) <u>the~LYING.PLACE</u> (הַמִּשְׁכָּב
ha'mish'kav) <u>HE</u> (הוּא *hu*) <u>OR</u> (אוֹ *o*) <u>UPON</u> (עַל *al*) <u>the~UTENSIL</u>
(הַכְּלִי *hak'li*) <u>WHICH</u> (אֲשֶׁר *a'sher*) <u>SHE</u> (הִוא *hi*) SETTLE^(V)*~ing*^{*(fs)*}
(יֹשֶׁבֶת *yo'she'vet*) <u>UPON~him</u> (עָלָיו *a'law*) <u>in~>~TOUCH</u>^(V)*~him*
(בְּנָגְעוֹ *bê'nag'o*) <u>in~him</u> (בוֹ *vo*) *he~will~*BE.DIRTY^(V) (יִטְמָא *yit'ma*)
<u>UNTIL</u> (עַד *ad*) <u>the~EVENING</u> (הָעָרֶב *ha'a'rev*) **RMT:** and if he is upon
the lying place or upon the utensil which she settled upon, with his
touch, he will be dirty until the evening,

15:24 <u>and~IF</u> (וְאִם *wê'im*) <u>>~LIE.DOWN</u>(V) (שָׁכֹב *sha'khov*) <u>he~will~</u>
<u>LIE.DOWN</u>(V) (יִשְׁכַּב *yish'kav*) <u>MAN</u> (אִישׁ *ish*) <u>AT~her</u> (אֹתָהּ *o'tah*)
<u>and~she~will~EXIST</u>(V) (וּתְהִי *ut'hi*) <u>REMOVAL~her</u> (נִדָּתָהּ *ni'da'tah*)
<u>UPON~him</u> (עָלָיו *a'law*) <u>and~he~did~BE.DIRTY</u>(V) (וְטָמֵא *wê'ta'mey*)
<u>SEVEN</u> (שִׁבְעַת *shiv'at*) <u>DAY~s</u> (יָמִים *ya'mim*) <u>and~ALL</u> (וְכָל *wê'khol*)
<u>the~LYING.PLACE</u> (הַמִּשְׁכָּב *ha'mish'kav*) <u>WHICH</u> (אֲשֶׁר *a'sher*) <u>he~</u>
<u>will~LIE.DOWN</u>(V) (יִשְׁכַּב *yish'kav*) <u>UPON~him</u> (עָלָיו *a'law*) <u>he~will~</u>
<u>BE.DIRTY</u>(V) (יִטְמָא *yit'ma*) **RMT:** and if a man will surely lie down
with her, and her removal existed upon him, then he will be dirty
seven days, and every lying place which he lies down upon will be
dirty,

15:25 <u>and~WOMAN</u> (וְאִשָּׁה *wê'i'shah*) <u>GIVEN.THAT</u> (כִּי *ki*) <u>he~will~</u>
<u>ISSUE</u>(V) (יָזוּב *ya'zuv*) <u>DISCHARGE</u> (זוֹב *zov*) <u>BLOOD~her</u> (דָּמָהּ
da'mah) <u>DAY~s</u> (יָמִים *ya'mim*) <u>ABUNDANT~s</u> (רַבִּים *ra'bim*) <u>in~NOT</u>
(בְּלֹא *bê'lo*) <u>APPOINTED.TIME</u> (עֶת *et*) <u>REMOVAL~her</u> (נִדָּתָהּ
ni'da'tah) <u>OR</u> (אוֹ *o*) <u>GIVEN.THAT</u> (כִי *khi*) <u>she~will~ISSUE</u>(V)
(תָזוּב *ta'zuv*) <u>UPON</u> (עַל *al*) <u>REMOVAL~her</u> (נִדָּתָהּ *ni'da'tah*) <u>ALL</u> (כָּל *kol*)
<u>DAY~s</u> (יְמֵי *yê'mey*) <u>DISCHARGE</u> (זוֹב *zov*) <u>DIRTY~her</u> (טֻמְאָתָהּ
tu'me'a'tah) <u>like~DAY~s</u> (כִּימֵי *ki'mey*) <u>REMOVAL~her</u> (נִדָּתָהּ
ni'da'tah) <u>she~will~EXIST</u>(V) (תִּהְיֶה *tih'yeh*) <u>DIRTY</u> (טְמֵאָה *tê'mey'ah*)
<u>SHE</u> (הִוא *hi*) **RMT:** and a woman that will issue a discharge of her
blood an abundance of days, not in the appointed time of her
removal, or that she will issue upon her removal, she will exist all the
days of the discharge of her dirtiness like the days of her removal,
she is dirty.

15:26 <u>ALL</u> (כָּל *kol*) <u>the~LYING.PLACE</u> (הַמִּשְׁכָּב *ha'mish'kav*) <u>WHICH</u>
(אֲשֶׁר *a'sher*) <u>she~will~LIE.DOWN</u>(V) (תִּשְׁכַּב *tish'kav*) <u>UPON~him</u>
(עָלָיו *a'law*) <u>ALL</u> (כָּל *kol*) <u>DAY~s</u> (יְמֵי *yê'mey*) <u>DISCHARGE~her</u> (זוֹבָהּ
zo'vah) <u>like~LYING.PLACE</u> (כְּמִשְׁכַּב *kê'mish'kav*) <u>REMOVAL~her</u> (נִדָּתָהּ
ni'da'tah) <u>he~will~EXIST</u>(V) (יִהְיֶה *yih'yeh*) <u>to~her</u> (לָהּ *lah*) <u>and~ALL</u>
(וְכָל *wê'khol*) <u>the~UTENSIL</u> (הַכְּלִי *hak'li*) <u>WHICH</u> (אֲשֶׁר *a'sher*) <u>she~</u>
<u>will~SETTLE</u>(V) (תֵּשֵׁב *tey'sheyv*) <u>UPON~him</u> (עָלָיו *a'law*) <u>DIRTY</u> (טָמֵא
ta'mey) <u>he~will~EXIST</u>(V) (יִהְיֶה *yih'yeh*) <u>like~DIRTY</u> (כְּטֻמְאַת
kê'tum'at) <u>REMOVAL~her</u> (נִדָּתָהּ *ni'da'tah*) **RMT:** Every lying place
which she lies down upon all the days of her discharge is like the
lying place of her removal, and every utensil which she settles upon
is dirty, he will be dirty like the dirtiness of her removal,

15:27 <u>and~ALL</u> (וְכָל *wê'khol*) <u>the~TOUCH</u>(V)<u>~ing</u>(ms) (הַנּוֹגֵעַ
ha'no'gey'a) <u>in~them</u>(m) (בָּם *bam*) <u>he~will~BE.DIRTY</u>(V) (יִטְמָא *yit'ma*)

and~*he~did~much~*WASH^(V) (וְכִבֶּס *wê'khi'bes*) GARMENT~s~him (בְּגָדָיו *bê'ga'daw*) and~*he~did~*BATHE^(V) (וְרָחַץ *wê'ra'hhats*) in~the~ WATER~s2 (בַּמַּיִם *ba'ma'yim*) and~*he~did~*BE.DIRTY^(V) (וְטָמֵא *wê'ta'mey*) UNTIL (עַד *ad*) the~EVENING (הָעָרֶב *ha'a'rev*) **RMT:** and everyone touching them will be dirty, and he will wash his garments in the waters and he will be dirty until the evening,

15:28 and~*IF* (וְאִם *wê'im*) *she~did~*BE.CLEAN^(V) (טָהֲרָה *ta'ha'rah*) from~DISCHARGE~her (מִזּוֹבָהּ *mi'zo'vah*) and~*she~did~*COUNT^(V) (וְסָפְרָה *wê'saph'rah*) to~her (לָהּ *lah*) SEVEN (שִׁבְעַת *shiv'at*) DAY~s (יָמִים *ya'mim*) and~*AFTER* (וְאַחַר *wê'a'hhar*) *she~will~*BE.CLEAN^(V) (תִּטְהָר *tit'har*) **RMT:** but if she was clean from her discharge and she counted seven days for herself, then after that she will be clean,

15:29 and~in~the~DAY (וּבַיּוֹם *u'vai'yom*) the~EIGHTH (הַשְּׁמִינִי *hash'mini*) *she~will~*TAKE^(V) (תִּקַּח *ti'qahh*) to~her (לָהּ *lah*) TWO (שְׁתֵּי *shê'tey*) TURTLEDOVE~s (תֹרִים *to'rim*) OR (אוֹ *o*) TWO (שְׁנֵי *shê'ney*) SON~s (בְּנֵי *bê'ney*) DOVE (יוֹנָה *yo'nah*) and~*she~did~ make~*COME^(V) (וְהֵבִיאָה *wê'hey'vi'ah*) AT~them^(m) (אוֹתָם *o'tam*) TO (אֶל *el*) the~ADMINISTRATOR (הַכֹּהֵן *ha'ko'heyn*) TO (אֶל *el*) OPENING (פֶּתַח *pe'tahh*) TENT (אֹהֶל *o'hel*) APPOINTED (מוֹעֵד *mo'eyd*) **RMT:** and in the eighth day she will take for herself two turtledoves or two sons of a dove and she will bring them to the administrator, to the opening of the appointed tent,

15:30 and~*he~did~*DO^(V) (וְעָשָׂה *wê'a'sah*) the~ADMINISTRATOR (הַכֹּהֵן *ha'ko'heyn*) AT (אֶת *et*) the~UNIT (הָאֶחָד *ha'e'hhad*) FAILURE (חַטָּאת *hha'tat*) and~*AT* (וְאֶת *wê'et*) the~UNIT (הָאֶחָד *ha'e'hhad*) ASCENSION.OFFERING (עֹלָה *o'lah*) and~*he~did~much~*COVER^(V) (וְכִפֶּר *wê'khi'per*) UPON~her (עָלֶיהָ *a'ley'ah*) the~ADMINISTRATOR (הַכֹּהֵן *ha'ko'heyn*) to~FACE~s (לִפְנֵי *liph'ney*) **YHWH** (יְהוָה *YHWH*) from~DISCHARGE (מִזּוֹב *mi'zov*) DIRTY~her (טֻמְאָתָהּ *tu'me'a'tah*) **RMT:** and the administrator will do the one for a failure and the other one for an ascension offering, and the administrator will make a covering upon her, to the face of **YHWH** because of the discharge of her dirtiness,

15:31 and~*you*^(mp)~*did~make~*DEDICATE^(V) (וְהִזַּרְתֶּם *wê'hi'zar'tem*) AT (אֶת *et*) SON~s (בְּנֵי *bê'ney*) Yisra'eyl (יִשְׂרָאֵל *yis'ra'eyl*) from~ DIRTY~them^(m) (מִטֻּמְאָתָם *mi'tum'a'tam*) and~*NOT* (וְלֹא *wê'lo*) *they*^(m)~*will~*DIE^(V) (יָמֻתוּ *ya'mu'tu*) in~DIRTY~them^(m) (בְּטֻמְאָתָם *bê'tum'a'tam*) in~>~BE.DIRTY^(V)~them^(m) (בְּטַמְּאָם *bê'tam'am*) AT (אֶת *et*) DWELLING~me (מִשְׁכָּנִי *mish'ka'ni*) WHICH (אֲשֶׁר *a'sher*) in~

MIDST~them(m) (בְּתוֹכָם bê'to'kham) **RMT:** and you will dedicate the sons of Yisra'eyl from their dirtiness and they will not die from being dirty in my dwelling which is in the midst of them.

15:32 THIS (זאת zot) TEACHING (תּוֹרַת to'rat) the~ISSUE(V)~ing(ms) (הַזָּב ha'zav) and~WHICH (וַאֲשֶׁר wa'a'sher) she~will~GO.OUT(V) (תֵּצֵא tey'tsey) FROM~him (מִמֶּנּוּ mi'me'nu) LYING.DOWN (שִׁכְבַת shikh'vat) SEED (זֶרַע ze'ra) to~DIRTY~her (לְטָמְאָה lê'tam'ah) in~her (בָהּ vah) **RMT:** This is the teaching of the one issuing, and from his laying down of seed which will go out from him, for her dirtiness is in her,

15:33 and~the~ILLNESS (וְהַדָּוָה wê'ha'da'wah) in~REMOVAL~her (בְּנִדָּתָהּ bê'ni'da'tah) and~the~ISSUE(V)~ing(ms) (וְהַזָּב wê'ha'zav) AT (אֶת et) DISCHARGE~him (זוֹבוֹ zo'vo) to~the~MALE (לַזָּכָר la'za'khar) and~to~the~FEMALE (וְלַנְּקֵבָה wê'lan'qey'vah) and~to~MAN (וּלְאִישׁ ul'ish) WHICH (אֲשֶׁר a'sher) he~will~LIE.DOWN(V) (יִשְׁכַּב yish'kav) WITH (עִם im) DIRTY (טְמֵאָה tê'mey'ah) **RMT:** and the illness in her removal, and the issuing of his discharge of the male or the female, and for a man which lies down with dirtiness,

Chapter 16

16:1 and~he~will~much~SPEAK(V) (וַיְדַבֵּר wai'da'beyr) **YHWH** (יְהוָה YHWH) TO (אֶל el) Mosheh (מֹשֶׁה mo'sheh) AFTER (אַחֲרֵי a'hha'rey) DEATH (מוֹת mot) TWO (שְׁנֵי shê'ney) SON~s (בְּנֵי bê'ney) Aharon (אַהֲרֹן a'ha'ron) in~>~COME.NEAR(V)~them(m) (בְּקָרְבָתָם bê'qa're'va'tam) to~FACE~s (לִפְנֵי liph'ney) **YHWH** (יְהוָה YHWH) and~they(m)~will~DIE(V) (וַיָּמֻתוּ wai'ya'mu'tu) **RMT:** and **YHWH** spoke to Mosheh after the death of the two sons of Aharon in their coming near to the face of **YHWH**,

16:2 and~he~will~SAY(V) (וַיֹּאמֶר wai'yo'mer) **YHWH** (יְהוָה YHWH) TO (אֶל el) Mosheh (מֹשֶׁה mo'sheh) !(ms)~much~SPEAK(V) (דַּבֵּר da'beyr) TO (אֶל el) Aharon (אַהֲרֹן a'ha'ron) BROTHER~you(ms) (אָחִיךָ a'hhi'kha) and~DO.NOT (וְאַל wê'al) he~will~COME(V) (יָבֹא ya'vo) in~ALL (בְכָל vê'khol) APPOINTED.TIME (עֵת eyt) TO (אֶל el) the~SPECIAL (הַקֹּדֶשׁ ha'qo'desh) from~HOUSE (מִבֵּית mi'beyt) to~the~TENT.CURTAIN (לַפָּרֹכֶת la'pa'ro'khet) TO (אֶל el) FACE~s (פְּנֵי pê'ney) the~LID (הַכַּפֹּרֶת ha'ka'po'ret) WHICH (אֲשֶׁר a'sher) UPON (עַל al) the~BOX (הָאָרֹן ha'a'ron) and~NOT (וְלֹא wê'lo) he~will~DIE(V) (יָמוּת ya'mut) GIVEN.THAT (כִּי ki) in~CLOUD (בֶּעָנָן be'a'nan) I~will~be~

115

SEE^(V) (אֶרְאֶה ey'ra'eh) UPON (עַל al) the~LID (הַכַּפֹּרֶת ha'ka'po'ret) **RMT:** and YHWH said to Mosheh, speak to Aharon your brother, and do not come in every appointed time to the special tent curtain of the house, to the face of the lid which is upon the box, and he will not die, given that I will be seen in the cloud upon the lid,

16:3 in~THIS (בְּזֹאת bê'zot) he~will~COME^(V) (יָבֹא ya'vo) Aharon (אַהֲרֹן a'ha'ron) TO (אֶל el) the~SPECIAL (הַקֹּדֶשׁ ha'qo'desh) in~ BULL (בְּפַר bê'phar) SON (בֶּן ben) CATTLE (בָּקָר ba'qar) to~FAILURE (לְחַטָּאת lê'hha'tat) and~BUCK (וְאַיִל wê'a'yil) to~ ASCENSION.OFFERING (לְעֹלָה lê'lah) **RMT:** In this, Aharon will come to the special place with a bull, a son of cattle, for a failure, and a buck for an ascension offering.

16:4 TUNIC (כְּתֹנֶת kê'to'net) STRAND (בַּד bad) SPECIAL (קֹדֶשׁ qo'desh) he~will~WEAR^(V) (יִלְבָּשׁ yil'bash) and~UNDERGARMENT~s (וּמִכְנְסֵי u'mikh'ne'sey) STRAND (בַד vad) they^(m)~will~EXIST^(V) (יִהְיוּ yih'yu) UPON (עַל al) FLESH~him (בְּשָׂרוֹ bê'sar'o) and~in~SASH (וּבְאַבְנֵט uv'av'neyt) STRAND (בַּד bad) he~will~GIRD.UP^(V) (יַחְגֹּר yahh'gor) and~in~TURBAN (וּבְמִצְנֶפֶת uv'mits'ne'phet) STRAND (בַּד bad) he~will~WIND.AROUND^(V) (יִצְנֹף yits'noph) GARMENT~s (בִּגְדֵי big'dey) SPECIAL (קֹדֶשׁ qo'desh) THEY^(m) (הֵם heym) and~he~did~ BATHE^(V) (וְרָחַץ wê'ra'hhats) in~the~WATER~s2 (בַּמַּיִם ba'ma'yim) AT (אֶת et) FLESH~him (בְּשָׂרוֹ bê'sar'o) and~he~did~WEAR^(V)~ them^(m) (וּלְבֵשָׁם ul'vey'sham) **RMT:** He will wear a special tunic of strand and undergarments of strand will exist upon his flesh, and he will gird up with a sash of strand, and he will wind around with a turban of strand, they are special garments, and he will bathe his flesh in the waters, and he will wear them,

16:5 and~from~AT (וּמֵאֵת u'mey'eyt) COMPANY (עֲדַת a'dat) SON~s (בְּנֵי bê'ney) Yisra'eyl (יִשְׂרָאֵל yis'ra'eyl) he~will~TAKE^(V) (יִקַּח yi'qahh) TWO (שְׁנֵי shê'ney) HAIRY.GOAT~s (שְׂעִירֵי sê'i'rey) SHE-GOAT~s (עִזִּים i'zim) to~FAILURE (לְחַטָּאת lê'hha'tat) and~BUCK (וְאַיִל wê'a'yil) UNIT (אֶחָד e'hhad) to~ASCENSION.OFFERING (לְעֹלָה lê'lah) **RMT:** and he will take from the company of the sons of Yisra'eyl two hairy goats of the she-goats for a failure and one buck for an ascension offering,

16:6 and~he~did~make~COME.NEAR^(V) (וְהִקְרִיב wê'hiq'riv) Aharon (אַהֲרֹן a'ha'ron) AT (אֶת et) BULL (פַּר par) the~FAILURE (הַחַטָּאת ha'hha'tat) WHICH (אֲשֶׁר a'sher) to~him (לוֹ lo) and~he~did~much~ COVER^(V) (וְכִפֶּר wê'khi'per) in~UNTIL~him (בַּעֲדוֹ ba'a'do) and~in~

UNTIL (וּבְעַד *uv'ad*) HOUSE~him (בֵּיתוֹ *bey'to*) **RMT:** and Aharon will bring near the bull of the failure which is for himself, and he will make a covering on his behalf and on behalf of his house,

16:7 and~*he~did~*TAKE^(V) (וְלָקַח *wê'la'qahh*) <u>AT</u> (אֶת *et*) <u>TWO</u> (שְׁנֵי *shê'ney*) the~HAIRY.GOAT~s (הַשְּׂעִירִם *has'i'rim*) and~*he~did~make~* <u>STAND</u>^(V) (וְהֶעֱמִיד *wê'he'e'mid*) <u>AT~them</u>^(m) (אֹתָם *o'tam*) to~FACE~s (לִפְנֵי *liph'ney*) **YHWH** (יְהֹוָה *Yh'WH*) <u>OPENING</u> (פֶּתַח *pe'tahh*) <u>TENT</u> (אֹהֶל *o'hel*) <u>APPOINTED</u> (מוֹעֵד *mo'eyd*) **RMT:** and he will take the two hairy goats and he will make them stand to the face of **YHWH**, at the opening of the appointed tent,

16:8 and~*he~did~*GIVE^(V) (וְנָתַן *wê'na'tan*) Aharon (אַהֲרֹן *a'ha'ron*) <u>UPON</u> (עַל *al*) <u>TWO</u> (שְׁנֵי *shê'ney*) the~HAIRY.GOAT~s (הַשְּׂעִירִם *has'i'rim*) <u>LOT</u>~s (גּוֹרָלוֹת *go'ra'lot*) <u>LOT</u> (גּוֹרָל *go'ral*)⁷⁵ <u>UNIT</u> (אֶחָד *e'hhad*) to~**YHWH** (לַיהוָה *la'YHWH*) and~<u>LOT</u> (וְגוֹרָל *wê'go'ral*) <u>UNIT</u> (אֶחָד *e'hhad*) to~Azazeyl (לַעֲזָאזֵל *la'a'za'zeyl*) **RMT:** and Aharon will place upon the two hairy goats lots, one lot is for **YHWH** and one lot is for Azazeyl⁷⁶,

16:9 and~*he~did~make~*COME.NEAR^(V) (וְהִקְרִיב *wê'hiq'riv*) Aharon (אַהֲרֹן *a'ha'ron*) <u>AT</u> (אֶת *et*) the~HAIRY.GOAT (הַשָּׂעִיר *ha'sa'ir*) <u>WHICH</u> (אֲשֶׁר *a'sher*) *he~did~*GO.UP^(V) (עָלָה *a'lah*) <u>UPON~him</u> (עָלָיו *a'law*) the~<u>LOT</u> (הַגּוֹרָל *ha'go'ral*) to~**YHWH** (לַיהוָה *la'YHWH*) and~ *he~did~*DO^(V)~him (וְעָשָׂהוּ *wê'a'sa'hu*) <u>FAILURE</u> (חַטָּאת *hha'tat*) **RMT:** and Aharon will bring near the hairy goat, which went up⁷⁷ upon him the lot for **YHWH**, and he will do him⁷⁸ as a failure,

16:10 and~the~HAIRY.GOAT (וְהַשָּׂעִיר *wê'ha'sa'ir*) <u>WHICH</u> (אֲשֶׁר *a'sher*) *he~did~*GO.UP^(V) (עָלָה *a'lah*) <u>UPON~him</u> (עָלָיו *a'law*) the~ <u>LOT</u> (הַגּוֹרָל *ha'go'ral*) to~Azazeyl (לַעֲזָאזֵל *la'a'za'zeyl*) *he~will~be~* much~STAND^(V) (יָעֳמַד *ya'a'mad*) <u>LIVING</u> (חַי *hhai*) to~FACE~s (לִפְנֵי *liph'ney*) **YHWH** (יְהֹוָה *YHW'H*) to~>~*much~*COVER^(V) (לְכַפֵּר *lê'kha'peyr*) <u>UPON~him</u> (עָלָיו *a'law*) to~>~*much~*SEND^(V) (לְשַׁלַּח *lê'sha'lahh*) <u>AT~him</u> (אֹתוֹ *o'to*) to~Azazeyl (לַעֲזָאזֵל *la'a'za'zeyl*) the~ <u>WILDERNESS</u>~unto (הַמִּדְבָּרָה *ha'mid'ba'rah*) **RMT:** and the hairy

---

⁷⁵ *Leningrad Codex:* גרלות

⁷⁶ Most translations have "scapegoat," but the context implies that this is the name of a person or other entity.

⁷⁷ Meaning the one that was "selected."

⁷⁸ That is, "offer him."

goat which went up[79] upon him the lot for Azazeyl, he will stand living to the face of **YHWH** to make a covering upon him, to send him for Azazeyl unto the wilderness,

16:11 and~*he~did~make~*COME.NEAR[(V)] (וְהִקְרִיב *wê'hiq'riv*) Aharon (אַהֲרֹן *a'ha'ron*) AT (אֶת *et*) BULL (פַּר *par*) the~FAILURE (הַחַטָּאת *ha'hha'tat*) WHICH (אֲשֶׁר *a'sher*) to~him (לוֹ *lo*) and~*he~did~much~*COVER[(V)] (וְכִפֶּר *wê'khi'per*) in~UNTIL~him (בַּעֲדֹו *ba'a'do*) and~in~UNTIL (וּבְעַד *uv'ad*) HOUSE~him (בֵּיתֹו *bey'to*) and~*he~did~SLAY*[(V)] (וְשָׁחַט *wê'sha'hhat*) AT (אֶת *et*) BULL (פַּר *par*) the~FAILURE (הַחַטָּאת *ha'hha'tat*) WHICH (אֲשֶׁר *a'sher*) to~him (לוֹ *lo*) **RMT:** and Aharon will bring near the bull of the failure which is for himself, and he will make a covering on behalf of himself and on behalf of his house, and he will slay the bull of the failure which is for himself,

16:12 and~*he~did~TAKE*[(V)] (וְלָקַח *wê'la'qahh*) FILLING (מְלֹא *mê'lo*) the~FIRE.PAN (הַמַּחְתָּה *ha'mahh'tah*) EMBER~s (גַּחֲלֵי *ga'hha'ley*) FIRE (אֵשׁ *eysh*) from~UPON (מֵעַל *mey'al*) the~ALTAR (הַמִּזְבֵּחַ *ha'miz'bey'ahh*) from~to~FACE~s (מִלִּפְנֵי *mi'liph'ney*) **YHWH** (יְהוָה *YHWH*) and~FILLING (וּמְלֹא *um'lo*) CUPPED.HAND~s~him (חָפְנָיו *hhaph'naw*) INCENSE.SMOKE (קְטֹרֶת *qê'to'ret*) AROMATIC.SPICE~s (סַמִּים *sa'mim*) SCRAWNY (דַּקָּה *da'qah*) and~*he~did~make~*COME[(V)] (וְהֵבִיא *wê'hey'vi*) from~HOUSE (מִבֵּית *mi'beyt*) to~the~TENT.CURTAIN (לַפָּרֹכֶת *la'pa'ro'khet*) **RMT:** and he will take the filling of the fire pan, the embers of the fire, from upon the altar from before the face of **YHWH**, and a filling of his cupped hand, incense smoke of scrawny aromatic spices, and he will bring inside to the tent curtain,

16:13 and~*he~did~GIVE*[(V)] (וְנָתַן *wê'na'tan*) AT (אֶת *et*) the~INCENSE.SMOKE (הַקְּטֹרֶת *haq'to'ret*) UPON (עַל *al*) the~FIRE (הָאֵשׁ *ha'eysh*) to~FACE~s (לִפְנֵי *liph'ney*) **YHWH** (יְהוָה *YHWH*) and~*he~did~much~COVER.OVER*[(V)] (וְכִסָּה *wê'khi'sah*) CLOUD (עֲנַן *a'nan*) the~INCENSE.SMOKE (הַקְּטֹרֶת *haq'to'ret*) AT (אֶת *et*) the~LID (הַכַּפֹּרֶת *ha'ka'po'ret*) WHICH (אֲשֶׁר *a'sher*) UPON (עַל *al*) the~EVIDENCE (הָעֵדוּת *ha'ey'dut*) and~NOT (וְלֹא *wê'lo*) he~will~DIE[(V)] (יָמוּת *ya'mut*) **RMT:** and he will place the incense smoke upon the fire to the face of **YHWH**, and the cloud of incense smoke will cover over the lid which is upon the evidence, and he will not die,

---

[79] Meaning the one that was "selected."

16:14 and~*he~did*~TAKE^(V) (וְלָקַח *wê'la'qahh*) from~BLOOD (מִדַּם *mi'dam*) the~BULL (הַפָּר *ha'par*) and~*he~did~make*~SPATTER^(V) (וְהִזָּה *wê'hi'zah*) in~FINGER~him (בְאֶצְבָּעוֹ *vê'ets'ba'o*) UPON (עַל *al*) FACE~s (פְּנֵי *pê'ney*) the~LID (הַכַּפֹּרֶת *ha'ka'po'ret*) EAST~unto (קֵדְמָה *qeyd'mah*) and~to~FACE~s (וְלִפְנֵי *wê'liph'ney*) the~LID (הַכַּפֹּרֶת *ha'ka'po'ret*) he~*will~make*~SPATTER^(V) (יַזֶּה *ya'zeh*) SEVEN (שֶׁבַע *she'va*) FOOTSTEP~s (פְּעָמִים *pê'a'mim*) FROM (מִן *min*) the~BLOOD (הַדָּם *ha'dam*) in~FINGER~him (בְּאֶצְבָּעוֹ *bê'ets'ba'o*) **RMT:** and he will take from the blood of the bull, and he will spatter with his finger upon the east face of the lid, and to the face of the lid he will spatter seven times from the blood with his finger,

16:15 and~*he~did*~SLAY^(V) (וְשָׁחַט *wê'sha'hhat*) AT (אֶת *et*) HAIRY.GOAT (שְׂעִיר *sê'ir*) the~FAILURE (הַחַטָּאת *ha'hha'tat*) WHICH (אֲשֶׁר *a'sher*) to~the~PEOPLE (לָעָם *la'am*) and~*he~did~make*~COME^(V) (וְהֵבִיא *wê'hey'vi*) AT (אֶת *et*) BLOOD~him (דָּמוֹ *da'mo*) TO (אֶל *el*) from~HOUSE (מִבֵּית *mi'beyt*) to~the~TENT.CURTAIN (לַפָּרֹכֶת *la'pa'ro'khet*) and~*he~did*~DO^(V) (וְעָשָׂה *wê'a'sah*) AT (אֶת *et*) BLOOD~him (דָּמוֹ *da'mo*) like~WHICH (כַּאֲשֶׁר *ka'a'sheyr*) he~*did*~DO^(V) (עָשָׂה *a'sah*) to~BLOOD (לְדַם *lê'dam*) the~BULL (הַפָּר *ha'par*) and~*he~did~make*~SPATTER^(V) (וְהִזָּה *wê'hi'zah*) AT~him (אֹתוֹ *o'to*) UPON (עַל *al*) the~LID (הַכַּפֹּרֶת *ha'ka'po'ret*) and~to~FACE~s (וְלִפְנֵי *wê'liph'ney*) the~LID (הַכַּפֹּרֶת *ha'ka'po'ret*) **RMT:** and he will slay the hairy goat of the failure which is for the people, and he will bring his blood to the inside, to the tent curtain, and he will do with his blood, just as he did to the blood of the bull, and he will spatter him upon the lid and to the face of the lid,

16:16 and~*he~did~much*~COVER^(V) (וְכִפֶּר *wê'khi'per*) UPON (עַל *al*) the~SPECIAL (הַקֹּדֶשׁ *ha'qo'desh*) from~DIRTY~s (מִטֻּמְאֹת *mi'tum'ot*) SON~s (בְּנֵי *bê'ney*) Yisra'eyl (יִשְׂרָאֵל *yis'ra'eyl*) and~from~OFFENSE~s~them^(m) (וּמִפִּשְׁעֵיהֶם *u'mi'pish'ey'hem*) to~ALL (לְכָל *lê'khol*) FAILURE~them^(m) (חַטֹּאתָם *hha'to'tam*) and~SO (וְכֵן *wê'kheyn*) he~*will*~DO^(V) (יַעֲשֶׂה *ya'a'seh*) to~TENT (לְאֹהֶל *lê'o'hel*) APPOINTED (מוֹעֵד *mo'eyd*) the~DWELL^(V)~ing^(ms) (הַשֹּׁכֵן *ha'sho'kheyn*) AT~them^(m) (אִתָּם *i'tam*) in~MIDST (בְּתוֹךְ *bê'tokh*) DIRTY~s~them^(m) (טֻמְאֹתָם *tum'o'tam*) **RMT:** and he will make a covering upon the special place because of the dirtiness of the sons of Yisra'eyl, and because of their offenses for all their failures, and so he will do this for the appointed tent dwelling with them in the midst of their dirtiness,

16:17 and~ALL (וְכָל wê'khol) HUMAN (אָדָם a'dam) NOT (לֹא lo) he~will~EXIST^(V) (יִהְיֶה yih'yeh) in~TENT (בְּאֹהֶל bê'o'hel) APPOINTED (מוֹעֵד mo'eyd) in~>~COME^(V)~him (בְּבֹאוֹ bê'vo'o) to~>~much~COVER^(V) (לְכַפֵּר lê'kha'peyr) in~the~SPECIAL (בַּקֹּדֶשׁ ba'qo'desh) UNTIL (עַד ad) >~GO.OUT^(V)~him (צֵאתוֹ tsey'to) and~he~did~much~COVER^(V) (וְכִפֶּר wê'khi'per) in~UNTIL~him (בַּעֲדוֹ ba'a'do) and~in~UNTIL (וּבְעַד uv'ad) HOUSE~him (בֵּיתוֹ bey'to) and~in~UNTIL (וּבְעַד uv'ad) ALL (כָּל kol) ASSEMBLY (קְהַל qê'hal) Yisra'eyl (יִשְׂרָאֵל yis'ra'eyl) **RMT:** and there will not exist any human in the appointed tent when he comes in to make a covering in the special place, until his going out, and he will make a covering on his behalf and on the behalf of his house and on behalf of all the assembly of Yisra'eyl,

16:18 and~he~will~GO.OUT^(V) (וְיָצָא wê'ya'tsa) TO (אֶל el) the~ALTAR (הַמִּזְבֵּחַ ha'miz'bey'ahh) WHICH (אֲשֶׁר a'sher) to~FACE~s (לִפְנֵי liph'ney) **YHWH** (יְהֹוָה YHWH) and~he~did~much~COVER^(V) (וְכִפֶּר wê'khi'per) UPON~him (עָלָיו a'law) and~he~did~TAKE^(V) (וְלָקַח wê'la'qahh) from~BLOOD (מִדַּם mi'dam) the~BULL (הַפָּר ha'par) and~from~BLOOD (וּמִדַּם u'mi'dam) the~HAIRY.GOAT (הַשָּׂעִיר ha'sa'ir) and~he~did~GIVE^(V) (וְנָתַן wê'na'tan) UPON (עַל al) HORN~s (קַרְנוֹת qar'not) the~ALTAR (הַמִּזְבֵּחַ ha'miz'bey'ahh) ALL.AROUND (סָבִיב sa'viv) **RMT:** and he will go out to the altar which is to the face of **YHWH**, and he will make a covering upon him, and he will take from the blood of the bull and from the blood of the hairy goat, and he will place them upon the horns of the altar all around,

16:19 and~he~did~make~SPATTER^(V) (וְהִזָּה wê'hi'zah) UPON~him (עָלָיו a'law) FROM (מִן min) the~BLOOD (הַדָּם ha'dam) in~FINGER~him (בְּאֶצְבָּעוֹ bê'ets'ba'o) SEVEN (שֶׁבַע she'va) FOOTSTEP~s (פְּעָמִים pê'a'mim) and~he~did~much~BE.CLEAN^(V)~him (וְטִהֲרוֹ wê'ti'ha'ro) and~he~did~much~SET.APART^(V)~him (וְקִדְּשׁוֹ wê'qid'sho) from~DIRTY~s (מִטֻּמְאֹת mi'tum'ot) SON~s (בְּנֵי bê'ney) Yisra'eyl (יִשְׂרָאֵל yis'ra'eyl) **RMT:** and he will spatter upon him from the blood with his finger seven times, and he will make him clean, and he will set him apart from the dirty ones of Yisra'eyl,

16:20 and~he~did~much~FINISH^(V) (וְכִלָּה wê'khi'lah) from~>~much~COVER^(V) (מִכַּפֵּר mi'ka'peyr) AT (אֶת et) the~SPECIAL (הַקֹּדֶשׁ ha'qo'desh) and~AT (וְאֶת wê'et) TENT (אֹהֶל o'hel) APPOINTED (מוֹעֵד mo'eyd) and~AT (וְאֶת wê'et) the~ALTAR (הַמִּזְבֵּחַ ha'miz'bey'ahh) and~he~did~make~COME.NEAR^(V) (וְהִקְרִיב wê'hiq'riv) AT (אֶת et) the~HAIRY.GOAT (הַשָּׂעִיר ha'sa'ir) the~LIVING (הֶחָי he'hhai)

120

RMT: and he will finish making a covering for the special place and the appointed tent and the altar, and he will bring near the living hairy goat,

16:21 and~_he~did_~SUPPORT^(V) (וְסָמַךְ _wê'sa'makh_) <u>Aharon</u> אַהֲרֹן _a'ha'ron_) <u>AT</u> (אֶת _et_) <u>TWO</u> שְׁתֵּי _shê'tey_) <u>HAND~him</u> יָדֹו _ya'do_)⁸⁰ <u>UPON</u> (עַל _al_) <u>HEAD</u> (רֹאשׁ _rosh_) the~HAIRY.GOAT הַשָּׂעִיר _ha'sa'ir_) the~<u>LIVING</u> (הַחַי _ha'hhai_) and~_he~did~self_THROW.THE.HAND^(V) (וְהִתְוַדָּה _wê'hit'wa'dah_) <u>UPON~him</u> עָלָיו _a'law_) <u>AT</u> (אֶת _et_) <u>ALL</u> כָּל _kol_) <u>TWISTEDNESS~s</u> (עֲוֹנֹת _a'o'not_) <u>SON~s</u> בְּנֵי _bê'ney_) Yisra'eyl יִשְׂרָאֵל _yis'ra'eyl_) and~<u>AT</u> (וְאֵת _wê'et_) <u>ALL</u> כָּל _kol_) <u>OFFENSE~s~</u> <u>them</u>^(m) פִּשְׁעֵיהֶם _pish'ey'hem_) to~<u>ALL</u> (לְכָל _lê'khol_) <u>FAILURE~</u> <u>them</u>^(m) (חַטֹּאתָם _hha'to'tam_) and~_he~did_~GIVE^(V) (וְנָתַן _wê'na'tan_) <u>AT~them</u>^(m) (אֹתָם _o'tam_) <u>UPON</u> (עַל _al_) <u>HEAD</u> (רֹאשׁ _rosh_) the~ HAIRY.GOAT הַשָּׂעִיר _ha'sa'ir_) and~_he~did~much~_SEND^(V) wê'shi'lahh) in~<u>HAND</u> (בְּיַד _bê'yad_) <u>MAN</u> (אִישׁ _ish_) <u>READY</u> (עִתִּי _i'ti_) the~WILDERNESS~unto (הַמִּדְבָּרָה _ha'mid'ba'rah_) **RMT:** and Aharon will support his two hands upon the head of the living hairy goat, and he will confess upon him all the twistedness of the sons of Yisra'eyl and all their offenses for all their failures, and he will place them upon the head of the hairy goat, and he will send it by the hand of a ready man unto the wilderness,

16:22 and~_he~did_~LIFT.UP^(V) (וְנָשָׂא _wê'na'sa_) the~HAIRY.GOAT (הַשָּׂעִיר _ha'sa'ir_) <u>UPON~him</u> עָלָיו _a'law_) <u>AT</u> (אֶת _et_) <u>ALL</u> כָּל _kol_) TWISTEDNESS~s~them^(m) (עֲוֹנֹתָם _a'o'no'tam_) <u>TO</u> (אֶל _el_) <u>LAND</u> (אֶרֶץ _e'rets_) <u>UNINHABITED</u> (גְּזֵרָה _gê'zey'rah_) and~_he~did~much~_SEND^(V) (וְשִׁלַּח _wê'shi'lahh_) <u>AT</u> (אֶת _et_) the~HAIRY.GOAT (הַשָּׂעִיר _ha'sa'ir_) in~ the~WILDERNESS (בַּמִּדְבָּר _ba'mid'bar_) **RMT:** and the hairy goat will lift up upon himself all their twistedness to the uninhabited land, and he will send the hairy goat into the wilderness,

16:23 and~_he~did_~COME^(V) (וּבָא _u'va_) <u>Aharon</u> אַהֲרֹן _a'ha'ron_) <u>TO</u> (אֶל _el_) <u>TENT</u> (אֹהֶל _o'hel_) <u>APPOINTED</u> (מוֹעֵד _mo'eyd_) and~_he~did_~ STRIP.OFF^(V) (וּפָשַׁט _u'pha'shat_) <u>AT</u> (אֶת _et_) <u>GARMENT~s</u> בִּגְדֵי _big'dey_) the~<u>STRAND</u> (הַבָּד _ha'bad_) <u>WHICH</u> (אֲשֶׁר _a'sher_) _he~did~_ WEAR^(V) (לָבַשׁ _la'vash_) in~>~COME^(V)~him (בְּבֹאוֹ _bê'vo'o_) <u>TO</u> (אֶל _el_) the~<u>SPECIAL</u> (הַקֹּדֶשׁ _ha qo'desh_) and~_he~did~make~_REST^(V)~them^(m) (וְהִנִּיחָם _wê'hi'ni'hham_) <u>THERE</u> (שָׁם _sham_) **RMT:** and Aharon will come to the appointed tent and he will strip off the garments of

---

⁸⁰ _Qere_ = יָדָיו.

121

strand which he wore in his coming to the special place, and he will make them rest there,

16:24 and~he~did~BATHE(V) (וְרָחַץ we'ra'hhats) AT (אֶת et) FLESH~ him (בְּשָׂרוֹ bê'sar'o) in~the~WATER~s2 (בַמַּיִם va'ma'yim) in~AREA (בְּמָקוֹם bê'ma'qom) UNIQUE (קָדוֹשׁ qa'dosh) and~he~did~WEAR(V) (וְלָבַשׁ wê'la'vash) AT (אֶת et) GARMENT~s~him (בְּגָדָיו bê'ga'daw) and~he~will~GO.OUT(V) (וְיָצָא wê'ya'tsa) and~he~did~DO(V) (וְעָשָׂה wê'a'sah) AT (אֶת et) ASCENSION.OFFERING~him (עֹלָתוֹ o'la'to) and~ AT (וְאֵת wê'et) ASCENSION.OFFERING (עֹלַת o'lat) the~PEOPLE (הָעָם ha'am) and~he~did~much~COVER(V) (וְכִפֶּר wê'khi'per) in~UNTIL~ him (בַּעֲדוֹ ba'a'do) and~in~UNTIL (וּבְעַד uv'ad) the~PEOPLE (הָעָם ha'am) **RMT:** and he will bathe his flesh in the waters in the unique area, and he will wear his garments, and he will go out and he will do his ascension offering and the ascension offering of the people, and he will make restitution on his behalf and on behalf of the people,

16:25 and~AT (וְאֵת wê'eyt) FAT (חֵלֶב hhey'lev) the~FAILURE (הַחַטָּאת ha'hha'tat) he~did~make~BURN.INCENSE(V) (יַקְטִיר yaq'tir) the~ALTAR~unto (הַמִּזְבֵּחָה ha'miz'bey'hhah) **RMT:** and the fat of the failure he will burn as incense upon the altar,

16:26 and~the~much~SEND(V)~ing(ms) (וְהַמְשַׁלֵּחַ wê'ham'sha'ley'ahh) AT (אֶת et) the~HAIRY.GOAT (הַשָּׂעִיר ha'sa'ir) to~Azazeyl (לַעֲזָאזֵל la'a'za'zeyl) he~will~WASH(V) (יְכַבֵּס yê'kha'beys) GARMENT~s~him (בְּגָדָיו bê'ga'daw) and~he~did~BATHE(V) (וְרָחַץ wê'ra'hhats) AT (אֶת et) FLESH~him (בְּשָׂרוֹ bê'sar'o) in~the~WATER~s2 (בַּמָּיִם ba'ma'yim) and~AFTER (וְאַחֲרֵי wê'a'hha'rey) SO (כֵן kheyn) he~will~COME(V) (יָבוֹא ya'vo) TO (אֶל el) the~CAMP (הַמַּחֲנֶה ha'ma'hha'neh) **RMT:** and the one sending the hairy goat for Azazeyl will wash his garments and he will bathe his flesh in the waters and after this he will come to the camp,

16:27 and~AT (וְאֵת wê'eyt) BULL (פַּר par) the~FAILURE (הַחַטָּאת ha'hha'tat) and~AT (וְאֵת wê'eyt) HAIRY.GOAT (שְׂעִיר sê'ir) the~ FAILURE (הַחַטָּאת ha'hha'tat) WHICH (אֲשֶׁר a'sher) he~did~be~ make~COME(V) (הוּבָא hu'va) AT (אֶת et) BLOOD~them(m) (דָּמָם da'mam) to~>~much~COVER(V) (לְכַפֵּר lê'kha'peyr) in~the~SPECIAL (בַּקֹּדֶשׁ ba'qo'desh) he~will~make~GO.OUT(V) (יוֹצִיא yo'tsi) TO (אֶל el) from~OUTSIDE (מִחוּץ mi'hhuts) to~the~CAMP (לַמַּחֲנֶה la'ma'hha'neh) and~they~did~CREMATE(V) (וְשָׂרְפוּ wê'sar'phu) in~ the~FIRE (בָאֵשׁ va'eysh) AT (אֶת et) SKIN~s~them(m) (עֹרֹתָם o'ro'tam) and~AT (וְאֶת wê'et) FLESH~them(m) (בְּשָׂרָם bê'sa'ram) and~AT (וְאֵת *wê'et*) DUNG~them(m) (פִּרְשָׁם *pir'sham*) **RMT:** and the bull of the failure, and the hairy goat of the failure, whose blood was brought to make a covering in the special place, he will bring it out to the outside of the camp, and they will cremate their skin and their flesh and their dung in the fire,

16:28 and~the~CREMATE(V)~ing(ms) (וְהַשֹּׂרֵף *wê'ha'so'reyph*) AT~ them(m) (אֹתָם *o'tam*) he~will~WASH(V) (יְכַבֵּס *yê'kha'beys*) GARMENT~s~him (בְּגָדָיו *bê'ga'daw*) and~he~did~BATHE(V) (וְרָחַץ *wê'ra'hhats*) AT (אֶת *et*) FLESH~him (בְּשָׂרוֹ *bê'sar'o*) in~the~WATER~s2 (בַּמָּיִם *ba'ma'yim*) and~AFTER (וְאַחֲרֵי *wê'a'hha'rey*) SO (כֵן *kheyn*) he~will~COME(V) (יָבוֹא *ya'vo*) TO (אֶל *el*) the~CAMP (הַמַּחֲנֶה *ha'ma'hha'neh*) **RMT:** and the one cremating them will wash his flesh in the waters, and after this he will come to the camp,

16:29 and~she~did~EXIST(V) (וְהָיְתָה *wê'hai'tah*) to~you(mp) (לָכֶם *la'khem*) to~CUSTOM (לְחֻקַּת *lê'hhu'qat*) DISTANT (עוֹלָם *o'lam*) in~ the~NEW.MOON (בַּחֹדֶשׁ *ba'hho'desh*) the~SEVENTH (הַשְּׁבִיעִי *hash'vi'i*) in~TENTH.ONE (בֶּעָשׂוֹר *be'a'sor*) to~the~NEW.MOON (לַחֹדֶשׁ *la'hho'desh*) you(mp)~will~AFFLICT(V) (תְּעַנּוּ *tê'a'nu*) AT (אֶת *et*) SOUL~s~you(mp) (נַפְשֹׁתֵיכֶם *naph'sho'tey'khem*) and~ALL (וְכָל *wê'khol*) BUSINESS (מְלָאכָה *mê'la'khah*) NOT (לֹא *lo*) you(mp)~will~ DO(V) (תַעֲשׂוּ *ta'a'su*) the~NATIVE (הָאֶזְרָח *ha'ez'rahh*) and~the~ IMMIGRANT (וְהַגֵּר *wê'ha'geyr*) the~IMMIGRATE(V)~ing(ms) (הַגָּר *ha'gar*) in~MIDST~you(mp) (בְּתוֹכְכֶם *bê'tokh'khem*) **RMT:** and she will exist for you for a distant custom, in the seventh new moon in the tenth one to the new moon[81] you will afflict your souls and you will not do any business, the native and the immigrant immigrating in your midst,

16:30 GIVEN.THAT (כִּי *ki*) in~the~DAY (בַיּוֹם *vai'yom*) the~THIS (הַזֶּה *ha'zeh*) he~will~much~COVER(V) (יְכַפֵּר *yê'kha'peyr*) UPON~you(mp) (עֲלֵיכֶם *a'ley'khem*) to~>~much~BE.CLEAN(V) (לְטַהֵר *lê'ta'heyr*) AT~ you(mp) (אֶתְכֶם *et'khem*) from~ALL (מִכֹּל *mi'kol*) FAILURE~s~you(mp) (חַטֹּאתֵיכֶם *hha'to'tey'khem*) to~FACE~s (לִפְנֵי *liph'ney*) YHWH (יְהוָה *YHWH*) you(mp)~will~BE.CLEAN(V) (תִּטְהָרוּ *tit'ha'ru*) **RMT:** given that in this day he will make restitution upon you to make you clean from all your failures, to the face of **YHWH** you will be clean.

16:31 CEASING (שַׁבַּת *sha'bat*) REST.PERIOD (שַׁבָּתוֹן *sha'ba'ton*) SHE (הִיא *hi*) to~you(mp) (לָכֶם *la'khem*) and~you(mp)~did~much~AFFLICT(V)

---

[81] That is the "tenth day of the new moon."

(וְעִנִּיתֶם we'i'ni'tem) AT (אֶת et) SOUL~s~you[mp] (נַפְשֹׁתֵיכֶם naph'sho'tey'khem) CUSTOM (חֻקַּת hhu'qat) DISTANT (עוֹלָם o'lam) **RMT:** She is a ceasing rest period for you, and you will afflict your souls, it is a distant custom,

16:32 and~he~did~much~COVER[(V)] (וְכִפֶּר we'khi'per) the~ ADMINISTRATOR (הַכֹּהֵן ha'ko'heyn) WHICH (אֲשֶׁר a'sher) he~will~ SMEAR[(V)] (יִמְשַׁח yim'shahh) AT~him (אֹתוֹ o'to) and~WHICH (וַאֲשֶׁר wa'a'sher) he~will~much~FILL[(V)] (יְמַלֵּא yê'ma'ley) AT (אֶת et) HAND~ him (יָדוֹ ya'do) to~>~much~ADORN[(V)] (לְכַהֵן lê'kha'heyn) UNDER (תַּחַת ta'hhat) FATHER~him (אָבִיו a'viw) and~he~did~WEAR[(V)] (וְלָבַשׁ wê'la'vash) AT (אֶת et) GARMENT~s (בִּגְדֵי big'dey) the~STRAND (הַבָּד ha'bad) GARMENT~s (בִּגְדֵי big'dey) the~SPECIAL (הַקֹּדֶשׁ ha'qo'desh) **RMT:** and the administrator, who smeared himself and filled his hand[82] to be adorned in place of his father, will make restitution, and he will wear the garments of strand, the special garments,

16:33 and~he~did~much~COVER[(V)] (וְכִפֶּר we'khi'per) AT (אֶת et) SANCTUARY (מִקְדַּשׁ miq'dash) the~SPECIAL (הַקֹּדֶשׁ ha'qo'desh) and~AT (וְאֶת wê'et) TENT (אֹהֶל o'hel) APPOINTED (מוֹעֵד mo'eyd) and~AT (וְאֶת wê'et) the~ALTAR (הַמִּזְבֵּחַ ha'miz'bey'ahh) he~will~ much~COVER[(V)] (יְכַפֵּר yê'kha'peyr) and~UPON (וְעַל wê'al) the~ ADMINISTRATOR~s (הַכֹּהֲנִים ha'ko'ha'nim) and~UPON (וְעַל wê'al) ALL (כָּל kol) PEOPLE (עַם am) the~ASSEMBLY (הַקָּהָל ha'qa'hal) he~ will~much~COVER[(V)] (יְכַפֵּר yê'kha'peyr) **RMT:** and he will make a covering for the special sanctuary, and the appointed tent and the altar he will make a covering, and upon the administrators and upon the people of the assembly he will make a covering,

16:34 and~she~did~EXIST[(V)] (וְהָיְתָה wê'hai'tah) THIS (זֹאת zot) to~ you[mp] (לָכֶם la'khem) to~CUSTOM (לְחֻקַּת lê'hhu'qat) DISTANT (עוֹלָם o'lam) to~>~much~COVER[(V)] (לְכַפֵּר lê'kha'peyr) UPON (עַל al) SON~s (בְּנֵי bê'ney) Yisra'eyl (יִשְׂרָאֵל yis'ra'eyl) from~ALL (מִכָּל mi'kol) FAILURE~them[(m)] (חַטֹּאתָם hha'to'tam) UNIT (אַחַת a'hhat) in~the~YEAR (בַּשָּׁנָה ba'sha'nah) and~he~will~DO[(V)] (וַיַּעַשׂ wai'ya'as) like~WHICH (כַּאֲשֶׁר ka'a'sheyr) he~did~much~DIRECT[(V)] (צִוָּה tsi'wah)

---

[82] To "fill the hand" is an idiom of uncertain meaning, but the same phrase is used in Akkadian to mean the placing of a relevant tool or insignia (such as a scepter for a king) in the hand of one being installed in a high office.

tsi'wah) **YHWH** (יְהוָה *YHWH*) **AT** (אֶת *et*) <u>Mosheh</u> (מֹשֶׁה *mo'sheh*)
RMT: and this will exist for you for a distant custom to make a
covering upon the sons of Yisra'eyl from all their failures once in the
year, and he will do just as **YHWH** directed Mosheh,

Chapter 17

17:1 <u>and~he~will~much~SPEAK</u>^(V) (וַיְדַבֵּר *wai'da'beyr*) **YHWH** (יְהוָה
YHWH) **TO** (אֶל *el*) <u>Mosheh</u> (מֹשֶׁה *mo'sheh*) <u>to~>~SAY</u>^(V) (לֵאמֹר
ley'mor) **RMT:** and YHWH spoke to Mosheh saying,

17:2 <u>!^(ms)~much~SPEAK</u>^(V) (דַּבֵּר *da'beyr*) **TO** (אֶל *el*) <u>Aharon</u> (אַהֲרֹן
a'ha'ron) <u>and~TO</u> (וְאֶל *wê'el*) <u>SON~s~him</u> (בָּנָיו *ba'naw*) <u>and~TO</u>
(וְאֶל *wê'el*) <u>ALL</u> (כָּל *kol*) <u>SON~s</u> (בְּנֵי *bê'ney*) <u>Yisra'eyl</u> (יִשְׂרָאֵל
yis'ra'eyl) <u>and~you^(ms)~did~SAY</u>^(V) (וְאָמַרְתָּ *wê'a'mar'ta*) <u>TO~them^(m)</u>
(אֲלֵיהֶם *a'ley'hem*) <u>THIS</u> (זֶה *zeh*) <u>the~WORD</u> (הַדָּבָר *ha'da'var*)
<u>WHICH</u> (אֲשֶׁר *a'sher*) <u>he~did~much~DIRECT</u>^(V) (צִוָּה *tsi'wah*) **YHWH**
(יְהוָה *YHWH*) <u>to~>~SAY</u>^(V) (לֵאמֹר *ley'mor*) **RMT:** speak to Aharon
and to his sons and to all the sons of Yisra'eyl, and you will say to
them this word which **YHWH** directed, saying,

17:3 <u>MAN</u> (אִישׁ *ish*) <u>MAN</u> (אִישׁ *ish*) <u>from~HOUSE</u> (מִבֵּית *mi'beyt*)
<u>Yisra'eyl</u> (יִשְׂרָאֵל *yis'ra'eyl*) <u>WHICH</u> (אֲשֶׁר *a'sher*) <u>he~will~SLAY</u>^(V)
(יִשְׁחַט *yish'hhat*) <u>OX</u> (שׁוֹר *shor*) <u>OR</u> (אוֹ *o*) <u>SHEEP</u> (כֶשֶׂב *khe'sev*) <u>OR</u>
(אוֹ *o*) <u>SHE-GOAT</u> (עֵז *eyz*) <u>in~the~CAMP</u> (בַּמַּחֲנֶה *ba'ma'hha'neh*) <u>OR</u>
(אוֹ *o*) <u>WHICH</u> (אֲשֶׁר *a'sher*) <u>he~will~SLAY</u>^(V) (יִשְׁחַט *yish'hhat*) <u>from~</u>
<u>OUTSIDE</u> (מִחוּץ *mi'hhuts*) <u>to~the~CAMP</u> (לַמַּחֲנֶה *la'ma'nha'neh*)
RMT: each man from the house of Yisra'eyl which will slay an ox or a
sheep or a she-goat in the camp, or which he will slay outside the
camp,

17:4 <u>and~TO</u> (וְאֶל *wê'el*) <u>OPENING</u> (פֶּתַח *pe'tahh*) <u>TENT</u> (אֹהֶל *o'hel*)
<u>APPOINTED</u> (מוֹעֵד *mo'eyd*) <u>NOT</u> (לֹא *lo*) <u>he~did~make~COME</u>^(V)~him
(הֱבִיאוֹ *he'vi'o*) <u>to~>~make~COME.NEAR</u>^(V) (לְהַקְרִיב *lê'naq'riv*)
<u>DONATION</u> (קָרְבָּן *qar'ban*) <u>to~YHWH</u> (לַיהוָה *la'YHWH*) <u>to~FACE~s</u>
(לִפְנֵי *liph'ney*) <u>DWELLING</u> (מִשְׁכַּן *mish'kan*) **YHWH** (יְהוָה *YHWH*)
<u>BLOOD</u> (דָּם *dam*) <u>he~will~be~THINK</u>^(V) (יֵחָשֵׁב *yey'hha'sheyv*) <u>to~</u>
<u>the~MAN</u> (לָאִישׁ *la'ish*) <u>the~HE</u> (הַהוּא *ha'hu*) <u>BLOOD</u> (דָּם *dam*) <u>he~</u>
<u>did~POUR.OUT</u>^(V) (שָׁפָךְ *sha'phakh*) <u>and~he~did~be~CUT</u>^(V) (וְנִכְרַת
wê'nikh'rat) <u>the~MAN</u> (הָאִישׁ *ha'ish*) <u>the~HE</u> (הַהוּא *ha'hu*) <u>from~</u>
<u>INSIDE</u> (מִקֶּרֶב *mi'qe'rev*) <u>PEOPLE~him</u> (עַמּוֹ *a'mo*) **RMT:** and did not
bring it to the opening of the appointed tent to bring near a

125

donation for **YHWH**, to the face of the dwelling of **YHWH**, blood is considered for the man, this is blood poured out, and this man will be cut from the inside of his people.

17:5 to~THAT (לְמַעַן *lê'ma'an*) WHICH (אֲשֶׁר *a'sher*) *they⁽ᵐ⁾~will~ make~COME*⁽ⱽ⁾ (יָבִיאוּ *ya'vi'u*) SON~s (בְּנֵי *bê'ney*) Yisra'eyl (יִשְׂרָאֵל *yis'ra'eyl*) AT (אֵת *et*) SACRIFICE~s~them⁽ᵐ⁾ (זִבְחֵיהֶם *ziv'hhey'hem*) WHICH (אֲשֶׁר *a'sher*) THEY⁽ᵐ⁾ (הֵם *heym*) SACRIFICE⁽ⱽ⁾~ing⁽ᵐᵖ⁾ (זֹבְחִים *zov'hhim*) UPON (עַל *al*) FACE~s (פְּנֵי *pê'ney*) the~FIELD (הַשָּׂדֶה *ha'sa'deh*) and~they~did~make~COME⁽ⱽ⁾~them⁽ᵐ⁾ (וֶהֱבִיאֻם *we'he'vi'um*) to~**YHWH** (לַיהוָה *la'YHWH*) TO (אֶל *el*) OPENING (פֶּתַח *pe'tahh*) TENT (אֹהֶל *o'hel*) APPOINTED (מוֹעֵד *mo'eyd*) TO (אֶל *el*) the~ADMINISTRATOR (הַכֹּהֵן *ha'ko'heyn*) and~they~did~SACRIFICE⁽ⱽ⁾ (וְזָבְחוּ *wê'zav'hhu*) SACRIFICE~s (זִבְחֵי *zav'hhey*) OFFERING.OF.RESTITUTION~s (שְׁלָמִים *shê'la'mim*) to~**YHWH** (לַיהוָה *la'YHWH*) AT~them⁽ᵐ⁾ (אוֹתָם *o'tam*) **RMT:** For that which the sons of Yisra'eyl will bring their sacrifices which they are sacrificing upon the face of the field, and they will bring them to **YHWH**, to the opening of the appointed tent, to the administrator, and they will sacrifice them as the sacrifices of the offering of restitutions to **YHWH**,

17:6 and~he~did~SPRINKLE⁽ⱽ⁾ (וְזָרַק *wê'za'raq*) the~ ADMINISTRATOR (הַכֹּהֵן *ha'ko'heyn*) AT (אֵת *et*) the~BLOOD (הַדָּם *ha'dam*) UPON (עַל *al*) ALTAR (מִזְבַּח *miz'bahh*) **YHWH** (יְהוָה *YHWH*) OPENING (פֶּתַח *pe'tahh*) TENT (אֹהֶל *o'hel*) APPOINTED (מוֹעֵד *mo'eyd*) and~he~did~make~BURN.INCENSE⁽ⱽ⁾ (וְהִקְטִיר *wê'hiq'tir*) the~FAT (הַחֵלֶב *ha'hhey'lev*) to~AROMA (לְרֵיחַ *lê'rey'ahh*) SWEET (נִיחֹחַ *ni'hho'ahh*) to~**YHWH** (לַיהוָה *la'YHWH*) **RMT:** and the administrator will sprinkle the blood upon the altar of **YHWH**, the opening of the appointed tent, and he will burn as incense the fat for a sweet aroma to **YHWH**,

17:7 and~NOT (וְלֹא *wê'lo*) *they⁽ᵐ⁾~will~SACRIFICE*⁽ⱽ⁾ (יִזְבְּחוּ *yiz'be'hhu*) YET.AGAIN (עוֹד *od*) AT (אֵת *et*) SACRIFICE~s~them⁽ᵐ⁾ (זִבְחֵיהֶם *ziv'hhey'hem*) to~the~HAIRY.GOAT~s (לַשְּׂעִירִם *las'i'rim*) WHICH (אֲשֶׁר *a'sher*) THEY⁽ᵐ⁾ (הֵם *heym*) BE.A.HARLOT⁽ⱽ⁾~ing⁽ᵐᵖ⁾ (זֹנִים *zo'nim*) AFTER~them⁽ᵐ⁾ (אַחֲרֵיהֶם *a'hha'rey'hem*) CUSTOM (חֻקַּת *hhu'qat*) DISTANT (עוֹלָם *o'lam*) *she~will~EXIST*⁽ⱽ⁾ (תִּהְיֶה *tih'yeh*) THIS (זֹאת *zot*) to~them⁽ᵐ⁾ (לָהֶם *la'hem*) to~ GENERATION~s~them⁽ᵐ⁾ (לְדֹרֹתָם *lê'do'ro'tam*) **RMT:** and they will not sacrifice ever again their sacrifices to the hairy goats, which they were harloting after, this will be a distant custom for them for their generations,

17:8 and~TO~them⁽ᵐ⁾ (וַאֲלֵהֶם *wa'a'ley'hem*) you⁽ᵐˢ⁾~will~SAY⁽ᵛ⁾ (תֹּאמַר *to'mar*) MAN (אִישׁ *ish*) MAN (אִישׁ *ish*) from~HOUSE (מִבֵּית *mi'beyt*) Yisra'eyl (יִשְׂרָאֵל *yis'ra'ey.*) and~FROM (וּמִן *u'min*) the~ IMMIGRANT (הַגֵּר *ha'geyr*) WHICH (אֲשֶׁר *a'sher*) he~will~ IMMIGRATE⁽ᵛ⁾ (יָגוּר *ya'gur*) in~M DST~them⁽ᵐ⁾ (בְּתוֹכָם *bê'to'kham*) WHICH (אֲשֶׁר *a'sher*) he~will~GO. JP⁽ᵛ⁾ (יַעֲלֶה *ya'a'leh*) ASCENSION.OFFERING (עֹלָה *o'lah*) OR (אוֹ *o*) SACRIFICE (זֶבַח *za'vahh*) **RMT:** and to them you will say, each man from the house of Yisra'eyl, and from the immigrant which immigrated in their midst, which will bring up an ascension offering or sacrifice,

17:9 and~TO (וְאֶל *wê'el*) OPENING (פֶּתַח *pe'tahh*) TENT (אֹהֶל *o'hel*) APPOINTED (מוֹעֵד *mo'eyd*) NOT (לֹא *lo*) he~will~make~COME⁽ᵛ⁾~him (יְבִיאֶנּוּ *yê'vi'e'nu*) to~>~DO⁽ᵛ⁾ (לַעֲשׂוֹת *la'a'sot*) AT~him (אֹתוֹ *o'to*) to~YHWH (לַיהוָה *la'YHWH*) and~he~did~be~CUT⁽ᵛ⁾ (וְנִכְרַת *wê'nikh'rat*) the~MAN (הָאִישׁ *ha'ish*) the~HE (הַהוּא *ha'hu*) from~ PEOPLE~s~him (מֵעַמָּיו *mey'a'maw*) **RMT:** and he will not bring him to the opening of the appointed tent to do[83] him for **YHWH**, this man will be cut from his peoples,

17:10 and~MAN (וְאִישׁ *wê'ish*) MAN (אִישׁ *ish*) from~HOUSE (מִבֵּית *mi'beyt*) Yisra'eyl (יִשְׂרָאֵל *yis'ra'eyl*) and~FROM (וּמִן *u'min*) the~ IMMIGRANT (הַגֵּר *ha'geyr*) the~IMMIGRATE⁽ᵛ⁾~ing⁽ᵐˢ⁾ (הַגָּר *ha'gar*) in~MIDST~them⁽ᵐ⁾ (בְּתוֹכָם *bê'to'kham*) WHICH (אֲשֶׁר *a'sher*) he~ will~EAT⁽ᵛ⁾ (יֹאכַל *yo'khal*) ALL (כָּל *kol*) BLOOD (דָּם *dam*) and~I~did~ GIVE⁽ᵛ⁾ (וְנָתַתִּי *wê'na'ta'ti*) FACE~s~me (פָּנַי *pha'nai*) in~the~SOUL (בַּנֶּפֶשׁ *ba'ne'phesh*) the~EAT⁽ᵛ⁾~ing⁽ᶠˢ⁾ (הָאֹכֶלֶת *ha'o'khe'let*) AT (אֶת *et*) the~BLOOD (הַדָּם *ha'dam*) and~I~did~make~CUT⁽ᵛ⁾ (וְהִכְרַתִּי *wê'hikh'ra'ti*) AT~her (אֹתָהּ *o'tah*) from~INSIDE (מִקֶּרֶב *mi'qe'rev*) PEOPLE~her (עַמָּהּ *a'mah*) **RMT:** and each man from the house of Yisra'eyl, and from the immigrant immigrating in your midst, that eats any blood, then I will place my face in the soul of the one eating the blood, and I will cause her[84] to be cut from inside her people,

17:11 GIVEN.THAT (כִּי *ki*) SOUL (נֶפֶשׁ *ne'phesh*) the~FLESH (הַבָּשָׂר *ha'ba'sar*) in~the~BLOOD (בַּדָּם *ba'dam*) SHE (הוּא *hi*) and~I (וַאֲנִי *wa'ani*) I~did~GIVE⁽ᵛ⁾~him (נְתַתִּיו *nê'ta'tiw*) to~you⁽ᵐᵖ⁾ (לָכֶם *la'khem*)

---

[83] That is to "sacrifice."

[84] Referring to the "soul," a feminine noun.

la'khem) UPON (עַל *al*) the~ALTAR (הַמִּזְבֵּחַ *ha'miz'bey'ahh*) to~>~ *much*~COVER^(V) (לְכַפֵּר *lê'kha'peyr*) UPON (עַל *al*) SOUL~s~you^(mp) (נַפְשֹׁתֵיכֶם *naph'sho'tey'khem*) GIVEN.THAT (כִּי *ki*) the~BLOOD (הַדָּם *ha'dam*) HE (הוּא *hu*) in~the~SOUL (בַּנֶּפֶשׁ *ba'ne'phesh*) he~will~ *much*~COVER^(V) (יְכַפֵּר *yê'kha'peyr*) **RMT:** given that the soul of flesh, she is in the blood, and I, I will give him to you upon the altar to make a covering upon your souls, given that the blood that is in the soul will make restitution.

17:12 UPON (עַל *al*) SO (כֵּן *keyn*) I~did~SAY^(V) (אָמַרְתִּי *a'mar'ti*) to~ SON~s (לִבְנֵי *liv'ney*) Yisra'eyl (יִשְׂרָאֵל *yis'ra'eyl*) ALL (כָּל *kol*) SOUL (נֶפֶשׁ *ne'phesh*) from~you^(mp) (מִכֶּם *mi'kem*) NOT (לֹא *lo*) you^(ms)~ will~EAT^(V) (תֹאכַל *to'khal*) BLOOD (דָּם *dam*) and~the~IMMIGRANT (וְהַגֵּר *wê'ha'geyr*) the~IMMIGRATE^(V)~ing^(ms) (הַגָּר *ha'gar*) in~ MIDST~you^(mp) (בְּתוֹכְכֶם *bê'tokh'khem*) NOT (לֹא *lo*) he~will~EAT^(V) (יֹאכַל *yo'khal*) BLOOD (דָּם *dam*) **RMT:** Therefore, I said to the sons of Yisra'eyl, every soul among you will not eat blood, and the immigrant immigrating in your midst will not eat blood,

17:13 and~MAN (וְאִישׁ *wê'ish*) MAN (אִישׁ *ish*) from~SON~s (מִבְּנֵי *mi'be'ney*) Yisra'eyl (יִשְׂרָאֵל *yis'ra'eyl*) and~FROM (וּמִן *u'min*) the~ IMMIGRANT (הַגֵּר *ha'geyr*) the~IMMIGRATE^(V)~ing^(ms) (הַגָּר *ha'gar*) in~MIDST~them^(m) (בְּתוֹכָם *bê'to'kham*) WHICH (אֲשֶׁר *a'sher*) he~ will~HUNT^(V) (יָצוּד *ya'tsud*) GAME (צֵיד *tseyd*) LIVING (חַיָּה *hhai'yah*) OR (אוֹ *o*) FLYER (עוֹף *oph*) WHICH (אֲשֶׁר *a'sher*) he~will~be~EAT^(V) (יֵאָכֵל *yey'a'kheyl*) and~he~did~POUR.OUT^(V) (וְשָׁפַךְ *wê'sha'phakh*) AT (אֶת *et*) BLOOD~him (דָּמוֹ *da'mo*) and~he~did~much~ COVER.OVER^(V)~him (וְכִסָּהוּ *wê'khi'sa'hu*) in~DIRT (בֶּעָפָר *be'a'phar*) **RMT:** and each man from the sons of Yisra'eyl, and from the immigrant immigrating in their midst, who will hunt living game or the flyer, will be eaten and he will pour out his blood, and he will cover it over with the dirt[85],

17:14 GIVEN.THAT (כִּי *ki*) SOUL (נֶפֶשׁ *ne'phesh*) ALL (כָּל *kol*) FLESH (בָּשָׂר *ba'sar*) BLOOD~him (דָּמוֹ *da'mo*) in~SOUL~him (בְנַפְשׁוֹ *vê'naph'sho*) HE (הוּא *hu*) and~I~will~SAY^(V) (וָאֹמַר *wa'o'mar*) to~ SON~s (לִבְנֵי *liv'ney*) Yisra'eyl (יִשְׂרָאֵל *yis'ra'eyl*) BLOOD (דַּם *dam*) ALL (כָּל *kol*) FLESH (בָּשָׂר *ba'sar*) NOT (לֹא *lo*) you^(mp)~will~EAT^(V) (תֹאכֵלוּ *to'khey'lu*) GIVEN.THAT (כִּי *ki*) SOUL (נֶפֶשׁ *ne'phesh*) ALL (כָּל *kol*) FLESH (בָּשָׂר *ba'sar*) BLOOD~him (דָּמוֹ *da'mo*) SHE (הִוא *hi*) ALL

---

[85] That is the "dust" of the ground where the blood is poured.

(כָּל kol) EAT^(V)~ing^(mp)~him אֹכְלָיו okh'law) _he~will~be~CUT_^(V) יִכָּרֵת yi'ka'reyt) **RMT:** given that the soul of all flesh is his blood, he is in his soul, and I said to the sons of Yisra'eyl, you will not eat the blood of all flesh, given that the soul of all flesh is blood, anyone eating him will be cut,

17:15 and~ALL (וְכָל wê'khol) SOUL (נֶפֶשׁ ne'phesh) WHICH (אֲשֶׁר a'sher) _she~will~EAT_^(V) תֹּאכַל to'khal) CARCASS (נְבֵלָה nê'vey'lah) and~TORN (וּטְרֵפָה ut'rey'phah) in~NATIVE (בָּאֶזְרָח ba'ez'rahh) and~in~the~IMMIGRANT (וּבַגֵּר u'va'geyr) and~he~did~much~WASH^(V) (וְכִבֶּס wê'khi'bes) GARMENT~s~im (בְּגָדָיו bê'ga'daw) and~he~did~BATHE^(V) (וְרָחַץ wê'ra'hhats) in~the~WATER~s2 (בַּמַּיִם ba'ma'yim) and~he~did~BE.DIRTY^(V) (וְטָמֵא wê'ta'mey) UNTIL (עַד ad) the~EVENING (הָעֶרֶב ah'e'rev) and~he~did~BE.CLEAN^(V) (וְטָהֵר wê'ta'har) **RMT:** and any soul who will eat a carcass and torn, by a native or by the immigrant, he will wash his garments and he will bathe in the waters, and he will be dirty until the evening and then he will be clean,

17:16 and~IF (וְאִם wê'im) NOT (לֹא lo) _he~will~WASH_^(V) yê'kha'beys) and~FLESH~him (וּבְשָׂרוֹ uv'sa'ro) NOT (לֹא lo) _he~will~BATHE_^(V) יִרְחָץ yir'hhats) and~he~did~LIFT.UP^(V) (וְנָשָׂא wê'na'sa) TWISTEDNESS~him (עֲוֹנוֹ a'o'no) **RMT:** but if he will not wash and he will not bathe his flesh, then he will lift up his twistedness,

Chapter 18

18:1 and~he~will~much~SPEAK^(v) (וַיְדַבֵּר wai'da'beyr) **YHWH** (יְהוָה YHWH) TO (אֶל el) Mosheh (מֹשֶׁה mo'sheh) to~>~SAY^(V) לֵאמֹר ley'mor) **RMT:** and **YHWH** spoke to Mosheh saying,

18:2 _I^(ms)~much~SPEAK_^(V) (דַּבֵּר da'beyr) TO (אֶל el) SON~s (בְּנֵי bê'ney) Yisra'eyl (יִשְׂרָאֵל yis'ra'eyl) and~you^(ms)~did~SAY^(V) (וְאָמַרְתָּ wê'a'mar'ta) TO~them^(m) (אֲלֵהֶם a'ley'hem) I (אֲנִי a'ni) **YHWH** (יְהוָה YHWH) Elohiym~you^(mp) (אֱלֹהֵיכֶם e'lo'hey'khem) **RMT:** speak to the sons of Yisra'eyl, and you will say to them, I am **YHWH** your Elohiym.

18:3 like~WORK (כְּמַעֲשֵׂה kê'ma'a'seyh) LAND (אֶרֶץ e'rets) Mits'rayim (מִצְרַיִם mits'ra'yim) WHICH (אֲשֶׁר a'sher) _you^(mp)~did~SETTLE_^(V) (יְשַׁבְתֶּם yê'shav'tem) _in_~her (בָהּ bah) NOT (לֹא lo) _you^(mp)~will~DO_^(V) (תַעֲשׂוּ ta'a'su) and~like~WORK (וּכְמַעֲשֵׂה ukh'ma'a'seyh) LAND (אֶרֶץ e'rets) Kena'an (כְּנַעַן kê'na'an) WHICH (אֲשֶׁר a'sher) I (אֲנִי a'ni) _make~COME_^(V)~ing^(ms) (מֵבִיא me'vi) AT~

you⁽ᵐᵖ⁾ (אֶתְכֶם et'khem) THERE~unto (שָׁמָּה sha'mah) NOT (לֹא lo)
you⁽ᵐᵖ⁾~will~DO⁽ⱽ⁾ (תַעֲשׂוּ ta'a'su) and~in~CUSTOM~s~them⁽ᵐ⁾
(וּבְחֻקֹּתֵיהֶם uv'hhu'qo'tey'hem) NOT (לֹא lo) you⁽ᵐᵖ⁾~will~WALK⁽ⱽ⁾
(תֵלֵכוּ tey'ley'khu) **RMT:** Like the work of the land of Mits'rayim that
you settled in, you will not do, and like the work of the land of
Kena'an that I am making you come unto, you will not do, and you
will not walk in their customs.

18:4 AT (אֶת et) DECISION~s~me (מִשְׁפָּטַי mish'pa'tai) you⁽ᵐᵖ⁾~will~
DO⁽ⱽ⁾ (תַעֲשׂוּ ta'a'su) and~AT (וְאֶת wê'et) CUSTOM~s~me (חֻקֹּתַי
hhu'qo'tai) you⁽ᵐᵖ⁾~will~SAFEGUARD⁽ⱽ⁾ (תִּשְׁמְרוּ tish'me'ru) to~>~
WALK⁽ⱽ⁾ (לָלֶכֶת la'le'khet) in~them⁽ᵐ⁾ (בָּהֶם ba'hem) I (אֲנִי a'ni)
YHWH (יְהוָה YHWH) Elohiym~you⁽ᵐᵖ⁾ (אֱלֹהֵיכֶם e'lo'hey'khem)
RMT: My decisions you will do, and my customs you will safeguard,
to walk in them, I am **YHWH** your Elohiym,

18:5 and~you⁽ᵐᵖ⁾~did~SAFEGUARD⁽ⱽ⁾ (וּשְׁמַרְתֶּם ush'mar'tem) AT (אֶת
et) CUSTOM~s~me (חֻקֹּתַי hhu'qo'tai) and~AT (וְאֶת wê'et)
DECISION~s~me (מִשְׁפָּטַי mish'pa'tai) WHICH (אֲשֶׁר a'sher) he~will~
DO⁽ⱽ⁾ (יַעֲשֶׂה ya'a'seh) AT~them⁽ᵐ⁾ (אֹתָם o'tam) the~HUMAN (הָאָדָם
ha'a'dam) and~he~did~LIVE⁽ⱽ⁾ (וָחַי wa'hhai) in~them⁽ᵐ⁾ (בָּהֶם
ba'hem) I (אֲנִי a'ni) **YHWH** (יְהוָה YHWH) **RMT:** and you will
safeguard my customs and my decisions, the human that does them
will then live in them, I am **YHWH**.

18:6 MAN (אִישׁ ish) MAN (אִישׁ ish) TO (אֶל el) ALL (כָּל kol) KIN
(שְׁאֵר shê'eyr) FLESH~him (בְּשָׂרוֹ bê'sar'o) NOT (לֹא lo) you⁽ᵐᵖ⁾~will~
COME.NEAR⁽ⱽ⁾ (תִקְרְבוּ tiq're'vu) to~>~much~REMOVE.THE.COVER⁽ⱽ⁾
(לְגַלּוֹת lê'ga'lot) NAKEDNESS (עֶרְוָה er'wah) I (אֲנִי a'ni) **YHWH** (יְהוָה
YHWH) **RMT:** Each man belonging to all the kin of his flesh, you will
not come near to remove the cover of nakedness, I am **YHWH**.

18:7 NAKEDNESS (עֶרְוַת er'wat) FATHER~you⁽ᵐˢ⁾ (אָבִיךָ a'vi'kha)
and~NAKEDNESS (וְעֶרְוַת wê'e're'wat) MOTHER~you⁽ᵐˢ⁾ (אִמְּךָ
im'kha) NOT (לֹא lo) you⁽ᵐˢ⁾~will~much~REMOVE.THE.COVER⁽ⱽ⁾
(תְגַלֵּה tê'ga'leyh) MOTHER~you⁽ᵐˢ⁾ (אִמְּךָ im'kha) SHE (הִוא hi) NOT
(לֹא lo) you⁽ᵐˢ⁾~will~much~REMOVE.THE.COVER⁽ⱽ⁾ (תְגַלֶּה tê'ga'leh)
NAKEDNESS~her (עֶרְוָתָהּ er'wa'tah) **RMT:** The nakedness of your
father and the nakedness of your mother, you will not remove the
cover, she is your mother, you will not remove the cover of her
nakedness.

18:8 NAKEDNESS (עֶרְוַת *er'wat*) WOMAN (אֵשֶׁת *ey'shet*) FATHER~
you^(ms) (אָבִיךָ *a'vi'kha*) NOT (לֹא *lo*) you^(ms)~will~much~
REMOVE.THE.COVER^(V) (תְגַלֵּה *tê'ga'leyh*) NAKEDNESS (עֶרְוַת *er'wat*)
FATHER~you^(ms) (אָבִיךָ *a'vi'kha*) SHE (הִוא *hi*) **RMT:** The nakedness of
the woman of your father you will not remove the cover, she is the
nakedness of your father.

18:9 NAKEDNESS (עֶרְוַת *er'wat*) SISTER~you^(ms) (אֲחוֹתְךָ *a'hhot'kha*)
DAUGHTER (בַת *vat*) FATHER~you^(ms) (אָבִיךָ *a'vi'kha*) OR (אוֹ *o*)
DAUGHTER (בַת *vat*) MOTHER~you^(ms) (אִמֶּךָ *i'me'kha*) KINDRED
(מוֹלֶדֶת *mo'le'det*) HOUSE (בַּיִת *ba'yit*) OR (אוֹ *o*) KINDRED (מוֹלֶדֶת
mo'le'det) OUTSIDE (חוּץ *hhuts*) NOT (לֹא *lo*) you^(ms)~will~much~
REMOVE.THE.COVER^(V) (תְגַלֶּה *tê'ga'leh*) NAKEDNESS~them^(f)
er'wa'tan) **RMT:** The nakedness of your sister, the daughter of your
father, or the daughter of your mother, the kindred of the house or
the kindred of outside, you will not remove the cover of their
nakedness.

18:10 NAKEDNESS (עֶרְוַת *er'wat*) DAUGHTER (בַּת *bat*) SON~you^(ms)
(בִּנְךָ *bin'kha*) OR (אוֹ *o*) DAUGHTER (בַת *vat*) DAUGHTER~you^(ms)
(בִּתְּךָ *bit'kha*) NOT (לֹא *lo*) you^(ms)~will~much~
REMOVE.THE.COVER^(V) (תְגַלֶּה *tê'ga'leh*) NAKEDNESS~them^(f)
er'wa'tan) GIVEN.THAT (כִּי *ki*) NAKEDNESS~you^(ms) (עֶרְוָתְךָ
er'wat'kha) THEY^(f) (הֵנָּה *heyn'nah*) **RMT:** The nakedness of the
daughter of your son or the daughter of your daughter, you will not
remove the cover of their nakedness, given that they are your
nakedness.

18:11 NAKEDNESS (עֶרְוַת *er'wat*) DAUGHTER (בַּת *bat*) WOMAN
(אֵשֶׁת *ey'shet*) FATHER~you^(ms) (אָבִיךָ *a'vi'kha*) KINDRED (מוֹלֶדֶת
mo'le'det) FATHER~you^(ms) (אָבִיךָ *a'vi'kha*) SISTER~you^(ms) (אֲחוֹתְךָ
a'hhot'kha) SHE (הִוא *hi*) NOT (לֹא *lo*) you^(ms)~will~much~
REMOVE.THE.COVER^(V) (תְגַלֶּה *tê'ga'leh*) NAKEDNESS~her (עֶרְוָתָהּ
er'wa'tah) **RMT:** The nakedness of the daughter of the woman of
your father, kindred of your father, she is your sister, you will not
remove the cover of her nakedness.

18:12 NAKEDNESS (עֶרְוַת *er'wat*) SISTER (אֲחוֹת *a'hhot*) FATHER~
you^(ms) (אָבִיךָ *a'vi'kha*) NOT (לֹא *lo*) you^(ms)~will~much~
REMOVE.THE.COVER^(V) (תְגַלֵּה *tê'ga'leyh*) KIN (שְׁאֵר *shê'eyr*)
FATHER~you^(ms) (אָבִיךָ *a'vi'kha*) SHE (הִוא *hi*) **RMT:** The nakedness of
the sister of your father, you will not remove the cover, she is the kin
of your father.

18:13 <u>NAKEDNESS</u> (עֶרְוַת *er'wat*) <u>SISTER</u> (אֲחוֹת *a'hhot*) <u>MOTHER~</u>
<u>you</u>^(ms) (אִמְּךָ *im'kha*) <u>NOT</u> (לֹא *lo*) *you^(ms)~will~much~*
<u>REMOVE.THE.COVER</u>^(V) (תְגַלֵּה *tê'ga'leyh*) <u>GIVEN.THAT</u> (כִּי *ki*) <u>KIN</u>
(שְׁאֵר *shê'eyr*) <u>MOTHER~you</u>^(ms) (אִמְּךָ *im'kha*) <u>SHE</u> (הִוא *hi*)
RMT: The nakedness of the sister of your mother, you will not
remove the cover, given that she is kin of your mother.

18:14 <u>NAKEDNESS</u> (עֶרְוַת *er'wat*) <u>BROTHER~of</u> (אֲחִי *a'hhi*) <u>FATHER~</u>
<u>you</u>^(ms) (אָבִיךָ *a'vi'kha*) <u>NOT</u> (לֹא *lo*) *you^(ms)~will~much~*
<u>REMOVE.THE.COVER</u>^(V) (תְגַלֵּה *tê'ga'leyh*) <u>TO</u> (אֶל *el*) <u>WOMAN~him</u>
(אִשְׁתּוֹ *ish'to*) <u>NOT</u> (לֹא *lo*) *you^(ms)~will~COME.NEAR*^(V) (תִקְרָב
teq'rav) <u>AUNT~you</u>^(ms) (דֹדָתְךָ *do'dat'kha*) <u>SHE</u> (הִוא *hi*) **RMT:** The
nakedness of the brother of your father, you will not remove the
cover, you will not come near to his woman, she is your aunt.

18:15 <u>NAKEDNESS</u> (עֶרְוַת *er'wat*) <u>DAUGHTER-IN-LAW~you</u>^(ms) (כַּלָּתְךָ
ka'lat'kha) <u>NOT</u> (לֹא *lo*) *you^(ms)~will~much~*REMOVE.THE.COVER^(V)
(תְגַלֵּה *tê'ga'leyh*) <u>WOMAN</u> (אֵשֶׁת *ey'shet*) <u>SON~you</u>^(ms) (בִּנְךָ *bin'kha*)
<u>SHE</u> (הִוא *hi*) <u>NOT</u> (לֹא *lo*) *you^(ms)~will~much~*REMOVE.THE.COVER^(V)
(תְגַלֵּה *tê'ga'leh*) <u>NAKEDNESS~her</u> (עֶרְוָתָהּ *er'wa'tah*) **RMT:** The
nakedness of your daughter-in-law, you will not remove the cover,
she is the woman of your son, you will not remove the cover of her
nakedness.

18:16 <u>NAKEDNESS</u> (עֶרְוַת *er'wat*) <u>WOMAN</u> (אֵשֶׁת *ey'shet*) <u>BROTHER~</u>
<u>you</u>^(ms) (אָחִיךָ *a'hhi'kha*) <u>NOT</u> (לֹא *lo*) *you^(ms)~will~much~*
<u>REMOVE.THE.COVER</u>^(V) (תְגַלֵּה *tê'ga'leyh*) <u>NAKEDNESS</u> (עֶרְוַת *er'wat*)
<u>BROTHER~you</u>^(ms) (אָחִיךָ *a'hhi'kha*) <u>SHE</u> (הִוא *hi*) **RMT:** The
nakedness of the woman of your brother, you will not remove the
cover, she is the nakedness of your brother.

18:17 <u>NAKEDNESS</u> (עֶרְוַת *er'wat*) <u>WOMAN</u> (אִשָּׁה *i'shah*) <u>and~</u>
<u>DAUGHTER~her</u> (וּבִתָּהּ *u'vi'tah*) <u>NOT</u> (לֹא *lo*) *you^(ms)~will~much~*
<u>REMOVE.THE.COVER</u>^(V) (תְגַלֵּה *tê'ga'leyh*) <u>AT</u> (אֶת *et*) <u>DAUGHTER</u> (בַּת
bat) <u>SON~her</u> (בְּנָהּ *bê'nah*) <u>and~AT</u> (וְאֶת *wê'et*) <u>DAUGHTER</u> (בַּת
bat) <u>DAUGHTER~her</u> (בִּתָּהּ *bi'tah*) <u>NOT</u> (לֹא *lo*) *you^(ms)~will~TAKE*^(V)
(תִקַּח *ti'qahh*) *to~>~much~*REMOVE.THE.COVER^(V) (לְגַלּוֹת *lê'ga'lot*)
<u>NAKEDNESS~her</u> (עֶרְוָתָהּ *er'wa'tah*) <u>KIN</u> (שַׁאֲרָה *sha'a'rah*) <u>THEY</u>^(f)
(הֵנָּה *heyn'nah*) <u>MISCHIEF</u> (זִמָּה *zi'mah*) <u>SHE</u> (הִוא *hi*) **RMT:** The
nakedness of a woman and her daughter, you will not remove the
cover, the daughter of her son and the daughter of her daughter,
you will not take to remove the cover of her nakedness, they are kin,
she is mischief,

18:18 and~WOMAN (וְאִשָּׁה *wê'i'shah*) TO (אֶל *el*) SISTER~her (אֲחֹתָהּ *a'hho'tah*) NOT (לֹא *lo*) you(ms)~will~TAKE(V) (תִקָּח *ti'qahh*) to~>~ PRESS.IN(V) (לִצְרֹר *lits'ror*) to~>~much~REMOVE.THE.COVER(V) (לְגַלּוֹת *lê'ga'lot*) NAKEDNESS~her (עֶרְוָתָהּ *er'wa'tah*) UPON~her (עָלֶיהָ *a'ley'ah*) in~LIVING~her (בְּחַיֶּיהָ *bê'hha'yey'ah*) **RMT:** and you will not take a woman to her sister to press in to remove the cover of her nakedness, upon her with her living,[86]

18:19 and~TO (וְאֶל *wê'el*) WOMAN (אִשָּׁה *i'shah*) in~REMOVAL (בְּנִדַּת *bê'ni'dat*) DIRTY~her (טֻמְאָתָהּ *tu'me'a'tah*) NOT (לֹא *lo*) you(ms)~will~COME.NEAR(V) (תִקְרַב *tiq'rav*) to~>~much~ REMOVE.THE.COVER(V) (לְגַלּוֹת *lê'ga'lot*) NAKEDNESS~her (עֶרְוָתָהּ *er'wa'tah*) **RMT:** and you will not come near to a woman in the removal of her dirtiness, to remove the cover of her nakedness,

18:20 and~TO (וְאֶל *wê'el*) WOMAN (אֵשֶׁת *ey'shet*) NEIGHBOR~ you(ms) (עֲמִיתְךָ *a'mit'kha*) NOT (לֹא *lo*) you(ms)~will~GIVE(V) (תִתֵּן *ti'teyn*) COPULATION~you(ms) (שְׁכָבְתְּךָ *shê'khav'te'kha*) to~SEED (לְזָרַע *lê'za'ra*) to~DIRTY~her (לְטָמְאָה *lê'tam'ah*) in~her (בָהּ *vah*) **RMT:** and you will not give copulation for seed to a woman of your neighbor, for her dirtiness is in her,

18:21 and~SEED~you(ms) (וּמִזַּרְעֲךָ *u'mi'zar'a'kha*) NOT (לֹא *lo*) you(ms)~will~GIVE(V) (תִתֵּן *ti'teyn*) to~>~make~CROSS.OVER(V) (לְהַעֲבִיר *lê'ha'a'vir*) to~the~Molekh (לַמֹּלֶךְ *la'mo'lekh*) and~NOT (וְלֹא *wê'lo*) you(ms)~will~much~DRILL(V) (תְחַלֵּל *tê'hha'leyl*) AT (אֶת *et*) TITLE (שֵׁם *sheym*) Elohiym~you(ms) (אֱלֹהֶיךָ *e'lo'hey'kha*) I (אֲנִי *a'ni*) **YHWH** (יְהוָה *YHWH*) **RMT:** and you will not give your seed to be made to cross over to Molekh, and you will not defile the title of your Elohiym, I am **YHWH**,

18:22 and~AT (וְאֶת *wê'et*) MALE (זָכָר *za'khar*) NOT (לֹא *lo*) you(ms)~ will~LIE.DOWN(V) (תִשְׁכַּב *tish'kav*) LYING.PLACE~s (מִשְׁכְּבֵי *mish'ke'vey*)[87] WOMAN (אִשָּׁה *i'shah*) DISGUSTING (תּוֹעֵבָה *to'ey'vah*) SHE (הוּא *hi*) **RMT:** and with a male you will not lie down in the lying places of a woman, this is disgusting,

---

[86] An alternate translation of this verse may be, "and you will not take a woman in addition to her sister to be her rival, to remove the cover of her nakedness, while her sister is still living,"

[87] A preposition like "on" or "in" appears to be missing before the "lying places of a woman."

18:23 and~in~ALL (וּבְכָל *uv'khol*) BEAST (בְּהֵמָה *bê'hey'mah*) NOT (לֹא *lo*) you(ms)~will~GIVE(V) (תִּתֵּן *ti'teyn*) COPULATION~you(ms) (שְׁכָבְתְּךָ *shê'khav'te'kha*) to~DIRTY~her (לְטָמְאָה *lê'tam'ah*) in~her (בָהּ *vah*) and~WOMAN (וְאִשָּׁה *wê'i'shah*) NOT (לֹא *lo*) you(ms)~will~STAND(V) (תַעֲמֹד *ta'a'mod*) to~FACE~s (לִפְנֵי *liph'ney*) BEAST (בְהֵמָה *vê'hey'mah*) to~>~BE.SQUARE(V)~her (לְרִבְעָהּ *lê'riv'ah*) UNNATURAL.MIX (תֶּבֶל *te'vel*) HE (הוּא *hu*) **RMT:** and you will not give your copulation in any beast, for her dirtiness is in her, and you will not stand a woman to the face of a beast for her to be squared[88], this is an unnatural mix,

18:24 DO.NOT (אַל *al*) you(mp)~will~self~BE.DIRTY(V) (תִּטַּמְּאוּ *ti'tam'u*) in~ALL (בְּכָל *bê'khol*) THESE (אֵלֶּה *ey'leh*) GIVEN.THAT (כִּי *ki*) in~ALL (בְכָל *vê'khol*) THESE (אֵלֶּה *ey'leh*) they~did~be~BE.DIRTY(V) (נִטְמְאוּ *nit'me'u*) the~NATION~s (הַגּוֹיִם *ha'go'yim*) WHICH (אֲשֶׁר *a'sher*) ! (אֲנִי *a'ni*) much~SEND(V)~ing(ms) (מְשַׁלֵּחַ *mê'sha'ley'ahh*) from~FACE~s~you(mp) (מִפְּנֵיכֶם *mi'pe'ney'khem*) **RMT:** and you will not make yourself dirty with all of these, given that with all these, the nations are dirty, which I am sending from your faces,

18:25 and~she~will~BE.DIRTY(V) (וַתִּטְמָא *wa'tit'ma*) the~LAND (הָאָרֶץ *ha'a'rets*) and~I~will~REGISTER(V) (וָאֶפְקֹד *wa'eph'qod*) TWISTEDNESS~her (עֲוֺנָהּ *a'o'nah*) UPON~her (עָלֶיהָ *a'ley'ah*) and~she~will~much~VOMIT(V) (וַתָּקִא *wa'ta'qi*) the~LAND (הָאָרֶץ *ha'a'rets*) AT (אֶת *et*) SETTLE(V)~ing(mp)~her (יֹשְׁבֶיהָ *yosh'vey'ah*) **RMT:** and the land was dirty, and I registered her twistedness upon her, and the land vomited her settlers,

18:26 and~you(mp)~did~SAFEGUARD(V) (וּשְׁמַרְתֶּם *ush'mar'tem*) YOU(mp) (אַתֶּם *a'tem*) AT (אֶת *et*) CUSTOM~s~me (חֻקֹּתַי *hhu'qo'tai*) and~AT (וְאֶת *wê'et*) DECISION~s~me (מִשְׁפָּטַי *mish'pa'tai*) and~NOT (וְלֹא *wê'lo*) you(mp)~will~DO(V) (תַעֲשׂוּ *ta'a'su*) from~ALL (מִכֹּל *mi'kol*) the~DISGUSTING~s (הַתּוֹעֵבֹת *ha'to'ey'vot*) the~THESE (הָאֵלֶּה *ha'ey'leh*) the~NATIVE (הָאֶזְרָח *ha'ez'rahh*) and~the~IMMIGRANT (וְהַגֵּר *wê'ha'geyr*) the~IMMIGRATE(V)~ing(ms) (הַגָּר *ha'gar*) in~MIDST~you(mp) (בְּתוֹכְכֶם *bê'tokh'khem*) **RMT:** and you, you will safeguard my customs and my decisions, and you will not do any of these disgusting things, the native and the immigrant immigrating in your midst,

---

[88] Meaning to be "on all fours" for procreation.

18:27 <u>GIVEN.THAT</u> (כִּי *ki*) <u>AT</u> (אֶת *et*) <u>ALL</u> (כָּל *kol*) the~
<u>DISGUSTING~s</u> (הַתּוֹעֵבֹת *ha'to'ey'vot*) the~THESE (הָאֵל *ha'eyl*) they~
<u>did~DO</u>^(V) (עָשׂוּ *a'su*) <u>MAN~s</u> (אַנְשֵׁי *an'shey*) the~LAND (הָאָרֶץ
ha'a'rets) <u>WHICH</u> (אֲשֶׁר *a'sher*) to~FACE~s~you^(mp) (לִפְנֵיכֶם
liph'ney'khem) and~she~will~BE.DIRTY^(V) (וַתִּטְמָא *wa'tit'ma*) the~
LAND (הָאָרֶץ *ha'a'rets*) **RMT:** given that all these disgusting things
the men of the land, which are to your faces, did, and the land will
be dirty,

18:28 <u>and~NOT</u> (וְלֹא *wê'lo*) she~will~make~VOMIT^(V) (תָקִיא *ta'qi*)
the~LAND (הָאָרֶץ *ha'a'rets*) AT~you^(mp) (אֶתְכֶם *et'khem*) in~much~
<u>DIRTY~you</u>^(mp) (בְּטַמַּאֲכֶם *bê'ta'ma'a'khem*) <u>AT~her</u> (אֹתָהּ *o'tah*) <u>like~</u>
<u>WHICH</u> (כַּאֲשֶׁר *ka'a'sheyr*) she~did~VOMIT^(V) (קָאָה *qa'ah*) <u>AT</u> (אֶת
et) the~NATION (הַגּוֹי *ha'goi*) <u>WHICH</u> (אֲשֶׁר *a'sher*) to~FACE~s~
you^(mp) (לִפְנֵיכֶם *liph'ney'khem*) **RMT:** and the land will not vomit you
when you make her dirty, like when she vomited the nation which is
to your faces,

18:29 <u>GIVEN.THAT</u> (כִּי *ki*) <u>ALL</u> (כָּל *kol*) <u>WHICH</u> (אֲשֶׁר *a'sher*) he~will~
<u>DO</u>^(V) (יַעֲשֶׂה *ya'a'seh*) from~ALL (מִכֹּל *mi'kol*) the~DISGUSTING~s
(הַתּוֹעֵבֹת *ha'to'ey'vot*)[89] the~THESE (הָאֵלֶּה *ha'ey'leh*) and~they~
<u>did~be~CUT</u>^(V) (וְנִכְרְתוּ *wê'nikh're'tu*) the~SOUL~s (הַנְּפָשׁוֹת
han'pha'shot) the~DO^(V)~ing^(fp) (הָעֹשֹׂת *ha'o'sot*) from~INSIDE (מִקֶּרֶב
mi'qe'rev) PEOPLE~them^(m) (עַמָּם *a'mam*) **RMT:** given that anyone
who will do all these disgusting things, then the souls doing this will
be cut from inside their people,

18:30 and~you^(mp)~did~SAFEGUARD^(V) (וּשְׁמַרְתֶּם *ush'mar'tem*) <u>AT</u>
(אֶת *et*) CHARGE~me (מִשְׁמַרְתִּי *mish'ma're'ti*) to~EXCEPT (לְבִלְתִּי
lê'vil'ti) >~DO^(V) (עֲשׂוֹת *a'sot*) from~CUSTOM~s (מֵחֻקּוֹת
mey'hhu'qot) the~DISGUSTING~s (הַתּוֹעֵבֹת *ha'to'ey'vot*) <u>WHICH</u>
(אֲשֶׁר *a'sher*) they~did~be~DO^(V) (נַעֲשׂוּ *na'a'su*) to~FACE~s~you^(mp)
(לִפְנֵיכֶם *liph'ney'khem*) and~NOT (וְלֹא *wê'lo*) you^(mp)~will~make~
<u>self~BE.DIRTY</u>^(V) (תִטַּמְּאוּ *ti'tam'u*) in~them^(m) (בָּהֶם *ba'hem*) <u>I</u> (אֲנִי
a'ni) **YHWH** (יְהוָה *YHWH*) Elohiym~you^(mp) (אֱלֹהֵיכֶם *e'lo'hey'khem*)
RMT: and you will safeguard my charge by not doing these
disgusting customs, which have been done to your faces, and you
will not make yourself dirty in them, I am **YHWH** your Elohiym,

---

[89] *Leningrad Codex:* התועבת

135

Chapter 19

19:1 *and~he~will~much~SPEAK*(V) (וַיְדַבֵּר *wai'da'beyr*) **YHWH** (יְהוָה *YHWH*) TO (אֶל *el*) Mosheh (מֹשֶׁה *mo'sheh*) *to~>~SAY*(V) (לֵּאמֹר *ley'mor*) **RMT:** and YHWH spoke to Mosheh saying,

19:2 *!(ms)~much~SPEAK*(V) (דַּבֵּר *da'beyr*) TO (אֶל *el*) ALL (כָּל *kol*) COMPANY (עֲדַת *a'dat*) SON~s (בְּנֵי *bê'ney*) Yisra'eyl (יִשְׂרָאֵל *yis'ra'eyl*) *and~you(ms)~did~SAY*(V) (וְאָמַרְתָּ *wê'a'mar'ta*) TO~them(m) (אֲלֵהֶם *a'ley'hem*) UNIQUE~s (קְדֹשִׁים *qê'do'shim*) *you(mp)~will~EXIST*(V) (תִּהְיוּ *tih'yu*) GIVEN.THAT (כִּי *ki*) UNIQUE (קָדֹושׁ *qa'dosh*) I (אֲנִי *a'ni*) **YHWH** (יְהוָה *YHWH*) Elohiym~you(mp) (אֱלֹהֵיכֶם *e'lo'hey'khem*) **RMT:** speak to all the company of the sons of Yisra'eyl and you will say to them, you will exist as unique ones, given that I, **YHWH** your Elohiym, am unique.

19:3 MAN (אִישׁ *ish*) MOTHER~him (אִמּוֹ *i'mo*) *and~FATHER~him* (וְאָבִיו *wê'a'viw*) *you(mp)~will~FEAR*(V) (תִּירָאוּ *ti'ra'u*) and~AT (וְאֶת *wê'et*) CEASING~s~me (שַׁבְּתֹתַי *sha'be'to'tai*) *you(mp)~will~SAFEGUARD*(V) (תִּשְׁמֹרוּ *tish'moru*) I (אֲנִי *a'ni*) **YHWH** (יְהוָה *YHWH*) Elohiym~you(mp) (אֱלֹהֵיכֶם *e'lo'hey'khem*) **RMT:** Each of you will fear his mother and his father, you will safeguard my ceasings, I am **YHWH** your Elohiym.

19:4 DO.NOT (אַל *al*) *you(mp)~will~TURN*(V) (תִּפְנוּ *tiph'nu*) TO (אֶל *el*) the~WORTHLESS~s (הָאֱלִילִים *ha'e'li'lim*)[90] and~Elohiym (וֵאלֹהֵי *wey'lo'hey*) CAST.IMAGE (מַסֵּכָה *ma'sey'khah*) NOT (לֹא *lo*) *you(mp)~will~DO*(V) (תַעֲשׂוּ *ta'a'su*) *to~you(mp)* (לָכֶם *la'khem*) I (אֲנִי *a'ni*) **YHWH** (יְהוָה *YHWH*) Elohiym~you(mp) (אֱלֹהֵיכֶם *e'lo'hey'khem*) **RMT:** You will not turn to the worthless ones and you will not make an Elohiym of a cast image for yourself, I am **YHWH** your Elohiym,

19:5 *and~GIVEN.THAT* (וְכִי *wê'khi*) *you(ms)~will~SACRIFICE*(V)~him (תִזְבְּחוּ *tiz'be'hhu*) SACRIFICE (זֶבַח *ze'vahh*) OFFERING.OF.RESTITUTION~s (שְׁלָמִים *shê'la'mim*) *to~YHWH* (לַיהוָה *la'YHWH*) *to~SELF-WILL~you(mp)* (לִרְצֹנְכֶם *lir'tson'khem*) *you(mp)~will~SACRIFICE*(V)~him (תִּזְבָּחֻהוּ *tiz'ba'hhu'hu*) **RMT:** and, given that you sacrifice him as a sacrifice of offering of restitutions to **YHWH**, by the will of yourself you will sacrifice him.

19:6 in~DAY (בְּיוֹם *bê'yom*) SACRIFICE~you(mp) (זִבְחֲכֶם *ziv'hha'khem*) *he~will~be~EAT*(V) (יֵאָכֵל *yey'a'kheyl*) and~from~MORROW (וּמִמָּחֳרָת

---

[90] *Leningrad Codex:* האלילם

u'mi'ma'hha'rat) and~the~*be*~LEAVE.BEHIND[(V)]~*ing*[(ms)] (וְהַנּוֹתָר
wê'ha'no'tar) UNTIL (עַד *ad*) DAY (יוֹם *yom*) the~THIRD הַשְּׁלִישִׁי
hash'li'shi) in~the~FIRE (בָּאֵשׁ *ba'eysh*) he~will~*be*~CREMATE[(V)]
(יִשָּׂרֵף *yi'sa'reyph*) **RMT:** In the day of your sacrifice he will be eaten,
and on the morrow, and what is being left behind until the third day
will be cremated in the fire,

19:7 and~IF (וְאִם *wê'im*) the~>~*be*~EAT[(V)] (הֵאָכֹל *hey'a'khol*) he~
will~*be*~EAT[(V)] (יֵאָכֵל *yey'a'kheyl*) in~the~DAY (בַּיּוֹם *ba'yom*) the~
THIRD (הַשְּׁלִישִׁי *hash'li'shi*) FOUL (פִּגּוּל *pi'gul*) HE (הוּא *hu*) NOT (לֹא
lo) he~will~*be*~ACCEPT[(V)] (יֵרָצֶה *yey'ra'tseh*) **RMT:** and if he will
surely be eaten in the third day, he is foul, he will not be accepted,

19:8 and~EAT[(V)]~*ing*[(mp)]~him (וְאֹכְלָיו *wê'okh'law*) TWISTEDNESS~him
(עֲוֹנוֹ *a'o'no*) he~will~LIFT.UP[(V)] (יִשָּׂא *yi'sa*) GIVEN.THAT (כִּי *ki*) AT
(אֶת *et*) SPECIAL (קֹדֶשׁ *qo'desh*) YHWH (יְהוָה *YHWH*) he~did~much~
DRILL[(V)] (חִלֵּל *hhi'leyl*) and~she~did~*be*~CUT[(V)] (וְנִכְרְתָה
wê'nikh're'tah) the~SOUL (הַנֶּפֶשׁ *ha'ne'phesh*) the~SHE (הַהִוא *ha'hi*)
from~PEOPLE~s~her (מֵעַמֶּיהָ *mey'a'mey'ah*) **RMT:** and the ones
eating him will have his twistedness lifted up, given that he defiled
the specialness of **YHWH**, that soul will be cut from her peoples,

19:9 and~in~>~SEVER[(V)]~you[(mp)] (וּבְקֻצְרְכֶם *uv'quts're'khem*) AT (אֶת
et) HARVEST (קְצִיר *qê'tsir*) LAND~you[(mp)] (אַרְצְכֶם *ar'tse'khem*) NOT
(לֹא *lo*) you[(ms)]~will~much~FINISH[(V)] (תְכַלֶּה *tê'kha'leh*) EDGE (פְּאַת
pê'at) FIELD~you[(ms)] (שָׂדְךָ *saa'kha*) to~>~SEVER[(V)] (לִקְצֹר *liq'tsor*)
and~GLEANINGS (וְלֶקֶט *wê'le'qet*) HARVEST~you[(ms)] (קְצִירְךָ
qê'tsir'kha) NOT (לֹא *lo*) you[(ms)]~will~much~PICK.UP[(V)] (תְלַקֵּט
tê'la'qeyt) **RMT:** and with your severing[91] of the harvest in your land,
you will not finish the edge of your field to sever it, and the gleanings
of your harvest you will not pick up,

19:10 and~VINEYARD~you[(ms)] (וְכַרְמְךָ *wê'khar'me'kha*) NOT (לֹא *lo*)
you[(ms)]~will~much~ROLL[(V)] (תְעוֹלֵל *tê'o'leyl*) and~FALLEN.GRAPE
(וּפֶרֶט *u'phe'ret*) VINEYARD~you[(ms)] (כַּרְמְךָ *kar'me'kha*) NOT (לֹא *lo*)
you[(ms)]~will~much~PICK.UP[(V)] (תְלַקֵּט *tê'la'qeyt*) to~AFFLICTION (לֶעָנִי
le'a'ni) and~to~IMMIGRANT (וְלַגֵּר *wê'la'geyr*) you[(ms)]~will~LEAVE[(V)]
(תַּעֲזֹב *ta'a'zov*) AT~them[(m)] (אֹתָם *o'tam*) I (אֲנִי *a'ni*) YHWH (יְהוָה
YHWH) Elohiym~you[(mp)] (אֱלֹהֵיכֶם *e'lo'hey'khem*) **RMT:** and your
vineyard you will not glean, and the fallen grapes of your vineyard

---

[91] That is the "reaping."

you will not pick up, you will leave them for the afflicted and for the immigrant, I am **YHWH** your Elohiym.

19:11 <u>NOT</u> (לֹא *lo*) <u>*you(ms)~will~STEAL(V)*</u> (תִּגְנֹבוּ *tig'no'vu*) <u>and~NOT</u> (וְלֹא *wê'lo*) <u>*you(mp)~will~much~DENY(V)*</u> (תְּכַחֲשׁוּ *tê'kha'hha'shu*) <u>and~NOT</u> (וְלֹא *wê'lo*) <u>*you(mp)~will~much~DEAL.FALSELY(V)*</u> (תְשַׁקְּרוּ *tê'shaq'ru*) <u>MAN</u> (אִישׁ *ish*) <u>in~the~NEIGHBOR~him</u> (בַּעֲמִיתוֹ *ba'a'mi'to*) **RMT:** You will not steal and you will not deal falsely and you will not deal falsely a man with his neighbor,

19:12 <u>and~NOT</u> (וְלֹא *wê'lo*) <u>*you(mp)~will~be~SWEAR(V)*</u> (תִשָּׁבְעוּ *ti'sha'va'u*) <u>in~TITLE~me</u> (בִשְׁמִי *vish'mi*) <u>to~the~FALSE</u> (לַשָּׁקֶר *la'sha'qer*) <u>and~*you(ms)~did~much~DRILL(V)*</u> (וְחִלַּלְתָּ *wê'hhi'lal'ta*) <u>AT</u> (אֶת *et*) <u>TITLE</u> (שֵׁם *sheym*) <u>Elohiym~you(ms)</u> (אֱלֹהֶיךָ *e'lo'hey'kha*) <u>I</u> (אֲנִי *a'ni*) **YHWH** (יְהֹוָה *YHWH*) **RMT:** and you will not swear with my title to falseness, and you will not defile my title Elohiym, I am **YHWH**.

19:13 <u>NOT</u> (לֹא *lo*) <u>*you(ms)~will~OPPRESS(V)*</u> (תַעֲשֹׁק *ta'a'shoq*) <u>AT</u> (אֶת *et*) <u>COMPANION~you(ms)</u> (רֵעֲךָ *rey'a'kha*) <u>and~NOT</u> (וְלֹא *wê'lo*) <u>*you(ms)~will~PLUCK.AWAY(V)*</u> (תִגְזֹל *tig'zol*) <u>NOT</u> (לֹא *lo*) <u>*you(ms)~will~STAY.THE.NIGHT(V)*</u> (תָלִין *ta'lin*) <u>MAKE(V)~ed(fs)</u> (פְּעֻלַּת *pê'u'lat*) <u>HIRELING</u> (שָׂכִיר *sa'khir*) <u>AT~you(ms)</u> (אִתְּךָ *it'kha*) <u>UNTIL</u> (עַד *ad*) <u>MORNING</u> (בֹּקֶר *bo'qer*) **RMT:** You will not oppress your companion and you will not pluck away[92], you will not stay the night[93] what is made[94] by your hireling until morning.

19:14 <u>NOT</u> (לֹא *lo*) <u>*you(ms)~will~much~BELITTLE(V)*</u> (תְקַלֵּל *tê'qa'leyl*) <u>SILENT</u> (חֵרֵשׁ *hhey'reysh*) <u>and~to~FACE~s</u> (וְלִפְנֵי *wê'liph'ney*) <u>BLIND</u> (עִוֵּר *i'weyr*) <u>NOT</u> (לֹא *lo*) <u>*you(ms)~will~GIVE(V)*</u> (תִתֵּן *ti'teyn*) <u>STUMBLING.BLOCK</u> (מִכְשֹׁל *mikh'shol*) <u>and~*you(ms)~did~FEAR(V)*</u> (וְיָרֵאתָ *wê'ya'rey'ta*) <u>from~Elohiym~you(ms)</u> (מֵאֱלֹהֶיךָ *mey'e'lo'hey'kha*) <u>I</u> (אֲנִי *a'ni*) **YHWH** (יְהֹוָה *YHWH*) **RMT:** You will not belittle a silent one, and to the face of blind you will not place a stumbling block, and you will fear your Elohiym, I am **YHWH**.

19:15 <u>NOT</u> (לֹא *lo*) <u>*you(mp)~will~DO(V)*</u> (תַעֲשׂוּ *ta'a'su*) <u>WICKED</u> (עָוֶל *a'wel*) <u>in~the~DECISION</u> (בַּמִּשְׁפָּט *ba'mish'pat*) <u>NOT</u> (לֹא *lo*) <u>*you(ms)~will~LIFT.UP(V)*</u> (תִשָּׂא *ti'sa*) <u>FACE~s</u> (פְנֵי *phê'ney*) <u>HELPLESS</u> (דָל *dal*)

---

[92] That is to "steal."

[93] That is to "keep for the night."

[94] That is the wages "made" by the hireling.

and~NOT (וְלֹא) *wê'lo*) you(ms)~will~GIVE.HONOR(V) (תֶהְדַּר *teh'dar*) FACE~s (פְּנֵי *pê'ney*) GREAT (גָדוֹל *ga'dol*) in~STEADFAST (בְּצֶדֶק *bê'tse'deq*) you(ms)~will~DECIDE(V) (תִּשְׁפֹּט *tish'pot*) NEIGHBOR~ you(ms) (עֲמִיתֶךָ *a'mi'te'kha*) **RMT:** You will not do wickedness in the decision, you will not lift up the face of the helpless and you will not give honor to the face of the great one, with steadfastness you will decide your neighbor.

19:16 NOT (לֹא *lo*) you(ms)~will~WALK(V) (תֵלֵךְ *tey'leykh*) TALEBEARER (רָכִיל *ra'khil*) in~PEOPLE~s~you(Ts) (בְּעַמֶּיךָ *bê'a'mey'kha*) NOT (לֹא *lo*) you(ms)~will~STAND(V) (תַעֲמֹד *ta'a'mod*) UPON (עַל *al*) BLOOD (דַּם *dam*) COMPANION~you(ms) (רֵעֶךָ *rey'e'kha*) I (אֲנִי *a'ni*) YHWH (יְהוָה *YHWH*) **RMT:** You will not walk as a talebearer with your people, you will not stand upon the blood of your companion, I am **YHWH**.

19:17 NOT (לֹא *lo*) you(ms)~will~HATE(V) (תִשְׂנָא *tis'na*) AT (אֶת *et*) BROTHER~you(ms) (אָחִיךָ *a'hhi'kha*) in~HEART~you(ms) (בִּלְבָבֶךָ *bil'va've'kha*) >~make~REBUKE(V) (הוֹכֵחַ *ho'khey'ahh*) you(ms)~will~ make~REBUKE(V) (תוֹכִיחַ *to'khi'ahh*) AT (אֶת *et*) NEIGHBOR~you(ms) (עֲמִיתֶךָ *a'mi'te'kha*) and~NOT (וְלֹא *wê'lo*) you(ms)~will~LIFT.UP(V) (תִשָּׂא *ti'sa*) UPON~him (עָלָיו *a'law*) FAILURE (חֵטְא *hheyt*) **RMT:** You will not hate your brother in your heart, you will certainly make a rebuking of your neighbor, and you will not lift up upon him failure,

19:18 NOT (לֹא *lo*) you(ms)~will~AVENGE(V) (תִקֹם *ti'qom*) and~NOT (וְלֹא *wê'lo*) you(ms)~will~KEEP(V) (תִטֹּר *ti'tor*) AT (אֶת *et*) SON~s (בְּנֵי *bê'ney*) PEOPLE~you(ms) (עַמֶּךָ *a'me'kha*) and~you(ms)~did~LOVE(V) (וְאָהַבְתָּ *wê'a'hav'ta*) to~COMPANION~you(ms) (לְרֵעֲךָ *lê'rey'a'kha*) like~THAT.ONE~you(ms) (כָּמוֹךָ *ka'mo'kha*) I (אֲנִי *a'ni*) YHWH (יְהוָה *YHWH*) **RMT:** and you will not avenge and you will not keep[95] the sons of your people, and you will love your companion like one of you, I am **YHWH**.

19:19 AT (אֶת *et*) CUSTOM~s~me (חֻקֹּתַי *hhu'qo'tai*) you(mp)~will~ SAFEGUARD(V) (תִּשְׁמֹרוּ *tish'moru*) BEAST~you(ms) (בְּהֶמְתְּךָ

---

[95] The Hebrew word meaning "keep" is defined as "to hold onto to preserve, protect or hold in reserve," but is problematic as it does not fit with the context. Many translations resolve this by adding the word "grudge," "keep a grudge," and it would appear that this Hebrew word, or a similar word, is missing from the text. The Greek *Septuagint* reads, "and you will not be angry," and may preserve a more correct Hebrew version.

bê'hem'te'kha) <u>NOT</u> (לֹא lo) you^(ms)~will~make~BE.SQUARE^(V) (תַרְבִּיעַ
tar'bi'a) <u>DIVERSE.KIND~s2</u> (כִּלְאַיִם kil'a'yim) <u>FIELD~you^(ms)</u> (שָׂדְךָ
sad'kha) <u>NOT</u> (לֹא lo) you^(ms)~will~SOW^(V) (תִזְרָע tiz'ra)
<u>DIVERSE.KIND~s2</u> (כִּלְאַיִם kil'a'yim) <u>and~GARMENT</u> (וּבֶגֶד u've'ged)
<u>DIVERSE.KIND~s2</u> (כִּלְאַיִם kil'a'yim) <u>LINSEY-WOOLSEY</u> (שַׁעַטְנֵז
sha'at'neyz) <u>NOT</u> (לֹא lo) he~will~GO.UP^(V) (יַעֲלֶה ya'a'leh) <u>UPON~
you^(ms)</u> (עָלֶיךָ a'ley'kha) **RMT:** My customs you will safeguard, your
beasts you will not cause to be squared⁹⁶ with diverse kinds, your
fields you will not sow with diverse kinds, and garments of diverse
kinds of linsey-woolsey you will not go up upon you⁹⁷,

19:20 <u>and~MAN</u> (וְאִישׁ wê'ish) <u>GIVEN.THAT</u> (כִּי ki) he~will~
LIE.DOWN^(V) (יִשְׁכַּב yish'kav) <u>AT</u> (אֶת et) <u>WOMAN</u> (אִשָּׁה i'shah)
LYING.DOWN (שִׁכְבַת shikh'vat) <u>SEED</u> (זֶרַע ze'ra) <u>and~SHE</u> (וְהִוא
wê'hi) <u>MAID</u> (שִׁפְחָה shiph'hhah) be~CONSORT^(V)~ing^(fs)
ne'hhe're'phet) <u>to~MAN</u> (לְאִישׁ lê'ish) <u>and~>~be~much~RANSOM^(V)</u>
(וְהָפְדֵּה wê'haph'deyh) <u>NOT</u> (לֹא lo) she~did~be~RANSOM^(V) (נִפְדָּתָה
niph'da'tah) <u>OR</u> (אוֹ o) <u>FREEDOM</u> (חֻפְשָׁה hhuph'shah) <u>NOT</u> (לֹא lo)
he~did~be~GIVE^(V) (נִתַּן ni'tan) <u>to~her</u> (לָהּ lah) <u>PUNISHMENT</u> (בִּקֹּרֶת
bi'qo'ret) she~will~EXIST^(V) (תִּהְיֶה tih'yeh) <u>NOT</u> (לֹא lo) they~will~
be~make~DIE^(V) (יוּמְתוּ yu'me'tu) <u>GIVEN.THAT</u> (כִּי ki) <u>NOT</u> (לֹא lo)
she~did~be~much~FREE^(V) (חֻפָּשָׁה hhu'pa'shah) **RMT:** and a man
that lies down with a woman for the laying down of seed, and she is
a maid, being a consort of a man and certainly not ransomed,
freedom will not be given her, there will be punishment, they will
not be made to die, given that she was not free,

19:21 <u>and~he~did~make~COME^(V)</u> (וְהֵבִיא wê'hey'vi) <u>AT</u> (אֶת et)
<u>GUILT~him</u> (אֲשָׁמוֹ a'sha'mo) <u>to~YHWH</u> (לַיהוָה la'YHWH) <u>TO</u> (אֶל el)
OPENING (פֶּתַח pe'tahh) <u>TENT</u> (אֹהֶל o'hel) <u>APPOINTED</u> (מוֹעֵד
mo'eyd) <u>BUCK</u> (אַיִל eyl) <u>GUILT</u> (אָשָׁם a'sham) **RMT:** and he will bring
his guilt to **YHWH** to the opening of the appointed tent, a buck of
guilt,

19:22 <u>and~he~did~much~COVER^(V)</u> (וְכִפֶּר wê'khi'per) <u>UPON~him</u>
(עָלָיו a'law) <u>the~ADMINISTRATOR</u> (הַכֹּהֵן ha'ko'heyn) <u>in~BUCK</u> (בְּאֵיל
bê'eyl) <u>the~GUILT</u> (הָאָשָׁם ha'a'sham) <u>to~FACE~s</u> (לִפְנֵי liph'ney)
YHWH (יְהוָה YHWH) <u>UPON</u> (עַל al) FAILURE~him (חַטָּאתוֹ hha'ta'to)
<u>WHICH</u> (אֲשֶׁר a'sher) he~did~FAIL^(V) (חָטָא hha'ta) <u>and~he~did~be~</u>

---

⁹⁶ Meaning to be "on all fours" for procreation.
⁹⁷ To "go up upon you" means to "wear."

FORGIVE^(V) (וְנִסְלַח wê'nis'lahh) to~him (לוֹ lo) from~FAILURE~him (מֵחַטָּאתוֹ mey'hha'ta'to) WHICH (אֲשֶׁר a'sher) he~did~FAIL^(V) (חָטָא hha'ta) **RMT:** and the administrator will make restitution upon him with the buck of guilt to the face of **YHWH**, concerning his failure which he failed, and he will be forgiven for him from his failure which he failed,

19:23 and~GIVEN.THAT (וְכִי wê'khi) you^(mp)~will~COME^(V) (תָבֹאוּ ta'vo'u) TO (אֶל el) the~LAND (הָאָרֶץ ha'a'rets) and~you^(mp)~did~ PLANT^(V) (וּנְטַעְתֶּם un'ta'tem) ALL (כָּל kol) TREE (עֵץ eyts) NOURISHMENT (מַאֲכָל ma'a'khal) and~you^(mp)~did~ CONSIDERED.UNCIRCUMCISED^(V) (וַעֲרַלְתֶּם wa'a'ral'tem) FORESKIN~ him (עָרְלָתוֹ ar'la'to) AT (אֶת et) PRODUCE~him (פִּרְיוֹ pir'yo) THREE (שָׁלֹשׁ sha'losh) YEAR~s (שָׁנִים sha'nim) he~will~EXIST^(V) (יִהְיֶה yih'yeh) to~you^(mp) (לָכֶם la'khem) FORESKIN~s (עֲרֵלִים a'rey'lim) NOT (לֹא lo) he~will~be~EAT^(V) (יֵאָכֵל yey'a'kheyl) **RMT:** and, given that you will come to the land, and you will plant every tree of nourishment, and you will consider uncircumcised his foreskin, his produce, three years he will exist to you as foreskin, he will not be eaten,

19:24 and~in~the~YEAR (וּבַשָּׁנָה u'va'sha'nah) the~FOURTH (הָרְבִיעִת har'vi'it) he~will~EXIST^(V) (יִהְיֶה yih'yeh) ALL (כָּל kol) PRODUCE~him (פִּרְיוֹ pir'yo) SPECIAL (קֹדֶשׁ qo'desh) SHINING~s (הִלּוּלִים hi'lu'lim) to~YHWH (לַיהוָה la'YHWH) **RMT:** and in the fourth year all his produce will exist as special, shining things to **YHWH**,

19:25 and~in~the~YEAR (וּבַשָּׁנָה u'va'sha'nah) the~FIFTH (הַחֲמִישִׁת ha'hha'mi'shit) you^(mp)~will~EAT^(V) (תֹּאכְלוּ tokh'lu) AT (אֶת et) PRODUCE~him (פִּרְיוֹ pir'yo) to~>~make~ADD^(V) (לְהוֹסִיף lê ho'siph) to~you^(mp) (לָכֶם la'khem) PRODUCTION~him (תְּבוּאָתוֹ tê'vu'a'to) I (אֲנִי a'ni) **YHWH** (יְהוָה YHWH) Elohiym~you^(mp) (אֱלֹהֵיכֶם e'lo'hey'khem) **RMT:** and in the fifth year you will eat his produce, his production will again be for you, I am **YHWH** your Elohiym.

19:26 NOT (לֹא lo) you^(mp)~will~EAT^(V) (תֹּאכְלוּ to'khe'lu) UPON (עַל al) the~BLOOD (הַדָּם ha'dam) NCT (לֹא lo) you^(mp)~will~much~ PREDICT^(V) (תְּנַחֲשׁוּ tê'na'hha'shu) and~NOT (וְלֹא wê'lo) you^(mp)~will~ much~CONJURE^(V) (תְעוֹנֵנוּ tê'o'ne'nu) **RMT:** You will not eat upon the blood, you will not predict, and you will not conjure.

19:27 NOT (לֹא lo) you^(mp)~will~ENCIRCLE^(V) (תַקִּפוּ ta'qi'phu) EDGE (פְּאַת pê'at) HEAD~you^(mp) (רֹאשְׁכֶם rosh'khem) and~NOT (וְלֹא)

wê'lo) <u>you</u>^(ms)*~will~make~*DAMAGE^(V) (תַּשְׁחִית *tash'hhit*) <u>AT</u> (אֶת *eyt*) <u>EDGE</u> (פְּאַת *pê'at*) <u>BEARD~you</u>^(ms) (זְקָנֶךָ *zê'qa'ne'kha*) **RMT:** You will not encircle the edge of your head, and you will not damage the edge of your beard,

19:28 <u>and~SLICING</u> (וְשֶׂרֶט *wê'se'ret*) <u>to~the~SOUL</u> (לָנֶפֶשׁ *la'ne'phesh*) <u>NOT</u> (לֹא *lo*) <u>you</u>^(mp)*~will~*GIVE^(V) (תִּתְּנוּ *tit'nu*) <u>in~FLESH~you</u>^(mp) (בִּבְשַׂרְכֶם *biv'sar'khem*) <u>and~WRITING</u> (וּכְתֹבֶת *ukh'to'vet*) <u>TATTOO</u> (קַעֲקַע *qa'a'qa*) <u>NOT</u> (לֹא *lo*) <u>you</u>^(mp)*~will~*GIVE^(V) (תִּתְּנוּ *tit'nu*) <u>in~you</u>^(mp) (בָּכֶם *ba'khem*) <u>I</u> (אֲנִי *a'ni*) **YHWH** (יְהוָה *YHWH*) **RMT:** and a slicing for the soul you will not give in your flesh, and a writing of a tattoo you not give in you, I am **YHWH**.

19:29 <u>DO.NOT</u> (אַל *al*) <u>you</u>^(ms)*~will~much~*DRILL^(V) (תְּחַלֵּל *tê'hha'leyl*) <u>AT</u> (אֶת *et*) <u>DAUGHTER~you</u>^(ms) (בִּתְּךָ *bit'kha*) <u>to~>~make~</u>BE.A.HARLOT^(V)*~her* (לְהַזְנוֹתָהּ *lê'haz'no'tah*) <u>and~NOT</u> (וְלֹא *wê'lo*) *she~will~*BE.A.HARLOT^(V) (תִזְנֶה *tiz'neh*) <u>the~LAND</u> (הָאָרֶץ *ha'a'rets*) <u>and~she~did~FILL</u>^(V) (וּמָלְאָה *u'mal'ah*) <u>the~LAND</u> (הָאָרֶץ *ha'a'rets*) <u>MISCHIEF</u> (זִמָּה *zi'mah*) **RMT:** You will not defile your daughter by making her be a harlot, and the land will not be a harlot, and the land will be filled with mischief.

19:30 <u>AT</u> (אֶת *et*) <u>CEASING~s~me</u> (שַׁבְּתֹתַי *sha'be'to'tai*) <u>you</u>^(mp)*~will~*SAFEGUARD^(V) (תִּשְׁמֹרוּ *tish'moru*) <u>and~SANCTUARY~me</u> (וּמִקְדָּשִׁי *u'miq'da'shi*) <u>you</u>^(mp)*~will~*FEAR^(V) (תִּירָאוּ *ti'ra'u*) <u>I</u> (אֲנִי *a'ni*) **YHWH** (יְהוָה *YHWH*) **RMT:** My ceasings you will safeguard and my sanctuary you will fear, I am **YHWH**.

19:31 <u>DO.NOT</u> (אַל *al*) <u>you</u>^(mp)*~will~*TURN^(V) (תִּפְנוּ *tiph'nu*) <u>TO</u> (אֶל *el*) <u>the~NECROMANCER~s</u> (הָאֹבֹת *ha'o'vot*) <u>and~TO</u> (וְאֶל *wê'el*) <u>the~KNOWER~s</u> (הַיִּדְּעֹנִים *hai'yid'o'nim*) <u>DO.NOT</u> (אַל *al*) <u>you</u>^(mp)*~will~much~*SEARCH.OUT^(V) (תְּבַקְשׁוּ *tê'vaq'shu*) <u>to~DIRTY~her</u> (לְטָמְאָה *lê'tam'ah*) <u>in~them</u>^(m) (בָהֶם *va'hem*) <u>I</u> (אֲנִי *a'ni*) **YHWH** (יְהוָה *YHWH*) <u>Elohiym~you</u>^(mp) (אֱלֹהֵיכֶם *e'lo'hey'khem*) **RMT:** You will not turn to the necromancers and you will not search out the knowers, for her dirtiness is in them, I am **YHWH** your Elohiym.

19:32 <u>from~FACE~s</u> (מִפְּנֵי *mip'ney*) <u>GRAY-HEADED</u> (שֵׂיבָה *sey'vah*) <u>you</u>^(ms)*~will~*RISE^(V) (תָּקוּם *ta'qum*) <u>and~you</u>^(ms)*~did~*GIVE.HONOR^(V) (וְהָדַרְתָּ *wê'ha'dar'ta*) <u>FACE~s</u> (פְּנֵי *pê'ney*) <u>BEARD</u> (זָקֵן *za'qeyn*) <u>and~you</u>^(ms)*~did~*FEAR^(V) (וְיָרֵאתָ *wê'ya'rey'ta*) <u>from~Elohiym~you</u>^(ms) (מֵאֱלֹהֶיךָ *mey'e'lo'hey'kha*) <u>I</u> (אֲנִי *a'ni*) **YHWH** (יְהוָה *YHWH*) **RMT:** You will rise to the face of gray-headed ones, and you will give honor to the face of bearded ones, and you will fear your Elohiym, I am **YHWH**,

19:33 and~GIVEN.THAT (וְכִי *wê khi*) he~will~IMMIGRATE[(V)] (יָגוּר *ya'gur*) AT~you[(ms)] (אִתְּךָ *it'kha*) IMMIGRANT (גֵּר *geyr*) in~LAND~ you[(mp)] (בְּאַרְצְכֶם *bê'ar'tse'khem*) NOT (לֹא *lo*) you[(mp)]~will~make~ SUPPRESS[(V)] (תוֹנוּ *to'nu*) AT~him (אֹתוֹ *o'to*) **RMT:** and, given that an immigrant will immigrate with you in your land, you will not cause him suppression.

19:34 like~NATIVE (כְּאֶזְרָח *kê'e'ze'rahh*) from~you[(mp)] (מִכֶּם *mi'kem*) he~will~EXIST[(V)] (יִהְיֶה *yih'yeh*) to~you[(mp)] (לָכֶם *la'khem*) the~ IMMIGRANT (הַגֵּר *ha'geyr*) the~IMMIGRATE[(V)]~ing[(ms)] (הַגָּר *ha'gar*) AT~you[(mp)] (אִתְּכֶם *it'khem*) and~you[(ms)]~did~LOVE[(V)] (וְאָהַבְתָּ *wê'a'hav'ta*) to~him (לוֹ *lo*) like~THAT.ONE~you[(ms)] (כָּמוֹךָ *ka'mo'kha*) GIVEN.THAT (כִּי *ki*) IMMIGRANT~s (גֵרִים *gey'rim*) you[(mp)]~did~EXIST[(V)] (הֱיִיתֶם *he'yi'tem*) in~LAND (בְּאֶרֶץ *bê'e'rets*) Mits'rayim (מִצְרָיִם *mits'ra'yim*) I (אֲנִי *a'ni*) **YHWH** (יְהוָה *YHWH*) Elohiym~you[(mp)] (אֱלֹהֵיכֶם *e'lo'hey'khem*) **RMT:** Like a native from you, he will exist with you, the immigrant immigrating with you, and you will love him like the ones of you, given that you existed as immigrants in the land of Mits'rayim, I am **YHWH** your Elohiym.

19:35 NOT (לֹא *lo*) you[(mp)]~will~DO[(V)] (תַעֲשׂוּ *ta'a'su*) WICKED (עָוֶל *a'wel*) in~the~DECISION (בַּמִּשְׁפָּט *ba'mish'pat*) in~the~ MEASUREMENT (בַּמִּדָּה *ba'mi'dah*) in~the~WEIGHT (בַּמִּשְׁקָל *ba'mish'qal*) and~in~the~QUANTITY (וּבַמְּשׂוּרָה *u'vam'su'rah*) **RMT:** You will not do wickedness in the decision, in the measurement, in the weight and in the quantity.

19:36 BALANCE~s2 (מֹאזְנֵי *moz'ney*) STEADFAST (צֶדֶק *tse'deq*) STONE~s (אַבְנֵי *av'ney*) STEADFAST (צֶדֶק *tse'deq*) EYPHAH (אֵיפַת *ey'phat*) STEADFAST (צֶדֶק *tse'deq*) and~HIYN (וְהִין *wê'hin*) STEADFAST (צֶדֶק *tse'deq*) he~will~EXIST[(V)] (יִהְיֶה *yih'yeh*) to~you[(mp)] (לָכֶם *la'khem*) I (אֲנִי *a'ni*) **YHWH** (יְהוָה *YHWH*) Elohiym~you[(mp)] (אֱלֹהֵיכֶם *e'lo'hey'khem*) WHICH (אֲשֶׁר *a'sher*) I~did~make~ GO.OUT[(V)] (הוֹצֵאתִי *ho'tsey'ti*) AT~you[(mp)] (אֶתְכֶם *et'khem*) from~ LAND (מֵאֶרֶץ *mey'e'rets*) Mits'rayim (מִצְרָיִם *mits'ra'yim*) **RMT:** Steadfast balances, steadfast stones[98], steadfast eyphah and a

---

[98] Measured stones were used in the balances for weights.

steadfast hiyn, he will exist for you, I am **YHWH** your Elohiym who caused you to go out from the land of Mits'rayim,

19:37 <u>and~you^(mp)~did~SAFEGUARD</u>^(V) (וּשְׁמַרְתֶּם *ush'mar'tem*) <u>AT</u> (אֵת *et*) <u>ALL</u> (כָּל *kol*) <u>CUSTOM~s~me</u> (חֻקֹּתַי *hhu'qo'tai*) <u>and~AT</u> (וְאֵת *wê'et*) <u>ALL</u> (כָּל *kol*) <u>DECISION~s~me</u> (מִשְׁפָּטַי *mish'pa'tai*) <u>and~ you^(mp)~did~DO</u>^(V) (וַעֲשִׂיתֶם *wa'a'si'tem*) <u>AT~them</u>^(m) (אֹתָם *o'tam*) <u>I</u> (אֲנִי *a'ni*) **YHWH** (יְהוָה *YHWH*) **RMT:** and you will safeguard all my customs and all my decisions, and you will do them, I am **YHWH**,

Chapter 20

20:1 <u>and~he~will~much~SPEAK</u>^(V) (וַיְדַבֵּר *wai'da'beyr*) **YHWH** (יְהוָה *YHWH*) <u>TO</u> (אֶל *el*) <u>Mosheh</u> (מֹשֶׁה *mo'sheh*) <u>to~>~SAY</u>^(V) (לֵּאמֹר *ley'mor*) **RMT:** and YHWH spoke to Mosheh saying,

20:2 <u>and~TO</u> (וְאֶל *wê'el*) <u>SON~s</u> (בְּנֵי *bê'ney*) <u>Yisra'eyl</u> (יִשְׂרָאֵל *yis'ra'eyl*) <u>you^(ms)~will~SAY</u>^(V) (תֹּאמַר *to'mar*) <u>MAN</u> (אִישׁ *ish*) <u>MAN</u> (אִישׁ *ish*) <u>from~SON~s</u> (מִבְּנֵי *mi'be'ney*) <u>Yisra'eyl</u> (יִשְׂרָאֵל *yis'ra'eyl*) <u>and~FROM</u> (וּמִן *u'min*) <u>the~IMMIGRANT</u> (הַגֵּר *ha'geyr*) <u>the~ IMMIGRATE</u>^(V)~<u>ing</u>^(ms) (הַגָּר *ha'gar*) <u>in~Yisra'eyl</u> (בְּיִשְׂרָאֵל *bê'yis'ra'eyl*) <u>WHICH</u> (אֲשֶׁר *a'sher*) <u>he~will~GIVE</u>^(V) (יִתֵּן *yi'teyn*) <u>from~SEED~him</u> (מִזַּרְעוֹ *mi'zar'o*) <u>to~the~Molekh</u> (לַמֹּלֶךְ *la'mo'lekh*) <u>>~DIE</u>^(V) (מוֹת *mot*) <u>he~will~be~make~DIE</u>^(V) (יוּמָת *yu'mat*) <u>PEOPLE</u> (עַם *am*) <u>the~LAND</u> (הָאָרֶץ *ha'a'rets*) <u>they</u>^(m)~<u>will~ KILL.BY.STONING</u>^(V)~<u>him</u> (יִרְגְּמֻהוּ *yir'ge'mu'hu*) <u>in~the~STONE</u> (בָאָבֶן *va'a'ven*) **RMT:** and to the sons of Yisra'eyl you will say, each man from the sons of Yisra'eyl and from the immigrant immigrating in Yisra'eyl, who give from his seed to Molekh, he will certainly be killed, the people of the land will kill him by stoning with the stone,

20:3 <u>and~I</u> (וַאֲנִי *wa'ani*) <u>I~will~GIVE</u>^(V) (אֶתֵּן *e'teyn*) <u>AT</u> (אֶת *et*) <u>FACE~s~me</u> (פָּנַי *pa'nai*) <u>in~the~MAN</u> (בָּאִישׁ *ba'ish*) <u>the~HE</u> (הַהוּא *ha'hu*) <u>and~I~did~make~CUT</u>^(V) (וְהִכְרַתִּי *wê'hikh'ra'ti*) <u>AT~him</u> (אֹתוֹ *o'to*) <u>from~INSIDE</u> (מִקֶּרֶב *mi'qe'rev*) <u>PEOPLE~him</u> (עַמּוֹ *a'mo*) <u>GIVEN.THAT</u> (כִּי *ki*) <u>from~SEED~him</u> (מִזַּרְעוֹ *mi'zar'o*) <u>he~did~GIVE</u>^(V) (נָתַן *na'tan*) <u>to~the~Molekh</u> (לַמֹּלֶךְ *la'mo'lekh*) <u>to~THAT</u> (לְמַעַן *lê'ma'an*) <u>he~did~BE.DIRTY</u>^(V) (טַמֵּא *ta'mey*) <u>AT</u> (אֶת *et*) <u>SANCTUARY~me</u> (מִקְדָּשִׁי *miq'da'shi*) <u>and~to~>~much~DRILL</u>^(V) (וּלְחַלֵּל *ul'hha'leyl*) <u>AT</u> (אֶת *et*) <u>TITLE</u> (שֵׁם *sheym*) <u>SPECIAL~me</u> (קָדְשִׁי *qad'shi*) **RMT:** and I, I will give my face in that man, and I will cause him to be cut from inside his people, given that from his seed he gave to Molekh, because of that he dirtied my sanctuary, and defiled my special title,

20:4 <u>and~IF</u> (וְאִם *wê'im*) <u>>~make~BE.OUT.OF.SIGHT</u>^(V) (הַעְלֵם *ha'leym*) <u>they^(m)~will~make~BE.OUT.OF.SIGHT</u>^(V) (יַעְלִימוּ *ya'li'mu*) <u>PEOPLE</u> (עַם *am*) <u>the~LAND</u> (הָאָרֶץ *ha'a'rets*) <u>AT</u> (אֶת *et*) <u>EYE~s2~them^(m)</u> (עֵינֵיהֶם *ay'ney'hem*) <u>FROM</u> (מִן *min*) <u>the~MAN</u> (הָאִישׁ *ha'ish*) <u>the~HE</u> (הַהוּא *ha'hu*) <u>in~>~GIVE</u>^(V)~him (בְּתִתּוֹ *bê'ti'to*) <u>from~SEED~him</u> (מִזַּרְעוֹ *mi'zar'o*) <u>to~the~Molekh</u> (לַמֹּלֶךְ *la'mo'lekh*) <u>to~EXCEPT</u> (לְבִלְתִּי *lê'vil'ti*) <u>>~make~DIE</u>^(V) (הָמִית *ha'mit*) <u>AT~him</u> (אֹתוֹ *o'to*) **RMT:** and if the people of the land will surely cause their eyes to be out of sight from that man, in his giving from his seed to Molekh, to not kill him,

20:5 <u>and~I~did~PLACE</u>^(V) (וְשַׂמְתִּי *wê'sam'ti*) <u>I</u> (אֲנִי *a'ni*) <u>AT</u> (אֶת *et*) <u>FACE~s~me</u> (פָּנַי *pa'nai*) <u>in~the~MAN</u> (בָּאִישׁ *ba'ish*) <u>the~HE</u> (הַהוּא *ha'hu*) <u>and~in~CLAN~him</u> (וּבְמִשְׁפַּחְתּוֹ *uv'mish'pahh'to*) <u>and~I~did~make~CUT</u>^(V) (וְהִכְרַתִּי *wê'hikh'ra'ti*) <u>AT~him</u> (אֹתוֹ *o'to*) <u>and~AT</u> (וְאֵת *wê'eyt*) <u>ALL</u> (כָּל *kol*) <u>the~BE.A.HARLOT</u>^(V)~ing^(mp) (הַזֹּנִים *ha'zo'nim*) <u>AFTER~him</u> (אַחֲרָיו *a'hha'raw*) <u>to~>~BE.A.HARLOT</u>^(V) (לִזְנוֹת *liz'not*) <u>AFTER</u> (אַחֲרֵי *a'hha'rey*) <u>the~Molekh</u> (הַמֹּלֶךְ *ha'mo'lekh*) <u>from~INSIDE</u> (מִקֶּרֶב *mi'qe'rev*) <u>PEOPLE~them^(m)</u> (עַמָּם *a'mam*) **RMT:** then I will place my face in that man and in his clan, and I will cause him and all the ones being a harlot after him, being a harlot after Molekh, to be cut from inside their people,

20:6 <u>and~the~SOUL</u> (וְהַנֶּפֶשׁ *wê'ha'ne'phesh*) <u>WHICH</u> (אֲשֶׁר *a'sher*) <u>she~will~TURN</u>^(V) (תִּפְנֶה *tiph'neh*) <u>TO</u> (אֶל *el*) <u>the~NECROMANCER~s</u> (הָאֹבֹת *ha'o'vot*) <u>and~TO</u> (וְאֶל *wê'el*) <u>the~KNOWER~s</u> (הַיִּדְּעֹנִים *hai'yid'o'nim*) <u>to~>~BE.A.HARLOT</u>^(v) (לִזְנוֹת *liz'not*)[99] <u>AFTER~them^(m)</u> (אַחֲרֵיהֶם *a'hha'rey'hem*) <u>and~I~did~GIVE</u>^(V) (וְנָתַתִּי *wê'na'ta'ti*) <u>AT</u> (אֶת *et*) <u>FACE~s~me</u> (פָּנַי *pa'nai*) <u>in~the~SOUL</u> (בַּנֶּפֶשׁ *ba'ne'phesh*) <u>the~SHE</u> (הַהִוא *ha'hi*) <u>and~I~did~make~CUT</u>^(V) (וְהִכְרַתִּי *wê'hikh'ra'ti*) <u>AT~him</u> (אֹתוֹ *o'to*) <u>from~INSIDE</u> (מִקֶּרֶב *mi'qe'rev*) <u>PEOPLE~him</u> (עַמּוֹ *a'mo*) **RMT:** and the soul that will turn to the necromancers and to the knowers, to be a harlot after them, then I will give my face in that soul, and I will cause him to be cut from inside his people,

20:7 <u>and~you^(mp)~did~self~SET.APART</u>^(V) (וְהִתְקַדִּשְׁתֶּם *wê'hit'qa'dish'tem*) <u>and~you^(mp)~did~EXIST</u>^(V) (וִהְיִיתֶם *wih'yi'tem*)

---

[99] *Leningrad Codex:* לזנת

UNIQUE~s (קְדֹשִׁים qê'do'shim) GIVEN.THAT (כִּי ki) I (אֲנִי a'ni) **YHWH** (יְהוָה YHWH) Elohiym~you[(mp)] (אֱלֹהֵיכֶם e'lo'hey'khem) **RMT:** and you will set yourself apart, and you will exist as unique ones, given that I am **YHWH** your Elohiym,

20:8 and~you[(mp)]~did~SAFEGUARD[(V)] (וּשְׁמַרְתֶּם ush'mar'tem) AT (אֵת et) CUSTOM~s~me (חֻקֹּתַי hhu'qo'tai) and~you[(mp)]~did~DO[(V)] (וַעֲשִׂיתֶם wa'a'si'tem) AT~them[(m)] (אֹתָם o'tam) I (אֲנִי a'ni) **YHWH** (יְהוָה YHWH) much~SET.APART[(V)]~ing[(ms)]~you[(ms)] (מְקַדִּשְׁכֶם mê'qa'dish'khem) **RMT:** and you will safeguard my customs, and you will do them, I am **YHWH** setting you apart,

20:9 GIVEN.THAT (כִּי ki) MAN (אִישׁ ish) MAN (אִישׁ ish) WHICH (אֲשֶׁר a'sher) he~will~much~BELITTLE[(V)] (יְקַלֵּל yê'qa'leyl) AT (אֶת et) FATHER~him (אָבִיו a'viw) and~AT (וְאֶת wê'et) MOTHER~him (אִמּוֹ i'mo) >~DIE[(V)] (מוֹת mot) he~will~be~make~DIE[(V)] (יוּמָת yu'mat) FATHER~him (אָבִיו a'viw) and~MOTHER~him (וְאִמּוֹ wê'i'mo) he~did~much~BELITTLE[(V)] (קִלֵּל qi'leyl) BLOOD~s~him (דָּמָיו da'maw) in~him (בּוֹ bo) **RMT:** given that each man which will belittle his father and his mother, he will certainly be killed, he belittled his father and his mother, his blood is on him,

20:10 and~MAN (וְאִישׁ wê'ish) WHICH (אֲשֶׁר a'sher) he~will~COMMIT.ADULTERY[(V)] (יִנְאַף yin'aph) AT (אֶת et) WOMAN (אֵשֶׁת ey'shet) MAN (אִישׁ ish) WHICH (אֲשֶׁר a'sher) he~will~COMMIT.ADULTERY[(V)] (יִנְאַף yin'aph) AT (אֶת et) WOMAN (אֵשֶׁת ey'shet)[100] COMPANION~him (רֵעֵהוּ rey'ey'hu) >~DIE[(V)] (מוֹת mot) he~will~be~make~DIE[(V)] (יוּמָת yu'mat) the~COMMIT.ADULTERY[(V)]~ing[(ms)] (הַנֹּאֵף ha'no'eyph) and~the~COMMIT.ADULTERY[(V)]~ing[(fs)] (וְהַנֹּאָפֶת wê'ha'no'a'phet) **RMT:** and a man that will commit adultery with the woman of his companion, will certainly be killed, the one committing adultery and the one committing adultery[101],

20:11 and~MAN (וְאִישׁ wê'ish) WHICH (אֲשֶׁר a'sher) he~will~LIE.DOWN[(V)] (יִשְׁכַּב yish'kav) AT (אֶת et) WOMAN (אֵשֶׁת ey'shet) FATHER~him (אָבִיו a'viw) NAKEDNESS (עֶרְוַת er'wat) FATHER~him (אָבִיו a'viw) he~did~much~REMOVE.THE.COVER[(V)] (גִּלָּה gi'lah) >~

---

[100] It appears that the phrase MAN WHICH he~will~COMMIT.ADULTERY AT WOMAN, is written twice by accident.

[101] The word "COMMIT.ADULTERY" is written twice, but one is referring to the "man" and the other is referring to the "woman."

DIE^(V) (מוֹת *mot*) *they~will~be~make~DIE*^(V) (יוּמְתוּ *yu'me'tu*) TWO~
them^(m) (שְׁנֵיהֶם *shê'ney'hem*) BLOOD~s~them^(m) (דְּמֵיהֶם
dê'mey'hem) in~them^(m) (בָּם *bam*) **RMT:** and the man that will lie
down with the woman of his father, he removed the cover of the
nakedness of his father, the two of them will certainly be killed, their
blood is on them,

20:12 and~MAN (וְאִישׁ *wê'ish*) WHICH (אֲשֶׁר *a'sher*) *he~will~*
LIE.DOWN^(V) (יִשְׁכַּב *yish'kav*) AT (אֶת *et*) DAUGHTER-IN-LAW~him
(כַּלָּתוֹ *ka'la'to*) >~DIE^(V) (מוֹת *mot*) *they~will~be~make~DIE*^(V) (יוּמְתוּ
yu'me'tu) TWO~them^(m) (שְׁנֵיהֶם *shê'ney'hem*) UNNATURAL.MIX
(תֶּבֶל *te'vel*) *they~did~DO*^(V) (עָשׂוּ *a'su*) BLOOD~s~them^(m) (דְּמֵיהֶם
dê'mey'hem) in~them^(m) (בָּם *bam*) **RMT:** and a man who will lie
down with his daughter-in-law, the two of them will certainly be
killed, they did an unnatural mix, their blood is on them,

20:13 and~MAN (וְאִישׁ *wê'ish*) WHICH (אֲשֶׁר *a'sher*) *he~will~*
LIE.DOWN^(V) (יִשְׁכַּב *yish'kav*) AT (אֶת *et*) MALE (זָכָר *za'khar*)
LYING.PLACE~s (מִשְׁכְּבֵי *mish'ke'vey*) WOMAN (אִשָּׁה *i'shah*)
DISGUSTING (תּוֹעֵבָה *to'ey'vah*) *they~did~DO*^(V) (עָשׂוּ *a'su*) TWO~
them^(m) (שְׁנֵיהֶם *shê'ney'hem*) >~DIE^(V) (מוֹת *mot*) *they~will~be~*
make~DIE^(V) (יוּמָתוּ *yu'ma'tu*) BLOOD~s~them^(m) (דְּמֵיהֶם
dê'mey'hem) in~them^(m) (בָּם *bam*) **RMT:** and a man who will lie
down with a male, lying places of a woman, the two of them did a
disgusting thing, they will certainly be killed, their blood is on them,

20:14 and~MAN (וְאִישׁ *wê'ish*) WHICH (אֲשֶׁר *a'sher*) *he~will~TAKE*^(V)
(יִקַּח *yi'qahh*) AT (אֶת *et*) WOMAN (אִשָּׁה *i'shah*) and~AT (וְאֶת
wê'et) MOTHER~her (אִמָּהּ *i'mah*) MISCHIEF (זִמָּה *zi'mah*) SHE (הִוא
hi) in~the~FIRE (בָּאֵשׁ *ba'eysh*) *they*^(m)*~will~CREMATE*^(V) (יִשְׂרְפוּ
yis're'phu) AT~him (אֹתוֹ *o'to*) and~AT~them^(f) (וְאֶתְהֶן *wê'et'hen*)
and~NOT (וְלֹא *wê'lo*) *she~will~EXIST*^(V) (תִהְיֶה *tih'yeh*) MISCHIEF
(זִמָּה *zi'mah*) in~MIDST~you^(mp) (בְּתוֹכְכֶם *bê'tokh'khem*) **RMT:** and a
man who will take a woman and her mother, this is mischief, they
will cremate him and them in the fire, and mischief will not exist in
your midst,

20:15 and~MAN (וְאִישׁ *wê'ish*) WHICH (אֲשֶׁר *a'sher*) *he~will~GIVE*^(V)
(יִתֵּן *yi'teyn*) COPULATION~him (שְׁכָבְתּוֹ *shê'khav'to*) in~BEAST
(בִּבְהֵמָה *biv'hey'mah*) >~DIE^(V) (מוֹת *mot*) *he~will~be~make~DIE*^(V)
(יוּמָת *yu'mat*) and~AT (וְאֶת *wê'et*) the~BEAST (הַבְּהֵמָה
ha'be'hey'mah) *they*^(m)*~will~KILL*^(V) (תַּהֲרֹגוּ *ta'ha'ro'gu*) **RMT:** and a

man who will give his copulation in a beast, he will certainly be killed, and they will kill the beast,

20:16 and~WOMAN (וְאִשָּׁה wê'i'shah) WHICH (אֲשֶׁר a'sher) you(ms)~will~COME.NEAR(V) (תִּקְרַב tiq'rav) TO (אֶל el) ALL (כָּל kol) BEAST (בְּהֵמָה bê'hey'mah) to~>~BE.SQUARE(V)~her (לְרִבְעָה lê'riv'ah) AT~her (אֹתָהּ o'tah) and~you(ms)~did~KILL(V) (וְהָרַגְתָּ wê'ha'rag'ta) AT (אֶת et) the~WOMAN (הָאִשָּׁה ha'i'shah) and~AT (וְאֶת wê'et) the~BEAST (הַבְּהֵמָה ha'be'hey'mah) >~DIE(V) (מוֹת mot) they~will~be~make~DIE(V) (יוּמָתוּ yu'ma'tu) BLOOD~s~them(m) (דְּמֵיהֶם dê'mey'hem) in~them(m) (בָּם bam) **RMT:** and a woman who will come near to any beast to be squared[102] with her, then you will kill the woman and the beast, they will certainly be killed, their blood is on them,

20:17 and~MAN (וְאִישׁ wê'ish) WHICH (אֲשֶׁר a'sher) he~will~TAKE(V) (יִקַּח yi'qahh) AT (אֶת et) SISTER~him (אֲחֹתוֹ a'hho'to) DAUGHTER (בַּת bat) FATHER~him (אָבִיו a'viw) OR (אוֹ o) DAUGHTER (בַת vat) MOTHER~him (אִמּוֹ i'mo) and~he~did~SEE(V) (וְרָאָה wê'ra'ah) AT (אֶת et) NAKEDNESS~her (עֶרְוָתָהּ er'wa'tah) and~SHE (וְהִיא wê'hi) you(ms)~will~SEE(V) (תִרְאֶה tir'eh) AT (אֶת et) NAKEDNESS~him (עֶרְוָתוֹ er'wa'to) KINDNESS (חֶסֶד hhe'sed) HE (הוּא hu) and~they~did~be~CUT(V) (וְנִכְרְתוּ wê'nikh're'tu) to~EYE~s2 (לְעֵינֵי lê'ey'ney) SON~s (בְּנֵי bê'ney) PEOPLE~them(m) (עַמָּם a'mam) NAKEDNESS (עֶרְוַת er'wat) SISTER~him (אֲחֹתוֹ a'hho'to) he~did~much~REMOVE.THE.COVER(V) (גִּלָּה gi'lah) TWISTEDNESS~him (עֲוֹנוֹ a'o'no) he~will~LIFT.UP(V) (יִשָּׂא yi'sa) **RMT:** and a man who will take his sister, the daughter of his father or the daughter of his mother, and he will see her nakedness, and she will see his nakedness, this is kindness[103], and they will be cut to the eyes of the sons of their people, he removed the cover of the nakedness of his sister, he will lift up his twistedness,

20:18 and~MAN (וְאִישׁ wê'ish) WHICH (אֲשֶׁר a'sher) he~will~LIE.DOWN(V) (יִשְׁכַּב yish'kav) AT (אֶת et) WOMAN (אִשָּׁה i'shah) ILLNESS (דָּוָה da'wah) and~he~did~much~REMOVE.THE.COVER(V) (וְגִלָּה wê'gi'lah) AT (אֶת et) NAKEDNESS~her (עֶרְוָתָהּ er'wa'tah) AT (אֶת et) FOUNTAIN~her (מְקֹרָהּ mê'qo'rah) he~did~make~

---

[102] Meaning to be "on all fours" for procreation.

[103] The context implies that the word KINDNESS (חסד / hhesed) is incorrect and may be a misspelling for another word, such as DIMINISH (חסר / hhaser), which is spelled almost the same.

UNCOVER^(V) (הֶעֱרָה *he'e'rah*) and~SHE (וְהִיא *wê'hi*)[104] *she~did~ much~REMOVE.THE.COVER*^(V) (גִּלְּתָה *gil'tah*) AT (אֶת *et*) FOUNTAIN (מְקוֹר *mê'qor*) BLOOD~s~her (דָּמֶיהָ *da'mey'ah*) and~they~did~be~ CUT^(V) (וְנִכְרְתוּ *wê'nikh're'tu*) TWO~them^(m) (שְׁנֵיהֶם *shê'ney'hem*) from~INSIDE (מִקֶּרֶב *mi'qe'rev*) PEOPLE~them^(m) (עַמָּם *a'mam*) **RMT:** and a man who will lay down with a woman of illness, and he will remove the cover of her nakedness, he caused the uncovering of her fountain, and she, she removed the cover of the fountain of her bloodshed, and the two of them will be cut from inside their people,

20:19 and~NAKEDNESS (וְעֶרְוַת *wê'e're'wat*) SISTER (אֲחוֹת *a'hhot*) MOTHER~you^(ms) (אִמְּךָ *im'kha*) and~SISTER (וַאֲחוֹת *wa'a'hhot*) FATHER~you^(ms) (אָבִיךָ *a'vi'kha*) NOT (לֹא *lo*) *you^(ms)~will~much~ REMOVE.THE.COVER*^(V) (תְגַלֵּה *tê'ga'leyh*) GIVEN.THAT (כִּי *ki*) AT (אֶת *et*) KIN~him (שְׁאֵרוֹ *shê'ey'ro*) he~did~make~UNCOVER^(V) (הֶעֱרָה *he'e'rah*) TWISTEDNESS~them^(m) (עֲוֹנָם *a'o'nam*) *they^(m)~will~ LIFT.UP*^(V) (יִשָּׂאוּ *yi'sa'u*) **RMT:** and the nakedness of the sister of your mother and the sister of your father, you will not remove the cover, given his kin he caused to be uncovered, they will lift up their twistedness,

20:20 and~MAN (וְאִישׁ *wê'ish*) WHICH (אֲשֶׁר *a'sher*) *he~will~ LIE.DOWN*^(V) (יִשְׁכַּב *yish'kav*) AT (אֶת *et*) AUNT~him (דֹּדָתוֹ *do'da'to*) NAKEDNESS (עֶרְוַת *er'wat*) UNCLE~him (דֹּדוֹ *do'do*) *he~did~much~ REMOVE.THE.COVER*^(V) (גִּלָּה *gi''ah*) FAILURE~them^(m) (חֶטְאָם *hhet'am*) *they^(m)~will~LIFT.UP*^(V) (יִשָּׂאוּ *yi'sa'u*) BARREN~s (עֲרִירִים *a'ri'rim*) *they^(m)~will~DIE*^(V) (יָמֻתוּ *ya'mu'tu*) **RMT:** and a man who will lay down with his aunt, he removed the cover of the nakedness of his uncle, they will lift up their failure, they will die barren,

20:21 and~MAN (וְאִישׁ *wê'ish*) WHICH (אֲשֶׁר *a'sher*) *he~will~TAKE*^(V) (יִקַּח *yi'qahh*) AT (אֶת *et*) WOMAN (אֵשֶׁת *ey'shet*) BROTHER~him (אָחִיו *a'hhiw*) REMOVAL (נִדָּה *ni'dah*) SHE (הִוא *hi*) NAKEDNESS (עֶרְוַת *er'wat*) BROTHER~him (אָחִיו *a'hhiw*) *he~did~much~ REMOVE.THE.COVER*^(V) (גִּלָּה *gi''ah*) BARREN~s (עֲרִירִים *a'ri'rim*) *they^(m)~will~EXIST*^(V) (יִהְיוּ *yih'yu*) **RMT:** and a man who will take the woman of his brother, this is a removal, he removed the cover of the nakedness of his brother, they will exist barren,

20:22 and~*you^(mp)~did~SAFEGUARD*^(V) (וּשְׁמַרְתֶּם *ush'mar'tem*) AT (אֶת *et*) ALL (כָּל *kol*) CUSTOM~s~me (חֻקֹּתַי *hhu'qo'tai*) and~AT (וְאֶת

---

[104] *Leningrad Codex:* והוא

wê'et) <u>ALL</u> (כָּל *kol*) <u>DECISION</u>~s~me (מִשְׁפָּטַי *mish'pa'tai*) and~
<u>you</u>⁽ᵐᵖ⁾~<u>did</u>~<u>DO</u>⁽ᵛ⁾ (וַעֲשִׂיתֶם *wa'a'si'tem*) <u>AT</u>~<u>them</u>⁽ᵐ⁾ (אֹתָם *o'tam*)
and~<u>NOT</u> (וְלֹא *wê'lo*) *she~will~make~*<u>VOMIT</u>⁽ᵛ⁾ (תָקִיא *ta'qi*) <u>AT</u>~
<u>you</u>⁽ᵐᵖ⁾ (אֶתְכֶם *et'khem*) <u>the</u>~<u>LAND</u> (הָאָרֶץ *ha'a'rets*) <u>WHICH</u> (אֲשֶׁר
a'sher) <u>I</u> (אֲנִי *a'ni*) *make~*<u>COME</u>⁽ᵛ⁾~*ing*⁽ᵐˢ⁾ (מֵבִיא *me'vi*) <u>AT</u>~<u>you</u>⁽ᵐᵖ⁾
(אֶתְכֶם *et'khem*) <u>THERE</u>~<u>unto</u> (שָׁמָּה *sha'mah*) <u>to</u>~>~<u>SETTLE</u>⁽ᵛ⁾
la'she'vet) <u>in</u>~<u>her</u> (בָּהּ *bah*) **RMT:** and you will safeguard all my
customs and all my decisions, and you will do them, and the land
that I brought you unto there to settle in will not vomit you,

20:23 <u>and</u>~<u>NOT</u> (וְלֹא *wê'lo*) <u>you</u>⁽ᵐᵖ⁾~<u>will</u>~<u>WALK</u>⁽ᵛ⁾ (תֵלְכוּ *teyl'khu*) <u>in</u>~
<u>CUSTOM</u> (בְּחֻקֹּת *bê'hhu'qot*) <u>the</u>~<u>NATION</u> (הַגּוֹי *ha'goi*) <u>WHICH</u> (אֲשֶׁר
a'sher) <u>I</u> (אֲנִי *a'ni*) *much~*<u>SEND</u>⁽ᵛ⁾~*ing*⁽ᵐˢ⁾ (מְשַׁלֵּחַ *mê'sha'ley'ahh*)
<u>from</u>~<u>FACE</u>~s~<u>you</u>⁽ᵐᵖ⁾ (מִפְּנֵיכֶם *mi'pe'ney'khem*) <u>GIVEN.THAT</u> (כִּי *ki*)
<u>AT</u> (אֶת *et*) <u>ALL</u> (כָּל *kol*) <u>THESE</u> (אֵלֶּה *ey'leh*) *they~did~*<u>DO</u>⁽ᵛ⁾ (עָשׂוּ
a'su) and~*I~will~*<u>LOATHE</u>⁽ᵛ⁾ (וָאָקֻץ *wa'a'quts*) <u>in</u>~<u>them</u>⁽ᵐ⁾ (בָּם *bam*)
RMT: and you will not walk in the customs of the nations which I am
sending from your faces, given that all these they did, and I loathed
them,

20:24 <u>and</u>~*I~will~*<u>SAY</u>⁽ᵛ⁾ (וָאֹמַר *wa'o'mar*) <u>to</u>~<u>you</u>⁽ᵐᵖ⁾ (לָכֶם *la'khem*)
<u>YOU</u>⁽ᵐᵖ⁾ (אַתֶּם *a'tem*) <u>you</u>⁽ᵐᵖ⁾~<u>will</u>~<u>POSSESS</u>⁽ᵛ⁾ (תִּירְשׁוּ *tir'shu*) <u>AT</u> (אֶת
et) <u>GROUND</u>~<u>them</u>⁽ᵐ⁾ (אַדְמָתָם *ad'ma'tam*) and~<u>I</u> (וַאֲנִי *wa'ani*) *I~
will~*<u>GIVE</u>⁽ᵛ⁾~<u>her</u> (אֶתְּנֶנָּה *et'ne'nah*) <u>to</u>~<u>you</u>⁽ᵐᵖ⁾ (לָכֶם *la'khem*) <u>to</u>~
<u>the</u>~>~<u>POSSESS</u>⁽ᵛ⁾ (לָרֶשֶׁת *la're'shet*) <u>AT</u>~<u>her</u> (אֹתָהּ *o'tah*) <u>LAND</u> (אֶרֶץ
e'rets) <u>ISSUE</u>⁽ᵛ⁾~*ing*⁽ᶠˢ⁾ (זָבַת *za'vat*) <u>FAT</u> (חָלָב *hha'lav*) and~<u>HONEY</u>
(וּדְבָשׁ *ud'vash*) <u>I</u> (אֲנִי *a'ni*) **YHWH** (יְהוָה *YHWH*) <u>Elohiym</u>~<u>you</u>⁽ᵐᵖ⁾
(אֱלֹהֵיכֶם *e'lo'hey'khem*) <u>WHICH</u> (אֲשֶׁר *a'sher*) *I~did~make~*
<u>SEPARATE</u>⁽ᵛ⁾ (הִבְדַּלְתִּי *hiv'dal'ti*) <u>AT</u>~<u>you</u>⁽ᵐᵖ⁾ (אֶתְכֶם *et'khem*) <u>FROM</u>
(מִן *min*) <u>the</u>~<u>PEOPLE</u>~s (הָעַמִּים *ha'a'mim*) **RMT:** and I said to you,
you, you will possess their ground and I will give her to you to
possess her, a land issuing fat and honey, I am **YHWH** your Elohiym
who caused you to be separated from the peoples,

20:25 <u>and</u>~<u>you</u>⁽ᵐᵖ⁾~<u>did</u>~make~<u>SEPARATE</u>⁽ᵛ⁾ (וְהִבְדַּלְתֶּם
wê'hiv'dal'tem) <u>BETWEEN</u> (בֵּין *beyn*) <u>the</u>~<u>BEAST</u> (הַבְּהֵמָה
ha'be'hey'mah) <u>the</u>~<u>CLEAN</u> (הַטְּהֹרָה *hat'ho'rah*) <u>to</u>~<u>the</u>~<u>DIRTY</u>
(לַטְּמֵאָה *lat'mey'ah*) and~<u>BETWEEN</u> (וּבֵין *u'veyn*) <u>the</u>~<u>FLYER</u> (הָעוֹף
ha'oph) <u>the</u>~<u>DIRTY</u> (הַטָּמֵא *ha'ta'mey*) <u>to</u>~<u>the</u>~<u>CLEAN</u> (לַטָּהֹר
la'ta'hor) <u>and</u>~<u>NOT</u> (וְלֹא *wê'lo*) <u>you</u>⁽ᵐᵖ⁾~<u>will</u>~*much~*<u>DETEST</u>⁽ᵛ⁾ (תְשַׁקְּצוּ
tê'shaq'tsu) <u>AT</u> (אֶת *et*) <u>SOUL</u>~s~<u>you</u>⁽ᵐᵖ⁾ (נַפְשֹׁתֵיכֶם
naph'sho'tey'khem) <u>in</u>~<u>the</u>~<u>BEAST</u> (בַּבְּהֵמָה *ba'be'hey'mah*) <u>and</u>~<u>in</u>~

the~FLYER (וּבָעוֹף u'va'oph) and~in~ALL (וּבְכֹל uv'khol) WHICH (אֲשֶׁר a'sher) she~will~TREAD⁽ⱽ⁾ (תִּרְמֹשׂ tir'mos) the~GROUND (הָאֲדָמָה ha'a'da'mah) WHICH (אֲשֶׁר a'sher) I~did~make~SEPARATE⁽ⱽ⁾ (הִבְדַּלְתִּי hiv'dal'ti) to~you⁽ᵐᵖ⁾ (לָכֶם la'khem) to~>~much~BE.DIRTY⁽ⱽ⁾ (לְטַמֵּא lê'ta'mey) **RMT:** and you will cause a separation between the clean beast to the dirty, and between the dirty flyer to the clean, and you will not make your souls detestable with the beast and with the flyer and with any that tread the ground which I separated for you for being dirty,

20:26 and~you⁽ᵐᵖ⁾~did~EXIST⁽ⱽ⁾ (וִהְיִיתֶם wih'yi'tem) to~me (לִי li) UNIQUE~s (קְדֹשִׁים qê'do'shim) GIVEN.THAT (כִּי ki) UNIQUE (קָדוֹשׁ qa'dosh) I (אֲנִי a'ni) **YHWH** (יְהוָה YHWH) and~I~will~make~ SEPARATE⁽ⱽ⁾ (וָאַבְדִּל wa'av'dil) AT~you⁽ᵐᵖ⁾ (אֶתְכֶם et'khem) FROM (מִן min) the~PEOPLE~s (הָעַמִּים ha'a'mim) to~>~EXIST⁽ⱽ⁾ (לִהְיוֹת lih'yot) to~me (לִי li) **RMT:** and you will exist for me as unique ones, given that I YHWH am unique, and I caused you to be separated from the people, to exist for me,

20:27 and~MAN (וְאִישׁ wê'ish) OR (אוֹ o) WOMAN (אִשָּׁה i'shah) GIVEN.THAT (כִּי ki) he~will~EXIST⁽ⱽ⁾ (יִהְיֶה yih'yeh) in~them⁽ᵐ⁾ (בָהֶם va'hem) NECROMANCER (אוֹב o'veyv) OR (אוֹ o) KNOWER (יִדְּעֹנִי yid'o'ni) >~DIE⁽ⱽ⁾ (מוֹת mot) they~will~be~make~DIE⁽ⱽ⁾ (יוּמָתוּ yu'ma'tu) in~the~STONE (בָּאֶבֶן ba'e'ven) they⁽ᵐ⁾~will~ KILL.BY.STONING⁽ⱽ⁾ (יִרְגְּמוּ yir'ge'mu) AT~them⁽ᵐ⁾ (אֹתָם o'tam) BLOOD~s~them⁽ᵐ⁾ (דְּמֵיהֶם dê'mev'hem) in~them⁽ᵐ⁾ (בָּם bam) **RMT:** and a man or woman who will exist in them a necromancer or a knower, they will certainly be killed with the stone, they will kill them by stoning, their blood is on them,

Chapter 21

21:1 and~he~will~SAY⁽ⱽ⁾ (וַיֹּאמֶר wai'yo'mer) **YHWH** (יְהוָה YHWH) TO (אֶל el) Mosheh (מֹשֶׁה mo'sheh) I⁽ᵐˢ⁾~SAY⁽ⱽ⁾ (אֱמֹר e'mor) TO (אֶל el) the~ADMINISTRATOR~s (הַכֹּהֲנִים ha'ko'ha'nim) SON~s (בְּנֵי bê'ney) Aharon (אַהֲרֹן a'ha'ron) and~you⁽ᵐˢ⁾~did~SAY⁽ⱽ⁾ (וְאָמַרְתָּ wê'a'mar'ta) TO~them⁽ᵐ⁾ (אֲלֵהֶם a'ley'hem) to~SOUL (לְנֶפֶשׁ lê'ne'phesh) NOT (לֹא lo) he~will~BE.DIRTY⁽ⱽ⁾ (יִטַּמָּא yi'ta'ma) in~ PEOPLE~s~him (בְּעַמָּיו bê'a'maw) **RMT:** and **YHWH** said to Mosheh, say to the administrators, the sons of Aharon, and you will say to them, he will not be dirty for a soul in his people.

21:2 GIVEN.THAT (כִּי ki) IF (אִם im) to~KIN~him (לִשְׁאֵרוֹ lish'ey'ro) the~NEAR (הַקָּרֹב ha'qa'rov) TO~him (אֵלָיו ey'law) to~MOTHER~him (לְאִמּוֹ lê'i'mo) and~to~FATHER~him (וּלְאָבִיו ul'a'viw) and~to~SON~him (וְלִבְנוֹ wê'liv'no) and~to~DAUGHTER~him (וּלְבִתּוֹ ul'vi'to) and~to~BROTHER~him (וּלְאָחִיו ul'a'hhiw) **RMT:** Instead, for his kin, the one near him, for his mother and for his father and for his son and for his daughter and for his brother,

21:3 and~to~SISTER~him (וְלַאֲחֹתוֹ wê'la'a'hho'to) the~VIRGIN (הַבְּתוּלָה ha'be'tu'lah) the~NEAR (הַקְּרוֹבָה haq'ro'vah) TO~him (אֵלָיו ey'law) WHICH (אֲשֶׁר a'sher) NOT (לֹא lo) she~did~EXIST(V) (הָיְתָה hai'tah) to~MAN (לְאִישׁ lê'ish) to~her (לָהּ lah) he~will~BE.DIRTY(V) (יִטָּמָא yi'ta'ma) **RMT:** and for his sister, the virgin, the one near to him, who does not have a man, for her he will be dirty.

21:4 NOT (לֹא lo) he~will~BE.DIRTY(V) (יִטָּמָא yi'ta'ma) MASTER (בַּעַל ba'al) in~PEOPLE~s~him (בְּעַמָּיו bê'a'maw) to~>~make~DRILL(V)~him (לְהֵחַלּוֹ lê'hey'hha'lo) **RMT:** A master in his people will not be dirty, to defile himself.

21:5 NOT (לֹא lo) he~will~make~MAKE.BALD(V)~her (יִקְרְחָה yiq're'hhah)[105] BALD.SPOT (קָרְחָה qar'hhah) in~HEAD~them(m) (בְּרֹאשָׁם bê'ro'sham) and~EDGE (וּפְאַת uph'at) BEARD~them(m) (זְקָנָם zê'qa'nam) NOT (לֹא lo) they(m)~will~much~SHAVE(V) (יְגַלֵּחוּ yê'ga'ley'hhu) and~in~FLESH~them(m) (וּבִבְשָׂרָם u'viv'sa'ram) NOT (לֹא lo) they(m)~will~SLICE(V) (יִשְׂרְטוּ yis're'tu) SLICING (שָׂרָטֶת sa'ra'tet) **RMT:** They will not make bald a bald spot on their head, and the edge of their beard they will not shave, and in their flesh they will not slice a slicing.

21:6 UNIQUE~s (קְדֹשִׁים qê'do'shim) they(m)~will~EXIST(V) (יִהְיוּ yih'yu) to~Elohiym~them(m) (לֵאלֹהֵיהֶם ley'lo'hey'hem) and~NOT (וְלֹא wê'lo) they(m)~will~much~DRILL(V) (יְחַלְּלוּ yê'hhal'lu) TITLE (שֵׁם sheym) Elohiym~them(m) (אֱלֹהֵיהֶם e'lo'hey'hem) GIVEN.THAT (כִּי ki) AT (אֶת et) FIRE.OFFERING~s (אִשֵּׁי i'shey) **YHWH** (יְהוָה YHWH) BREAD (לֶחֶם le'hhem) Elohiym~them(m) (אֱלֹהֵיהֶם e'lo'hey'hem) THEY(m) (הֵם heym) make~COME.NEAR(V)~ing(mp) (מַקְרִיבִם maq'ri'vim) and~they~did~EXIST(V) (וְהָיוּ wê'hai'u) SPECIAL (קֹדֶשׁ qo'desh) **RMT:** They will exist as unique ones to their Elohiym, and they will not defile the title of their Elohiym, given that the fire

---

[105] Qere = יִקְרְחוּ.

offerings of **YHWH**, the bread of their Elohiym, they are bringing near, and they will be special.

21:7 WOMAN (אִשָּׁה *i'shah*) BE.A.HARLOT^(V)~ing^(fs) (זֹנָה *zo'nah*) and~ DRILLED (וַחֲלָלָה *wa'hha'la'lah*) NOT (לֹא *lo*) they^(m)~will~TAKE^(V) (יִקָּחוּ *yi'qa'hhu*) and~WOMAN (וְאִשָּׁה *wê'i'shah*) CAST.OUT^(V)~ed^(fs) (גְּרוּשָׁה *gê'ru'shah*) from~MAN~her (מֵאִישָׁהּ *mey'i'shah*) NOT (לֹא *lo*) they^(m)~will~TAKE^(V) (יִקָּחוּ *yi'qa'hhu*) GIVEN.THAT (כִּי *ki*) UNIQUE (קָדֹשׁ *qa'dosh*) HE (הוּא *hu*) to~Elohiym~him (לֵאלֹהָיו *ley'lo'haw*) **RMT:** A woman being a harlot and drilled they will not take, and a woman cast out from her man they will not take, given that he is unique to his Elohiym,

21:8 and~you^(ms)~did~much~SET.APART^(V)~him (וְקִדַּשְׁתּוֹ *wê'qi'dash'to*) GIVEN.THAT (כִּי *ki*) AT (אֶת *et*) BREAD (לֶחֶם *le'hhem*) Elohiym~you^(ms) (אֱלֹהֶיךָ *e'lo'hey'kha*) HE (הוּא *hu*) make~ COME.NEAR^(V)~ing^(ms) (מַקְרִיב *maq'riv*) UNIQUE (קָדֹשׁ *qa'dosh*) he~ will~EXIST^(V) (יִהְיֶה *yih'yeh*) to~you^(fs) (לָךְ *lakh*) GIVEN.THAT (כִּי *ki*) UNIQUE (קָדוֹשׁ *qa'dosh*) I (אֲנִי *a'ni*) **YHWH** (יְהוָה *YHWH*) much~ SET.APART^(V)~ing^(ms)~you^(ms) (מְקַדִּשְׁכֶם *mê'qa'dish'khem*) **RMT:** and you will set him apart, given that the bread of your Elohiym he is bringing near, he exists unique for you, given that unique am I, **YHWH**, the one setting you apart,

21:9 and~DAUGHTER (וּבַת *u'vat*) MAN (אִישׁ *ish*) ADMINISTRATOR (כֹּהֵן *ko'heyn*) GIVEN.THAT (כִּי *ki*) she~will~be~DRILL^(V) (תֵחֵל *tey'hheyl*) to~>~BE.A.HARLOT^(V) (לִזְנוֹת *liz'not*) AT (אֶת *et*) FATHER~ her (אָבִיהָ *a'vi'ah*) SHE (הִיא *hi*) much~DRILL^(V)~ing^(fs) (מְחַלֶּלֶת *mê'hha'le'let*) in~the~FIRE (בָּאֵשׁ *ba'eysh*) you^(ms)~will~CREMATE^(V) (תִּשָּׂרֵף *ti'sa'reyph*) **RMT:** and the daughter of each administrator that will be defiled by being a harlot, she is defiling her father, you will cremate in the fire,

21:10 and~the~ADMINISTRATOR (וְהַכֹּהֵן *wê'ha'ko'heyn*) the~GREAT (הַגָּדוֹל *ha'ga'dol*) from~BROTHER~s~him (מֵאֶחָיו *mey'e'hhaw*) WHICH (אֲשֶׁר *a'sher*) he~will~be~make~POUR.DOWN^(V) (יוּצַק *yu'tsaq*) UPON (עַל *al*) HEAD~him (רֹאשׁוֹ *ro'sho*) OIL (שֶׁמֶן *she'men*) the~OINTMENT (הַמִּשְׁחָה *ha'mish'hhah*) and~he~did~much~FILL^(V) (וּמִלֵּא *u'mi'ley*) AT (אֶת *et*) HAND~him (יָדוֹ *ya'do*) to~>~WEAR^(V) (לִלְבֹּשׁ *lil'bosh*) AT (אֶת *et*) the~GARMENT~s (הַבְּגָדִים *ha'be'ga'dim*) AT (אֶת *et*) HEAD~him (רֹאשׁוֹ *ro'sho*) NOT (לֹא *lo*) he~will~LOOSE^(V) (יִפְרָע *yiph'ra*) and~GARMENT~s~him (וּבְגָדָיו *uv'ga'daw*) NOT (לֹא *lo*) he~will~RIP^(V) (יִפְרֹם *yiph'rom*) **RMT:** and the great administrator from his brothers, which will have poured the oil of the ointment down upon his head, and he will fill his hand[106] to wear the garments, he will not loose his head, and his garments he will not rip,

21:11 and~UPON (וְעַל *wê'al*) ALL (כָּל *kol*) SOUL~s (נַפְשֹׁת *naph'shot*) DIE[(V)]~ing[(ms)] (מֵת *meyt*) NOT (לֹא *lo*) he~will~COME[(V)] (יָבֹא *ya'vo*) to~FATHER~him (לְאָבִיו *lê'a'viw*) and~to~MOTHER~him (וּלְאִמּוֹ *ul'i'mo*) NOT (לֹא *lo*) he~will~BE.DIRTY[(V)] (יִטַּמָּא *yi'ta'ma*) **RMT:** and he will not come upon any soul of the dying, for his father and for his mother he will not be dirty,

21:12 and~FROM (וּמִן *u'min*) the~SANCTUARY (הַמִּקְדָּשׁ *ha'miq'dash*) NOT (לֹא *lo*) he~will~GO.OUT[(V)] (יֵצֵא *yey'tsey*) and~NOT (וְלֹא *wê'lo*) he~will~much~DRILL[(V)] (יְחַלֵּל *yê'hha'leyl*) AT (אֵת *eyt*) SANCTUARY (מִקְדַּשׁ *miq'dash*) Elohiym~him (אֱלֹהָיו *e'lo'haw*) GIVEN.THAT (כִּי *ki*) DEDICATION (נֵזֶר *ney'zer*) OIL (שֶׁמֶן *she'men*) OINTMENT (מִשְׁחַת *mish'hhat*) Elohiym~him (אֱלֹהָיו *e'lo'haw*) UPON~him (עָלָיו *a'law*) I (אֲנִי *a'ni*) YHWH (יְהוָה *YHWH*) **RMT:** and from the sanctuary he will not go out, and he will not defile the sanctuary of his Elohiym, given that the dedication of oil of ointment of his Elohiym is upon him, I am **YHWH**,

21:13 and~HE (וְהוּא *wê'hu*) WOMAN (אִשָּׁה *i'shah*) in~VIRGINITY~s~her (בִבְתוּלֶיהָ *viv'tu'ley'ah*) he~will~TAKE[(V)] (יִקָּח *yi'qahh*) **RMT:** and he, he will take a woman in her virginity.

21:14 WIDOW (אַלְמָנָה *al'ma'nah*) and~CAST.OUT[(V)]~ed[(fs)] (וּגְרוּשָׁה *ug'ru'shah*) and~DRILLED (וַחֲלָלָה *wa'hha'la'lah*) BE.A.HARLOT[(V)]~ing[(fs)] (זֹנָה *zo'nah*) AT (אֶת *et*) THESE (אֵלֶּה *ey'leh*) NOT (לֹא *lo*) he~will~TAKE[(V)] (יִקָּח *yi'qahh*) GIVEN.THAT (כִּי *ki*) IF (אִם *im*) VIRGIN (בְּתוּלָה *bê'tu'lah*) from~PEOPLE~s~him (מֵעַמָּיו *mey'a'maw*) he~will~TAKE[(V)] (יִקָּח *yi'qahh*) WOMAN (אִשָּׁה *i'shah*) **RMT:** A widow and a casted out one and a drilled one, one being a harlot, he will not take these, but if there is a virgin from his people he will take a woman,

---

[106] To "fill the hand" is an idiom of uncertain meaning, but the same phrase is used in Akkadian to mean the placing of a relevant tool or insignia (such as a scepter for a king) in the hand of one being installed in a high office.

21:15 and~NOT (וְלֹא *wê'lo*) he~will~much~DRILL[V] (יְחַלֵּל *yê'hha'leyl*) SEED~him (זַרְעוֹ *zar'o*) in~PEOPLE~s~him (בְּעַמָּיו *bê'a'maw*) GIVEN.THAT (כִּי *ki*) I (אֲנִי *a'ni*) **YHWH** (יְהוָה *YHWH*) much~SET.APART[V]~ing[ms]~him (מְקַדְּשׁוֹ *mê'qad'sho*) **RMT:** and he will not defile his seed in his people, given that I am **YHWH** setting him apart,

21:16 and~he~will~much~SPEAK[V] (וַיְדַבֵּר *wai'da'beyr*) **YHWH** (יְהוָה *YHWH*) TO (אֶל *el*) Mosheh (מֹשֶׁה *mo'sheh*) to~>~SAY[V] (לֵּאמֹר *ley'mor*) **RMT:** and **YHWH** spoke to Mosheh saying,

21:17 !(ms)~much~SPEAK[V] (דַּבֵּר *da'beyr*) TO (אֶל *el*) Aharon (אַהֲרֹן *a'ha'ron*) to~>~SAY[V] (לֵאמֹר *ley'mor*) MAN (אִישׁ *ish*) from~SEED~you(ms) (מִזַּרְעֲךָ *mi'zar'a'kha*) to~GENERATION~s~them(m) (לְדֹרֹתָם *lê'do'ro'tam*) WHICH (אֲשֶׁר *a'sher*) he~will~EXIST[V] (יִהְיֶה *yih'yeh*) in~him (בוֹ *vo*) BLEMISH (מוּם *mum*) NOT (לֹא *lo*) he~will~COME.NEAR[V] (יִקְרַב *yiq'rav*) to~>~make~COME.NEAR[V] (לְהַקְרִיב *lê'haq'riv*) BREAD (לֶחֶם *le'hhem*) Elohiym~him (אֱלֹהָיו *e'lo'haw*) **RMT:** speak to Aharon saying, a man from your seed to their generations who will exist in him a blemish, he will not come near to bring near the bread of his Elohiym,

21:18 GIVEN.THAT (כִּי *ki*) ALL (כָל *khol*) MAN (אִישׁ *ish*) WHICH (אֲשֶׁר *a'sher*) in~him (בוֹ *bo*) BLEMISH (מוּם *mum*) NOT (לֹא *lo*) he~will~COME.NEAR[V] (יִקְרָב *yiq'rav*) MAN (אִישׁ *ish*) BLIND (עִוֵּר *i'weyr*) OR (אוֹ *o*) LAME (פִּסֵּחַ *phi'sey'ahh*) OR (אוֹ *o*) PERFORATE[V]~ed(ms) (חָרֻם *hha'rum*) OR (אוֹ *o*) BE.SUPERFLUOUS[V]~ed(ms) (שָׂרוּעַ *sa'ru'a*) **RMT:** given that every man who in him is a blemish, he will not come near, a blind man or a lame one or a perforated[107] one or one being superfluous,

21:19 OR (אוֹ *o*) MAN (אִישׁ *ish*) WHICH (אֲשֶׁר *a'sher*) he~will~EXIST[V] (יִהְיֶה *yih'yeh*) in~him (בוֹ *vo*) SHATTERING (שֶׁבֶר *she'ver*) FOOT (רָגֶל *ra'gel*) OR (אוֹ *o*) SHATTERING (שֶׁבֶר *she'ver*) HAND (יָד *yad*) **RMT:** or a man who exists in him a shattering of the foot or a shattering of the hand,

21:20 OR (אוֹ *o*) HUNCHBACK (גִבֵּן *gi'beyn*) OR (אוֹ *o*) SCRAWNY (דַק *daq*) OR (אוֹ *o*) CATARACT (תְּבַלֻּל *tê'va'lul*) in~EYE~him (בְּעֵינוֹ *bê'ey'no*) OR (אוֹ *o*) IRRITATION (גָרָב *ga'rav*) OR (אוֹ *o*) SKIN.SORE (יַלֶּפֶת *ya'le'phet*) OR (אוֹ *o*) CRUMBLED (מְרוֹחַ *mê'ro'ahh*) TESTICLES

---

[107] Of uncertain meaning.

(אָשֶׁךְ a'shekh) **RMT:** or a hunchback or scrawny or a cataract in his eye or an irritation or a skin sore or crumbled testicles.

21:21 <u>ALL</u> (כָּל kol) <u>MAN</u> (אִישׁ ish) <u>WHICH</u> (אֲשֶׁר a'sher) <u>in~him</u> (בּוֹ bo) <u>BLEMISH</u> (מוּם mum) <u>from~SEED</u> (מִזֶּרַע mi'ze'ra) <u>Aharon</u> (אַהֲרֹן a'ha'ron) <u>the~ADMINISTRATOR</u> (הַכֹּהֵן ha'ko'heyn) <u>NOT</u> (לֹא lo) <u>he~ will~DRAW.NEAR</u>[V] (יִגַּשׁ yi'gash) <u>to~>~make~COME.NEAR</u>[V] (לְהַקְרִיב lê'haq'riv) <u>AT</u> (אֶת et) <u>FIRE.OFFERING~s</u> (אִשֵּׁי i'shey) **YHWH** (יְהוָה YHWH) <u>BLEMISH</u> (מוּם mum) <u>in~him</u> (בּוֹ bo) <u>AT</u> (אֶת eyt) <u>BREAD</u> (לֶחֶם le'hhem) <u>Elohiym~him</u> (אֱלֹהָיו e'lo'haw) <u>NOT</u> (לֹא lo) <u>he~will~DRAW.NEAR</u>[V] (יִגַּשׁ yi'gash) <u>to~>~make~COME.NEAR</u>[V] (לְהַקְרִיב lê'haq'riv) **RMT:** Every man, which is in him a blemish, from the seed of Aharon the administrator, will not draw near to bring near the fire offerings of **YHWH**, a blemish is in him, he will not draw near to bring near the bread of his Elohiym.

21:22 <u>BREAD</u> (לֶחֶם le'hhem) <u>Elohiym~him</u> (אֱלֹהָיו e'lo'haw) <u>from~ SPECIAL~s</u> (מִקָּדְשֵׁי mi'qad'shey) <u>the~SPECIAL~s</u> (הַקֳּדָשִׁים ha'qa'da'shim) <u>and~FROM</u> (וּמִן u'min) <u>the~SPECIAL~s</u> (הַקֳּדָשִׁים ha'qa'da'shim) <u>he~will~EAT</u>[V] (יֹאכֵל yo'kheyl) **RMT:** The bread of his Elohiym, from the very special ones, and from the special ones, he will eat.

21:23 <u>SURELY</u> (אַךְ akh) <u>TO</u> (אֶל el) <u>the~TENT.CURTAIN</u> (הַפָּרֹכֶת ha'pa'ro'khet) <u>NOT</u> (לֹא lo) <u>he~will~COME</u>[V] (יָבֹא ya'vo) <u>and~TO</u> (וְאֶל wê'el) <u>the~ALTAR</u> (הַמִּזְבֵּחַ ha'miz'bey'ahh) <u>NOT</u> (לֹא lo) <u>he~ will~DRAW.NEAR</u>[V] (יִגַּשׁ yi'gash) <u>GIVEN.THAT</u> (כִּי ki) <u>BLEMISH</u> (מוּם mum) <u>in~him</u> (בּוֹ bo) <u>and~NOT</u> (וְלֹא wê'lo) <u>he~will~much~DRILL</u>[V] (יְחַלֵּל yê'hha'leyl) <u>AT</u> (אֶת et) <u>SANCTUARY~s~me</u> (מִקְדָּשַׁי miq'da'shai) <u>GIVEN.THAT</u> (כִּי ki) <u>I</u> (אֲנִי a'ni) **YHWH** (יְהוָה YHWH) <u>from~>~much~SET.APART</u>[V]<u>~them</u>[m] (מְקַדְּשָׁם mê'qad'sham) **RMT:** Surely, to the tent curtain he will not come and to the altar he will not draw near, given that a blemish is in him, and he will not defile my sanctuaries, given that I am **YHWH**, setting them apart,

21:24 <u>and~he~will~much~SPEAK</u>[V] (וַיְדַבֵּר wai'da'beyr) <u>Mosheh</u> (מֹשֶׁה mo'sheh) <u>TO</u> (אֶל el) <u>Aharon</u> (אַהֲרֹן a'ha'ron) <u>and~TO</u> (וְאֶל wê'el) <u>SON~s~him</u> (בָּנָיו ba'naw) <u>and~TO</u> (וְאֶל wê'el) <u>ALL</u> (כָּל kol) <u>SON~s</u> (בְּנֵי bê'ney) <u>Yisra'eyl</u> (יִשְׂרָאֵל yis'ra'eyl) **RMT:** and Mosheh spoke to Aharon and to his sons and to all the sons of Yisra'eyl,

Chapter 22

22:1 and~he~will~much~SPEAK^(V) (וַיְדַבֵּר *wai'da'beyr*) **YHWH** (יְהוָה YHWH) TO (אֶל *el*) Mosheh (מֹשֶׁה *mo'sheh*) to~>~SAY^(V) (לֵּאמֹר *ley'mor*) **RMT:** and **YHWH** spoke to Mosheh saying,

22:2 !^(ms)~much~SPEAK^(V) (דַּבֵּר *da'beyr*) TO (אֶל *el*) Aharon (אַהֲרֹן *a'ha'ron*) and~TO (וְאֶל *wê'el*) SON~s~him (בָּנָיו *ba'naw*) and~ they^(m)~will~be~DEDICATE^(V) (וְיִנָּזְרוּ *wê'yi'naz'ru*) from~SPECIAL~s (מִקַּדְשֵׁי *mi'qad'shey*) SON~s (בְנֵי *vê'ney*) Yisra'eyl (יִשְׂרָאֵל *yis'ra'eyl*) and~NOT (וְלֹא *wê'lo*) they^(m)~will~much~DRILL^(V) (יְחַלְּלוּ *yê'hhal'lu*) AT (אֶת *et*) TITLE (שֵׁם *sheym*) SPECIAL~me (קָדְשִׁי *qad'shi*) WHICH (אֲשֶׁר *a'sher*) THEY^(m) (הֵם *heym*) make~SET.APART^(V)~ing^(mp) (מַקְדִּשִׁים *maq'di'shim*) to~me (לִי *li*) I (אֲנִי *a'ni*) **YHWH** (יְהוָה YHWH) **RMT:** speak to Aharon and to his sons, and they will be dedicated from the special things of the sons of Yisra'eyl, and they will not defile my special title, which they are setting apart for me, I am **YHWH**.

22:3 !^(ms)~SAY^(V) (אֱמֹר *e'mor*) TO~them^(m) (אֲלֵהֶם *a'ley'hem*) to~ GENERATION~s~you^(mp) (לְדֹרֹתֵיכֶם *lê'do'ro'tey'khem*) ALL (כָּל *kol*) MAN (אִישׁ *ish*) WHICH (אֲשֶׁר *a'sher*) he~will~COME.NEAR^(V) (יִקְרַב *yiq'rav*) from~ALL (מִכָּל *mi'kol*) SEED~you^(mp) (זַרְעֲכֶם *zar'a'khem*) TO (אֶל *el*) the~SPECIAL~s (הַקֳּדָשִׁים *ha'qa'da'shim*) WHICH (אֲשֶׁר *a'sher*) they^(m)~will~make~SET.APART^(V) (יַקְדִּישׁוּ *yaq'di'shu*) SON~s (בְנֵי *vê'ney*) Yisra'eyl (יִשְׂרָאֵל *yis'ra'eyl*) to~YHWH (לַיהוָה *la'YHWH*) and~DIRTY~him (וְטֻמְאָתוֹ *wê'tum'a'to*) UPON~him (עָלָיו *a'law*) and~she~did~be~CUT^(V) (וְנִכְרְתָה *wê'nikh're'tah*) the~SOUL (הַנֶּפֶשׁ *ha'ne'phesh*) the~SHE (הַהִוא *ha'hi*) from~to~FACE~s~me (מִלְּפָנַי *mi'le'pha'nai*) I (אֲנִי *a'ni*) **YHWH** (יְהוָה YHWH) **RMT:** Say to them, to your generations, every man from all your seed that will come near to the special things, which the sons of Yisra'eyl will set apart for **YHWH**, and his dirtiness is upon him, and that soul will be cut from before my face, I am **YHWH**.

22:4 MAN (אִישׁ *ish*) MAN (אִישׁ *ish*) from~SEED (מִזֶּרַע *mi'ze'ra*) Aharon (אַהֲרֹן *a'ha'ron*) and~HE (וְהוּא *wê'hu*) INFECT^(V)~ed^(ms) (צָרוּעַ *tsa'ru'a*) OR (אוֹ *o*) ISSUE^(V)~ing^(ms) (זָב *zav*) in~the~SPECIAL~s (בַּקֳּדָשִׁים *ba'qa'da'shim*) NOT (לֹא *lo*) he~will~EAT^(V) (יֹאכַל *yo'khal*) UNTIL (עַד *ad*) WHICH (אֲשֶׁר *a'sher*) he~will~BE.CLEAN^(V) (יִטְהָר *yit'har*) and~the~TOUCH^(V)~ing^(ms) (וְהַנֹּגֵעַ *wê'ha'no'gey'a*) in~ALL (בְּכָל *bê'khol*) DIRTY (טְמֵא *tê'mey*) SOUL (נֶפֶשׁ *ne'phesh*) OR (אוֹ *o*) MAN (אִישׁ *ish*) WHICH (אֲשֶׁר *a'sher*) she~will~GO.OUT^(V) (תֵּצֵא *tê'tsey*) *tey'tsey)* FROM~him (מִמֶּנּוּ *mi'me'nu*) LYING.DOWN (שִׁכְבַת *shikh'vat)* SEED (זָרַע *za'ra)* **RMT:** Each man from the seed of Aharon and is infected or issuing, he will not eat the special things, until he is clean, and anyone touching a dirty soul or a man that had the lying down of seed going out from him,

22:5 OR (אוֹ *o)* MAN (אִישׁ *ish)* WHICH (אֲשֶׁר *a'sher)* *he~will~* TOUCH⁽ᵛ⁾ (יִגַּע *yiga)* in~ALL (בְּכָל *bê'khol)* SWARMER (שֶׁרֶץ *she'rets)* WHICH (אֲשֶׁר *a'sher)* *he~will~*BE.DIRTY⁽ᵛ⁾ (יִטְמָא *yit'ma)* to~him (לוֹ *lo)* OR (אוֹ *o)* in~HUMAN (בְּאָדָם *vê'a'dam)* WHICH (אֲשֶׁר *a'sher)* *he~ will~*BE.DIRTY⁽ᵛ⁾ (יִטְמָא *yit'ma)* to~him (לוֹ *lo)* to~ALL (לְכֹל *lê'khol)* DIRTY~him (טֻמְאָתוֹ *tu'm'a'to)* **RMT:** or a man that touched any swarmer that is dirty to him, or with a human that is dirty to him to all his dirtiness.

22:6 SOUL (נֶפֶשׁ *ne'phesh)* WHICH (אֲשֶׁר *a'sher)* *she~will~*TOUCH⁽ᵛ⁾ (תִּגַּע *ti'ga)* in~him (בּוֹ *bo)* and~she~did~BE.DIRTY⁽ᵛ⁾ (וְטָמְאָה *wê'tam'ah)* UNTIL (עַד *ad)* the~EVENING (הָעָרֶב *ha'a'rev)* and~NOT (וְלֹא *wê'lo)* *he~will~*EAT⁽ᵛ⁾ (יֹאכַל *yo'khal)* FROM (מִן *min)* the~ SPECIAL~s (הַקֳּדָשִׁים *ha'qa'da'shim)* GIVEN.THAT (כִּי *ki)* IF (אִם *im)* *he~did~*BATHE⁽ᵛ⁾ (רָחַץ *ra'hhats)* FLESH~him (בְּשָׂרוֹ *bê'sar'o)* in~the~ WATER~s2 (בַּמָּיִם *ba'ma'yim)* **RMT:** A soul that touches in him, then she¹⁰⁸ will be dirty until the evening, and he will not eat from the special things, unless he bathed his flesh in the waters,

22:7 and~he~did~COME⁽ᵛ⁾ (וּבָא *u'va)* the~SUN (הַשֶּׁמֶשׁ *ha'she'mesh)* and~he~did~BE.CLEAN⁽ᵛ⁾ (וְטָהֵר *wê'ta'har)* and~AFTER (וְאַחַר *wê'a'hhar)* *he~will~*EAT⁽ᵛ⁾ (יֹאכַל *yo'khal)* FROM (מִן *min)* the~ SPECIAL~s (הַקֳּדָשִׁים *ha'qa'da'shim)* GIVEN.THAT (כִּי *ki)* BREAD~him (לַחְמוֹ *lahh'mo)* HE (הוּא *hu)* **RMT:** and the sun came¹⁰⁹, and he will be clean, and afterward he will eat from the special things, given that he is his bread.

22:8 CARCASS (נְבֵלָה *nê'vey'lah)* and~TORN (וּטְרֵפָה *ut'rey'phah)* NOT (לֹא *lo)* *he~will~*EAT⁽ᵛ⁾ (יֹאכַל *yo'khal)* to~DIRTY~her (לְטָמְאָה *lê'tam'ah)* in~her (בָהּ *vah)* I (אֲנִי *a'ni)* YHWH (יְהֹוָה *YHWH)* **RMT:** A carcass or a torn one he will not eat, for her dirtiness is in her, I am **YHWH,**

---

¹⁰⁸ Referring to the "soul," a feminine noun.
¹⁰⁹ This Hebrew word can also imply the "going down" of the sun.

22:9 and~*they~did*~SAFEGUARD^(V) (וְשָׁמְרוּ *wê'sham'ru*) AT (אֶת *et*) CHARGE~me (מִשְׁמַרְתִּי *mish'ma're'ti*) and~NOT (וְלֹא *wê'lo*) they^(m)~ *will*~LIFT.UP^(V) (יִשְׂאוּ *yis'u*) UPON~him (עָלָיו *a'law*) FAILURE (חֵטְא *hheyt*) and~*they~did*~DIE^(V) (וּמֵתוּ *u'mey'tu*) in~him (בוֹ *vo*) GIVEN.THAT (כִּי *ki*) he~will~much~DRILL^(V)~her (יְחַלְלֻהוּ *yê'hhal'lu'hu*) I (אֲנִי *a'ni*) **YHWH** (יְהוָה *YHWH*) from~>~much~ SET.APART^(V)~them^(m) (מְקַדְּשָׁם *mê'qad'sham*) **RMT:** and they will safeguard my charge and they will not lift up upon him failure, and they will die in him if he defiles her, I am **YHWH** setting them apart,

22:10 and~ALL (וְכָל *wê'khol*) BE.STRANGE^(V)~*ing*^(ms) (זָר *zar*) NOT (לֹא *lo*) he~*will*~EAT^(V) (יֹאכַל *yo'khal*) SPECIAL (קֹדֶשׁ *qo'desh*) SETTLER (תּוֹשָׁב *to'shav*) ADMINISTRATOR (כֹהֵן *ko'heyn*) and~HIRELING (וְשָׂכִיר *wê'sa'khir*) NOT (לֹא *lo*) he~*will*~EAT^(V) (יֹאכַל *yo'khal*) SPECIAL (קֹדֶשׁ *qo'desh*) **RMT:** and anyone being a stranger will not eat the special thing, a settler of the administrator or a hireling will not eat the special thing,

22:11 and~ADMINISTRATOR (וְכֹהֵן *wê'kho'heyn*) GIVEN.THAT (כִּי *ki*) he~*will*~PURCHASE^(V) (יִקְנֶה *yiq'neh*) SOUL (נֶפֶשׁ *ne'phesh*) MATERIAL (קִנְיָן *qin'yan*) SILVER~him (כַּסְפּוֹ *kas'po*) HE (הוּא *hu*) he~*will*~EAT^(V) (יֹאכַל *yo'khal*) in~him (בוֹ *bo*) and~BORN (וִילִיד *wi'lid*) HOUSE~him (בֵיתוֹ *bey'to*) THEY^(m) (הֵם *heym*) *they*^(m)~*will*~EAT^(V) (יֹאכְלוּ *yokh'lu*) in~BREAD~him (בְלַחְמוֹ *vê'lahh'mo*) **RMT:** and the administrator that will purchase a soul, he is the material of his purchase, he will eat with him, and the ones born of his house, they will eat his bread,

22:12 and~DAUGHTER (וּבַת *u'vat*) ADMINISTRATOR (כֹהֵן *ko'heyn*) GIVEN.THAT (כִּי *ki*) she~*will*~EXIST^(V) (תִהְיֶה *tih'yeh*) to~MAN (לְאִישׁ *lê'ish*) BE.STRANGE^(V)~*ing*^(ms) (זָר *zar*) SHE (הִוא *hi*) in~OFFERING (בִּתְרוּמַת *bit'ru'mat*) the~SPECIAL~s (הַקֳּדָשִׁים *ha'qa'da'shim*) NOT (לֹא *lo*) she~*will*~EAT^(V) (תֹאכֵל *to'kheyl*) **RMT:** and the daughter of the administrator that will exist to a man being a stranger, she will not eat the special offering,

22:13 and~DAUGHTER (וּבַת *u'vat*) ADMINISTRATOR (כֹהֵן *ko'heyn*) GIVEN.THAT (כִּי *ki*) she~*will*~EXIST^{V)} (תִהְיֶה *tih'yeh*) WIDOW (אַלְמָנָה *al'ma'nah*) and~CAST.OUT^(V)~*ed*^(fs) (וּגְרוּשָׁה *ug'ru'shah*) and~SEED (וְזֶרַע *wê'ze'ra*) WITHOUT (אֵין *eyn*) to~her (לָהּ *lah*) and~*she~did*~ TURN.BACK^(V) (וְשָׁבָה *wê'sha'vah*) TO (אֶל *el*) HOUSE (בֵּית *beyt*) FATHER~her (אָבִיהָ *a'vi'ah*) like~YOUNG.AGE~s~her (כִּנְעוּרֶיהָ *kin'ur'yah*) from~BREAD (מִלֶּחֶם *mi'le'hhem*) FATHER~her (אָבִיהָ *a'vi'ah*) she~*will*~EAT^(V) (תֹאכֵל *to'kheyl*) and~ALL (וְכָל *wê'khol*)

BE.STRANGE(V)~*ing(ms)* (זָר *zar*) NOT (לֹא *lo*) *he~will~*EAT(V) (יֹאכַל *yo'khal*) in~him (בּוֹ *bo*) **RMT:** and the daughter of the administrator that will exist as a widow or is casted out or is without seed, and she is returned to the house of her father like in her young age, from the bread of her father she will eat, and anyone being a stranger will not eat with him,

22:14 and~MAN (וְאִישׁ *wê'ish*) GIVEN.THAT (כִּי *ki*) *he~will~*EAT(V) (יֹאכַל *yo'khal*) SPECIAL (קֹדֶשׁ *qo'desh*) in~ERROR (בִּשְׁגָגָה *bish'ga'gah*) and~*he~will~*ADD(V) (וְיָסַף *wê'ya'saph*) FIVE~him (חֲמִשִׁיתוֹ *hha'mi'shi'to*) UPON~him (עָלָיו *a'law*) and~*he~did~*GIVE(V) (וְנָתַן *wê'na'tan*) to~the~ADMINISTRATOR (לַכֹּהֵן *la'ko'heyn*) AT (אֶת *et*) the~SPECIAL (הַקֹּדֶשׁ *ha'qo'desh*) **RMT:** and a man that will eat the special thing in error, then he will add his fifth part upon him and he will give to the administrator with the special thing,

22:15 and~NOT (וְלֹא *wê'lo*) *they(m)~will~much~*DRILL(V) (יְחַלְּלוּ *yê'hhal'lu*) AT (אֶת *et*) SPECIAL~s (קָדְשֵׁי *qad'shey*) SON~s (בְּנֵי *bê'ney*) Yisra'eyl (יִשְׂרָאֵל *yis'ra'eyl*) AT (אֵת *eyt*) WHICH (אֲשֶׁר *a'sher*) *they(m)~will~make~*RAISE.UP(V) (יָרִימוּ *ya'ri'mu*) to~**YHWH** (לַיהוָה *la'YHWH*) **RMT:** and the sons of Yisra'eyl will not defile the special things that they raise up to **YHWH**,

22:16 and~*they~did~make~*LIFT.UP(V) (וְהִשִּׂיאוּ *wê'hi'si'u*) AT~them(m) (אוֹתָם *o'tam*) TWISTEDNESS (עֲוֹן *a'won*) GUILT (אַשְׁמָה *ash'mah*) in~>~EAT(V)~them(m) (בְּאָכְלָם *bê'akh'lam*) AT (אֶת *et*) SPECIAL~s~them(m) (קָדְשֵׁיהֶם *qad'shey'hem*) GIVEN.THAT (כִּי *ki*) I (אֲנִי *a'ni*) **YHWH** (יְהוָה *YHWH*) from~>~*much~*SET.APART(V)~them(m) (מְקַדְּשָׁם *mê'qad'sham*) **RMT:** and they will lift them up, the twistedness of guilt, in their eating their special things, given that I am **YHWH** setting them apart,

22:17 and~*he~will~much~*SPEAK(V) (וַיְדַבֵּר *wai'da'beyr*) **YHWH** (יְהוָה *YHWH*) TO (אֶל *el*) Mosheh (מֹשֶׁה *mo'sheh*) to~>~SAY(V) (לֵאמֹר *ley'mor*) **RMT:** and **YHWH** spoke to Mosheh saying,

22:18 *I(ms)~much~*SPEAK(V) (דַּבֵּר *da'beyr*) TO (אֶל *el*) Aharon (אַהֲרֹן *a'ha'ron*) and~TO (וְאֶל *wê'el*) SON~s~him (בָּנָיו *ba'naw*) and~TO (וְאֶל *wê'el*) ALL (כָּל *kol*) SON~s (בְּנֵי *bê'ney*) Yisra'eyl (יִשְׂרָאֵל *yis'ra'eyl*) and~*you(ms)~did~*SAY(V) (וְאָמַרְתָּ *wê'a'mar'ta*) TO~them(m) (אֲלֵהֶם *a'ley'hem*) MAN (אִישׁ *ish*) MAN (אִישׁ *ish*) from~HOUSE (מִבֵּית *mi'beyt*) Yisra'eyl (יִשְׂרָאֵל *yis'ra'eyl*) and~FROM (וּמִן *u'min*) the~IMMIGRANT (הַגֵּר *ha'geyr*) in~Yisra'eyl (בְּיִשְׂרָאֵל *bê'yis'ra'eyl*)

WHICH (אֲשֶׁר *a'sher*) _he~will~make~COME.NEAR_^(v) (יַקְרִיב *yaq'riv*) DONATION~him (קָרְבָּנוֹ *qar'ba no*) to~ALL (לְכָל *lê'khol*) VOW~s~ them(m) (נִדְרֵיהֶם *nid'rey'hem*) and~to~ALL (וּלְכָל *ul'khol*) FREEWILL.OFFERING~them(m) (נִדְבוֹתָם *nid'vo'tam*) WHICH (אֲשֶׁר *a'sher*) _they_(m)~_will~make~COME.NEAR_^(v) (יַקְרִיבוּ *yaq'ri'vu*) to~ YHWH (לַיהוָה *la'YHWH*) to~ASCENSION.OFFERING (לְעֹלָה *lê'lah*) **RMT:** speak to Aharon and to his sons, and to the sons of Yisra'eyl, and you will say to them, each man from the house of Yisra'eyl and from the immigrant in Yisra'eyl, which will bring near his donation for all their vows and for all their freewill offerings, which they bring near to **YHWH** for an ascension offering.

22:19 to~SELF-WILL~you(mp) (לִרְצֹנְכֶם *lir'tson'khem*) WHOLE (תָּמִים *ta'mim*) MALE (זָכָר *za'khar*) in~the~CATTLE (בַּבָּקָר *ba'ba'qar*) in~ the~SHEEP~s (בַּכְּשָׂבִים *bak'sa'vim*) and~in~the~SHE-GOAT~s (וּבָעִזִּים *u'va'i'zim*) **RMT:** For yourself, a whole male of the cattle, of the sheep and[110] of the she-goats.

22:20 ALL (כֹּל *kol*) WHICH (אֲשֶׁר *a'sher*) in~him (בּוֹ *bo*) BLEMISH (מוּם *mum*) NOT (לֹא *lo*) _you_(mp)~_will~make~COME.NEAR_^(v) (תַקְרִיבוּ *taq'riv'u*) GIVEN.THAT (כִּי *ki*) NOT (לֹא *lo*) to~SELF-WILL (לְרָצוֹן *lê'ra'tson*) _he~will~EXIST_^(v) (יִהְיֶה *yih'yeh*) to~you(mp) (לָכֶם *la'khem*) **RMT:** All that have in him a blemish you will not bring near, given that he will not exist for you for yourself,

22:21 and~MAN (וְאִישׁ *wê'ish*) GIVEN.THAT (כִּי *ki*) _he~will~make~ COME.NEAR_^(v) (יַקְרִיב *yaq'riv*) SACRIFICE (זֶבַח *ze'vahh*) OFFERING.OF.RESTITUTION~s (שְׁלָמִים *shê'la'mim*) to~YHWH (לַיהוָה *la'YHWH*) to~>~much~PERFORM^(v) (לְפַלֵּא *lê'pha'ley*) VOW (נֶדֶר *ne'der*) OR (אוֹ *o*) to~FREEWILL.OFFERING (לִנְדָבָה *lin'da'vah*) in~ the~CATTLE (בַּבָּקָר *ba'ba'qar*) OR (אוֹ *o*) in~the~FLOCKS (בַּצֹּאן *va'tson*) WHOLE (תָּמִים *ta'mim*) _he~will~EXIST_^(v) (יִהְיֶה *yih'yeh*) to~ SELF-WILL (לְרָצוֹן *lê'ra'tson*) ALL (כָּל *kol*) BLEMISH (מוּם *mum*) NOT (לֹא *lo*) _he~will~EXIST_^(v) (יִהְיֶה *yin'yeh*) in~him (בּוֹ *bo*) **RMT:** and a man that will bring near a sacrifice of offerings of restitution to **YHWH**, to perform a vow or for a freewill offering in the cattle or in the flocks, he will exist whole, to be accepted not any blemish will exist in him.

22:22 BLINDNESS (עַוֶּרֶת *a'we're't*) OR (אוֹ *o*) CRACK^(v)~_ed_(ms) (שָׁבוּר *sha'vur*) OR (אוֹ *o*) CUT.SHARPLY^(v)~_ed_(ms) (חָרוּץ *hha'ruts*) OR (אוֹ *o*)

---

[110] The prefix meaning "and" can also mean "or."

ULCER (יַבֶּלֶת ya'be'let) OR (אוֹ o) IRRITATION (גָרָב ga'rav) OR (אוֹ o) SKIN.SORE (יַלֶּפֶת ya'le'phet) NOT (לֹא lo) you(mp)~will~make~ COME.NEAR(V) (תַקְרִיבוּ taq'riv'u) THESE (אֵלֶּה ey'leh) to~**YHWH** (לַיהוָה la'YHWH) and~FIRE.OFFERING (וְאִשֶּׁה wê'i'sheh) NOT (לֹא lo) you(mp)~will~GIVE(V) (תִתְּנוּ tit'nu) from~them(m) (מֵהֶם mey'hem) UPON (עַל al) the~ALTAR (הַמִּזְבֵּחַ ha'miz'bey'ahh) to~**YHWH** (לַיהוָה la'YHWH) **RMT:** Blindness or cracked or cut sharply or an ulcer or an irritation or a skin sore, you will not bring these near to **YHWH**, and a fire offering you will not give from them upon the altar to **YHWH**,

22:23 and~OX (וְשׁוֹר wê'shor) and~RAM (וָשֶׂה wa'seh) BE.SUPERFLUOUS(V)~ed(ms) (שָׂרוּעַ sa'ru'a) and~DEFORM(V)~ed(ms) (וְקָלוּט wê'qa'lut) FREEWILL.OFFERING (נְדָבָה nê'da'vah) you(ms)~ will~DO(V) (תַּעֲשֶׂה ta'a'seh) AT~him (אֹתוֹ o'to) and~to~VOW (וּלְנֵדֶר ul'ney'der) NOT (לֹא lo) he~will~be~ACCEPT(V) (יֵרָצֶה yey'ra'tseh) **RMT:** and an ox or a ram, being superfluous or deformed, that you will make freewill offering of him, or for a vow, will not be accepted.

22:24 and~PRESS.FIRMLY(V)~ed(ms) (וּמָעוּךְ u'ma'ukh) and~SMASH(V)~ ed(ms) (וְכָתוּת wê'kha'tut) and~DRAW.AWAY(V)~ed(ms) (וְנָתוּק wê'na'tuq) and~CUT(V)~ed(ms) (וְכָרוּת wê'kha'rut) NOT (לֹא lo) you(mp)~will~make~COME.NEAR(V) (תַקְרִיבוּ taq'riv'u) to~**YHWH** (לַיהוָה la'YHWH) and~in~LAND~you(mp) (וּבְאַרְצְכֶם uv'ar'tse'khem) NOT (לֹא lo) you(mp)~will~DO(V) (תַעֲשׂוּ ta'a'su) **RMT:** Or pressed firmly or smashed or drawn away or cut, you will not bring near to **YHWH**, and in your land you will not do,

22:25 and~from~HAND (וּמִיַּד u'mi'yad) SON (בֶּן ben) FOREIGNER (נֵכָר ney'khar) NOT (לֹא lo) you(mp)~will~make~COME.NEAR(V) (תַקְרִיבוּ taq'riv'u) AT (אֶת et) BREAD (לֶחֶם le'hhem) Elohiym~ you(mp) (אֱלֹהֵיכֶם e'lo'hey'khem) from~ALL (מִכָּל mi'kol) THESE (אֵלֶּה ey'leh) GIVEN.THAT (כִּי ki) CORRUPTION~them(m) (מָשְׁחָתָם mash'hha'tam) in~them(m) (בָּהֶם ba'hem) BLEMISH (מוּם mum) in~ them(m) (בָּם bam) NOT (לֹא lo) they(m)~will~be~ACCEPT(V) (יֵרָצוּ yey'ra'tsu) to~you(mp) (לָכֶם la'khem) **RMT:** and from the hand of the son of a foreigner you will not bring near the bread of your Elohiym from any of these, given that their corruption is in them, a blemish is in them, they will not be accepted for you,

22:26 and~he~will~much~SPEAK(V) (וַיְדַבֵּר wai'da'beyr) **YHWH** (יְהוָה YHWH) TO (אֶל el) Mosheh (מֹשֶׁה mo'sheh) to~>~SAY(V) (לֵאמֹר ley'mor) **RMT:** and YHWH spoke to Mosheh saying,

22:27 <u>OX</u> (שׁוֹר shor) <u>OR</u> (אוֹ o) <u>SHEEP</u> (כֶּשֶׂב khe'sev) <u>OR</u> (אוֹ o) <u>SHE-GOAT</u> (עֵז eyz) <u>GIVEN.THAT</u> (כִּי ki) <u>he~will~be~BRING.FORTH</u>^(V) יִוָּלֵד yi'wa'leyd) <u>and~he~did~EXIST</u>^(V) (וְהָיָה wê'hai'yah) <u>SEVEN</u> (שִׁבְעַת shiv'at) <u>DAY~s</u> (יָמִים ya'mim) <u>UNDER</u> (תַּחַת ta'hhat) <u>MOTHER~him</u> (אִמּוֹ i'mo) <u>and~from~DAY</u> (וּמִיּוֹם u'mi'yom) <u>the~EIGHTH</u> הַשְּׁמִינִי hash'mini) <u>and~FURTHER</u> (וָהָלְאָה wa'hal'ah) <u>he~will~be~ACCEPT</u>^(V) (יֵרָצֶה yey'ra'tseh) <u>to~DONATION</u> (לְקָרְבַּן lê'qar'ban) <u>FIRE.OFFERING</u> (אִשֶּׁה i'sheh) <u>to~YHWH</u> (לַיהוָה la'YHWH) **RMT:** an ox or sheep or she-goat that will be brought forth, will exist seven days under his mother, and from the eighth day and further will be accepted for a donation of a fire offering for **YHWH**,

22:28 <u>and~OX</u> (וְשׁוֹר wê'shor) <u>OR</u> (אוֹ o) <u>RAM</u> (שֶׂה seh) <u>AT~him</u> (אֹתוֹ o'to) <u>and~AT</u> (וְאֶת wê'et) <u>SON~him</u> (בְּנוֹ bê'no) <u>NOT</u> (לֹא lo) <u>you^(ms)~will~SLAY</u>^(V) (תִשְׁחֲטוּ tish'hha'tu) <u>in~DAY</u> (בְּיוֹם bê'yom) <u>UNIT</u> (אֶחָד e'hhad) **RMT:** and an ox or a ram, you will not slay him and his son in one day,

22:29 <u>and~GIVEN.THAT</u> (וְכִי wê'khi) <u>you^(ms)~will~SACRIFICE</u>^(V)~him (תִזְבְּחוּ tiz'be'hhu) <u>SACRIFICE</u> (זֶבַח ze'vahh) <u>THANKS</u> (תּוֹדָה to'dah) <u>to~YHWH</u> (לַיהוָה la'YHWH) <u>to~SELF-WILL~you^(mp)</u> לִרְצֹנְכֶם lir'tson'khem) <u>you^(ms)~will~SACRIFICE</u>^(V)~him (תִזְבָּחוּ tiz'ba'hhu) **RMT:** and when you will sacrifice him as a sacrifice of thanks to **YHWH**, you will sacrifice him by your own will.

22:30 <u>in~the~DAY</u> (בַּיּוֹם ba'yom) <u>the~HE</u> (הַהוּא ha'hu) <u>he~will~be~EAT</u>^(V) (יֵאָכֵל yey'a'kheyl) <u>NOT</u> (לֹא lo) <u>you^(mp)~will~make~LEAVE.BEHIND</u>^(V) (תוֹתִירוּ to'ti'ru) <u>FROM~him</u> (מִמֶּנּוּ mi'me'nu) <u>UNTIL</u> (עַד ad) <u>MORNING</u> (בֹּקֶר bo'qer) <u>I</u> (אֲנִי a'ni) **YHWH** (יְהוָה YHWH) **RMT:** In that day he will be eaten, you will not leave anything behind from him until morning, I am **YHWH**,

22:31 <u>and~you^(mp)~did~SAFEGUARD</u>^(V) (וּשְׁמַרְתֶּם ush'mar'tem) <u>DIRECTIVE~s~me</u> (מִצְוֹתַי mits'o'tai) <u>and~you^(mp)~did~DO</u>^(V) (וַעֲשִׂיתֶם wa'a'si'tem) <u>AT~them^(m)</u> (אֹתָם o'tam) <u>I</u> (אֲנִי a'ni) **YHWH** (יְהוָה YHWH) **RMT:** and you will safeguard my directives, and you will do them, I am **YHWH**,

22:32 <u>and~NOT</u> (וְלֹא wê'lo) <u>you^(mp)~will~much~DRILL</u>^(V) תְחַלְלוּ tê'hhal'lu) <u>AT</u> (אֶת et) <u>TITLE</u> (שֵׁם shêym) <u>SPECIAL~me</u> (קָדְשִׁי qad'shi) <u>and~I~did~be~SET.APART</u>^(V) (וְנִקְדַּשְׁתִּי wê'niq'dash'ti) <u>in~MIDST</u> (בְּתוֹךְ bê'tokh) <u>SON~s</u> (בְּנֵי bê'ney) <u>Yisra'eyl</u> (יִשְׂרָאֵל yis'ra'eyl) <u>I</u> (אֲנִי a'ni) **YHWH** (יְהוָה YHWH) <u>much~SET.APART</u>^{(V)~}

ing^(ms)~you^(ms)) מְקַדִּשְׁכֶם *mê'qa'dish'khem*) **RMT:** and you will not defile my special title, and I will be set apart in the midst of the sons of Yisra'eyl, I am **YHWH** setting you apart.

22:33 the~*make*~GO.OUT^(V)~*ing*^(ms) (הַמּוֹצִיא *ha'mo'tsi*) AT~you^(mp) (אֶתְכֶם *et'khem*) from~LAND (מֵאֶרֶץ *mey'e'rets*) Mits'rayim (מִצְרַיִם *mits'ra'yim*) to~>~EXIST^(V) (לִהְיוֹת *lih'yot*) to~you^(mp) (לָכֶם *la'khem*) to~Elohiym (לֵאלֹהִים *ley'lo'him*) I (אֲנִי *a'ni*) **YHWH** (יְהֹוָה *YHWH*) **RMT:** The one causing you to go out from the land of Mits'rayim, to exist for you for Elohiym, I am **YHWH**,

Chapter 23

23:1 and~*he*~*will*~*much*~SPEAK^(V) (וַיְדַבֵּר *wai'da'beyr*) **YHWH** (יְהֹוָה *YHWH*) TO (אֶל *el*) Mosheh (מֹשֶׁה *mo'sheh*) to~>~SAY^(V) (לֵאמֹר *ley'mor*) **RMT:** and **YHWH** spoke to Mosheh saying,

23:2 *l*^(ms)~*much*~SPEAK^(V) (דַּבֵּר *da'beyr*) TO (אֶל *el*) SON~s (בְּנֵי *bê'ney*) Yisra'eyl (יִשְׂרָאֵל *yis'ra'eyl*) and~*you*^(ms)~*did*~SAY^(V) (וְאָמַרְתָּ *wê'a'mar'ta*) TO~them^(m) (אֲלֵהֶם *a'ley'hem*) APPOINTED~s (מוֹעֲדֵי *mo'a'dey*) **YHWH** (יְהֹוָה *YHWH*) WHICH (אֲשֶׁר *a'sher*) you^(mp)~*will*~CALL.OUT^(V) (תִּקְרְאוּ *tiq're'u*) AT~them^(m) (אֹתָם *o'tam*) MEETING~s (מִקְרָאֵי *miq'ra'ey*) SPECIAL (קֹדֶשׁ *qo'desh*) THESE (אֵלֶּה *ey'leh*) THEY^(m) (הֵם *heym*) APPOINTED~s (מוֹעֲדָי *mo'a'dey*) **RMT:** speak to the sons of Yisra'eyl, and you will say to them, the appointed times of **YHWH** that you will call out, these are special meetings, they are appointed times.

23:3 SIX (שֵׁשֶׁת *shey'shet*) DAY~s (יָמִים *ya'mim*) she~*will*~be~DO^(V) (תֵּעָשֶׂה *tey'a'seh*) BUSINESS (מְלָאכָה *mê'la'khah*) and~in~the~DAY (וּבַיּוֹם *u'vai'yom*) the~SEVENTH (הַשְּׁבִיעִי *hash'vi'i*) CEASING (שַׁבָּת *sha'bat*) REST.PERIOD (שַׁבָּתוֹן *sha'ba'ton*) MEETING (מִקְרָא *miq'ra*) SPECIAL (קֹדֶשׁ *qo'desh*) ALL (כָּל *kol*) BUSINESS (מְלָאכָה *mê'la'khah*) NOT (לֹא *lo*) you^(mp)~*will*~DO^(V) (תַעֲשׂוּ *ta'a'su*) CEASING (שַׁבָּת *sha'bat*) SHE (הִוא *hi*) to~**YHWH** (לַיהֹוָה *la'YHWH*) in~ALL (בְּכֹל *bê'khol*) SETTLING~s~you^(mp) (מוֹשְׁבֹתֵיכֶם *mosh'vo'tey'khem*) **RMT:** Six days business will be done, and in the seventh day is a ceasing rest period, a special meeting, no business will be done, she is a ceasing for **YHWH** in all your settling places.

23:4 THESE (אֵלֶּה *ey'leh*) APPOINTED~s (מוֹעֲדֵי *mo'a'dey*) **YHWH** (יְהֹוָה *YHWH*) MEETING~s (מִקְרָאֵי *miq'ra'ey*) SPECIAL (קֹדֶשׁ *qo'desh*) WHICH (אֲשֶׁר *a'sher*) you^(mp)~*will*~CALL.OUT^(V) (תִּקְרְאוּ *tiq're'u*)

tiq're'u) AT~them(m) (אֹתָם o'tam) in~APPOINTED~them(m) (בְּמוֹעֲדָם bê'mo'a'dam) **RMT:** These are the appointed times of **YHWH**, special meetings which you will call out in their appointed time.

23:5 in~the~NEW.MOON (בַּחֹדֶשׁ ba'hho'desh) the~FIRST (הָרִאשׁוֹן ha'ri'shon) in~FOUR (בְּאַרְבָּעָה bê'ar'ba'ah) TEN (עָשָׂר a'sar) to~the~NEW.MOON (לַחֹדֶשׁ la'hho'desh) BETWEEN (בֵּין beyn) the~EVENING~s2 (הָעַרְבָּיִם ha'ar'ba'yim) Pesahh (פֶּסַח pe'sahh) to~YHWH (לַיהוָה la'YHWH) **RMT:** In the first new moon, on the fourteenth[111] of the new moon, between the evenings[112], is the Pesahh for **YHWH**,

23:6 and~in~the~FIVE (וּבַחֲמִשָּׁה u'va'hha'mi'shah) TEN (עָשָׂר a'sar) DAY (יוֹם yom) to~the~NEW.MOON (לַחֹדֶשׁ la'hho'desh) the~THIS (הַזֶּה ha'zeh) FEAST (חַג hhag) the~UNLEAVENED.BREAD~s (הַמַּצּוֹת ha'ma'tsot) to~YHWH (לַיהוָה la'YHWH) SEVEN (שִׁבְעַת shiv'at) DAY~s (יָמִים ya'mim) UNLEAVENED.BREAD~s (מַצּוֹת ma'tsot) you(mp)~will~EAT(V) (תֹּאכֵלוּ to'khey'lu) **RMT:** and on the fifteenth day of this new moon is the feast of unleavened bread for **YHWH**, seven days you will eat unleavened bread.

23:7 in~the~DAY (בַּיּוֹם ba'yom) the~FIRST (הָרִאשׁוֹן ha'ri'shon) MEETING (מִקְרָא miq'ra) SPECIAL (קֹדֶשׁ qo'desh) he~will~EXIST(V) (יִהְיֶה yih'yeh) to~you(mp) (לָכֶם lc'khem) ALL (כָּל kol) BUSINESS (מְלָאכֶת mê'le'khet) SERVICE (עֲבֹדָה a'vo'dah) NOT (לֹא lo) you(mp)~will~DO(V) (תַעֲשׂוּ ta'a'su) **RMT:** In the first day a special meeting will exist for you, you will not do any business of service,

23:8 and~you(mp)~did~make~COME.NEAR(V) (וְהִקְרַבְתֶּם wê'hiq'rav'tem) FIRE.OFFERING (אִשֶּׁה i'sheh) to~**YHWH** (לַיהוָה la'YHWH) SEVEN (שִׁבְעַת shiv'at) DAY~s (יָמִים ya'mim) in~the~DAY (בַּיּוֹם ba'yom) the~SEVENTH (הַשְּׁבִיעִי hash'vi'i) MEETING (מִקְרָא miq'ra) SPECIAL (קֹדֶשׁ qo'desh) ALL (כָּל kol) BUSINESS (מְלָאכֶת mê'le'khet) SERVICE (עֲבֹדָה a'vo'dah) NOT (לֹא lo) you(mp)~will~DO(V) (תַעֲשׂוּ ta'a'su) **RMT:** and you will bring near a fire offering to **YHWH**

---

[111] The word "day" may be missing from the text (compare with Lev 23:6).

[112] As the word for "evening" is written in the double plural. This is literally translated as "between the 'two' evenings," but is of uncertain meaning. It may be the time between sunset and dark or between sunrise (as the word ערב literally means the "mixing" of light) and sunset.

seven days, in the seventh day is a special meeting, you will not do any business of service,

23:9 and~he~will~much~SPEAK[(V)] (וַיְדַבֵּר *wai'da'beyr*) **YHWH** (יְהוָה *YHWH*) TO (אֶל *el*) Mosheh (מֹשֶׁה *mo'sheh*) to~>~SAY[(V)] (לֵּאמֹר *ley'mor*) **RMT:** and YHWH spoke to Mosheh saying,

23:10 !(ms)~much~SPEAK[(V)] (דַּבֵּר *da'beyr*) TO (אֶל *el*) SON~s (בְּנֵי *bê'ney*) Yisra'eyl (יִשְׂרָאֵל *yis'ra'eyl*) and~you(ms)~did~SAY[(V)] (וְאָמַרְתָּ *wê'a'mar'ta*) TO~them(m) (אֲלֵהֶם *a'ley'hem*) GIVEN.THAT (כִּי *ki*) you(mp)~will~COME[(V)] (תָבֹאוּ *ta'vo'u*) TO (אֶל *el*) the~LAND (הָאָרֶץ *ha'a'rets*) WHICH (אֲשֶׁר *a'sher*) I (אֲנִי *a'ni*) GIVE[(V)]~ing(ms) (נֹתֵן *no'teyn*) to~you(mp) (לָכֶם *la'khem*) and~you(mp)~did~SEVER[(V)] (וּקְצַרְתֶּם *uq'tsar'tem*) AT (אֶת *et*) HARVEST~her (קְצִירָהּ *qê'tsi'rah*) and~you(mp)~did~make~COME[(V)] (וַהֲבֵאתֶם *wa'ha'vey'tem*) AT (אֶת *et*) SHEAF (עֹמֶר *o'mer*) SUMMIT (רֵאשִׁית *rey'shit*) HARVEST~you(mp) (קְצִירְכֶם *qê'tsir'khem*) TO (אֶל *el*) the~ADMINISTRATOR (הַכֹּהֵן *ha'ko'heyn*) **RMT:** speak to the sons of Yisra'eyl, and you will say to them, when you will come to the land that I am giving to you, and you will sever her harvest, and you will bring a sheaf of the summit of your harvest to the administrator,

23:11 and~he~did~WAVE[(V)] (וְהֵנִיף *wê'hey'niph*) AT (אֶת *et*) the~SHEAF (הָעֹמֶר *ha'o'mer*) to~FACE~s (לִפְנֵי *liph'ney*) **YHWH** (יְהוָה *YHWH*) to~SELF-WILL~you(mp) (לִרְצֹנְכֶם *lir'tson'khem*) from~MORROW (מִמָּחֳרַת *mi'ma'hha'rat*) the~CEASING (הַשַּׁבָּת *ha'sha'bat*) he~will~make~WAVE[(V)]~him (יְנִיפֶנּוּ *yê'ni'phe'nu*) the~ADMINISTRATOR (הַכֹּהֵן *ha'ko'heyn*) **RMT:** and he will wave the sheaf to the face of **YHWH** for your own will, on the morrow of the ceasing the administrator will make his waving,

23:12 and~you(mp)~did~DO[(V)] (וַעֲשִׂיתֶם *wa'a'si'tem*) in~DAY (בְּיוֹם *bê'yom*) >~make~WAVE[(V)]~you(mp) (הֲנִיפְכֶם *ha'niph'khem*) AT (אֶת *et*) the~SHEAF (הָעֹמֶר *ha'o'mer*) SHEEP (כֶּבֶשׂ *ke'ves*) WHOLE (תָּמִים *ta'mim*) SON (בֶּן *ben*) YEAR~him (שְׁנָתוֹ *shê'na'to*) to~ASCENSION.OFFERING (לְעֹלָה *lê'lah*) to~**YHWH** (לַיהוָה *la'YHWH*) **RMT:** and in the day you make your waving of the sheaf, a whole sheep, a son of his year, is for an ascension offering to **YHWH**,

23:13 and~DEPOSIT~him (וּמִנְחָתוֹ *u'min'hha'to*) TWO (שְׁנֵי *shê'ney*) ONE.TENTH~s (עֶשְׂרֹנִים *es'ro'nim*) FLOUR (סֹלֶת *so'let*) MIX[(V)]~ed(fs) (בְּלוּלָה *bê'lu'lah*) in~the~OIL (בַשֶּׁמֶן *va'she'men*) FIRE.OFFERING (אִשֶּׁה *i'sheh*) to~**YHWH** (לַיהוָה *la'YHWH*) AROMA (רֵיחַ *rey'ahh*)

SWEET (נִיחֹחַ *ni'hho'ahh*) and~POURING~her (וְנִסְכֹּה *wê'nis'koh*) WINE (יַיִן *ya'yin*) FOURTH (רְבִיעִת *rê'vi'it*) the~HIYN (הַהִין *ha'hin*) **RMT:** and his deposit is two tenths of flour mixed in the oil, a fire offering to **YHWH**, a sweet aroma, and her[113] pouring of wine, a fourth of a hiyn,

23:14 and~BREAD (וְלֶחֶם *wê'le'hhem*) and~ROASTED.GRAIN (וְקָלִי *wê'qa'li*) and~PLANTATION (וְכַרְמֶל *wê'khar'mel*) NOT (לֹא *lo*) you[(mp)]~will~EAT[(V)] (תֹאכְלוּ *to'khe'lu*) UNTIL (עַד *ad*) BONE (עֶצֶם *e'tsem*) the~DAY (הַיּוֹם *hai'yom*) the~THIS (הַזֶּה *ha'zeh*) UNTIL (עַד *ad*) >~make~COME[(V)]~you[(mp)] (הֲבִיאֲכֶם *ha'vi'a'khem*) AT (אֶת *et*) DONATION (קָרְבַּן *qar'ban*) Elohiym~you[(mp)] (אֱלֹהֵיכֶם *e'lo'hey'khem*) CUSTOM (חֻקַּת *hhu'qat*) DISTANT (עוֹלָם *o'lam*) to~GENERATION~s~you[(mp)] (לְדֹרֹתֵיכֶם *lê'do'ro'tey'khem*) in~ALL (בְּכֹל *bê'khol*) SETTLING~s~you[(mp)] (מֹשְׁבֹתֵיכֶם *mosh'vo'tey'khem*) **RMT:** and bread and roasted grain and plantation crops you will not eat, until the bone of the day[114] that you bring the donation of your Elohiym, a distant custom for your generations in all your settlings,

23:15 and~you[(mp)]~did~COUNT[(v)] (וּסְפַרְתֶּם *us'phar'tem*) to~you[(mp)] (לָכֶם *la'khem*) from~MORROW (מִמָּחֳרַת *mi'ma'hha'rat*) the~ CEASING (הַשַּׁבָּת *ha'sha'bat*) from~DAY (מִיּוֹם *mi'yom*) >~make~ COME[(V)]~you[(mp)] (הֲבִיאֲכֶם *ha'vi'a'khem*) AT (אֶת *et*) SHEAF (עֹמֶר *o'mer*) the~WAVING (הַתְּנוּפָה *hat'nu'phah*) SEVEN (שֶׁבַע *she'va*) CEASING~s (שַׁבָּתוֹת *sha'ba'tot*) WHOLE~s (תְּמִימֹת *tê'mi'mot*) they[(f)]~ will~EXIST[(V)] (תִּהְיֶינָה *tih'yey'nan*) **RMT:** and you will count for you from the morrow of the ceasing from the day you bring the sheaf of the waving, seven whole ceasings exist.

23:16 UNTIL (עַד *ad*) from~MORROW (מִמָּחֳרַת *mi'ma'hha'rat*) the~ CEASING (הַשַּׁבָּת *ha'sha'bat*) the~SEVENTH (הַשְּׁבִיעִת *ha'she'vi'it*) you[(mp)]~will~COUNT[(V)] (תִּסְפְּרוּ *tis'pe'ru*) FIVE~s (חֲמִשִּׁים *hha'mi'shim*) DAY (יוֹם *yom*) and~you[(mp)]~did~make~COME.NEAR[(V)] (וְהִקְרַבְתֶּם *wê'hiq'rav'tem*) DEPOSIT (מִנְחָה *min'hhah*) NEW (חֲדָשָׁה *hha'da'shah*) to~YHWH (לַיהוָה *la'YHWH*) **RMT:** Unto the morrow of the seventh ceasing, you will count fifty days, and you will bring near a new deposit for **YHWH**.

---

[113] The "her" is probably referring to the "deposit," a feminine word.
[114] "Bone of this day" is an idiom of uncertain meaning, but may mean "this very same day" or the "middle of this day."

23:17 from~SETTLING~s~you^(mp) (מִמּוֹשְׁבֹתֵיכֶם *mi'mosh'vo'tey'khem*) you^(mp)~will~make~COME^(V) (תָּבִיאוּ *ta'vi'u*) BREAD (לֶחֶם *le'hhem*) WAVING (תְּנוּפָה *tê'nu'phah*) TWO (שְׁתַּיִם *shê'ta'yim*) TWO (שְׁנֵי *shê'ney*) ONE.TENTH~s (עֶשְׂרֹנִים *es'ro'nim*) FLOUR (סֹלֶת *so'let*) they^(f)~will~EXIST^(V) (תִּהְיֶינָה *tih'yey'nah*) LEAVENED.BREAD (חָמֵץ *hha'meyts*) they^(f)~will~be~BAKE^(V) (תֵּאָפֶינָה *tey'a'phey'nah*) FIRST-FRUIT~s (בִּכּוּרִים *bi'ku'rim*) to~YHWH (לַיהוָה *la'YHWH*) **RMT:** From your settlings you will bring the bread of waving, two, two tenths of flour, they will exist as leavened bread, they will be baked, first-fruits for **YHWH**,

23:18 and~you^(mp)~did~make~COME.NEAR^(V) (וְהִקְרַבְתֶּם *wê'hiq'rav'tem*) UPON (עַל *al*) the~BREAD (הַלֶּחֶם *ha'le'hhem*) SEVEN (שִׁבְעַת *shiv'at*) SHEEP~s (כְּבָשִׂים *kê'va'sim*) WHOLE~s (תְּמִימִם *tê'mi'mim*) SON~s (בְּנֵי *bê'ney*) YEAR (שָׁנָה *sha'nah*) and~BULL (וּפַר *u'phar*) SON (בֶּן *ben*) CATTLE (בָּקָר *ba'qar*) UNIT (אֶחָד *e'hhad*) and~BUCK~s (וְאֵילִם *wê'ey'lim*) TWO (שְׁנָיִם *shê'na'yim*) they^(m)~will~EXIST^(V) (יִהְיוּ *yih'yu*) ASCENSION.OFFERING (עֹלָה *o'lah*) to~YHWH (לַיהוָה *la'YHWH*) and~DEPOSIT~them^(m) (וּמִנְחָתָם *u'min'hha'tam*) and~POURING~s~them^(m) (וְנִסְכֵּיהֶם *wê'nis'key'hem*) FIRE.OFFERING (אִשֵּׁה *i'sheyh*) AROMA (רֵיחַ *rey'ahh*) SWEET (נִיחֹחַ *ni'hho'ahh*) to~YHWH (לַיהוָה *la'YHWH*) **RMT:** and you will bring near upon the bread seven whole sheep, sons of a year, and one bull, son of cattle, and two bucks, they will exist as ascension offerings for **YHWH**, and their deposit and their pourings are a fire offering, a sweet aroma to **YHWH**,

23:19 and~you^(mp)~did~DO^(V) (וַעֲשִׂיתֶם *wa'a'si'tem*) HAIRY.GOAT (שְׂעִיר *sê'ir*) SHE-GOAT~s (עִזִּים *i'zim*) UNIT (אֶחָד *e'hhad*) to~FAILURE (לְחַטָּאת *lê'hha'tat*) and~TWO (וּשְׁנֵי *ush'ney*) SHEEP~s (כְבָשִׂים *khê'va'sim*) SON~s (בְּנֵי *bê'ney*) YEAR (שָׁנָה *sha'nah*) to~SACRIFICE (לְזֶבַח *lê'ze'vahh*) OFFERING.OF.RESTITUTION~s (שְׁלָמִים *shê'la'mim*) **RMT:** and you will do one hairy goat of the she-goats for a failure and two sheep, sons of a year, for a sacrifice of offering of restitution,

23:20 and~he~did~WAVE^(V) (וְהֵנִיף *wê'hey'niph*) the~ADMINISTRATOR (הַכֹּהֵן *ha'ko'heyn*) AT~them^(m) (אֹתָם *o'tam*) UPON (עַל *al*) BREAD (לֶחֶם *le'hhem*) the~FIRST-FRUIT~s (הַבִּכּוּרִים *ha'bi'ku'rim*)[115] WAVING (תְּנוּפָה *tê'nu'phah*) to~FACE~s (לִפְנֵי *li'phney*)

---

[115] *Leningrad Codex:* הבכרים

liph'ney) **YHWH** (יְהוָה *YHWH*) UPON (עַל *al*) TWO (שְׁנֵי *shê'ney*)
SHEEP~s (כְּבָשִׂים *kê'va'sim*) SPECIAL (קֹדֶשׁ *qo'desh*) they(m)~will~
EXIST(V) (יִהְיוּ *yih'yu*) to~**YHWH** (לַיהוָה *la'YHWH*) to~the~
ADMINISTRATOR (לַכֹּהֵן *la'ko'heyn*) **RMT:** and the administrator will
wave them with the bread of the first-fruits, waving to the face of
YHWH, concerning the two sheep, they will exist special for **YHWH**
and for the administrator,

23:21 and~you(mp)~did~CALL.OUT(V) (וּקְרָאתֶם *uq'ra'tem*) in~BONE
(בְּעֶצֶם *bê'e'tsem*) the~DAY (הַיּוֹם *hai'yom*) the~THIS (הַזֶּה *ha'zeh*)
MEETING (מִקְרָא *miq'ra*) SPECIAL (קֹדֶשׁ *qo'desh*) he~will~EXIST(V)
(יִהְיֶה *yih'yeh*) to~you(mp) (לָכֶם *la'khem*) ALL (כָּל *kol*) BUSINESS
(מְלֶאכֶת *mê'le'khet*) SERVICE (עֲבֹדָה *a'vo'dah*) NOT (לֹא *lo*) you(mp)~
will~DO(V) (תַעֲשׂוּ *ta'a'su*) CUSTOM (חֻקַּת *hhu'qat*) DISTANT (עוֹלָם
o'lam) in~ALL (בְּכֹל *bê'khol*) SETTLING~s~you(mp) מוֹשְׁבֹתֵיכֶם
mosh'vo'tey'khem) to~GENERATION~s~you(mp) (לְדֹרֹתֵיכֶם
lê'do'ro'tey'khem) **RMT:** and you will call out in the bone of that
day[116], he will exist as a special meeting, you will not do any business
of service, a distant custom in all your settlings to your generations,

23:22 and~in~>~SEVER(V)~you(mp) (וּבְקֻצְרְכֶם *uv'quts're'khem*) AT (אֶת
et) HARVEST (קְצִיר *qê'tsir*) LAND~you(mp) (אַרְצְכֶם *ar'tse'khem*) NOT
(לֹא *lo*) you(ms)~will~much~FINISH(V) (תְכַלֶּה *tê'kha'leh*) EDGE (פְּאַת
pê'at) FIELD~you(ms) (שָׂדְךָ *sad'kha*) in~>~SEVER(V)~you(ms) בְּקֻצְרֶךָ
bê'quts're'kha) and~GLEANINGS (וְלֶקֶט *wê'le'qet*) HARVEST~you(ms)
(קְצִירְךָ *qê'tsir'kha*) NOT (לֹא *lo*) you(ms)~will~much~PICK.UP(V)
tê'la'qeyt) to~AFFLICTION (לֶעָנִי *le'a'ni*) and~to~IMMIGRANT (וְלַגֵּר
wê'la'geyr) you(ms)~will~LEAVE(V) (תַעֲזֹב *ta'a'zov*) AT~them(m) (אֹתָם
o'tam) I (אֲנִי *a'ni*) **YHWH** (יְהוָה *YHWH*) Elohiym~you(mp)
e'lo'hey'khem) **RMT:** and in your severing of the harvest of your land,
you will not finish the edge of your field, in your severing and
gleanings of your harvest you will not pick up, they are for the
afflicted and for the immigrant, you will leave them, I am **YHWH**
your Elohiym,

23:23 and~he~will~much~SPEAK(V) (וַיְדַבֵּר *wai'da'beyr*) **YHWH** (יְהוָה
YHWH) TO (אֶל *el*) Mosheh (מֹשֶׁה *mo'sheh*) to~>~SAY(V) (לֵאמֹר
ley'mor) **RMT:** and **YHWH** spoke to Mosheh saying,

---

[116] "Bone of this day" is an idiom of uncertain meaning, but may
mean "this very same day" or the "middle of this day."

23:24 !(ms)~*much*~SPEAK(V) (דַּבֵּר *da'beyr*) TO (אֶל *el*) SON~s (בְּנֵי *bê'ney*) Yisra'eyl (יִשְׂרָאֵל *yis'ra'eyl*) to~>~SAY(V) (לֵאמֹר *ley'mor*) in~ the~NEW.MOON (בַּחֹדֶשׁ *ba'hho'desh*) the~SEVENTH (הַשְּׁבִיעִי *hash'vi'i*) in~UNIT (בְּאֶחָד *bê'e'hhad*) to~the~NEW.MOON (לַחֹדֶשׁ *la'hho'desh*) he~will~EXIST(V) (יִהְיֶה *yih'yeh*) to~you(mp) (לָכֶם *la'khem*) REST.PERIOD (שַׁבָּתוֹן *sha'ba'ton*) REMEMBRANCE (זִכְרוֹן *zikh'ron*) SIGNAL (תְּרוּעָה *tê'ru'ah*) MEETING (מִקְרָא *miq'ra*) SPECIAL (קֹדֶשׁ *qo'desh*) **RMT**: speak to the sons of Yisra'eyl saying, in the seventh new moon, on the first of the new moon is a rest period, it will exist for you as a remembrance of a signal, a special meeting.

23:25 ALL (כָּל *kol*) BUSINESS (מְלֶאכֶת *mê'le'khet*) SERVICE (עֲבֹדָה *a'vo'dah*) NOT (לֹא *lo*) you(mp)~will~DO(V) (תַעֲשׂוּ *ta'a'su*) and~you(mp)~ did~make~COME.NEAR(V) (וְהִקְרַבְתֶּם *wê'hiq'rav'tem*) FIRE.OFFERING (אִשֶּׁה *i'sheh*) to~YHWH (לַיהוָה *la'YHWH*) **RMT**: You will not do any business of service and you will bring near a fire offering to YHWH,

23:26 and~he~will~*much*~SPEAK(V) (וַיְדַבֵּר *wai'da'beyr*) YHWH (יהוה YHWH) TO (אֶל *el*) Mosheh (מֹשֶׁה *mo'sheh*) to~>~SAY(V) (לֵאמֹר *ley'mor*) **RMT**: and YHWH spoke to Mosheh saying,

23:27 SURELY (אַךְ *akh*) in~TENTH.ONE (בֶּעָשׂוֹר *be'a'sor*) to~the~ NEW.MOON (לַחֹדֶשׁ *la'hho'desh*) the~SEVENTH (הַשְּׁבִיעִי *hash'vi'i*) the~THIS (הַזֶּה *ha'zeh*) DAY (יוֹם *yom*) the~ATONEMENT~s (הַכִּפֻּרִים *ha'ki'pu'rim*) HE (הוּא *hu*) MEETING (מִקְרָא *miq'ra*) SPECIAL (קֹדֶשׁ *qo'desh*) he~will~EXIST(V) (יִהְיֶה *yih'yeh*) to~you(mp) (לָכֶם *la'khem*) and~you(mp)~did~*much*~AFFLICT(V) (וְעִנִּיתֶם *wê'i'ni'tem*) AT (אֵת *et*) SOUL~s~you(mp) (נַפְשֹׁתֵיכֶם *naph'sho'tey'khem*) and~you(mp)~did~ make~COME.NEAR(V) (וְהִקְרַבְתֶּם *wê'hiq'rav'tem*) FIRE.OFFERING (אִשֶּׁה *i'sheh*) to~YHWH (לַיהוָה *la'YHWH*) **RMT**: surely, on the tenth of this seventh new moon is a day of atonements, he will exist for you as a special meeting and you will afflict your souls, and you will bring near a fire offering to YHWH,

23:28 and~ALL (וְכָל *wê'khol*) BUSINESS (מְלָאכָה *mê'la'khah*) NOT (לֹא *lo*) you(mp)~will~DO(V) (תַעֲשׂוּ *ta'a'su*) in~BONE (בְּעֶצֶם *bê'e'tsem*) the~DAY (הַיּוֹם *hai'yom*) the~THIS (הַזֶּה *ha'zeh*) GIVEN.THAT (כִּי *ki*) DAY (יוֹם *yom*) ATONEMENT~s (כִּפֻּרִים *ki'pu'rim*) HE (הוּא *hu*) to~>~ *much*~COVER(V) (לְכַפֵּר *lê'kha'peyr*) UPON~you(mp) (עֲלֵיכֶם *a'ley'khem*) to~FACE~s (לִפְנֵי *liph'ney*) YHWH (יהוה YHWH) Elohiym~ you(mp) (אֱלֹהֵיכֶם *e'lo'hey'khem*) **RMT**: and you will not do any business in the bone of this day[117], given that he is a day of atonements to make restitution upon you to the face of **YHWH** your Elohiym,

23:29 GIVEN.THAT (כִּי *ki*) ALL (כָּל *khol*) the~SOUL (הַנֶּפֶשׁ *ha'ne'phesh*) WHICH (אֲשֶׁר *a'sher*) NOT (לֹא *lo*) *she~will~be~much~* AFFLICT[(V)] (תְעֻנֶּה *tê'u'neh*) in~BONE (בְּעֶצֶם *bê'e'tsem*) the~DAY (הַיּוֹם *hai'yom*) the~THIS (הַזֶּה *hc'zeh*) and~*she~did~be~CUT*[(V)] (וְנִכְרְתָה *wê'nikh're'tah*) from~PEOPLE~s~her (מֵעַמֶּיהָ *mey'a'mey'ah*) **RMT:** given that any soul that is not afflicted in the bone of this day[118] will be cut from her people.

23:30 and~ALL (וְכָל *wê'khol*) the~SOUL (הַנֶּפֶשׁ *ha'ne'phesh*) WHICH (אֲשֶׁר *a'sher*) *you*[(ms)]*~will~DO*[(V)] (תַּעֲשֶׂה *ta'a'seh*) ALL (כָּל *kol*) BUSINESS (מְלָאכָה *mê'la'khah*) in~BONE (בְּעֶצֶם *bê'e'tsem*) the~DAY (הַיּוֹם *hai'yom*) the~THIS (הַזֶּה *ha'zeh*) and~*I~did~make~PERISH*[(V)] (וְהַאֲבַדְתִּי *wê'ha'a'vad'ti*) AT (אֶת *et*) the~SOUL (הַנֶּפֶשׁ *ha'ne'phesh*) the~SHE (הַהִוא *ha'hi*) from~INSIDE (מִקֶּרֶב *mi'qe'rev*) PEOPLE~her (עַמָּהּ *a'mah*) **RMT:** and any soul that does business in the bone of this day, then I will cause that soul to perish from inside her people.

23:31 ALL (כָּל *kol*) BUSINESS (מְלָאכָה *mê'la'khah*) NOT (לֹא *lo*) *you*[(mp)]*~will~DO*[(V)] (תַעֲשׂוּ *ta'a'su*) CUSTOM (חֻקַּת *hhu'qat*) DISTANT (עוֹלָם *o'lam*) to~GENERATION~s~*you*[(mp)] (לְדֹרֹתֵיכֶם *lê'do'ro'tey'khem*) in~ALL (בְּכֹל *bê'khol*) SETTLING~s~*you*[(mp)] (מֹשְׁבֹתֵיכֶם *mosh'vo'tey'khem*) **RMT:** You will not do any business, a distant custom for your generations in all your settlings.

23:32 CEASING (שַׁבַּת *sha'bat*) REST.PERIOD (שַׁבָּתוֹן *sha'ba'ton*) HE (הוּא *hu*) to~*you*[(mp)] (לָכֶם *la'khem*) and~*you*[(mp)]*~did~much~* AFFLICT[(V)] (וְעִנִּיתֶם *wê'i'ni'tem*) AT (אֶת *et*) SOUL~s~*you*[(mp)] (נַפְשֹׁתֵיכֶם *naph'sho'tey'khem*) in~NINE (בְּתִשְׁעָה *bê'tish'ah*) to~the~ NEW.MOON (לַחֹדֶשׁ *la'hho'desh*) in~the~EVENING (בָּעֶרֶב *ba'e'rev*) from~EVENING (מֵעֶרֶב *mey'e'rev*) UNTIL (עַד *ad*) EVENING (עֶרֶב *e'rev*) *you*[(mp)]*~will~CEASE*[(V)] (תִּשְׁבְּתוּ *tish'be'tu*) CEASING~*you*[(mp)] (שַׁבַּתְּכֶם *sha'bat'khem*) **RMT:** He is a ceasing of rest period for you,

---

[117] "Bone of this day" is an idiom of uncertain meaning, but may mean "this very same day" or the "middle of this day."
[118] "Bone of this day" is an idiom of uncertain meaning, but may mean "this very same day" or the "middle of this day."

and you will afflict your souls in the ninth of the new moon in the evening, from evening until evening[119] you will cease your ceasings,

23:33 and~*he~will~much*~SPEAK[(V)] וַיְדַבֵּר *wai'da'beyr* **YHWH** (יְהוָה *YHWH*) TO (אֶל *el*) Mosheh (מֹשֶׁה *mo'sheh*) to~>~SAY[(V)] (לֵאמֹר *ley'mor*) **RMT:** and YHWH spoke to Mosheh saying,

23:34 !*(ms)~much*~SPEAK[(V)] (דַּבֵּר *da'beyr*) TO (אֶל *el*) SON~s (בְּנֵי *bê'ney*) Yisra'eyl (יִשְׂרָאֵל *yis'ra'eyl*) to~>~SAY[(V)] (לֵאמֹר *ley'mor*) in~ the~FIVE (בַּחֲמִשָּׁה *ba'hha'mi'shah*) TEN (עָשָׂר *a'sar*) DAY (יוֹם *yom*) to~the~NEW.MOON (לַחֹדֶשׁ *la'hho'desh*) the~SEVENTH (הַשְּׁבִיעִי *hash'vi'i*) the~THIS (הַזֶּה *ha'zeh*) FEAST (חַג *hhag*) the~BOOTH~s (הַסֻּכּוֹת *ha'su'kot*) SEVEN (שִׁבְעַת *shiv'at*) DAY~s (יָמִים *ya'mim*) to~ **YHWH** (לַיהֹוָה *le'YHWH*) **RMT:** speak to the sons of Yisra'eyl saying, in the fifteenth day of this seventh new moon, a feast of booths, seven days for **YHWH**.

23:35 in~the~DAY (בַּיּוֹם *ba'yom*) the~FIRST (הָרִאשׁוֹן *ha'ri'shon*) MEETING (מִקְרָא *miq'ra*) SPECIAL (קֹדֶשׁ *qo'desh*) ALL (כָּל *kol*) BUSINESS (מְלֶאכֶת *mê'le'khet*) SERVICE (עֲבֹדָה *a'vo'dah*) NOT (לֹא *lo*) *you(mp)~will~*DO[(V)] (תַעֲשׂוּ *ta'a'su*) **RMT:** On the first day is a special meeting, you will not do any business of service.

23:36 SEVEN (שִׁבְעַת *shiv'at*) DAY~s (יָמִים *ya'mim*) *you(mp)~will~ make~*COME.NEAR[(V)] (תַּקְרִיבוּ *taq'ri'vu*) FIRE.OFFERING (אִשֶּׁה *i'sheh*) to~**YHWH** (לַיהֹוָה *la'YHWH*) in~the~DAY (בַּיּוֹם *ba'yom*) the~ EIGHTH (הַשְּׁמִינִי *hash'mini*) MEETING (מִקְרָא *miq'ra*) SPECIAL (קֹדֶשׁ *qo'desh*) *he~will~*EXIST[(V)] (יִהְיֶה *yih'yeh*) to~you(mp) (לָכֶם *la'khem*) and~*you(mp)~did~make~*COME.NEAR[(V)] (וְהִקְרַבְתֶּם *wê'hiq'rav'tem*) FIRE.OFFERING (אִשֶּׁה *i'sheh*) to~**YHWH** (לַיהֹוָה *la'YHWH*) CONFERENCE (עֲצֶרֶת *a'tse'ret*) SHE (הוא *hi*) ALL (כָּל *kol*) BUSINESS (מְלֶאכֶת *mê'le'khet*) SERVICE (עֲבֹדָה *a'vo'dah*) NOT (לֹא *lo*) *you(mp)~ will~*DO[(V)] (תַעֲשׂוּ *ta'a'su*) **RMT:** Seven days you will bring near a fire offering to YHWH, on the eighth day, a special meeting will exist for you, and you will bring near a fire offering to **YHWH**, she is a conference, you will not do any business of service.

23:37 THESE (אֵלֶּה *ey'leh*) APPOINTED~s (מוֹעֲדֵי *mo'a'dey*) **YHWH** (יְהוָה *YHWH*) WHICH (אֲשֶׁר *a'sher*) *you(mp)~will~*CALL.OUT[(V)] (תִּקְרְאוּ *tiq're'u*) AT~them(m) (אֹתָם *o'tam*) MEETING~s (מִקְרָאֵי *miq'ra'ey*)

---

[119] The phrase "from the evening until evenings" is of uncertain meaning, but may be the time between sunset and dark.

SPECIAL (קֹדֶשׁ qo'desh) to~>~make~COME.NEAR[V] (לְהַקְרִיב)
lê'haq'riv) FIRE.OFFERING (אִשֶּׁה i'sheh) to~YHWH (לַיהוָה la'YHWH)
ASCENSION.OFFERING (עֹלָה o'lah) and~DEPOSIT (וּמִנְחָה
u'min'hhah) SACRIFICE (זֶבַח ze'vahh) and~POURING~s (וּנְסָכִים
un'sa'khim) WORD (דְּבַר dê'var) DAY (יוֹם yom) in~DAY~him (בְּיוֹמוֹ
bê'yo'mo) **RMT:** These are the appointed times of **YHWH** that you
will call them out, special meetings to bring near a fire offering to
YHWH, an ascension offering and a deposit, a sacrifice and pourings,
a thing of a day in his day.

23:38 from~to~STRAND (מִלְּבַד mi'le'vad)[120] CEASING~s (שַׁבְּתֹת
sha'be'tot) **YHWH** (יְהוָה YHWH) and~from~to~STRAND (וּמִלְּבַד
u'mil'vad) CONTRIBUTION~s~you[mp] (מַתְּנוֹתֵיכֶם mat'no'tey'khem)
and~from~to~STRAND (וּמִלְּבַד u'mil'vad) ALL (כָּל kol) VOW~s~
you[mp] (נִדְרֵיכֶם nid'rey'khem) and~from~to~STRAND (וּמִלְּבַד
u'mil'vad) ALL (כָּל kol) FREEWILL.OFFERING~you[mp] (נִדְבוֹתֵיכֶם
nid'vo'tey'khem)[121] WHICH (אֲשֶׁר a'sher) you[mp]~will~GIVE[V] (תִּתְּנוּ
tit'nu) to~YHWH (לַיהוָה la'YHWH) **RMT:** Apart from the ceasings of
YHWH, and besides your contributions, and besides all your vows,
and besides all your freewill offerings, which you will give to **YHWH**.

23:39 SURELY (אַךְ akh) in~the~FIVE (בַּחֲמִשָּׁה ba'hha'mi'shah) TEN
(עָשָׂר a'sar) DAY (יוֹם yom) to~the~NEW.MOON (לַחֹדֶשׁ la'hho'desh)
the~SEVENTH (הַשְּׁבִיעִי hash'vi'i) in~>~GATHER[V]~you[mp] (בְּאָסְפְּכֶם
bê'as'pe'khem) AT (אֶת et) PRODUCTION (תְּבוּאַת tê'vu'at) the~
LAND (הָאָרֶץ ha'a'rets) you[mp]~will~HOLD.A.FEAST[V] (תָּחֹגּוּ
ta'hho'gu) AT (אֶת et) FEAST (חַג hhag) **YHWH** (יְהוָה YHWH) SEVEN
(שִׁבְעַת shiv'at) DAY~s (יָמִים ya'mim) in~the~DAY (בַּיּוֹם ba'yom)
the~FIRST (הָרִאשׁוֹן ha'ri'shon) REST.PERIOD (שַׁבָּתוֹן sha'ba'ton)
and~in~the~DAY (וּבַיּוֹם u'vai'yom) the~EIGHTH (הַשְּׁמִינִי hash'mini)
REST.PERIOD (שַׁבָּתוֹן sha'ba'ton) **RMT:** Surely, on the fifteenth day
of the seventh new moon, in the gathering of your production of the
land, you will hold a feast, a feast of **YHWH**, seven days, on the first
day is a rest period, and on the eighth day is a rest period,

23:40 and~you[mp]~did~TAKE[V] (וּלְקַחְתֶּם ul'qahh'tem) to~you[mp]
(לָכֶם la'khem) in~the~DAY (בַּיּוֹם ba'yom) the~FIRST (הָרִאשׁוֹן
ha'ri'shon) PRODUCE (פְּרִי pê'ri) TREE (עֵץ eyts) HONOR (הָדָר ha'dar)
PALM~s (כַּפֹּת ka'pot) DATE.PALM~s (תְּמָרִים tê'ma'rim) and~

---

[120] An idiom meaning "apart from."
[121] *Leningrad Codex*: נדבתיכם

BOUGH (וַעֲנַף wa'a'naph) TREE (עֵץ eyts) THICK.WOVEN (עָבֹת a'vot) and~WILLOW~s (וְעַרְבֵי wê'ar'vey) WADI (נָחַל na'hhal) and~ REJOICING~you(mp) (וּשְׂמַחְתֶּם us'mahh'tem) to~FACE~s (לִפְנֵי liph'ney) **YHWH** (יהוה YHWH) Elohiym~you(mp) (אֱלֹהֵיכֶם e'lo'hey'khem) SEVEN (שִׁבְעַת shiv'at) DAY~s (יָמִים ya'mim)
RMT: and you will take for you in the first day produce of an honorable tree, palms of the date palms and a bough of a thick woven tree, and willows of the wadi, and your rejoicing to the face of **YHWH** your Elohiym, seven days,

23:41 and~you(mp)~did~HOLD.A.FEAST(V) (וְחַגֹּתֶם wê'hha'go'tem) AT~ him (אֹתוֹ o'to) FEAST (חַג hhag) to~**YHWH** (לַיהוָה la'YHWH) SEVEN (שִׁבְעַת shiv'at) DAY~s (יָמִים ya'mim) in~the~YEAR (בַּשָּׁנָה ba'sha'nah) CUSTOM (חֻקַּת hhu'qat) DISTANT (עוֹלָם o'lam) to~ GENERATION~s~you(mp) (לְדֹרֹתֵיכֶם lê'do'ro'tey'khem) in~the~ NEW.MOON (בַּחֹדֶשׁ ba'hho'desh) the~SEVENTH (הַשְּׁבִיעִי hash'vi'i) you(mp)~will~HOLD.A.FEAST(V) (תָּחֹגּוּ ta'hho'gu) AT~him (אֹתוֹ o'to)
RMT: and you will hold his feast, a feast to **YHWH**, seven days in the year, a distant custom for your generations, in the seventh new moon you will hold his feast.

23:42 in~the~BOOTH~s (בַּסֻּכֹּת ba'su'kot) you(mp)~will~SETTLE(V) (תֵּשְׁבוּ teysh'vu) SEVEN (שִׁבְעַת shiv'at) DAY~s (יָמִים ya'mim) ALL (כָּל kol) the~NATIVE (הָאֶזְרָח ha'ez'rahh) in~Yisra'eyl (בְּיִשְׂרָאֵל bê'yis'ra'eyl) they(m)~will~SETTLE(V) (יֵשְׁבוּ yeysh'vu) in~the~BOOTH~s (בַּסֻּכֹּת ba'su'kot) **RMT:** You will settle in the booths seven days, every native in Yisra'eyl will settle in the booths.

23:43 to~THAT (לְמַעַן lê'ma'an) they(m)~will~KNOW(V) (יֵדְעוּ yeyd'u) GENERATION~s~you(mp) (דֹרֹתֵיכֶם do'ro'tey'khem) GIVEN.THAT (כִּי ki) in~the~BOOTH~s (בַּסֻּכּוֹת va'su'kot) I~did~be~make~ TURN.BACK(V) (הוֹשַׁבְתִּי ho'shav'ti) AT (אֶת et) SON~s (בְּנֵי bê'ney) Yisra'eyl (יִשְׂרָאֵל yis'ra'eyl) in~>~make~GO.OUT(V)~me (בְּהוֹצִיאִי bê'ho'tsi'i) AT~them(m) (אוֹתָם o'tam) from~LAND (מֵאֶרֶץ mey'e'rets) Mits'rayim (מִצְרָיִם mits'ra'yim) I (אֲנִי a'ni) **YHWH** (יְהוָה YHWH) Elohiym~you(mp) (אֱלֹהֵיכֶם e'lo'hey'khem) **RMT:** So that your generations will know that in the booths I made the sons of Yisra'eyl turn back in my bringing them out from the land of Mits'rayim, I am **YHWH** your Elohiym,

23:44 and~he~will~much~SPEAK(V) (וַיְדַבֵּר wai'da'beyr) Mosheh (מֹשֶׁה mo'sheh) AT (אֶת et) APPOINTED~s (מֹעֲדֵי mo'a'dey) **YHWH** (יְהוָה YHWH) TO (אֶל el) SON~s (בְּנֵי bê'ney) Yisra'eyl (יִשְׂרָאֵל yis'ra'eyl)

yis'ra'eyl) **RMT:** and Mosheh spoke about the appointed times of **YHWH** to the sons of Yisra'eyl,

Chapter 24

24:1 and~he~will~much~SPEAK^(V) וַיְדַבֵּר) wai'da'beyr) **YHWH** (יְהוָה) YHWH) TO (אֶל el) Mosheh (מֹשֶׁה mo'sheh) to~>~SAY^(V) (לֵאמֹר) ley'mor) **RMT:** and **YHWH** spoke to Mosheh saying,

24:2 !^(ms)~much~DIRECT^(V) צַו) tsaw) AT (אֶת et) SON~s (בְּנֵי bê'ney) Yisra'eyl (יִשְׂרָאֵל yis'ra'eyl) and~they^(m)~will~TAKE^(V) (וְיִקְחוּ) wê'yiq'hhu) TO~you^(ms) (אֵלֶיךָ ey'ley'kha) OIL (שֶׁמֶן she'men) OLIVE (זַיִת za'yit) REFINED (זָךְ zakh) SMASHED (כָּתִית ka'tit) to~the~ LUMINARY (לַמָּאוֹר la'ma'or) to~>~^make~GO.UP^(V) (לְהַעֲלֹת) lê'ha'a'lot) LAMP (נֵר neyr) CONTINUALLY (תָּמִיד ta'mid) **RMT:** direct the sons of Yisra'eyl, and they will take to you refined olive oil, smashed for the luminary[122], to make the lamp continually go up[123].

24:3 from~OUTSIDE (מִחוּץ mi'hhuts) to~TENT.CURTAIN (לְפָרֹכֶת) lê'pha'ro'khet) the~EVIDENCE (הָעֵדֻת ha'ey'dut) in~TENT (בְּאֹהֶל bê'o'hel) APPOINTED (מוֹעֵד mo'eyd) he~will~ARRANGE^(V) (יַעֲרֹךְ) ya'a'rokh) AT~him (אֹתוֹ o'to) Aharon (אַהֲרֹן a'ha'ron) from~ EVENING (מֵעֶרֶב mey'e'rev) UNTIL (עַד ad) MORNING (בֹּקֶר bo'qer) to~FACE~s (לִפְנֵי liph'ney) **YHWH** (יְהוָה YHWH) CONTINUALLY (תָּמִיד ta'mid) CUSTOM (חֻקַּת hhu'qat) D STANT (עוֹלָם o'lam) to~ GENERATION~s~you^(mp) (לְדֹרֹתֵיכֶם lê'do'ro'tey'khem) **RMT:** From the outside of the tent curtain of the evidence, in the appointed tent, Aharon will arrange him, from the evening until morning, to the face of **YHWH** continually, a distant custom for your generations.

24:4 UPON (עַל al) the~LAMPSTAND (הַמְּנֹרָה ham'no'rah) the~ CLEAN (הַטְּהֹרָה hat'ho'rah) he~will~ARRANGE^(V) (יַעֲרֹךְ ya'a'rokh) AT (אֶת et) the~LAMP~s (הַנֵּרוֹת ha'ney'rot) to~FACE~s (לִפְנֵי liph'ney) **YHWH** (יְהוָה YHWH) CONTINUALLY (תָּמִיד ta'mid) **RMT:** Upon the clean lampstand he will arrange the lamps to the face of **YHWH** continually,

24:5 and~you^(ms)~did~TAKE^(V) (וְלָקַחְתָּ wê'la'qahh'ta) FLOUR (סֹלֶת so'let) and~you^(ms)~did~BAKE^(V) (וְאָפִיתָ wê'a'phi'ta) AT~her (אֹתָהּ o'tah) TWO (שְׁתֵּים shê'teym) TEN (עֶשְׂרֵה es'reyh) PIERCED.BREAD~s

---

[122] Meaning the "lamps."
[123] Meaning to "burn."

(חַלּוֹת hha'lot) <u>TWO</u> (שְׁנֵי shê'ney) <u>ONE.TENTH~s</u> (עֶשְׂרֹנִים es'ro'nim) *he~will~EXIST*[(V)] (יִהְיֶה yih'yeh) <u>the~PIERCED.BREAD</u> (הַחַלָּה ha'hha'lah) <u>the~UNIT</u> (הָאֶחָת ha'e'hhat) **RMT:** and you will take flour and you will bake twelve pierced breads, two tenths will exist in one pierced bread,

24:6 <u>and~you</u>[(ms)]<u>~did~PLACE</u>[(V)] (וְשַׂמְתָּ wê'sam'ta) <u>AT~them</u>[(m)] (אוֹתָם o'tam) <u>TWO</u> (שְׁתַּיִם shê'ta'yim) <u>from~ARRANGEMENT~s</u> (מַעֲרָכוֹת ma'a'ra'khot) <u>SIX</u> (שֵׁשׁ sheysh) <u>the~IN.LINE</u> (הַמַּעֲרָכֶת ha'ma'a'ra'khet) <u>UPON</u> (עַל al) <u>the~TABLE</u> (הַשֻּׁלְחָן ha'shul'hhan) <u>the~CLEAN</u> (הַטָּהֹר ha'ta'hor) <u>to~FACE~s</u> (לִפְנֵי liph'ney) **YHWH** (יְהוָה YHWH) **RMT:** and you will place them in two arrangements, six in a line upon the clean table to the face of **YHWH**,

24:7 <u>and~you</u>[(ms)]<u>~did~GIVE</u>[(V)] (וְנָתַתָּ wê'na'ta'ta) <u>UPON</u> (עַל al) <u>the~IN.LINE</u> (הַמַּעֲרֶכֶת ha'ma'a're'khet) <u>FRANKINCENSE</u> (לְבֹנָה lê'vo'nah) <u>REFINED</u> (זַכָּה za'kah) <u>and~she~did~EXIST</u>[(V)] (וְהָיְתָה wê'hai'tah) <u>to~the~BREAD</u> (לַלֶּחֶם la'le'hhem) <u>to~MEMORIAL</u> (לְאַזְכָּרָה lê'az'ka'rah) <u>FIRE.OFFERING</u> (אִשֶּׁה i'sheh) <u>to~YHWH</u> (לַיהוָה la'YHWH) **RMT:** and you will place refined frankincense upon the line, and she will exist for the bread for a memorial, a fire offering to **YHWH**.

24:8 <u>in~DAY</u> (בְּיוֹם bê'yom) <u>the~CEASING</u> (הַשַּׁבָּת ha'sha'bat) <u>in~DAY</u> (בְּיוֹם bê'yom) <u>the~CEASING</u> (הַשַּׁבָּת ha'sha'bat) *he~will~ARRANGE*[(V)]<u>~him</u> (יַעַרְכֶנּוּ ya'ar'khe'nu) <u>to~FACE~s</u> (לִפְנֵי liph'ney) **YHWH** (יְהוָה YHWH) <u>CONTINUALLY</u> (תָּמִיד ta'mid) <u>from~AT</u> (מֵאֵת mey'eyt) <u>SON~s</u> (בְּנֵי bê'ney) <u>Yisra'eyl</u> (יִשְׂרָאֵל yis'ra'eyl) <u>COVENANT</u> (בְּרִית bê'rit) <u>DISTANT</u> (עוֹלָם o'lam) **RMT:** In the ceasing day[124] he will arrange him to the face of **YHWH** continually, from the sons of Yisra'eyl, a distant covenant,

24:9 <u>and~she~did~EXIST</u>[(V)] (וְהָיְתָה wê'hai'tah) <u>to~Aharon</u> (לְאַהֲרֹן lê'a'ha'ron) <u>and~to~SON~s~him</u> (וּלְבָנָיו ul'va'naw) <u>and~they~did~EAT</u>[(V)]<u>~him</u> (וַאֲכָלֻהוּ wa'a'kha'lu'hu) <u>in~AREA</u> (בְּמָקוֹם bê'ma'qom) <u>UNIQUE</u> (קָדֹשׁ qa'dosh) <u>GIVEN.THAT</u> (כִּי ki) <u>SPECIAL</u> (קֹדֶשׁ qo'desh) <u>SPECIAL~s</u> (קָדָשִׁים qa'da'shim) <u>HE</u> (הוּא hu) <u>to~him</u> (לוֹ lo) <u>from~FIRE.OFFERING~s</u> (מֵאִשֵּׁי mey'i'shey) **YHWH** (יְהוָה YHWH) <u>CUSTOM</u> (חָק hhaq) <u>DISTANT</u> (עוֹלָם o'lam) **RMT:** and she will exist for Aharon and for his sons, and they will eat him in the unique area, given that

---

[124] The phrase "in the ceasing day" is duplicated, either by accident or for the purpose of identifying "every ceasing day."

he is special of specials[125] for him. from the fire offerings of **YHWH**, it is a distant custom,

24:10 and~he~will~GO.OUT[(V)] (וַיֵּצֵא *wai'yey'tsey*) <u>SON</u> (בֶּן *ben*) <u>WOMAN</u> (אִשָּׁה *i'shah*) <u>Yisra'eyl~of</u> (יִשְׂרְאֵלִית *yis're'ey'lit*) <u>and~HE</u> (וְהוּא *wê'hu*) <u>SON</u> (בֶּן *ben*) <u>MAN</u> (אִישׁ *ish*) <u>Mits'rayim~of</u> (מִצְרִי *mits'ri*) <u>in~MIDST</u> (בְּתוֹךְ *bê'tokh*) <u>SON~s</u> (בְּנֵי *bê'ney*) <u>Yisra'eyl</u> (יִשְׂרָאֵל *yis'ra'eyl*) <u>and~they</u>[(m)]<u>~will~be~STRUGGLE</u>[(V)] (וַיִּנָּצוּ *wai'yi'na'tsu*) <u>in~the~CAMP</u> (בַּמַּחֲנֶה *ba'ma'hha'neh*) <u>SON</u> (בֶּן *ben*) <u>the~Yisra'eyl~of</u> (הַיִּשְׂרְאֵלִית *hai'yis're'ey'lit*) <u>and~MAN</u> (וְאִישׁ *wê'ish*) <u>the~Yisra'eyl~of</u> (הַיִּשְׂרְאֵלִי *hai'yis're'ey'li*) **RMT:** and a son of a woman, one of Yisra'eyl, went out, and he is a son of a man, one of Mits'rayim, in the midst of the sons of Yisra'eyl, and they were struggling in the camp, the son, one of Yisra'eyl, and the man, one of Yisra'eyl,

24:11 and~he~will~PIERCE.THROUGH[(V)] (וַיִּקֹּב *wai'yi'qov*) <u>SON</u> (בֶּן *ben*) <u>the~WOMAN</u> (הָאִשָּׁה *ha'i'shah*) <u>the~Yisra'eyl~of</u> (הַיִּשְׂרְאֵלִית *hai'yis're'ey'lit*) <u>AT</u> (אֶת *et*) <u>the~TITLE</u> (הַשֵּׁם *ha'sheym*) <u>and~he~will~much~BELITTLE</u>[(V)] (וַיְקַלֵּל *wai'qa'leyl*) <u>and~they</u>[(m)]<u>~will~make~COME</u>[(V)] (וַיָּבִיאוּ *wai'ya'vi'u*) <u>AT~him</u> (אֹתוֹ *o'to*) <u>TO</u> (אֶל *el*) <u>Mosheh</u> (מֹשֶׁה *mo'sheh*) <u>and~TITLE</u> (וְשֵׁם *wê'sheym*) <u>MOTHER~him</u> (אִמּוֹ *i'mo*) <u>Sh'lomiyt</u> (שְׁלֹמִית *shê'lo'mit*) <u>DAUGHTER</u> (בַּת *bat*) <u>Divriy</u> (דִּבְרִי *div'ri*) <u>to~BRANCH</u> (לְמַטֵּה *lê'ma'teyh*) <u>Dan</u> (דָן *dan*) **RMT:** and the son of the woman, the one of Yisra'eyl, pierced through the title, and he belittled it, and they brought him to Mosheh, and the title of his mother is Sh'lomiyt, daughter of Divriy, belonging to the branch of Dan,

24:12 and~they[(m)]~will~make~REST[(V)]~him (וַיַּנִּיחֻהוּ *wai'ya'ni'hhu'hu*) <u>in~the~CUSTODY</u> (בַּמִּשְׁמָר *ba'mish'mar*) <u>to~>~SPREAD.OUT</u>[(V)] (לִפְרֹשׁ *liph'rosh*) <u>to~them</u>[(m)] (לָהֶם *la'hem*) <u>UPON</u> (עַל *al*) <u>MOUTH</u> (פִּי *pi*) **YHWH** (יְהוָה *YHWH*) **RMT:** and they will make him rest in the custody, to spread out to them by the mouth of **YHWH**,

24:13 and~he~will~much~SPEAK[(V)] (וַיְדַבֵּר *wai'da'beyr*) **YHWH** (יְהוָה *YHWH*) <u>TO</u> (אֶל *el*) <u>Mosheh</u> (מֹשֶׁה *mo'sheh*) <u>to~>~SAY</u>[(V)] (לֵאמֹר *ley'mor*) **RMT:** and **YHWH** spoke to Mosheh saying,

---

[125] The phrase "special of specials" means a "very special thing, one or place."

24:14 !⁽ᵐᵖ⁾~*make*~GO.OUT⁽ⱽ⁾ (הוֹצֵא *ho'tsey*) AT (אֶת *et*) the~*much*~
BELITTLE⁽ⱽ⁾~*ing*⁽ᵐˢ⁾ (הַמְקַלֵּל *ham'qa'leyl*) TO (אֶל *el*) from~OUTSIDE
(מִחוּץ *mi'hhuts*) to~the~CAMP (לַמַּחֲנֶה *la'ma'hha'neh*) and~*they*~
did~SUPPORT⁽ⱽ⁾ (וְסָמְכוּ *wê'sam'khu*) ALL (כָּל *khol*) the~HEAR⁽ⱽ⁾~
ing⁽ᵐᵖ⁾ (הַשֹּׁמְעִים *ha'shom'im*) AT (אֶת *et*) HAND~s2~them⁽ᵐ⁾ (יְדֵיהֶם
yê'dey'hem) UPON (עַל *al*) HEAD~him (רֹאשׁוֹ *ro'sho*) and~*they*~*did*~
KILL.BY.STONING⁽ⱽ⁾ (וְרָגְמוּ *wê'rag'mu*) AT~him (אֹתוֹ *o'to*) ALL (כָּל
kol) the~COMPANY (הָעֵדָה *ha'ey'dah*) **RMT:** bring out the belittling
one to the outside of the camp, and all the ones hearing will support
their hands upon his head, and all the company will kill him by
stoning,

24:15 and~TO (וְאֶל *wê'el*) SON~s (בְּנֵי *bê'ney*) Yisra'eyl (יִשְׂרָאֵל
yis'ra'eyl) you⁽ᵐˢ⁾~*will*~*much*~SPEAK⁽ⱽ⁾ (תְּדַבֵּר *tê'da'beyr*) to~>~SAY⁽ⱽ⁾
(לֵאמֹר *ley'mor*) MAN (אִישׁ *ish*) MAN (אִישׁ *ish*) GIVEN.THAT (כִּי *ki*)
he~*will*~*much*~BELITTLE⁽ⱽ⁾ (יְקַלֵּל *yê'qa'leyl*) Elohiym~him (אֱלֹהָיו
e'lo'haw) and~he~*did*~LIFT.UP⁽ⱽ⁾ (וְנָשָׂא *wê'na'sa*) FAILURE~him
(חֶטְאוֹ *hhet'o*) **RMT:** and to the sons of Yisra'eyl you will speak
saying, each man that will belittle his Elohiym, and he will lift up his
failure,

24:16 and~PIERCE.THROUGH⁽ⱽ⁾~*ing*⁽ᵐˢ⁾ (וְנֹקֵב *wê'no'qeyv*) TITLE (שֵׁם
sheym) **YHWH** (יְהוָה *YHWH*) >~DIE⁽ⱽ⁾ (מוֹת *mot*) he~*will*~be~*make*~
DIE⁽ⱽ⁾ (יוּמָת *yu'mat*) >~KILL.BY.STONING⁽ⱽ⁾ (רָגוֹם *ra'gom*) they⁽ᵐ⁾~
will~KILL.BY.STONING⁽ⱽ⁾ (יִרְגְּמוּ *yir'ge'mu*) in~him (בוֹ *vo*) ALL (כָּל
kol) the~COMPANY (הָעֵדָה *ha'ey'dah*) like~the~IMMIGRANT (כַּגֵּר
ka'geyr) like~NATIVE (כָּאֶזְרָח *ka'ez'rahh*) in~>~PIERCE.THROUGH⁽ⱽ⁾~
him (בְּנָקְבוֹ *bê'naq'vo*) TITLE (שֵׁם *sheym*) he~*will*~be~*make*~DIE⁽ⱽ⁾
(יוּמָת *yu'mat*) **RMT:** and the one piercing through the title of **YHWH**
will surely be killed, all the company will surely kill him by stoning,
like the immigrant, like a native, in his piercing through the title, he
will be killed,

24:17 and~MAN (וְאִישׁ *wê'ish*) GIVEN.THAT (כִּי *ki*) he~*will*~*make*~
HIT⁽ⱽ⁾ (יַכֶּה *ya'keh*) ALL (כָּל *kol*) SOUL (נֶפֶשׁ *ne'phesh*) HUMAN (אָדָם
a'dam) >~DIE⁽ⱽ⁾ (מוֹת *mot*) he~*will*~be~*make*~DIE⁽ⱽ⁾ (יוּמָת *yu'mat*)
RMT: and a man that will attack any soul of a human will certainly be
killed,

24:18 and~*make*~HIT⁽ⱽ⁾~*ing*⁽ᵐˢ⁾ (וּמַכֵּה *u'ma'keyh*) SOUL (נֶפֶשׁ
ne'phesh) BEAST (בְהֵמָה *bê'hey'mah*) he~*will*~*much*~
MAKE.RESTITUTION⁽ⱽ⁾~her (יְשַׁלְּמֶנָּה *yê'shal'me'nah*) SOUL (נֶפֶשׁ
ne'phesh) UNDER (תַּחַת *ta'hhat*) SOUL (נָפֶשׁ *na'phesh*) **RMT:** and the

one attacking a soul of a beast will make restitution for her, a being in place of a beast,

24:19 and~MAN (וְאִישׁ wê'ish) GIVEN.THAT (כִּי ki) he~will~GIVE^(V) (יִתֵּן yi'teyn) BLEMISH (מוּם mum) in~the~NEIGHBOR~him (בַּעֲמִיתוֹ ba'a'mi'to) like~WHICH (כַּאֲשֶׁר ka'a'sheyr) he~did~DO^(V) (עָשָׂה a'sah) SO (כֵּן keyn) he~will~be~DO^(V) (יֵעָשֶׂה yey'a'seh) to~him (לוֹ lo) **RMT:** and a man that will give a blemish to his neighbor, just as he did so, will be done to him.

24:20 SHATTERING (שֶׁבֶר she'ver) UNDER (תַּחַת ta'hhat) SHATTERING (שֶׁבֶר she'ver) EYE (עַיִן a'yin) UNDER (תַּחַת ta'hhat) EYE (עַיִן a'yin) TOOTH (שֵׁן sheyn) UNDER (תַּחַת ta'hhat) TOOTH (שֵׁן sheyn) like~WHICH (כַּאֲשֶׁר ka'a'sheyr) he~will~GIVE^(V) (יִתֵּן yi'teyn) BLEMISH (מוּם mum) in~the~HUMAN (בָּאָדָם ba'a'dam) SO (כֵּן keyn) he~will~be~GIVE^(V) (יִנָּתֶן yi'na'ten) in~him (בּוֹ bo) **RMT:** Shattering in place of shattering, eye in place of eye, tooth in place of tooth, just as he will place a blemish in the human, so will he be placed in him,

24:21 and~make~HIT^(V)~ing^(ms) (וּמַכֵּה u'ma'keyh) BEAST (בְהֵמָה vê'hey'mah) he~will~much~MAKE.RESTITUTION^(V)~her (יְשַׁלְּמֶנָּה yê'shal'me'nah) and~make~HIT^(V)~ing^(ms) (וּמַכֵּה u'ma'keyh) HUMAN (אָדָם a'dam) he~will~be~make~DIE^(V) (יוּמָת yu'mat) **RMT:** and the one attacking a beast, he will make restitution for her, and the one hitting a human will be killed.

24:22 DECISION (מִשְׁפָּט mish'pat) UNIT (אֶחָד e'hhad) he~will~ EXIST^(V) (יִהְיֶה yih'yeh) to~you^(mp) (לָכֶם la'khem) like~the~ IMMIGRANT (כַּגֵּר ka'geyr) like~NATIVE (כָּאֶזְרָח ka'ez'rahh) he~will~ EXIST^(V) (יִהְיֶה yih'yeh) GIVEN.THAT (כִּי ki) I (אֲנִי a'ni) YHWH (יְהוָה YHWH) Elohiym~you^(mp) (אֱלֹהֵיכֶם e'lo'hey'khem) **RMT:** One decision will exist for you, like the immigrant like the native he will exist, given that I am **YHWH** your Elohiym,

24:23 and~he~will~much~SPEAK^(V) (וַיְדַבֵּר wai'da'beyr) Mosheh (מֹשֶׁה mo'sheh) TO (אֶל el) SON~s (בְּנֵי bê'ney) Yisra'eyl (יִשְׂרָאֵל yis'ra'eyl) and~they^(m)~will~make~GO.OUT^(V)~him (וַיּוֹצִיאוּ wai'yo'tsi'u) AT (אֶת et) the~much~BELITTLE^(V)~ing^(ms) (הַמְקַלֵּל ham'qa'leyl) TO (אֶל el) from~OUTSIDE (מִחוּץ mi'hhuts) to~the~ CAMP (לַמַּחֲנֶה la'ma'hha'neh) and~they^(m)~will~KILL.BY.STONING^(V) (וַיִּרְגְּמוּ wai'yir'ge'mu) AT~him (אֹתוֹ o'to) STONE (אָבֶן a'ven) and~ SON~s (וּבְנֵי uv'ney) Yisra'eyl (יִשְׂרָאֵל yis'ra'eyl) they~did~DO^(V) (עָשׂוּ a'su) *a'su*) like~WHICH (כַּאֲשֶׁר *ka'a'sheyr*) *he~did~much~*DIRECT^(V) (צִוָּה *tsi'wah*) **YHWH** (יְהוָה *YHWH*) AT (אֵת *et*) Mosheh (מֹשֶׁה *mo'sheh*) **RMT:** and Mosheh spoke to the sons of Yisra'eyl, and they brought out the belittling one to the outside of the camp, and killed him by stoning with stones, and the sons of Yisra'eyl did just as **YHWH** directed Mosheh,

Chapter 25

25:1 and~*he~will~much~*SPEAK^(V) (וַיְדַבֵּר *wai'da'beyr*) **YHWH** (יְהוָה *YHWH*) TO (אֶל *el*) Mosheh (מֹשֶׁה *mo'sheh*) in~HILL (בְּהַר *bê'har*) Sinai (סִינַי *si'nai*) to~>~SAY^(V) (לֵאמֹר *ley'mor*) **RMT:** and **YHWH** spoke to Mosheh in the hill of Sinai saying,

25:2 !^(ms)~*much~*SPEAK^(V) (דַּבֵּר *da'beyr*) TO (אֶל *el*) SON~s (בְּנֵי *bê'ney*) Yisra'eyl (יִשְׂרָאֵל *yis'ra'eyl*) and~*you*^(ms)~*did~*SAY^(V) (וְאָמַרְתָּ *wê'a'mar'ta*) TO~them^(m) (אֲלֵהֶם *a'ley'hem*) GIVEN.THAT (כִּי *ki*) *you*^(mp)~*will~*COME^(V) (תָבֹאוּ *ta'vo'u*) TO (אֶל *el*) the~LAND (הָאָרֶץ *ha'a'rets*) WHICH (אֲשֶׁר *a'sher*) I (אֲנִי *a'ni*) GIVE^(V)~*ing*^(ms) (נֹתֵן *no'teyn*) to~*you*^(mp) (לָכֶם *la'khem*) and~*she~did~*CEASE^(V) (וְשָׁבְתָה *wê'shav'tah*) the~LAND (הָאָרֶץ *ha'a'rets*) CEASING (שַׁבָּת *sha'bat*) to~**YHWH** (לַיהוָה *la'YHWH*) **RMT:** speak to the sons of Yisra'eyl and you will say to them, given that you will come to the land which I am giving to you, and the land will cease a ceasing for **YHWH**.

25:3 SIX (שֵׁשׁ *sheysh*) YEAR~s (שָׁנִים *sha'nim*) *you*^(ms)~*will~*SOW^(V) (תִּזְרַע *tiz'ra*) FIELD~*you*^(ms) (שָׂדֶךָ *sa'de'kha*) and~SIX (וְשֵׁשׁ *wê'sheysh*) YEAR~s (שָׁנִים *sha'nim*) *you*^(ms)~*will~*PLUCK^(V) (תִּזְמֹר *tiz'mor*) VINEYARD~*you*^(ms) (כַּרְמֶךָ *kar'me'kha*) and~*you*^(ms)~*did~*GATHER^(V) (וְאָסַפְתָּ *wê'a'saph'ta*) AT (אֶת *et*) PRODUCTION~her (תְּבוּאָתָהּ *tê'vu'a'tah*) **RMT:** Six years you will sow your field, and six years you will pluck your vineyard and you will gather her production,

25:4 and~in~the~YEAR (וּבַשָּׁנָה *u'va'sha'nah*) the~SEVENTH (הַשְּׁבִיעִת *ha'she'vi'it*) CEASING (שַׁבַּת *sha'bat*) REST.PERIOD (שַׁבָּתוֹן *sha'ba'ton*) *he~will~*EXIST^(V) (יִהְיֶה *yih'yeh*) to~the~LAND (לָאָרֶץ *la'a'rets*) CEASING (שַׁבָּת *sha'bat*) to~**YHWH** (לַיהוָה *la'YHWH*) FIELD~*you*^(ms) (שָׂדְךָ *sad'kha*) NOT (לֹא *lo*) *you*^(ms)~*will~*SOW^(V) (תִזְרָע *tiz'ra*) and~VINEYARD~*you*^(ms) (וְכַרְמְךָ *wê'khar'me'kha*) NOT (לֹא *lo*) *you*^(ms)~*will~*PLUCK^(V) (תִזְמֹר *tiz'mor*) **RMT:** and in the seventh year a ceasing rest period will exist for the land, a ceasing for **YHWH**, you will not sow your field, and you will not pluck your vineyard.

25:5 <u>AT</u> (אֶת־ *eyt*) <u>AFTER.GROWTH</u> (סְפִיחַ *sê'phi'ahh*) <u>HARVEST~</u> <u>you</u>^(ms) (קְצִירְךָ *qê'tsir'kha*) <u>NOT</u> (לֹא *lo*) <u>you</u>^(ms)~*will*~<u>SEVER</u>^(V) (תִקְצוֹר *tiq'tsor*) <u>and~AT</u> (וְאֶת־ *wê'et*) <u>GRAPE</u>~s (עִנְּבֵי *in'vey*) <u>DEDICATED~</u> <u>you</u>^(ms) (נְזִירֶךָ *nê'zi're'kha*) <u>NOT</u> (לֹא *lo*) <u>you</u>^(ms)~*will*~<u>FENCE.IN</u>^(V) (תִבְצֹר *tiv'tsor*) <u>YEAR</u> (שְׁנַת *shê'nat*) <u>REST.PERIOD</u> (שַׁבָּתוֹן *sha'ba'ton*) <u>he~*will*~EXIST</u>^(V) (יִהְיֶה *yih'yeh*) <u>to~the~LAND</u> (לָאָרֶץ *la'a'rets*) **RMT:** You will not sever the after growth of your harvest, you will not fence in the grapes of your dedicated place, a year of a rest period will exist for the land,

25:6 <u>and~she~did~EXIST</u>^(V) (וְהָיְתָה *wê'hai'tah*) <u>CEASING</u> (שַׁבַּת *sha'bat*) <u>the~LAND</u> (הָאָרֶץ *ha'a'rets*) <u>to~you</u>^(mp) (לָכֶם *la'khem*) <u>to~</u> <u>FOOD</u> (לְאָכְלָה *lê'akh'lah*) <u>to~you</u>^{ms} (לְךָ *lê'kha*) <u>and~to~SERVANT~</u> <u>you</u>^(ms) (וּלְעַבְדְּךָ *ul'av'de'kha*) <u>and~to~BONDWOMAN~you</u>^(ms) (וְלַאֲמָתֶךָ *wê'la'a'ma'te'kha*) <u>and~to~HIRELING~you</u>^(ms) (וְלִשְׂכִירְךָ *wê'lis'khir'kha*) <u>and~to~SETTLER~you</u>^(ms) (וּלְתוֹשָׁבְךָ *ul'to'shav'kha*) <u>the~IMMIGRATE</u>^(V)<u>~ing</u>^(mp) (הַגָּרִים *ha'ga'rim*) <u>WITH~you</u>^(fs) (עִמָּךְ *i'makh*) **RMT:** and a ceasing of the land will exist for you for food, for you and for your servants and for your bondwoman and for your hireling and for your settlers immigrating with you,

25:7 <u>and~to~BEAST~you</u>^(ms) (וְלִבְהֶמְתְּךָ *wê'liv'hem'te'kha*) <u>and~to~</u> <u>the~LIVING</u> (וְלַחַיָּה *wê'la'hhai'yah*) <u>WHICH</u> (אֲשֶׁר *a'sher*) <u>in~LAND~</u> <u>you</u>^(ms) (בְּאַרְצֶךָ *bê'ar'tse'kha*) <u>she~will~EXIST</u>^(V) (תִהְיֶה *tih'yeh*) <u>ALL</u> (כָל *khol*) <u>PRODUCTION~her</u> (תְבוּאָתָהּ *tê'vu'a'tah*) <u>to~>~EAT</u>^(V) (לֶאֱכֹל *le'e'khol*) **RMT:** and for your beast and for the living ones[126] which are in your land, all of her production will exist for eating,

25:8 <u>and~you</u>^(ms)<u>~did~COUNT</u>^(V) (וְסָפַרְתָּ *wê'saph're'ta*) <u>to~you</u>^(ms) (לְךָ *lê'kha*) <u>SEVEN</u> (שֶׁבַע *she'va*) <u>CEASING</u>~s (שַׁבְּתֹת *sha'be'tot*) <u>YEAR</u>~s (שָׁנִים *sha'nim*) <u>SEVEN</u> (שֶׁבַע *she'va*) <u>YEAR</u>~s (שָׁנִים *sha'nim*) <u>SEVEN</u> (שֶׁבַע *she'va*) <u>FOOTSTEP</u>~s (פְּעָמִים *pê'a'mim*) <u>and~they~did~EXIST</u>^(V) (וְהָיוּ *wê'hai'u*) <u>to~you</u>^(ms) (לְךָ *lê'kha*) <u>DAY</u>~s (יְמֵי *yê'mey*) <u>SEVEN</u> (שֶׁבַע *she'va*) <u>CEASING</u>~s (שַׁבְּתֹת *sha'be'tot*) <u>the~YEAR</u>~s (הַשָּׁנִים *ha'sha'nim*) <u>NINE</u> (תֵּשַׁע *tey'sha*) <u>and~FOUR</u>~s (וְאַרְבָּעִים *wê'ar'ba'im*) <u>YEAR</u> (שָׁנָה *sha'nah*) **RMT:** and you will count for yourself seven

---

[126] A euphemism for the wild animals.

ceasings of years, seven years seven times, and days of seven ceasings of years will exist for you, nine and forty years,

25:9 and~you(ms)~did~make~CROSS.OVER(V) (וְהַעֲבַרְתָּ wê'ha'a'var'ta) RAM.HORN (שׁוֹפָר sho'phar) SIGNAL (תְּרוּעָה tê'ru'ah) in~the~ NEW.MOON (בַּחֹדֶשׁ ba'hho'desh) the~SEVENTH (הַשְּׁבִעִי hash'vi'i) in~TENTH.ONE (בֶּעָשׂוֹר be'a'sor) to~the~NEW.MOON (לַחֹדֶשׁ la'hho'desh) in~DAY (בְּיוֹם bê'yom) the~ATONEMENT~s (הַכִּפֻּרִים ha'ki'pu'rim) you(ms)~will~make~CROSS.OVER(V) (תַּעֲבִירוּ ta'a'vi'ru) RAM.HORN (שׁוֹפָר sho'phar) in~ALL (בְּכָל bê'khol) LAND~you(mp) (אַרְצְכֶם ar'tse'khem) **RMT:** and you will make the ram horn a signal to cross over in the tenth one of the seventh new moon, on the day of atonements you will make the ram horn cross over in all your land,

25:10 and~you(mp)~did~much~SET.APART(V) (וְקִדַּשְׁתֶּם wê'qi'dash'tem) AT (אֶת eyt) YEAR (שְׁנַת shê'nat) the~FIVE~s (הַחֲמִשִּׁים ha'hha'mi'shim) YEAR (שָׁנָה sha'nah) and~you(mp)~did~ CALL.OUT(V) (וּקְרָאתֶם uq'ra'tem) FREE.FLOWING (דְּרוֹר dê'ror) in~ the~LAND (בָּאָרֶץ ba'a'rets) to~ALL (לְכָל lê'khol) SETTLE(V)~ing(mp)~ her (יֹשְׁבֶיהָ yosh'vey'ah) JUBILEE (יוֹבֵל yo'veyl) SHE (הִוא hi) she~ will~EXIST(V) (תִּהְיֶה tih'yeh) to~you(mp) (לָכֶם la'khem) and~you(mp)~ did~TURN.BACK(V) (וְשַׁבְתֶּם wê'shav'tem) MAN (אִישׁ ish) TO (אֶל el) HOLDINGS~him (אֲחֻזָּתוֹ a'hhu'za'to) and~MAN (וְאִישׁ wê'ish) TO (אֶל el) CLAN~him (מִשְׁפַּחְתּוֹ mish'pahh'to) you(mp)~will~TURN.BACK(V) (תָּשֻׁבוּ ta'shu'vu) **RMT:** and you will set apart the year, the fiftieth year, and you will call out a free flowing in the land to all her settlers, she, she will exist for you as a jubilee, and you will turn back a man to his holdings, and a man to his clan you will turn back.

25:11 JUBILEE (יוֹבֵל yo'veyl) SHE (הִוא hi) YEAR (שְׁנַת shê'nat) the~ FIVE~s (הַחֲמִשִּׁים ha'hha'mi'shim) YEAR (שָׁנָה sha'nah) she~will~ EXIST(V) (תִּהְיֶה tih'yeh) to~you(mp) (לָכֶם la'khem) NOT (לֹא lo) you(mp)~will~SOW(V) (תִזְרָעוּ tiz'ra'u) and~NOT (וְלֹא wê'lo) you(mp)~ will~SEVER(V) (תִקְצְרוּ tiq'tse'ru) AT (אֶת et) AFTER.GROWTH~her (סְפִיחֶיהָ sê'phi'hhey'ah) and~NOT (וְלֹא wê'lo) you(mp)~will~ FENCE.IN(V) (תִבְצְרוּ tiv'tse'ru) AT (אֶת et) DEDICATED~s~her (נְזִרֶיהָ nê'zi'rey'ah) **RMT:** She is a jubilee year, the fiftieth year will exist for you, you will not sow, and you will not sever her after growth, and you will not fence in her dedicated places,

25:12 GIVEN.THAT (כִּי ki) JUBILEE (יוֹבֵל yo'veyl) SHE (הִוא hi) SPECIAL (קֹדֶשׁ qo'desh) she~will~EXIST(V) (תִּהְיֶה tih'yeh) to~you(mp)

(לָכֶם la'khem) <u>FROM</u> (מִן min) the~FIELD (הַשָּׂדֶה ha'sa'deh) you(mp)~
<u>will~EAT</u>(V) (תֹּאכְלוּ tokh'lu) <u>AT</u> (אֶת et) PRODUCTION~her (תְּבוּאָתָהּ
tê'vu'a'tah) **RMT:** given that she is a special jubilee, she will exist for
you, from the field you will eat her production.

25:13 <u>in~YEAR</u> (בִּשְׁנַת bish'nat) the~JUBILEE (הַיּוֹבֵל hai'yo'veyl) the~
THIS (הַזֹּאת ha'zot) you(mp)~will~URN.BACK(V) (תָּשֻׁבוּ ta'shu'vu)
MAN (אִישׁ ish) <u>TO</u> (אֶל el) HOLDINGS~him (אֲחֻזָּתוֹ a'hhu'za'to)
RMT: In the year of this jubilee you will turn a man to his holdings,

25:14 <u>and~GIVEN.THAT</u> (וְכִי wê'khi) you(mp)~will~SELL(V) (תִמְכְּרוּ
tim'ke'ru) <u>MERCHANDISE</u> (מִמְכָּר mim'kar) to~the~NEIGHBOR~
you(ms) (לַעֲמִיתֶךָ la'a'mi'te'kha) OR (אוֹ o) >~PURCHASE(V) (קָנֹה
qa'noh) from~HAND (מִיַּד mi'yad) NEIGHBOR~you(ms) (עֲמִיתֶךָ
a'mi'te'kha) <u>DO.NOT</u> (אַל al) you(mp)~will~make~SUPPRESS(V) (תּוֹנוּ
to'nu) MAN (אִישׁ ish) <u>AT</u> (אֶת et) BROTHER~him (אָחִיו a'hhiw)
RMT: and, given that you will sell merchandise to your neighbor, or
purchase from the hand of your neighbor, you will not make a man
suppressed by his brother.

25:15 <u>in~NUMBER</u> (בְּמִסְפַּר bê'mis'par) YEAR~s (שָׁנִים sha'nim)
<u>AFTER</u> (אַחַר a'hhar) the~JUBILEE (הַיּוֹבֵל hai'yo'veyl) you(ms)~will~
PURCHASE(V) (תִּקְנֶה tiq'neh) from~AT (מֵאֵת mey'eyt) NEIGHBOR~
you(ms) (עֲמִיתֶךָ a'mi'te'kha) in~NUMBER (בְּמִסְפַּר bê'mis'par) YEAR~s
(שְׁנֵי shê'ney) PRODUCTION~s (תְבוּאֹת tê'vut) he~will~SELL(V) (יִמְכָּר
yim'kar) to~you(fs) (לָךְ lakh) **RMT:** By the number of years after the
jubilee you will purchase from your neighbor, by the number of
years he will sell productions to you.

25:16 <u>to~MOUTH</u> (לְפִי lê'phi) ABUNDANCE (רֹב rov) the~YEAR~s
(הַשָּׁנִים ha'sha'nim) you(ms)~will~make~INCREASE(V) (תַּרְבֶּה tar'beh)
ACQUIRED~him (מִקְנָתוֹ miq'na'to) and~to~MOUTH (וּלְפִי ul'phi) >~
BE.LESS(V) (מְעֹט mê'ot) the~YEAR~s (הַשָּׁנִים ha'sha'nim) you(ms)~will~
make~BE.LESS(V) (תַּמְעִיט tam'it) ACQUIRED~him (מִקְנָתוֹ miq'na'to)
GIVEN.THAT (כִּי ki) NUMBER (מִסְפַּר mis'par) PRODUCTION~s
(תְבוּאֹת tê'vu'ot) HE (הוּא hu) SELL(V)~ing(ms) (מֹכֵר mo'kheyr) to~
you(fs) (לָךְ lakh) **RMT:** By the mouth[127] of an abundance of years you
will make his acquirings increase, and by the mouth of the lesser
years you will make his acquirings less, given that the number of
productions he is selling to you,

---

[127] Meaning "according to."

25:17 and~NOT (וְלֹא wê'lo) you(mp)~will~make~SUPPRESS(V) תוֹנוּ to'nu) MAN (אִישׁ ish) AT (אֶת et) NEIGHBOR~him (עֲמִיתוֹ a'mi'to) and~you(ms)~did~FEAR(V) (וְיָרֵאתָ wê'ya'rey'ta) from~Elohiym~you(ms) (מֵאֱלֹהֶיךָ mey'e'lo'hey'kha) GIVEN.THAT (כִּי ki) I (אֲנִי a'ni) **YHWH** (יְהוָה YHWH) Elohiym~you(mp) (אֱלֹהֵיכֶם e'lo'hey'khem) **RMT:** and you will not make a man suppressed by his neighbor, and you will fear your Elohiym, given that I am **YHWH** your Elohiym,

25:18 and~you(mp)~did~DO(V) (וַעֲשִׂיתֶם wa'a'si'tem) AT (אֶת et) CUSTOM~s~me (חֻקֹּתַי hhu'qo'tai) and~AT (וְאֶת wê'et) DECISION~s~ me (מִשְׁפָּטַי mish'pa'tai) you(mp)~will~SAFEGUARD(V) (תִּשְׁמְרוּ tish'me'ru) and~you(mp)~did~DO(V) (וַעֲשִׂיתֶם wa'a'si'tem) AT~them(m) (אֹתָם o'tam) and~you(mp)~did~SETTLE(V) (וִישַׁבְתֶּם wi'shav'tem) UPON (עַל al) the~LAND (הָאָרֶץ ha'a'rets) to~the~SAFELY (לָבֶטַח la've'tahh) **RMT:** and you will do my customs, and my decisions you will safeguard, and you will do them, and you will settle upon the land in safety,

25:19 and~she~did~GIVE(V) (וְנָתְנָה wê'nat'nah) the~LAND (הָאָרֶץ ha'a'rets) PRODUCE~her (פִּרְיָהּ pir'yah) and~you(mp)~did~EAT(V) (וַאֲכַלְתֶּם wa'a'khal'tem) to~SATISFACTION (לָשֹׂבַע la'so'va) and~ you(mp)~did~SETTLE(V) (וִישַׁבְתֶּם wi'shav'tem) to~the~SAFELY (לָבֶטַח la've'tahh) UPON~her (עָלֶיהָ a'ley'ah) **RMT:** and the land will give her produce, and you will eat to satisfaction, and you will settle safely upon her,

25:20 and~GIVEN.THAT (וְכִי wê'khi) you(mp)~will~SAY(V) תֹאמְרוּ to'me'ru) WHAT (מַה mah) we~will~EAT(V) (נֹאכַל no'khal) in~the~ YEAR (בַּשָּׁנָה ba'sha'nah) the~SEVENTH (הַשְּׁבִיעִת ha'she'vi'it) THOUGH (הֵן heyn) NOT (לֹא lo) we~will~SOW(V) (נִזְרָע niz'ra) and~ NOT (וְלֹא wê'lo) we~will~GATHER(V) (נֶאֱסֹף ne'e'soph) AT (אֶת et) PRODUCTION~s~him (תְּבוּאָתֵנוּ tê'vu'a'tey'nu) **RMT:** and, given that you will say, what will we eat in the seventh year, though we will not sow and we will not gather his productions,

25:21 and~I~did~much~DIRECT(V) (וְצִוִּיתִי wê'tsi'wi'ti) AT (אֶת et) PRESENT~me (בִּרְכָתִי bir'kha'ti) to~you(mp) (לָכֶם la'khem) in~the~ YEAR (בַּשָּׁנָה ba'sha'nah) the~SIXTH (הַשִּׁשִׁית ha'shi'shit) and~she~ did~DO(V) (וְעָשָׂת wê'a'sat) AT (אֶת et) the~PRODUCTION (הַתְּבוּאָה hat'vu'ah) to~THREE (לִשְׁלֹשׁ lish'losh) the~YEAR~s (הַשָּׁנִים ha'sha'nim) **RMT:** then I will direct my presents to you in the sixth year, and she will do the production for the three years,

25:22 and~you*(mp)*~did~SOW*(v)* (וּזְרַעְתֶּם uz'ra'e'tem) AT (אֵת eyt) the~YEAR (הַשָּׁנָה ha'sha'nah) the~EIGHTH (הַשְּׁמִינִת hash'mi'nit) and~you*(mp)*~did~EAT*(v)* (וַאֲכַלְתֶּם wa'a'khal'tem) FROM (מִן min) the~PRODUCTION (הַתְּבוּאָה hat'vu'ah) SLEEPING (יָשָׁן ya'shan) UNTIL (עַד ad) the~YEAR (הַשָּׁנָה ha'sha'nah) the~NINTH (הַתְּשִׁיעִת hat'shi'it) UNTIL (עַד ad) !*(ms)*~COME*(v)* (בּוֹא bo) PRODUCTION~her (תְּבוּאָתָהּ tê'vu'a'tah) you*(mp)*~will~EAT*(v)* (תֹּאכְלוּ tokh'lu) SLEEPING (יָשָׁן ya'shan) **RMT:** and you will sow the eighth year, and you will eat from the stored production until the ninth year, until her production comes, you will eat what is stored,

25:23 and~the~LAND (וְהָאָרֶץ wê'ha'a'rets) NOT (לֹא lo) she~will~ be~SELL*(v)* (תִמָּכֵר ti'ma'kheyr) to~PERMANENT (לִצְמִתֻת lits'mi'tut) GIVEN.THAT (כִּי ki) to~me (לִי li) the~LAND (הָאָרֶץ ha'a'rets) GIVEN.THAT (כִּי ki) IMMIGRANT~s (גֵרִים gey'rim) and~SETTLER~s (וְתוֹשָׁבִים wê'to'sha'vim) YOU*(mp)* (אַתֶּם a'tem) BY~me (עִמָּדִי i'ma'di) **RMT:** and the land will not be sold permanently, given that the land belongs to me, given that you are immigrants and settlers with me,

25:24 and~in~ALL (וּבְכֹל uv'khol) LAND (אֶרֶץ e'rets) HOLDINGS~ you*(mp)* (אֲחֻזַּתְכֶם a'hhu'zat'khem) REDEMPTION (גְּאֻלָּה gê'u'lah) you*(mp)*~will~GIVE*(v)* (תִּתְּנוּ tit'nu) to~the~LAND (לָאָרֶץ la'a'rets) **RMT:** and in all the land of your holdings, you will give redemption to the land,

25:25 GIVEN.THAT (כִּי ki) he~will~BE.LOW*(v)* (יָמוּךְ ya'mukh) BROTHER~you*(ms)* (אָחִיךָ a'hhi'kha) and~he~did~SELL*(v)* (וּמָכַר u'ma'khar) from~HOLDINGS~him (מֵאֲחֻזָּתוֹ mey'a'hhu'za'to) and~ he~did~COME*(v)* (וּבָא u'va) REDEEM*(v)*~ing*(ms)*~him (גֹּאֲלוֹ go'a'lo) the~NEAR (הַקָּרֹב ha'qa'rov) TO~him (אֵלָיו ey'law) and~he~did~ REDEEM*(v)* (וְגָאַל wê'ga'al) AT (אֵת eyt) MERCHANDISE (מִמְכַּר mim'kar) BROTHER~him (אָחִיו a'hhiw) **RMT:** given that your brother will be low, and he will sell his holdings, and a near one to him will come redeeming him, and he will redeem the merchandise of his brother,

25:26 and~MAN (וְאִישׁ wê'ish) GIVEN.THAT (כִּי ki) NOT (לֹא lo) he~ will~EXIST*(v)* (יִהְיֶה yih'yeh) to~him (לוֹ lo) REDEEM*(v)*~ing*(ms)* (גֹּאֵל go'eyl) and~she~did~make~OVERTAKE*(v)* (וְהִשִּׂיגָה wê'hi'si'gah) HAND~him (יָדוֹ ya'do) and~he~did~FIND*(v)* (וּמָצָא u'ma'tsa) like~ SUFFICIENT (כְּדֵי kê'dey) REDEMPTION~him (גְאֻלָּתוֹ gê'u'la'to)

RMT: and a man that will not exist for him a redeemer, and his hand will reach, and he will find as sufficient his redemption,

25:27 and~he~did~much~THINK$^{(V)}$ (וְחִשַּׁב *wê'hhi'shav*) AT (אֶת *et*) YEAR~s (שְׁנֵי *shê'ney*) MERCHANDISE~him (מִמְכָּרוֹ *mim'ka'ro*) and~ he~did~make~TURN.BACK$^{(V)}$ (וְהֵשִׁיב *wê'hey'shiv*) AT (אֶת *et*) the~ EXCEED$^{(V)}$~ing$^{(ms)}$ (הָעֹדֵף *ha'o'deyph*) to~the~MAN (לָאִישׁ *la'ish*) WHICH (אֲשֶׁר *a'sher*) he~did~SELL$^{(V)}$ (מָכַר *ma'khar*) to~him (לוֹ *lo*) and~he~did~TURN.BACK$^{(V)}$ (וְשָׁב *wê'shav*) to~HOLDINGS~him (לַאֲחֻזָּתוֹ *la'a'hhu'za'to*) **RMT:** and he will plan the years of his merchandise, and he will make the exceedings turn back to the man which he sold to him, and he will turn back to his holdings,

25:28 and~IF (וְאִם *wê'im*) NOT (לֹא *lo*) she~did~FIND$^{(V)}$ (מָצְאָה *mats'ah*) HAND~him (יָדוֹ *ya'do*) SUFFICIENT (דֵּי *dey*) >~make~ TURN.BACK$^{(V)}$ (הָשִׁיב *ha'shiv*) to~him (לוֹ *lo*) and~he~did~EXIST$^{(V)}$ (וְהָיָה *wê'hai'yah*) MERCHANDISE~him (מִמְכָּרוֹ *mim'ka'ro*) in~HAND (בְּיַד *bê'yad*) the~PURCHASE$^{(V)}$~ing$^{(ms)}$ (הַקֹּנֶה *ha'qo'neh*) AT~him (אֹתוֹ *o'to*) UNTIL (עַד *ad*) YEAR (שְׁנַת *shê'nat*) the~JUBILEE (הַיּוֹבֵל *hai'yo'veyl*) and~he~will~GO.OUT$^{(V)}$ (וְיָצָא *wê'ya'tsa*) in~the~JUBILEE (בַּיֹּבֵל *bai'yo'veyl*) and~he~did~TURN.BACK$^{(V)}$ (וְשָׁב *wê'shav*) to~ HOLDINGS~him (לַאֲחֻזָּתוֹ *la'a'hhu'za'to*) **RMT:** and if his hand did not find sufficiency to turn back to him, then his merchandise will exist in the hand of the one purchasing him, until the year of the jubilee, and he will go out in the jubilee, and he will turn back to his holdings,

25:29 and~MAN (וְאִישׁ *wê'ish*) GIVEN.THAT (כִּי *ki*) he~will~SELL$^{(V)}$ (יִמְכֹּר *yim'kor*) HOUSE (בֵּית *beyt*) SETTLING (מוֹשַׁב *mo'shav*) CITY (עִיר *ir*) RAMPART (חוֹמָה *hho'mah*) and~she~did~EXIST$^{(V)}$ (וְהָיְתָה *wê'hai'tah*) REDEMPTION~him (גְּאֻלָּתוֹ *gê'u'la'to*) UNTIL (עַד *ad*) >~ BE.WHOLE$^{(V)}$ (תֹּם *tom*) YEAR (שְׁנַת *shê'nat*) MERCHANDISE~him (מִמְכָּרוֹ *mim'ka'ro*) DAY~s (יָמִים *ya'mim*) she~will~EXIST$^{(V)}$ (תִּהְיֶה *tih'yeh*) REDEMPTION~him (גְּאֻלָּתוֹ *gê'u'la'to*) **RMT:** and a man that will sell a settling house of the city rampart, then his redemption will exist until the year be whole for his merchandise, the days his redemption will exist,

25:30 and~IF (וְאִם *wê'im*) NOT (לֹא *lo*) he~will~be~REDEEM$^{(V)}$ (יִגָּאֵל *yi'ga'eyl*) UNTIL (עַד *ad*) >~FILL$^{(V)}$ (מְלֹאת *mê'lot*) to~him (לוֹ *lo*) YEAR (שָׁנָה *sha'nah*) WHOLE (תְמִימָה *tê'mi'mah*) and~he~did~RISE$^{(V)}$ (וְקָם *wê'qam*) the~HOUSE (הַבַּיִת *ha'ba'yit*) WHICH (אֲשֶׁר *a'sher*) in~the~

CITY (בָּעִיר ba'ir) WHICH (אֲשֶׁר a'sher) NOT (לֹא lo)[128] RAMPART (חֹמָה hho'mah) to~PERMANENT (לַצְמִיתֻת lats'mi'tut) to~ PURCHASE[(V)]~ing[(ms)] (לַקֹּנֶה la'qo'neh) AT~him (אֹתוֹ o'to) to~ GENERATION~s~him (לְדֹרֹתָיו lê'do'ro'taw) NOT (לֹא lo) he~will~ GO.OUT[(V)] (יֵצֵא yey'tsey) in~the~JUBILEE (בַּיֹּבֵל bai'yo'veyl) **RMT:** and if he will not be able to redeem until his filling of a whole year, then the house, which is in the city that belongs to him in the rampart, will rise to permanence to his purchaser to his generations, he will not go out in the jubilee,

25:31 and~HOUSE~s (וּבָתֵּי u'va'tey) the~COURTYARD~s (הַחֲצֵרִים ha'hha'tsey'rim) WHICH (אֲשֶׁר a'sher) WITHOUT (אֵין eyn) to~ them[(m)] (לָהֶם la'hem) RAMPART (חֹמָה hho'mah) ALL.AROUND (סָבִיב sa'viv) UPON (עַל al) FIELD (שְׂדֵה sê'deyh) the~LAND (הָאָרֶץ ha'a'rets) he~will~be~THINK[(V)] (יֵחָשֵׁב yey'hha'sheyv) REDEMPTION (גְּאֻלָּה gê'u'lah) she~will~EXIST[(V)] (תִּהְיֶה tih'yeh) to~him (לֹו lo) and~ in~the~JUBILEE (וּבַיֹּבֵל u'vai'yo'veyl) he~will~GO.OUT[(V)] (יֵצֵא yey'tsey) **RMT:** and the courtyard houses that are without a rampart all around, he will be considered upon the field of the land, redemption will exist for him, and in the jubilee, he will go out,

25:32 and~CITY~s (וְעָרֵי wê'a'rey) the~Lewi~s (הַלְוִיִּם hal'wi'yim) HOUSE~s (בָּתֵּי ba'tey) CITY~s (עָרֵי a'rey) HOLDINGS~them[(m)] (אֲחֻזָּתָם a'hhu'za'tam) REDEMPTION (גְּאֻלַּת gê'u'lat) DISTANT (עוֹלָם o'lam) she~will~EXIST[(V)] (תִּהְיֶה tih'yeh) to~Lewi~s (לַלְוִיִּם la'le'wi'yim) **RMT:** and the cities of the ones of Lewi, houses of the cities of their holdings, redemption of distance will exist to the ones of Lewi,

25:33 and~WHICH (וַאֲשֶׁר wa'a'sher) he~will~REDEEM[(V)] (יִגְאַל yig'al) FROM (מִן min) the~Lewi~s (הַלְוִיִּם hal'wi'yim) and~he~will~ GO.OUT[(V)] (וְיָצָא wê'ya'tsa) MERCHANDISE (מִמְכַּר mim'kar) HOUSE (בַּיִת ba'yit) and~CITY (וְעִיר wê'ir) HOLDINGS~him (אֲחֻזָּתוֹ a'hhu'za'to) in~the~JUBILEE (בַּיֹּבֵל bai'yo'veyl) GIVEN.THAT (כִּי ki) HOUSE~s (בָתֵּי va'tey) CITY~s (עָרֵי a'rey) the~Lewi~s (הַלְוִיִּם hal'wi'yim) SHE (הוּא hi) HOLDINGS~them[(m)] (אֲחֻזָּתָם a'hhu'za'tam) in~MIDST (בְּתוֹךְ bê'tokh) SON~s (בְּנֵי bê'ney) Yisra'eyl (יִשְׂרָאֵל yis'ra'eyl) **RMT:** and that which he will redeem from the ones of Lewi, and he will go out, the merchandise of the house and the city of his holdings, in the jubilee, given that the houses of the cities of

---

[128] *Qere* = לֹו (to him).

the ones of Lewi, she is their holdings in the midst of the sons of Yisra'eyl,

25:34 and~FIELD (וּשְׂדֵה *us'deyh*) OPEN.SPACE (מִגְרַשׁ *mig'rash*) CITY~s~them^(m) (עָרֵיהֶם *a'rey'hem*) NOT (לֹא *lo*) he~will~be~SELL^(V) (יִמָּכֵר *yi'ma'kheyr*) GIVEN.THAT (כִּי *ki*) HOLDINGS (אֲחֻזַּת *a'hhu'zat*) DISTANT (עוֹלָם *o'lam*) HE (הוּא *hu*) to~them^(m) (לָהֶם *la'hem*) **RMT:** and the fields of the open spaces of their cities will not be sold, given that he is a distant holdings for them,

25:35 and~GIVEN.THAT (וְכִי *wê'khi*) he~will~BE.LOW^(V) (יָמוּךְ *ya'mukh*) BROTHER~you^(ms) (אָחִיךָ *a'hhi'kha*) and~she~did~TOTTER^(V) (וּמָטָה *u'ma'tah*) HAND~him (יָדוֹ *ya'do*) WITH~you^(fs) (עִמָּךְ *i'makh*) and~you^(ms)~did~make~SEIZE^(V) (וְהֶחֱזַקְתָּ *wê'he'hhe'zaq'ta*) in~him (בּוֹ *bo*) IMMIGRANT (גֵּר *geyr*) and~SETTLER (וְתוֹשָׁב *wê'to'shav*) and~he~did~LIVE^(V) (וָחַי *wa'hhai*) WITH~you^(fs) (עִמָּךְ *i'makh*) **RMT:** and, given that your brother will be low, and his hand will totter with you, and you will seize him, immigrant and settler, and he will live with you.

25:36 DO.NOT (אַל *al*) you^(ms)~will~TAKE^(V) (תִּקַּח *ti'qahh*) from~AT~ him (מֵאִתּוֹ *mey'i'to*) USURY (נֶשֶׁךְ *ne'shekh*) and~INTEREST (וְתַרְבִּית *wê'tar'bit*) and~you^(ms)~did~FEAR^(V) (וְיָרֵאתָ *wê'ya'rey'ta*) from~ Elohiym~you^(ms) (מֵאֱלֹהֶיךָ *mey'e'lo'hey'kha*) and~LIVING (וְחֵי *wê'hhey*) BROTHER~you^(ms) (אָחִיךָ *a'hhi'kha*) WITH~you^(fs) (עִמָּךְ *i'makh*) **RMT:** You will not take from him usury and interest, and you will fear your Elohiym, and your brother is living with you.

25:37 AT (אֶת *et*) SILVER~you^(ms) (כַּסְפְּךָ *kas'pe'kha*) NOT (לֹא *lo*) you^(ms)~will~GIVE^(V) (תִּתֵּן *ti'teyn*) to~him (לוֹ *lo*) in~USURY (בְּנֶשֶׁךְ *bê'ne'shekh*) and~in~GREAT.NUMBER (וּבְמַרְבִּית *uv'mar'bit*) NOT (לֹא *lo*) you^(ms)~will~GIVE^(V) (תִּתֵּן *ti'teyn*) FOODSTUFF~you^(ms) (אָכְלֶךָ *akh'le'kha*) **RMT:** You will not give your silver to him in usury, and you will not give your foodstuff in great number.

25:38 I (אֲנִי *a'ni*) **YHWH** (יְהוָה *YHWH*) Elohiym~you^(mp) (אֱלֹהֵיכֶם *e'lo'hey'khem*) WHICH (אֲשֶׁר *a'sher*) I~did~make~GO.OUT^(V) (הוֹצֵאתִי *ho'tsey'ti*) AT~you^(mp) (אֶתְכֶם *et'khem*) from~LAND (מֵאֶרֶץ *mey'e'rets*) Mits'rayim (מִצְרָיִם *mits'ra'yim*) to~>~GIVE^(V) (לָתֵת *la'teyt*) to~you^(mp) (לָכֶם *la'khem*) AT (אֶת *et*) LAND (אֶרֶץ *e'rets*) Kena'an (כְּנַעַן *kê'na'an*) to~>~EXIST^(V) (לִהְיוֹת *lih'yot*) to~you^(mp) (לָכֶם *la'khem*) to~Elohiym (לֵאלֹהִים *ley'lo'him*) **RMT:** I am **YHWH** your

Elohiym, who made you go out from the land of Mits'rayim, to give to you the land of Kena'an, to exist for you for Elohiym,

25:39 and~GIVEN.THAT (וְכִי *wê'khi*) he~will~BE.LOW⁽ⱽ⁾ (יָמוּךְ *ya'mukh*) BROTHER~you⁽ᵐˢ⁾ (אָחִיךָ *a'hhi'kha*) WITH~you⁽ᶠˢ⁾ (עִמָּךְ *i'makh*) and~he~did~be~SELL⁽ⱽ⁾ (וְנִמְכַּר *wê'nim'kar*) to~you⁽ᶠˢ⁾ (לָךְ *lakh*) NOT (לֹא *lo*) you⁽ᵐˢ⁾~will~SERVE⁽ⱽ⁾ (תַעֲבֹד *ta'a'vod*) in~him (בּוֹ *bo*) SERVICE (עֲבֹדַת *a'vo'dat*) SERVANT (עָבֶד *a'ved*) **RMT:** and, given that your brother will be low with you, and he will be sold to you, you will not serve with him, as service of a servant¹²⁹.

25:40 like~HIRELING (כְּשָׂכִיר *kê'sa'khir*) like~SETTLER (כְּתוֹשָׁב *kê'to'shav*) he~will~EXIST⁽ⱽ⁾ (יִהְיֶה *yih'yeh*) WITH~you⁽ᶠˢ⁾ (עִמָּךְ *i'makh*) UNTIL (עַד *ad*) YEAR (שְׁנַת *shê'nat*) the~JUBILEE (הַיֹּבֵל *hai'yo'veyl*) he~will~SERVE⁽ⱽ⁾ (יַעֲבֹד *ya'a'vod*) WITH~you⁽ᶠˢ⁾ (עִמָּךְ *i'makh*) **RMT:** Like a hireling, like a settler, he will exist with you until the year of the jubilee, he will serve with you,

25:41 and~he~will~GO.OUT⁽ⱽ⁾ (וְיָצָא *wê'ya'tsa*) from~WITH~you⁽ᵐˢ⁾ (מֵעִמָּךְ *mey'i'makh*) HE (הוּא *hu*) and~SON~s~him (וּבָנָיו *u'va'naw*) WITH~him (עִמּוֹ *i'mo*) and~he~did~TURN.BACK⁽ⱽ⁾ (וְשָׁב *wê'shav*) TO (אֶל *el*) CLAN~him (מִשְׁפַּחְתּוֹ *mish'pahh'to*) and~TO (וְאֶל *wê'el*) HOLDINGS (אֲחֻזַּת *a'hhu'zat*) FATHER~s~him (אֲבֹתָיו *a'vo'taw*) he~will~TURN.BACK⁽ⱽ⁾ (יָשׁוּב *ya'shuv*) **RMT:** and he will go out from with you, he and his sons with him, and he will turn back to his clan, and to the holdings of his fathers he will turn back,

25:42 GIVEN.THAT (כִּי *ki*) SERVANT~s~me (עֲבָדַי *a'va'dai*) THEY⁽ᵐ⁾ (הֵם *heym*) WHICH (אֲשֶׁר *a'sher*) I~did~make~GO.OUT⁽ⱽ⁾ (הוֹצֵאתִי *ho'tsey'ti*) AT~them⁽ᵐ⁾ (אֹתָם *o'tam*) from~LAND (מֵאֶרֶץ *mey'e'rets*) Mits'rayim (מִצְרָיִם *mits'ra'yim*) NOT (לֹא *lo*) they⁽ᵐ⁾~will~be~SELL⁽ⱽ⁾ (יִמָּכְרוּ *yi'makh'ru*) MERCHANDISE (מִמְכֶּרֶת *mim'ke'ret*) SERVANT (עָבֶד *a'ved*) **RMT:** given that they are my servants, which I made them go out from the land of Mits'rayim, they will not be sold as merchandise, a servant.

25:43 NOT (לֹא *lo*) you⁽ᵐˢ⁾~will~RULE⁽ⱽ⁾ (תִרְדֶּה *tir'deh*) in~him (בוֹ *vo*) in~WHIP (בְּפָרֶךְ *bê'pha'rekh*) and~you⁽ᵐˢ⁾~did~FEAR⁽ⱽ⁾ (וְיָרֵאתָ *wê'ya're'ta*)

---

¹²⁹ The Hebrew verb תעבד is written in the *qal* form, but may be in error and should have been written in the *hiphil* form. In which case this phrase would be translated as "you will not make him serve in the service of a servant."

wê'ya'rey'ta) <u>from~Elohiym~you</u>(ms) (מֵאֱלֹהֶיךָ *mey'e'lo'hey'kha*)
RMT: You will not rule in him with a whip, and you will fear your
Elohiym,

25:44 <u>and~SERVANT~you</u>(ms) (וְעַבְדְּךָ *wê'av'de'kha*) <u>and~</u>
<u>BONDWOMAN~you</u>(ms) (וַאֲמָתְךָ *wa'a'mat'kha*) <u>WHICH</u> (אֲשֶׁר *a'sher*)
they(m)*~will~*EXIST(V) (יִהְיוּ *yih'yu*) <u>to~you</u>(fs) (לָךְ *lakh*) <u>from~AT</u> (מֵאֵת
mey'eyt) <u>the~NATION~s</u> (הַגּוֹיִם *ha'go'yim*) <u>WHICH</u> (אֲשֶׁר *a'sher*)
<u>ALL.AROUND~s~you</u>(mp) (סְבִיבֹתֵיכֶם *sê'vi'vo'tey'khem*) <u>from~them</u>(m)
(מֵהֶם *mey'hem*) *you*(ms)*~will~*PURCHASE(V) (תִּקְנוּ *tiq'nu*) <u>SERVANT</u>
(עֶבֶד *e'ved*) <u>and~BONDWOMAN</u> (וְאָמָה *wê'a'mah*) **RMT:** and your
servant and your bondwoman, which will exist for you from the
nations that are all around you, from them you will purchase a
servant and a bondwoman,

25:45 <u>and~ALSO</u> (וְגַם *wê'gam*) <u>from~SON~s</u> (מִבְּנֵי *mi'be'ney*) <u>the~</u>
<u>SETTLER~s</u> (הַתּוֹשָׁבִים *ha'to'sha'vim*) <u>the~IMMIGRATE</u>(V)*~ing*(mp)
(הַגָּרִים *ha'ga'rim*) <u>WITH~you</u>(mp) (עִמָּכֶם *i'ma'khem*) <u>from~them</u>(m)
(מֵהֶם *mey'hem*) *you*(ms)*~will~*PURCHASE(V) (תִּקְנוּ *tiq'nu*) <u>and~CLAN~</u>
<u>them</u>(m) (וּמִמִּשְׁפַּחְתָּם *u'mi'mish'pahh'tam*) <u>WHICH</u> (אֲשֶׁר *a'sher*)
<u>WITH~you</u>(mp) (עִמָּכֶם *i'ma'khem*) <u>WHICH</u> (אֲשֶׁר *a'sher*) *they~did~*
*make~*BRING.FORTH(V) (הוֹלִידוּ *ho'li'du*) <u>in~LAND~you</u>(mp) (בְּאַרְצְכֶם
bê'ar'tse'khem) <u>and~they~did~</u>EXIST(V) (וְהָיוּ *wê'hai'u*) <u>to~you</u>(mp)
(לָכֶם *la'khem*) <u>to~HOLDINGS</u> (לַאֲחֻזָּה *la'a'hhu'zah*) **RMT:** and also
from the sons of the immigrating settlers with you, from them you
will purchase, and their clan that is with you, which they brought
forth in your land, and they will exist for you for holdings,

25:46 <u>and~you</u>(mp)*~will~self~*INHERIT(V) (וְהִתְנַחַלְתֶּם
wê'hit'na'hhal'tem) <u>AT~them</u>(m) (אֹתָם *o'tam*) <u>to~SON~s~you</u>(mp)
(לִבְנֵיכֶם *liv'ney'khem*) <u>AFTER~you</u>(mp) (אַחֲרֵיכֶם *a'hha'rey'khem*) <u>to~</u>
<u>the~>~POSSESS</u>(V) (לָרֶשֶׁת *la're'shet*) <u>HOLDINGS</u> (אֲחֻזָּה *a'hhu'zah*)
<u>to~DISTANT</u> (לְעֹלָם *lê'o'lam*) <u>in~them</u>(m) (בָּהֶם *ba'hem*) *you*(mp)*~will~*
<u>SERVE</u>(V) (תַּעֲבֹדוּ *ta'a'vo'du*) <u>and~in~BROTHER~s~you</u>(mp)
uv'a'hhey'khem) <u>SON~s</u> (בְּנֵי *bê'ney*) Yisra'eyl (יִשְׂרָאֵל *yis'ra'eyl*) <u>MAN</u>
(אִישׁ *ish*) <u>in~BROTHER~him</u> (בְּאָחִיו *bê'a'hhiw*) <u>NOT</u> (לֹא *lo*) *you*(ms)*~*
*will~*RULE(V) (תִרְדֶּה *tir'deh*) <u>in~him</u> (בוֹ *vo*) <u>in~WHIP</u> (בְּפָרֶךְ
bê'pha'rekh) **RMT:** and you will inherit them for your sons after you,
for the possessing of holdings, for a distant time with them you will
serve, and with your brothers, the sons of Yisra'eyl, each with his
brother, you will not rule in him with a whip,

25:47 and~GIVEN.THAT (וְכִי wê'khi) _she~will~make~OVERTAKE_^(V) (תַשִּׂיג ta'sig) HAND (יַד yad) IMMIGRANT (גֵּר geyr) and~SETTLER (וְתוֹשָׁב wê'to'shav) WITH~you^(fs) (עִמָּךְ i'makh) and~he~did~ BE.LOW^(V) (וּמָךְ u'makh) BROTHER~you^(ms) (אָחִיךָ a'hhi'kha) WITH~ him (עִמּוֹ i'mo) and~he~did~be~SELL^(V) (וְנִמְכַּר wê'nim'kar) to~ IMMIGRANT (לְגֵר lê'geyr) SETTLER (תוֹשָׁב to'shav) WITH~you^(fs) (עִמָּךְ i'makh) OR (אוֹ o) to~OFFSHOOT (לְעֵקֶר lê'ey'qer) CLAN (מִשְׁפַּחַת mish'pa'hhat) IMMIGRANT (גֵּר geyr) **RMT:** and, given that the hand of an immigrant and the settler with you will reach, and your brother with him will be low, and he will be sold to an immigrant settling with you, or to an offshoot of the clan of an immigrant.

25:48 AFTER (אַחֲרֵי a'hha'rey) _he~did~be~SELL_^(V) (נִמְכַּר nim'kar) REDEMPTION (גְּאֻלָּה gê'u'lah) _she~will~EXIST_^(V) (תִּהְיֶה tih'yeh) to~ him (לוֹ lo) UNIT (אֶחָד e'hhad) from~BROTHER~s~him (מֵאֶחָיו mey'e'hhaw) _he~will~REDEEM_^(V)~him (יִגְאָלֶנּוּ yig'a'le'nu) **RMT:** After he was sold, redemption will exist for him, one of his brothers will redeem him.

25:49 OR (אוֹ o) UNCLE~him (דֹדוֹ do'do) OR (אוֹ o) SON (בֶן ven) UNCLE~him (דֹדוֹ do'do) _he~will~REDEEM_^(V)~him (יִגְאָלֶנּוּ yig'a'le'nu) OR (אוֹ o) from~REMAINS (מִשְּׁאֵר mish'eyr) FLESH~him (בְּשָׂרוֹ bê'sar'o) from~CLAN~him (מִמִּשְׁפַּחְתּוֹ mi'mish'pahh'to) _he~will~ REDEEM_^(V)~him (יִגְאָלֶנּוּ yig'a'le'nu) OR (אוֹ o) _she~did~make~ OVERTAKE_^(V) (הִשִּׂיגָה hi'si'gah) HAND~him (יָדוֹ ya'do) and~he~did~ be~REDEEM^(V) (וְנִגְאָל wê'nig'al) **RMT:** Or his uncle, or a son of his uncle, will redeem him, or from the remains of his flesh from his clan will redeem him, or his hand will reach and he will be redeemed,

25:50 and~he~did~much~THINK^(V) (וְחִשַּׁב wê'hhi'shav) WITH (עִם im) PURCHASE^(V)~ing^(ms)~him (קֹנֵהוּ qo'ney'hu) from~YEAR (מִשְּׁנַת mi'she'nat) _>~be~SELL_^(V)~him (הִמָּכְרוֹ hi'makh'ro) to~him (לוֹ lo) UNTIL (עַד ad) YEAR (שְׁנַת shê'nat) the~JUBILEE (הַיֹּבֵל hai'yo'veyl) and~he~did~EXIST^(V) (וְהָיָה wê'hai'yah) SILVER (כֶּסֶף ke'seph) MERCHANDISE~him (מִמְכָּרוֹ mim'ka'ro) in~NUMBER (בְּמִסְפַּר bê'mis'par) YEAR~s (שָׁנִים sha'nim) like~DAY~s (כִּימֵי ki'mey) HIRELING (שָׂכִיר sa'khir) _he~will~EXIST_^(V) (יִהְיֶה yih'yeh) WITH~him (עִמּוֹ i'mo) **RMT:** and he will plan with his purchaser from the year of his being sold to him until the year of the jubilee, and the silver of his merchandise will exist with the number of years like the days of a hireling that will exist with him.

25:51 <u>IF</u> (אִם *im*) <u>YET.AGAIN</u> (עוֹד *od*) <u>ABUNDANT</u> (רַבּוֹת *ra'bot*) in~ the~YEAR~s (בַּשָּׁנִים *ba'sha'nim*) to~MOUTH~them[f] (לְפִיהֶן *lê'phi'hen*) *he~will~make~*TURN.BACK[V] (יָשִׁיב *ya'shiv*) <u>REDEMPTION~him</u> (גְּאֻלָּתוֹ *gê'u'la'to*) <u>from~SILVER</u> (מִכֶּסֶף *mi'ke'seph*) <u>ACQUIRED~him</u> (מִקְנָתוֹ *miq'na'to*) **RMT:** If there is yet an abundance in years, by their mouth he will cause to turn back his redemption from the silver of his acquiring,

25:52 <u>and~IF</u> (וְאִם *wê'im*) <u>SMALL.AMOUNT</u> (מְעַט *mê'at*) *he~did~ be~*REMAIN[V] (נִשְׁאַר *nish'ar*) in~the~YEAR~s (בַּשָּׁנִים *ba'sha'nim*) <u>UNTIL</u> (עַד *ad*) <u>YEAR</u> (שְׁנַת *shê'nat*) <u>the~JUBILEE</u> (הַיֹּבֵל *hai'yo'veyl*) *and~he~did~much~*THINK[V] (וְחִשַּׁב *wê'hhi'shav*) to~him (לוֹ *lo*) like~ MOUTH (כְּפִי *kê'phi*) YEAR~s~him (שָׁנָיו *sha'naw*) *he~will~make~* TURN.BACK[V] (יָשִׁיב *ya'shiv*) <u>AT</u> (אֶת *et*) <u>REDEMPTION~him</u> (גְּאֻלָּתוֹ *gê'u'la'to*) **RMT:** and if a small amount will remain in the years until the year of the jubilee, then he will plan with him, according to the mouth of his years, he will make his redemption turn back.

25:53 <u>like~HIRELING</u> (כִּשְׂכִיר *kis'khir*) <u>YEAR</u> (שָׁנָה *sha'nah*) <u>in~YEAR</u> (בְּשָׁנָה *bê'sha'nah*) *he~will~*EXIST[V] (יִהְיֶה *yih'yeh*) <u>WITH~him</u> (עִמּוֹ *i'mo*) <u>NOT</u> (לֹא *lo*) *he~will~*RULE[V]~him (יִרְדֶּנּוּ *yir'de'nu*) in~WHIP (בְּפֶרֶךְ *bê'phe'rekh*) to~EYE~s2~you[ms] (לְעֵינֶיךָ *lê'ey'ney'kha*) **RMT:** Like a hireling, year by year, he will exist with him, he will not rule him with a whip to your eyes,

25:54 <u>and~IF</u> (וְאִם *wê'im*) <u>NOT</u> (לֹא *lo*) *he~will~be~*REDEEM[V] (יִגָּאֵל *yi'ga'eyl*) in~THESE (בְּאֵלֶּה *bê'ey'leh*) *and~he~will~*GO.OUT[V] (וְיָצָא *wê'ya'tsa*) in~YEAR (בִּשְׁנַת *bish'nat*) the~JUBILEE (הַיֹּבֵל *hai'yo'veyl*) <u>HE</u> (הוּא *hu*) and~SON~s~him (וּבָנָיו *u'va'naw*) <u>WITH~him</u> (עִמּוֹ *i'mo*) **RMT:** and if he will not be redeemed by these, then he will go out in the year of the jubilee, he and his sons with him,

25:55 <u>GIVEN.THAT</u> (כִּי *ki*) <u>to~me</u> (לִי *li*) <u>SON~s</u> (בְנֵי *vê'ney*) Yisra'eyl (יִשְׂרָאֵל *yis'ra'eyl*) <u>SERVANT~s</u> (עֲבָדִים *a'va'dim*) SERVANT~s~me (עֲבָדָי *a'va'dai*) <u>THEY</u>[m] (הֵם *heym*) <u>WHICH</u> (אֲשֶׁר *a'sher*) *I~did~ make~*GO.OUT[V] (הוֹצֵאתִי *ho'tsey'ti*) AT~them[m] (אוֹתָם *o'tam*) <u>from~LAND</u> (מֵאֶרֶץ *mey'e'rets*) Mits'rayim (מִצְרָיִם *mits'ra'yim*) I (אֲנִי *a'ni*) YHWH (יְהוָה *YHWH*) Elohiym~you[mp] (אֱלֹהֵיכֶם *e'lo'hey'khem*) **RMT:** given that to me are the sons of Yisra'eyl are servants, they are my servants, which I made them go out from the land of Mits'rayim, I am **YHWH** your Elohiym.

Chapter 26

26:1 NOT (לֹא *lo*) you^(mp)~will~DO^(V) (תַעֲשׂוּ *ta'a'su*) to~you^(mp) (לָכֶם *la'khem*) WORTHLESS~s (אֱלִילִם *e'li'lim*) and~SCULPTURE (וּפֶסֶל *u'phe'sel*) and~MONUMENT (וּמַצֵּבָה *u'ma'tsey'vah*) NOT (לֹא *lo*) you^(mp)~will~make~RISE^(V) (תָקִימוּ *ta'qi'mu*) to~you^(mp) (לָכֶם *la'khem*) and~STONE (וְאֶבֶן *wê'e'ven*) IMAGERY (מַשְׂכִּית *mas'kit*) NOT (לֹא *lo*) you^(mp)~will~GIVE^(V) (תִתְּנוּ *tit'nu*) in~LAND~you^(mp) (בְּאַרְצְכֶם *bê'ar'tse'khem*) to~>~self~BEND.DOWN^(V) (לְהִשְׁתַּחֲוֺת *lê'hish'ta'hha'ot*) UPON~her (עָלֶיהָ *a'ley'ah*) GIVEN.THAT (כִּי *ki*) I (אֲנִי *a'ni*) **YHWH** (יְהוָה *YHWH*) Elohiym~you^(mp) (אֱלֹהֵיכֶם *e'lo'hey'khem*) **RMT:** You will not make for you worthless ones, and sculpture and monument you will not make rise for you, and stone of imagery you will not place in your land to bow yourself down upon her, given that I am **YHWH** your Elohiym.

26:2 AT (אֶת *et*) CEASING~s~me (שַׁבְּתֹתַי *sha'be'to'tai*) you^(mp)~will~SAFEGUARD^(V) (תִּשְׁמֹרוּ *tish'moru*) and~SANCTUARY~me (וּמִקְדָּשִׁי *u'miq'da'shi*) you^(mp)~will~FEAR^(V) (תִּירָאוּ *ti'ra'u*) I (אֲנִי *a'ni*) **YHWH** (יְהוָה *YHWH*) **RMT:** My ceasings you will safeguard, and my sanctuary you will fear, I am **YHWH**.

26:3 IF (אִם *im*) in~CUSTOM~s~me (בְּחֻקֹּתַי *bê'hhu'qo'tai*) you^(mp)~will~WALK^(V) (תֵּלֵכוּ *tey'ley'khu*) and~AT (וְאֶת *wê'et*) DIRECTIVE~s~me (מִצְוֺתַי *mits'o'tai*) you^(mp)~will~SAFEGUARD^(V) (תִּשְׁמְרוּ *tish'me'ru*) and~you^(mp)~did~DO^(V) (וַעֲשִׂיתֶם *wa'a'si'tem*) AT~them^(m) (אֹתָם *o'tam*) **RMT:** If in my customs you will walk, and my directives you will safeguard, and you will do them,

26:4 and~I~did~GIVE^(V) (וְנָתַתִּי *wê'na'ta'ti*) RAIN.SHOWER~s~you^(mp) (גִשְׁמֵיכֶם *gish'mey'khem*) in~APPOINTED.TIME~them^(m) (בְּעִתָּם *bê'i'tam*) and~she~did~GIVE^(V) (וְנָתְנָה *wê'nat'nah*) the~LAND (הָאָרֶץ *ha'a'rets*) PRODUCT~her (יְבוּלָהּ *yê vu'lah*) and~TREE (וְעֵץ *wê'eyts*) the~FIELD (הַשָּׂדֶה *ha'sa'deh*) he~will~GIVE^(V) (יִתֵּן *yi'teyn*) PRODUCE~him (פִּרְיוֹ *pir'yo*) **RMT:** then I will give your rain showers in their appointed time, and the land will give her produce, and the tree of the field will give his produce,

26:5 and~he~did~make~OVERTAKE^(V) (וְהִשִּׂיג *wê'hi'sig*) to~you^(mp) (לָכֶם *la'khem*) THRESHING (דַּיִשׁ *da'yish*) AT (אֶת *et*) VINTAGE (בָּצִיר *ba'tsir*) and~VINTAGE (וּבָצִיר *u'va'tsir*) he~will~make~OVERTAKE^(V) (יַשִּׂיג *ya'sig*) AT (אֶת *et*) SEED (זֶרַע *za'ra*) and~you^(mp)~did~EAT^(V) (וַאֲכַלְתֶּם *wa'a'khal'tem*) BREAD~you^(mp) (לַחְמְכֶם *lahh'me'khem*) to~

SATISFACTION (שֹׂבַע la'so'va) and~you(mp)~did~SETTLE(V) (וִישַׁבְתֶּם wi'shav'tem) to~the~SAFELY (לָבֶטַח la've'tahh) in~LAND~you(mp) (בְּאַרְצְכֶם bê'ar'tse'khem) **RMT:** and the threshing will overtake the vintage for you, and the vintage will overtake the seed, and you will eat your bread to satisfaction, and you will settle safely in the land,

26:6 and~I~did~GIVE(V) (וְנָתַתִּי wê'na'ta'ti) COMPLETENESS (שָׁלוֹם sha'lom) in~the~LAND (בָּאָרֶץ ba'a'rets) and~you(mp)~did~ LIE.DOWN(V) (וּשְׁכַבְתֶּם ush'khav'tem) and~WITHOUT (וְאֵין wê'eyn) make~TREMBLE(V)~ing(ms) (מַחֲרִיד ma'hha'rid) and~I~did~make~ CEASE(V) (וְהִשְׁבַּתִּי wê'hish'ba'ti) LIVING (חַיָּה hhai'yah) DYSFUNCTIONAL (רָעָה ra'ah) FROM (מִן min) the~LAND (הָאָרֶץ ha'a'rets) and~SWORD (וְחֶרֶב wê'hhe'rev) NOT (לֹא lo) you(ms)~will~ CROSS.OVER(V) (תַעֲבֹר ta'a'vor) in~LAND~you(mp) (בְּאַרְצְכֶם bê'ar'tse'khem) **RMT:** and I will give completeness in the land, and you will lay down, and without trembling, and I will make the dysfunctional living ones[130] cease from the land, and the sword will not cross over in your land,

26:7 and~you(mp)~did~PURSUE(V) (וּרְדַפְתֶּם ur'daph'tem) AT (אֶת et) ATTACK(V)~ing(mp)~you(mp) (אֹיְבֵיכֶם oy'vey'khem) and~they~did~ FALL(V) (וְנָפְלוּ wê'naph'lu) to~FACE~s~you(mp) (לִפְנֵיכֶם liph'ney'khem) to~SWORD (לֶחָרֶב le'hha'rev) **RMT:** and you will pursue your attackers, and they will fall to your faces by the sword,

26:8 and~they~did~PURSUE(V) (וְרָדְפוּ wê'rad'phu) from~you(mp) (מִכֶּם mi'kem) FIVE (חֲמִשָּׁה hha'mi'shah) HUNDRED (מֵאָה mey'ah) and~HUNDRED (וּמֵאָה u'mey'ah) from~you(mp) (מִכֶּם mi'kem) MYRIAD (רְבָבָה rê'va'vah) they(m)~will~PURSUE(V) (יִרְדֹּפוּ yir'do'phu) and~they~did~FALL(V) (וְנָפְלוּ wê'naph'lu) ATTACK(V)~ing(mp)~you(mp) (אֹיְבֵיכֶם oy'vey'khem) to~FACE~s~you(mp) (לִפְנֵיכֶם liph'ney'khem) to~SWORD (לֶחָרֶב le'hha'rev) **RMT:** and five from you will pursue a hundred, and a hundred from you will pursue a myriad, and your attackers will fall to your faces by the sword,

26:9 and~I~did~TURN(V) (וּפָנִיתִי u'pha'ni'ti) TO~you(mp) (אֲלֵיכֶם a'ley'khem) and~I~did~make~REPRODUCE(V) (וְהִפְרֵיתִי wê'hiph'rey'ti) AT~you(mp) (אֶתְכֶם et'khem) and~I~did~make~INCREASE(V) (וְהִרְבֵּיתִי wê'hir'bey'ti) AT~you(mp) (אֶתְכֶם et'khem) and~I~did~make~RISE(V) (וַהֲקִימֹתִי wa'ha'qi'mo'ti) AT (אֶת et) COVENANT~me (בְּרִיתִי bê'ri'ti) AT~you(mp) (אִתְּכֶם it'khem) **RMT:** and I will turn to you, and I will

---

[130] A euphemism for wild beasts.

make you reproduce, and I will make you increase, and I will make my covenant rise with you,

26:10 and~you(mp)~did~EAT(V) (וַאֲכַלְתֶּם wa'a'khal'tem) SLEEPING (יָשָׁן ya'shan) be~SLEEP(V)~ing(ms) (נוֹשָׁן no'shan) and~SLEEPING (וְיָשָׁן wê'ya'shan) from~FACE~s (מִפְּנֵי mip'ney) NEW (חָדָשׁ hha'dash) you(mp)~will~make~GO.OUT(V) (תּוֹצִיאוּ to'tsi'u) **RMT:** and you will eat the stores that are being stored, and you will make the storage go out from the face of the new ones,

26:11 and~I~did~GIVE(V) (וְנָתַתִּי wê'na'ta'ti) DWELLING~me (מִשְׁכָּנִי mish'ka'ni) in~MIDST~you(mp) (בְּתוֹכְכֶם bê'tokh'khem) and~NOT (וְלֹא wê'lo) she~will~CAST.AWAY(V) (תִגְעַל tig'al) SOUL~me (נַפְשִׁי naph'shi) AT~you(mp) (אֶתְכֶם et'khem) **RMT:** and I will place my dwelling in your midst, and my soul will not cast you away,

26:12 and~I~did~self~WALK(V) (וְהִתְהַלַּכְתִּי wê'hit'ha'lakh'ti) in~MIDST~you(mp) (בְּתוֹכְכֶם bê'tokh'khem) and~I~did~EXIST(V) (וְהָיִיתִי wê'hai'yi'ti) to~you(mp) (לָכֶם la'khem) to~Elohiym (לֵאלֹהִים ley'lo'him) and~YOU(mp) (וְאַתֶּם wê'a'tem) you(mp)~will~EXIST(V) (תִּהְיוּ tih'yu) to~me (לִי li) to~PEOPLE (לְעָם lê'am) **RMT:** and I will walk myself in your midst, and I will exist for you for Elohiym, and you, you will exist for me for a people.

26:13 I (אֲנִי a'ni) **YHWH** (יְהֹוָה YHWH) Elohiym~you(mp) (אֱלֹהֵיכֶם e'lo'hey'khem) WHICH (אֲשֶׁר a'sher) I~did~make~GO.OUT(V) (הוֹצֵאתִי ho'tsey'ti) AT~you(mp) (אֶתְכֶם et'khem) from~LAND (מֵאֶרֶץ mey'e'rets) Mits'rayim (מִצְרַיִם mits'ra'yim) from~>~EXIST(V) (מִהְיֹת mih'yot) to~them(m) (לָהֶם la'hem) SERVANT~s (עֲבָדִים a'va'dim) and~I~will~CRACK(V) (וָאֶשְׁבֹּר wa'esh'bor) POLE~s (מֹטֹת mo'tot) YOKE~you(mp) (עֻלְּכֶם ul'khem) and~I~will~make~WALK(V) (וָאוֹלֵךְ wa'o'leykh) AT~you(mp) (אֶתְכֶם et'khem) VERTICAL (קוֹמְמִיּוּת qom'mi'yut) **RMT:** I am **YHWH** your Elohiym who made you go out from the land of Mits'rayim, from existing for them as servants, and I will crack the poles of your yoke, and I will make you walk vertical,

26:14 and~IF (וְאִם wê'im) NOT (לֹא lo) you(mp)~will~HEAR(V) (תִּשְׁמְעוּ tish'me'u) to~me (לִי li) and~NOT (וְלֹא wê'lo) you(mp)~will~DO(V) (תַעֲשׂוּ ta'a'su) AT (אֵת eyt) ALL (כָּל kol) the~DIRECTIVE~s (הַמִּצְוֹת ha'mits'ot) the~THESE (הָאֵלֶּה ha'ey'leh) **RMT:** but if you will not listen to me, and you will not do all these directives,

26:15 and~IF (וְאִם wê'im) in~CUSTOM~s~me (בְּחֻקֹּתַי bê'hhu'qo'tai) you(mp)~will~REJECT(V) (תִּמְאָסוּ tim'a'su) and~IF (וְאִם wê'im) AT (אֶת et *et*) DECISION~s~me (מִשְׁפָּטַי *mish'pa'tai*) *she~will~*CAST.AWAY^(V) (תִּגְעַל *tig'al*) SOUL~you^(ms) (נַפְשְׁכֶם *naph'she'khem*) to~EXCEPT (לְבִלְתִּי *lê'vil'ti*) >~DO^(V) (עֲשׂוֹת *a'sot*) AT (אֶת *et*) ALL (כָּל *kol*) DIRECTIVE~s~me (מִצְוֹתַי *mits'o'tai*) to~>~make~BREAK^(V)~you^(mp) (לְהַפְרְכֶם *lê'haph're'khem*) AT (אֶת *et*) COVENANT~me (בְּרִיתִי *bê'ri'ti*) **RMT:** and if you will reject my customs, and if your soul will cast away my decisions, to not do all my directives to cause you to break my covenant.

26:16 MOREOVER (אַף *aph*) I (אֲנִי *a'ni*) *I~will~*DO^(V) (אֶעֱשֶׂה *e'e'seh*) THIS (זֹאת *zot*) to~you^(mp) (לָכֶם *la'khem*) and~*I~did~make~* REGISTER^(V) (וְהִפְקַדְתִּי *wê'hiph'qad'ti*) UPON~you^(mp) (עֲלֵיכֶם *a'ley'khem*) DISMAY (בֶּהָלָה *be'ha'lah*) AT (אֶת *et*) the~ CONSUMPTION (הַשַּׁחֶפֶת *ha'sha'hhe'phet*) and~AT (וְאֶת *wê'et*) the~ FEVER (הַקַּדַּחַת *ha'qa'da'hhat*) *much~*FINISH^(V)~*ing*^(fp) (מְכַלּוֹת *mê'kha'lot*) EYE~s2 (עֵינַיִם *ey'na'yim*) and~*make~*SORROW^(V)~*ing*^(fp) (וּמְדִיבֹת *um'di'vot*) SOUL (נָפֶשׁ *na'phesh*) and~you^(mp)~did~SOW^(V) (וּזְרַעְתֶּם *uz'ra'e'tem*) to~the~EMPTY (לָרִיק *la'riq*) SEED~you^(mp) (זַרְעֲכֶם *zar'a'khem*) and~*they~did~*EAT^(V)~him (וַאֲכָלֻהוּ *wa'a'kha'lu'hu*) ATTACK^(V)~*ing*^(mp)~you^(mp) (אֹיְבֵיכֶם *oy'vey'khem*) **RMT:** Moreover, I will do this to you, and I will make register upon you dismay, the consumption and the fever, a finishing of the eyes, and making the soul sorrowful, and you will sow your seed to emptiness, and your attackers will eat him,

26:17 and~*I~did~*GIVE^(V) (וְנָתַתִּי *wê'na'ta'ti*) FACE~s~me (פָּנַי *pha'nai*) in~you^(mp) (בָּכֶם *ba'khem*) and~you^(mp)~did~be~SMITE^(V) (וְנִגַּפְתֶּם *wê'ni'gaph'tem*) to~FACE~s (לִפְנֵי *liph'ney*) ATTACK^(V)~ *ing*^(mp)~you^(mp) (אֹיְבֵיכֶם *oy'vey'khem*) and~*they~did~*RULE^(V) (וְרָדוּ *wê'ra'du*) in~you^(mp) (בָכֶם *va'khem*) HATE^(V)~*ing*^(mp)~you^(mp) (שֹׂנְאֵיכֶם *son'ey'khem*) and~you^(mp)~did~FLEE^(V) (וְנַסְתֶּם *wê'nas'tem*) and~ WITHOUT (וְאֵין *wê'eyn*) PURSUE^(V)~*ing*^(ms) (רֹדֵף *ro'deyph*) AT~you^(mp) (אֶתְכֶם *et'khem*) **RMT:** and I will place my face with you, and you will be smitten at the face of your attackers, and your haters will rule over you, and you will flee without anyone pursuing you,

26:18 and~IF (וְאִם *wê'im*) UNTIL (עַד *ad*) THESE (אֵלֶּה *ey'leh*) NOT (לֹא *lo*) you^(mp)~will~HEAR^(V) (תִּשְׁמְעוּ *tish'me'u*) to~me (לִי *li*) and~*I~ did~*ADD^(V) (וְיָסַפְתִּי *wê'ya'saph'ti*) to~>~much~CORRECT^(V)~her (לְיַסְּרָה *lê'yas'rah*) AT~you^(mp) (אֶתְכֶם *et'khem*) SEVEN (שֶׁבַע *she'va*) UPON (עַל *al*) FAILURE~s~you^(mp) (חַטֹּאתֵיכֶם *hha'to'tey'khem*)

RMT: and if unto these you will not listen to me, then I will add seven times upon your failures to correct you,

26:19 and~/~did~CRACK[V] (וְשָׁבַרְתִּי wê'sha'var'ti) AT (אֶת et) MAJESTY (גָּאוֹן gê'on) BOLDNESS~you[mp] (עֻזְּכֶם uz'khem) and~/~did~GIVE[V] (וְנָתַתִּי wê'na'ta'ti) AT (אֶת et) SKY~s2~you[mp] (שְׁמֵיכֶם sh'mey'khem) like~IRON (כַּבַּרְזֶל ka'bar'zel) and~AT (וְאֶת wê'et) LAND~you[mp] (אַרְצְכֶם ar'tse'khem) like~the~BRASS (כַּנְּחֻשָׁה kan'hhu'shah) **RMT:** and I will crack the majesty of your boldness, and I will make your skies like iron and your land like brass,

26:20 and~he~did~BE.WHOLE[V] (וְתַם wê'tam) to~the~EMPTY (לָרִיק la'riq) STRENGTH~you[mp] (כֹּחֲכֶם ko'hha'khem) and~NOT (וְלֹא wê'lo) she~will~GIVE[V] (תִתֵּן ti'teyn) LAND~you[mp] (אַרְצְכֶם ar'tse'khem) AT (אֶת et) PRODUCT~her (יְבוּלָהּ yê'vu'lah) and~TREE (וְעֵץ wê'eyts) the~LAND (הָאָרֶץ ha'a'rets) NOT (לֹא lo) he~will~GIVE[V] (יִתֵּן yi'teyn) PRODUCE~him (פִּרְיוֹ pir'yo) **RMT:** and your strength will be whole in emptiness, and your land will not give her produce, and the tree of the land will not give his produce,

26:21 and~IF (וְאִם wê'im) you[mp]~will~WALK[V] (תֵּלְכוּ teyl'khu) WITH~me (עִמִּי i'mi) CONTRARY (קֶרִי qe'ri) and~NOT (וְלֹא wê'lo) you[mp]~will~CONSENT[V] (תֹאבוּ to'vu) to~>~HEAR[V] (לִשְׁמֹעַ lish'mo'a) to~me (לִי li) and~/~did~ADD[V] (וְיָסַפְתִּי wê'ya'saph'ti) UPON~you[mp] (עֲלֵיכֶם a'ley'khem) HITTING (מַכָּה ma'kah) SEVEN (שֶׁבַע she'va) like~FAILURE~s~you[mp] (כְּחַטֹּאתֵיכֶם kê'hha'to'tey'khem) **RMT:** and if you will walk contrary with me, and you will not consent to listen to me, then I will add a hitting upon you seven times according to your failures,

26:22 and~/~did~make~SEND[V] (וְהִשְׁלַחְתִּי wê'hish'lahh'ti) in~you[mp] (בָכֶם va'khem) AT (אֶת et) LIVING (חַיַּת hhai'yat) the~FIELD (הַשָּׂדֶה ha'sa'deh) and~she~did~much~BE.CHILDLESS[V] (וְשִׁכְּלָה wê'shik'lah) AT~you[mp] (אֶתְכֶם et'khem) and~she~did~make~CUT[V] (וְהִכְרִיתָה wê'hikh'ri'tah) AT (אֶת et) BEAST~you[mp] (בְּהֶמְתְּכֶם bê'hem'te'khem) and~she~did~make~BE.LESS[V] (וְהִמְעִיטָה wê'him'i'tah) AT~you[mp] (אֶתְכֶם et'khem) and~they~did~be~DESOLATE[V] (וְנָשַׁמּוּ wê'na'sha'mu) ROAD~s (דַּרְכֵיכֶם dar'khey'khem) **RMT:** and I will cause to send among you living ones of the field[131], and she[132] will

---

[131] The "living ones of the field" is a euphemism for "wild animals."
[132] The "she" is referring to the word "living," a singular feminine noun.

make you be childless, and she will make you be less, and the roads will be desolate,

26:23 and~IF (וְאִם *wê'im*) in~THESE (בְּאֵלֶּה *bê'ey'leh*) NOT (לֹא *lo*) you(ms)~will~be~CORRECT(V) (תִוָּסְרוּ *ti'was'ru*) to~me (לִי *li*) and~ you(mp)~did~WALK(V) (וַהֲלַכְתֶּם *wa'ha'lakh'tem*) WITH~me (עִמִּי *i'mi*) CONTRARY (קֶרִי *qe'ri*) **RMT:** and if in these you will not be corrected for me, and you will walk contrary with me,

26:24 and~I~did~WALK(V) (וְהָלַכְתִּי *wê'ha'lakh'ti*) MOREOVER (אַף *aph*) I (אֲנִי *a'ni*) WITH~you(mp) (עִמָּכֶם *i'ma'khem*) in~CONTRARY (בְּקֶרִי *bê'qe'ri*) and~I~did~make~HIT(V) (וְהִכֵּיתִי *wê'hi'key'ti*) AT~ you(mp) (אֶתְכֶם *et'khem*) ALSO (גַּם *gam*) I (אָנִי *a'ni*) SEVEN (שֶׁבַע *she'va*) UPON (עַל *al*) FAILURE~s~you(mp) (חַטֹּאתֵיכֶם *hha'to'tey'khem*) **RMT:** then moreover I, I will walk contrary with you, and I, also I, will attack you seven times over your failures,

26:25 and~I~will~make~COME(V) (וְהֵבֵאתִי *wê'hey'vey'ti*) UPON~ you(mp) (עֲלֵיכֶם *a'ley'khem*) SWORD (חֶרֶב *hhe'rev*) AVENGE(V)~ing(fs) (נֹקֶמֶת *no'qe'met*) VENGEANCE (נָקָם *nê'qam*) COVENANT (בְּרִית *bê'rit*) and~you(mp)~did~be~GATHER(V) (וְנֶאֱסַפְתֶּם *wê'ne'e'saph'tem*) TO (אֶל *el*) CITY~s~you(mp) (עָרֵיכֶם *a'rey'khem*) and~I~did~much~ SEND(V) (וְשִׁלַּחְתִּי *wê'shi'lahh'ti*) EPIDEMIC (דֶבֶר *de'ver*) in~MIDST~ you(mp) (בְּתוֹכְכֶם *bê'tokh'khem*) and~you(mp)~did~be~GIVE(V) (וְנִתַּתֶּם *wê'ni'ta'tem*) in~HAND (בְּיַד *bê'yad*) ATTACK(V)~ing(ms) (אוֹיֵב *o'yeyv*) **RMT:** and I will bring upon you a sword, avenging vengeance of a covenant, and you will be gathered to your cities, and I will send an epidemic in your midst, and you will be given into the hand of the attackers.

26:26 in~>~CRACK(V)~me (בְּשִׁבְרִי *bê'shiv'ri*) to~you(mp) (לָכֶם *la'khem*) BRANCH (מַטֵּה *ma'teyh*) BREAD (לֶחֶם *le'hhem*) and~they~ will~BAKE(V) (וְאָפוּ *wê'a'phu*) TEN (עֶשֶׂר *e'ser*) WOMAN~s (נָשִׁים *na'shim*) BREAD~you(mp) (לַחְמְכֶם *lahh'me'khem*) in~OVEN (בְּתַנּוּר *bê'ta'nur*) UNIT (אֶחָד *e'hhad*) and~they~did~make~TURN.BACK(V) (וְהֵשִׁיבוּ *wê'hey'shi'vu*) BREAD~you(mp) (לַחְמְכֶם *lahh'me'khem*) in~ the~WEIGHT (בַּמִּשְׁקָל *ba'mish'qal*) and~you(mp)~did~EAT(V) (וַאֲכַלְתֶּם *wa'a'khal'tem*) and~NOT (וְלֹא *wê'lo*) you(mp)~will~BE.SATISFIED(V) (תִשְׂבָּעוּ *tis'ba'u*) **RMT:** In my cracking your branch of bread, and ten women will bake your bread in one oven, and they will make your bread turn back by the weight, and you will eat, but you will not be satisfied,

26:27 and~IF (וְאִם wê'im) in~THIS (בְּזֹאת bê'zot) NOT (לֹא lo) you(mp)~will~HEAR(V) (תִשְׁמְעוּ tish'me'u) to~me (לִי li) and~you(mp)~ did~WALK(V) (וַהֲלַכְתֶּם wa'ha'lakh'tem) WITH~me (עִמִּי i'mi) in~ CONTRARY (בְּקֶרִי bê'qe'ri) **RMT:** and if in this you will not listen to me, and you will walk contrary with me,

26:28 and~I~did~WALK(V) (וְהָלַכְתִּי wê'ha'lakh'ti) WITH~you(mp) (עִמָּכֶם i'ma'khem) in~FURY (בַּחֲמַת ba'hha'mat) CONTRARY (קֶרִי qe'ri) and~I~did~much~CORRECT(V) (וְיִסַּרְתִּי wê'yi'sar'ti) AT~you(mp) (אֶתְכֶם et'khem) MOREOVER (אַף aph) I (אָנִי a'ni) SEVEN (שֶׁבַע she'va) UPON (עַל al) FAILURE~s~you(mp) (חַטֹּאתֵיכֶם hha'to'tey'khem) **RMT:** then I will walk contrary with you in a fury, and moreover I, I will correct you seven times over your failures,

26:29 and~you(mp)~did~EAT(V) (וַאֲכַלְתֶּם wa'a'khal'tem) FLESH (בְּשַׂר bê'sar) SON~s~you(mp) (בְּנֵיכֶם bê'ney'khem) and~FLESH (וּבְשַׂר uv'sar) DAUGHTER~s~you(mp) (בְּנֹתֵיכֶם bê'no'tey'khem) you(mp)~will~ EAT(V) (תֹּאכֵלוּ to'khey'lu) **RMT:** and you will eat the flesh of your sons, and the flesh of your daughters you will eat,

26:30 and~I~did~make~DESTROY(V) (וְהִשְׁמַדְתִּי wê'hish'mad'ti) AT (אֶת et) PLATFORM~s~you(mp) (בָּמֹתֵיכֶם ba'mo'tey'khem) and~I~did~ make~CUT(V) (וְהִכְרַתִּי wê'hikh'ra'ti) AT (אֶת et) SUN.IDOL~s~you(mp) (חַמָּנֵיכֶם hha'ma'ney'khem) and~I~did~GIVE(V) (וְנָתַתִּי wê'na'ta'ti) AT (אֶת et) CORPSE~s~you(mp) (פִּגְרֵיכֶם pig'rey'khem) UPON (עַל al) CORPSE~s (פִּגְרֵי pig'rey) IDOL~s~you(mp) (גִּלּוּלֵיכֶם gi'lu'ley'khem) and~she~did~CAST.AWAY(V) (וְגָעֲלָה wê'ga'a'lah) SOUL~me (נַפְשִׁי naph'shi) AT~you(mp) (אֶתְכֶם et'khem) **RMT:** and I will cause your platforms to be destroyed, and I will cause your sun idols to be cut, and I will place your corpses upon the corpses of your idols, and my soul will cast you away,

26:31 and~I~did~GIVE(V) (וְנָתַתִּי wê'na'ta'ti) AT (אֶת et) CITY~s~ you(mp) (עָרֵיכֶם a'rey'khem) DRIED.OUT (חָרְבָּה hhar'bah) and~I~did~ make~DESOLATE(V) (וַהֲשִׁמּוֹתִי wa'ha'shi'mo'ti) AT (אֶת et) SANCTUARY~s~you(mp) (מִקְדְּשֵׁיכֶם miq'de'shey'khem) and~NOT (וְלֹא wê'lo) I~will~make~SMELL(V) (אָרִיחַ a'ri'ahh) in~AROMA (בְּרֵיחַ bê'rey'ahh) SWEET~you(mp) (נִיחֹחֲכֶם ni'hho'hha'khem) **RMT:** and I will make your cities dried out, and I will make your sanctuaries desolate, and I will not smell your sweet aroma,

26:32 and~I~did~make~DESOLATE(V) (וַהֲשִׁמֹּתִי wa'ha'shi'mo'ti) I (אֲנִי a'ni) AT (אֶת et) the~LAND (הָאָרֶץ ha'a'rets) and~they~did~

DESOLATE^(V) (וְשָׁמְמוּ *wê'sham'mu*) UPON~her (עָלֶיהָ *a'ley'ah*) ATTACK^{(V)~}ing^{(mp)~}you^(mp) (אֹיְבֵיכֶם *oy'vey'khem*) the~SETTLE^{(V)~}ing^(mp) (הַיֹּשְׁבִים *hai'yosh'vim*) in~her (בָּהּ *bah*) **RMT:** and I, I, will make the land desolate, and your attackers settling in her will desolate her,

26:33 and~AT~you^(mp) (וְאֶתְכֶם *wê'et'khem*) *I~will~much~*DISPERSE^(V) (אֱזָרֶה *e'za'reh*) in~the~NATION~s (בַגּוֹיִם *va'go'yim*) and~*I~did~make~*DRAW.OUT^(V) (וַהֲרִיקֹתִי *wa'ha'ri'qo'ti*) AFTER~you^(mp) (אַחֲרֵיכֶם *a'hha'rey'khem*) SWORD (חָרֶב *hha'rev*) and~she~did~EXIST^(V) (וְהָיְתָה *wê'hai'tah*) LAND~you^(mp) (אַרְצְכֶם *ar'tse'khem*) DESOLATE (שְׁמָמָה *shê'ma'mah*) and~CITY~s~you^(mp) (וְעָרֵיכֶם *wê'a'rey'khem*) they^{(m)~}will~EXIST^(V) (יִהְיוּ *yih'yu*) DRIED.OUT (חָרְבָּה *hhar'bah*) **RMT:** and I will disperse you in the nations, and I will make the sword draw out after you, and your land will exist desolate, and your cities will exist dried out.

26:34 AT.THAT.TIME (אָז *az*) she~will~ACCEPT^(V) (תִּרְצֶה *tir'tseh*) the~LAND (הָאָרֶץ *ha'a'rets*) AT (אֶת *et*) CEASING~s~her (שַׁבְּתֹתֶיהָ *sha'be'to'tey'ah*) ALL (כֹּל *kol*) DAY~s (יְמֵי *yê'mey*) >~be~make~DESOLATE^{(V)~}her (הֳשַׁמָּה *ha'sha'mah*) and~YOU^(mp) (וְאַתֶּם *wê'a'tem*) in~LAND (בְּאֶרֶץ *bê'e'rets*) ATTACK^{(V)~}ing^{(mp)~}you^(mp) (אֹיְבֵיכֶם *oy'vey'khem*) AT.THAT.TIME (אָז *az*) she~will~CEASE^(V) (תִּשְׁבַּת *tish'bat*) the~LAND (הָאָרֶץ *ha'a'rets*) and~she~did~make~ACCEPT^(V) (וְהִרְצָת *wê'hir'tsat*) AT (אֶת *et*) CEASING~s~her (שַׁבְּתֹתֶיהָ *sha'be'to'tey'ah*) **RMT:** At that time the land will accept her ceasings all the days of her being desolate, and you will be in the land of your attackers, at that time the land will cease, and she will accept her ceasings.

26:35 ALL (כָּל *kol*) DAY~s (יְמֵי *yê'mey*) >~be~make~DESOLATE^{(V)~}her (הֳשַׁמָּה *ha'sha'mah*) she~will~CEASE^(V) (תִּשְׁבֹּת *tish'bot*) AT (אֵת *eyt*) WHICH (אֲשֶׁר *a'sher*) NOT (לֹא *lo*) she~did~CEASE^(V) (שָׁבְתָה *shav'tah*) in~CEASING~s~you^(mp) (בְּשַׁבְּתֹתֵיכֶם *bê'sha'be'to'tey'khem*) in~>~SETTLE^{(V)~}you^(mp) (בְּשִׁבְתְּכֶם *bê'shiv'te'khem*) UPON~her (עָלֶיהָ *a'ley'ah*) **RMT:** All the days of her being made desolate, she will cease, because she did not cease with your ceasings with you settling upon her,

26:36 and~the~be~REMAIN^{(V)~}ing^(mp) (וְהַנִּשְׁאָרִים *wê'ha'nish'a'rim*) in~you^(mp) (בָּכֶם *ba'khem*) and~*I~will~make~*COME^(V) (וְהֵבֵאתִי *wê'hey'vey'ti*) FAINT (מֹרֶךְ *mo'rekh*) in~HEART~them^(m) (בִּלְבָבָם *bil'va'vam*) in~LAND~s (בְּאַרְצֹת *bê'ar'tsot*) ATTACK^{(V)~}ing^{(ms)~}s~

them^(m)

them^(m) (אֹיְבֵיהֶם *oy'vey'hem*) and~he~did~PURSUE^(V) (וְרָדַף *wê'ra'daph*) AT~them^(m) (אֹתָם *o'tam*) VOICE (קוֹל *qol*) LEAF (עָלֶה *a'leh*) be~TWIRL^(V)~ing^(ms) (נִדָּף *ni'daph*) and~they~did~FLEE^(V) (וְנָסוּ *wê'na'su*) FLEEING (מְנֻסַת *mê'nu'sat*) SWORD (חֶרֶב *hhe'rev*) and~they~did~FALL^(V) (וְנָפְלוּ *wê'naph'lu*) and~WITHOUT (וְאֵין *wê'eyn*) PURSUE^(V)~ing^(ms) (רֹדֵף *ro'deyph*) **RMT:** and the ones remaining in you, then I will bring faintness in their heart in the lands of their attackers, and the voice of a leaf twirling will pursue them, and they will flee, fleeing the sword, and they will fall and without a pursuer,

26:37 and~they~did~TOPPLE^(V) (וְכָשְׁלוּ *wê'khash'lu*) MAN (אִישׁ *ish*) in~BROTHER~him (בְאָחִיו *bê'a'hhiw*) like~from~FACE~s (כְּמִפְּנֵי *kê'mi'pe'ney*) SWORD (חֶרֶב *hhe'rev*) and~PURSUE^(V)~ing^(ms) (וְרֹדֵף *wê'ro'deyph*) WITHOUT (אָיִן *a'yin*) and~NOT (וְלֹא *wê'lo*) she~will~EXIST^(V) (תִהְיֶה *tih'yeh*) to~you^(mp) (לָכֶם *la'khem*) HIGH.PLACE (תְּקוּמָה *tê'qu'mah*) to~FACE~s (לִפְנֵי *liph'ney*) ATTACK^(V)~ing^(mp)~you^(mp) (אֹיְבֵיכֶם *oy'vey'khem*) **RMT:** and they will topple, each with his brother, as from the face of a sword, and without a pursuer, and a high place will not exist for you to the face of your attackers,

26:38 and~you^(mp)~did~PERISH^(V) (וַאֲבַדְתֶּם *wa'a'vad'tem*) in~the~NATION~s (בַּגּוֹיִם *ba'go'yim*) and~she~did~EAT^(V) (וְאָכְלָה *wê'akh'lah*) AT~you^(mp) (אֶתְכֶם *et'khem*) LAND (אֶרֶץ *e'rets*) ATTACK^(V)~ing^(mp)~you^(mp) (אֹיְבֵיכֶם *oy'vey'khem*) **RMT:** and you will perish in the nations, and the land of your attackers will eat you,

26:39 and~the~be~REMAIN^(V)~ing^(mp) (וְהַנִּשְׁאָרִים *wê'ha'nish'a'rim*) in~you^(mp) (בָּכֶם *ba'khem*) they^(m)~will~be~ROT^(V) (יִמַּקּוּ *yi'ma'qu*) in~the~TWISTEDNESS~them^(m) (בַּעֲוֹנָם *ba'a'o'nam*) in~LAND~s (בְּאַרְצֹת *bê'ar'tsot*) ATTACK^(V)~ing^(mp)~you^(mp) (אֹיְבֵיכֶם *oy'vey'khem*) and~MOREOVER (וְאַף *wê'aph*) in~the~TWISTEDNESS~s (בַּעֲוֹנֹת *ba'a'o'not*) FATHER~s~them^(m) (אֲבֹתָם *a'vo'tam*) AT~them^(m) (אִתָּם *i'tam*) they^(m)~will~be~ROT^(V) (יִמָּקּוּ *yi'ma'qu*) **RMT:** and the ones remaining in you, they will be rotted in their twistedness in the lands of your attackers, and moreover, in the twistedness of their fathers with them, they will be rotted,

26:40 and~they~did~self~THROW.THE.HAND^(V) (וְהִתְוַדּוּ *wê'hit'wa'du*) AT (אֶת *et*) TWISTEDNESS~them^(m) (עֲוֹנָם *a'o'nam*) and~AT (וְאֶת *wê'et*) TWISTEDNESS (עֲוֹן *a'won*) FATHER~s~them^(m) (אֲבֹתָם *a'vo'tam*) in~TRANSGRESSION~them^(m) (בְּמַעֲלָם *bê'ma'a'lam*) WHICH (אֲשֶׁר *a'sher*) they~did~TRANSGRESS^(V) (מָעֲלוּ *ma'a'lu*) in~me (בִי *vi*) and~MOREOVER (וְאַף *wê'aph*) WHICH (אֲשֶׁר *a'sher*)

a'sher) _they~did~WALK_(V) (הָלְכוּ hal'khu) <u>WITH~me</u> (עִמִּי i'mi) <u>in~</u>
<u>CONTRARY</u> (בְּקֶרִי bê'qe'ri) **RMT:** and they will confess their
twistedness and the twistedness of their fathers, in their
transgression that they transgressed in me, and moreover that they
walked contrary with me.

26:41 <u>MOREOVER</u> (אַף aph) <u>I</u> (אֲנִי a'ni) _I~will~WALK_(V) (אֵלֵךְ
ey'leykh) <u>WITH~them</u>(m) (עִמָּם i'mam) <u>in~CONTRARY</u> (בְּקֶרִי bê'qe'ri)
and~_I~will~make~COME_(V) (וְהֵבֵאתִי wê'hey'vey'ti) <u>AT~them</u>(m) (אֹתָם
o'tam) <u>in~LAND</u> (בְּאֶרֶץ bê'e'rets) _ATTACK_(V)~_ing_(ms)~s~them(m)
(אֹיְבֵיהֶם oy'vey'hem) <u>OR</u> (אוֹ o) <u>AT.THAT.TIME</u> (אָז az) _he~will~be~_
<u>LOWER</u>(V) (יִכָּנַע yi'ka'na) <u>HEART~them</u>(m) (לְבָבָם lê'va'vam) <u>the~</u>
<u>UNCIRCUMCISED</u> (הֶעָרֵל he'ar'eyl) and~<u>AT.THAT.TIME</u> (וְאָז wê'az)
they(m)~_will~ACCEPT_(V) (יִרְצוּ yir'tsu) <u>AT</u> (אֶת et) <u>TWISTEDNESS~</u>
<u>them</u>(m) (עֲוֺנָם a'o'nam) **RMT:** Moreover I, I will walk contrary with
them, and I brought them in the land of their attackers, or at that
time their uncircumcised heart will be lowered, and at that time they
will accept their twistedness,

26:42 and~_I~did~REMEMBER_(V) (וְזָכַרְתִּי wê'za'khar'ti) <u>AT</u> (אֶת et)
<u>COVENANT~me</u> (בְּרִיתִי bê'ri'ti) <u>Ya'aqov</u> (יַעֲקוֹב ya'a'qov) <u>and~</u>
<u>MOREOVER</u> (וְאַף wê'aph) <u>AT</u> (אֶת et) <u>COVENANT~me</u> (בְּרִיתִי
bê'ri'ti) <u>Yits'hhaq</u> (יִצְחָק yits'hhaq) and~<u>MOREOVER</u> (וְאַף wê'aph)
<u>AT</u> (אֶת et) <u>COVENANT~me</u> (בְּרִיתִי bê'ri'ti) <u>Avraham</u> (אַבְרָהָם
av'ra'ham) _I~will~REMEMBER_(V) (אֶזְכֹּר ez'kor) and~<u>the~LAND</u>
(וְהָאָרֶץ wê'ha'a'rets) _I~will~REMEMBER_(V) (אֶזְכֹּר ez'kor) **RMT:** and I
will remember my covenant with Ya'aqov, and moreover my
covenant with Yits'hhaq, and moreover my covenant with Avraham I
will remember, and I will remember the land,

26:43 and~<u>the~LAND</u> (וְהָאָרֶץ wê'ha'a'rets) _she~will~be~LEAVE_(V)
(תֵּעָזֵב tey'a'zeyv) <u>from~them</u>(m) (מֵהֶם mey'hem) and~_she~will~_
<u>ACCEPT</u>(V) (וְתִרֶץ wê'ti'rets) <u>AT</u> (אֶת et) <u>CEASING~s~her</u> (שַׁבְּתֹתֶיהָ
sha'be'to'tey'ah) _in~>~be~make~DESOLATE_(V) (בָּהְשַׁמָּה bah'sha'mah)
<u>from~them</u>(m) (מֵהֶם mey'hem) and~<u>THEY</u>(m) (וְהֵם wê'heym) _they_(m)~
will~ACCEPT(V) (יִרְצוּ yir'tsu) <u>AT</u> (אֶת et) <u>TWISTEDNESS~them</u>(m)
(עֲוֺנָם a'o'nam) <u>SEEING.AS</u> (יַעַן ya'an) and~<u>in~SEEING.AS</u>
uv'ya'an) <u>in~DECISION~s~me</u> (בְּמִשְׁפָּטַי bê'mish'pa'tai) _they~did~_
<u>REJECT</u>(V) (מָאָסוּ ma'a'su) and~<u>AT</u> (וְאֶת wê'et) <u>CUSTOM~s~me</u>
(חֻקֹּתַי hhu'qo'tai) _she~did~CAST.AWAY_(V) (גָּעֲלָה ga'a'lah) <u>SOUL~</u>
<u>them</u>(m) (נַפְשָׁם naph'sham) **RMT:** and the land will be left from
them, and she will accept her ceasings in being made desolate from

them, and they will accept their twistedness, seeing as, and in seeing as in my directions they rejected, and my customs their soul casted away,

26:44 and~MOREOVER (וְאַף wê'aph) ALSO (גַם gam) THIS (זאת zot) in~>~EXIST(V)~them(m) (בִּהְיוֹתָם bih'yo'tam) in~LAND (בְּאֶרֶץ bê'e'rets) ATTACK(V)~ing(ms)~s~them(m) (אֹיְבֵיהֶם oy'vey'hem) NOT (לֹא lo) I~did~REJECT(V)~them(m) (מְאַסְתִּים mê'as'tim) and~NOT (וְלֹא wê'lo) I~did~CAST.AWAY(V)~them(m) (גְעַלְתִּים gê'al'tim) to~>~much~ FINISH(V)~them(m) (לְכַלֹּתָם lê'kha'lo'tam) to~>~make~BREAK(V) (לְהָפֵר lê'ha'pheyr) COVENANT~me (בְּרִיתִי bê'ri'ti) AT~them(m) (אִתָּם i'tam) GIVEN.THAT (כִּי ki) I (אֲנִי a'ni) **YHWH** (יְהוָה YHWH) Elohiym~ them(m) (אֱלֹהֵיהֶם e'lo'hey'hem) **RMT:** and moreover, also this, in their existing in the land of their attackers, I did not reject them, and I did not cast them away to finish them by breaking my covenant with them, given that I am **YHWH** their Elohiym,

26:45 and~I~did~REMEMBER(V) (וְזָכַרְתִּי wê'za'khar'ti) to~them(m) (לָהֶם la'hem) COVENANT (בְּרִית bê'rit) FIRST~s (רִאשֹׁנִים ri'sho'nim) WHICH (אֲשֶׁר a'sher) I~did~make~GO.OUT(V) (הוֹצֵאתִי ho'tsey'ti) AT~ them(m) (אֹתָם o'tam) from~LAND (מֵאֶרֶץ mey'e'rets) Mits'rayim (מִצְרַיִם mits'ra'yim) to~EYE~s2 (לְעֵינֵי lê'ey'ney) the~NATION~s (הַגּוֹיִם ha'go'yim) to~>~EXIST(V) (לִהְיוֹת lih'yot)[133] to~them(m) (לָהֶם la'hem) to~Elohiym (לֵאלֹהִים ley'lo'him) I (אֲנִי a'ni) **YHWH** (יְהוָה YHWH) **RMT:** and I remembered for them the covenant of the first ones that I brought out from the and of Mits'rayim to the eyes of the nations, to exist for them as Elohiym, I am **YHWH**.

26:46 THESE (אֵלֶּה ey'leh) the~CUSTOM~s (הַחֻקִּים ha'hhu'qim) and~the~DECISION~s (וְהַמִּשְׁפָּטִים wê'ha'mish'pa'tim) and~the~ TEACHING~s (וְהַתּוֹרֹת wê'ha'to'rot) WHICH (אֲשֶׁר a'sher) he~did~ GIVE(V) (נָתַן na'tan) **YHWH** (יְהוָה YHWH) BETWEEN~him (בֵּינוֹ bey'no) and~BETWEEN (וּבֵין u'veyn) SON~s (בְּנֵי bê'ney) Yisra'eyl (יִשְׂרָאֵל yis'ra'eyl) in~HILL (בְּהַר bê'har) Sinai (סִינַי si'nai) in~HAND (בְּיַד bê'yad) Mosheh (מֹשֶׁה mo'sheh) **RMT:** These are the customs and the decisions and the teachings that **YHWH** gave between him and between the sons of Yisra'eyl on the hill of Sinai by the hand of Mosheh,

---

[133] *Leningrad Codex*: להיות

Chapter 27

27:1 and~*he~will~much~*SPEAK^(V) (וַיְדַבֵּר *wai'da'beyr*) **YHWH** (יְהוָה YHWH) <u>TO</u> (אֶל *el*) <u>Mosheh</u> (מֹשֶׁה *mo'sheh*) <u>to~>~SAY</u>^(V) (לֵּאמֹר *ley'mor*) **RMT:** and YHWH spoke to Mosheh saying,

27:2 !^(ms)~*much~*SPEAK^(V) (דַּבֵּר *da'beyr*) <u>TO</u> (אֶל *el*) <u>SON</u>~s (בְּנֵי *bê'ney*) <u>Yisra'eyl</u> (יִשְׂרָאֵל *yis'ra'eyl*) and~*you*^(ms)~*did~*SAY^(V) (וְאָמַרְתָּ *wê'a'mar'ta*) <u>TO~them</u>^(m) (אֲלֵהֶם *a'ley'hem*) <u>MAN</u> (אִישׁ *ish*) <u>GIVEN.THAT</u> (כִּי *ki*) *he~will~make~*PERFORM^(V) (יַפְלִא *yaph'li*) <u>VOW</u> (נֶדֶר *ne'der*) <u>in~ARRANGEMENT~you</u>^(ms) (בְּעֶרְכְּךָ *bê'er'ke'kha*) <u>SOUL</u>~s (נְפָשֹׁת *nê'pha'shot*) <u>to~YHWH</u> (לַיהוָה *la'YHWH*) **RMT:** speak to the sons of Yisra'eyl and you will say to them, a man that will perform a vow, by your valuation souls belong to **YHWH**,

27:3 and~*he~did~*EXIST^(V) (וְהָיָה *wê'hai'yah*) <u>ARRANGEMENT~you</u>^(ms) (עֶרְכְּךָ *er'ke'kha*) <u>the~MALE</u> (הַזָּכָר *ha'za'khar*) <u>from~SON</u> (מִבֶּן *mi'ben*) <u>TEN</u>~s (עֶשְׂרִים *es'rim*) <u>YEAR</u> (שָׁנָה *sha'nah*) and~*UNTIL* (וְעַד *wê'ad*) <u>SON</u> (בֶּן *ben*) <u>SIX</u>~s (שִׁשִּׁים *shi'shim*) <u>YEAR</u> (שָׁנָה *sha'nah*) and~*he~did~*EXIST^(V) (וְהָיָה *wê'hai'yah*) <u>ARRANGEMENT~you</u>^(ms) (עֶרְכְּךָ *er'ke'kha*) <u>FIVE</u>~s (חֲמִשִּׁים *hha'mi'shim*) <u>SHEQEL</u> (שֶׁקֶל *she'qel*) <u>SILVER</u> (כֶּסֶף *ke'seph*) <u>in~SHEQEL</u> (בְּשֶׁקֶל *bê'she'qel*) <u>the~SPECIAL</u> (הַקֹּדֶשׁ *ha'qo'desh*) **RMT:** and your valuation will exist, the male, from a son of twenty years and until a son of sixty years, and your valuation will exist, fifty sheqels of silver, by the special sheqel,

27:4 and~*IF* (וְאִם *wê'im*) <u>FEMALE</u> (נְקֵבָה *nê'qey'vah*) <u>SHE</u> (הִוא *hi*) and~*he~did~*EXIST^(V) (וְהָיָה *wê'hai'yah*) <u>ARRANGEMENT~you</u>^(ms) (עֶרְכְּךָ *er'ke'kha*) <u>THREE</u>~s (שְׁלֹשִׁים *shê'lo'shim*) <u>SHEQEL</u> (שָׁקֶל *sha'qel*) **RMT:** and if she is a female, your valuation will exist of thirty sheqels,

27:5 and~*IF* (וְאִם *wê'im*) <u>from~SON</u> (מִבֶּן *mi'ben*) <u>FIVE</u> (חָמֵשׁ *hha'meysh*) <u>YEAR</u>~s (שָׁנִים *sha'nim*) and~*UNTIL* (וְעַד *wê'ad*) <u>SON</u> (בֶּן *ben*) <u>TEN</u>~s (עֶשְׂרִים *es'rim*) <u>YEAR</u> (שָׁנָה *sha'nah*) and~*he~did~*EXIST^(V) (וְהָיָה *wê'hai'yah*) <u>ARRANGEMENT~you</u>^(ms) (עֶרְכְּךָ *er'ke'kha*) <u>the~MALE</u> (הַזָּכָר *ha'za'khar*) <u>TEN</u>~s (עֶשְׂרִים *es'rim*) <u>SHEQEL</u>~s (שְׁקָלִים *shê'qa'lim*) and~*to~the~FEMALE* (וְלַנְּקֵבָה *wê'lan'qey'vah*) <u>TEN</u> (עֲשֶׂרֶת *a'se'ret*) <u>SHEQEL</u>~s (שְׁקָלִים *shê'qa'lim*) **RMT:** and if from a son of five years and until a son of twenty years, and your valuation will exist, the male, twenty sheqels, and for the female, ten sheqels,

27:6 and~*IF* (וְאִם *wê'im*) <u>from~SON</u> (מִבֶּן *mi'ben*) <u>NEW.MOON</u> (חֹדֶשׁ *hho'desh*) and~*UNTIL* (וְעַד *wê'ad*) <u>SON</u> (בֶּן *ben*) <u>FIVE</u> (חָמֵשׁ *hha'meysh*)

hha'meysh) YEAR~s (שָׁנִים sha'nim) and~he~did~EXIST[V] (וְהָיָה
wê'hai'yah) ARRANGEMENT~you[ms] (עֶרְכְּךָ er'ke'kha) the~MALE
(הַזָּכָר ha'za'khar) FIVE (חֲמִשָּׁה hha'mi'shah) SHEQEL~s (שְׁקָלִים
shê'qa'lim) SILVER (כֶּסֶף ka'seph) and~to~the~FEMALE (וְלַנְּקֵבָה
wê'lan'qey'vah) ARRANGEMENT~you[ms] (עֶרְכְּךָ er'ke'kha) THREE
(שְׁלֹשֶׁת shê'lo'shet) SHEQEL~s (שְׁקָלִים shê'qa'lim) SILVER (כָּסֶף
ka'seph) **RMT:** and if from a son of a new moon and until a son of
five years, then your valuation will exist, the male, five sheqels of
silver, and to the female your valuation is three sheqels of silver,

27:7 and~IF (וְאִם wê'im) from~SCN (מִבֶּן mi'ben) SIX~s (שִׁשִּׁים
shi'shim) YEAR (שָׁנָה sha'nah) and~UPWARD~unto (וָמַעְלָה
wa'ma'lah) IF (אִם im) MALE (זָכָר za'khar) and~he~did~EXIST[V]
(וְהָיָה wê'hai'yah) ARRANGEMENT~you[ms] (עֶרְכְּךָ er'ke'kha) FIVE
(חֲמִשָּׁה hha'mi'shah) TEN (עָשָׂר a'sar) SHEQEL (שֶׁקֶל sha'qel) and~
to~the~FEMALE (וְלַנְּקֵבָה wê'lan'qey'vah) TEN (עֲשָׂרָה a'sa'rah)
SHEQEL~s (שְׁקָלִים shê'qa'lim) **RMT:** and if from a son of sixty years
and upward, if a male, then your valuation will exist, fifteen sheqels,
and for the female, ten sheqels,

27:8 and~IF (וְאִם wê'im) he~did~BE.LOW[V] (מָךְ makh) HE (הוּא hu)
from~ARRANGEMENT~you[ms] (מֵעֶרְכֶּךָ mey'er'ke'kha) and~he~did~
make~STAND[V]~him (וְהֶעֱמִידוֹ wê'he'e'mi'do) to~FACE~s (לִפְנֵי
liph'ney) the~ADMINISTRATOR (הַכֹּהֵן ha'ko'heyn) and~he~did~
make~ARRANGE[V] (וְהֶעֱרִיךְ wê'he e'rikh) AT~him (אֹתוֹ o'to) the~
ADMINISTRATOR (הַכֹּהֵן ha'ko'heyn) UPON (עַל al) MOUTH (פִּי pi)
WHICH (אֲשֶׁר a'sher) she~will~make~OVERTAKE[V] (תַּשִּׂיג ta'sig)
HAND (יַד yad) the~MAKE.A.VOW[V]~ing[ms] (הַנֹּדֵר ha'no'deyr) he~
will~make~ARRANGE[V]~him (יַעֲרִיכֶנּוּ ya'a'ri'khe'nu) the~
ADMINISTRATOR (הַכֹּהֵן ha'ko'heyn) **RMT:** and if he be low from
your valuation, then he will make him stand to the face of the
administrator, and the administrator will value him by the mouth[134]
of what the hand making a vow will overtake, the administrator will
value him,

27:9 and~IF (וְאִם wê'im) BEAST (בְּהֵמָה bê'hey'mah) WHICH (אֲשֶׁר
a'sher) they[m]~will~make~COME.NEAR[V] (יַקְרִיבוּ yaq'ri'vu) FROM~
her (מִמֶּנָּה mi'me'nah) DONATION (קָרְבָּן qar'ban) to~YHWH (לַיהֹוָה
la'YHWH) ALL (כֹּל kol) WHICH (אֲשֶׁר a'sher) he~will~GIVE[V] (יִתֵּן
yi'teyn) FROM~him (מִמֶּנּוּ mi'me'nu) to~YHWH (לַיהֹוָה la'YHWH)

---

[134] The phrase "by the mouth" means "according to."

*he~will~*EXIST^(V) (יִהְיֶה *yih'yeh*) SPECIAL (קֹדֶשׁ *qo'desh*) **RMT:** and if a beast that they will bring near, a donation for **YHWH**, all that he will give from him belong to **YHWH**, he will exist special.

27:10 NOT (לֹא *lo*) *he~will~make~*PASS.OVER^(V)*~him* (יַחֲלִיפֶנּוּ *ya'hha'li'phe'nu*) *and~*NOT (וְלֹא *wê'lo*) *he~will~make~*CONVERT^(V) (יָמִיר *ya'mir*) AT~him (אֹתוֹ *o'to*) FUNCTIONAL (טוֹב *tov*) *in~* DYSFUNCTIONAL (בְּרָע *bê'ra*) OR (אוֹ *o*) DYSFUNCTIONAL (רָע *ra*) *in~* FUNCTIONAL (בְּטוֹב *bê'tov*) *and~*IF (וְאִם *wê'im*) *>~make~* CONVERT^(V) (הָמֵר *ha'meyr*) *he~will~make~*CONVERT^(V) (יָמִיר *ya'mir*) BEAST (בְּהֵמָה *bê'hey'mah*) *in~*BEAST (בִּבְהֵמָה *biv'hey'mah*) *and~he~ did~*EXIST^(V) (וְהָיָה *wê'hai'yah*) HE (הוּא *hu*) *and~*EXCHANGE~him (וּתְמוּרָתוֹ *ut'mu'ra'to*) *he~will~*EXIST^(V) (יִהְיֶה *yih'yeh*) SPECIAL (קֹדֶשׁ *qo'desh*) **RMT:** He will not pass him over, and he will not convert him, a functional for a dysfunctional or a dysfunction for a functional, and if he convert beast for a beast, and he will exist, he and his exchange will exist special,

27:11 *and~*IF (וְאִם *wê'im*) ALL (כָּל *kol*) BEAST (בְּהֵמָה *bê'hey'mah*) DIRTY (טְמֵאָה *tê'mey'ah*) WHICH (אֲשֶׁר *a'sher*) NOT (לֹא *lo*) *they^(m)~ will~make~*COME.NEAR^(V) (יַקְרִיבוּ *yaq'ri'vu*) FROM~her (מִמֶּנָּה *mi'me'nah*) DONATION (קָרְבָּן *qar'ban*) *to~*YHWH (לַיהוָה *la'YHWH*) *and~he~did~make~*STAND^(V) (וְהֶעֱמִיד *wê'he'e'mid*) AT (אֶת *et*) *the~* BEAST (הַבְּהֵמָה *ha'be'hey'mah*) *to~*FACE~s (לִפְנֵי *liph'ney*) *the~* ADMINISTRATOR (הַכֹּהֵן *ha'ko'heyn*) **RMT:** and if any dirty beast, which they will not bring her near for a donation to **YHWH**, then he will make the beast stand to the face of the administrators,

27:12 *and~he~did~make~*ARRANGE^(V) (וְהֶעֱרִיךְ *wê'he'e'rikh*) *the~* ADMINISTRATOR (הַכֹּהֵן *ha'ko'heyn*) AT~her (אֹתָהּ *o'tah*) BETWEEN (בֵּין *beyn*) FUNCTIONAL (טוֹב *tov*) *and~*BETWEEN (וּבֵין *u'veyn*) DYSFUNCTIONAL (רָע *ra*) *like~*ARRANGEMENT~you^(ms) (כְּעֶרְכְּךָ *kê'er'ke'kha*) *the~*ADMINISTRATOR (הַכֹּהֵן *ha'ko'heyn*) SO (כֵּן *keyn*) *he~will~*EXIST^(V) (יִהְיֶה *yih'yeh*) **RMT:** and the administrator will value her between the functional and the dysfunctional, like your valuation of the administrator, so he will exist,

27:13 *and~*IF (וְאִם *wê'im*) *>~*REDEEM^(V) (גָּאֹל *ga'ol*) *he~will~* REDEEM^(V)*~her* (יִגְאָלֶנָּה *yig'a'le'nah*) *and~he~will~*ADD^(V) (וְיָסַף *wê'ya'saph*) FIFTH~him (חֲמִישִׁתוֹ *hha'mi'shi'to*) UPON (עַל *al*) ARRANGEMENT~you^(ms) (עֶרְכֶּךָ *er'ke'kha*) **RMT:** but if he will surely redeem her, and he will add a fifth of him upon your valuation,

27:14 and~MAN (וְאִישׁ wê'ish) GIVEN.THAT (כִּי ki) he~will~make~ SET.APART[(V)] (יַקְדִּשׁ yaq'dish) AT (אֶת et) HOUSE~him (בֵּיתוֹ bey'to) SPECIAL (קֹדֶשׁ qo'desh) to~**YHWH** (לַיהוָה la'YHWH) and~he~did~ make~ARRANGE[(V)]~him (וְהֶעֱרִיכוֹ wê'he'e'ri'kho) the~ ADMINISTRATOR (הַכֹּהֵן ha'ko'heyn) BETWEEN (בֵּין beyn) FUNCTIONAL (טוֹב tov) and~BETWEEN (וּבֵין u'veyn) DYSFUNCTIONAL (רָע ra) like~WHICH (כַּאֲשֶׁר ka'a'sheyr) he~will~ make~ARRANGE[(V)] (יַעֲרִיךְ ya'a'rikh) AT~him (אֹתוֹ o'to) the~ ADMINISTRATOR (הַכֹּהֵן ha'ko'heyn) SO (כֵּן keyn) he~will~RISE[(V)] (יָקוּם ya'qum) **RMT:** and a man that will make his house set apart as special for **YHWH**, and the administrator will value him between the functional and dysfunctional, just as the administrator will value him, so he will rise,

27:15 and~IF (וְאִם wê'im) the~make~SET.APART[(V)]~ing[(ms)] (הַמַּקְדִּישׁ ha'maq'dish) he~will~REDEEM[(V)] (יִגְאַל yig'al) AT (אֶת et) HOUSE~ him (בֵּיתוֹ bey'to) and~he~will~ADD[(V)] (וְיָסַף wê'ya'saph) FIFTH (חֲמִישִׁת hha'mi'shit) SILVER (כֶּסֶף ke'seph) ARRANGEMENT~you[(ms)] (עֶרְכְּךָ er'ke'kha) UPON~him (עָלָיו a'law) and~he~did~EXIST[(V)] (וְהָיָה wê'hai'yah) to~him (לוֹ lo) **RMT:** and if the one making set apart will redeem his house, then he will add a fifth of silver of your valuation upon him, and he will exist for him,

27:16 and~IF (וְאִם wê'im) from~FIELD (מִשְׂדֵה mis'deyh) HOLDINGS~ him (אֲחֻזָּתוֹ a'hhu'za'to) he~will~make~SET.APART[(V)] (יַקְדִּישׁ yaq'dish) MAN (אִישׁ ish) to~**YHWH** (לַיהוָה la'YHWH) and~he~did~ EXIST[(V)] (וְהָיָה wê'hai'yah) ARRANGEMENT~you[(ms)] (עֶרְכְּךָ er'ke'kha) to~MOUTH (לְפִי lê'phi) SEED~him (זַרְעוֹ zar'o) SEED (זֶרַע ze'ra) HHOMER (חֹמֶר hho'mer) BARLEY~s (שְׂעֹרִים sê'o'rim) in~the~FIVE~s (בַּחֲמִשִּׁים ba'hha'mi'shim) SHEQEL (שֶׁקֶל she'qel) SILVER (כָּסֶף ka'seph) **RMT:** and if from the field of his holdings a man will set it apart for **YHWH**, then your valuation will exist by the mouth[135] of his seed, the seed of a hhomer of barleys with fifty sheqels of silver.

27:17 IF (אִם im) from~YEAR (מִשְּׁנַת mi'she'nat) the~JUBILEE (הַיֹּבֵל hai'yo'veyl) he~will~make~SET.APART[(V)] (יַקְדִּישׁ yaq'dish) FIELD~him (שָׂדֵהוּ sa'dey'hu) like~ARRANGEMENT~you[(ms)] (כְּעֶרְכְּךָ kê'er'ke'kha) he~will~RISE[(V)] (יָקוּם ya'qum) **RMT:** If from the year of the jubilee, he will make his field set apart, like your valuation he will rise,

---

[135] Meaning "according to."

27:18 <u>and~IF</u> (וְאִם *wê'im*) <u>AFTER</u> (אַחַר *a'hhar*) <u>the~JUBILEE</u> (הַיֹּבֵל *hai'yo'veyl*) <u>he~will~make~SET.APART</u>(V) (יַקְדִּישׁ *yaq'dish*) <u>FIELD~him</u> (שָׂדֵהוּ *sa'dey'hu*) <u>and~he~did~much~THINK</u>(V) (וְחִשַּׁב *wê'hhi'shav*) <u>to~him</u> (לוֹ *lo*) <u>the~ADMINISTRATOR</u> (הַכֹּהֵן *ha'ko'heyn*) <u>AT</u> (אֶת *et*) <u>the~SILVER</u> (הַכֶּסֶף *ha'ke'seph*) <u>UPON</u> (עַל *al*) <u>MOUTH</u> (פִּי *pi*) <u>the~YEAR~s</u> (הַשָּׁנִים *ha'sha'nim*) <u>the~be~LEAVE.BEHIND</u>(V)~<u>ing</u>(fp) (הַנּוֹתָרֹת *ha'no'ta'rot*) <u>UNTIL</u> (עַד *ad*) <u>YEAR</u> (שְׁנַת *shê'nat*) <u>the~JUBILEE</u> (הַיֹּבֵל *hai'yo'veyl*) <u>and~he~did~be~TAKE.AWAY</u>(V) (וְנִגְרַע *wê'nig'ra*) <u>from~ARRANGEMENT~you</u>(ms) (מֵעֶרְכֶּךָ *mey'er'ke'kha*) **RMT:** but if after the jubilee, he will make his field set apart, then the administrator will plan for him, the silver by the mouth[136] of the years being left behind until the year of the jubilee, then he will be taken away from your valuation,

27:19 <u>and~IF</u> (וְאִם *wê'im*) <u>>~REDEEM</u>(V) (גָּאֹל *ga'ol*) <u>he~will~REDEEM</u>(V) (יִגְאַל *yig'al*) <u>AT</u> (אֶת *et*) <u>the~FIELD</u> (הַשָּׂדֶה *ha'sa'deh*) <u>the~make~SET.APART</u>(V)~<u>ing</u>(ms) (הַמַּקְדִּישׁ *ha'maq'dish*) <u>AT~him</u> (אֹתוֹ *o'to*) <u>and~he~will~ADD</u>(V) (וְיָסַף *wê'ya'saph*) <u>FIVE</u> (חֲמִשִׁית *hha'mi'shit*) <u>SILVER</u> (כֶּסֶף *ke'seph*) <u>ARRANGEMENT~you</u>(ms) (עֶרְכְּךָ *er'ke'kha*) <u>UPON~him</u> (עָלָיו *a'law*) <u>and~he~did~RISE</u>(V) (וְקָם *wê'qam*) <u>to~him</u> (לוֹ *lo*) **RMT:** and if he will surely redeem the field, the one making him set apart, then he will add a fifth of the silver of your valuation, and he will rise for him,

27:20 <u>and~IF</u> (וְאִם *wê'im*) <u>NOT</u> (לֹא *lo*) <u>he~will~REDEEM</u>(V) (יִגְאַל *yig'al*) <u>AT</u> (אֶת *et*) <u>the~FIELD</u> (הַשָּׂדֶה *ha'sa'deh*) <u>and~IF</u> (וְאִם *wê'im*) <u>he~did~SELL</u>(V) (מָכַר *ma'khar*) <u>AT</u> (אֶת *et*) <u>the~FIELD</u> (הַשָּׂדֶה *ha'sa'deh*) <u>to~MAN</u> (לְאִישׁ *lê'ish*) <u>OTHER</u> (אַחֵר *a'hheyr*) <u>NOT</u> (לֹא *lo*) <u>he~will~be~REDEEM</u>(V) (יִגָּאֵל *yi'ga'eyl*) <u>YET.AGAIN</u> (עוֹד *od*) **RMT:** and if he will not redeem the field, or if he will sell the field to another man, he will not be redeemed again,

27:21 <u>and~he~did~EXIST</u>(V) (וְהָיָה *wê'hai'yah*) <u>the~FIELD</u> (הַשָּׂדֶה *ha'sa'deh*) <u>in~>~GO.OUT</u>(V)~<u>him</u> (בְּצֵאתוֹ *bê'tsey'to*) <u>in~the~JUBILEE</u> (בַיֹּבֵל *vai'yo'veyl*) <u>SPECIAL</u> (קֹדֶשׁ *qo'desh*) <u>to~YHWH</u> (לַיהוָה *la'YHWH*) <u>like~FIELD</u> (כִּשְׂדֵה *kis'deyh*) <u>the~ASSIGNED</u> (הַחֵרֶם *ha'hhey'rem*) <u>to~the~ADMINISTRATOR</u> (לַכֹּהֵן *la'ko'heyn*) <u>she~will~EXIST</u>(V) (תִּהְיֶה *tih'yeh*) <u>HOLDINGS~him</u> (אֲחֻזָּתוֹ *a'hhu'za'to*) **RMT:** and the field will exist in his going out in the jubilee, special to

---

[136] The phrase "by the mouth" means "according to."

YHWH, like the assigned field, his holdings will exist for the administrator,

27:22 and~IF (וְאִם wê'im) AT (אֶת et) FIELD (שְׂדֵה sê'deyh) ACQUIRED~him (מִקְנָתוֹ miq'na'to) WHICH (אֲשֶׁר a'sher) NOT (לֹא lo) from~FIELD (מִשְּׂדֵה mis'deyh) HOLDINGS~him (אֲחֻזָּתוֹ a'hhu'za'to) he~will~make~SET.APART[V] (יַקְדִּישׁ yaq'dish) to~YHWH (לַיהוָה la'YHWH) **RMT:** and if a field acquired of him, which is not from the field of his holdings, he will set it apart for **YHWH**,

27:23 and~he~did~much~THINK[V] (וְחִשַּׁב wê'hhi'shav) to~him (לוֹ lo) the~ADMINISTRATOR (הַכֹּהֵן ha'ko'heyn) AT (אֵת eyt) WORTH (מִכְסַת mikh'sat) the~ARRANGEMENT~you[ms] (הָעֶרְכְּךָ ha'er'ke'kha) UNTIL (עַד ad) YEAR (שְׁנַת shê'nat) the~JUBILEE (הַיֹּבֵל hai'yo'veyl) and~he~did~GIVE[V] (וְנָתַן wê'na'tan) AT (אֶת et) the~ARRANGEMENT~you[ms] (הָעֶרְכְּךָ ha'er'ke'kha) in~the~DAY (בַּיּוֹם ba'yom) the~HE (הַהוּא ha'hu) SPECIAL (קֹדֶשׁ qo'desh) to~YHWH (לַיהוָה la'YHWH) **RMT:** and the administrator will plan for him the worth of your arrangement until the year of the jubilee, and he will give your arrangement in that day, special for **YHWH**.

27:24 in~YEAR (בִּשְׁנַת bish'nat) the~JUBILEE (הַיּוֹבֵל hai'yo'veyl) he~will~TURN.BACK[V] (יָשׁוּב ya'shuv) the~FIELD (הַשָּׂדֶה ha'sa'deh) to~the~WHICH (לַאֲשֶׁר la'a'sheyr) he~did~PURCHASE[V]~him (קָנָהוּ qa'na'hu) from~AT~him (מֵאִתּוֹ mey'i'to) to~the~WHICH (לַאֲשֶׁר la'a'sheyr) to~him (לוֹ lo) HOLDINGS (אֲחֻזַּת a'hhu'zat) the~LAND (הָאָרֶץ ha'a'rets) **RMT:** In the year of the jubilee he will turn back the field to whom he purchased him from, to who belonged to him the holdings of the land,

27:25 and~ALL (וְכָל wê'khol) ARRANGEMENT~you[ms] (עֶרְכְּךָ er'ke'kha) he~will~EXIST[V] (יִהְיֶה yih'yeh) in~SHEQEL (בְּשֶׁקֶל bê'she'qel) the~SPECIAL (הַקֹּדֶשׁ ha'qo'desh) TEN~s (עֶשְׂרִים es'rim) GERAH (גֵּרָה gey'rah) he~will~EXIST[V] (יִהְיֶה yih'yeh) the~SHEQEL (הַשָּׁקֶל ha'sha'qel) **RMT:** and all your arrangements will exist by the special sheqel, twenty gerahs will be the sheqel.

27:26 SURELY (אַךְ akh) FIRSTBORN (בְּכוֹר bê'khor) WHICH (אֲשֶׁר a'sher) he~will~be~much~BE.FIRSTBORN[V] (יְבֻכַּר yê'vu'kar) to~YHWH (לַיהוָה la'YHWH) in~BEAST (בִּבְהֵמָה biv'hey'mah) NOT (לֹא lo) he~will~make~SET.APART[V] (יַקְדִּישׁ yaq'dish) MAN (אִישׁ ish) AT~him (אֹתוֹ o'to) IF (אִם im) OX (שׁוֹר shor) IF (אִם im) RAM (שֶׂה seh) to~YHWH (לַיהוָה la'YHWH) HE (הוּא hu) **RMT:** Only the firstborn, which will be the firstborn for **YHWH** in the beasts, a man will not set him apart if of the ox, if of the ram, he belongs to **YHWH**,

27:27 and~IF (וְאִם *wê'im*) in~the~BEAST (בַּבְּהֵמָה *ba'be'hey'mah*) the~DIRTY (הַטְּמֵאָה *hat'mey'ah*) and~he~did~RANSOM(V) (וּפָדָה *u'pha'dah*) in~ARRANGEMENT~you(ms) (בְעֶרְכֶּךָ *vê'er'ke'kha*) and~he~will~ADD(V) (וְיָסַף *wê'ya'saph*) FIVE~him (חֲמִשִׁתוֹ *hha'mi'shi'to*) UPON~him (עָלָיו *a'law*) and~IF (וְאִם *wê'im*) NOT (לֹא *lo*) he~will~be~REDEEM(V) (יִגָּאֵל *yi'ga'eyl*) and~he~did~be~SELL(V) (וְנִמְכַּר *wê'nim'kar*) in~ARRANGEMENT~you(ms) (בְּעֶרְכֶּךָ *bê'er'ke'kha*) **RMT:** and if in the dirty beast, and he will ransom by your arrangement, then he will add five parts of him upon him, and if he will not be redeemed, he will be sold by your arrangement.

27:28 SURELY (אַךְ *akh*) ALL (כָּל *kol*) ASSIGNED (חֵרֶם *hhey'rem*) WHICH (אֲשֶׁר *a'sher*) he~will~make~ASSIGN(V) (יַחֲרִם *ya'hha'rim*) MAN (אִישׁ *ish*) to~**YHWH** (לַיהוָה *la'YHWH*) from~ALL (מִכָּל *mi'kol*) WHICH (אֲשֶׁר *a'sher*) to~him (לוֹ *lo*) from~HUMAN (מֵאָדָם *mey'a'dam*) and~BEAST (וּבְהֵמָה *uv'hey'mah*) and~from~FIELD (וּמִשְׂדֵה *u'mis'deyh*) HOLDINGS~him (אֲחֻזָּתוֹ *a'hhu'za'to*) NOT (לֹא *lo*) he~will~be~SELL(V) (יִמָּכֵר *yi'ma'kheyr*) and~NOT (וְלֹא *wê'lo*) he~will~be~REDEEM(V) (יִגָּאֵל *yi'ga'eyl*) ALL (כָּל *kol*) ASSIGNED (חֵרֶם *hhey'rem*) SPECIAL (קֹדֶשׁ *qo'desh*) SPECIAL~s (קָדָשִׁים *qa'da'shim*) HE (הוּא *hu*) to~**YHWH** (לַיהוָה *la'YHWH*) **RMT:** Only all the assigned, which a man assigned for **YHWH**, from all that belongs to him, from the human and the beast and from the field of his holdings, he will not be sold, and he will not be redeemed, every assigned one is a special of special[137], he belongs to **YHWH**.

27:29 ALL (כָּל *kol*) ASSIGNED (חֵרֶם *hhey'rem*) WHICH (אֲשֶׁר *a'sher*) he~will~be~make~ASSIGN(V) (יָחֳרַם *ya'hha'ram*) FROM (מִן *min*) the~HUMAN (הָאָדָם *ha'a'dam*) NOT (לֹא *lo*) he~will~be~RANSOM(V) (יִפָּדֶה *yi'pa'deh*) >~DIE(V) (מוֹת *mot*) he~will~be~make~DIE(V) (יוּמָת *yu'mat*) **RMT:** Every assigned one that will be assigned from the human, he will not be ransomed, he must surely be killed,

27:30 and~ALL (וְכָל *wê'khol*) TENTH.PART (מַעְשַׂר *ma'sar*) the~LAND (הָאָרֶץ *ha'a'rets*) from~SEED (מִזֶּרַע *mi'ze'ra*) the~LAND (הָאָרֶץ *ha'a'rets*) from~PRODUCE (מִפְּרִי *mi'pe'ri*) the~TREE (הָעֵץ *ha'eyts*) to~**YHWH** (לַיהוָה *la'YHWH*) HE (הוּא *hu*) SPECIAL (קֹדֶשׁ *qo'desh*) to~

---

[137] The phrase "special of specials" means a "very special thing, one or place."

YHWH (לַיהוָה *la'YHWH*) **RMT:** and all the tenth part of the land, from the seed of the land, from the produce of the tree, belong to **YHWH**, he is special for **YHWH**,

27:31 and~IF (וְאִם *wê'im*) >~REDEEM[V] (גָּאֹל *ga'ol*) he~will~ REDEEM[V] (יִגְאַל *yig'al*) MAN (אִישׁ *ish*) from~TENTH.PART~him (מִמַּעַשְׂרוֹ *mi'ma'as'ro*) FIVE~Tim (חֲמִישִׁתוֹ *hha'mi'shi'to*) he~will~ make~ADD[V] (יֹסֵף *yo'seyph*) UPON~him (עָלָיו *a'law*) **RMT:** and if a man will surely redeem from his tenth part, he will add a fifth of him upon him,

27:32 and~ALL (וְכָל *wê'khol*) TENTH.PART (מַעְשַׂר *ma'sar*) CATTLE (בָּקָר *ba'qar*) and~FLOCKS (וָצֹאן *wa'tson*) ALL (כֹּל *kol*) WHICH (אֲשֶׁר *a'sher*) he~will~CROSS.OVER[N] (יַעֲבֹר *ya'a'vor*) UNDER (תַּחַת *ta'hhat*) the~STAFF (הַשָּׁבֶט *ha'sha've'ṭ*) the~TENTH (הָעֲשִׂירִי *ha'a'si'ri*) he~ will~EXIST[V] (יִהְיֶה *yih'yeh*) SPECIAL (קֹדֶשׁ *qo'desh*) to~**YHWH** (לַיהוָה *la'YHWH*) **RMT:** and all the tenth part of the cattle and the flocks, all that will cross over under the staff[138], the tenth will exist special for **YHWH**.

27:33 NOT (לֹא *lo*) he~will~much~INVESTIGATE[V] (יְבַקֵּר *yê'va'qeyr*) BETWEEN (בֵּין *beyn*) FUNCTIONAL (טוֹב *tov*) to~the~ DYSFUNCTIONAL (לָרַע *la'ra*) and~NOT (וְלֹא *wê'lo*) he~will~make~ CONVERT[V]~him (יְמִירֶנּוּ *yê'mi're'nu*) and~IF (וְאִם *wê'im*) >~make~ CONVERT[V] (הָמֵר *ha'meyr*) he~will~make~CONVERT[V]~him (יְמִירֶנּוּ *yê'mi're'nu*) and~he~did~EXIST[V] (וְהָיָה *wê'hai'yah*) HE (הוּא *hu*) and~EXCHANGE~him (וּתְמוּרָתוֹ *ut'mu'ra'to*) he~will~EXIST[V] (יִהְיֶה *yih'yeh*) SPECIAL (קֹדֶשׁ *qo'desh*) NOT (לֹא *lo*) he~will~be~REDEEM[V] (יִגָּאֵל *yi'ga'eyl*) **RMT:** He will not investigate between the functional and the dysfunctional, and he will not convert him, but if he will surely convert him, then he and his exchange will exist as special, he will not be redeemed.

27:34 THESE (אֵלֶּה *ey'leh*) the~DIRECTIVE~s (הַמִּצְוֹת *ha'mits'ot*) WHICH (אֲשֶׁר *a'sher*) he~did~much~DIRECT[V] (צִוָּה *tsi'wah*) **YHWH** (יְהוָה *YHWH*) AT (אֶת *et*) Mosheh (מֹשֶׁה *mo'sheh*) TO (אֶל *el*) SON~s (בְּנֵי *bê'ney*) Yisra'eyl (יִשְׂרָאֵל *yis'ra'eyl*) in~HILL (בְּהַר *bê'har*) Sinai (סִינָי *si'nai*) **RMT:** These are the directives that **YHWH** directed Mosheh to the sons of Yisra'eyl in the hill of Sinai,

---

[138] Livestock was counted when they passed under the staff of the shepherd as they entered the gate.

www.ingramcontent.com/pod-product-compliance
Lightning Source LLC
Chambersburg PA
CBHW052038090426
42739CB00010B/1958